MW01063692

BERNSTEIN MEETS BROADWAY

Geoffrey Block, Series Editor

Series Board

Stephen Banfield   Jeffrey Magee
Tim Carter   Carol J. Oja
Kim Kowalke   Larry Starr

BERNSTEIN MEETS BROADWAY

Collaborative Art in a Time of War

CAROL J. OJA

OXFORD
UNIVERSITY PRESS

OXFORD
UNIVERSITY PRESS

Oxford University Press is a department of the
University of Oxford. It furthers the University's objective
of excellence in research, scholarship, and education
by publishing worldwide.

Oxford   New York
Auckland   Cape Town   Dar es Salaam   Hong Kong   Karachi
Kuala Lumpur   Madrid   Melbourne   Mexico City   Nairobi
New Delhi   Shanghai   Taipei   Toronto

With offices in
Argentina   Austria   Brazil   Chile   Czech Republic   France   Greece
Guatemala   Hungary   Italy   Japan   Poland   Portugal   Singapore
South Korea   Switzerland   Thailand   Turkey   Ukraine   Vietnam

Oxford is a registered trade mark of Oxford University Press
in the UK and certain other countries.

Published in the United States of America by
Oxford University Press
198 Madison Avenue, New York, NY 10016

© Oxford University Press 2014

This volume is published with the generous support of the Dragan Plamenac Endowment
of the American Musicological Society and the Claire and Barry Brook Endowment of the
American Musicological Society, both funded in part by the National Endowment for
the Humanities and the Andrew W. Mellon Foundation.

Library of Congress Cataloging-in-Publication Data
Oja, Carol J., 1953–, author.
Bernstein meets Broadway : collaborative art in a time of war/
Carol J. Oja.
pages   cm
Includes bibliographical references and index.
ISBN 978-0-19-986209-2 (hardcover : alk. paper)
1. Bernstein, Leonard, 1918–1990—Criticism and interpretation.
2. Musicals—New York (State)—New York—20th century—History and criticism.
3. Bernstein, Leonard, 1918–1990. On the town.   I. Title.
ML410.B566O43   2014
792.609747'109044—dc23
2013043497

1 3 5 7 9 8 6 4 2

Printed in the United States of America
on acid-free paper

To ZOE *and* WYNN

and the memory of MARK TUCKER

CONTENTS

• • •

FOREWORD

* * *

In Carol J. Oja's *Bernstein Meets Broadway: Collaborative Art in a Time of War* we learn how a quartet of young, exuberant talents and children of Jewish immigrants, Leonard Bernstein, Jerome Robbins, Betty Comden, and Adolph Green, came together to produce their own urban landmark show, less than two years after *Oklahoma!* From his meteoric rise to fame in the early 1940s to the end of his life, Bernstein (1918–1990), the man who meets Broadway in Oja's title, remained one of the most famous musicians in the world and one of the best-known Americans in any domain. As a composer, Bernstein created a wide range of classically oriented compositions as well as four remarkable Broadway musicals: *On the Town* (1944), *Wonderful Town* (1953), *Candide* (1956), and *West Side Story* (1957).

Nine months before *On the Town* danced onto Broadway on December 28, 1944, Bernstein met the young choreographer Jerome Robbins, and the two teamed up to create the ballet *Fancy Free*, which premiered on April 18, 1944. Over the next two decades, along with more ground-breaking ballets, Robbins would boldly and permanently transform the possibilities of dance choreography on Broadway with various collaborators, including Irving Berlin (*Miss Liberty, Call Me Madam*), Richard Rodgers and Oscar Hammerstein (*The King and I*), Jule Styne and Stephen Sondheim (*Gypsy*), Jerry Bock and Sheldon Harnick (*Fiddler on the Roof*), and Bernstein and Sondheim (*West Side Story*).

As readers will discover in Oja's second chapter, even before *Fancy Free* Bernstein had met Comden and Green. Here we also meet the Village Vanguard nightclub act called The Revuers, an act launched in 1938 that consisted of Comden and Green and their friend Judy Tuvim, the future Judy Holliday, while their versatile friend Bernstein makes an occasional appearance as their pianist. Comden and Green, like Bernstein and Robbins newcomers to Broadway in 1944, would go on to create a series of acclaimed shows, including *Wonderful Town* with Bernstein, and screenplays and songs for such acclaimed musical films as *On the Town, Singin' in the Rain,* and *The Band Wagon.* As late as the early 1990s they managed to create yet another hit show, *The Will Rogers Follies,* with music by Cy Coleman. But as with Bernstein and Robbins, Comden and Green's first Broadway stop was *On the Town.*

Oja's *Bernstein Meets Broadway* is the first major study of this illustrious quartet's spectacular Broadway debut, a highly regarded and yet, undeservedly, less well known show than Rodgers and Hammerstein's contemporaneous *Oklahoma!* or Berlin's *Annie Get Your Gun.* The original production was directed by the legendary George Abbott. Abbott perhaps smoothed the way for a wacky and clever show comparable to his pioneering directing and writing work with the classic team of Rodgers and Hart and another young choreographer, none other than George Balanchine, in the 1930s. Loaded with a dizzying array of dance styles, *On the Town* is about three sailors seeking sex, companionship, and perhaps even love during a mere twenty-four hours of shore leave. The show opens with a song that has become one of the most recognizable and joyous of all city anthems, "New York, New York" ("It's a helluva town!"). At a moment of reflection near its close audiences could also shed tears at the deeply poignant farewell for the sailors and their new girlfriends, the quartet "Some Other Time," whose opening chords served jazz pianist Bill Evans as the harmonic foundation for his "Peace Piece" and "Flamenco Sketches" in the late 1950s.

As Oja relates in her Introduction (from which all the quotations of this Foreword are taken), "Bernstein is at the center of the action, but he becomes part of a collective process—enough so that the narrative moves past him for extended periods." In fact, Oja's book is chock full of discoveries based on previously unexplored archival terrain that go far beyond the central creative quartet, including newly available digitized articles from the vital African American newspapers of the time from which a "new vision emerges of the world of performance, exposing the degree to which white viewpoints have dominated historical perceptions." In one especially gripping chapter Oja tells the story of the path-breaking Japanese American dancer Sono Osato (interviewed for this book), who graced the show as the elusive and desirable Miss Turnstiles, the "Exotic Ivy Smith." Ironically, at the same time, her father, an immigrant to the United States, unsuccessfully fought internment and harassment by the U.S. government and was unable to attend his daughter's opening night.

As much as any scholar writing today, Oja possesses the skill, perspective, and, yes, pizzazz necessary to make meaningful connections between social and artistic forces come to life, creating a musical history that is both engrossing and powerful. Readers will learn from Oja that actions, onstage and off, can speak louder than words (or plots). Despite limits to the show's "daring" as it "fabricated a vision of urban interracial fellowship," the many signs of desegregation in its racially mixed dance chorus and the fact that African American conductor Everett Lee led the all-white orchestra during the second half of the show's run offered a new way to see what a musical can mean to a nation at war abroad and in the midst of racial conflicts at home.

Readers of *Bernstein Meets Broadway* will also learn about the symbiotic but independent compositional genesis of *On the Town* as it developed from *Fancy Free*, which Oja explores provocatively but persuasively for its "gay interpretation" in both its dance and plot subtexts. We even learn the striking untold story of the "initial inspiration" for *Fancy Free*, a 1934 painting by Paul Cadmus, which paints a "bisexual message" that "holds the key to the ballet's multiple narratives, as well as the interplay of personal and professional relationships among its collaborators."

In her efforts to explore the complex and far-ranging and eclectic social contexts and racial politics of *On the Town*, Oja does not neglect to include generous chapters on the interrelationship between the musical and dramatic components of the show as exhibited in Bernstein's rich musical score and the ways the nightclub scenes in Act II demonstrate biographical connections to the earlier nightclub experiences of Comden and Green as well as those remarkable new visions of racial representation.

Carol Oja is the author of *Making Music Modern: New York in the 1920s* (Oxford University Press, 2000), a book that received the Society for American Music's

"Oscar" for the best book of its year. Previously, Oja produced the major study of the composer Colin McPhee (Smithsonian Press, 1990; paperback, University of Illinois Press, 2004), which like *Making Music Modern* received an ASCAP Deems Taylor Award. Joined by Judith Tick, Oja coedited *Copland and His World* (Princeton University Press, 2005), and she also coedited *Crosscurrents: American and European Music in Interaction, 1900–2000* (The Boydell Press, 2014), together with Felix Meyer, Wolfgang Rathert, and Anne C. Shreffler.

An imaginative scholar informed by a deep understanding of music and its social meanings and an engaging writer, in *Bernstein Meets Broadway* Oja has written a book that will delight scholars and general readers alike. In short, it's a helluva good read.

GEOFFREY BLOCK
Series Editor, Broadway Legacies

ACKNOWLEDGMENTS

• • •

Books take flight as vague ideas become life-absorbing passions, and sometimes an especially meaningful experience provides the initial inspiration. For me, that impetus came through an interlinked seminar and festival at Harvard University in 2006. Together with my colleague Kay Kaufman Shelemay, I team-taught a seminar titled "Before *West Side Story*: Leonard Bernstein's Boston," in which we guided students in hands-on research about Bernstein's childhood experiences in the Boston area. A public festival followed, which I co-directed with the New York–based conductor Judith Clurman, and the entire event was brilliantly produced by Jack Megan and Tom Lee from Harvard's Office for the Arts. Through those experiences, I had the privilege of getting to know the Bernstein family, including Leonard's children Jamie, Nina, and Alexander, his brother Burton, and his childhood friend Sid Ramin, and I entered into a rewarding relationship with the Leonard Bernstein Office in New York City, especially with Marie Carter, vice president for licensing and publishing; Paul Epstein, senior vice president; and Craig Urquhart, senior consultant, public relations and promotion. I also got to know Humphrey Burton, biographer of Bernstein and noted classical music broadcaster in Britain; his work has been fundamental to my own research.

I am grateful to them all and to many others as well. Norman Hirschy, editor of music books at Oxford University Press, and Geoffrey Block, series editor of OUP's Broadway Legacies, believed in this project when the concept was just beginning to take shape, and both have generously offered critiques and assistance. Working with Norm has been thoroughly gratifying. I have benefited hugely from his sharp-eyed editorial recommendations, responsibility about deadlines, and abundant goodwill. I am also grateful for the exceptional expertise of my production editor Joellyn Ausanka, publicist Owen Keiter, and marketing assistant Taylor Coe. Woytek Rynczak typeset my musical examples.

I am equally fortunate to have friends and colleagues who have given insightful readings of individual chapters, including Thomas F. DeFrantz, Lynn Garafola, Charles Hiroshi Garrett, Andrew Gordon, Andrea Most, Christopher Reynolds, Thomas L. Riis, Anne Shreffler, Larry Starr, and Stacy Wolf. Discerning comments on the entire manuscript came from Jeffrey Magee, Kay Kaufman Shelemay, Judith Tick, and Susan Ware. Each of these readers was extraordinarily helpful, freely sharing their reactions and their time. Discussions with the Musical Theater Forum, a loosely constructed working group initially formed by me and Stacy Wolf, have also been stimulating. Its members have included George Burrows, Lynn Garafola, Liza Gennaro, Raymond Knapp, Jeffrey Magee, David Savran, Dominic Symonds, Tamsen Wolff, and Elizabeth Wollman, together with a shifting roster of graduate students. At the same time, my writers' group in the Boston area—including Carol Bundy, Kathleen Dalton, Carla Kaplan, and Susan Ware—has been downright transformative, critiquing just about every word of this manuscript. I am also grateful to colleagues and friends at Harvard, including

Janet Beizer, Lizabeth Cohen, Nancy Cott, and Dean of Arts and Humanities Diana Sorensen. Judith Clurman, who directed musical performances in Harvard's Bernstein festival, has been an invaluable source of information about American musical theater and of performer contacts. And my dear friend Carol Southard, a theater aficionado, has shared her immense knowledge from years of experience.

Interviews are central to this book, and I am grateful to those who shared memories of a Broadway production from long ago. They include Sono Osato Elmaleh and her husband, Victor Elmaleh; George Gaynes; Jean Handy; Billie Allen Henderson and her niece Candace Allen; Everett Lee and his son Everett Lee Jr.; Aza Bard McKenzie and her son Richard; Allyn Ann McLerie; Phyllis Newman; Harold Prince; and Stephen Sondheim.

I benefited from the advice of exceptional library professionals, beginning with Mark Eden Horowitz, senior music specialist in the Music Division of the Library of Congress. Mark processed the immense Leonard Bernstein Collection, and he has been proactive on multiple fronts: contacting me when new archival materials arrived, suggesting obscure corners of the collection that I might otherwise have missed, and sharing the text of his own lecture about On the Town, which he presented at Catholic University in 2011. I am also grateful to Sarah Adams, Liza Vick, Robert Dennis, Andrew Wilson, and Kerry Carwile Masteller of the Eda Kuhn Loeb Music Library at Harvard, as well as Frederic Burchsted at Harvard's Widener Library. I have worked most closely with Liza, who has a wizard's gift for untangling knotty research questions. Other librarians and archivists who have generously answered queries include Heidi Coleman, photo archivist at the Noguchi Museum; Sylvia Curtis, dance librarian at the University of California at Santa Barbara; Jeni Dahmus, archivist of the Juilliard School; Emily Ferrigno, of the Yale Music Library; Cynthia Fife-Townsel, of the Harsh Research Collection at the Chicago Public Library; Scott M. Forsythe, of the National Archives at Chicago; Gino Francesconi, of the Carnegie Hall Archives and Museum; Laurel Fujisawa, of the Chicago Japanese American Historical Society; Jane Gottlieb, librarian at the Juilliard School; Barbara Haws, director of the New York Philharmonic Archives; Karen Kanemoto, of the Japanese American Service Committee Legacy Center Archives and Library in Chicago; Doug Litts, of the Smithsonian American Art Museum; Anne Mar, assistant college archivist, Occidental College; Jean Mishima, president, Chicago Japanese American Historical Society; Jane Nakasako, of the Hirasaki National Resource Center at the Japanese American National Museum in Los Angeles; Charles Perrier, of the Jerome Robbins Dance Collection, New York Public Library; Rosemarie Romano, of the Norman F. Bourke Memorial Library, Cayuga Community College, Auburn, New York; Robert Sloane, art reference librarian, Chicago Public Library; Martin Tuohy, National Archives and Records Administration, Great Lakes Region; Frank Villella, archivist, Chicago Symphony Orchestra; and Zack Wilske, USCIS History Office, U.S. Citizenship and Immigration Services.

Thanks are also due to the following: Samuel Baltimore, independent researcher at the Library of Congress; Tamar Barzel, Wellesley College; Paul De Angelis, editor; Sylvia Chong, American Studies, University of Virginia; Joanna Dee Das, Ph.D.

candidate at Columbia University; Eddy Determeyer, Dutch jazz scholar who shared an interview with J. Flash Riley; Annegret Fauser, University of North Carolina; Aryeh Finklestein, cantor at Congregation Mishkan Tefila, Newton, Massachusetts; Stacy Frierson, Promotion Department of Boosey & Hawkes; David Hajdu, biographer of Billy Strayhorn, who provided an interview transcript with Dorcas Neal, wife of the dancer Frank Neal; Deborah Jowitt, biographer of Jerome Robbins, who generously shared contact information for dancers in *On the Town*; Bruce Kellner, executor of the Carl Van Vechten Estate; Paul Laird, University of Kansas; Ingrid Monson, Harvard University; Howard Pollack, University of Houston; Larry Rosenthal, scholar of left-wing literature at Wellesley College; Allen Shawn, who was writing his own Bernstein book as mine emerged; Steve Takasugi, Boston-based composer who shared insights about the Japanese American experience; Jim Steichen, Ph.D. candidate at Princeton University, who gave me a tip about interviewing Aza Bard; Frank van Straten, director emeritus of the Performing Arts Museum in Melbourne, who shared information about the baritone Robert Chisholm; and Michael Zande, company manager of *Encores!* at City Center in New York. I want to single out Greg Robinson, Université du Québec à Montréal and *Nichi Bei Times*, who is an eminent historian of Japanese Americans. He responded with exceptional generosity to an email from a stranger (me), sharing research tips about Sono Osato, her father, and the Japanese American community during World War II.

In a busy academic life, fellowship support is essential in order to clear time for research and writing. I started this book—in an exploratory way—while on the faculty of the College of William and Mary, which solidly supports research, and Harvard has also provided crucial assistance. I was fortunate to receive a Fellowship for University Teachers from the National Endowment for the Humanities and a residency at the Susan and Donald Newhouse Center for the Humanities at Wellesley College. Tim Peltason was director of the Newhouse Center during my year there, and he created a lively interdisciplinary community. The film theorist Laura Mulvey, Birkbeck College, University of London, and legal scholar Margaret Burnham, Northeastern University, were also in residence that year, and I learned much from conversations with them. I finished this project under a fellowship from the Guggenheim Foundation, at the same time as I began another.

Clearing permissions has been a daunting task in a book with multiple protagonists. I extend special thanks to Marie Carter, Leonard Bernstein Office; Jessica Conflitti, Warner/Chappell Music; Mark Merriman, Estate of Betty Comden; Christopher Pennington, Jerome Robbins Rights Trust; and John White, Boosey & Hawkes.

Many Harvard students have been involved in this book, both directly and indirectly. Elizabeth Craft compiled the discography and videography in the concluding appendix. Emily Abrams Ansari worked as teaching fellow for the Bernstein seminar, while Ryan Raul Bañagale, Sheryl Kaskowitz, and Drew Massey were galvanizing forces in that class. Marc Gidal offered advice about Latin American musical styles. A number of students—both undergraduates and graduate students—have either helped with research or simply been available for stimulating conversations about Bernstein or American music in general. In addition to those mentioned above, they include Davide Ceriani, Glenda Goodman, Jack Hamilton, Aaron Hatley, Hannah Lewis, Lucille Mok, Matthew Mugmon, Benjamin Ory, Paige Pavonne, Anna Rice, Anne Searcy, Michael Uy, Stephen Vider, and Micah Wittmer. In the final stretch, Monica Hershberger and Samuel Parler gave expert assistance with checking footnotes.

In a generous gesture of friendship, R. Allen Lott read proofs of the book with a keen attention to detail. I am also grateful to Saralyn Fosnight for help with proofreading.

Finally, I want to thank my family, who makes everything possible. That includes my mother, Helen Oja; my parents-in-law, Carolyn and Len Tucker; and my children, Zoe and Wynn, who are boundless sources of joy. Zoe transcribed some interviews for this book. This project was under way as she and Wynn were in high school, then college. I wrap up this litany of gratitude with a shout-out to William Lazonick for the model of his brilliant and ethical scholarship and for his patience in listening to me chatter on about Lenny and Betty and Adolph and Jerry.

BERNSTEIN MEETS BROADWAY

INTRODUCTION

* * *

I was deeply immersed in *West Side Story* when I fell for *On the Town*. That is, while writing a book that encompassed the most famous Broadway musical by Leonard Bernstein—if not the most famous of all time—I began a series of extraordinary conversations with participants in *On the Town*, the first Broadway collaboration of Bernstein, Jerome Robbins, Betty Comden, and Adolph Green. It debuted in 1944. *On the Town* is by no means as well known as *West Side Story*, but it laid the groundwork for Bernstein's influential theater style, and it raises unexpected insights into the historical moment when it first appeared. I talked with the ballet dancer Sono Osato, who starred in the show and is now elderly and living in New York City. I also spoke with the New York–based dancer, actress, and director Billie Allen and with the conductor Everett Lee, who settled in Sweden decades ago. All three brought me face-to-face with a forgotten side of *On the Town*: it employed a mixed-race cast as a way of tackling Jim Crow segregation, not through a plot with a message but rather through decisions in casting and representation. Osato is Japanese American, and Allen and Lee are both African American. I wanted to understand the complex questions raised by the show's first production, and *On the Town* became the centerpiece of this book. While there have been many important studies of black performing artists—reflecting wide-ranging disciplinary perspectives and especially focusing on jazz—little has been written about the process of desegregation as it took place across different types of performance, including the Broadway musical. *On the Town* provides an opportunity to jump-start that history.

In the show's original production, Sono Osato starred as Ivy Smith, a character shaped with an intentionally ambiguous racial identity, and she did so while her father, a Japanese national, was battling wartime detainment by the U.S. government. Few Asian Americans had preceded her on Broadway. Halfway into the show's run, Everett Lee took over at the podium, becoming one of the first African Americans to conduct an all-white orchestra in a mainstream Broadway production. Lee had the ironic task of leading the orchestra every night in "The Star-Spangled Banner," an affirmation of patriotism that opened Broadway musicals during the war, and he did so even as his rights as a citizen were constricted on a daily basis by a northern version of Jim Crow segregation, which limited access to education, jobs, and public spaces. Billie Allen joined *On the Town*'s mixed-race dance chorus toward the end of its Broadway run, then for its road tour. That chorus was deployed in ways that pushed back against racial stereotypes common at the time on stage and screen. *On the Town* eschewed blackface, and it steered clear of bandanas, maids, and butlers. Instead, black dancers in sailor costumes stood alongside their white comrades, and there was mixed-race dancing, some of which required training in ballet. These staging decisions fabricated a vision of urban interracial fellowship. They imagined an alternative to the segregated U.S. military of World War II, and they offered an early case of what has become known as color-blind casting. Yet there were limits to the show's daring: its script did not include anti-racist rhetoric, and it did not specify any of the racially progressive staging decisions that were central to the original production.

In this book, *On the Town* becomes the hub of a cultural history that reconstructs a collaborative, activist performance community at the height of World War II. It does so by exploring the work of a talented team of twentysomethings who were establishing themselves in New York City. Bernstein, Robbins, Comden, and Green were then young and undiscovered—by no means the creative titans they later became—and they launched *On the Town* by attracting the veteran director George Abbott to guide their vision. Ultimately, Robbins and Bernstein collaborated on *West Side Story*; Robbins was a central force in *The King and I*, *Gypsy*, and *Fiddler on the Roof*; and Comden and Green wrote scripts and/or lyrics for a string of major Broadway shows and Hollywood films, including *Singin' in the Rain*, *Wonderful Town*, and *Bells Are Ringing*. They excelled in devising sophisticated works for a broad audience.

Back in the early 1940s, however, these artists were emerging voices, filled with the zest and daring of youth. All were the children of Jewish immigrants, and all embraced left-wing passions of the Depression and World War II years. With limberness and imagination, they delighted in crossing artistic boundaries, darting between concert halls, ballet companies, Broadway theaters, and nightclubs. At the same time, they seized opportunities to work in mixed-race venues, and they used comedy to inject left-wing politics into their art. Collectively and individually, they shaped an edgy style that conveyed progressive political visions while attaining box-office success, and they did so in an era just before the repressions of the Red Scare dampened such idealistic creative spirits.

On the Town was by no means a one-off phenomenon. Rather, it was the product of two streams of creative collaboration, growing out of the ballet *Fancy Free* and out of nightclub skits developed by The Revuers, a comedy team that included Comden and Green and sometimes Bernstein. This unlikely-seeming combination of performance genres and venues is central to the story told here. *Fancy Free* was the very first collaboration between Bernstein and Robbins. With the same basic plotline that was soon to inspire *On the Town*, the ballet featured sailors on shore leave in wartime New York City, aiming to capture the city's street life and its potential for a devil-may-care fling during a reprieve from battles on land and at sea. Its premiere took place at the old Metropolitan Opera House on April 18, 1944, just short of nine months before *On the Town*, and it was a surprise hit, emerging in an era when dance enjoyed enormous popularity in the United States. "We were shocked opening night. We were absolutely floored by it,"

Robbins recalled years later about the debut of their first ballet. "We didn't know it was going to be what it was.... Because suddenly where I had—Up until that point where I was sort of wanting to get in, suddenly I was not only in, but sought after.... It was a shocking change. From nothing to—to everything."[1]

A few years before *Fancy Free*, The Revuers had launched their nightclub act at the Village Vanguard. Made up of performers who included not only Comden and Green but also Judy Tuvim, who was soon to gain fame under the name Judy Holliday, The Revuers wrote and performed their own material, and Bernstein was occasionally their pianist. Their skits were essentially mini-musicals. As they struggled to gain traction for their compelling comedic style, they ventured into radio, recordings, early television, and film. The group attracted considerable attention, but it never took off in a resounding way, resulting in what Comden later described as a "precarious and terminal nightclub career."[2]

All this artistic activity took place during a global conflict that directly affected most American families. A major international port during World War II, New York City took measures to avert enemy attack, and in 1944 the lights remained dimmed along Broadway at night, as they had been since the spring immediately after Pearl Harbor. At the same time, European exiles had flooded into the city, including the Ballet Russe de Monte Carlo and the composer Kurt Weill; both had a direct impact on figures involved with *On the Town*. Emigrés also brought with them a European model of sophisticated nightclubs without racial barriers.

This collaborative moment was possible because Bernstein, Green, and Robbins were exempted from military service. The Selective Training and Service Act of 1940 required male citizens between twenty-one and thirty-six to register for the draft, and the age span widened to between eighteen and sixty-five after Pearl Harbor.[3] Even though historical memory renders World War II as a time of national unity, the draft yielded striking inequities, and not all eligible males served. Two of the military's thorniest issues centered around racial segregation of the troops and a policy of screening out gays during psychological evaluations at induction centers.[4] Many artists and entertainers enlisted, such as composer Marc Blitzstein, bandleader Artie Shaw, and dancer Gene Kelly. Yet there were famous exemptions, notably Frank Sinatra.[5] In Bernstein's case, he was classified as IV-F because of asthma. In the summer of 1941, he wrote to his good friend Aaron Copland suggesting that his classification had been granted to support his professional aspirations: "The particular doctor who examined me insisted on preserving the cultural foundations of [the] USA, not killing all the musicians. And so I am in class IV! Go, attend to your career, said the great M.D., & that will be yr. greatest service."[6] Robbins was also classified IV-F, in his case because of sexual orientation. When asked in an interview with his draft board if he "ever had a homosexual experience," Robbins apparently replied, "Last night," thus triggering an exclusion.[7] For reasons not entirely clear, Adolph Green was exempted from service as well, while Betty Comden's husband, Siegfried Schutzman (who later took the name Steven Kyle), enlisted and served.[8]

As the "Good War" raged on, Americans from all walks of life pitched in to contribute, if not through military service then through citizen-initiated projects such as Bundles for Britain, in which American women knitted sweaters to be shipped to Allied soldiers overseas. Bernstein, Robbins, Comden, and Green supported the troops through performance, doing so in an era of high popularity for war themes, whether in musicals such as Irving Berlin's *This Is the Army* (1941) or films such as *Casablanca, Thousands Cheer,* or *Stage Door Canteen* (all 1943). *Fancy Free* and *On the Town* both contributed to this broad-based civic engagement. There was a twist, however: at the same time as these two works asserted patriotism, they also registered dissent, albeit with breathtaking virtuosity and zany comedy.

• • •

Bernstein Meets Broadway: Collaborative Art in a Time of War unfolds in three overarching sections. Ballet and Nightclubs puts high and low art side by side, exploring the energetic boundary crossings that characterized both the ballet *Fancy Free* and comedy skits by The Revuers. With *Fancy Free*, I argue that the show delivered gendered messages grounded in a tight network of personal and professional relationships, and I consider the emergence of Bernstein's distinctive voice as a composer in relation to Robbins's choreographic style. Nightclub skits by The Revuers are then explored in terms of their politically inflected brand of comedy and their strong tie to new media. A nexus of aesthetic and ideological threads bound together *Fancy Free* and The Revuers, including montage, parody, dynamic collaborations, and sheer delight in blurring cultural categories, genres, and ethnic groups.

Broadway and Racial Politics, the book's second major section, puts *On the Town* at the center of a multifaceted cultural history. A chronicle of the show's genesis sets the scene for the ensuing chapters, exploring how its key personnel nimbly navigated the high-low continuum and how the creative process unfolded. I then pose a series of questions about the struggle for racial equality in performance during World War II. What did it mean to have a mixed-race cast in 1944? Who were the performers of color in *On the Town*, and how did they get artistic training within the constraints of Jim Crow? Collective biography becomes a means of probing those issues. First, the remarkable story of Sono Osato intertwines her father's persecution and detention during World War II as a Japanese national, her history with the Ballet Russe de Monte Carlo, and the handling of her racial identity in *On the Town*. Then I consider the desegregation of *On the Town* amid a cluster of signal moments in the racial history of performance in New York City. When the show opened, to cite one striking example, no black singer had yet been featured in a production of the Metropolitan Opera—a barrier that did not fall until 1955. Biographies of the African American performers in *On the Town* then probe the careers of Everett Lee, Royce Wallace, Frank Neal, Flash Riley, and Billie Allen, demonstrating how African American performing artists outside of jazz navigated Jim Crow segregation. During World War II, African American critics reviewed contemporary theater, concerts, and nightclubs in black newspapers, and they perceived an America different from the one covered by their white colleagues at the *New York Times* or *Chicago Tribune*. They relentlessly reported to their readership—that is, the black community— about racial advances and injustices onstage, and they wrote revealingly about black artists. Musical Style, the book's final section, ponders Bernstein's compositional voice in *On the Town*, a voice that ultimately became known around the world. Confronting the norms of Broadway, Bernstein conceived a style that relished unexpected conjunctions. The language of swing and the blues inflected his music, as did parody techniques developed by The Revuers. Allusions to opera and operetta also appeared, yielding an aesthetic of montage. Whether writing for a ballet or for Broadway, Bernstein approached orchestras as flexible entities, at times fulfilling traditional expectations and at others reconfiguring the instrumentation to simulate a swing band or Latin ensemble. A final chapter circles back to nightclubs, with a focus on the club-hopping scene in Act II of *On the Town*. Not only did that scene reflect early experiences of The Revuers, but it also went through extensive revisions, in part to grapple with racial representation. In the process, it exposed much about the tension between idealistic political goals and pragmatic decisions made during a fast-paced editing process.

● ● ●

All in all, this book explores *On the Town* through the multilevel collaborative process that brought it into being, arguing that the high-low interchange and interracial networks reflected among its conductors, dancers, singers, and crew mirrored—even empowered—its hybrid aesthetic. A broad-ranging cultural history grows out of close readings, extensive archival research, interviews with surviving cast members, and a detailed exploration of performances. An interartistic framework results, bringing classical ballet, nightclubs, musical theater, social dance, concert music, opera, and radio into conversation with one another. Many central figures in the show regularly crossed boundaries as they worked in related environments. Bernstein is at the center of the action, but he becomes part of a collective process—enough so that the narrative moves past him for extended periods. These young artists were experimenting with ways to fuse commercially successful entertainment with socially responsible content and casting decisions, finding amiable means of encoding themes considered transgressive in wartime America. In the lingo of today's academic discourse, this is a microhistory—that is, a study that focuses intensely on a group of key historical moments to illuminate broad-ranging cultural and artistic questions.

Research for this book has been as diverse and adaptive as the subject itself, and I found myself forging new modes of archival exploration as one type of source led to another. Many of the sources are both unconventional and newly accessible through the digital revolution. Even a decade ago, I could not have written a book with such a detailed focus on race in performance. The personal archives of Leonard Bernstein, Betty Comden, Adolph Green, and Jerome Robbins have been catalogued fully, and the papers of Peggy Clark provided an important source for reconstructing the details of who did what onstage, especially through her remarkable production flow charts. Most important, digitization has opened up access to historically black newspapers published across the United States and to entertainment-industry magazines such as *Variety*, *Billboard*, and *The Stage*, making these publications fully searchable for the first time. These developments have taken place since the mid-1990s—accelerating even more since the early

2000s—and they have resulted in a massive democratizing of research, making it possible to gain information across racial boundaries. As detailed data surface from black newspapers, a new vision emerges of the world of performance, exposing the degree to which white viewpoints have dominated historical perceptions. Finding biographical information about figures such as the black singer Lonny Jackson, for example, who played a cop in *On the Town*, previously would have required cranking through thousands of pages of microfilm, randomly searching for needles in haystacks. With digitization—and the good fortune to be connected with a major university library that can afford subscriptions to those services—a researcher can now cast a wide net and turn up surprising results.

A fundamental goal for me has been to shape this book, in part, as a kind of historical ethnography in which the voices of the era's participants could be heard. I have tried to be especially aware of representing as broad a range of voices as possible. As research progressed, a matrix of print sources and personal relationships grew before my eyes, and nonlinear tangents abounded. Archival research led to interviews with surviving cast members and their families, especially Billie Allen, Everett Lee, Phyllis Newman, and Sono Osato, and engagement with audio and film sources as well as radio transcripts transported me into the realm of American entertainment during World War II. Viewing a silent film of *Fancy Free*, shot from the balcony of the old Metropolitan Opera House, was especially moving.

Putting *On the Town*, *Fancy Free*, and The Revuers side by side opens a fresh perspective on the performing arts in New York City during World War II. It reveals the fitful process through which racial desegregation was being achieved in the performing arts, and it provides a case study of the impact of Japanese internment policies on the world of performance. When Bernstein, Comden, Green, and Robbins set out to desegregate their first Broadway show, they were by no means cashing in on power and celebrity accrued over the course of long careers. Rather, they were newcomers taking a daring but controlled leap, with no guarantee of what the outcome might be.

BALLET AND NIGHTCLUBS

1
YOUTHFUL CELEBRITY AND PERSONAL FREEDOM
Breaking Out with *Fancy Free*

* * *

But Jerry's Fancy Free—*when you left the theater you saw the same thing that you saw onstage. Same kind of behavior. And all these innocent boys coming, swarming into New York. They'd never been there, I mean. It just captured the time we were in really brilliantly for someone who was—what was he? Twenty-four, twenty-five years old.*
—Sono Osato, the original Ivy in On the Town

It may not be blank verse, but it is indisputably art.
—*John Martin, dance critic for the* New York Times

On April 18, 1944, a rousing new ballet appeared in New York City. Titled *Fancy Free*, it lasted twenty-five minutes and featured three sailors cutting loose in the city. "The ballet," as Bernstein later put it, was "strictly young America of 1944."[1] World War II was in full force, with the Allies gaining ground in Europe, and D-Day took place six weeks later. Angling for women in a bar, the sailors of *Fancy Free* faced the inconvenient fact that only two gals appeared to be available, and the men competed to attract their attention. The sailors were also unabashedly close to one another. At times they migrated across the stage as a tight unit, almost cartoon-like. At others they executed dazzling solos to captivate their prey and entertain themselves, seeming a bit like adolescents showing off. They ingeniously mixed movements from ballet, vaudeville, gymnastics, social dance, and street life. Popeye met Petipa as American popular culture mingled with the legacy of Russian ballet. The sailors' performances were virtuosic, and they played for laughs.

Fancy Free is "a rare little genre masterpiece—young, human, tender and funny," enthused John Martin, dance critic of the *New York Times*.[2] The work was produced by Ballet Theatre, an American troupe that was then barely five years old. Audiences responded so ecstatically that extra performances were added, and the ballet's twenty-five-year-old creators, composer Leonard Bernstein and choreographer Jerome Robbins, became overnight sensations, with coverage in New York's major newspapers and across the country. *Time* magazine dubbed *Fancy*

Free "the surprise hit of Manhattan's booming ballet season."[3] From the perspective of the twenty-first century, when ballet, opera, orchestras, and other exalted institutions of high art struggle to retain cultural capital, it is striking to reflect on an era when a new ballet could become a popular hit. During World War II "ballet in the United States had a bright moment of eagerness and glory," observed the esteemed dance critic Edwin Denby. There was "a burst of dance talent."[4]

Just as remarkable as its success, *Fancy Free* thrived on negotiating multiple borders simultaneously. *Fancy Free* was about twentysomethings in a time of war, about transience, risk taking, and the sheer fun of popular culture. It focused on New York City, balancing high art with popular entertainment to produce a here-and-now aesthetic. As its sailors danced arm in arm enacting a primary plotline about the pursuit of women, they also hovered in a hazy space between gay and heterosexual encounters, and this "modern, free-style, jive ballet" was conceived within a historically European artistic realm that crossed racial boundaries.[5] It incorporated a recording of the blues at the opening—thus transporting pop-music technology onto the hallowed stage of the Metropolitan Opera House—and it engaged with Afro-Cuban traditions. Even though *Fancy Free*'s crossing of racial boundaries was modest in scope, it paved the way for a different set of bold steps in *On the Town*—steps that also were delivered in a burst of raucous entertainment.

Fancy Free has since become a classic of American ballet. After its premiere, the dance remained in continuous performance by Ballet Theatre, with a number of landmarks over time. In 1946, Decca issued a recording conducted by Bernstein, which filled four 78s and included extraordinary liner notes by Agnes de Mille, choreographer of the ballet *Rodeo* and of the musical *Oklahoma!*[6] Slightly older than Robbins, de Mille was a strong role model and mentor for him. In 1949 Ballet Theatre reassembled the original cast of *Fancy Free* onstage.[7] A decade later, the work traveled to Moscow with the American Ballet Theatre (ABT), as the company had been newly named, as part of a Cold War cultural exchange program, and in 1974 ABT celebrated the work's thirtieth birthday.[8] Then in 1980, New York City Ballet staged a revival billed as a "facsimile of the original."[9] Over the years, *Fancy Free* has attracted some of the great male stars of dance, including Mikhail Baryshnikov, Fernando Bujones, Eliot Feld, Peter Martins, and Damian Woetzel. It remains in the active repertory of ballet companies around the world. Within scholarship and criticism about dance, *Fancy Free* has been discussed at regular intervals.[10]

The first production of *Fancy Free* is central to the story told here, opening up issues of performance, collaborative creativity, and personal expression. The work's balletic plot and music are considered side by side for the first time. *Fancy Free* met established expectations for a new ballet of its day while amiably pushing back against social and artistic norms. Its rollicking sense of artistic fusion grew out of the personal and professional flexibilities of its creative team, and it had the capacity to tell different stories to different members of the audience. In a city coping with the disruptions of war, *Fancy Free* beamed out the energy and progressive optimism of youth, displaying onstage some of the "social readjustment" that war could yield.[11] In the process, it launched the stage careers of two of the twentieth century's most powerful artistic figures.

GENESIS OF A HIT: BERNSTEIN AND ROBBINS
EMERGE ONSTAGE

An exuberant sense of shared inspiration emanated from *Fancy Free*, and its youthful energy struck critics as distinctive. "*Fancy Free* was prepared and executed in an exemplary spirit of collaboration among friends who were all about the same age," wrote the dance historian George Amberg in 1949, five years after the ballet's premiere. "They were fully successful," he continued, "for the ballet conveys the impression of being all of a piece and of one mind, tightly coherent and perfectly integrated, from the opening sounds of a melancholy voice to the last wild chase into the wings."[12] It was a "happy collaboration," declared Agnes de Mille.[13]

In 1943, as *Fancy Free* was being developed, Leonard Bernstein and Jerome Robbins—the two linchpins in the collaboration—were rising to prominence with lightning speed. They shared parallel family histories as children of Ukrainian Jewish immigrants, with fathers who had successfully established businesses in the United States, and they also had a love of theater deep in their veins. *Fancy Free*'s other central creative force was the scene designer Oliver Smith, whose career had recently been launched with set designs for *Rodeo* (1942).

Bernstein produced some of his best work as a collaborative composer, and his musical experiences fluidly blended high art and popular culture from the very beginning. Jewish artistic networks were crucial to the connections that Bernstein made, as was his adolescent experience of listening to a wide range of programs on the radio. He deliberately cultivated an ecumenical aesthetic, and his dashing good looks and charisma onstage made him a natural celebrity from the moment he emerged in public.

Born in 1918 and raised in Boston, Bernstein studied classical piano like many upper-middle-class young people of his day, and he also grew passionate about musical theater, primarily through directing summertime neighborhood productions near his family's second home in Sharon, Massachusetts. Jewish summer camps were also part of the mix. During the summer of 1937, Bernstein served as a counselor at Camp Onota in the Berkshires. There he directed musical activities, staging productions of Gilbert and Sullivan's *The Pirates of Penzance* and Gershwin's *Of Thee I Sing*, and he met his lifelong friend Adolph Green.[14] Theater also became an important part of his undergraduate experience at Harvard (1935–39), most notably the final semester of his senior year, when Bernstein directed a student production of Marc Blitzstein's angry yet witty *The Cradle Will Rock*, which was then just two years old. This production brought Bernstein into the realm of agitprop—that is, theater intended as agitating propaganda—and it acquainted him firsthand with Blitzstein's distinctive compositional voice, which became a potent model for Bernstein's own music. He then completed a master's degree in conducting at the Curtis Institute of Music in Philadelphia.

One set of sketches for *Fancy Free* includes a page titled "7 Solos by Coleman Hawkins/Leonard Bernstein," and it attests to Bernstein's strong ties to the worlds of jazz and popular music. Bernstein arranged these solos by the famous

African American tenor saxophonist during the winter of 1942–43—three years out of Harvard—when he worked as an arranger and staff composer for Harms-Witmark, the country's foremost publisher of popular music.[15] Bernstein earned $25 a week and published under the name "Lenny Amber."[16] In addition to transcribing jazz improvisations, he also made piano arrangements of music by Raymond Scott, the composer and bandleader whose music appeared in a slew of early cartoons. Bernstein had enjoyed Scott's music even before reaching New York City, as correspondence with his sister, Shirley, shows. The two siblings loved a good joke. Around 1940, Shirley wrote to her brother about Scott's "wonderful" radio performances, encouraging him to tune in to Scott's *Concert in Rhythm* on Tuesday nights at 9:30 p.m. on WEEI. It "begins like a symphonic concert, orchestra tuning up, low-voiced announcer," Shirley described. "He says, 'The audience applauds as Mr. Scott mounts the podium. He lifts his baton.'...At which time the orchestra strikes up a wonderful arrangement of 'Just a Gigolo,' a sensation when he swings out instead of soberly conducting a sedate overture."[17]

For Bernstein, the conventions of classical music and the fast-changing trends of the commercial world mixed freely. At the same time as he placed high value on entertainment, comedy, and broad-based appeal, he was trying to establish himself as a composer of classical music and conductor of symphony orchestras. "I do get diffused," wrote Bernstein to Aaron Copland in a 1943 letter outlining the broad-ranging opportunities he was juggling in the period leading up to *Fancy Free*.[18] A few years later, Bernstein recalled the diversity of his activities in this early period. "I had a job with a jazz-publishing firm in New York. I had always liked and played jazz, and now it came in handy," Bernstein wrote. "I wasn't wildly happy, but I was eating....Of course, it [sic] wasn't always just practicing [at the piano]. I loved to improvise, to pick out jazz that I heard on the radio, and to read—anything and everything I could lay hands on—symphonies, Italian operas, marches, or Tip-Toe through the Tulips, which was the great favorite of the time."[19]

At the same time, Bernstein's career as a conductor gained momentum, especially when he became assistant conductor of the New York Philharmonic in 1943. He made a sensational debut on November 14 of that year, when Bruno Walter, the orchestra's music director, called in sick, and Bernstein stepped in to conduct a concert that was broadcast nationally over the radio. His performance was so electrifying that it was reviewed on the front page of the *New York Times*.[20] Bernstein also composed concert music, and Symphony No. 1, *Jeremiah*, his first major orchestral work, had its premiere in January 1944, with Bernstein conducting the Pittsburgh Symphony Orchestra.

Jerome Robbins was born the same year as Bernstein, and he brought to *Fancy Free* a comparable background that mingled high and low. Robbins had formative experiences at Camp Tamiment in the Pocono Mountains, "the summer borscht-circuit place," as he later called it.[21] The camp included the Tamiment Playhouse, which Robbins recalled as "an extraordinary training field." There he learned to mix and match, linking ballet, entertainment, comedy, and theater. "We had to do three different shows each week," Robbins continued. "There was a big revue on Saturday night. There was a nightclub show—on Thursday night, I think. And on one other night there was a sort of vaudeville-style show."[22] At Tamiment, Robbins made his first attempts at choreography. "That's where I first started to do little sketches of things," he recalled.[23]

As a young professional, before working in ballet, Robbins danced in the chorus of several Broadway shows, including *Great Lady*, a musical by Frederick Loewe that ran for a couple of weeks in December 1938 and starred Norma Terris, who eleven years earlier had played the role of Magnolia in the original production of *Show Boat*. *Great Lady* was "where I first met Mr. Balanchine," Robbins remembered, referring to the great Russian choreographer George Balanchine, who had immigrated to the United States five years earlier.[24] The dance chorus of *Great Lady* included Alicia Alonso, Nora Kaye, and other dancers who, like Robbins, became major figures in American ballet. Robbins also appeared with some of the same dancers in *Stars in Your Eyes* of 1939, with lyrics by Dorothy Fields and music by Arthur Schwartz.[25]

In the summer of 1940, Robbins made his first appearance in the corps of Ballet Theatre, a company that had been formed the previous year and "marked a culmination of a series of efforts to establish an American ballet."[26] As dance experienced a wave of popularity, American choreographers such as Eugene Loring and Agnes de Mille were producing new works to broad-based acclaim. At the same time, the interactions among American and Russian artists fueled the growth of ballet in the United States. Ballet Theatre established a reputation for producing ballets of considerable "dramatic power," as the critic Irving Kolodin noted, making it possible for an individual star to realize her potential "as a kind of actress-in-the-dance."[27] Amid this surge of new productions and young performers, Robbins stood out as startlingly gifted, with a delicious sense of humor onstage. In 1941 he starred in Ballet Theatre's new production of *Three Virgins and a Devil*, choreographed by de Mille.[28] There he was hailed "for the style and authority" that he brought to his role as the Youth.[29] The next year, he danced the lead role in Ballet Theatre's production of *Petrushka*, with its famous score by Igor Stravinsky. Robbins learned this iconic role from Mikhail Fokine, the work's original choreographer, who was among the war refugees in New York City.[30] "He liked me and encouraged me tremendously and gave me things to dance and taught me Petroushka," Robbins recalled of Fokine. "In all fairness I must say I was the third Petroushka in the line of Petroushkas when he first taught it ... and he was very inspiring to work with."[31]

During these early years with Ballet Theatre, Robbins proposed a series of ideas for new productions, without success. "Well, I had sort of been propagandizing Ballet Theatre to do ballets, and when I think about them now they were rather ambitious," Robbins offered decades later. "They were four-act, full-length, mostly Americana themes somehow or other, and who was it, I think Chujoy, who said 'why don't you get together a small ballet with a few people.'"[32] Anatole Chujoy was a leading New York–based dance writer and editor.

In June 1943, when Robbins "had almost given up hope of ever having a real chance," as de Mille recounted, he successfully pitched the idea for *Fancy Free* to the management of Ballet Theatre.[33] Over the course of the following months, Robbins looked for a composer to realize his vision; at this point, he did not know Bernstein. "I took it to a lot of people who turned it down," Robbins recalled.[34] His notebooks for *Fancy Free* show that he considered quite a range of composers. They included Paul Nordoff, who had composed for Martha Graham's company; Norman Dello Joio and Vincent Persichetti, who were primarily classical composers with an accessible style; Les Baxter, who was a pop musician and composer, singing in the 1940s with Mel Tormé's Mel-Tones; and Jerome Moross, Alec Wilder, and Morton Gould, who were crossover figures, with work combining Broadway, pop songs, and classical traditions.[35]

Robbins credited Persichetti with recommending Bernstein as a good match. Bernstein, at the time, was living "in the honeycomb" of Carnegie Hall. "At the end of a long corridor, noisy with voice and piano teachers, [he] kept a small studio," recounted de Mille.[36] Sometimes he played for dance classes.[37] At first Robbins made an unsuccessful attempt to locate Bernstein; then he obtained a correct address from stage designer Oliver Smith. As Robbins later recalled, Smith introduced the two men: "Lenny played me part of his yet unplayed *Jeremiah* symphony. I gave him my scenario to read. We decided to go ahead and work."[38] Robbins's notes for *Fancy Free* list Bernstein's address as "Carnegie Hall, N.Y./Studio 803."[39]

On November 14, 1943—by coincidence the very day when Bernstein made his unexpected debut with the New York Philharmonic—a notice about the collaboration of Bernstein and Robbins appeared in the *New York Times*.[40] Three days earlier, Bernstein had written to J. Alden Talbot, managing director of Ballet Theatre: "I have begun the music of the ballet and I am suddenly teeming with ideas. I think it is going to be a lot of fun."[41] He and Robbins had no commission fee to subsidize the time involved in composition and choreography. Rather, they squeezed creative activity into busy performance schedules. A manuscript short score is dated December 30, 1943, and the published score gives the work's ultimate completion date as April 10, 1944.[42] For the final two months of 1943, Robbins was on tour with Ballet Theatre, traveling through the Northeast and Midwest, and Bernstein was absorbing the sudden fame from his premiere with the Philharmonic.[43] In early 1944, Bernstein was also on the move, traveling to Pittsburgh for the premiere of his *Jeremiah* Symphony in January, then to Boston three weeks later for a second performance of the work with the Boston Symphony Orchestra. Robbins's typescript ballet scenario interpolated verbal descriptions of the music, carefully explaining to Bernstein exactly how the music should sound. There were indications like "Fast, explosive, jolly, rollicking. A bang-away start" and "Slow...relaxed, music should have literal meanings as far as specific action is concerned."[44] During this period, Bernstein, as his biographer Humphrey Burton recounts, "made piano duet disc recordings of the numbers as he wrote them and mailed them to Robbins."[45] Aaron Copland served as second pianist on those recordings. At this point, there was no hint of the stunning success that lay ahead for Bernstein and Robbins with *Fancy Free*. They were so unproven as collaborators that they did not sign a final contract with Ballet Theatre until April 4, 1944, just two weeks before the ballet had its debut. Robbins received $10 for each public performance, and he was still using his parents' address in New Jersey.[46]

Fancy Free "opened cold without so much as a preview," reported *Dance Magazine*, and the audience response was extraordinary.[47] "So untried was the ballet," continued the same critic, "that the applause and laughter that broke out spontaneously from the audience during the performance came as a distinct surprise. Nor had rehearsals prepared anyone for the tremendous ovation." "The set drew a gasp and applause," recalled de Mille. "The volume of the reaction nearly threw them [the dancers] off their counts.... At the conclusion there was a genuine ovation with approximately twenty curtains and a house cheering from its heart."[48] The work was "so big a hit," chronicled Edwin Denby, "that the young participants all looked a little dazed as they took their bows."[49]

Fancy Free scored such a success that Ballet Theatre extended its season by a couple of weeks so that the work could be shown an additional twelve times, with Bernstein conducting. "I'm still not over it," exclaimed Bernstein in a letter to Aaron Copland. "Hurok has added numerous extra performances of FF & I'm to conduct them all, & for a fabulous fee."[50] Then manager of Ballet Theatre, Sol Hurok was one of the country's preeminent managers of the performing arts. According to a report in *Time*, *Fancy Free* was also performed for "troops at camps around Manhattan."[51] One year later the ballet was acclaimed in *Dance*

Leonard Bernstein, Sol Hurok, and Jerome Robbins on the stage set of Fancy Free, *probably 1944. Unidentified photographer*. Jerome Robbins Photograph Collection, New York Public Library for the Performing Arts, Astor, Lenox, and Tilden Foundations.

Magazine as "the leading success of modern ballet in America, literally taking the country by storm."[52]

THE PLEASURE OF ARCHIVAL FOOTAGE

The original cast of *Fancy Free* drew on core dancers in Ballet Theatre, all of whom were as young as Robbins and Bernstein. They included Rex Cooper as Bartender, Harold Lang, John Kriza, and Robbins as Three Sailors, Muriel Bentley as the Brunette, Janet Reed as the Red-Head, and Shirley Eckl as the Blonde.[53] Lincoln Kirstein described the men as "flashy and magnetic character dancers" (in classical ballet, character dancers enact folk and national traditions), and he called Bentley and Reed "excellent comediennes as well as classical ballerinas."[54] The generic nature of the character names in *Fancy Free*—for example, the Red-Head and the Bartender—link to Mister Mister and Editor Daily in Blitzstein's *The Cradle Will Rock*.

Fancy Free enacted a common scene in wartime New York, as its three sailors tried to pick up girls in a bar while they roughhoused among themselves. They are simultaneously best friends and competitors, while the ballet's women are pert and self-confident. Overall the plot of the ballet has a rounded form, ending in much the same way as it opened, as the sailors try their luck with yet another woman.

Jerome Robbins, Harold Lang, John Kriza, Janet Reed, and Muriel Bentley in front of the original set for Fancy Free *by Oliver Smith.* Photofest Digital Archive.

The original Ballet Theatre production comes alive through a silent film that was shot in 1944–45.[55] Viewing it, a person can almost slip into a seat at the old Metropolitan Opera House and experience a sense of time travel. The old Met was a landmark building at Broadway and 39th Street that was demolished in 1966. The film was "taken from the balcony of the Met," Robbins later recalled. "It's a fuzzy, grainy film, and sometimes you can't tell which sailor is which, but Shirley [Eckl]'s accuracy and projection is amazing."[56] Despite the grainy segments, this film conveys Robbins's sky-high standards. I watched it at a viewing station in the Jerome Robbins Dance Division of the New York Public Library at Lincoln Center, where I simultaneously plugged into my iPod so as to sync the film with a recording of *Fancy Free*. Doing so made it possible to reconstruct the fused experience of dance and music, albeit with a bit of stopping and starting.

Most strikingly, the film conveys how *Fancy Free* approached dance as comedy. The sailors use lots of whole-body movements, and the film makes clear how they navigate the stage as a joined-at-the-hip threesome, giving the work its cartoon-like character. They're all legs. Their near fusion as bodies in motion is also presaged by the five tap dancers of the film *Black and Tan Fantasy* of 1929, which featured Duke Ellington and his orchestra.[57] Oliver Smith's set for *Fancy Free* is beautiful in its simplicity, with a solitary bar in the left foreground against a backdrop of New York City with lights ablaze. Visually, it positions the innocence and vulnerability of the soldiers against the alluring city, a playground brimming with risks. It is reminiscent of the late-night lunch counter in Edward Hopper's famous *Nighthawks* of 1942, sharing Hopper's sense of nocturnal solitude in a refuge from the surrounding social space.

Throughout footage of the ballet, there is easy camaraderie among the sailors, even when they are in the midst of rough-and-tumble disagreements. These guys have a relationship so close that it is safe to tangle. Near the opening, they use an upward-sweeping arm motion, which was later made famous with choreographed movements for *On the Town*'s "New York, New York."

There is much sexualized dancing in the film of *Fancy Free*. The section titled "Enter Two Girls," for example, incorporates hip swinging and seductive movements for the women. Similarly, the "Pas de Deux" between the Third Sailor (Robbins) and the Red-Head (Janet Reed) is a sensual sequence in which the lovers draw closer and tighter as the music becomes slower and more sinuous. This scene soars with choreographed ballroom dancing, inspired by the world of Fred Astaire and Ginger Rogers. With the "Competition Scene" that follows, it becomes clear that three guys plus two girls means someone will come up short. Even though the men get aggressive as they strive to attract a woman, they also seem vulnerable. "Girls security vs mens uneasiness," wrote Robbins in manuscript notes for the ballet.[58] In other words, sailors don't always win—a message with strong resonance for wartime audiences.

Three virtuosic variations begin with "Galop," and the First Sailor (Harold Lang) spins off into an exhibitionist frenzy. He does the splits, dances on the bar, and somersaults all over the stage, frenetically trying to win his gal. His strategy is reminiscent of a little boy showing off on a playground. The Second Sailor (John Kriza) moves lyrically in "Waltz," more like Astaire than a vaudeville performer.

The three sailors in Fancy Free *moving as a cartoon-like unit, with Shirley Eckl (the Blonde) on the right. Photograph by Fred Fehl, courtesy of Gabriel Pinski.* Jerome Robbins Photograph Collection, New York Public Library for the Performing Arts, Astor, Lenox, and Tilden Foundations.

He takes huge slides across the stage, with exaggerated leg movements. Yet he too picks up steam as he pushes toward his goal, jumping over bar stools before winding up in slow motion. Finally Robbins steps out for "Danzón."[59] He tosses finger snaps over his shoulders with panache, and his gestures are the most sexualized of the three, with sinuous hip swings and jaw-dropping leaps. At the end of the sequence, he jumps to the top of a bar stool and then lands in a squat on the floor for the final razzle-dazzle chord of that segment.

The sailors wind up the ballet with a fight behind the bar, tripping each other, tumbling all over the place, and generally indulging in slapstick. At a certain point, they sit on bar stools again as a new girl walks in—a surprise entrance, with a suggestion that everything is fluid, especially human relationships in a time of war. They lean over as a Popeye-like trio to watch her, affirming the tightness of their male bond, which ultimately trumps all else.

"MY BUDDY": *THE FLEET'S IN!* AND *FANCY FREE*

Ballet Theatre's program for the original production of *Fancy Free* articulated no dramatic detail to translate the action onstage for the audience. Rather, it gave a spare outline for the work's scenario, with the same kind of epigrammatic writing that was later used for *West Side Story*:

FANCY FREE
A ballet in one act concerning three sailors on shore leave . . .
Time: The present, a hot summer night
Place: New York City, a side street[60]

Separately from the published program, Robbins developed a detailed verbal scenario for the ballet, which describes both the dramatic action and music. It was
published in George Amberg's *Ballet in America: The Emergence of an American Art*
in 1949.[61]

None of these early documents credits the ballet's initial inspiration, which
came from *The Fleet's In!*, a controversial painting by Paul Cadmus (see page 22)
that holds the key to the ballet's multiple narratives, as well as the interplay of
personal and professional relationships among its collaborators. In the early
1940s, Robbins's close friend Mary Hunter, director of the American Actors
Company, brought the painting to his attention. *The Fleet's In!* was at the time
somewhat notorious as a volatile and sexualized work of art.[62] It had been produced as part of the government's Public Works of Art Project (later folded into
the Works Progress Administration), and it provoked a nationally publicized
scandal in 1934 when it was scheduled to be part of an exhibit of Public Works of
Art at the Corcoran Gallery in Washington, D.C. The painting was pulled from the
show—indeed, it was withdrawn from public circulation—and a famous case of
censorship resulted.[63] Admiral Hugh Rodman, retired commander in chief of the
Navy's Pacific Fleet, condemned the painting as an "insult to the enlisted men of
the American Navy." He decried it as portraying "a most disgraceful, sordid, dis-
reputable, drunken brawl," complaining of its evocation of "streetwalkers and
denizens of the red-light district."[64]

The painting is set along a stone wall on Riverside Drive in Manhattan, a location described by Kirstein as "a strip of public land bordering the broad
Hudson, [which] was then a fast and happy hunting ground for sailors on
summer liberty with their casual pickups, male or female."[65] Cadmus uses bold
colors to render voluptuous bodies, and the painting essentially divides into
three sections. "A solidity of firm flesh and muscle swells the flush health within
the tightness of navy blues and whites," wrote Kirstein about *Shore Leave*, a related painting by Cadmus from the previous year.[66] On the left of *The Fleet's In!*
an elderly woman walks her dog, appearing to have landed in the wrong place at
the wrong time, and a young woman with a very tight skirt has her back to the
viewer, leaning to the side while exchanging a cigarette with one of the sailors.
In that same group, the arm of a reclining sailor is draped across the lap of his
buddy. Is he passed out? Making himself available for an erotic encounter?
A civilian in a business suit sits to the left. He has blond hair and a red necktie,
and a counternarrative starts to emerge, as uncovered by recent historians of art and
gender. The color of the civilian's hair and tie were part of "a common code at the
time for signaling the homosexuality of its wearer," writes art historian Jonathan
Weinberg.[67] According to this interpretation, *The Fleet's In!* not only depicts women
flirting with sailors but also suggests a romantic connection among the males.

Paul Cadmus, The Fleet's In!, *1934, oil on canvas*. Navy Art Collection, Naval History and Heritage Command, Washington, D.C. Created for the Public Works of Art Project (later part of the Works Progress Administration) and in the public domain.

In the center segment of the painting, a sailor wraps his legs around the hips of a woman, perhaps having sex, while she roughly pushes his face away. On the right, a group of three women and two sailors greet one another, with the buttocks of another sailor and a woman in the background. The painting constructs "a complex knot of desire," according to art historian Richard Meyer, in which "three separate kinds of investment—homosocial, homosexual, and heterosexual—swirl around the figure of the sleeping sailor."[68] Censorship of *The Fleet's In!* produced a firestorm in national news outlets during the 1930s. Admiral Rodman levied no direct charge of homoerotic representation, yet press coverage generated a "double discourse," as Meyer puts it, in which "the artist's homosexuality was occasionally alluded to by journalists" but "such references remained strictly within the register of connotation."[69]

As a gay man and an artist with strong ties to the world of ballet, Cadmus is central to the story behind *Fancy Free*. His sister, Fidelma, married Lincoln Kirstein, director of Ballet Caravan, which was the other main up-and-coming ballet troupe in New York. Kirstein was a patron of Cadmus, and decades later he wrote a book about the artist.[70] In 1937 Cadmus designed sets and "comic-strip clothes" for Ballet Caravan's production of *Filling Station*, with music by Virgil Thomson and choreography by Lew Christensen. With its "contemporary background" and "virtuosity and showmanship," as Kirstein described the work in an important manifesto titled *Blast at Ballet* (1937), *Filling Station* was among a core cluster of American ballets that inspired *Fancy Free*.[71] Christensen had long experience in "big-time vaudeville," as Kirstein pointed out, and Robbins also combined wide-ranging types of performance. All these forces, from Cadmus to Christensen to Kirstein, converged to inspire *Fancy Free*.

As a result, Robbins's ballet can be viewed as operating in simultaneous spheres, with a primary story of boy meets girl that addressed a broad audience and a gay narrative directed to those who knew the signals. When Agnes de Mille reported the audience's reaction on opening night, she might have been responding to a gendered reception. "The Metropolitan Opera House was jammed with standees five deep," de Mille noted. "From the entrance of the sailors and the first measures of their brilliant, explosive, precise cavorting the audience sat up sharp in delighted attention. Then it began to roar with deep, male laughs—not the female titters that usually reward dancing."[72] Focusing on those "deep, male laughs" and on the intensity of the sailors' closeness in *Fancy Free* reinforces an alternative reading in tandem with the ballet's dominant straight story. Male bonding characterizes the ballet as strongly as does the sailors' pursuit of women.[73] The men ultimately fail in capturing the women's attention. There is passing contact between the sexes, but no real relationship and no sense of successful heterosexual coupling. While the primary male-female plot of the ballet features these disrupted liaisons, the male-male subplot depicts stable relationships unruffled by external forces.

Robbins's typewritten scenario, filed away with his archive at the New York Public Library at Lincoln Center, includes segments open to gay interpretations. This is especially the case with the beginning and ending of the ballet. When the three sailors first "explode onto the stage," as Robbins described it, they are characterized in terms of their closeness to one another and the degree to which they are completely comfortable with that fact.[74] These traits are packaged by Robbins as a standard part of military camaraderie, and the phrase "my buddy" turns up:

> One should feel immediately that the three are good friends, used to bumming around together, used to each other's guff...that they are in the habit of spending their time as a trio, and that, under all their rough and tumble exterior, there is a real affection for each other, a kind of "my buddy" feeling.[75]

After the sailors take their three solos, "the girls really get to work on them," Robbins continues, and there is "a fast kind of finale-coda dance...The dance becomes hotter, almost a furious lindy hop."[76] The sailors toss the two girls around, then temporarily lose track of the women. They are palpably physical and completely fixated on their male comrades:

> The boys become more violent in their contact with one another; they push, and shove and nudge until finally it happens—one shoves another too hard and a fight breaks out.... The boys are in a heap on the floor, arms, legs, heads, bodies entangled and weaving; grunts, groans, heaves and swings, kicks and jerks—they struggle and pant and pull and push. Suddenly one gets flung off the pile, and he rolls fast across the floor, hitting the two girls in the shins and knocking them flat. Ignoring them completely, he dives back into the melee. The girls help each other to their feet, shocked and furious. They rub their sore spots and stamp their feet for attention, to no avail: the men are too busy fighting.[77]

Robbins's sailors thus abandon the women while wrestling, oblivious that the women are clamoring for their attention. Furthermore, the "heap" of sailors on the floor has all the earmarks of a vaudeville sequence. It is a pantomimed fight, complete with shoving and hitting. The scene involves a striking degree of male fixation, with women relegated to the sidelines.

Sailors provided an ideal medium for conveying the double message of Robbins's ballet. A fixture on the streets of New York City during World War II, they were enjoying heroic depictions in American popular culture at large. Sailors also sent a well-established set of signals to the male gay community, with a long history of being perceived as "young and manly, unattached, and unconstrained by conventional morality," according to historian George Chauncey.[78] At the same time, antigay codes of conduct were being strictly enforced during World War II, which meant that the homoerotic strain in Robbins's narrative pushed back against military directives of the day. The psychological tests at induction centers built an "antihomosexual wall" around the military, writes historian Allan Bérubé.[79] While these policies resulted in a military exemption for some potential recruits, such as Robbins, they were not so stringent as to prevent other gay men and women from being inducted, and those soldiers and sailors essentially went undercover to serve alongside heterosexual troops.

Bérubé's landmark study of gay culture during World War II, for which he interviewed scores of gay veterans, essentially documents the scene evoked in

The sailors fight with one another while Muriel Bentley and Janet Reed watch from the sidelines. Photograph by Fred Fehl, courtesy of Gabriel Pinski. Jerome Robbins Photograph Collection, New York Public Library for the Performing Arts, Astor, Lenox, and Tilden Foundations.

Fancy Free, revealing striking parallels between real life and the ballet. Bérubé describes "intermission at the ballet" as a prime site for gay male soldiers and civilians to cruise: "Male GIs who packed the standing-room section in the Metropolitan Opera House in New York City, which for years had been a gay male cruising mecca, pressed their bodies together several deep against the rail."[80] Shore leave provided an opportunity for being open about one's sexuality, and gay bars gained special prominence during World War II, moving "closer to the center of gay life." "The gay crowd found a little more freedom off base than they could in the barracks or service clubs," Bérubé writes. He describes cruising in gay bars as "quiet and covert, but still charged with erotic possibilities," and he quotes a soldier who recalled that "the approaches" at gay bars "were all extremely indirect," saying he had "to try to figure out what the nuance was" in each new setting. Furthermore, Bérubé analyzes the physical space of gay-friendly bars as being laid out to accommodate a range of sexual orientations. The Astor Bar near Times Square, "one of New York City's primary meeting places," provided just such flexibility, according to another soldier interviewed by Bérubé: "One side of the large oval bar was gay, and the other was straight. It was pretty obvious what was going on."

Fancy Free gave those gay GIs at the Metropolitan Opera House a staged vision of their own lives by dramatizing a bar where hetero- and homosexual partnering happened in overlapping spheres, where "nuance" governed one's self-presentation. It conveyed the fragility of wartime liaisons, and it placed youth at center stage.

"The whole attitude of so many young people at that time was very disoriented," remembered dancer Janet Reed. "We were uprooted, and although we had a very carefree attitude, we were also very tentative about relationships....Our attitude was one of wanting to be close to one another but knowing that it couldn't last."[81] *Fancy Free*'s brilliance lay in communicating those profound insecurities through comedy, music, and dance.

PERSONAL NARRATIVES MEET ARTISTIC VISIONS

A gay interpretation of *Fancy Free* reaches even further. For one thing, the ballet not only enacted the bisexual message of *The Fleet's In!* but also performed the gay identity of its male dancers and creative team. As it happened, Robbins, Bernstein, and Oliver Smith all were involved in gay relationships during this period, and John Kriza and Harold Lang—the other two male dancers in the original production of *Fancy Free*—were gay as well. The links between these personal identities and *Fancy Free* were central to the work's conception, and intimate relationships among the cast and creative team extended in multiple directions. Gore Vidal later recalled that Bernstein claimed "he had been in bed with the entire original cast of *Fancy Free*."[82] "He meant the men," responded dancer Janet Reed in an interview with Greg Lawrence, a biographer of Robbins.[83] Robbins too had multiple romantic liaisons with core figures from *Fancy Free*. "Well, you know, as with any ballet after its first performances, it's hard for other people who dance it to catch all the intimate qualities that happened while you first worked on it," Robbins later reflected. "I think the hardest thing is to find the warmth and intimacy that the original cast had with each other, that relationship of three buddies who always bummed around together, always had this terrific affection and support for each other—who knew each other well."[84]

Personally, Robbins negotiated both sides of the gendered messages conveyed by his sailors. In public, he presented himself as straight, and his artistic work often focused on all-American, heterosexual imagery. He also had relationships with women. At the same time, he was actively gay, albeit covert and cautious. Lawrence chronicles this ambivalence, observing at one point: "His attitude toward his sexuality would remain so conflicted that it would be his relationships, engagements and near-engagements with women that he would present to the world, while his affairs with men remained as clandestine as possible."[85] Yet in private documents, including notes for *Fancy Free* and correspondence with lovers, Robbins dropped the mask. Sketches penned on stationery from hotels where he stayed while on tour with Ballet Theatre in late 1943 show sailors in motion; presumably he was recording ideas for *Fancy Free*. These drawings are remarkably kinetic and choreographic, with no women in sight. The sensuality of the bodies is palpable, and one drawing appears at the end of a love letter (see page 27). There the personal and professional are quite literally entangled. Robbins writes first as a choreographer, describing how "little pieces o/music,

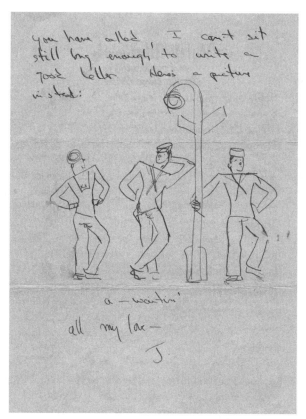

Drawing of sailors from a letter written by Robbins in 1943. Jerome Robbins Personal Papers, New York Public Library for the Performing Arts, Astor, Lenox, and Tilden Foundations. Permission of the Jerome Robbins Rights Trust.

stray ideas, costumes & opening nights, all go spinning around my head forever & ever." He then shifts gears to call the recipient "baby" and refers to a recent phone conversation. The drawing at the end shows three sailors clustered in stylized postures around a lamppost, just as in the opening of *Fancy Free*. The letter ends with "A-waitin' All my love—J."[86]

The first page of the letter is missing, so we cannot know the recipient. But there are multiple possibilities. To start with, Robbins had an intimate relationship during this period with *Fancy Free*'s scene designer, Oliver Smith. Although details are limited, suggestive traces exist. In the notebook of ideas for *Fancy Free* where Robbins lists possible composers, he mentions Smith on one page, simply naming him. Another page features a drawing of a nude male dancer, in midleap and with an erection. An arrow from the initials J.R. (written upside down) points to the drawing.[87] A separate document—a letter from Smith to "Jerry" dated August 8, 1944—chronicles their romantic involvement several months after the ballet's premiere. The opening paragraph is unambiguously addressed to a romantic partner, with sexual references and direct affirmation of being in love.

The rest of the letter migrates between romantic gestures and details of "a layout for the show," which at that point meant *On the Town*.[88]

Lawrence speculates that Robbins had affairs with John Kriza and Harold Lang while *Fancy Free* was emerging.[89] In interviews with Lawrence, various dancers associated with Ballet Theatre attested to these romances, although many were sharing hunches. Kriza was "the real love of Jerry's life then," asserted dancer Shaun O'Brien, and Lawrence quotes others who also believed that Kriza and Robbins had an affair.[90] Janet Reed inserted Harold Lang into the mix, recalling that he was bisexual and suggesting that a romantic tie to Robbins would have been strategic. "He [Lang] was very ambitious," Reed stated, "and it seemed to me that any homosexual relationship he had was for getting ahead. But Jerry didn't have anything to gain, whereas they [Lang and Kriza] had everything to gain from him."[91] Fellow dancers also suspected a romantic relationship between Robbins and Bernstein. "They had a kind of brief encounter," declared the dancer Richard D'Arcy, "an affair just in that early period when they were doing *Fancy Free*." D'Arcy believed it happened "when the score was being written."[92]

Bernstein had many male lovers at the time, even as he, like Robbins, also had significant relationships with women. Some of his boyfriends were connected to the world of ballet, others were not. Bernstein's biographer Humphrey Burton noted "the sheer volume of his sexual and social life," and personal correspondence at the Library of Congress confirms a large number of relationships of great intensity.[93] Letters from Lang to Bernstein, written from May through July of 1944, are among them. Lang was in California after the premiere of *Fancy Free*, and he voiced the same sentiment repeatedly: "I miss you so much already. Please miss me a bit."[94] The letters make clear that the two men had been involved romantically, but Lang seems more invested in the relationship than Bernstein. Perhaps it was the "ambition" that Janet Reed observed. Lang also alluded to the high volume of Bernstein's love affairs: "I'll bet you're hitting the same head-splitting pace 'socially' as when I left."[95]

During this period, Bernstein also had a major romantic relationship with the composer Aaron Copland. While not directly involved in *Fancy Free*, Copland was central to the work's conception, providing a model with his own ballet scores and serving as second pianist on the recordings of *Fancy Free* that were made by Bernstein as the work was in progress. Considerable correspondence exists between Bernstein and Copland, beginning in the late 1930s.[96] Bernstein repeatedly attests to being in "love" with Copland, and Copland too uses deeply intimate language.[97] On a couple of occasions, the appeal of military men factor into their exchanges. "VT [Virgil Thomson] always said that wartime was a wonderful time for tail," wrote Copland to Bernstein at some point during World War II.[98] In another letter, written in July 1943, Copland wrote enthusiastically about Bernstein's "wonderful letters," calling them "the I miss you I adore you kind, while sailors and marines flit through the background in a general atmosphere of moral decay."[99]

Even though work had not yet begun on *Fancy Free*, Copland attested to the erotic power of sailors within gay culture of the day. Dance was also on his mind, for he mentioned having "started a ballet for Martha Graham," a landmark project that became *Appalachian Spring*.

Fancy Free's connection to this web of gay relationships was one manifestation of its overall aesthetic, which aimed to represent life during World War II as realistically as possible. Robbins and his creative team strove for a perceptible urban flavor, as well as to convey sheer delight with contemporary popular culture, and their vision grew out of a nearly ethnographic focus on the bustling life of city streets. This graphic depiction was manifested in multiple ways. The scenario states, for example, that "the girls should wear actual street dresses," that the set "should represent a city street," and that the sailors should "dance down the street."[100] George Amberg called *Fancy Free* "a group picture as it were, of typical young Americans."[101] Robbins's colleagues from Ballet Theatre who starred in the original production remembered Robbins as an acute observer who collected ideas from the daily life around him. "When we were in New York, between rehearsals and performances [with Ballet Theatre] at the old Met," stated Harold Lang, "often Jerry, Muriel, and I would be wandering around Times Square and Jerry would point out, 'Did you ever see one or two sailors? No, you always see three. There are always three together.'"[102] Janet Reed concurred: "Jerry picked up on everything that was going on all around us. I didn't actually witness this, but someone, Johnny or Jerry, told me that the little episode in Jerry's solo, the rumba, where he pretends to dance with a girl who isn't there—someone told me he got the idea from seeing a drunken soldier pick up a chair in a bar and dance with it as though it were a girl."[103]

One means of injecting realism into the ballet was to include social dances that were popular during the war. Robbins later recalled that the dance types in *Fancy Free* included "the Lindy of course. Boogie-woogie. Shorty George." He remembered incorporating "steps...that I actually saw sailors do in a bar."[104] Muriel Bentley, who danced the Brunette, added to these recollections. "I remember, from my sojourn with Ballet Theatre, all of us going to a lot of parties, and that Jerry would watch the people dance. It's incredible. It's constant research with Jerry," Bentley stated. "At that party he would stand at the side—he still does—and watch how the people dance and how they are and what they are."[105] As a result, *Fancy Free* employed "dance-hall practice," observed the *New York Times*.[106] Edwin Denby concurred: the ballet made "all sorts of references to our normal dance-hall steps, as they are done from Roseland to the Savoy: trucking, the boogie, knee drops, even a round-the-back done in slow motion."[107] The 1940s was the decade of a "dance craze," as dance scholar Chrystelle Trump Bond has described it, with "the new swing music inspir[ing] the creation of new dances."[108] Arthur Murray's dance studios formed a nationwide forum for learning the latest steps, and USO clubs sponsored dances for servicemembers "to make new friends and to avoid loneliness," as a contemporary dance magazine put it.[109]

Equally striking was *Fancy Free*'s inclusion of gymnastics, which was familiar to the worlds of vaudeville, film, nightclubs, and jazz-tap. In the first of the sailors' three solos, Harold Lang brought down the house with a "brilliant acrobatic turn, with splits like those of the Berry Brothers," Edwin Denby reported.[110] The

Berry Brothers were a famous African American dance trio, performing regularly at Harlem's Cotton Club. The splits were not only their signature but also that of the equally famous Nicholas Brothers, who delivered a dazzling sequence of splits in the film *Stormy Weather*, which opened in November 1943, while *Fancy Free* was being conceived. Robbins added that Lang landed "straight down with the feet—one in front and one in back, and the arms out to the side. When he landed he looked like a jack."[111] Robbins also did the splits in the ballet. These virtuosic acrobatic segments lent *Fancy Free* a playful physicality, and they represented one way in which the work drew upon black popular culture for inspiration.

Fancy Free also employed aspects of collaborative choreography. Robbins was clearly in charge, and he devised the initial scenario. Yet his fellow dancers bore witness to brainstorming with him while on tour with Ballet Theatre in late 1943, contributing ideas and movements.[112] The critic Tobi Tobias asked Robbins when he brought in "actual bodies to work on," as part of a remarkable interview with Robbins and the original cast of *Fancy Free*. Robbins replied, "On this tour. And with my best friends then. I teamed around with Johnny Kriza and Harold Lang and Muriel Bentley and Janet Reed. It was sort of like working with your home team."[113] Indeed, Robbins was fully immersed in conceptualizing his new ballet while on the road. "We were in Bloomington, Indiana, walking down the street on the way to the theater," recalled Janet Reed, who played the Red-Head, "and Jerry said, 'I wonder what would happen if'—and he described the girl running and suddenly jumping and the boy catching her. . . . I let him walk on ahead a little ways and I said, 'You mean like this?' and I ran down the street and jumped

Robbins doing the splits. Unidentified photographer. Jerome Robbins Photograph Collection, New York Public Library for the Performing Arts, Astor, Lenox, and Tilden Foundations.

at him. And he had to drop his bag to catch me. That's in the pas de deux we did together."[114]

As part of this collaborative conception, Robbins tailored each character to fit the dancer for whom the role was conceived. "Robbins had chosen his cast carefully," Agnes de Mille later observed. The dancers were "young, and with the exception of Janet Reed, untried talents of great potential ability who were not so sure of themselves that they would snub his first efforts."[115] Robbins himself later described each of the characters in detail, tightly linking them to the dancer for whom they were originally devised. The First Sailor in the ballet, according to Robbins, was "the most bawdy, boisterous of the three." Robbins continued, "He exploits the extrovert vulgarity of sailors, the impudence and loudness, the get-me-how-good-I-am type."[116] Harold Lang, who inaugurated the role, "had a formidable technique," Robbins recalled. "Not a classical, *danseur noble* technique, but still a very strong one, and yet he was unusually limber."[117] The Second Sailor's personality was "more naïve, lovable," according to Robbins. "There is more warmth, humor and almost a wistfulness about him."[118] Decades later, Robbins reflected back on how that role was shaped for John Kriza: "Johnny's variation is certainly based on Johnny.... Well there was an incredible sweetness about that man. And not in an icky way. He was generally nice and kindhearted and light. And wistful."[119]

Finally, the "keynote" of the Third Sailor was "intensity." He uses "swift and sudden movements, a strong passion and violence and attractive quality of flashiness and smoldering."[120] Robbins himself danced the role, later describing it as "a sort of a New York sharpie...Latin influenced." When asked if that was how he perceived himself at the time, Robbins replied, "No, that's how I decided to make that character. Spanish dancing and character dancing were close to me and I was good at them, so maybe I threw it that way, for myself."[121] The dancer Sono Osato affirmed that Robbins made a striking impression in the Third Sailor's solo: "Jerry was agile, graceful, and poignant, insinuating a spirit into the rhumba-dancing sailor that I have never seen equaled."[122]

Meanwhile, each of the women who danced in *Fancy Free* described their characters to critic Tobi Tobias. Muriel Bentley said of the Brunette: "That role is me—the first girl.... She was sharp, she was knowing, she was not a whore, she was bright...Patent leather. Jerry used to describe that girl as patent leather. Black hair, slicked up, and carrying a red pocketbook." Janet Reed concurred: "Muriel's movement was more big city—sharp and staccato; she was a real rhythmic virtuoso." Reed's own character (the Red-Head) was, as Reed recalled, "a little softer, sweeter. Long red hair hanging loose. Every girl I saw do it after me I thought was too tough and hard, consciously trying to be sexy." For Robbins, the difference in the two female characters was defined by the geographic origins of the original dancers: "Muriel's a New Yorker; Janet isn't. In a way that sums it up."[123]

Fancy Free also established yet another essential trait of Robbins's work, which was a capacity to express human relationships. As the dancer and choreographer Robert LaFosse once put it, the Robbins ballets are all "about a community of people."[124] This had both civic and interpersonal dimensions. At the same time, *Fancy Free* had "an intimately personal character," as the ballet critic George

Amberg observed. "It develops and moves along like a spirited conversation between the performers, informally inviting and including the audience behind the footlights." He concluded, "The true significance of this work is the revelation of democratic human relationships."[125] *Fancy Free* grew out of Robbins's close ties with his fellow dancers, and the final version managed to convey those bonds—to shape its story as a dynamic interaction among a cluster of distinctive individuals. As Robbins stated in "Thoughts on Choreography," a typescript account of a conversation in 1954 with the dance historian Selma Jeanne Cohen: "Dance is performed by human beings and deals with human values, so in no way can it ever be impersonal. Using a form like ballet does not crush personal expression but rather brings it out, makes it communicable."[126]

Perhaps most fundamentally, *Fancy Free* consciously breached any perceived divide between high art and popular culture, yet the result firmly fit into the world of "ballet." " 'Fancy Free' is utterly colloquial," observed John Martin in the *New York Times*, "but it would be a serious mistake to consider it for that reason as merely vaudeville highjinks." It employed "jazz idioms" and incorporated "the techniques of the popular theatre in terms of timing," yet was "nevertheless an artistic entity and a modern ballet in the best sense of the phrase."[127]

CROSSING OVER WITH "BIG STUFF" AND BILLIE HOLIDAY

When the curtain rose on the first production of *Fancy Free*, the audience at the old Metropolitan Opera House did not hear a pit orchestra, which would have followed a long-established norm in ballet. Rather, a recorded vocal blues wafted from the stage. Those attending must have been caught by surprise, as they were drawn into a contemporary sound world. The song was "Big Stuff," with music and lyrics by Bernstein. It had been conceived with the African American jazz singer Billie Holiday in mind, even though it ended up being recorded for the production by Bernstein's sister, Shirley.[128] At that early point in Bernstein's career, he lacked the cultural and fiscal capital to hire anyone as famous as Holiday. The melody and piano accompaniment for "Big Stuff" contained bent notes and lilting rhythms basic to urban blues (Example 1.1), and the lyrics summoned up the blues as an animate force, following a standard rhetorical mode for the genre:

> So you cry, "What's it about, Baby?"
> You ask why the blues had to go and pick you.[129]

Talk of going "down to the shore" vaguely referred to the sailors of *Fancy Free*, as the lyrics became sexually explicit:

> So you go down to the shore, kid stuff.
> Don't you know there's honey in store for you, Big Stuff?
> Let's take a ride in my gravy train;
> The door's open wide,
> Come in from out of the rain.

"Big Stuff" spoke to youth in the audience by alluding to contemporary popular culture. It boldly injected an African American commercial idiom into a predominantly white high-art performance sphere, and its raunchiness enhanced the sexual provocations of *Fancy Free*. "Big Stuff" also blurred distinctions between acoustic and recorded sound. It marked Bernstein as a crossover composer, with the talent to write a pop song and the temerity to unveil it within a high-art context.

Billie Holiday was "one of [Bernstein's] idols," according to Humphrey Burton.[130] He admired her brilliance as a performer, and he was also sympathetic to her progressive politics. In 1939, Holiday first recorded "Strange Fruit," a song about a lynching that became one of her signatures. With biracial and left-leaning roots, "Strange Fruit" was written by the white teacher and social activist Abel Meeropol. Holiday performed "Strange Fruit" nightly at Café Society, a club that enforced a progressive desegregationist agenda both onstage and in the audience.[131] Those performances marked "the beginning of the civil rights movement," recalled the famed record producer Ahmet Ertegun (founder of Atlantic Records).[132] Barney Josephson, who ran Café Society, famously declared, "I wanted a club where blacks and whites worked together behind the footlights and sat together out front."[133]

Bernstein had experience on both sides of Café Society's footlights. In the early 1940s, he performed there occasionally with The Revuers, and he played excerpts from *The Cradle Will Rock* in at least one evening session with Marc Blitzstein.[134] Bernstein also hung out at the club with friends, including Judy Tuvim, Betty Comden, and Adolph Green, listening to the jazz pianist Teddy Wilson and boogie-woogie pianists Pete Johnson and Albert Ammons.[135] Thus Bernstein had ample opportunities to witness the intentional "blurring of cultural categories, genres, and ethnic groups" that historian David Stowe has called the "dominant theme" of Café Society.[136]

Robbins also had an affinity for the work of Billie Holiday. In the summer of 1940, he choreographed Holiday's recording of "Strange Fruit" and performed it with the dancer Anita Alvarez at Camp Tamiment. "*Strange Fruit* was one of the most dramatic and heart-breaking dances I have ever seen—a masterpiece," remembered Dorothy Bird, a dancer there that summer.[137]

As a result of these experiences, the music of Billie Holiday had crossed the paths of both Robbins and Bernstein before "Big Stuff" opened their first ballet. While Billie Holiday's voice was not heard the evening of *Fancy Free*'s premiere, only seven months passed before she recorded "Big Stuff" with the Toots Camarata Orchestra on November 8, 1944. The fact that Holiday made this recording so soon after the premiere of *Fancy Free* bore witness to the rapid rise of Bernstein's clout within the music industry. Over the next two years, Holiday made six more recordings of "Big Stuff," and when Bernstein issued the first recording of *Fancy Free* with the Ballet Theatre Orchestra in 1946, Holiday's rendition of "Big Stuff" opened the disc.[138] Both she and Bernstein recorded for the Decca label. Holiday recorded her final three takes of "Big Stuff" for Decca on March 13, 1946, and that label released *Fancy Free* the same year.

Musically, "Big Stuff" links closely to the worlds of George Gershwin and Harold Arlen, whose songs drew on African American idioms. Like some of the most beloved songs by these composers—whether Arlen's "Stormy Weather" of 1933 or Gershwin's "Summertime" of 1935 from *Porgy and Bess*—"Big Stuff" used a standard thirty-two-bar song form. With a tempo indication of "slow & blue," "Big Stuff" has a lilting one-bar riff in the bass, a classic formulation for a jazz-based popular song of the day. The riff retains its shape throughout, as is also typical, while its internal pitch structure shifts in relation to the harmonic motion. Both the accompaniment and melody are drenched with signifiers of the blues, especially with chromatically altered third, fourth, sixth, and seventh scale degrees, and the overall downward motion of the melody is also characteristic of the blues, with a weighted sense of being ultimately earthbound.

The published score for *Fancy Free* states that the recording of "Big Stuff" "can be interrupted at any point by the entrance of the orchestra."[139] From the moment the orchestra cuts loose, it delivers a hard-driving "jump theme"—that is, an up-tempo riff common to swing bands of the late 1930s and 1940s (as in Count Basie's "One o'Clock Jump" of 1937).[140] Those opening measures provide a bridge from the blues-saturated recording of "Big Stuff" to a work that merges the sounds of big-band jazz with a spectrum of orchestral styles, ranging from radio and cartoons to the modernist ballets of the early twentieth century. In a sense, it transfers the concept of Raymond Scott's radio show *Concert in Rhythm* to the ballet, treating the orchestra as a flexible mechanism that can deliver both drama and comedy.

Today, we have lost track of the degree to which the term "orchestra" in the 1940s was extraordinarily versatile. In an era before rock, "orchestras," broadly defined, were the principal instrumental ensembles for public music performance. Most of the major big bands used the term, as in the Duke Ellington Orchestra, the Count Basie Orchestra, or the Stan Kenton Orchestra, and orchestras with large string sections also assumed widely varying functions. Standard symphonies, such as the New York Philharmonic or the Philadelphia Orchestra, carried high cultural prestige. But there were also studio orchestras associated with major radio stations, recording companies, and film companies, as well as theater orchestras, "pops" orchestras, and hybrid "symphonic jazz" ensembles that backed major jazz and pop soloists of the day, whether on recordings or in glistening hotel ballrooms. Many of the same players migrated among these interrelated musical worlds, and individual orchestras sometimes took on more than one function, most notably the Boston Symphony Orchestra, which regularly flipped its identity and its repertory to become the Boston Pops.

Blending these visions of an orchestra was one of the central ways in which Bernstein constructed the musical style of *Fancy Free*. Akin to sampling, as practiced in the late twentieth and early twenty-first centuries, Bernstein developed a compositional technique in which he stitched together a mélange of musical references, often mimicking—sometimes parodying—the spectrum of styles involved, and he intentionally used different modes of orchestration to establish the core identity for each of those musical styles.[141] His music is all newly composed, which differentiates it from the literal transfer of today's mediated sampling. As a result, he did not often quote existing material but rather simulated genres and styles. One model of doing so came from operetta, which relied consistently on parody, and Bernstein's close friends in The Revuers made parodies and spoofs a central force in their skits. New media of the 1930s and 1940s also played a conceptual role in *Fancy Free*, for Bernstein's compositional technique relied on fusing seemingly dissimilar sources. In part that technique grew from his experiences with radio programs and cartoons, where the music often shifted gears rapidly to illustrate action. In theatrical terms, the score to *Fancy Free* accompanies pantomime, highlighting the action onstage and making the plot comprehensible.

Fancy Free has seven movements, including three variations within Part VI. The sections of the main work are all three minutes or shorter, each with the capacity to fit on one side of a 78 rpm recording. Here are the sections:

"Big Stuff": prerecorded blues prologue
I. Enter Three Sailors
II. Scene at the Bar
III. Enter Two Girls
IV. Pas de Deux
V. Competition Scene
VI. Variation I (Galop)
VI. Variation II (Waltz)
VI. Variation III (Danzón)
VII. Finale

The diverse musical realms referenced in *Fancy Free* can be grouped into the following categories: big-band jazz and solo jazz piano; melodramatic action music of radio shows, cartoons, and film; honky-tonk piano; and the great ballet scores of Copland, Stravinsky, and other composers associated with the heyday of the Ballet Russe de Monte Carlo, Ballet Theatre, and other famous ballet companies of the era. Plus, the "Danzón" movement—the one danced by Robbins's sailor—stands out stylistically, providing a view of Bernstein's early tie to Latin musical traditions, a linkage that proved to have future importance for *West Side Story*.

Fancy Free established yet another lifelong trait of Bernstein's compositional style: his works for the stage—including many of his highly memorable tunes—had mass-market accessibility, yet they are complex and challenging to perform. He employed the rhythms, melodic gestures, and formal structures of commercial popular music, yet he played with their norms, altering phrase lengths and subverting rhythmic and harmonic expectations.

JAZZ AND MUSICAL MONTAGE

Jazz suffuses major sections of the score to *Fancy Free*, becoming one of the central musical building blocks in an overall structure of montage. A cinematic technique, montage provided a conceptual tool through which Bernstein's score could animate shifts in the action of the ballet by toggling from one musical idea to another, often with abrupt contrasts, and it enabled a kind of artifice in which Bernstein's score could position itself as being *about* jazz.[142] To achieve this effect, Bernstein cut and spliced various jazz styles, achieving a "witty synthesis of jazz then in fashion," as Lincoln Kirstein perceived it at the time.[143] It "employs jazz idioms at will," declared John Martin.[144] "Synthesizing" and "employing" were attained in part through flexibly handling the orchestra, embedding a big band and solo jazz piano amid an otherwise traditional ballet orchestra.[145] The orchestra for *Fancy Free* has a "rhythm section"—that is, a traditional jazz cluster of percussion, piano, and bass—and the handling of instrumentation provided a means to cross genre boundaries. Significantly, however, no jazz musicians were hired to perform the ballet. Rather Bernstein relied on classically trained musicians in the Ballet Theatre orchestra, which meant that they dealt with unusual demands. "Aaron Copland on hearing the opening measures [of *Fancy Free*] rattled off by Bernstein's magic fingers laughed aloud," reported de Mille, "and after wiping his glasses gave his young protégé a brief summary of his own experiences in getting American syncopation from symphony men."[146]

The jump theme that opens "Enter Three Sailors" (first movement) follows a classic big-band style, heralded by rim shots in the percussion and commencing with the brass and rhythm sections playing a four-bar riff (Example 1.2, page 38). That riff, in turn, yields one of the principal thematic cells of the entire work.[147] The rhythm of the opening employs a syncopated swing that was a signature of its era. In a manuscript short score for the piece, Bernstein gave performance instructions that show he was aware of crossing barriers between musical worlds: "The signs — • — • over consecutive eighth-notes indicate a slight exaggeration in rhythm, almost as though they were written ♩ ♪ ♪ ♩ ♪ . These must be observed rigidly in order to make any jazz effect at all."[148] "Rigidly" was an odd word for describing the need to attain rhythmic suppleness, yet it conveyed to symphonic musicians that the rhythmic swing of a jazz ensemble was fundamental to the work's overall character.

There are bursts of solo-piano writing in *Fancy Free* that evoke jazz-piano improvisation. In his scenario for the ballet, Robbins asked for "hot boogie-woogie" piano, but Bernstein's music does not have the percussive, hard-pounding left hand associated with boogie-woogie.[149] Rather, the piano in *Fancy Free* swings loosely, with a tendency toward obsessive repetition. It signifies urban popular culture and provides an aural counterpart to the replication of swing steps and sidewalk movements that Robbins incorporated in his choreography. Here too simulation most aptly defines the jazz-piano writing. Bernstein's musical material does not appear to quote the work of celebrated jazz pianists of the day but rather employs the same blend of original composition and mimicry as in "Big Stuff." A prominent influence on those solo piano passages was the music of George Gershwin, where in works such as Concerto in F the piano score fuses two worlds of virtuosity—that of a jazz instrumentalist taking a solo and that of a classical player being featured in a concerto.

In *Fancy Free*, the piano often serves as part of the rhythm section for the score's "big band," then erupts into solo passages, many of which are brief and episodic— flashy components of the overall montage. This is the case with "Enter Three Sailors," where the piano is initially part of the four-bar big-band riff (starting at m. 6) and a piano solo then grows out of the same pattern (Example 1.3, page 39).[150] The piano plays a key role in narrating the action, especially with a series of melodramatic glissandi just after the middle of the first movement (mm. 108–15) that are followed by a truncated clip of the opening riff (mm. 116–19).

Piano is especially prominent in "Enter Two Girls" (third movement), which has a tempo indication of "fast and hot." This is the section that Robbins characterized as "boogie-woogie": "Sudden, loud, change of tempo and mood. Hot, boogie-woogie influence, which quiets down to being insistent with sudden hot loud licks."[151] The orchestra is in big-band mode, and as in the first movement, the

piano emerges from the rhythm section to drive the movement as a whole. Midway through, a static piano riff injects a segment of protominimalist frenzy (Example 1.4, page 40). At this point, abruptly clipped sectionalism becomes paramount, as the score dramatizes rapid changes of action and mood. In what quickly became a signature trait, Bernstein disrupts the regular repetitions and structural norms of well-known popular idioms, continually shifting the accents and the length of individual

Example 1.3. "Enter Three Sailors," from Fancy Free, mm. 22–26.
Piano and percussion only.

patterns. A key cell gets hammered out through much of the movement (e.g., m. 239, clarinets), yet it mutates continually through shifting internal subdivisions, accents, and meters. Toward the end, the pace shifts abruptly to "adagio subito (twice as slow)," with a low and lumbering segment in the trombones, reeds, and violins that could just as easily have been written to accompany the action in a cartoon (mm. 304ff.). As Robbins states in his scenario, the music makes a "transition" to the "next quality." He continues: "As they [the sailors] leave, slowly, music dies and alters."[152]

Jazz also energizes "Pas de Deux" (fourth movement), which essentially presents a theme and variations on "Big Stuff," merging a big-band sound with a distended orchestral waltz. "There are moments of casualness," as prescribed in Robbins's scenario, "mixed in with sudden moments of heat and intensity."[153] These emotional shifts are conveyed vividly in the music. Partway through, there is a full-blown orchestral presentation of "Big Stuff" (m. 362).

In "Competition Scene," a montage structure dominates action-based writing, which is filled with musical tropes of conflict and high drama. The movement is segmented and rapidly shifting, and it has roots in melodrama and film. This is the point in the scenario where the sailors intensify their bid to attract the women, and it immediately precedes the three variations, where each sailor will strut his stuff. "Variation I (Galop)" is another rapidly changing, cinematically spliced movement. It shifts from mimicking the energetic action music of cartoons to allusions to the music of Stravinsky, whose ballets were standard fare for Ballet Theatre. "Galop" has the brittle, slightly off-kilter character of Petrushka, the same ballet in which Robbins starred with Ballet Theatre, and it is frenetic, as the music essentially fuels the extreme gymnastics of Harold Lang. "Variation II (Waltz)" is gentler and more lyrical, while offering yet another version of modernist tropes. No standard waltz appears; rather, the well-known dance rhythm is distorted with continually shifting accents and meters. "Variation III (Danzón)" adds Afro-Cuban traditions into the mix, and classical ballet is evoked when the gentle Latin rhythm

Example 1.4. "Enter Two Girls," from Fancy Free, *mm. 257–62.*

in the flutes abruptly concludes on a crisp chord, parodying similar cadences in well-known works such as Tchaikovsky's *Nutcracker*.

COMPOSING "MY BUDDY": THE SHADOW OF AARON COPLAND IN *FANCY FREE*

Allusions to the ballet scores of Aaron Copland form another crucial component of the musical montage in *Fancy Free*. At times, the references are so literal as to be jarring. Bernstein and Robbins shared a stiff challenge—that is, to distinguish *Fancy Free* from recent successful American ballets, such as

Rodeo (choreography by de Mille) and *Billy the Kid* (Eugene Loring), both of which had much-admired scores by Copland. Those ballets signaled a new era of collaboration between American composers and choreographers. Both valorized the American frontier, frequently incorporating folk tunes and conveying nostalgia for an idealized rural past.

Thus the up-to-the-minute scenario in *Fancy Free* gave Bernstein an opportunity to forge his own compositional style separate from Copland's, and in many ways he did so, especially through the work's foundation in jazz and its hyperspliced conception. Yet even so, Copland's voice rings out repeatedly in *Fancy Free* as a prominent component of the overall montage. References to Copland's music are especially striking in three of the movements: the secondary theme of "Enter Three Sailors," much of "Scene at the Bar," and "Finale." Copland recognized that his voice was audible in *Fancy Free*, complaining to Bernstein that the ballet was "hopelessly married" to his own *Rodeo*. "I'd better watch out that people don't say my new one [*Appalachian Spring*] shows Bernstein influences!" Copland continued sarcastically, "It's amusing to ruminate on where it will all end—but right now it makes a question mark as big as your piano."[154]

Bernstein handled the Copland-inflected sections in a way that paralleled his adaptations of swing-era jazz: he simulated Copland's style rather than quoting it directly. Given that the two men had a deep personal relationship, such mimicry contributed to the ballet's overall double discourse, essentially composing their liaison into the fabric of the work. While a queer reading of *Fancy Free*'s plot foregrounds how the ballet action animates the sailors' intimacy with one another, an analogous interpretation of Bernstein's score offers a way of hearing the sections that resonate with Copland's sound. In the years immediately leading up to *Fancy Free*, Bernstein's relationship with Copland was central to his romantic life, despite the distraction of other affairs. "I can't stop writing you," Bernstein confessed to Copland in September 1942.[155] Or that same year: "I'm not at all interested in seeing anybody. . . . you're the only one that persists and persists, come hell or high water. And I love you and miss you as much as I did the first month I knew you, and always will."[156] Thus when the voice of Copland spoke out at specific points in *Fancy Free*— doing so audibly, unmistakably—it had the capacity to deliver a private message, albeit one that also exasperated Copland.

Copland's very distinctive compositional style appears in "Enter Three Sailors," the first movement of the ballet, where a falling four-note melodic idea yields a secondary theme (first appearing in m. 27), which I am calling the "Copland cell." It grows out of the opening big-band material, and soon it is showcased with the kind of spare voicings and spacious construction that were Copland's signature. It is also thoroughly symmetrical, dividing an octave with descending major seconds at either end (Example 1.5a, page 42). Throughout "Enter Three Sailors," this four-note Copland cell generates other materials, employing a process that is similar to the opening, where jazz riffs generate thematic ideas. Near the end of "Enter Three Sailors" (m. 131ff.), the full orchestra presents the Copland cell with a sense of expansiveness, even as it is interrupted by fragments of the jazz riff. "The matter of chord spacing may possibly turn out to be one of the great musical contributions of the last few decades," wrote the composer and critic Arthur Berger, crediting Copland as being "close to Stravinsky" in spearheading this development.[157] Of the many examples Berger cites of characteristic chord spacings by Copland, he includes the opening of the "Lento Molto" from *Two Pieces for String Quartet* (1928) (Example 1.5b), which Bernstein closely parallels in the Copland cell of "Enter Three Sailors" (Example 1.5a).[158]

Example 1.5a. *"Enter Three Sailors," from* Fancy Free, *mm. 38–39. Cello and bass only.*

Example 1.5b. *Aaron Copland, Lento Molto from* Two Pieces for String Quartet *(1928), mm. 3–4, with pickup. As reproduced in Arthur Berger's* Aaron Copland *(New York: Oxford University Press, 1953), 67.*

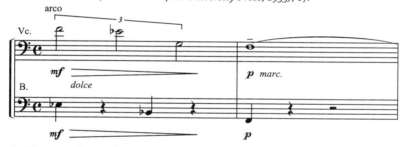

In "Scene at the Bar," Copland's voice soars even more prominently, with some segments suggesting that Bernstein had merged quite thoroughly with his mentor. "Slow, relaxed...music should have literal meanings as far as specific action is concerned," instructs Robbins's scenario. The sailors, Robbins continues, "saunter toward the bar.... They order up three beers which the bartender serves. They pick up their glasses and clink them together in a mutual toast."[159] The description continues with words such as "satisfaction," "mutual," and "relaxation" highlighting the camaraderie among the three men.

"Scene at the Bar" is quiet and contemplative, built on the Copland cell introduced in "Enter Three Sailors," and Copland's lean sound again dominates. The instrumentation is chamber-like, and the woodwinds are deployed in a manner reminiscent of Copland, starting with clarinet (Example 1.6). Soon the instrumentation shifts to flute, oboe, and bassoon (beginning at m. 190). Bernstein's stitched-together structure continues amid all this tenderness, with two saucy interjections of the piano riff (first at m. 184, then at m. 194). Here Bernstein imitates Copland's sound, but he also inserts his own, as though in a compositional conversation.

Example 1.6. "Scene at the Bar," from Fancy Free, mm. 165–70.

The third major segment inspired by Copland appears in "Finale," which overall is extremely sectional and action-based. It opens by evoking a chase scene, then joins together crisp fragments of the first movement's jazz riff (m. 915) and the Copland cell (m. 923). A sense of montage intensifies, and an especially striking piano solo appears toward the end (mm. 993ff.), which references Copland's Piano Concerto at the same time as it conveys the improvised fluidity of jazz. There jazz dominates, with the Copland cell relegated to brief interjections (e.g., m. 998). At this point, the roles of the two composers have shifted from Copland commanding the narrative to Bernstein gaining a primary position. Yet a sense of dialogue remains.

Annotations in Bernstein's manuscript piano short score demonstrate how the music for *Fancy Free* was modeled on that for a melodrama or cartoon. There,

Example 1.7. Manuscript short score of "Finale," from Fancy Free, *page VII–8. Bernstein Collection B15/F8.*

he labeled "Finale" as "(Boogie-woogie, fight, and pantomime),'" and dramatic instructions are indicated with the kind of balloons used in a comic strip. They include "[aches and groans]," "(what dopes!)," and "[They go back to the bar]" (Example 1.7).[160] These directives relate to the fight scene in the closing part of Robbins's scenario, where the sailors focus obsessively on one another, ending up in a pile of bodies on the floor. There is an aspect of camp to this movement, as male bodies and exaggerated physicality are preened with abandon.

Throughout *Fancy Free*, the most striking Copland moments coincide with segments of the narrative that highlight the physical connectedness of the sailors, making both Copland and his sound world an integral component of the ballet's overall identity. Viewed from this perspective, Bernstein composed one of his most revered mentors and lovers into his first ballet score, valorizing their relationship in sound at the same time as he also asserted a separate identity that was young, urban, and unabashedly tied to contemporary popular music.

FANCY FREE'S "DANZÓN": EXPLORING AFRO-CUBAN MUSIC WITH COPLAND

"Danzón" of *Fancy Free*—the solo danced by Robbins as the Third Sailor—adds yet another layer to the ties binding Bernstein and Copland, at the same time as its implications extend deep into Bernstein's career. This movement offers a perspective on Bernstein's emerging crossover aesthetic and his growing awareness of contemporary racial politics. Yet in many ways it is the most conservative movement of *Fancy Free*, yielding an exception to the score's overall reliance on urban big bands and montage. Robbins's sailor had "a feeling of the Spanish or Latin about him," according to the scenario, and Bernstein drew on Latin traditions in the score.[161] He turned to his own "Conch Town," an earlier incomplete draft of a ballet, for the primary motive of "Danzón," and "Conch Town," in turn, had a history tied to experiences he and Copland shared in exploring the music of Cuba, in part as heard in Key West, Florida. Robbins, Bernstein, and Copland were by no means alone in taking notice of Latin America during World War II. This was the era of Roosevelt's Good Neighbor Policy, when cultural and diplomatic ties south of the border were actively cultivated. "With Europe's warfare thrusting the Americas closer together," reported the *New York Times* in 1940, "with radio spreading Latin music through the ether, with dancing teachers everywhere encouraging the rumba, and with Hollywood preparing to glorify Latin America on the screen, it looks as though . . . the South American Way will spread to every part of the land."[162]

Agnes de Mille described Bernstein's score as reflecting just this sort of syncretism, incorporating "a rhumba" that was "performed with the syncopation and innuendo of a New Yorker bred on Harlem rhythms." She also credited the movement with folkloric authenticity, saying it was "based on a direct quotation from a Cuban Danzon."[163] In describing sources for the movement, Robbins and Bernstein each singled out different parts of its lineage. "My variation [in *Fancy Free*],"

Robbins in the "Danzón." Photograph by Fred Fehl. Courtesy of Gabriel Pinski.

Robbins told an interviewer, "is really based on a *danzón*—a Mexican dance—but we call it the rumba."[164] Bernstein identified his source for the movement's music as a "Cuban pattern," adding that Robbins's sailor drew upon "seductive Latin American gestures, grotesquely parodied."[165] The notion of parody came in part from the exoticism common to classical ballet, as in the national dances of *Swan Lake* and *The Nutcracker*, where stereotyped gestures depicted national traits.[166] In choreographing "Danzón," Robbins drew on that well-established realm, which connected with his flair for character dancing.

Bernstein constructed *Fancy Free*'s "Danzón" in a rondo form, with two main thematic areas. It has a traditional overall design, and its principal link to compositional techniques in the rest of the ballet comes with the use of a riff, which appears immediately in the rhythm section and recurs for structural demarcation (Example 1.8).[167]

Other traditional Cuban traits appear in Bernstein's score, including the bass line, which draws upon a *cinquillo* rhythmic pattern (3 + 3 + 2), using wood blocks to generate the sound of claves. Bernstein's version emulates a common variant of a *tresillo cubano* rhythm by suppressing the second "3" in the pattern.[168] The A section layers this rhythm with an imitation of a traditional *orquesta típica*—defined as "a Latin American ensemble that integrates 'typical' or regional instruments with standard European orchestral instruments."[169] Commercial Cuban versions of this type of ensemble favored winds, and Bernstein's rendering included flutes, clarinets, strings, trumpet, and timpani, adding yet another type of

Example 1.8. *"Danzón," from* Fancy Free, *mm. 737–39.*

"orchestra" to the multiple versions exhibited in *Fancy Free*. The harmonic motion of the bass in this section also fits with Cuban norms, with tonic on the downbeat and dominant on the fourth beat. The B section features a trumpet solo, and as in the traditional *danzón*, the section differs substantially enough from A so as to form a trio. Bernstein handled these Cuban materials in his own distinctive way, especially by varying the phrase lengths of standard forms that normally fall into four- or eight-bar units. This pliability happens mildly but consistently in

"Danzón." The lengths of the various A sections are ten bars, fifteen bars, twelve bars, and fifteen bars. The B sections fill twelve bars, then ten.

Copland and Bernstein had already been exploring Latin music together for some time. In 1938, when Bernstein was an undergraduate at Harvard and their relationship was just beginning, he and Copland attended a performance of Copland's *El Salón México* by the Boston Symphony Orchestra. Copland "stayed in the guest quarters of Eliot House where I lived," Bernstein recalled, and they bonded so strongly over the piece that they gave it a nickname: "We went to the performance of *Saloon*, as we used to call it—'Play the old *Saloon*.'"[170] Bernstein's identification with *El Salón México* was deep. "It's going to be hard to keep this from being a fan letter," Bernstein wrote to Copland effusively after the Boston performance. "I still don't sleep much from the pounding of

in my head. In any event, it's a secure feeling to know we have a master in America." For Bernstein, *El Salón México* provided an inspiring model for negotiating left-wing politics, on one hand, and rigid notions of cultural importance, on the other. "[Clifford] Odets, true to form, thinks the Salon Mexico 'light,'" Bernstein wrote to Copland, referring to the famed left-wing playwright. "This angers me terrifically. I wish these people could see that a composer is just as *serious* when he writes a work, even if the piece is not deaftist (that Worker word again) and Weltschmerzy and misanthropic and long. 'Light piece,' indeed. I tremble when I think of producing something like the Salon."[171] With "deaftist" Bernstein was likely indulging in his love of wordplay, suggesting that leftists turned a deaf ear to work that was rhythmic, tuneful, and void of an overt political message. Three years later Bernstein again engaged actively with *El Salón México*, preparing arrangements for solo piano and two pianos, both of which were published.[172]

Bernstein also knew Copland's *Danzón Cubano* very well. A work based in the same Afro-Cuban genre as *Fancy Free*, *Danzón Cubano* included "four simple Cuban dances—simple from a melodic standpoint," according to Copland, "but with polyrhythms and the syncopated beat typical of the Cuban *danzón*." He termed it "a genuine tourist souvenir."[173] Bernstein joined Copland in giving a premiere of the two-piano version of the work in New York in December 1942. Copland had traveled to Key West and then Havana in the spring of 1941, and he did so alone, with exuberant reports to Bernstein. He was then in the process of separating from his longtime companion Victor Kraft.[174] "It's a crazily mixed-up city with skins of all colors, clothes of all varieties, and everybody jabbering away at top speed," Copland wrote from Havana.[175] "I wish you were here to share the music with me," he opined in another letter, revealing not only their personal tie but also their shared love for Latin music:

I have a slightly frustrated feeling in not being able to discuss it with anyone, and a sinking feeling that no one but you and I would think it so much fun. Anyway, I'm bringing back a few records, but they are only analogous to Guy Lombardo versions of the real thing. I've sat for hours on end in 5 cents a dance joints, listening. Finally the band in one place got the idea, and invited me up to the band platform. "Usted músico?" Yes, says I. What a music factory it is! Thirteen black men and me—quite a piquant scene. The thing I like most is the quality of voice when the Negroes sing down here. It does things to me—it's so sweet and moving. And just think, no serious Cuban composer is using any of this.[176]

From the vantage point of the twenty-first century, the words "serious" and "using" carry the sting of colonial conquest. Yet for an American composer in the early 1940s, these ethical considerations were nowhere in sight. Rather, within the context of left-wing politics of the era, an interest in working-class musical traditions in the Caribbean—especially those connected with black and mixed-race Latinos—conveyed a progressive impulse, reflecting empathy for the poor and oppressed. Furthermore, Afro-Cuban styles offered a way to push back against the demand for complexity in modernist circles, as well as against the cultural arrogance of the concert-music world at large. At the same time, Copland did not miss an opportunity to tantalize Bernstein by pointing out that he was hanging out with "black men."

For Bernstein, Cuban traditions offered a way to both connect with and separate from his teacher and lover. Ultimately, his "Danzón" has quite a different character than the two-piano version of Copland's *Danzón Cubano*. The latter is over twice as long, and it is lyrical and more intentionally folkloric. Bernstein's "Danzón," by contrast, has a pronounced rhythmic swing and an overall spirit that derives from commercial popular idioms.

Key West offered a site that bound together Bernstein, Copland, and musical traditions of Latin America. In yet another letter to Bernstein, written during this same trip in the spring of 1941, Copland described the enticements of Key West, once again with a homoerotic edge. "Incredible place," Copland wrote to Bernstein. "You'd love it. Population: part Cuban, part Negro, part Sailor, part Marine, and a few Americans. But only juke box music, so I'm going to Havana on Monday."[177] Sailors played a role in fantasies about Key West. That same year the playwright Tennessee Williams became a regular visitor to the city as it gained fame for its gay culture. And while "juke box music" held minimal appeal for Copland, it was exactly what Bernstein valued.

In August 1941, Bernstein made his own trip to Key West. He loved the place, and it was there that he made his first attempt at composing a ballet, which happened two years before *Fancy Free* was even an idea.[178] "I was crazy about Cuban music. The ballet was to be called 'Conch Town.' It never got finished," Bernstein later recalled. Many residents of Key West referred to themselves as "Conchs," although the term literally denotes residents of the city who immigrated from the Bahamas. "[The ballet] was always lying around and part of it got used in 'West Side,'" Bernstein continued. "It's on the jukebox when Anita is being taunted in the drugstore. Also in that ballet was a tune that became 'America.'"[179] What Bernstein fails to mention is that another part of "Conch Town," separate from what fed into "America," became the basis for "Danzón" in *Fancy Free*.[180]

At the same time as Bernstein was writing "Conch Town," he was gaining exposure to urban bands from Cuba, as broadcast on the radio in Key West.[181] This was the "great age of Cuban radio," according to scholar Ned Sublette, when Havana had "thirty-four medium-wave radio stations," with signals that could travel at night as far as New York City.[182] As a result, an American musician could absorb the sounds of Cuba from the comfort of his Manhattan apartment or during an escape to Florida, bearing witness to the power and importance of radio during the 1930s and 1940s. Key West was "made up of a conglomeration of races speaking English and Spanish, each influenced by Negro dialects," as described in *The WPA Guide to Florida*, published in 1939. "About one-fourth of the population is descended from Cubans and Spaniards."[183]

In the short score of "Conch Town" that survives at the Library of Congress, themes from *West Side Story* and "Danzón" are juxtaposed frequently and freely, yielding a text that appears to have been snipped apart when constructing these

Example 1.9a. "Danzón," from Fancy Free, *mm. 744–48. Flutes only.*

Example 1.9b. Manuscript of "Conch Town," first two systems of page 6.
Bernstein Collection B9/F13.

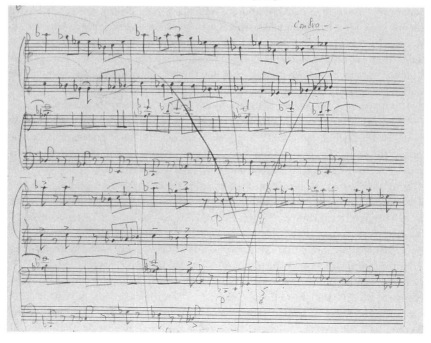

later scores. A version of the opening theme of "Danzón" appears several pages into "Conch Town" (compare Example 1.9a to Example 1.9b), where it has been crossed out. The same material recurs at later points in the manuscript.

* * *

Viewed as a whole, the score to *Fancy Free* fused a remarkably broad spectrum of cultural and artistic references, splicing together a blues-inflected pop song with ballet, big-band jazz with signifiers of Stravinsky and Tchaikovsky, the sound worlds of Aaron Copland and Billie Holiday with Afro-Cuban traditions. Startling juxtapositions resulted, all intended to generate an up-to-the-minute aural collage, essentially refracting through a composer's creativity the experience of flipping a radio dial or changing discs on a turntable, exposing listeners to a range of musical styles experienced by audiences of the 1940s. This kind of montage represented the essence of Bernstein's emerging compositional style. Within this aesthetic, the transnational, biracial world of a nightclub such as Café Society attained parity with the artistic expectations of the old Metropolitan Opera House. High-low cultural divisions were breached gleefully, and musical parody became an equal-opportunity technique.

Amid these cultural negotiations, gay identities were performed onstage, albeit within plotlines that could be read in various ways, depending on the inclination of the viewer. Audiences could take in a charming artistic rendition of a common wartime scene, with sailors on leave playfully competing for the attention of women in a bar, or they could savor a counternarrative in which "buddies" cavorted with one another, indulging in comical physicality and the sheer pleasure of male comradeship. Personal identities fused with artistic visions, as Robbins, Bernstein, Oliver Smith, John Kriza, and Harold Lang all engaged in gay relationships, including with one another. Added to that, the patriarchal presence of Aaron Copland offered musical models to be both emulated and countered at the same time as Copland and Bernstein were experiencing deep personal intimacy. Transgressing one contemporary boundary—whether it marked sexual identity, musical genre, or cultural hierarchy—yielded an opening to push past another. At the same time, *Fancy Free* did not deliver political manifestos. Its goal was entertainment.

Race also lurked around the edges of *Fancy Free*, largely by conjuring up Billie Holiday's voice on the recording of "Big Stuff" at the opening of the ballet. Plus there were evocations of big-band and solo-piano jazz. *Fancy Free* depicted New York City during World War II as a multiracial site, and it asserted parity between mechanized music and live performance. Yet there were racial compromises in the original production of *Fancy Free*: the recording of "Big Stuff" projected the voice of Bernstein's little sister Shirley, no black dancers took part, and no black musicians were in the pit. As a result, African American culture appeared via proxy, filtered through white performers.

Brand-new collaborators when they worked on *Fancy Free*, Robbins and Bernstein immediately achieved a kind of artistic combustion. Not only did crossing borders quickly become central to their personal and creative identities, but they also simultaneously devised a way to reach broad-ranging audiences. Many more negotiations—cultural, political, commercial—lay ahead.

2

FROM NIGHTCLUBS TO BROADWAY
The Revuers, Comedy Skits, and Left-Wing Politics
● ● ●

I like The Revuers the best by far,
Why aren't the kiddies more popular?
On Sundays I'd like to tune in on their show,
But I can't seem to get me a radio.
—The Revuers on NBC radio, November 3, 1940

While *Fancy Free* was establishing Bernstein and Robbins as a talented new creative team, a parallel collaboration had been unfolding in New York City between
Betty Comden and Adolph Green. In 1938, six years before *Fancy Free*, they joined
up with three friends to launch a nightclub act called The Revuers, a group hailed
at the time for writing and performing "the cleverest, sauciest and altogether
most entertaining topical skits we have seen in a year of midnight travels."[1] Now
and then Bernstein served as their pianist. While *Fancy Free* eventually bequeathed to *On the Town* an exceptional focus on ballet, The Revuers—via
Comden and Green—brought hands-on experience with writing scripts for commercial entertainment and with performing in mixed-race venues.

Like Bernstein and Robbins, The Revuers cleverly bridged the worlds of classical music, progressive political causes, and the latest pop-culture hits. Their skits
drew upon an eclectic range of topics, from revered European operas and the classics of Western literature to radio, movies, operetta, contemporary journalism,
pulp fiction, and the latest shenanigans in Washington, D.C. Each skit amounted
to "a 40-minute musical comedy," reported the progressive mass-market magazine *Collier's Weekly* in 1939, "with an opening chorus, a master of ceremonies, . . .
songs, and hilarious parodies."[2] While never didactic, these "brash youngsters"
delivered "social satire," according to the *Daily Worker*, and they performed in a
wide range of settings, starting out in nightclubs and eventually moving into
radio, early television, film, and variety shows.[3] Notably, their act was covered in
the left-wing press, including not only the *Daily Worker* but also *New Masses*, and
they performed at benefits for political causes. Perhaps most striking was their
commitment to challenging the racial segregation that defined contemporary

performance. They did so by consistently appearing in clubs that welcomed all, regardless of race, whether onstage or in the audience.

While The Revuers are legendary in the history of American entertainment, they have not been the subject of extensive historical writing, and their commitment to addressing civil rights issues within the world of performance has gone completely unnoticed. By the late 1940s and early 1950s, the anti-Communist purges of the House Un-American Activities Committee (HUAC) and the Senate Permanent Subcommittee on Investigations, chaired by Senator Joseph McCarthy, came close to their circle, with varying consequences. The Revuers preceded these turbulent events with a period of youthful innovation and idealism. They devised their act with an eye to professional success, and they also hoped to contribute to social change. The group broke apart in the winter of 1943–44 after five jam-packed years. Soon afterward Comden and Green were recruited to write the book and lyrics for *On the Town*. Not only had The Revuers given them experience in writing scripts, but it also provided training in performance— skills that Comden and Green then brought to the Broadway stage.

LAUNCHING THE REVUERS

A series of lightning-quick developments in the late 1930s mobilized The Revuers, bringing them together through shared social and professional circles. "The five of us were not a group to begin with," wrote Comden. "The only thing we had in common was that we were unemployed, and we knew each other vaguely from meetings in casting offices, agencies and drugstores."[4] In addition to Comden and Green, the group included Judy Tuvim, John Frank, and Al Hammer. Julian Claman sometimes handled props but was not consistently part of the ensemble.[5] Comden and Frank often took turns accompanying at the piano, and others occasionally sat at the keyboard. Bernstein was the most noteworthy of that group, but the pianists also included Roger Vaughn and Eddie Heywood Jr.[6]

Comden and Green were both children of Jewish immigrants, raised in the outer boroughs of New York City. Born Basya Cohen in Brooklyn in 1917, Comden came from a middle-class family. Her father, Leo Cohen, who immigrated from the border area between Russia and Poland, was a lawyer, and her mother, Rebecca Sadvoransky Cohen, was a teacher. Comden attended the Brooklyn Ethical Culture School and Erasmus Hall High School. As a child she changed her first name to Betty, then as an adult she changed her last name, too.[7] "I went to NYU, where I majored in dramatic art," she recalled, "and somebody brought Adolph down to meet me when I was still a student. Then we kind of remet after I got out of school and started making the rounds of the offices"—this occurred as each looked for work in the theater.[8] She graduated from New York University in 1938 and was twenty-one when The Revuers started up. Working as an actress was one thing— lots of women did that—but it was an entirely different matter to write scripts and lyrics. Doing so meant entering a man's world, and up until that time only a few women had succeeded in that realm, notably Dorothy Fields.

The Revuers: Adolph Green, John Frank, Betty Comden, Al Hammer, Judy Tuvim.
Photofest Digital Archive.

Adolph Green was born in 1914. "I'm from the East Bronx," Green later stated, "that's the Clifford Odets, have-a-piece-of-fruit Bronx."[9] With that statement, Green identified with a famous line from Odets's *Awake and Sing!* of 1935, a play that explored assimilation and intergenerational struggles within a Jewish immigrant family—a scene resonant with Green's own background.[10] His parents, Daniel Green and Helen Weiss Green, had immigrated from Hungary, and the family did not attain the same middle-class status as the Cohens.[11] Adolph attended P.S. 39 in the Bronx, where he had an early experience in the theater, playing "the villainous dwarf in *Snow White*."[12] He then attended DeWitt Clinton High School, where he wrote poetry and graduated in 1934, in the middle of the Depression. His next step was to work as a runner on Wall Street, "carting bonds around for tycoons," as the *Daily Worker* colorfully described it.[13] He also worked for a carpet company, doing floor measurements. "I was just an unemployed fellow who hoped he would get into the theater somewhere," Green recalled.[14] When Green met Bernstein in the summer of 1937 at Camp Onota in the Berkshire Mountains, he had gone there only to be in a production of *The Pirates of Penzance*, stated Green's wife, the actress Phyllis Newman: "Adolph couldn't afford to go to the camp, but one of the kids there brought him up to be in the thing." Green had a capacious memory. "He knew every piece of classical music probably extant," Newman recalls.[15] "He can rattle off the casts of almost any picture made since the Twenties," reported the *New York Times*, "and can sing the background score of every Chaplin film."[16]

Betty Comden in the early 1940s. Photofest Digital Archive.

When Green later recounted his first meeting with Comden, he echoed her story, adding Judy Tuvim into the mix. Green's account conveys how intensely these young people were building their networks and how quickly The Revuers took shape:

> Betty and I met, as she just said, at NYU, and later I met her [again] on my rounds looking for work in the theater. I had recently met a young girl of sixteen, Judy Holliday, just out of high school. She somehow got involved with a little Greenwich Village nightclub where the owner said, "Do you know any people who could put on a show here?" and she said, "Yes." She had met me, and I ran into Betty and I said, "Look, we can work. We can do a night's work in this place, the Village Vanguard. We'll get five dollars apiece, and no one will ever have to know about it!"[17]

Tuvim joined John Frank and Al Hammer as the other core members of The Revuers. All three emerged from left-wing performance circles in New York during the late 1930s, and all ended up in Hollywood, with varying degrees of success. Born in 1921, Tuvim had been an organizer for the American Student Union, and she had a connection with Orson Welles's Mercury Theatre, working at the switchboard.[18] In the early days of The Revuers, Tuvim was described as "the group's sparkplug," and she was a gifted actress, reputed to have a photographic memory.[19] She was "actively involved in more social causes than the others," according to historian Milly S. Barranger.[20] Her affiliations included the Stop Censorship Committee, the Civil Rights Congress, and the World Federation of Democratic Youth, many with ties to the American Communist Party. She later became a major Hollywood star, winning an Oscar in 1950 for *Born Yesterday* and appearing in seventeen films and television series.[21] In 1956, Comden and Green wrote the successful Broadway show *Bells Are Ringing* expressly for Holliday. Jule Styne composed the score, and Robbins directed and choreographed.

John Frank, who often served as master of ceremonies for The Revuers, also had a deep political commitment. He attended NYU, where he met Comden, and he joined the Peasant Singers, which reportedly performed folk songs in twenty-eight different languages.[22] Al Hammer, meanwhile, had worked in the garment district and spent time in the Youth Theatre, the New Labor Theatre, and the International Workers Order. He eventually ended up in Hollywood, appearing in more than seventy films and television series, often in uncredited roles.[23]

In late 1938, while the country was still deep in the Depression and radical politics retained a prominent voice, the new group kicked off its act. They called themselves The Village Vanguard or The Vanguard, after the now-famous nightclub in New York's Greenwich Village, which had opened not long before and provided their home base. The group was singled out immediately as being "highly talented," and it was called a "seedling collective," signaling its progressive politics.[24] The members garnered praise for the originality of their sketches and the wry skill of their delivery. Within a few months, they had been reviewed in the *New York Times* and the *Daily Worker*. "Without benefit of sets or equipment, they are currently drawing back the curtain on some of the wittiest sketches in town," reported the *Times*. "Their wit stabs everywhere," the article continued, "not merely the political scene but the foibles and fancies of anyone from Chairman Dies to Noel Coward. A few days ago they were satirizing the newspapers, this week Hollywood."[25] The group was crafting its skits very quickly, putting on a new show every month.[26] Decades later, Comden acknowledged that fiscal constraints made it necessary to write their own skits: "We couldn't afford to buy material.... We had no money to pay royalties, so we started to write."[27] Throughout the winter of 1938–39, the group continued performing at the Village Vanguard in a cramped space with a makeshift stage, as other opportunities started to emerge. "It's all—quotes—like a dream—unquotes. Exciting as hell," exclaimed Green in a letter to Bernstein that spring. "But I'm not in the dough yet . . . But Gott zei donk, I'm making a little salary. I've lost about 25 pounds, so I'm no longer a rolly-polly-Adolph, just a flabby Adolph." At some point in the spring of 1939, the group renamed itself The Revuers.[28]

Socially conscious entertainment enjoyed a peak period during the late 1930s, notably in Marc Blitzstein's *The Cradle Will Rock,* which opened in June 1937. For The Revuers, as for Bernstein, that show was inspirational. Comden recalled that they "got together and put on excerpts from Blitzstein's *The Cradle Will Rock*" at an early point in their stint at the Vanguard.[29] After that, she continued, "we began to write our own material."[30] *The Cradle Will Rock* was essentially skit-based, structured as a series of vignettes about the struggle to unionize steelworkers. Each scene focused on a different resident of Steeltown, U.S.A., and virtue and evil were sharply delineated. Those representing organized labor were the good guys, and those from management were very bad. In May 1939, when Bernstein mounted his production of *The Cradle Will Rock* at Harvard, Green wrote to wish him "good luck." He continued: "I hope Blitzstein is there. He told me about it, and I was going to come up, but I can't get Saturday off."[31] In an interview decades later, Green stated categorically that he "worshiped" Blitzstein "from *Cradle*."[32] That summer Green and Bernstein shared a sublet in New York City, together with Julian Claman of The Revuers. Before taking the place, Green pitched its advantages to Bernstein: "It's got swell furnishing, it's got a phonograph-radio, it's got a good grand piano…on 55th St. near 6th Ave."[33] That summer, Bernstein started hanging out regularly with the group at the Village Vanguard, learning their skits and sometimes taking over at the piano.

Skit-based formats were popular during the late 1930s, and another model for The Revuers was *Pins and Needles*, produced by the International Ladies' Garment Workers' Union. It had a long run in New York City (November 1937 to June 1940), and it was an ideological successor to *The Cradle Will Rock*. *Pins and Needles* started out at the Labor Stage on West 39th Street, and its central composer-lyricist was Harold Rome together with other writers, including Blitzstein, providing material. The sketches were frequently updated in relation to current events.[34] Another inspiration for The Revuers was the Theatre Arts Committee Cabaret, a group of "actor-activists" that presented skits, political satires, songs, and speeches from May 1937 to April 1940.[35] Blitzstein was on its executive committee. One of its skits, "Gone with the Movie Rights," parodied *Gone with the Wind*, the hit film of 1939. According to theater scholar Michael Greenwald, this skit provided "an iconoclastic commentary on Hollywood's commercialism." In it, Scarlett O'Hara learned the nasty realities of the movie business from talent scouts while her parents looked on. "Her Daddy threatens to shoot the film-makers for corrupting his 'L'il Girl,'" writes Greenwald.[36] The Revuers wrote a skit titled "The Reader's Digest," which included their own lampoon of *Gone with the Wind*.

As The Revuers gathered steam, they quickly carved out a distinctive identity in the world of left-leaning skits. Or as Judy Tuvim said in comparing their routines to *Pins and Needles*, "Ours are a little different."[37] They were learning on the job. During the 1938–39 season, when The Revuers enjoyed their first flush of success, they were described as being young and "a little amateurish."[38] In part, the Vanguard's cramped and "not-too-sumptuous" basement performance space imposed constraints.[39] The Vanguard was "a dump," as one critic indelicately put it.[40] Their skits were essentially mini-productions, presented "on a packing-box stage before a six-foot home-made backdrop," reported Otis Ferguson in the *New Republic*.[41] In discussing The Revuers, he gave a sense of their youthful inexperience and sheer brilliance:

> Their shows are ragged and in many ways an illustration of how merely speaking a line is as far from putting it over as no line at all. Singly, they haven't anything like the talent either. In the short fellow with the intense dumb stare [Adolph Green] they possibly have one natural future comedian. But

collectively—conceiving, working out, presenting their material—they have a conception of stage ends and means that you could shop around for all year without matching . . .

I won't try to describe the acts, for I found that one of their most notorious numbers had been so well described in the prints that when I finally caught the show, it fell as flat as bed linen, from anticipation of the absurd and unexpected—"Young Man with a Kazoo." But I can say that you could hardly go and be disappointed . . . The body of the thing may falter, but the spirit is unmistakably there and all to the good.[42]

Theodore Strauss, who was nightclub critic for the *New York Times*, made a similar observation: "The comparatively inexperienced performances of the players are overshadowed by the brilliance of the songs and lines."[43] As a result, the group was "one of the minor rages of the town," according to *New Masses*.[44]

In September 1939, The Revuers moved to the stylish Rainbow Room at the top of Rockefeller Center, and that same fall, Bernstein began a master's program in conducting at the Curtis Institute of Music in Philadelphia.[45] "We began in the cellar—the Village Vanguard—and in less than six months we were up 65 floors atop the glamorous RCA building in the magnificent Rainbow Room," Green later recounted with dramatic flair. "And less than a year after that, we were back at the Village Vanguard."[46] His description not only produced a major laugh when delivered to an audience, but it was completely accurate. The Revuers started out with a bang in their new location, attracting exceptionally positive press, especially considering their relative obscurity. Ultimately, though, their gig at the Rainbow Room lasted only briefly. "Their material failed—in a spectacular fashion—to register," reported the *New York Times*.[47]

Yet there was hope. During their start-up year at the Village Vanguard, The Revuers had been signed by the William Morris Agency, which was among the most prominent in the entertainment business.[48] Still, their trajectory continued to career up and down, with high-profile engagements followed by periods of struggle. In later years, Comden and Green coined the term "Revuers' luck" for professional misfortunes that came their way.[49] Even though this early period was not easy, it produced valuable experience. Broadcast media became an important source of revenue and broad-based exposure, as The Revuers landed jobs on radio, early TV, and film. Bernstein took part in some of these appearances, marking his debut on television and recordings—realms of performance and mass dissemination that would ultimately make him one of the most famous classical musicians of the second half of the twentieth century.

From March 5 through November 3, 1940, The Revuers had a weekly spot on NBC radio.[50] "The job that worked them the hardest was a thirty-week stretch on radio," reported Ferguson, "and it was the job most productive for us [i.e., their fans], because they had to work up a completely new half-hour of material every week, and out of that came some of their best ideas."[51] Yet that success, too, ended up having limits. "They clicked," according to one reporter. "A sponsor and big money loomed. Then—the station changed hands. They were out on their ears."[52] Some of their skits might have worked better in the theater, or so Bernstein's sister, Shirley, reported after tuning in to catch the group in November 1939: "I heard Adolph 2 weeks ago. Is that number something new. I don't think they're as good on the radio as in person," she wrote to her big brother. "You've got to see Adolph to appreciate him."[53]

The Revuers recorded two experimental television broadcasts as well, including one in 1939 on DuMont Television, which was one of the earliest TV networks, and another on June 1, 1940, on NBC.[54] The latter was an hour-long program, with Bernstein at the piano and Aaron Copland turning pages for him. Ferguson mentioned their work on television but rued that "I can hardly report on [them], as television where I saw it was not even in its first infancy and kept hopping around or blotting out."[55]

In May 1940, The Revuers made a 78 rpm recording on the Musicraft label, and again Bernstein was at the piano. "In the snappy, breezy vein of our own day is the work of The Revuers," reported the *New York Times*. "Their *Night Life in New York, No. 2* (Musicraft, six twelve-inch sides, $5) contains *The Girl with the Two Left Feet*, and on the sixth side, *Joan Crawford Fan Club*. We found the 'Joan Crawford Fan Club' a deliciously satirical item. 'The Girl with the Two Left Feet' has its moments, but it probably needs to be seen as well as heard."[56] Bernstein accompanied these two skits.[57] "Swell about recording with the Reviewers [sic]—$35 ain't hay," wrote Shirley Bernstein to her brother. "Hey! Save that 35 dollars and spend it on me."[58] Musicraft was a company with a progressive agenda. Founded in 1937, the next year it released Blitzstein's *The Cradle Will Rock*, the first original-cast recording.[59] Just as notably, Musicraft became a leader in building a mixed-race catalogue, including recordings by African American artists such as Teddy Wilson and Leadbelly.[60]

As The Revuers struggled to gain consistent traction, the surrounding political climate shifted from left-wing activism to wartime crisis. They were on a vaudeville program in Maplewood, New Jersey (September 1940), immediately before appearing at Radio City Music Hall (October 1940). Then they returned to the Village Vanguard in January 1941, staying through at least June, although it is unclear if this was a continuous engagement.[61] After that there were periods with long gaps, and then a first-rate booking would unexpectedly come along. "Suddenly we caught on," Green recalled. "We got several splendid reviews, and people started coming down like mad—distinguished people of the theater and letters and the arts—and I said, 'My God, where did this come from?'" Yet their success was not reliable. "We were discovered," Green continued, "but we were 'too smart' for the average audiences. We went through long periods of unemployment."[62] In mid-August 1941, Green wrote to Bernstein: "The Revuers are long gone from the Vanguard. Our future looks promising, but indefinite. Oy!"[63] The following September (1942), Bernstein told Copland, "The Revuers are all depressed."[64]

Next, The Revuers headed for Hollywood. In July 1943, the *New York Times* reported that they had been "signed for a spot" in a film titled *Duffy's Tavern*.[65] By then, they were reduced to a group of four, with John Frank in "defense work."[66] As soon as they arrived in California, the film deal collapsed. But they obtained a four-week engagement at the Trocadero nightclub in Hollywood. In a newsy letter to Bernstein, Green sketched the scene with his delicious sense of humor:

Dollink Leonard, . . . Forgive me for not writing sooner. As always was the case with The Revuers we have been through parlous times. I'll give a brief resumé.

The day we arrived, our agent, Kurt Frings told us that "Duffy's Tavern" was off. The varied producers had quarreled—but, said Kurt, this was a good thing because now we were free to receive really good offers. We opened at the New Trocadero & were sensational, so sensational that the owner let us go after 4 weeks because he figured that now that he was doing a landslide business, it would continue so without us. At this point we realized that no movie company wanted us. Too smart, they said.[67]

Green recounted a series of disappointments as they tried to get a movie contract: "First M.G.M. turned us down. Then everybody turned us down all the way down the line, including dinky little Universal, who screen-tested us and said we stank." Then their agent got them an audition at 20th Century Fox. "It seems that 20th was the one company that hadn't caught us at the Trocadero," Green quipped to Bernstein. "Oh god, we said, an audition, how horrible." At first their tryout did not go well. "For four numbers no one smiled. We noticed that a number of them wanted to laugh, but had to stifle it, because [Darryl] Zanuck [studio executive and producer] didn't look happy or pleased," Green continued. "Then suddenly it happened. D.Z. grinned. HE GRINNED!! Then he chuckled. CHUCKLED!! From that second on we were in. Everybody there roared & rolled & clutched their sides with helpless laughter. We did number after number & they screamed."

They signed a contract "that very day," Green continued, for a film that turned out to be *Greenwich Village*. It was planned, as he put it, as "a super-duper all-dancing, all-technicolor, all Alice-Faye picture with a minimum guarantee of 6 weeks at a very fine figure indeed . . . We're going to do Bazooka [a skit with the full title "The Baroness Bazooka"] in it, plus a new spot which should be something stupid about the Vie de Boheme of Greenwich Village." Green concluded, "Hollywood is the weirdest country in the world."

Despite those early hopes, *Greenwich Village* did not turn out as planned. Alice Faye, who was then one of the celebrities under contract at 20th Century Fox, was nowhere to be seen. Instead, Don Ameche and Carmen Miranda starred. Ameche and Faye had frequently appeared together as co-stars, notably in *Alexander's Ragtime Band* (1938). Most disappointingly, The Revuers only made a cameo appearance in the film. "If you turn away from the screen for a moment, and I hope you do," Betty Comden later quipped, "you are likely to miss my pallid frightened face in blazing Technicolor flashing briefly across the screen."[68] The film is set in a nightclub, presumably in the Village, and The Revuers are included in a party scene, after which Adolph Green performs in a barbershop rendition of "When You Wore a Tulip."

Greenwich Village was released on September 27, 1944, and it was judged as "battling against the odds" with "the most meager sort of material."[69] Fans of The Revuers were disappointed. Writing in *New Masses*, the critic Joseph Foster claimed that the film had little to do with the Village, "either as a geographical location or a state of mind," although it incorporated a leftist landmark with "a shot of Webster Hall (where New Masses has been holding its annual Artists and

The Revuers hamming it up: Adolph Green and Judy Tuvim, Betty Comden and Al Hammer. Photofest Digital Archive.

Writers Ball for thirty-three years, the next one on December 2—adv[ertisement])."
As for The Revuers, Foster must have blinked when they appeared on-screen:
"I waited and waited and sat to the very end of the picture, but they never did
appear."[70]

Despite these shortcomings, *Greenwich Village* contains fascinating moments
in relation to *On the Town* and also to *Wonderful Town* (1953). The film includes an
appearance by the Four Step Brothers, a famed black tap dance group that had
worked with Duke Ellington, among others. Also, Carmen Miranda's performance of "I'm Just Wild About Harry" employs her usual markers of exoticism,
with an extravagant hat and a blend of Portuguese and English, in which Portuguese is treated like scat. In terms of *On the Town*, the setting of her performance
is noteworthy: she sings the song in a nightclub, Danny's Den, and she does so
with a Latin beat, all presaging the nightclub scene of *On the Town*. *Greenwich Village* also found its way into *Wonderful Town*, which opened with a bus of tourists.
In *Greenwich Village*, the guide proclaims, "You are now in the heart of Greenwich
Village," a concept—even specific language—that reappeared in the opening
number of the later Broadway show by Comden, Green, and Bernstein.

While in Los Angeles, The Revuers took part in a broadcast on Armed Forces
Radio (January 1944), and around that time the group broke up.[71] By then Judy
Tuvim had changed her name to Judy Holliday, and she and Alvin Hammer stayed
in Hollywood, launching careers in film and television. Comden and Green went
back to New York. Green later recalled this period as a low point in his professional

life. He and Comden drew upon it for the screenplay for *The Band Wagon*, a film from 1953 starring Fred Astaire. In one scene from *The Band Wagon*, Astaire returns to New York as a washed-up movie star and dances up a ramp in Grand Central Station, which replicated Green's own experience in the late winter and early spring of 1944. "Many years ago, I, too, had walked ruefully, but definitely not jauntily, up the ramp at Grand Central, lugging a heavy, battered suitcase which contained all my worldly goods," Green recalled, "and I, too, had just returned from Los Angeles, an unemployed nightclub performer, broke, discouraged, and conspicuously unknown." He continued: "As I reached the gates, ready to exit into a hostile and indifferent world, I was greeted by the sight of my performing partner, Betty Comden (also recently returned to New York), carrying a large banner reading: The Adolph Green Fan Club. It was a moment I will cherish forever."[72]

After returning to New York from Hollywood, Comden and Green went back to club dates, now working as a group of two, and in late May, Green alone participated in a New York tribute to the conductor Serge Koussevitzky, honoring him for his twenty years as director of the Boston Symphony Orchestra and for his exceptional record of performing music by American composers. Bernstein was a protégé of Koussevitzky. An account of the testimonial event appeared in the *New York Times*: "The side-splitting take-off of Koussevitzky for one, and Copland for another, 'Sacha Pizzekaski,' [was performed] by the incomparable virtuoso humorist Adolph Green, with Leonard Bernstein at the piano."[73]

RACE AND PERFORMANCE CHOICES

During the early 1940s, the racial segregation of performers in music, dance, and theater was implemented informally but consistently, even in a liberal cultural center such as New York City. It is remarkable, therefore, that The Revuers steadily opted to appear in mixed-race venues, contributing to a growing movement to achieve racial equality in performance. The group was gaining momentum just as a small but important group of New York nightclubs with a mixed-race agenda were opening up, and it was within those performance spaces that The Revuers shaped their identity as entertainers.

The Village Vanguard was the first such site. The club's programming was diverse in multiple dimensions, including folk musicians (Leadbelly famously began playing there in 1941), jazz (including Sidney Bechet and Mary Lou Williams, among many others), and comedy and cabaret acts (like The Revuers). For a time in the early 1940s, the Vanguard employed a resident trio of African American musicians, which consisted of pianist Eddie Heywood Jr., drummer Zutty Singleton, and clarinetist Jimmy Hamilton. They were on hand regularly to play for dancing and accompany guest performers.[74] When The Revuers appeared at the Vanguard in 1941, they were onstage with Heywood and his trio. As a result, The Revuers were reviewed in the *Amsterdam News*, where Dan Burley called them "about the classiest grey act I've ever seen," adding that Heywood's piano playing was "something to talk about."[75] Max Gordon, owner of the Vanguard, recalled going with Heywood and Tuvim to Reuben's Restaurant on 58th Street for a "late sandwich" after an evening's performance, and his story reveals the racial gauntlets of segregation. Tuvim "had the cabbie stop in front of the place, told us to wait, she'd be right back, because she had an important errand to perform inside," Gordon recounted. "I found out later what her errand was. She wanted to make sure there was a table available in the place. She put the headwaiter on the spot so that there'd be no hassle, no embarrassment, no turndown at the door when we walked in with Eddie Heywood, a jazz musician in our party, a black man who was playing at the Vanguard."[76]

Café Society was equally important to The Revuers' development. A mixed-race club with strong ties to the political left, Café Society opened in 1938, not far from the Village Vanguard. Two years later, it established an uptown branch on 58th Street near Park Avenue, and The Revuers performed in both locations.[77] The club provided "some of the finest Negro musical talent" in New York City, as the *New York Times* stated. Its "unofficial advisor" was John H. Hammond Jr., the famous record producer, talent scout, and civil rights activist.[78] This was the same club where Billie Holiday's performances of "Strange Fruit" became a ritual and where Bernstein performed excerpts of *The Cradle Will Rock* with Blitzstein. In addition to Holiday, Café Society's central core of black artists included the African American piano virtuoso Hazel Scott, the Golden Gate Quartet, and the pianists Teddy Wilson, Meade "Lux" Lewis, Albert Ammons, and Pete Johnson.

Café Society's influential patrons helped The Revuers break into the entertainment business. "It all began about 2-½ months ago, when we did a guest booking for an Actors' Party at Café Society," Green wrote to Bernstein in May 1939. "Herman Shumlin & Arthur Kober & others were there & they went nuts about us," Green enthused. "So since then everything happened. Publicity—all kinds— New Yorker, N.Y. Times, Post, Journal-American, Masses, The Worker, all over. Everyone in Theatre has been to see us. And composers—anyway—Blitzstein, Copeland [*sic*], Paul Bowles, Jerry Moross, etc. etc. They're swell people, too."[79] Shumlin was a Broadway director and producer, and Kober was a humorist. Bowles was a novelist and composer (his wife was the novelist Jane Bowles), and Moross was among the composers whom Robbins would soon consider for *Fancy Free*. At this early date—that is, one year after The Revuers had been founded and while Bernstein was still finishing at Harvard—these young people were just getting to know performing artists and intellectuals who would soon be part of their inner circle.[80]

One of The Revuers' more remarkable performances occurred as part of a concert titled "From Swing to Shostakovich," sponsored by Café Society at Carnegie Hall on April 11, 1943. Part of a series of concerts at Carnegie Hall that aimed for both black-white and high-low rapprochements, this event was intended to bridge racial divides. In 1938, Benny Goodman and his orchestra performed there with African American musicians from the orchestras of Count Basie and Duke Ellington, among others. It was a famous event, and its live recording is one of the best-selling jazz records of all time. Other mixed-race concerts at Carnegie Hall included "From Spirituals to Swing," produced by John H. Hammond Jr., in 1938 and 1939, and "From Bach to Boogie-Woogie," also produced by Hammond, in

1941 and 1943. In November 1943, seven months after "From Swing to Shostakovich," the Duke Ellington Orchestra gave a famous Carnegie Hall concert.

In addition to sponsorship by Café Society, "From Swing to Shostakovich" was organized as a benefit for the Ambijan Committee for Emergency Aid to the Soviet Union. The Soviet Union and the United States were allies in the war against Hitler and Mussolini, and the Ambijan Committee—or the American Committee for the Settlement of Jews in Birobidjan—was "composed of Jewish residents of the [New York] metropolitan area."[81] It advocated the relocation of Jews to the Jewish Autonomous Region of the Soviet Union, an area known as Birobidjan, located some five thousand miles east of Moscow.

"From Swing to Shostakovich" had the character of a variety show, mixing an array of different kinds of performers in a program of jazz standards, left-wing tunes, and "jazzed" classics, especially pieces by Russian composers.[82] "Jazzing" works from the European concert repertory was a popular practice at the time, undertaken both by highbrow virtuosi such as the violinist Jascha Heifetz and by jazz and popular musicians. Hazel Scott was renowned for jazzing the classics. At "From Swing to Shostakovich," the Hazel Scott Trio, including Sid Catlett on drums and Johnny Williams on bass, jazzed three Preludes (Nos. 10, 13, and 24) by Dmitri Shostakovich. They also jazzed Bach's C-Major Invention and performed "Hazel's Boogie-Woogie."[83] Pianist Albert Ammons, best known for playing boogie-woogie, performed "Timoshenko Torch," honoring Semyon Timoshenko, commander of the Red Army during the German invasion of the Soviet Union. Kenneth Spencer, a black actor and baritone who was soon to sing the role of Joe in the 1946 revival of *Show Boat*, performed a diverse group that included "Meadow Land" (which was identified as a "Red Army Song"), Hall Johnson's "City Called Heaven," and Rachmaninoff's "In the Silence of Night." The Golden Gate Quartet delivered a performance that fused traditional gospel repertory with political messages. Their numbers included "Hush," one of their signature gospel tunes, together with "Stalin Wasn't Stallin'," which was identified on the printed program as a "topical spiritual by Willie Johnson." The latter was recorded that same year on Okeh Records, one of the most successful race labels.[84] In the midst of all this music, The Revuers performed two of their skits: "The Baroness Bazooka" and "Banshee Sisters." "It was a long program, running into midnight, what with speeches," reported the *New York Times*. After this concert, "all of the proceeds [were] to be contributed for watches for the Soviet army and for doctors and nurses at the front."[85]

Benefit concerts were popular during the 1930s and 1940s, offering a grass-roots format in which star performers helped raise money for left-wing causes. The Revuers participated in many such events. In March 1941, they appeared with Hazel Scott and the Golden Gate Quartet at the District Reporters Association's "annual frolic." In May 1942, they performed together with the black actor Avon Long at a party for Russian war relief at the Lafayette Hotel. In October 1942, they were onstage in Carnegie Hall at a concert titled "Stars for Democracy, Presented by Allied Voters Against Coudert," which included the Russian pianists Josef and Rosina Lhévinne, the actress Margo, the singer and actress Libby Holman, and the actor Morris Carnovsky.[86] This last event was staged to protest the Rapp-Coudert Committee, which was formed by the New York state legislature to examine "subversive activities" in the state's schools and colleges.[87] The City College of New York was a target. Although benefit concerts played a significant role in the history of performance, they have been little studied by historians. Many of the performers who took part in them ended up facing profound ramifications for their political alliances. Hazel Scott, for one, was called in by HUAC to testify in 1950. She had her own television show at the time, which was canceled, and her career was severely affected overall.

The Blue Angel on East 55th Street in New York City was the other high-profile mixed-race club where Comden and Green performed. They appeared there in 1944 after their disappointment in California. "Adolph and I had returned here [New York] to accept an offer to appear as a group of two, at the Blue Angel," Comden recalled.[88] They did so as "the desperate remnants" of The Revuers.[89] Sharing the values of Café Society, the "elegant" Blue Angel had opened the previous year. It was managed by Herbert Jacoby, an émigré who previously ran the famous Boeuf sur le Toit in Paris, and Max Gordon of the Village Vanguard, the same person who helped launch The Revuers. In his memoir, Gordon recounted the racial politics in which the Blue Angel emerged, focusing on a moment when he hired the black singer Pearl Bailey and the white comedian Irwin Corey to appear on stage together. "In 1943 you had to think twice before bringing a black woman to the smart Upper East Side of Manhattan," Gordon stated.[90] Like the mixed-race concerts at Carnegie Hall, the shows at the Blue Angel freely combined different genres, races, and ethnicities among its acts. On opening night, the club featured the French singer Claude Alphand, the harpsichordist Sylvia Marlowe, and the Venezuelan singer Hector Monteverde.[91]

The Blue Angel joined a succession of Old World venues in New York City—places such as La Vie Parisienne and Le Ruban Bleu—that provided a cultural haven for war exiles. *Time* described the Blue Angel's opening-night audience as "a swarm of De Gaullist refugees and friends."[92] These clubs transported liberal European values about race to the United States. Lorraine Gordon, wife of co-manager Max Gordon, later reflected on the exceptional egalitarian spirit of the Blue Angel, which she highlighted in terms of both race and sexual orientation. "Perhaps the most important thing . . . was the utter absence of racism on or off its little stage," Gordon wrote. "Blue Angel audiences were always mixed audiences. . . . There were many strata of nightlife in the city then, and Blue Angel regulars were a rarefied breed, very New York, mostly East Siders—smart, clever, well-dressed, and with a real knowledge of good entertainment. Plenty of gays, there were always lots of guys at the bar."[93]

In the spring of 1943, while working at Harms-Witmark, Bernstein had been approached about making an appearance at the Blue Angel. The opportunity came at a point in his career when he had not decided whether to focus on the concert world or on popular music, and his breakout success with the New York Philharmonic was still six months in the future (occurring that November). "Jacoby really wants me bad in his new night club (the Blue Angel), & wants to build me, etc. comme impresario," Bernstein reported in a letter to Aaron Copland that spring.[94] Copland, however, was intent on directing Bernstein toward a career as a conductor. "I keep being properly impressed by all the offers, interests, contracts, personalities that flit through your life," Copland wrote to his protégé. "But don't forget *our* party line—you're heading for conductoring in a big way—and everybody and everything that doesn't lead there is an excrescence on the body politic."[95] During this emergent stage of Bernstein's career, Copland repeatedly admonished him to stick with classical music, while Adolph Green nudged him toward commercial entertainment.[96] "But strictly between us, where's all that long-haired stuff going to get you?" Green asked his friend in the early fall of 1943 when Bernstein's appointment as assistant conductor of the New York Philharmonic had just been announced. "You don't want to end up on the shit end of the stick. You'd better get on that gravy train, soon. But—nice goin', kid."[97]

In April or May 1944, while Comden and Green were performing at the Blue Angel, the idea for collaborating with Bernstein on a Broadway show took hold. Both comedians attended the debut of *Fancy Free*, which happened around the same time, and one evening that spring, Bernstein brought to the nightclub a group of potential associates, including the scene designer Oliver Smith and the producer Paul Feigay. "We were at the Blue Angel at the time," Comden later recalled, "and Leonard got us the job to write the book and lyrics for *On the Town*— and that's how we began."[98] Thus a crucial step toward building a creative team for *On the Town* took place in a mixed-race nightclub.

SAMPLING SKITS

The Revuers' skits can still make a person laugh, and their offbeat style emerges vividly from transcripts of radio broadcasts and from recordings. Scripts exist for some of their skits.[99] I am most fascinated with listening to their material, and I have relied primarily on sound sources for the discussion here. Since their style of comedy was performance-based, it is most vividly appreciated through hearing their voices, their timing, their interactions with one another. The skits were essentially structured as mini-musicals, fusing a broad span of theater genres that included operetta, stand-up comedy, and vaudeville. In retrospect, they appear as a precursor to *Saturday Night Live*, hilariously riffing on conditions in the contemporary world.

The Revuers' skits were tightly written, performed against the backdrop of a melodramatic instrumental accompaniment. Onstage and in recordings, the accompaniment came from a single piano or a small jazz combo, and on the radio it was performed by an orchestra. The Revuers mixed together the great works of Western culture—whether in literature or music—with references to commercial entertainment of the day, especially pop songs and the movies. Their style fused swing with parodies of operetta. Consistently, they tossed in references to the plight of the poor and working class, often with an absurd twist. Their lyrics are dense with names and cultural allusions, and language tends to spill out in a chaotic jumble. The group played to an educated New York audience that could grasp high-end references. Ancient and modern, great art and street life—all zip by in outlandish, lickety-split conjunctions. Some of the references were so much of the moment that exploring them today involves a bit of sleuthing to unravel their original contexts. Race is virtually absent from the scripts.

Musically, the skits stretched on a fairly seamless continuum that ranged from rhythmicized speech to patter (i.e., sung speech) to straight-out song, all of which the group composed themselves. When The Revuers burst into song, they used super-simple melodies, with lots of repetition and a narrow range. The melodic simplicity could have been cloying, even idiotic-sounding, but instead it became an effective part of their shtick, as they commented on contemporary culture with a calculated naïveté. Sometimes they parodied well-known tunes and added new texts. "They were fairly elementary tunes," observed a retrospective assessment in the *New York Times*, "for they had to fit the four chords" that were at the core of Comden's piano repertory. She often accompanied the group, both in performance and as they developed new material. "I've always felt, though," Adolph Green told the *Times*, "that Betty with two more chords would have put us over the top."[100] A handwritten sheet of notes by Comden and Green, which lists ten of their sketches, gives the keys in which they were performed: C major, D major, F major, and A major.[101]

Comden and Green often took highbrow roles in the skits. Both could summon up a commanding vocal presence and an elevated elocution using trilled *r*'s as though intoning Shakespearean monologues. Yet they also nimbly negotiated a range of personas, as when Comden put on a thick Brooklyn accent in "The Girl with the Two Left Feet." Green was a baritone buffo, and Comden was a mezzo. Both vaulted now and then to operatically inflected high notes, using them for comic effect. Sometimes Judy Tuvim did so, too, although she largely played a squeaky-voiced, clueless ingénue whose punch line often delivered the smartest quip of the skit. John Frank assumed the role of a calm, level-headed force—a regular sort of guy in the midst of eccentric characters. And Al Hammer played droll parts, with his characters often down-in-the-mouth and powerless, albeit hilariously.

The format for The Revuers' nightclub skits transferred effectively to the radio and back again. In the NBC series *Fun with The Revuers*, the skits were the centerpiece of a thirty-minute program, with two breaks of two to three minutes for a guest singer and, of course, commercials. The shows were aired on Sundays at 9:30 p.m., and they followed a standard format. They started with an opening gambit presented over a vamp in the orchestra. The rhythmic punch of their delivery is so engaging that the text transcribed below pales in comparison to the radio transmission:

[Rhythmic speech:]
TUVIM: I'm Judy, and my hair is up.
      One Revuer.
COMDEN: I'm Betty and my hair is down.
TUVIM & COMDEN: Two Revuers.
HAMMER: I'm Alvin and my hair is red.

The Revuers on NBC Radio. Clockwise from top left: Judy Tuvim, Adolph Green, Betty Comden, Al Hammer. John Frank is in the center. Photofest Digital Archive.

TUVIM, COMDEN, & HAMMER: Three Revuers.
GREEN: I'm Adolph and my hair is brown.
TUVIM, COMDEN, HAMMER, & GREEN: Four Revuers.
FRANK: I'm John and that is all there is.
ALL: Five Revuers.
[Sung:]
ALL: That's all: there are five of us!
We are The Revuers.
There are five Revuers.
Plink plank plunk.[102]

The skit of the day then began. At approximately the ten-minute and twenty-minute junctures, a male or female crooner delivered a current popular song, with The Revuers providing a clever transition from their skit to the tune. The singers included Kenny Gardner, who made his name performing with Guy Lombardo and His Royal Canadians; Dinah Shore, who was then launching her career and also had her own NBC program; Gwen Williams, who frequently appeared on NBC; and Marion Kaye, another radio vocalist. The Revuers recorded live in the studio with a full orchestra. Norman Cloutier's orchestra performed for their first episode and Paul Lavalle's orchestra for all the rest. Like the singers, Cloutier and Lavalle both made their careers on radio, and they—or a professional arranger at NBC—generated imaginative orchestral arrangements for The Revuers' material. The episode titled "20th Anniversary of Radio" (aired on November 3, 1940), for example, included an orchestral theme and variations on "Pop Goes the Weasel" that was exceptionally fetching.[103] Generally, however, the role of the orchestra was similar to that of the soundtrack in a cartoon, with music dramatizing the action.

The Revuers' zany fusion of high art with mass-disseminated cultural products comes through brilliantly in "The Reader's Digest," which lampoons the famous magazine that published condensed books and marketed them to homes across the country. In 1958, Comden and Green recreated "The Reader's Digest" as part of a two-person revue titled *A Party with Comden and Green*.[104] Hence the extant audio version of that particular skit includes two voices, not the original five. "The Reader's Digest" sketches the fast-paced demands of modern life as a way of explaining the need to save time by reading condensed books, and the setup corresponds structurally to the verse of a popular song. Comedy is delivered in part through intentionally awkward rhymes, which are part of the tongue-in-cheek quality of The Revuers' style. Each section has its own very limited melodic pattern, and two of the melodic segments are repeated. Each melodic pattern (labeled A, B, and C below) has no more than four notes. Comden and Green sing the verse together:

[A] In these days of hurly burly,
Everyone must hurry.
[A] There's no time for reading books,
But you don't have to worry.
[B] You may not have the time, but perhaps you'll
Learn to take your culture in a capsule.
[C] For though the field of literature's immense,
There's a magazine that knows how to condense.
[C¹] Don't sweat for weeks and weeks over just one book,
The Reader's Digest gives it to you in one look!

The rhymes parody bad poetry, and they are a hallmark of The Revuers' style. Since those rhymes are fully performance-based, appreciating their wacky wonders means being able to hear the unconventional word rhythms and pronunciations. "Hurly burly," "hurry," and "worry" offer a mild example. Even better are "perhaps you'll" and "capsule," which involve pronouncing "capsule" with a long *u*. One model for this style of rhyme comes from the late nineteenth-century lyrics of W. S. Gilbert (of the team Gilbert and Sullivan), and segments from *The Mikado* offer a useful parallel. In the following text, sung by the character Ko-ko, the word "chances" rhymes with "re-cog-ni-zan-ces" and "tran-ces":

> Taken from the county jail
> By a set of curious chances,
> Liberated then on bail
> On my own recognizances;
> Wafted by a fav'ring gale
> As one sometimes is in trances.

And here is Yum-Yum, another character from *The Mikado*, with an oompah accompaniment and rhymes that accentuate the absurdity of the text:

> Here's a how-de-do!
> If I marry you,
> When your time has come to perish,
> Then the maiden whom you cherish
> Must be slaughter'd too![105]

Incorporating The Revuers' own version of this type of word play, "The Reader's Digest" skewers the concept of digest-length literature, with a chorus that spews out absurdly compact versions of famous books, juxtaposing classics of Western literature with recent best-sellers. There are two iterations of the chorus, and the text is different in each, except for the concluding two-line proclamation. Comden and Green largely alternate performing the segments, and they conclude most of them by shouting together, "The *end!*" (see Table 2.1).

Most of the books mentioned in "The Reader's Digest," like *Romeo and Juliet* and *Gone with the Wind*, remain well known. Others had their fame in the late 1930s and early 1940s. *How to Win Friends and Influence People* was a best-seller by Dale Carnegie from 1936, and *The Starting of Mankind* inserts itself into debates about evolution. It might refer to *The Origin of Mankind* of 1935, by Ambrose Fleming, who was a creationist, or perhaps to Darwin's *The Origin of Species*—or both. The section about *Les Misérables* provides the clumsiest (hence funniest) example of the comic use of rhyme: "doer," "poor," and "sewer." In *The Starting of Mankind*, "vertebrate," "you'll get ate," and "stood up straight" run a close second. With the segment that spoofed Hitler's manifesto *Mein Kampf*, Green spins off into a demonic frenzy, which begins with German-sounding nonsense syllables and ends with a string of absolutist statements of the sort that were Hitler's trademark. At that point, "The *end!*" has a twist—marking not just the conclusion of a supercondensed book but the urgent need to vanquish Hitler's reign of terror.[106] And the final tag—"That's all you have to know, the *Reader's Digest* told us so"—lampoons a culture that blithely shrinks down complex texts and ideas, delivering them to coffee tables from sea to shining sea.

Table 2.1. "The Reader's Digest" by The Revuers: transcription of the lyrics for two choruses

Abbreviations: sp (spoken), su (sung)

First Chorus:	Second Chorus:
COMDEN	COMDEN

[sp] *Gone with the Wind!*
[su] Scarlett O'Hara's a spoiled pet,
    She wants everything that she
        can get,
    The one thing she can't get is Rhett.
	[sp] *Les Misérables!*
	[su] Jean Valjean no evildoer,
	    Stole some bread 'cause he was
	        poor,
	    A detective chased him through
	        a sewer.

COMDEN & GREEN	COMDEN & GREEN
[sp] The *end!*	[sp] The *end!*
GREEN	GREEN

[sp] *The Complete Works of Sigmund Freud!*
    Things you did when just a kid
    Are still with you, don't keep them hid.
    You love your wife, but oh you id!
	[sp] *War and Peace!*
	[su] Napoleon did not beware,
	[sp/su] He attacked the Russian bear.
	    He came home on his derrière.

COMDEN & GREEN	COMDEN & GREEN
[sp] The *end!*	[sp] The *end!*
COMDEN & GREEN	COMDEN
[sp] *Romeo and Juliet!*	[sp] *How to Win Friends and Influence People!*
COMDEN	
[su] Juliet loved her Romeo,	[su] Confidence you must not lack,
GREEN	[sp/su] Slap each stranger on the back,
[su] Romeo loved his Juliet so,	Greet 'em with a "Hello Mac!" "Hello Mac!" "Hello Mac!" "Hello Mac!" "Hello Mac!" "Hello Mac!"
COMDEN & GREEN	GREEN
[sp] They both got killed, [su] That's all you have to know. [sp] The *end!*	[sp] The *end!*
GREEN	GREEN
[sp] *The Starting of Mankind!*	[sp] *Mein Kampf!*

(continued)

Table 2.1. Continued

First Chorus:	Second Chorus:
[su] At first there was no vertebrate,	[sp] [A blast of pseudo-German gibberish]
[sp] The rule was eat or you'll get ate,	Das ist schlecht,
	Der alles gut,
[sp/su] Then man came along and stood up straight.	Das ist ganze alles.
COMDEN & GREEN	COMDEN
[su] The *end!*	[su] Oy[?]. The *end!*
COMDEN & GREEN	COMDEN & GREEN
[su] That's all you have to know, *The Reader's Digest* told us so.	[su] That's all you have to know, *The Reader's Digest* told us so.

Another skit by The Revuers, "The Girl with the Two Left Feet," shows how the group shaped political messages through comedy. It appeared on the Musicraft recording of 1940, with Bernstein at the piano.[107] As a result, the sound sources are contemporaneous with The Revuers' heyday. "The Girl with the Two Left Feet" lasts twenty-two minutes, taking up five sides of the Musicraft recording. It is essentially a mini-musical, including a fast-paced succession of numbers and an absurdly jam-packed plot—so overfull that it takes a lot of focus to follow the main thread. A frenetic blend of operetta, swing, and soap operas, with a plot that takes wildly improbable twists and turns, its main subject is the absurdity of Hollywood celebrity. But it cleverly embeds a political message as well by focusing on a girl who is so ultra-left-wing that she has "two left feet." That image also carried a connotation of being clumsy.

Exploring "The Girl with the Two Left Feet" in detail offers another view of The Revuers' style. The skit opens in Plowman's Japanese Theatre, spoofing both the famed Grauman's Chinese Theatre in Hollywood and the tendency in the late 1930s and early 1940s to valorize Americana (hence the word "Plowman"). It comically critiques Hollywood for taking itself too seriously. The opening number (sung by Judy Tuvim) sets the theme with a burst of exoticized pentatonicism, evoking Japan as filtered through *The Mikado*. It plays with rhymes, as in "The Reader's Digest": note the word "premiere" in the first section of the opener, which is pronounced in three syllables. The texts that follow have been transcribed from the 1940 Musicraft recording.

In Hollywood there's a theater
Known as Plowman's Japanese,
Home of movie premiere,
Quite spectacular affair.

The skit's main characters include a Hollywood producer, Mr. Cecil Mille DeB (spoofing the great film director and producer Cecil B. DeMille). There is also his wife, Lamar Lamour (spoofing the actress Dorothy Lamour), who has a thick French accent, and Roger Merrill, a Hollywood star. Comden plays Lamour, Green plays DeB, and John Frank might be playing Merrill.[108] DeB's studio stages a media event to celebrate the premiere of a film starring Merrill and Lamour, and Merrill is scheduled to set his footprints in concrete at Plowman's Japanese Theatre, joining the illustrious stars who have been honored there. Merrill arrives with an entourage of studio handlers, and he finds that the concrete prepared for his footprints instead has prints of "two left feet"—and they are those of a girl! The whole group sings a catchy swing number, "What Lady Left Two Left Feet," which serves as a kind of Greek chorus commenting on the scene. The recorded performance is spunky and engaging:

What lady left two left feet,
Two left feet in the soft concrete?
Who's that unknown girl
Who ruined the great premiere?

What lady left two left feet,
Two left feet in the soft concrete?
Who's that unknown girl
The unknown girl
The unknown girl
Who ruined the great premiere?[109]

To a galloping tune in the style of Gilbert and Sullivan, Roger Merrill declares, "I'm off to find the girl with the two left feet." A fast section of patter ensues, and Mr. DeB declares melodramatically that "Hollywood is doomed," while he starts questioning workers in the studio to find out what happened. Briefly distracted from his mission, he sings a duet with his wife, Lamar Lamour, who reflects narcissistically on "the mystery of me." She adds, "I am a perfection of rare perfection." Mr. DeB then questions Mr. Tomato, a working-class Italian concrete mixer who prepares the footprint squares, trying to find out what he knows about the episode. Mr. Tomato sings a brief operatically inflected ditty, tossing off exclamations of "Pagliacci!" and "Funiculà, funiculì"—the former a reference to the beloved opera by Leoncavallo and the latter an inverted parody of the famous Neapolitan folk song "Funiculì, Funiculà."

Next, an usher at the theater is questioned: Miss Macy Deluxe, played by Comden.[110] Like Mr. Tomato, she represents the working class, with a thick Brooklyn accent, and she defends herself in a fast-paced song with jazz inflections. There is wordplay with "bottom" and "top," "down" and "up" as she describes a life of struggling with social mobility. The twists in language playfully assert that while many workers try hard to succeed, they do not necessarily pull it off.

I'm a uniformed attendant,
Work at Plowman's Japanese,

Started out right at the bottom
From the top of the second balcony,
Wo-ho, oo that balcony.

I had higher aspirations,
Just to show you what I mean.
I persuaded Mr. Plowman
To elevate me to the lower mezzanine,
You know, oo that mezzanine.

[Bridge]
I rose right up up
Down to the orchestra,
Finally I was there.
Then I won that position
As gold club attendant at the concrete square.

At the premiere for Roger Merrill,
I removed the cloth with greatest care.
Imagine my surprise and consternation
When I saw those two left footprints lying there.
Wo-ho, gee I got a scare,
Woo-oo, listen Mr. DeB,
Wo-ho, don't you blame poor me.

I'm innocent, I repeat.
Find the girl, find the girl with the two left feet.[111]

The police are called in to locate the culprit, and they question suspects, hurling accusations before the evidence has been assembled. Officer Mulligan, who is an Irish cop (a tenor, probably performed by John Frank), sings a lovely Irish air, contending that the imprints of left feet were produced by "pixies" (elves). That theory is quickly dismissed, and a national search ensues to find the culprit: "Calling all cars, be on the lookout for girl with two left feet."

Suddenly Mary Rose, played by Judy Tuvim, knocks on Roger Merrill's door, demurely confessing, "I'm the girl with the two left feet." She too is a working gal—a squeaky-voiced waitress on the movie lot—and she introduces herself in song: "Worshipping the film stars is the only joy I got." She says she has been Merrill's fan for a long time: "I've loved you from your 'extra' days until your great premiere." She succinctly describes how her feet happened to land in the concrete: "I looked, I loved, I slipped." Merrill then abruptly and improbably declares, "I believe your story, and in fact I love you." He accompanies her to a kind of inquisition by a board of producers, who grill her about the atrocity she has committed. They find her "guilty, guilty, guilty." Her punishments are proclaimed:

One. She will be denied membership in every fan club.
Two. She will be barred from every movie house in the country.
Three. She is banished from Hollywood forever.[112]

Then with a madcap plot twist, Mary Rose is declared to be a movie star. Since her footprints are in Plowman's Theatre, she must be famous! The group again sings "The Girl with the Two Left Feet," and a string of characters appears in a final succession of rapid-fire numbers as the style shifts to a swinging Gilbert and Sullivan. First a male commentator announces the marriage of Roger Merrill and the girl with the two left feet:

> The former Rose Marie
> Is Mary Rose Rose Marie Merrill now.
> La la la . . . [etc.],

Then Mary Rose sums up her new position in life:

> I was once a movie fan,
> And worshipped from afar.
> I fell into the soft concrete,
> And now I am a star.
>
> Oh, I love Roger, he loves me.
> Our married life is sweet.
> I owe my fame not to my fate,
> But to the two left feet.[113]

A swing chorus injects a couple of lines, and Lamar Lamour proclaims once again in song that she is "the greatest artist of the silver screen": "All my pictures pack ze house." We learn that Roger Merrill and Mary Rose now have footprints side by side at Plowman's Japanese Theatre, and the number concludes with a swing chorus:

> There's a story that's quite complete
> Of the girl with the two left feet.

"The Girl with the Two Left Feet" is a brilliant comic number, directing its parodies in a dizzying number of directions. *Pins and Needles* and leftist theater enter with a focus on workers. *Hot Mikado,* an all-black jazzed production of the famed operetta that was staged at the New York World's Fair in 1939, hovers in the background, especially when The Revuers swing the style of Gilbert and Sullivan in a manner reminiscent of jazz vocal groups of the era. "The Girl with the Two Left Feet" also yields a mash-up of ethnic humor, with pre–Pearl Harbor Japanese exoticism, a French movie star with a thick accent, an Italian concrete worker, and an Irish cop. When Mary Rose faces harsh questioning, with an assumption of guilt and a verdict of banishment from Hollywood, the script gestures to the House Un-American Activities Committee. In 1938, the committee had targeted the Federal Theatre Project, charging that it had strong ties to Communists, which marked the end of the project; that same year HUAC leveled accusations against the film industry. Yet even with these accusations and indictments, the political climate remained open enough in 1940 for The Revuers to perform flippant commentaries about political witch hunting and do so with some degree of freedom.

Bernstein's piano accompaniment in "The Girl with the Two Left Feet" is fascinating to parse. He must have been improvising, perhaps from a lead sheet. He was clearly comfortable with supplying melodramatic punctuation to the action, and he was adept at shifting stylistic gears very quickly—a warm-up for the proto-sampling techniques that he used in *Fancy Free*. He drew upon well-known pop-music tropes for various ethnicities, such as a pentatonic stereotype for the Japanese. Some of his accompaniment employed the kind of stock musical gestures used to narrate silent films, radio, and staged melodramas. His most striking segments occurred in the jazzy numbers, as in the title song and its various reprises. He also indulged in a few chromatic orgies, where he strayed far from the usual harmonic script of The Revuers. One such case accompanied the narcissistic rant of Lamar Lamour, with arpeggiated chromatic clusters in the bass.

A few other themes characterized The Revuers' skits. Empathy for the working poor appeared frequently, as in the setup for "Nightlife," which aired on NBC on September 29, 1940.[114] The skit portrayed a group of young people sitting around their apartment on a Saturday night, trying to figure out which nightclub to attend. At the opening, John Frank rents a tuxedo so he can be properly attired for the adventure, a sign that he cannot afford to own one. As Green declares in the skit, "We just didn't have the clothes." At midnight, Frank starts turning into a pumpkin because he has forgotten to return the tux. Ultimately, the group ends up forgetting about their plans and staying at home, representing average folks on a limited budget.

Another kooky politicized moment turns up in "World's Fair," which was performed both on NBC radio on May 14, 1940, and in The Revuers' foray into experimental television on June 16, 1940.[115] This skit captured some attention, principally for a number titled "The World's Fair Is Unfair," sung by Judy Tuvim, who was "dressed in a flowing white robe and the spiked crown of the Statue of Liberty."[116] "The World's Fair Is Unfair" is a bluesy torch song in which Tuvim complains that she, playing the Statue of Liberty, has been abandoned for the newest tourist sensation, the World's Fair, which had opened the previous year in Queens, New York. A protest follows, with the group singing, "We're picketing the fair." Concern for workers enters the skit at another point as well, with a song performed by "the people who push the chairs"—that is, the workers who have the tedious job of carting visitors around the fair grounds.

Abrupt juxtapositions of high and low culture were also among The Revuers' core strategies. "Joan Crawford Fan Club," which was included on the 1940 recording with Bernstein at the piano, pokes fun at the mindless valorizing of Hollywood celebrities, and it provides an example of the group's witty high-low cultural conjunctions. The skit opens with a musical setting that emulates a solemn hymn, with lyrics lampooning the absurdities of celebrity worship:

We love Joan Crawford,
For she is the epitome
Of what every girl would like to be,
And so to pay her fealty
We formed a Joan society.[117]

Another example of The Revuers' focus on high-low crossover is "The World of Music," which aired on June 18, 1940. Taking the listener "from Bach to Brahms to Basin Street," as the final line of the opening number puts it, the skit parodies the range of musical styles that were popular in the United States. Tuvim sings a number redolent of "The Reader's Digest," which juxtaposes major figures in European music and literature with references to American popular culture. Most are ripped completely out of context. The melody is simple and repetitive over an oompah accompaniment:

Oh how I love you,
And how you love me. Ain't love.
We're just like the lovers in old history. Grand.
Like Romeo and Juliet
And Tristan and Isolde
And Pélleas and Mélisande
And Romulus and Remus
And Horn and Hardart
And Amos and Andy
And Simon and Schuster
And Orson and Welles.[118]

In one segment of the "The World of Music," a singing teacher named Papa Rubato tells a story about his "most famous pupil," a singer named Larynx Tonsil, who is facing a crisis as he tries to uphold the Western classical tradition. Larynx is a baritone launching a concert career, and he gives a concert in Carnegie Hall, where he follows a trend of the day of placing the classics on the main program and singing a folk song or popular ditty for an encore. In this case, it is "Shortnin' Bread," a popular minstrel tune from the turn of the twentieth century, which uses black dialect. Critics rave about the encore while ignoring the rest of the program, much to Larynx's distress. He then takes "a triumphal tour" to Boston's Symphony Hall and the Hollywood Bowl, and he laments to Papa Rubato: "I'm so miserable. I studied for twenty years, I studied the classics so that I could give great music to the world, and now the only thing I sing is—you know what. I'm asked to sing it everywhere I go. At concerts. On the radio. At private parties. In the bathtub. What shall I do?" Papa Rubato advises him to "close the door." Larynx then decides to rent Yankee Stadium for a massive concert. "He papered the house with 80,000 people," an announcer in the skit states, "and swore he would sing exactly what he wanted to sing." Larynx begins with the aria "Largo al factotum" from The Barber of Seville, but with each line of Italian he dissolves into "Shortnin' Bread." At one point he sings: "Figaro, Figaro; Figa-bread, shortnin-ro."

Like the usherette in "The Girl with the Two Left Feet," Larynx finds that movement up the social ladder can be fickle, and he tumbles down to the working class, with John Frank declaring: "And so they led him away, poor fellow. And now he's a singing waiter in Weehawken—that's on the Jersey side." Thus Larynx was defeated—even destroyed—by attempting to champion the great works of Western music.

Despite Larynx's misfortune, "The World of Music" ends with a kind of musical détente, as The Revuers sing a number that asks musicians from the high and low sides of the artistic divide to "shake hands" with one another. The following lyric is performed over a five-note scale in the accompaniment:

> Benny Goodman, shake hands with Brahms.
> Schirmer and Sons, shake hands with Harms.
> Bach with Abe Liman, [unclear] with Grieg,
> We're forming a cosmic musicians' league.
> If the turtle shell can make a lute,
> And a piece of reed can make a flute,
> Then it must follow as the night does day
> That music is definitely here to stay.[119]

This closing segment also provides an example of the kinds of jam-packed texts that became part of Comden and Green's artistic identity as lyricists. "Schirmer" refers to G. Schirmer, a major publisher of classical music, and Harms was the same pop-music publisher that employed Bernstein for a year. Abe Liman was a big-band leader of the day. And the cultural disjunctions embedded in the rhymes again contribute to the comedy.

Rapid delivery was also critical to The Revuers' tool kit, and examples occur throughout the skits. One such case illustrates yet again their fascination with high-low intersections. Max Gordon recalled a performance at the Village Vanguard with Adolph Green singing and John Frank at the piano: "Adolph steps forward and sings out Grieg's [sic] 'Flight of the Bumblebee' in one minute flat—which brings the house down."[120] In one swoop, Green showed off his prodigious command of classical music and his virtuosity as a comedian.

POINTING TO THE FUTURE

With the passage of time, the skits of The Revuers have receded from the spotlight, becoming little known and not readily available. Once retrieved, those mini-musicals turn out to be fascinating, and they have strong resonances in the mature work of Comden, Green, and Bernstein. Employing an ecumenical sense of parody, they lampooned musics of all sorts, and they commented on a culture where classical music and commercial genres coexisted yet competed for attention. The musical language and performance style of swing were at the core of their material, and their mode of social satire was thoroughly good-humored and non-confrontational, if a bit opaque at times. While all five Revuers originally appear to have been involved in the creative process, Comden and Green were the two who ultimately made a career writing for stage shows and films. As for Bernstein, he was not consistently part of The Revuers' creative team, yet he was thoroughly familiar with their material, both from occasional stints as their accompanist and from watching them in action. Comden later reminisced that Bernstein was so intimately connected with The Revuers that he knew their skits "better than we did."[121] While her claim might have sounded a bit hyperbolic, Bernstein said basically the same thing about his tie to the group: "And I know all that stuff, or I came to know it, by heart, because they were very dear friends of mine, along with Judy Holliday and the other members of the group...So sometimes I sat in with them for fun and accompanied them."[122]

Later works by Bernstein (alone) and by Bernstein, Comden, and Green (together) resonate with The Revuers' material. Bernstein's one-act opera *Trouble in Tahiti* (1952), with its jazzy but cynical narration of married life in the suburbs, is anchored by a Greek chorus that swings its message, as in "The Girl with the Two Left Feet." *Wonderful Town* (1953), with a score by Bernstein and lyrics by Comden and Green, has multiple ties to The Revuers. "My Darlin' Eileen" uses musical tropes of Irishness and is sung by a chorus of Irish cops, in yet another allusion to "The Girl with the Two Left Feet" (where there is a single Irish policeman). "What a Waste," sung by *Wonderful Town*'s Bob Baker, recalls Larynx Tonsil of the skit "Nightlife" as it tells of aspiring artists who have been trampled by the harsh cruelties of New York City. The fourth verse of "What a Waste" features a working-class "kid from Cape Cod" who was a "marvelous singer—big baritone," and it concludes with razzle-dazzle vocal pirouettes:

Kid from Cape Cod
Fisherman's family,
Marvelous singer—big baritone—
Rented his boat,
Paid for his lessons,
Starved for his studies,
Down to the bone.
Came to New York,
Aimed at the opera—
Sing "Rigoletto" his wish.
At the Fulton market now he yells "Fish!"[123]

Larynx performed the *Barber of Seville*, not *Rigoletto*, and he too was crushed by the system, ending up as a singing waiter in New Jersey rather than as a singing fishmonger. "What a Waste" also revisits the many parodies of operatic vocal pyrotechnics that were tossed off by The Revuers.

On a fundamental level, listening to The Revuers' skits offers a clear perspective on one means by which Bernstein honed his compositional technique of parody and montage. Through formative artistic experiences with this group of friends, he gained hands-on experience in combining seemingly dissimilar musical styles while poking fun at iconic symbols from classical music. He came of age in a performance environment where his young colleagues were having a whale of a good time venturing beyond conventional genre boundaries, and he joined them in the journey, drawing on their comedic aesthetic for his own compositional voice. It was an environment of open-mindedness about what constituted "good" music, with popular and classical idioms cross-pollinating imaginatively. Just as important, The Revuers' decision to appear in mixed-race venues, sometimes with Bernstein at the keyboard, positioned them as part of a movement that was intent on providing equitable opportunity for performers of color. There, too, actions from this early stage of their careers had strong resonances in the years ahead.

BROADWAY AND RACIAL POLITICS

3

CREATING A BROADWAY MUSICAL
The Conception and Debut of
On the Town

* * *

*Though Robbins dances in many ballets besides his own, he is not happy
in the* Swan Lake–Sylphides *kind of thing. He wants to talk in terms of
radio, swing, newsreels and more than anything else—theater.*
—PM: New York Daily (1944)

*He never thought about whether a thing was pop
or serious, just whether it was good.*
—Betty Comden about Leonard Bernstein

On the Town opened on December 28, 1944, just eight months after the debut of
Fancy Free and Bernstein's visit to the Blue Angel, and the new show by no means
followed a conventional formula for a Broadway musical. Blending the conceptual
framework and comic energy of a nightclub act with a contemporary ballet, *On
the Town* achieved its joyous esprit from unorthodox aesthetic mergers. At the
same time it challenged audiences on hot-button social and political issues of the
day, albeit playfully. Given the financial pressures of Broadway, *On the Town*
instantly raised the stakes for Bernstein, Comden, Green, Robbins, and their collaborators. Just about everyone involved, with the exception of the famed director George Abbott, had little or no Broadway experience. "We turned up at
work via subway for a nickel," recalled Comden and Green about their modest
status at the time.[1]

While the success of *Fancy Free* had taken its creative team by surprise, that of
On the Town was less of a shock but still greater than expected. This time the reception was far more broad-based and financially lucrative. " 'On the Town' is the
freshest and most engaging musical show to come this way since the golden day
of 'Oklahoma!' " reported the *New York Times* the morning after its premiere.
"Everything about it is right."[2] A chorus of acclaim continued in the press, consistently recognizing the show's "high-spirited, youthful vitality," as the left-wing
newspaper *PM* put it. That particular critic also grasped the fundamental fusions
that made the show so remarkable: "Bernstein bridges the gap between [the] Tin

Pan Alley idiom and Copland-Stravinsky so successfully that the highly expert ballet music and the smart Broadway songs seem to be all of a piece."[3] As Comden and Green later observed, the show was "a maverick fitting into no particular theatrical category."[4]

On the Town appeared within a group of stage and film musicals about the military that relieved wartime anxieties with comic entertainment. Its predecessors included the film *The Gang's All Here* (1943) and stage productions such as *This Is the Army* (Irving Berlin, 1942; film in 1943), *Let Freedom Sing* (Harold J. Rome and Sam Locke, 1942), and *Something for the Boys* (Cole Porter and Herbert and Dorothy Fields, 1943). *This Is the Army* had a mixed-race cast, but it included on-stage segregation and stereotypes from blackface minstrelsy, with "racial dynamics" that "looked both forward and backward," writes historian Jeffrey Magee.[5]

On the Town established its own position amid these predecessors. For one thing, it combined a war musical with screwball comedy—that is, a form of comedy commonly associated with films of the 1930s. *Bringing Up Baby*, for example, which starred Katharine Hepburn and Cary Grant (1938), delivered madcap antics with strong female characters. Screwball comedies combined "the sophisticated, fast-paced dialogue of the romantic comedy" with "the zany action, comic violence and kinetic energy of slapstick comedy," according to one film scholar.[6] Added to that, *On the Town* incorporated references to the comic genre of opera buffa, as in Mozart's *The Marriage of Figaro*, which also had fast-paced action, with improbable twists in the plot. To a certain extent, *On the Town* merged opera buffa and screwball comedy with camp, passing the mixture through the filter of The Revuers. *On the Town* also incorporated an exceptional amount of ballet, with some scenes danced and sung rather than spoken. And its score combined music "in the popular vein," according to scene designer Oliver Smith, with writing that was "highly sophisticated."[7] Politically, the show reflected deliberate decisions in equitable racial representation and in depicting its female characters as feisty and independent.

On the Town ran for nearly fourteen months, closing on February 2, 1946, after 462 performances.[8] A national tour began on February 4, 1946, traveling to Baltimore, Philadelphia, Pittsburgh, Detroit, and Chicago, where it ended on April 27, 1946.[9] In 1949, a Hollywood film of *On the Town* appeared, starring Gene Kelly and Frank Sinatra. In many dimensions, the film was a different creature from the Broadway show. Comden and Green wrote a new script, and much of Bernstein's music was replaced with songs by Roger Edens. Choreography was by Gene Kelly, and there was no mixed-race casting. Yet the film gained its own iconic status, with an even broader viewership than the Broadway production.

On the Town has been produced occasionally in the ensuing decades, but it has by no means become a staple among American musicals. A revival in 1959 at the Carnegie Hall Playhouse included Pat Carroll as Hildy and Harold Lang as Gabey. Lang had danced the role of the First Sailor in the original *Fancy Free*.[10] A major Broadway revival of *On the Town* took place in 1971, with Donna McKechnie, Bernadette Peters, and Phyllis Newman as female leads, with a run that lasted only seventy-three performances.[11] Another memorable revival occurred in 1998, led by the distinguished African American director George C. Wolfe with choreography by Eliot Feld. It had sixty-nine performances, moving to Broadway after opening in Central Park. And in 2008, New York's City Center staged the show as part of its brilliant Encores! series.

The first production of *On the Town* is the focus of this chapter. The tale of the show's conception has become a standard part of Broadway lore, especially since its creative team went on to such illustrious careers.[12] Yet despite the show's instantly recognizable name, little has been known about the issues raised by its inaugural staging and its refractions of life in wartime New York. The show's plot and creative process, its original cast and production team, its Boston preview and Broadway launching, and its reconception as a film are explored here, offering a framework for the ensuing chapters, which delve into race, representation, and wartime politics, especially in relation to racial segregation of the military and the Japanese internment camps. The show's hiring practices placed high priority on racial and gender equity, and the career choices of its cast and production team represented crossover as fully as the show's artistic conception. In terms of personnel and aesthetics, *On the Town* navigated high-low balances with joy and imagination.

CONTEMPORARY PLOT AND CHARACTERS

On the Town is set on the streets of New York City during World War II. The city was then a site that soldiers passed through on their way from one point on the globe to another. "We wanted them to come off as people," Comden and Green wrote of the characters in their show. "No matter how extravagantly treated, we wanted them to possess the qualities and attitudes of the service men we had seen coming to the city for the first time, and at least touch on the frantic search for gaiety and love, and the terrific pressure of time that war brings."[13] At the same time, the show's mixed-race cast imagines an America of open-minded inclusion, free of racial bias and boundaries. All of this is delivered through a jam-packed plot, with lots of characters, fast-paced patter, and an intentionally exaggerated sense of hustle and bustle—all inheritances from The Revuers.

As the show opens, three sailors emerge at dawn from their ship, which is docked at the Brooklyn Navy Yard, and they set off on the subway for a twenty-four-hour leave that takes them all over the city, from Carnegie Hall and the Museum of Natural History to Times Square, a string of nightclubs, and Coney Island. More than anything, the soldiers want romance, and they soon discover that the women they meet are highly independent and sexually aggressive. There are six main characters who ultimately form three romantic couples: Ivy and Gabey, Hildy and Chip, and Claire and Ozzie.

Two of the female characters—Ivy Smith and Hildy Esterhazy—are working gals just like Miss Macy Deluxe, the usher in The Revuers' "The Girl with the Two Left Feet." Played originally by Sono Osato, Ivy is an aspiring singer and dancer who is crowned Miss Turnstiles for the month, a spin on the title Miss Subways,

Cris Alexander (Chip) and Nancy Walker (Hildy) in the scene in Hildy's apartment (Act I, Scene 10). Photofest Digital Archive.

which was a beauty pageant run by the City of New York beginning in 1941. Ivy earns a living as a cooch dancer, and she aspires to rise up the employment ladder, aiming for more legitimate realms of performance. Ivy basically fits the character type of an ingénue. Hildy, played by Nancy Walker, is tough as nails and drives a cab, which was a surprisingly common job for women during the war years.[14] Hildy's "objective is sex, plain and simple," states a document in Comden and Green's papers, and she fits a comedy character type of an "unruly woman."[15] Plus, her full name, Bruennhilde Esterhazy, glances back to The Revuers. Lovers of classical music will instantly recognize the two spoofs that it fuses: Brünnhilde, a character from Wagner's opera cycle *Der Ring des Nibelungen*, and Esterházy, the family of Hungarian nobility who served as patrons of the composer Franz Josef Haydn.[16]

Meanwhile, Claire, played by Betty Comden, is an anthropologist doing research at the Museum of Natural History. Well educated and perhaps even affluent, Claire represents an upper-class counterpart to Hildy's rough-edged bravado. Yet she, too, is sexually aggressive and seemingly oblivious to the social codes for romance, and her character's name also has roots in parodies by The Revuers: Claire De Loone spoofs *Clair de Lune*, a popular late nineteenth-century piano work by Claude Debussy, which continues to be played by thousands (if not millions) of young piano students around the world. The spelling "Loone" gives the

John Battles (Gabey) and Sono Osato (Ivy) in front of Oliver Smith's set for the
Coney Island roller coaster (Act II, Scene 5). Photofest Digital Archive.

name an absurd twist, with a suggestion of being "loony" or perhaps even tied to
Looney Tunes, the famous animated cartoon series.

In sharp contrast, the male characters appear as naïfs from the hinterlands,
emblematic of how New Yorkers viewed the unsophisticated servicemen who
came to the city from far-flung farms and small towns across the country. Chip,
played by Cris Alexander, is methodical, with an obsessive streak, as he doggedly
tries to get his buddies to stick to the sightseeing plan he has devised for the day.
Hailing from Illinois, he uses a guidebook so outdated that some of its landmarks
no longer exist. "Holy smoke," Chip declares near the opening of the show. "I've
never been anywhere bigger than Peoria."[17] His character name represents another high-low hodgepodge. Initially he introduces himself to Hildy as "John Of-
fenblock," alluding to Jacques Offenbach, the nineteenth-century composer of
operettas, and his nickname is a pun on the phrase "chip off the old block."[18]

Ozzie, played by Adolph Green, hails from Scranton, Pennsylvania, where
"everybody's covered with coal dust," and he brashly discloses an eye for women:
"I wanna see the beauties of the city, too, but I mean the kind with legs!" He is a
bit more streetwise then the other guys, although fundamentally ingenuous.
Finally, Gabey, played by John Battles, is a clean-cut dreamer, raised on a farm
somewhere in the middle of the continent. "I want one special girl," he declares
with dopey idealism, right before falling in love with an image of Ivy as displayed

Betty Comden (Claire) and Adolph Green (Ozzie) in the scene at the Museum of Natural History (Act I, Scene 6). Photofest Digital Archive.

in a subway poster. Chip and Ozzie pitch in to help Gabey find the woman pictured there, and their pursuit ultimately defines the day. Other characters enter along the way, including Madame Maude P. Dilly, Ivy's alcoholic vocal coach; Lucy Schmeeler, Hildy's homely roommate, who wheezes from a head cold; and Pitkin, a comic cuckold, who is engaged to Claire and is essentially a basso buffo.

Act I takes place in an ever-shifting series of locations in Manhattan. By doing so, it follows a tried-and-true plot device that reached back to *A Trip to Chinatown* (1914) and Irving Berlin's *Watch Your Step* (1914)—shows that were well enough known by Bernstein to be included later in his *Omnibus* television special "American Musical Comedy.[19] Starting in the Brooklyn Navy Yard, a dockworker evokes a Gershwin-like spiritual with "I Feel Like I'm Not Out of Bed Yet," and the sailors burst onto the pier with the now famous "New York, New York" before taking the subway into Manhattan. Each scene yields a different site in the city. At a beauty pageant, Ivy is crowned Miss Turnstiles for the month. Then Hildy tries to pick up Chip, singing the hilariously raunchy "Come Up to My Place," and Ozzie meets Claire at the Museum of Natural History, where he clumsily destroys a rare dinosaur and the two of them sing "I Get Carried Away." At that point, Gabey still has not located Ivy, and he performs "Lonely Town" on a bench at the edge of Central Park. He finally gets lucky when he pursues Ivy to the studios of Carnegie Hall, where she is having a voice lesson. Ivy sings "Do, Re, Do (Carnegie

Hall Pavane)" while standing on her head. Claire and Ozzie take off for Claire's apartment, where Pitkin delivers "I Understand" for the first time. The scene then shifts to Hildy's apartment, where she sings the lusty "I Can Cook Too" as she tries to seduce Chip. The first act culminates in Times Square, where Gabey exuberantly performs "Lucky to Be Me." He has arranged to meet Ivy there, and life is good—that is, until Ivy fails to show up. The entire cast assembles onstage for a rousing first-act finale: the ballet "Sailors on the Town," which takes place in Times Square and has come to be known as the "Times Square Ballet." It is a major segment of dance—a glorious tribute to the vitality and diversity of the population that gathered around the clock during World War II in one of the pulse centers of the Western world.

Act II opens as the five principals (minus Ivy) go to a series of three nightclubs, trying to cheer up Gabey and find him a new girl. At each club, a song is featured, first "So Long," then "I'm Blue," and finally "You Got Me." Pitkin appears toward the end of each nightclub segment, and he repeatedly gets stuck with the tab. Pitkin is treated with utter disrespect by Claire, his fiancée, who is having a romp with Ozzie. In multiple iterations of "I Understand," Pitkin at first lamely excuses Claire's infidelities but ultimately declares that in fact he does *not* understand her behavior—at which point he hooks up with sneezy Lucy Schmeeler. Claire, Ozzie, Hildy, Chip, and Gabey then take off on the subway for Coney Island, where a "dream ballet" ensues, featuring Ivy. This segment plugs into the vogue for extended segments of narrative dance, most notably in *Oklahoma!* (choreographed by Agnes de Mille) and the film *Stormy Weather* (choreographed by Katherine Dunham). During "Gabey in the Playground of the Rich," Gabey finally locates Ivy in a nightclub, where she is exposed as a cooch dancer. Toward the end of the show, the poignant number "Some Other Time" abruptly injects a moment of profound seriousness amid all the hilarity. The sailors then return to their ship, and the women disappear into the crowds of wartime New York as a new batch of sailors begins another day of leave.

COLLABORATION, TIMELINE, PROCESS

On the Town grew out of a remarkable burst of collaboration, as Bernstein, Comden, Green, and Robbins attested repeatedly over the years, and the process that produced their first Broadway show became an appealing topic for interviewers. "We worked very hard," Bernstein later recalled. "We were all 25 years old, you know, we were nothing but energy then."[20] In a separate interview, he added, "I remember the initial spontaneous fun of collaborating."[21] The others affirmed the intensity and pleasure of working together, with a strong sense of mutual trust. "If you're lucky enough to be with people who respond to one another the way we all did, and feel about each other the way we all felt," Betty Comden reminisced, "there is no borderline where one department ends and the other begins. There's never any defensive feeling about that, either.... We talked out everything that was in the show."[22]

The idea of launching a show seems to have originated with Oliver Smith, the scene designer and collaborator with Robbins on *Fancy Free*. After Smith and Paul Feigay—the show's two producers—accompanied Bernstein to the Blue Angel, discussions commenced about the show's thematic focus. "We had a meeting with Oliver in the Russian Tea Room," Green recalled. "We asked him, 'What do you see?' He said, 'Well, I see a scene—Coney Island. I see some scenes in the Museum of Natural History.' Oliver is, after all, a designer. So we decided we'd try our best to weave the story around those settings."[23] Yet Comden stated that the core premise of sailors on leave was initially up for negotiation. "We all sat down to figure out what this show should be, then it didn't start out definitely as being three sailors," Comden recalled. "But we eventually came full circle and came back to that but we discussed all kinds of ideas, three this three that, five that, twelve those."[24]

For a time, the group considered an opera, not a musical, but quickly shifted gears. "Lenny and Jerry didn't jump at [the idea of a show]," Smith offered. "There was a lot of resistance in the beginning. They wanted to do something perhaps more serious."[25] One article at the time stated that the creative team "dropped...their original plan for a serious book," and it quoted Bernstein as saying, "[You] can't do a serious opera about three sailors on furlough." He also attested that the show fell into place when they agreed "to avoid the monumental."[26] Over the years, however, Bernstein continued to defend the idea that his first show had a "serious" component. *On the Town* "is funny, light-hearted, satirical—but not really terribly satirical," he stated in one interview. "It was a very serious show from a structural point of view and from the point of view of everybody's contribution and the integration of the esthetic elements. The subject matter was light, but the show was serious."[27]

The collaborative process was intense:

> **ROBBINS:** "To start with, Betty and Adolph did a very rough outline of the show, and then we collaborated. They did the writing, but we all talked about plots, what could happen, where the story should go, whenever we could grab time together, in New York or Hollywood or wherever...."
>
> **COMDEN:** "Lenny was in on the book discussions, too. We all planned everything together...."
>
> **ROBBINS:** "We spent a lot of time together."
>
> **COMDEN:** "On every step of the story and every idea in it."
>
> **ROBBINS:** "George Abbott wasn't in on it yet."[28]

Accounts from the creative team consistently emphasized the speed with which the project took shape, and priority continued to be placed on the integration of words, music, plot, and dance. "The ballet [*Fancy Free*] opened sometime in the early spring and then we started working on the show in early May and it went into rehearsal in October," Comden recalled in an interview with the conductor Lehman Engel.[29] Green corrected her to say it was November, not October, and she amiably agreed. Whatever the details, these young people pulled together a full evening of entertainment in a remarkably short time. In terms of integrating the various components of the show—the concept that Rodgers and Hammer-

Leonard Bernstein, Adolph Green, Betty Comden, and Jerome Robbins at work on On the Town. *Photofest Digital Archive.*

stein's *Oklahoma!* had brought to public attention the previous year—the creative team of *On the Town* asserted the importance of this ideal over and over. In early December, for example, not long before the show opened in previews, Comden and Green talked with a reporter who then summarized their thoughts: "Hammerstein is one of their idols.... Like Hammerstein, they want to combine music, ballet, story in one cohesive whole."[30] An interview with Oliver Smith similarly emphasized the fusion of plot and dance as crucial, saying that their goal had been to avoid "a chorus line and show girls and the usual ingredients of the big, handsome but unoriginal musicals."[31]

Press of the day confirmed a lickety-split conception, and a publicity machine was in place that prompted a range of newspapers to print the same basic information, as documented by clippings in Bernstein's scrapbooks. On June 2, 1944, just six and a half weeks after the premiere of *Fancy Free*, a contract was signed between Feigay and Smith as producers and Comden, Green, Robbins, and Bernstein as authors, with an agreement that the new show was to open "before the 26th day of January 1945."[32] The show already was titled *On the Town*. By June 7, just five days later, both the *New York Times* and *Variety* announced that "a group of youngsters" was writing a new musical, which "will be placed in rehearsal late in August."[33] On July 3, an article stated that lyrics for *On the Town* would be supplied "by John Latouche, until recently a member of the Seabees," which was a construction battalion of the U.S. Navy. At that point, rehearsals for the show had been "put back to September for a late October opening."[34] Latouche's involvement in the show never materialized, but it was an intriguing possibility. He had written lyrics for works featuring African American performers, including "Ballad for Americans" (composed by Earl Robinson), which argued for a racially inclusive view of American citizenship and was performed frequently by Paul Robeson, beginning in 1939. Latouche also was lyricist for the all-black musical *Cabin in the Sky*, composed by Vernon Duke. The stage version opened in 1940, and the film appeared in 1943. The possibility of having Latouche write for *On the Town* might have come through Oliver Smith. The two men had worked together previously on *Rhapsody*, an operetta by Fritz Kreisler, with lyrics by Latouche and scene designs by Smith. *Rhapsody* opened in early November 1944 and lasted less than two weeks.[35] As development of *On the Town* kicked into full gear, however, Comden and Green ended up writing the lyrics.

Initial conception of the show took place over the summer of 1944, while the creative team also tended to the mundane demands of life. In June, Bernstein underwent surgery to have his "septum undeviated," as Comden and Green put it, while Green checked himself into an adjoining bed to have his tonsils removed.[36] The two were to be "operated upon the same day, in the same hospital, by the same doctor," according to press reports, setting up a comical scenario, and there was a tongue-in-cheek projection that "during their stay in the hospital, they'll finish the new show they're writing."[37] That same summer Bernstein, Comden, Green, and Robbins retreated to New Hampshire to write. "I feel you all worked very hard up in New Hampshire," Smith wrote to Robbins in early August, "and accomplished somewhat of a miracle in such a short time."[38] Bernstein then traveled to California in August with Ballet Theatre for performances of *Fancy Free*, and he composed on the move, writing to his assistant Helen Coates from San Francisco: "I'm staying at a nice ordinary rooming house where a friend of mine lives. There's a Steinway here, and nobody home all day, so I've been working on the show. And having a wonderful time."[39] The next stop was Los Angeles, where Bernstein conducted at the Hollywood Bowl. Robbins was there, too, and Comden and Green arrived on August 4. They had a rental house but needed a place to stay the first night. So Comden cabled ahead to ask Bernstein, "May Adolph & I live with you one glorious day[?]"[40] On August 16, Bernstein reported to Aaron Copland, "We're getting a show done by leaps & bounds. It's amazing how hard it is—such an unwieldy thing to juggle."[41]

A letter from Oliver Smith to Robbins, written during the August work session in California—the same letter that reveals their intimate personal relationship—gives considerable detail about where the process stood. Smith was in New York City, and Robbins was in California:

> I have done a layout for the show, and in the next letter, I will include sketches of all the sets, in rough pencil; I've got some wonderful ideas, and know you

can work with them beautifully. Everything is progressing from this end well, although of course no casting can be done until you return.

I feel very well pleased with the first draft and feel it contains all the elements of a terrific show, fresh, creative, and successful. I am terribly excited about what you will do; the excitement here in the city is terrific and the grapevine reports excellent; however we are playing down advance publicity as much as possible at this point.... However, we all collaborate beautifully, and I know that is why things moved so fast.

I think the action is too complicated now, the entire script needs considerable tightening, more humor, and if possible certain simultaneous scenes, which would render it less choppy in pace. If possible, I would also like to cut down on the scenery[,] if possible, and do some scenes just with lights. My Coney Island scene is a dream, very funny, and yet very beautiful, and slightly lascivious at the same time. You will love it. I'm not describing it, I shall let sketches do that, but it is very simple, will leave almost the entire stage free for dancing.[42]

In September, the creative team was back in New York, where they were "pruning and cutting, and cutting and pruning," Comden and Green reported. They were also trying to please their financial underwriters, "giving performances in Lenny's living room for our panic-stricken backers."[43] The next major step involved finding a director. Smith and Feigay aimed high from the outset. They started by approaching Lawrence Langner of the Theatre Guild, who had produced innovative new works for the American stage, including *Porgy and Bess* (1935) and *Oklahoma!* (1943). Langner, however, "fell asleep during the audition," Smith later recalled. They then went to Elia Kazan, whose productions included Clifford Odets's *Waiting for Lefty* (1935) and Kurt Weill's *One Touch of Venus* (1943). There, too, they were rejected.[44]

Still aiming for the top, Smith and Feigay next turned to the seasoned director George Abbott. With a career stretching back to the early years of the century, including major achievements such as *The Boys from Syracuse* (1938) and *Pal Joey* (1940), Abbott was a titan on Broadway, and it is remarkable that this young group of collaborators had the audacity to approach him. "I met with them," Abbott later recounted, "and listened to the material. They were a very engaging crew, the kind of people I like to work with—eager, emotional, enthusiastic."[45] The *New York Times* asked Abbott why he was doing the show. "I like the kids," Abbott replied.[46] And so the production immediately gained fiscal heft and artistic credibility. "Well we became a reality when George Abbott came in as director," Betty Comden remembered. "All of us had never done a show before, a first for everybody, and he got real excited about it and I think that was one of the reasons it was able to be put together so quickly. He had dates and time limitations.... He did it all very quickly."[47] Once Abbott was on board, cash flowed, as Smith recalled: "We had some front money, which was partially put up by Lucia Chase," who was one of the founders of Ballet Theatre. "But until we had George Abbott to direct it," Smith continued, "we couldn't raise a nickel. And then finally when George Abbott came in...we had the money the very next day—over-subscribed three times."[48]

Abbott paid attention to *On the Town* in part because he was "a great enthusiast of ballet," recalled Smith. "He'd seen *Fancy Free*."[49] Backers of the show also reflected its crossover appeal, hailing from diverse corners of the music and entertainment industry. "An unusual Hollywood-Broadway deal" was drawn up, in which "two screen companies...assist in financing the same production," reported the *Times*.[50] Both Metro and RKO invested in the show substantially, according to that report. From the world of ballet, funders included not only Lucia Chase but also George de Cuevas, a ballet impresario of Chilean birth who was married to Margaret Rockefeller Strong.[51] Another backer was Mrs. George Hamlin Shaw (Florence Shaw), who had the inclinations of a socialite feminist, having greeted "mail-order immigrant brides" on the docks of New York. She later became a close friend of Bernstein and a patron of the New York Philharmonic.[52] Backers hailing from the popular entertainment business included the Broadway producer George Somnes, as well as Herman Starr, Bernstein's advocate and boss at Harms-Witmark, an affiliate of Warner Brothers.[53]

From the moment Abbott became director, "he was papa," declared Bernstein—or "Mr. Abbott," as he was famously known.[54] Abbott immediately began helping the creative team wrestle the script and score into shape. Comden and Green claimed they had already rewritten the show once and that Abbott had them do so a second time—"in six days," according to Green.[55] Draft scripts for *On the Town* document this early stage of conception. Changes included dropping a structure reminiscent of *The Cradle Will Rock*, with a prologue set in a night court. "All the characters were screaming at one another or yelling," Green recalled. "The judge says, 'One at a time! What happened?'" The action then proceeded via flashbacks, and ended back in night court. All these devices were central to *The Cradle Will Rock*. A much-recounted tussle between Abbott and the young writers ensued. "So we [i.e., the creative team] got together at Lenny's and we said, 'Look here, it can't be done without that prologue. We're going down to Abbott's office and tell him so. We're going to lay down the law,'" Green continued. "So we went to Radio City and saw him in his office. We told him how necessary the prologue was to the show. He said, 'Well, OK. Good. I tell you what: I'll make you a proposition. You either have the prologue—or you have me.' And we left so happy. The decision had been taken out of our hands."[56] Another structural change had to do with eliminating "a series of scenes between big scenes, in which an old woman ran across the stage," Abbott stated in an interview with Lehman Engel. "I wanted that out," Abbott continued. "And they were very stubborn about it. And I finally said 'Well, you have to choose between the old woman and...' So they gave in."[57] A page of suggestions for the show, presumably written by Abbott, ends with: "In general...simplify...keep people real."[58]

Other changes had to do with trimming the amount of music and dance, as well as pacing the material. Abbott steered the creative team away from a "serious" work, and he "showed them that many of their ideas—like having three songs succeed each other with no intervening dialogue—simply weren't feasible for a Broadway show."[59] With dance, changes took place during rehearsals. "*On the Town*...was very dancy, with a lot of musical numbers, and when they went on the stage, a lot of them didn't work," Robbins recalled. "That was a shock to me.

It was the first time I learned the lesson that one's work in a musical is not alone on the stage—what comes right before and after it can affect it.... The master of it all was Mr. Abbott.... He stepped right in, took my second act ballet—which I thought was terrific, I still believe in the conception of it—cut it right down the middle and put a scene in between the halves. The ballet was a dream image of what Coney Island was going to be like, and then the reality of it. I wanted to contrast them, but he said, 'No, we have to cut this.'"[60]

Bernstein auditioned singers on October 19, 1944, and rehearsals began on November 13.[61] Allyn Ann McLerie, who was in the dance chorus and took the role of Ivy when the show went on tour, recalls that rehearsals took place at Labor Stage, the same location where *Pins and Needles* had appeared.[62] Initially, the show was booked at the International Theatre at Columbus Circle, which had recently reopened and wasn't exactly at the center of the Broadway scene.[63] George de Cuevas, the ballet impresario among the backers of *On the Town*, ran the International. The venue soon got upgraded to the Adelphi Theatre at 152 West 54th Street, which had a larger seating capacity and sufficient backstage equipment.[64] This was a sign of confidence about the new production.

In mid-November, Comden, Green, and Bernstein returned to a nightclub, this time Le Ruban Bleu, where they presented a preview of *On the Town* at "a gala cocktail party" celebrating the club's eighth anniversary.[65] The event provided solid promotion for their upcoming premiere. Another major piece of advance publicity came on November 26 when a caricature by the famed Al Hirschfeld appeared in the *New York Times*, depicting the show in rehearsal.[66] Momentum was clearly building for a Broadway opening in late December.

DRAMATIS PERSONAE, CROSSOVER NETWORKS

A simple handwritten to-do list, jotted down on Bernstein's sketches for *On the Town*, vividly captures the newness of his fame, as well as the ways in which balancing high art and popular music defined daily life:

Post office
Judson
Starr
Carnegie Hall[67]

In other words, he was not too famous to run his own errands to the post office, and his immediate tasks had to do with powerful forces in different sectors of the music business: Arthur Judson, manager of the New York Philharmonic, and Herman Starr at Harms-Witmark. "Carnegie Hall" could have signaled various possibilities, from a completely mundane issue related to the modest studio apartment that Bernstein rented there to a major career-enhancing opportunity. While Bernstein balanced parallel projects in classical and popular music, mentors such as Copland and Koussevitzky continued to apply pressure on him to avoid the temptations of commercial entertainment. Bernstein resisted them in order to write *On the Town*. As the show approached its Boston preview, he boldly invited Koussevitzky to walk over to the Colonial Theatre from Symphony Hall.[68] "He liked it," Bernstein told a reporter soon after the show opened, "but he was furious with me. He gave me a three-hour lecture the next day on the way I was going."[69] Years later, Bernstein recalled that Koussevitzky came backstage and said, "Good boy, Lenushka, it is a noble jezz [*sic*]." Betty Comden briskly added to that memory: "But don't do it again."[70]

When Bernstein and his colleagues set out to hire a cast and production team, they selected people with backgrounds that were similarly broad-ranging, including a significant number who straddled high and low realms of performance. Doing so enabled the aesthetic fusions that distinguished the show. Like the creative team, most of the show's personnel were in their twenties, which meant that *On the Town* represented their first big break on Broadway. They added up to a fascinating group of people. There were a few gay romantic relationships embedded among the personnel, as had been the case with *Fancy Free*, but they did not seem to define the show or its aesthetic in the same all-embracing way. (One notable exception was the score for the ballet "The Presentation of Miss Turnstiles," discussed in Chapter 7.) On the whole, *On the Town* was produced by a larger, more diverse group of artists than had been the case with *Fancy Free*. Plus the prominent presence of Betty Comden and Adolph Green shifted gender balances within the creative team.

The careers of the core personalities involved in *On the Town* reveal the extraordinarily tight networks that formed quickly and served some of these young people for a lifetime. Crossover credentials started with Paul Feigay and Oliver Smith, who as producers and originators of *On the Town* shaped the fundamental character of the team being assembled. Both were twenty-six at the time. Feigay went on to have a career that bridged opera, ballet, Broadway musicals, and television. Prior to *On the Town*, Feigay started out as a designer, with his earliest projects in New York including work on murals for the World's Fair.[71] Then he became assistant director of the New Opera Company, at the time an active troupe in New York City.[72] That company produced *Rosalinda* on Broadway, a remake of *Die Fledermaus* that opened in October 1942 and ran for over a year.[73] Feigay was *Rosalinda*'s associate stage manager, and Smith was scene designer. Feigay "gave Smith the scene designing assignment that led to their mutual admiration society," reported the *New York Times*.[74] For a time after *On the Town*, they continued to work together, developing *Billion Dollar Baby* (1945) with Comden and Green and the composer Morton Gould while the Broadway run of *On the Town* continued. In the 1950s, Feigay became associate producer of the *Omnibus* television series, working especially on its ballet productions, including Copland's *Rodeo*.[75] During that same period, Bernstein's appearances on *Omnibus* were turning him into a television celebrity.

Oliver Smith was a similarly flexible creative artist and producer whose major performance passions spanned musical theater, ballet, and opera. His sets for *On the Town* garnered high praise. "Mr. Smith's effects, even when they verge on the spectacular, are achieved with remarkable economy," observed one reviewer.[76] Smith moved to New York City in 1939, where he earned a living as an usher at the

Roxy Theatre.[77] This was only five years before *Fancy Free* and *On the Town*. Smith designed sets for the original production of *Rodeo* by the Ballet Russe de Monte Carlo, and after *On the Town* he too was involved with *Billion Dollar Baby*. In 1945, Smith became co-director of Ballet Theatre with Lucia Chase, and he designed sets for a string of major Broadway shows, including *Candide*, *West Side Story*, and *Flower Drum Song*. He also designed for opera, including a production of *La Traviata* at the Metropolitan Opera (1957) and Copland's *The Tender Land* at the New York City Opera (Robbins directed that production in 1954).[78]

Max Goberman, *On the Town*'s musical director, also navigated work in various performance genres, and he received exceptional notices for the high quality of *On the Town*'s orchestra.[79] Like Bernstein, Goberman studied at the Curtis Institute under Fritz Reiner. His earliest conducting engagements included work for the Works Progress Administration and for left-wing benefit shows.[80] In 1941, Goberman made his debut with the orchestra of Ballet Theatre, and he continued to work in ballet for many years.[81] His politics aligned with those of the show's creative team, and he appears to have joined the American Communist Party. In 1957, Goberman was called in to testify before HUAC as part of an investigation of Local 802 of the American Federation of Musicians, where another witness named him as a party member, and Goberman pleaded the Fifth Amendment.[82] Just two months later, Goberman was hired as the conductor for *West Side Story*.[83]

Proudly identified in the souvenir program for *On the Town* as "the first of her sex to stage-manage a large-scale Broadway musical," Peggy Clark stands out among those hired for the show.[84] Whether or not her appointment marked a first, it certainly was exceptional for the day, and Clark worked her way up the ladder within the crew. Initially she did drawings for Oliver Smith's set designs.[85] Then during out-of-town previews she was technical assistant (as opposed to technical director), while Larry Bolton was stage manager.[86] By opening night, she had become technical director and stage manager, and Bolton was listed as general stage manager.[87] From documents in Clark's papers, it is clear she handled myriad tasks for the show, with a keen attention to detail. She assigned the cast to dressing rooms, rehearsed new understudies and actors, managed scenery and props, oversaw the lights, and made sure that everyone in the cast and orchestra was in the right place at the right time. She designed the cover for the show's souvenir program as well (see page 99). Like so many women during World War II, Clark also took on considerable war work, largely through Stage Door Canteen, where she and Emeline Roche designed the performance space.[88] Sponsored by the American Theatre Wing, the Stage Door Canteen opened in March 1942 in the building of the 44th Street Theatre—the same theater to which *On the Town* moved in June 1945.[89] The Canteen was a mixed-race social and performance facility in terms of its social dancing, its entertainers, and the soldiers who attended.[90]

Together with so many others from *On the Town*, Clark went on to *Billion Dollar Baby* (as technical director) and subsequently became one of "the first great lighting designers of the modern era."[91] She designed the lighting for such major productions as *Beggar's Holiday*, *Brigadoon*, *Gentlemen Prefer Blondes*, *Pal Joey*, *Wonderful Town*, *Threepenny Opera*, *Auntie Mame*, *Bells Are Ringing*, *Flower Drum*

Peggy Clark in a publicity photograph taken during the 1940s by G. Maillard Kessière.
© Billy Rose Theatre Division, The New York Public Library for the Performing Arts,
Astor, Lenox, and Tilden Foundations.

Song, and *Bye Bye Birdie*. By the end of her career, Clark had nearly eighty shows
to her credit. "Lighting design was women's work," claimed fellow designer Tharon
Musser. "There was just no money there, and women could live with that better
than men."[92]

While the production team of *On the Town* mostly worked in both high art and
commercial entertainment, the cast did not fit this profile as consistently. Yet
they were all young, and many were new to Broadway at the time.

Sono Osato and Nancy Walker, the two leads, complemented each other brilliantly, serving as a physical embodiment of the show's aesthetic. They had "the
only two dressing rooms on the stage level" of the Adelphi Theatre, signaling their
status.[93] Both were gifted comedians, with radically different personal styles and
professional backgrounds. "The heart of the show…is Sono Osato, the en-
chanting little dancer of Mary Martin's 'One Touch of Venus,'" commented the
Boston critic Peggy Doyle during out-of-town previews. But it was pairing Osato
with Walker that made the difference. "She and Hollywood comedienne, Nancy
Walker, pretty nearly walked away with the show last night," continued Doyle.
"They are excellent foils for each other, the fragile, lovely dancer and the glib,
clowning, sturdily constructed zaney from screenland."[94] Comden and Green recalled that the two women had been hired by the end of August 1944—the period
when Comden, Green, Robbins, and Bernstein spent time in California writing an
early draft of the show.[95]

Design by Peggy Clark for the cover of the souvenir program for On the Town. *Peggy Clark Collection, Music Division, Library of Congress. © Douglas Clark.*

Walker "was probably the most experienced veteran of Broadway in the cast," wrote Osato in her autobiography.[96] "Experience" was a relative term, for Walker was then twenty-two. She was tiny at 4´11˝, with a long face and red hair.[97] The child of the vaudevillians Myrtle Lawler and Dewey Barto, Walker had made her Broadway debut in *Best Foot Forward* (1941), directed by George Abbott. She also appeared in the Hollywood version of the same show, as well as the film musicals *Girl Crazy* and *Broadway Rhythm*, all released in 1943–44. Walker delivered physical comedy, thrusting her body around the stage, wearing pants that fell just below the knee, and ambushing her male prey with a robust slapstick approach to romance. She could deliver a song with aplomb, having started her career with hopes of being a torch singer. "She can shrill out a ballad like 'Come Up to My Place' with all the harshness of a Coney Island barker and all the verve of—well, Nancy Walker," declared one critic.[98] Another observed that Walker's performance of that number "nightly booms throughout the Adelphi Theatre."[99] On Broadway, Walker later appeared in *Pal Joey* and *Do Re Mi*, and she gained renown on television for the role of Ida Morgenstern (Rhoda's mother) on *The Mary Tyler Moore Show* and subsequently on *Rhoda*.

Betty Comden and Adolph Green both made their Broadway stage debut with *On the Town*. "He and Betty Comden were a wonderful team," recalled George Abbott. "Reposed, where Adolph was exuberant, she was a dark, quiet girl possessing more than her share of handsome sex appeal."[100] Their roles involved broad humor and caricature, with which Comden and Green had considerable experience from The Revuers. Like others in *On the Town*, they got sidetracked with *Billion Dollar Baby* during the middle of the run, yet they kept returning to perform their roles as Claire and Ozzie. On July 12, 1945, they reportedly began a two-week vacation from appearing in *On the Town* to "collaborate on a new musical book." They ended up being gone for most of the month.[101]

Before *On the Town*, John Battles, who played Gabey, had been in the chorus of *Something for the Boys* (1943); then he had a small part in *Follow the Girls* (1944).[102] Battles was exceptionally handsome, and he later went on to star in Rodgers and Hammerstein's *Allegro* (1947), where his "candor and innocence" were deemed to be "admirable and effective."[103] The role of Gabey was dewy-eyed, representing "our boys," as World War II lingo put it. Early in the run of *On the Town*, as three letters document, Battles was having an intense affair with Bernstein. Battles wrote fervently of being in love and of the lingering sensations of their sexual encounters.[104] He talked of studying voice, and of hanging out after the show with Shirley Bernstein, who appeared in the chorus of *On the Town* as "Shirley Ann Burton." "Thanks for your letter," Battles says at one point. "Tried to write you yesterday in the dressing room but it became impossible with everyone dropping in." Given the small number of extant letters, it is impossible to know how long the affair lasted or if Bernstein was as emotionally involved as Battles. In 1948, Battles left the United States to work with the Dublin Gate Theatre, and he married that same year. He returned to New York five years later to work in television.[105]

Cris Alexander, who played Chip, was an eclectic artist who acted on Broadway and also had a career as a photographer, with a special focus on ballet. A native of Oklahoma, Alexander came to New York in 1938, where he set up a photography studio and also studied acting.[106] *On the Town* marked his Broadway debut, and the show's *Playbill* featured his photograph of the cast. Alexander went on to take occasional stage roles, notably in *Wonderful Town* (1953), where he played Frank Lippencott, a bumbling drugstore owner, and *Auntie Mame* (1956). Alexander was gay, and in the early 1940s, his boyfriend was the dancer John Butler, who was in the dance chorus of *On the Town*. John Battles referred to the couple in one of his letters to Bernstein.[107] Ultimately, Alexander formed a life relationship with Shaun O'Brien, famed character dancer with the New York City Ballet.[108]

Chris Alexander

THE PLAYBILL

REGISTERED IN U. S. PATENT OFFICE

FOR THE ADELPHI THEATRE

Cover of The Playbill *for* On the Town *at the Adelphi Theatre. Includes a photograph of the cast, taken by Cris Alexander.* Photofest Digital Archive.

Finally, Robert Chisholm, who sang the role of Judge Pitkin W. Bridgework—the basso buffo who gets jilted by Claire—was an Australian baritone trained in London. He was one of the first hires for *On the Town*.[109] Chisholm was older than the rest of the cast, having made his Broadway debut in 1927 in the operetta *Golden Dawn* (Otto Harbach and Oscar Hammerstein II), which boasted "several of the finest singing voices to be heard on the dramatic stage," according to the *New York Times*. There Chisholm sang alongside Louise Hunter, a lyric soprano who had performed with the Metropolitan Opera, and both were singled out as having "trained, full voices of a quality rarely heard in musical entertainments."[110] Notable moments in Chisholm's long career included playing Macheath in the New York production of *Threepenny Opera* (1933) and King Arthur in *A Connecticut Yankee* (1943).[111] Like others in the cast of *On the Town*, he went on to perform in *Billion Dollar Baby*. His career apparently stalled in the early 1950s, and it culminated in a London production of *My Fair Lady* in 1958.[112] Operetta was at the core of Chisholm's performance world.

SOCIAL ANATOMY OF A BOSTON PREVIEW
AND BROADWAY RUN

After undergoing rehearsals in New York City and presenting an abbreviated sketch of the show at Le Ruban Bleu, the cast and crew headed to Boston for a tryout at the Colonial Theatre. In the 1940s, a pre-Broadway test run traditionally took place in Boston, New Haven, and/or Philadelphia, offering an opportunity to refine the show in front of an audience and away from New York critics. Looking back at *On the Town*'s Boston preview, Bernstein puzzled over how "a bunch of neophytes like us" pulled it off. "It was a wonder that it succeeded the way it did," Bernstein reminisced to Lehman Engel, "because we had only ten days out of town in Boston. Period. But we did make a lot of changes in Boston, yes."[113] Tickets went on sale in Boston the morning of December 4, and the company arrived there on December 10.[114] The ten-day run opened on December 13, although critics were asked to wait until the following night to write their reviews. Last-minute refinements had been implemented when the cast reached Boston, and the request not to review the December 13 show cited "the many scenes in the show and the fact that the scene shifters had had insufficient time to assemble the sets for the performance—although they worked 48 hours without sleep."[115] Critics were then asked to give yet another night's reprieve. "After two previews, the formal opening of the show took place on December 15 at the Colonial Theatre—that is to say, the reviewers were invited to this third performance," reported Boston's *Christian Science Monitor*. "The reason for the belated hospitality, it was explained, was that George Abbott, the director, considered that the piece was not ready earlier for critical appraisal."[116]

Not only was Boston a standard site for trying out Broadway shows, it also happened to be Bernstein's hometown, and coverage of *On the Town*'s preview reflected deep pride and solid support for a native son. It also demonstrated the balancing act that this talented young musician continued to negotiate. Bernstein's father owned a business in Boston—the Bernstein Hair Company, a wholesale supplier of beauty products and wigs. Leonard had grown up within a community of upwardly mobile Jewish immigrants, attending the famous Boston Latin School before Harvard.[117] When *On the Town* arrived, praise for Bernstein in the Boston press was lavish and proudly articulated. For the *Jewish Advocate*, a Boston publication, he was "Boston's own musical ball-of-fire."[118] For the *Boston Post*, he was the "Roxbury

Maestro."[119] The *Providence Journal* called him a "Boy Wonder"—this after Bernstein conducted the Boston Symphony Orchestra in mid-November 1944, only weeks before the opening of *On the Town*'s preview.[120] Jules Wolffers, music critic for the *Jewish Advocate*, was also wowed by Bernstein's appearance with the Boston Symphony Orchestra. "I have previously expressed the opinion that Bernstein would be numbered among the greatest conductors of his generation," Wolffers wrote. "Far from changing my opinion, last week's program served to confirm it anew."[121]

On December 13, 1944, when the initial public performance of *On the Town* took place in Boston, it was a gala event, with "fans" of Bernstein having "bought out the opening night house." The "distinguished audience" had purchased tickets long in advance. "Those who owned fur coats were wrapped to the ears in them," reported the *Boston Traveler*, "against the icy wind which swept across the Common."[122] That initial performance was staged as a "benefit first-night," sponsored by the relatively new Institute of Modern Art, and the *Boston Herald* reminded its readers of the museum's recent history with Bernstein. "In the spring of 1941, the Institute of Modern Art conducted at Jordan Hall the first performance in Boston of Aaron Copeland's [sic] 'Second Hurricane,'" recalled the *Herald*. "And Leonard Bernstein rehearsed, directed and conducted the little opera, which really constituted his debut in the professional field."[123] Besides this "first-night" with the Institute of Modern Art, a dinner in Bernstein's honor took place two days later (December 15) at the Copley Plaza Hotel. The event was a benefit sponsored by the Joint Anti-Fascist Refugee Committee, founded in 1941 and dedicated to supplying humanitarian aid for refugees of the Spanish Civil War.[124] This Anti-Fascist Committee was later targeted by HUAC as a Communist front. The program honoring Bernstein included Jules Wolffers of the *Jewish Advocate*, together with George Abbott, and Richard Linsley, representing the United Electrical Workers. The young composer Lukas Foss, who had been a Curtis classmate of Bernstein, accompanied soprano Rae Muscanto, who performed "selections chosen from [Bernstein's] compositions."[125] During the period of *On the Town*'s Boston preview, the local sculptor Beatrice Paipert, whose work had previously been exhibited at Symphony Hall, was sculpting a bust of Bernstein.[126]

When *On the Town* had its official Boston opening night on December 15, 1944, local critics raved about the show's "aura of ballet," its "rhythmic and brassy music," and its "brilliant score, far more interesting than the average musical comedy."[127] There were criticisms, too, of the show being "too long, too loose" and "sometimes a little coarse," as the production continued to evolve from night to night.[128] Although the exact dimensions and timing of the revision process are difficult to trace, some aspects are known. For one thing, the show was trimmed down. "At the official opening the show did not quite live up to its possibilities," reported the *Christian Science Monitor*, "but at a second viewing, this week, it had been cut and tightened. It was much livelier, and the plot was clarified and unified. One dull scene had been eliminated. Sono Osato's role had been expanded to give the principal dancer more opportunity as the romantic lead."[129] As part of this process, there was a cluster of revisions toward the end of Act I. "Intermission Number," which took place in a theater lobby before the "Times Square

Flier for the preview of On the Town *at the Colonial Theatre in Boston, December 1944.*
Harvard Theatre Collection, Houghton Library, Harvard University.

Ballet," was cut at some point before the New York premiere.[130] Also deleted were
"Pick Up Song" and "Penny Arcade Boy," which in Boston surrounded "Sailors on
the Town" (i.e., the Times Square scene).

Another major change came with adding the ballad "Some Other Time." "This
one we had to write in Boston, writing most of the night," Comden recalled. "We
were in the window of a music store, because that was the only place we could find
a piano we could use. We needed a special song, and we found it there, in that
window, in the middle of the night."[131] That episode—which made for a very good
story—must have occurred in the days immediately before December 13, because
"Some Other Time" is included in programs for the Boston preview.

COLONIAL THEATRE

— BOSTON —

Direction L. A. B. Amusement Corp.

DECEMBER 13 TO 23RD

OLIVER SMITH & PAUL FEIGAY

Present

"ON THE TOWN"

With

Sono	Nancy	Betty	Adolph
OSATO	**WALKER**	**COMDEN**	**GREEN**
John	Robert	Cris	Ray
BATTLES	**CHISHOLM**	**ALEXANDER**	**HARRISON**

Book by BETTY COMDEN & ADOLPH GREEN
Based on an idea by Jerome Robbins
Music by LEONARD BERSTEIN
Lyrics by Betty Comden & Adolph Green
Additional lyrics by Leonard Bernstein
Musical Numbers and Choreography staged by JEROME ROBBINS
Production designed by OLIVER SMITH
Costumes designed by ALVIN COLT
Orchestrations by Leonard Bernstein & Hershy Kay
Musical Director: MAX GOBERMAN

PRODUCTION DIRECTED BY GEORGE ABBOTT

CAST

1st WORKMAN	MARTIN SAMETH
2nd WORKMAN	FRANK MILTON
3rd WORKMAN	HERBERT GREENE
OZZIE	ADOLPH GREEN
CHIP	CRIS ALEXANDER
SAILOR	LYLE CLARK
Gabey	JOHN BATTLES
ANDY	FRANK WESTBROOK
TOM	RICHARD D'ARCY
GADOLPHIN	FLORENCE MacMICHAEL
GADOLPHIN, JR.	MARION KOHLER
BILL POSTER	LARRY BOLTON
LITTLE OLD LADY	MAXINE ARNOLD
POLICEMAN	LONNY JACKSON
S. UPERMAN	MILTON TAUBMAN
HILDY	NANCY WALKER
POLICEMAN	ROGER TREAT
FIGMENT	REMO BUFANO
CLAIRE	BETTY COMDEN
MAUDE P. DILLY	SUSAN STEELL
IVY	SONO OSATO
LUCY SCHMEELER	ALICE PEARCE

Program for the preview of On the Town *at the Colonial Theater in Boston, December 1944. Peggy Clark Collection, Music Division, Library of Congress.*

The final Boston tryout performance took place on December 23, and the show opened on Broadway five days later. As that major moment approached, the young creative team confessed raw fear. "We're scared," declared Adolph Green.[132] "It sure gives you a panicky feeling," said Bernstein.[133] "I'll probably be hiding under one of the seats or wandering around lost." The show's reception in Boston filtered down to New York, with the *Herald Tribune* reporting that "Boston drama critics were unanimously favorable to 'On the Town.'"[134] A publicity machine was in place to generate a positive vibe. A caricature in the *New York Times* by Al Hirschfeld showed the five principals seated around a nightclub table as an elegantly elongated Sono Osato flowed into the image.[135] Photos and interviews promoting the show appeared in multiple New York papers, and ticket sales were strong.[136] The "admission scale" for opening-night tickets ranged from $1.20 to $12. After that, "from Monday through Friday nights the top will be $5.40; on Saturday nights $6."[137]

On the Town was an immediate hit, with a rave review in the *New York Times*— the paper whose critical evaluation mattered most. Lewis Nichols, the *Times*'s drama critic, grasped the show's high-low combustion. "'On the Town' even has a literate book, which for once instead of stopping the action dead speeds it merrily on its way," wrote Nichols. "'On the Town' is a perfect example of what a well-knit fusion of the respectable arts can provide for the theatre."[138] Rave reviews also appeared in a string of major national publications, including *Newsweek*, *Time*, *Life*, and *Mademoiselle*.[139] The show played to capacity houses, entering an extended run.[140]

The famed producer and director Hal Prince attended *On the Town* as a college student. "I saw it nine times, in very short order. I thought the show had a kind of bubble and real joyfulness that was extraordinary. A kind of innocence," Prince recalled. "I thought the music was unprecedented in terms of modern musical theater. And I thought the dance—certainly I'd not seen dance like that in what was considered Broadway musical theater . . . So I saw it nine times because I knew it was something extremely unique about how it all came together and . . . created an odd mix that actually worked."[141]

After five months at the Adelphi Theatre (152 W. 54th Street), *On the Town* moved on June 4, 1945, to the 44th Street Theatre (216 W. 44th Street). The Adelphi was not "air-cooled," and Peggy Clark declared the 44th Street Theatre to be "more convenient" in terms of backstage operations.[142] On July 30, the show moved again—this time to the Martin Beck Theatre (302 W. 45th Street), known today as the Al Hirschfeld Theatre, and it stayed there until the end of the run.[143]

Broadway shows are most often explored in terms of openings and closings, with little sense of what happened during the course of the run. But every show involves a community of people with illnesses, internal conflicts, and interactions with the world around them, which in this case not only included promotion of the show but also special civic obligations in the midst of World War II. The life of *On the Town*'s first Broadway production can be chronicled in part through "Showlog," which was a column in *Billboard* that offered week-by-week developments for major Broadway productions and delivered its information in telegraphic prose using insider lingo. The papers of stage manager Peggy Clark are also valuable, especially for agendas for benefit performances.

Radio played an important role in marketing the show, as was increasingly the case for Broadway productions overall during the mid-1940s. "Star guesting on such programs as Mary Margaret McBride, Bessie Beattie, Adrienne Ames and other fem spielers has proved its worth at Broadway box offices," wrote *Billboard*.[144] Headliners from *On the Town* were among the guests on these very radio programs. On January 10, 1945, not quite two weeks after the show opened, Osato and Bernstein were on the air with McBride, and on January 25 Comden and Green appeared with Maggie McNellis.[145] Other radio appearances included Robbins, Comden, and Green on Bessie Beattie's show (January 8) and Comden and Green with Alma Kitchell (March 2).[146] After these initial waves of publicity, radio appearances diminished. Then on August 26, the day after Osato left for a two-week vacation, her replacement, Nelle Fisher, appeared on the *Solitaire* program (on WEAF, an NBC station), presumably to alleviate potential concerns about Osato's absence.[147]

Cast changes and personnel issues occurred during the run. A major problem developed early on with Susan Steell, who originally played the role of Madame Maude P. Dilly, Ivy's alcoholic singing teacher. Steell reportedly had a real-life drinking problem. Osato had been studying voice with Steell as the show was being developed, and the character of Madame Dilly was modeled on Osato's tales about the experience. "I was very happy indeed to receive your interesting report on the life of a stage manager at the Adelphi," wrote George Abbott to Peggy Clark in early February 1945, five weeks into the show's run. By then, Abbott had left to direct the film *Kiss and Tell* in Hollywood. Abbott continued: "Since that date, I understand the situation has become even more complicated by Madam Steele's [*sic*] lapse to the bottle. That's too bad. I am sure the old girl made a very great effort to stay sober, but it's just beyond her."[148] "Showlog" fills in the conclusion to this story. Steell was absent from the show on January 23, 1945, and Zamah Cunningham replaced her on February 5.[149]

Another personnel issue occurred only two weeks into the run, when Remo Bufano, a celebrated puppeteer who had been playing the walk-on role of Figment, left for the West Coast because of an "MGM deal," according to "Showlog."[150] Then in February, John Battles was ill for a time, and Abbott wrote to Clark about having heard "that Peerless John Battles has finally collapsed but that Samoff is very good. I should think it would be a pleasure to hear that strong voice in the part."[151] Abbott probably meant Marten Sameth (not Samoff), who appears on Clark's list of understudies.[152] Sameth was a trained singer, and he continued to give recitals at least into the 1950s.[153]

Clark also handled issues that arose backstage. "May I say, since the subject of your authority is brought up, that the reports all point to the fact that you have excellent discipline backstage and this does not surprise me," Abbott wrote in early February 1945, when the run was just over a month old. "But I suppose you realize you are rather breaking ground, since there has for a long time existed a theory that a woman could be an assistant, but not the commanding officer, backstage."[154] There had been difficulties handling Jerome Robbins, who was a notoriously difficult artistic figure. Abbott's language is oblique enough so that the dimensions of the episode are unclear: "I am glad you stopped Robbins from directing the book. I think, as a matter of fact, he has pretty good sense about such things, but it's none of his business, and he might as well be kept in his place. It doesn't help your authority if you are directing them and he has told them something else."

Billboard also revealed that Robbins danced Ray Harrison's role at least twice, which meant performing the extended dream ballet that Harrison danced with Osato in Act II.[155] There were homey touches, too, such as when Comden's "artist-husband" painted her dressing room, or when the "current 'Miss Subways,'" who was a waitress at Schrafft's Restaurant on 57th Street, "partied" Osato and Green.[156] Plus there were illnesses, injuries, and competing professional opportunities. In June, Nancy Walker almost left the cast for a throat operation, then was said to be "undergoing treatment" instead.[157] In June and July, Osato was out with a "fractured rib."[158] Comden and Green left the cast on September 19 to work on *Billion Dollar Baby*—this after their extended vacation to write the script. They returned toward the end of the Broadway run, after *Billion Dollar Baby* had its debut, and they went on the road with *On the Town*.[159]

The show's cast also gave numerous performances for the military. Doing so was standard for Broadway productions during World War II, but *On the Town* had a special tie to war work because of Peggy Clark's involvement with Stage Door Canteen. On February 8, 1945, for example, the cast appeared at Stage Door Canteen for a one-hour performance beginning at 6:00 p.m. "That hour belongs to the show that comes down and they can do whatever they please," wrote Elizabeth Morgan of Stage Door Canteen in a letter to Charles Harris. "Some bring their chorus, orchestra and principals. Some wear costumes, some come in street clothes. In other words, it is up to you to do anything you like."[160] *On the Town*'s orchestra took part in that February performance, and a week later *Billboard* reported that the show began "an entertainment program for Stage Door Canteen on alternate Thursdays."[161] Clark's notes include an outline for an "abridged version" of *On the Town* for a Stage Door Canteen show on June 14, once again with orchestra.[162] Other events for the military included a "complete and unabridged" performance of the show for GIs at St. Albans Hospital on March 11, an abridged performance at Halloran General Hospital on May 6, and a performance at Mitchel Field on June 24.[163] Judging from the meticulous arrangements made by Peggy Clark, the cast and crew of *On the Town* contributed vigorously to the war effort, and those volunteer performances delivered the same high-level professional standards as for Broadway audiences.

Through all this, the war continued through its various stages. "It's funny," Clark wrote to a friend on May 14, 1945, "V-E Day didn't make much difference to people, except Times Square was sort of splattery." Victory in Europe Day had occurred on May 8, almost a week before her letter. "Since the lifting of the Curfew," Clark continued, "and the return of Lights to Broadway, people are really beginning to realize that we've won something."[164] At that point, fighting persisted in the Pacific.

When *On the Town* closed its Broadway run on February 2, 1946, it ended strong, having had "a highly successful career and a total of 462 showings."[165] The show then hit the road for three months, traveling as far west as Chicago. The first stop was Ford's Theatre in Baltimore (February 4–9). Then came the Forrest Theatre in Philadelphia (February 11–March 2), the Nixon Theatre in Pittsburgh (March 4–9), the Cass Theatre in Detroit (March 24–30), and the Shubert Great Northern Theatre in Chicago (April 1–27).[166] Betty Comden and Adolph Green toured with the show, as did Nancy Walker and Allyn Ann McLerie, who had taken over the role of Ivy late in the New York run.[167] Zamah Cunningham continued as Madame Maude P. Dilly. All the other principals were replaced from the Broadway run: Don Miller took the role of Chip, Loren Welch became Gabey, and Lee Edwards was Pitkin.[168] Comden went with the company to Baltimore and Philadelphia, then left the show and was replaced in Pittsburgh by Xenia Bank.[169] Green stayed with the cast until April 20, nearly at the end of its time in Chicago.[170]

On the Town's mixed-race dance chorus was part of its touring cast, and African American newspapers took notice. Baltimore's *Afro-American* predicted that "colored members of its cast will get a shock, not only in the theatre but from the town's tradition as well."[171] There, too, casting replacements had occurred. Flash Riley and Frank Neal stayed on from the Broadway troupe, while Billie Allen and Hilda Seine were new to the cast.[172] The society column of Baltimore's *Afro-American* reported that Seine was a "house guest of Dr. and Mrs. Leslie Jones," and in fact all black members of the cast must have stayed in private homes, given the restrictions of southern segregation. According to the Norfolk, Virginia, *New Journal and Guide*, Billie Allen's mother traveled to Baltimore from Richmond to view her daughter in the show, and she "was guest of the Leonard Gibsons of Carrolton Avenue."[173] Baltimore was the only southern city on the show's tour.

In Chicago, African Americans in the cast were singled out by the *Chicago Defender*, the local black paper. "'ON THE TOWN' the swellegant show at Great Northern, has several Negroes, Lonnie Johnson and Frank Neal, in the cast. FLASH! They're billed as Americans too so see the show if you can."[174] While Neal was a dancer, Johnson was a singer, and both men had strong ties to Chicago.

Otherwise, the tour was fairly routine, with largely positive reviews in local newspapers, as chronicled in Bernstein's scrapbooks. By the time the show opened in Chicago on April 1, however, it was struggling financially. "'On the Town' has gone over gaily at the Great Northern," reported the *Chicago Daily Tribune*.[175] Yet the show appeared to be exhausting its potential market and perhaps quickly becoming out of date after the war ended. On April 17, Paul Feigay, in his capacity as one of the show's producers, wrote to "all persons receiving royalties," asking them to "waive" royalties "retroactive to the opening of the run in Chicago and until such time as we start again operating at a profit."[176] Feigay detailed the financial status of the road tour:

> As you know the business of ON THE TOWN on the road has been very disappointing everywhere in spite of the terrific notices. Up to date we have personally

lost over $50,000.00, in getting the show ready for the road and the losses on the road. The first week in Chicago the loss was $6,300.00, and then last week we lost $1,600.00, and that was due to the fact that we did not charge off any but cash bills.... We have used up our entire surplus cash.

The Chicago run closed ten days later.[177]

Recordings also played a significant role in extending the life of *On the Town* beyond Broadway. Two early releases featured studio arrangements, and neither had the impact of a full-fledged original-cast album. *On the Town*'s first recording was issued by RCA Victor, and Leonard Bernstein was the only person involved from the original production. Recorded in Victor's studio in February and March 1945, the discs featured Bernstein conducting ballet music from the show, together with choral arrangements of selected vocal numbers performed by the "Victor Chorale and On the Town Orchestra," conducted by Robert Shaw and featuring new arrangements (see the Appendix for a full list of titles). Shaw, who later became an exceptionally influential American choral conductor, was then beginning his career. The On the Town Orchestra must have been the house ensemble in the Victor Studios (rather than the pit orchestra from the show). The Victor recording appeared in May 1945. *Victor Record News* put the release on its cover, and New York's *PM* newspaper featured a photo of Mayor Fiorello La Guardia accepting a copy of it for the library of "his pet project, the High School of Music and Art" (which was named for La Guardia).[178]

Sono Osato and Leonard Bernstein presenting the Victor recording of
On the Town *to Mayor La Guardia. Photograph by Dan Keleher.*
It was published in PM, *May 9, 1945.* Photofest Digital Archive.

Sono Osato "looks on," while Bernstein "autographs the album for the Mayor." This is a striking cultural moment, for La Guardia had not been perceived as a friend of Japanese Americans living in New York City.[179]

The concept of an original-cast recording was fairly new. After Musicraft released *The Cradle Will Rock* in 1938, Decca Records became the leader in original-cast releases, starting with *Porgy and Bess* (1940) and Berlin's *This Is the Army* (1942).[180] Decca's recording of *Oklahoma!* was the most successful of these early ventures, featuring fifteen numbers from the show, including the overture and finale. The original cast performed, and the original conductor (Jay Blackton) was at the podium.[181] In the spring of 1946, Decca released a recording of *On the Town*. While not ambitiously covering the bulk of the major tunes from the show—as Decca had done with *Oklahoma!*—the company still marketed *On the Town* as one of its "Original Cast Show Albums."[182] Strictly speaking, however, the Decca recording of *On the Town* was a modified version of an original-cast production.[183] It featured "I Can Cook Too" and "Ya Got Me" with Nancy Walker and "I Get Carried Away" with Betty Comden and Adolph Green. The rest of the numbers were performed by outsiders, and most had new arrangements. The Broadway star Mary Martin sang "Lonely Town" and "Lucky to Be Me," which had originally been assigned to Gabey, the lead male character. Hiring Martin must have compensated for the show's lack of celebrity performers. The opening of the show— "I Feel Like I'm Not Out of Bed Yet" and "New York, New York"—was performed by the Lyn Murray Chorus and Orchestra. Murray was a conductor and arranger whose Lyn Murray Singers were featured on CBS radio's *Your Hit Parade*. Other conductors on the release were Leonard Joy and Tutti Camarata, who were active in the studio orchestras of radio and record companies.

All this time—through the long Broadway run, the road tour, and the release of two recordings of the show—Bernstein continued to pursue his career as a conductor and composer of concert music. He became director of the New York City Symphony Orchestra in October 1945, and he also traveled around the country as a guest conductor. A recording of his Symphony No. 1, *Jeremiah*, was issued in February 1945 and reviewed in early 1946, not long before the Decca release of *On the Town*.[184]

HOLLYWOOD RECONCEPTION

The next stage in the life of *On the Town* came with a film released by MGM in New York City on December 8, 1949, nearly five years after the Broadway premiere.[185] The film's opening performance of "New York, New York" by Gene Kelly, Frank Sinatra, and Jules Munshin was shot at the Brooklyn Navy Yard, and much of the filming was done on location in New York City, enhancing the verisimilitude that had been valued in the Broadway version. The basic narrative of the stage show remained intact, with a focus on three sailors enjoying a day of shore leave.[186]

Yet beyond that central framework, the film diverged substantively from its stage origins. Like the Victor and Decca recordings, the film glossed over the show's multilayered high-low fusions, instead producing a mainstream piece of commercial entertainment. Rather than gender parity among a group of six leads, male sailors became the main stars, with Kelly as Gabey, Sinatra as Chip, and Munshin as Ozzie. The assertive female voices of the stage production receded to become more coquettish. Vera-Ellen played Ivy, Betty Garrett was Hildy, and Ann Miller was Claire. Just as strikingly, the mixed-race images of street life in New York City were erased in the film to depict a thoroughly Caucasian population— that is, until the nightclub scene, where a series of exotic floor shows enacted long-standing stereotypes, which were familiar in film musicals of the day. Thus Ivy no longer emerged in the body of a Japanese American dancer but rather through a blond-haired Hollywood personality. As a result, the romance of Ivy and Gabey had nothing to do with cultural difference. Rather, the couple were now strikingly similar, especially since a plot twist in the film has them hailing from the same midwestern town. Comden and Green adapted the stage script for the film, Gene Kelly did the choreography (with uncredited assistance from Jeanne Coyne, Carol Haney, and Alex Romero), and Kelly directed the film together with Stanley Donen.[187]

Many other changes took place. In the museum scene of the film, when Ozzie clumsily destroys a valuable dinosaur, the slapstick event becomes the reason for multiple pursuits by the police, who repeatedly try to capture the person who did the damage. The resulting scenes include a Godzilla-like segment at the top of the Empire State Building, where Munshin hangs perilously over the edge, staring

Betty Garrett (Hildy) and Frank Sinatra (Chip), Ann Miller
(Claire) and Jules Munshin (Ozzie), Vera-Ellen (Ivy) and Gene Kelly
(Gabey) in On the Town, *MGM film, 1949. Photofest Digital Archive.*

with raw fear at traffic eighty-six floors below while hiding from the police who interrogate Sinatra, Kelly, and the women. There is also a fast-paced car chase scene, with Hildy at the wheel, and it is followed by a campy attempt by Kelly, Sinatra, and Munshin to conceal themselves from the police by cross-dressing as cooch dancers.[188] Another difference from the stage show has to do with the style of dance, which leans in the film toward tap and soft-shoe more than extensions of ballet and the Lindy Hop. Plus, rather than depicting a series of thwarted (or frustrated) romances, all three couples in the film kiss and cuddle with abandon.

Bernstein's voice as a composer was also systematically submerged in the film, either by replacing his work with new arrangements of his tunes by MGM personnel or by substituting entirely new numbers by Roger Edens. The film's vocal arrangements were by Saul Chaplin and its orchestrations by Conrad Salinger, both major Hollywood figures. The following Bernstein songs were retained from the stage show: "I Feel Like I'm Not Out of Bed Yet," "New York, New York," and "Come Up to My Place." Plus his ballet music for "The Presentation of Miss Turnstiles" and for the dream ballet, "Gabey in the Playground of the Rich," was adapted for the film.[189] With the latter, the narrative thrust was completely different, and the segment had a new title, "A Day in New York." Years later, Gene Kelly recalled a collaborative process between himself and Bernstein in which they shared "musical data . . . re the adjusting of 'On the Town' ballet for the screen."[190] By " 'On the Town' ballet," Kelly must have been referring to "A Day in New York." Notably, the beautiful ballads "Some Other Time" and "Lonely Town" were omitted.

The bulk of the songs in the film were not by Bernstein but by Roger Edens. They included "Prehistoric Man," "Main Street," "You're Awful," "On the Town," "Count on Me," and "That's All There Is, Folks."[191] When asked decades later why the score of On the Town was changed so "radically" for the film, Comden responded: "At the time, MGM and Louis B. Mayer thought that the Bernstein score was too difficult. It wouldn't happen today, but they thought that the music was too symphonic and too classical and that audiences wouldn't understand it." Green continued, "We were under contract to MGM." Comden concluded: "There wasn't much we could do about it. We were very unhappy about it. The only part of the movie we really liked is the opening, which is terrific—and wonderfully shot at the Brooklyn Navy Yard."[192] Given that Bernstein's musical presence in the film was severely diluted, he kept some distance from it. An article in Theatre Arts that appeared seven months after the film's release stated bluntly: "It substituted a mediocre score for Bernstein's music to such an extent that the busy composer-conductor and pianist hasn't even bothered to see it."[193]

The film's racial retrenchment is especially apparent in the exoticized spectacle of the three nightclub scenes. On one hand, those segments follow the basic outline of the stage show. On the other, they stand out starkly against the thorough whiteness of the rest of the film. The first nightclub scene in the film takes place in the Club Sambacabana—a Latin club—and ends with a jungle dance, complete with a variety of drums. That segment riffs on jungle tropes in earlier film musicals, notably the "African Dance" of Bill "Bojangles" Robinson in Stormy Weather (1943), where he nimbly leaps across the tops of drums. The next stop on the nightclub circuit in the film is Club Dixieland, where a black chorus line performs to an all-white audience in a racially segregated club. Finally, there is Club Shanghai, which features an Asian chorus line in another segregated performance space. Another change in the film had to do with eliminating the comic character Pitkin. Instead, Lucy Schmeeler, the sneezing date with whom Pitkin connects after dumping Claire in the stage version, hooks up briefly and unsuccessfully with Gabey. Pitkin's character was probably too operatic for Hollywood.

Critics of the day seemed to grasp the compromises that turned the film into entertainment for a wide audience. On the day of its release, the *Los Angeles Times* reported that the film was "far more synthetic than original," with "synthetic" as a euphemism for imitating the conventions of recent films, especially *Anchors Aweigh*, a sailor film of 1945 that also started Sinatra and Kelly. The article continued, "It is likely audiences just seeking entertainment will not object to that."[194] The *New York Times* concurred, albeit with milder language: "Some major changes have been made in the amiable show which caused such a buzz when it opened on Broadway five years ago."[195]

Despite these artistic compromises, the film of *On the Town* is a fascinating cultural document, especially for the blueprint it provided for the much more famous *Singin' in the Rain* (1952), which again had a script by Comden and Green, direction by Gene Kelly and Stanley Donen, and Kelly as one of the stars. *On the Town* also yielded an iconic segment of film footage, with Sinatra, Kelly, and Munshin projecting American ebullience and self-confidence as they sang "New York, New York." The trio gesticulate energetically to such phrases as "New York, New York, it's a wonderful town. The Bronx is up, and the Battery's down."[196] That scene turned *On the Town* into a widely viewed and emblematic moment in the American cultural experience, and it is important to recognize that the "America" greeted by the film was different from the place it had been when the stage show emerged. By 1949, not only had World War II been won, but the United States was entering a period of unprecedented growth and cultural ascendancy. It was also a more volatile political era, especially for left-leaning artists. Two years earlier the famous "Hollywood Ten" had appeared before the House Un-American Activities Committee, charged with Communist affiliations, and they had refused to answer questions, resulting in prison sentences for contempt of Congress and subsequent blacklisting by the Hollywood studios. At the same time, the civil rights movement was challenging rigid Jim Crow restrictions with increasing effectiveness. In an analysis of racial representation in Hollywood films of this era, the critic Donald Bogle has talked of "the schizophrenic 1940s." On one hand, "problem pictures," such as *Home of the Brave* (1949), confronted racial segregation squarely.[197] On the other, many films—including *On the Town*—ignored race entirely.

Within such a climate, the racial idealism of the stage version of *On the Town* was reconfigured in the film to accommodate new realities, emerging in a world where "a maverick fitting into no particular theatrical category"—as Comden and Green had described the stage version—needed to settle into a safe zone, familiar to its audiences.[198] In the process, the film toned down a work that had been proudly conceived as an amalgam of Broadway musicals, pop songs, ballet, swing dance, and operetta, turning it into straight-out easy-access entertainment.

A JAPANESE AMERICAN STAR DURING WORLD WAR II
Sono Osato and "Exotic Ivy Smith"
* * *

Your life [as a dancer] is made up of entertaining, performing, and taking care of yourself. There is not much time for learning. Some of us may not know what went on at Bretton Woods, or understand high finance, but we have feelings. We feel what is going on deeply. We know where we stand. There is such a great flood of liberal feeling in the theatre these days—and in Hollywood too—such a great good feeling for what is right.
—*Sono Osato, April 1945*

Several bold personnel decisions marked the debut production of *On the Town*, and the most visible one involved casting the dancer Sono Osato in the starring role of Ivy Smith. The role required a gifted dancer, and Osato brought extensive experience with the Ballet Russe de Monte Carlo and Ballet Theatre. "There was more dancing in [*On the Town*] than, I think, even *West Side Story*," observed Jerome Robbins decades later. "It was almost totally a dance show."[1] Everett Lee, who became the show's conductor midway through its run, called it a "ballet-musical."[2] Yet Osato also brought to *On the Town* her family heritage. That is, she was *nisei*—the child of a Japanese national—which carried dark implications in wartime America. Her Japanese father had immigrated to the United States in the early years of the century, and her mother was European American. Immediately after the Japanese attack on Pearl Harbor, her father became one of some 120,000 Americans of Japanese ancestry who were interned, yet Sono continued to achieve ever greater success on the public stage. *On the Town* was in midrun when the bombings of Hiroshima and Nagasaki took place in August 1945.

Hiring Sono Osato occurred during a violent war with Japan, when racial prejudice and war hysteria against the Japanese were intense and systematic in the United States, yielding both "official and unofficial discrimination."[3] Furthermore, casting an actress of *any* Asian background stood out mightily in the context of Broadway, where the last Asian female in a featured role had probably been the Chinese American Anna May Wong in 1930.[4] In interviews with me, Sono Osato recalled that it was "very strange, very strange" to headline a Broadway show amid geopolitical strife that had a direct impact on her family, and in *Distant Dances*, her forthright and fascinating memoir, she marveled at the improbable-seeming situation in which she found herself with *On the Town*:

> It was amazing to me that, at the height of a world war fought over the most vital political, moral, and racial issues, a Broadway musical should feature, and have audiences unquestionably accept, a half-Japanese as an All-American Girl. This is probably the most indelible impression I have had of the magic of the theatre. I could never have been accepted as Ivy Smith in films or, later, on television. Only the power of illusion created between performers and audiences across the footlights can transcend political preference, moral attitudes, and racial prejudice.[5]

In this chapter, I explore the racial, political, and artistic meanings that surround the appearance of Sono Osato in *On the Town* and the ways in which the role of Ivy Smith was written to accommodate Osato's personal identity. Just as the show's African American dancers did not play black characters and avoided racial stereotypes of the day, so too Ivy was not defined in the script as being Japanese American. The result is an interwoven saga of Broadway casting, stage representation, first-class ballet companies, and the persecution of one Japanese national during World War II. Grasping the details of Shoji Osato's case is crucial to understand the risk undertaken in hiring his daughter. The creative team of *On the Town* shaped the presentation of Sono's race enigmatically, at times reracializing her character, and as the war dragged on, offstage she became increasingly active politically, which had a profound impact on her subsequent career.

Sono Osato's starring role in *On the Town* represented a major moment in the racial history of the American musical, especially within the context of the wartime campaign against the "Japs," as the era's lurid lingo put it. It represented a substantial gamble for the creative and production teams of the show at the same time as it turned Osato into a symbol of success for Japanese American advocacy groups. Viewed against the backdrop of World War II, choosing Osato to be the star was a subversive act.

INTRODUCING SONO OSATO AS IVY

In Scene 2 of *On the Town*, as Chip, Ozzie, and Gabey ride the subway from the Brooklyn Navy Yard, they notice a poster proclaiming "Meet Exotic Ivy Smith," which sports a photo of a stunning young woman who has just been named Miss Turnstiles for the month. Gabey immediately falls in love with the image in what is essentially a pin-up. While on the train, the three sailors talk with Bill Poster, a man who is literally posting the bill that features Miss Turnstiles. Poster's generic character name could have come straight out of *The Cradle Will Rock*, and his conversation with the sailors sets up the enigma that defines Ivy:

OZZIE: Oh, boy—I'd love to meet her.
CHIP: Obviously an upper class society girl.

GABEY: Fellas, she reminds me of Minnie Frenchley [a girl back home]....

BILL POSTER (Reading [from the poster]): Now look at that for an all-round creature: "Ivy's a home-loving type who likes to go out night-clubbing."

GABEY (Reading): Gee—she loves the Navy.

BILL POSTER: Yeah—but her heart belongs to the Army... "She's not a career girl, but she is studying singing and ballet at Carnegie Hall and painting at the Museum. She is a frail and flowerlike girl—who's a champion at polo, tennis, and shotput."[6]

Even before Ivy stepped into view, the audience knew that she represented a bundle of contradictions. She is home-loving, yet a nightclub crawler. She spurns being a career woman, yet has aspirations as a performer and artist. She is frail, yet a champion at shotput! Traditional Broadway humor is at work, albeit with an unusual purpose.

Two scenes later, Sono Osato finally appears onstage during "Presentation of Miss Turnstiles" (Act I, Scene 4), a scene where she says nothing but dances mightily. "A line of GIRLS sways in, backs to the audience," instructs the script, against a backdrop proclaiming "Meet Miss Turnstiles: Exotic Ivy Smith." Then the ANNOUNCER proclaims, "Miss Turnstiles for June!" He intones:

Every month some lucky little New York miss is chosen Miss Turnstiles for the month. She's got to be beautiful. She's got to be just an average girl, and most important of all, she's got to ride the subway.... Beautiful, brilliant, average, a typical New Yorker.

A spotlight shines on Ivy Smith, who pantomimes her surprise at being chosen as she "turns around with a happy 'Who, me?' expression." (In some productions, Ivy speaks those two words.) The ANNOUNCER then states, "YES, YOU!! Ivy Smith!" He launches into a sung introduction of Ivy, and he affirms her populist, patriotic qualities, reiterating the same bundle of oppositional traits outlined on the poster:

She's a home-loving girl,
But she loves high society's whirl.
She adores the Army, the Navy as well,
At poetry and polo she's swell.

An extended ballet follows. A scenario for it appears in the script, and the dance takes up the bulk of the scene, as Ivy pirouettes with a series of men whose role is to help "glamourize and publicize MISS TURNSTILES." This is a dance about celebrity.

The PHOTOGRAPHER, the REPORTER, the DESIGNER and ASSISTANT back off, and IVY and A SERIES OF MALE ADMIRERS as delineated in the lyric [HOME-LOVING TYPE, PLAYBOY, SOLDIER, SAILOR, AESTHETE, ATHLETE] do a satiric dance based on the contradictory attributes that Miss Turnstiles seems to possess: IVY does a brief pas-de-deux with each of them and a final dance with them ALL.[7]

A series of comedic dance vignettes enact these various visions of Ivy at the same time as they embed a tension between this fictional character and the real-life identity of Sono Osato. In shaping Ivy, the creative team of *On the Town* constructed a character who was simultaneously "exotic" and "an average girl." "A typical New Yorker." An "all-round creature." Defined as being both different from someone who was fully European American and part of the country's essence, her character had a chameleon-like identity that lay in the eyes of the beholder. Having Osato in the lead meant that Gabey was not only headed for a fling but flirting with what was then termed miscegenation. Even more than that, in the midst of an all-out war, he was pursuing a gal with a familial connection to the enemy.

Over the course of the show, Ivy is featured in three major dances. In addition to "Presentation of Miss Turnstiles," they include "Do, Re, Do" (Act I, Scene 8, also known as "Carnegie Hall Pavane") and the expansive ballet "Dream Coney Island" (Act II, Scene 3), which is part of a protracted narrative arc, ranging from Gabey's fantasies about Ivy as he rides on a subway car to the harsh reality of exposing her as a cooch dancer in a Coney Island dive.

No film footage exists of Osato's onstage performances in *On the Town*, and the very limited footage from the original production features Allyn Ann McLerie as Ivy.[8] Yet written accounts convey Osato's impact onstage. She brought to the show both extensive experience in ballet and a flair for comedy, drawing upon

Sono Osato and John Battles in On the Town. *Photofest Digital Archive.*

pantomime and caricature to inspire laughter. Edwin Denby, the famed American dance critic, called her "a warm-hearted comedienne," a dancer "with brilliant rhythm and a brilliant sense of shades of character."[9] By the time of *On the Town*, Osato had performed a secondary role in another musical comedy, *One Touch of Venus*, where she had been hugely successful. Even before that, a talent for comedy was singled out in reviews of her performances with the Ballet Russe de Monte Carlo and Ballet Theatre. "Sono has great beauty, a pert, distinctive presence, quick and clever understanding of character, and real ability as a mime," wrote a Chicago critic as early as 1937.[10] In *On the Town*, she did not dance *en pointe*, as one feature writer went out of her way to make clear.[11]

Not only was Osato talented at comedy and satire, but also her stunning face and sensuous body brought depth and complexity to her stage persona. "She's got to be beautiful," intoned the Announcer at the ceremony selecting Miss Turnstiles. Comedy did not traditionally go hand in hand with female glamour and sexual allure. Even more strikingly, Osato's long black hair and biracial features countered conventional notions of American beauty, as constructed during the 1940s. Perhaps as a strategy to confront Osato's divergence from those norms, her physical appearance was featured in the show's plot, thereby heading off any critique by boldly co-opting perceptions of her identity. Osato was consistently labeled as "exotic" in both the script and the press.[12] Given the long tradition of exoticizing that was fundamental to opera, the ballet, and musical theater, it provided a way of drawing Osato into the realm of historically grounded—even conventional—stage practices.

SONO OSATO AND AMERICAN BEAUTY

One of the remarkable aspects of featuring a young woman of mixed-race heritage in *On the Town* had to do with connecting Osato to the American ritual of beauty pageants, an arena carefully controlled during the 1940s as the province of white women of European Christian heritage. Two obvious real-life models for the Miss Turnstiles competition were Miss America, a national pageant that originated in 1921, and, more directly, Miss Subways, a New York City contest begun in 1941. At the moment when Osato appeared in *On the Town*, beauty pageants were just beginning to admit cultural difference. In the 1941 Miss America pageant, a Native American woman represented the state of Oklahoma, and in September 1945, nine months into the run of *On the Town*, Bess Myerson, a Bronx native, won the contest, becoming the first person of Jewish heritage to take the title. Like the character of Ivy Smith, Myerson was both artistically gifted and beautiful. No women of Asian ancestry competed for the title of Miss America until 1948.[13] At the same time, African American women were barred from the contest for decades. Initially the exclusion was tacit, and in the 1930s it was inscribed into the pageant's written policy. The first African American woman to enter the national Miss America pageant did so at the very late date of 1970.

Meanwhile, the title of Miss Subways originated during World War II out of a commercial impulse, aiming to "prove that the subways could be a successful

Photograph of Sono Osato, undated. Photofest Digital Archive.

advertising medium."[14] The contest quickly became a local cultural event—"a familiar sight for us straphangers riding the NYC subways," as one memoirist recalls. "It was all . . . good, clean fun. Because of the resultant publicity one winner received over 200 marriage proposals."[15] Just as with Miss Turnstiles, winners of Miss Subways held the title for one month. The contest featured women of exceptional beauty, and as of 1944, all the winners had been of European descent. Looking back on the history of Miss Subways, Betty Comden later mused about its restrictive racial demographics: "There were never any black Miss Subways, or Puerto Rican or Oriental or even Jewish," declared Comden. "And of course, Sono Osato was a very exotic-looking girl. She would not have been a typical Miss Subways of that period."[16] Racial progress came sooner with Miss Subways than with Miss America, however. In 1947 an African American won the title, and two years later an Asian American did so.[17]

NISEI IN INTERWAR AMERICA

The audaciousness of hiring Sono Osato to play the role of a beauty queen emerges in sharp relief against her family's history. In the early twentieth century, Asian immigrants had only limited legal protection in the United States, with laws denying the attainment of citizenship. Once World War II began, the few legal rights that did exist were suspended for the Japanese, disrupting families and communities quickly and harshly. Exploring Osato's early years also underscores the degree to which *On the Town*'s ballet pedigree was solid gold. These two plot strands are jarringly incongruous, yet they converged in the life of this gorgeous young dancer.

Born in 1919 in Omaha, Nebraska, Sono Osato was the child of a mixed-race marriage. Her father, Shoji Osato, was an immigrant from Akita, Japan, who came to the United States at age twenty, just before the San Francisco earthquake of 1906.[18] First he picked strawberries in California, and then he began developing skills as a photographer. "After working from coast to coast," his daughter recalled in her memoir, "he finally settled in Omaha, where he opened his own studio."[19] Meanwhile, her mother, Frances Fitzpatrick (born around 1899), was of Irish and French-Canadian descent. Frances had talent as an actress, which went unrealized, but she found other ways to assert her individuality, being considered "daringly modern" in her day.[20] "She was fascinated by everything Japanese and at eighteen decorated the Oriental Room of the Blackstone Hotel in Omaha, which her father [an architect] had designed," Sono stated.[21] The Blackstone was built in 1915.[22] Sono's parents met there when Shoji was having dinner with Sessue Hayakawa and his wife, who were traveling through town. Hayakawa was one of the few Asian film stars of the day. Frances and Shoji met again a few days later and "fell in love on the spot," according to Sono.[23] Because of antimiscegenation laws in Nebraska, they went to Iowa to be married, and Frances Fitzpatrick Osato probably lost her U.S. citizenship in the process. A 1907 law declared that "any American woman who marries a foreigner shall take the nationality of her husband," and Frances would have gained nothing from the Cable Act of 1922, which "asserted the principle of 'independent citizenship' for married women without implementing it fully," writes historian Nancy F. Cott.[24] The manifest for a ship that arrived in New York on September 25, 1929 from Cherbourg, France, lists Frances Osato's nationality as Japanese.[25]

In 1925, the Osatos moved to Chicago, where Frances's family was based. At the time, Chicago had a fairly small Japanese community—nothing like the major presence it would assume after World War II. Two years after settling there, Sono, her mother, and her siblings suddenly took off for France. They stayed in Europe—without her father—for two years. While abroad, Sono saw Serge Diaghilev's famous Ballets Russes during a performance in Monte Carlo. She was then around nine, and she recalled lying in bed that night and thinking, "I wanted to be on that stage in that theatre, dancing with those people."[26] Sono's first personal connection with the Ballets Russes—specifically with a successor company called the Ballet Russe de Monte Carlo—came not in France, however, but rather in Chicago, after her family had resettled at home. There in 1934, at age fourteen, she had a successful audition during a U.S. tour by the company.[27] She had been studying ballet since age ten with Berenice Holmes and Adolph Bolm, two major dance figures in Chicago.[28] The Ballet Russe de Monte Carlo was led by Colonel Wassily de Basil, and Léonide Massine was its star dancer and choreographer. Suddenly the teenage Sono was working with some of the best professionals in the business, most of whom had gone into exile in France during the Russian Revolution. Colonel de Basil "suggested that I take a Russian name," Sono remembered. "I refused," she continued. "'Sono is like Sonia,' I said respectfully but firmly, 'and

Osato looks just right next to Obidenna's name.' He must have been rather surprised at the vehement reaction of a 'little girl,' and...my name remained my own," although she was nicknamed "Osatchka" within the troupe.[29] Ironically enough, her "unusual name" became an asset in a profession where the exotic was valued.

Back in Chicago, Frances and Shoji Osato attained some prominence in the city's small Japanese American community. Shoji at first distinguished himself as a photographer, producing "notable pictures of Chicago cityscapes," and he contributed photographs to a book by the Chicago-based artist Oskar Hansen, who later created the now-famous sculptures adorning the Hoover Dam.[30] One of Shoji's cityscapes appeared in the *Chicago Evening Post's Magazine of the Art World* in 1926, showing a view of Michigan Avenue shot from the Art Institute plaza. A caption described the photo as being "unusual in both composition and 'feeling.'" Shoji clearly had an artistic gift, right down to his signature in the lower left corner of the image, where the *t* has the flair of Japanese kanji.[31] In 1936 Frances and Shoji got attention in the local press for opening a traditional Japanese tea garden in a bamboo building that had been constructed by the government of Japan for the Chicago World's Fair of 1933 (the fair known as "A Century of Progress"). The teahouse was built on the Wooded Island in Chicago's Jackson Park and dubbed "House of Friendly Neighbors" as a way of promoting cultural ties between Japan and the United States.[32] After the fair closed, the building was "given to the park board by Shoji Osato, a Japanese resident of Chicago," reported the *Chicago Daily Tribune*.[33] When the inaugural tea was held, there were "native girls serving," as chronicled in the *Tribune*, and Teru Osato (Sono's younger sister) was among them.[34] The Japanese consul Sadao Iguchi attended.[35]

Photograph of Michigan Avenue by Shoji Osato, as published in the
Chicago Evening Post's Magazine of the Art World, *July 6, 1926.*
Courtesy of the Smithsonian Institution Libraries.

Teru Osato (right) in the Osatos' tea garden in Chicago. As published in the Chicago Daily Tribune, *June 16, 1936.*

Frances Osato had a strong commitment to the tea garden. In July 1939, as the *Chicago Daily Tribune* reported, she invited sixty women there for lunch to meet "Mrs. Oshikawa, head of a flower arrangement school in Tokio," who was visiting Chicago.[36] As it turned out, 1939 was a late date to be hosting functions that proclaimed a tie to Japan. Two years earlier, Japan had invaded China, and it continued a violent occupation there while gearing up to widen the hostilities.

A DEVELOPING ARTIST

While Shoji and Frances ran their tea garden and became a presence within Chicago's small Japanese community, Sono continued to grow artistically within the transnational world of the Ballet Russe de Monte Carlo. Both she and her family became adept at crossing cultural boundaries, and she added genre boundaries into the mix, moving from the world of ballet to that of Broadway in a prolonged but high-flying leap.

Osato's career with the Ballet Russe de Monte Carlo lasted until 1941. With a home base in Monte Carlo, this modern ballet company toured western Europe, venturing also to the United States, Australia, and South America during the 1930s. In April 1934, when Osato joined on, the Ballet Russe de Monte Carlo was in the midst of its first visit to the United States since Diaghilev's Ballets Russes had toured in 1916–17. According to the *New York Times*, the company then included fifty-three Russian dancers.[37] At fourteen, Osato was reported to be its "youngest, and its first American, member."[38] To be singled out in this way, Osato clearly had exceptional talent.

In a somewhat self-deprecating assessment, Osato later speculated that her exoticism led de Basil to hire her. "'It was my strange looks again," she told a reporter for the New York newspaper *PM*. "I couldn't dance very well, but I had a good ear and learned quickly and I was well-built. But it was really because I was funny looking that de Basil took me."[39] If by "funny looking" Osato meant that she looked Japanese, then there was some truth to her perception. Osato's first role was as the "little Japanese boy" in *Union Pacific*, a ballet choreographed by Massine in 1934 and set to a libretto by the American poet and writer Archibald MacLeish.[40] Like Anna May Wong, who was slotted into roles depicting Chinese or Chinese American women, Osato initially danced a role tied to her own race. Since she took part in the premiere of *Union Pacific* on April 6, 1934, during the troupe's season in New York City, Massine must have been casting the dance as the troupe passed through Chicago.[41] The role involved having to "wiggle" through a crowd of "rival laborers and bargirls" while serving drinks to customers. "Later in the scene, when a fight broke out," Osato recalled, "I whacked some of them over the head with a bottle. 'Make hit real,' Massine instructed me, 'but don't hurt dancers.'"[42]

During seven years with the company, Osato entered a life of "constant travel and interminable work," according to ballet critic John Gruen.[43] It was also one of exceptional artistic experiences. "Monte Carlo was my talisman," Osato remembered. "I had crossed America and the Atlantic to become part of the Diaghilev heritage as a dancer." It was "thrilling."[44] By 1937, there were reportedly five Americans in the company, and a year later there were ten.[45] It was a peripatetic life. "There is a constant packing and unpacking of cases as they move from city to city, stopping only for a few nights en route to their ultimate Mecca, New York, where . . . they stay for a season of some three weeks or so," observed one critic.[46] While in New York City, the Ballet Russe performed at the old Metropolitan Opera House. They also toured the country: Philadelphia, Cincinnati, Chicago, Omaha, Boise, Seattle, Portland (Oregon), Los Angeles. "We lived this vagabond life, . . . dancing our 'ham-and-eggs' programs to the point of boredom," Osato recalled.[47] In 1938, a schism in the company's leadership produced two separate troupes, yielding the Ballet Russe de Monte Carlo (led by Massine) and the Original Ballet Russe (led by de Basil).[48] Osato stayed with de Basil's company. The result generated a competitive scene, with a confusing overlap in names.

Osato was "one of the company's youngest dancers," according to *Time* magazine, where she was also described as being "by far its most exotic looking."[49] Becoming a star within the organization proved difficult. "I was dancing considerably better as the months passed. . . . The more I danced, the better I danced," Osato stated. Yet the company was "large," she acknowledged, and "solo roles were hard to come by."[50] During an eight-month season in Australia during 1939–40, when she was around twenty, she stepped out of secondary roles to take one of the principal parts in *Les Sylphides*, a *ballet blanc* in which all the women wore pointe shoes and long white tutus.[51] In October 1940, while on tour in Los Angeles, Osato was featured in the role of Beauty in the U.S. premiere of *La Lutte Eternelle*, choreographed by Igor Schwezoff.[52] That same month, when the Original Ballet Russe opened in Chicago, she was hailed "as a dancer of extensive experience."[53]

One of Osato's signature roles with the Ballet Russe became the Siren in *Le Fils Prodigue (The Prodigal Son)*, which premiered in December 1938 when the troupe was in Australia.[54] The role of the Siren was initially danced by Tamara Grigorieva, and Osato stepped into it by the summer of 1939. Her partner was David Lichine, who was also the work's choreographer.[55] After a performance of that ballet at Covent Garden in the summer of 1939, the *Daily Telegraph* called her dancing "the great event of the evening." The review continued: "Cold at first, she became, as the scene went on, more and more possessed by her part, till at the climax, the identification was almost terrifying."[56] When she performed the role in New York City the following year, the response was just as strong. "[Lichine's] performance of the chief role is brilliant and tireless," reported John Martin in the *New York Times*. "But no less excellent is Sono Osato as the siren. Her exotic beauty and her grasp of the mood and manner of the choreographer make her completely and delightfully right. Nor does she falter at the technical demands that are made upon her."[57] "My strongest memory of [*The Prodigal Son*]," recalled the Ballet Russe's impresario, Sol Hurok, "is the exciting performance given by Sono Osato as the exotic siren."[58] Notably, both John Martin and Sol Hurok labeled Osato as "exotic."

Then in 1941, while the Original Ballet Russe was in residence in New York City, having sought exile there during the war, Osato hit a wall with the organization, in terms of both her pay and the slow pace of her advancement. "I was tired of replacing people who fell ill, of never having sufficient rehearsal time, and of the very hard working conditions," Osato remembered, "I gave the management two weeks to come through with a new contract. The two weeks passed and I had received no communication. I came to realize that this was the end for me. I couldn't go on. I remember going to the theater that night, of taking my make-up, all my Woolworth jewelry, all my false hair and tights, and packing them in a suitcase. I quietly slipped out the stage door."[59] Osato was essentially a demi-caractère dancer with the Ballet Russe, and she never performed lead roles from the company's classical repertory. "Probably no one who ever worked for the de Basil Ballet ended up without a financial grievance," observes a historian of the organization. "Everyone was cheated, one way or another, or at least *felt* cheated."[60] A sense of entropy infected the troupe, as Sol Hurok recalled: "With the 1940–1941 season, deterioration had set in at the vitals of the Monte Carlo Ballet Russe. . . . The dancers themselves were no longer interested. They day-dreamed of Broadway musicals; they night-dreamed of the hills of Hollywood and film contracts."[61]

During the winter of 1940–41, Osato started to establish herself as an independent public personality. A fascinating promotional letter by a publicist named Barry Hyams was sent to a writer at the *New York Post*, providing an inside view of how Osato's image as a transnational artist was being managed. The letter was written in November 1940, one year before Pearl Harbor, and facets of Osato's biography were spun into promotional lingo, including her mixed-race heritage and a childhood visit to meet her father's family in Japan, a traumatic trip that took place during the Great Kanto Earthquake of 1923:

Dear Miss Bussang:

The young international "heart beat" I introduced you to over the phone is Sono Osato, Japanese-Irish denizen of Chicago. She comes by her name legitimately thru her father who was Shoji Osato, artist photographer. Her mother, a Fitzpatrick from the Emerald Isle, is the daughter of the man who planned Canberra, capitol city of the Commonwealth of Australia.

Sono herself is a cultural League of Nations—what with her origin, her mastery of French and her membership in the Russian Ballet. Exotic in real life as an odalisque in Scheherazade or as the Siren in Prodigal Son (one of her favorite roles), Sono's Chicago English and brisk American manner is as exhilarating as football weather. The only living Japanese classical ballet dancer, upon arrival with the company in Chicago in October, she was offered a job as a night club hula dancer by a dance band leader who saw her photograph. Needless to say she turned it down because she prefers being a part of the sixteen different nationalities presented in the Ballet Russe whom she invites for Sukiyaki dinner with "shoes off," typical Japanese style. Her penchant for being a part of "a crazy Russian Company," among whom she has never felt race prejudice and with whom she converses in Russian, English or French, plus a little Polish, has made her forget Japanese. . . . Her most vivid memory is the 1923 earthquake in Yokohama when she was but three years of age.

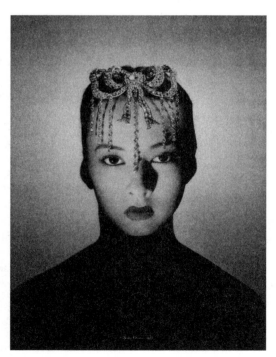

Sono Osato, 1937. Photograph by George Platt Lynes.
© Estate of George Platt Lynes.

These are the facts—why don't you mull them over a bit and let's have dinner on Friday. Will you call me?

Sincerely,
Barry Hyams
Associate Press Representative[62]

Osato was essentially being marketed as a "hybrid, cosmopolitan, Westernized female"—a phrase that comes from Shirley Jennifer Lim's analysis of the persona shaped by actress Anna May Wong. Lim writes of Wong as having "exploit[ed] the space of agency between exoticism and cosmopolitanism."[63] A generation younger than Wong, Osato seemed to be completely comfortable and supple in achieving that same balance. More than that, she was good at it. Boosted by

Isamu Noguchi with Sono Osato and Noguchi's bust of Osato, 1940. Photograph by Eliot Elisofon. © 2013 The Isamu Noguchi Foundation and Garden Museum, New York/Artists Rights Society (ARS), New York.

Hyams's publicity efforts and a growing reputation in New York City, Osato increasingly emerged as a public figure, and photographs document a celebrity on the rise. In the *New York Times*, one image in 1940 featured her in a tutu and *en pointe*, with the caption "Ballet on the Wing," and another in March 1941 was titled "Sono Osato, an Action Study."[64] Visual artists also responded to Osato's beauty. In 1937, George Platt Lynes, the famed fashion photographer who did extensive work with dancers, produced at least two photographs of Osato—one a dramatically exquisite head shot (see page 126) and the other a full-body portrait.[65] In 1940, the eminent Japanese American artist Isamu Noguchi sculpted a bust of Osato (see page 127).[66] Noguchi had strong ties in the dance world through collaborations with Martha Graham that began in the mid-1930s, and he, like Osato, was one of the best-known *nisei* of the day.

BALLET THEATRE AND THE CASE OF SHOJI OSATO, "ALIEN ENEMY"

During the winter of 1940–41, as Sono entered a transitional phase in her career that would soon lead to *On the Town*, World War II gained intensity, and the United States drew closer to direct engagement. In the late summer of 1940, the Germans began massive bombings in Britain, and Germany, Italy, and Japan signed the Tripartite Pact that September. In April 1941, the United States—while still maintaining neutrality—began sea patrols in the Atlantic, and in August it declared an oil embargo against Japan, essentially cutting off 80 percent of Japan's oil imports. While Sono pursued her professional goals, a parallel series of events was unfolding in Chicago, where her father's status as a Japanese national increasingly brought him under scrutiny. At times, the sagas of father and daughter collided. But there were also implausible-seeming stretches when Sono's career flourished. By the time of *On the Town*'s premiere, Sono personified the ways in which the show positioned itself in relation to the politics of war, yet largely stayed under the radar in doing so.

In the winter of 1940–41, immediately after Sono left the Ballet Russe de Monte Carlo, she spent six months studying at the School of American Ballet in New York City (essentially during the first half of 1941), as many dancers from the Ballet Russe did at the time.[67] That fall, she officially began dancing with Ballet Theatre when it was very new. Four years later, Ballet Theatre was to give its premiere of Robbins's and Bernstein's *Fancy Free*. Just as Osato became part of Ballet Theatre in 1941, this thoroughly American troupe gained a major Russian inflection as members of "one or both Ballets Russes" joined its ranks—all among the artists then displaced from Europe. A headline in the *New York Times* proclaimed "Russe and Near Russe" in describing the character of ballet performance in New York City that season.[68] German (Gerald) Sevastianov became Ballet Theatre's director, Antal Dorati stepped in as its conductor, and Sol Hurok was its new manager. All had worked previously with de Basil's company. Thus even though Osato had left the Ballet Russe during the previous season, she remained at least partly within its ranks as transplanted to Ballet Theatre. In the early fall of 1941 Ballet Theatre traveled to Mexico City "to prepare the new works," as Hurok recalled, and Osato went along, as documented in a vaccination certificate in the archives of Ballet Theatre.[69] On November 12, 1941, Ballet Theatre was back in New York to open its season, and Osato was among its soloists, together with Nora Kaye, Lucia Chase, Jerome Robbins, and others. They worked as the second string of dancers, while the principals were Irina Baronova, Alicia Markova, and Anton Dolin.[70] John Martin of the *New York Times* bemoaned the impact on Ballet Theatre of its new Russian leadership. "The whole direction of the company has been altered, and the original purpose of the Ballet Theatre can be said to have been abandoned altogether," Martin complained.[71]

During Ballet Theatre's spring 1942 season in New York, a high point for both Osato and the company came with the premiere of Antony Tudor's *Pillar of Fire*, which was unveiled in April and immediately became, as Agnes de Mille put it, "one of the theatrical landmarks of our era."[72] The stars were Nora Kaye and Hugh Laing. Osato was one of the Lovers-in-Experience and Jerome Robbins was among the lovers' partners. "All [are] as near perfection as can be asked," reported Martin.[73] Another of Osato's signature roles with the troupe was that of the Lilac Fairy in *Princess Aurora*, a distillation by Dolin (after the original by Marius Petipa) drawn from *The Sleeping Beauty*.[74]

With Ballet Theatre, then, Osato attracted considerable attention, yet once again she never reached its highest echelon. Even so, her celebrity in the United States was growing, inspired by her "exotic beauty," as journalists repeatedly continued to note.[75] In April 1942, a stunning photo of her appeared on the cover of *Peacock Alley*, a glossy magazine issued by the luxurious Waldorf Astoria Hotel. The photo also appeared inside the magazine, with the caption "Sono Osato, exotic soloist of the Ballet Theatre, will be seen in the newest Fokine hit, *Russian Soldier*, during the Ballet Season at the Metropolitan."[76] Not only does this cover photo chronicle Osato's rise as a ballerina, but it also shows that she had become a darling of photojournalists and fashion photographers. In another case, Osato modeled a dress by Pattullo Modes, with the following caption: "Worn by Sono Osato, the Half-American, Half-Japanese Ballerina of the Ballet Theatre" (although undated, the photo must have appeared in 1941 or 1942; see page 130).[77] Again there is a parallel with Anna May Wong, who has been described as having "used modern fashion to claim beauty, humanity, and modernity for Chinese Americans" and to attain "fame, and therefore power in her career."[78] So too with Osato, who at the opening of the 1940s created a space in which her beauty, including its Japanese qualities, became an asset, one that she could use to promote her ambitions as a dancer.

Yet for Osato, the same Japanese heritage that had produced rhapsodic exclamations about her "exotic beauty" began to spell trouble when Ballet Theatre went on tour in the months after Pearl Harbor, and her family faced a deepening crisis in Chicago. Shoji and Frances continued to run the Japanese Tea Garden in Chicago's Jackson Park until it was "forced to close" as a result of World War II, according to historian Alice Murata.[79] Even before Pearl Harbor, Shoji's identity as a Japanese American, which he had capitalized on as a means of earning a living,

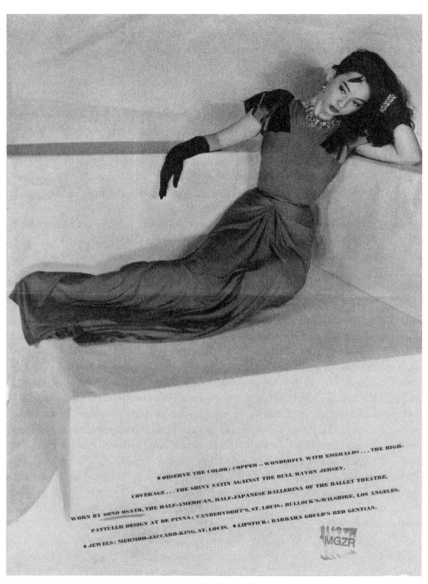

Sono Osato modeling a dress by Pattullo Modes. Dance Clipping Files, New York Public Library at Lincoln Center, Astor, Lenox, and Tilden Foundations.

had begun to generate problems. In October 1938, as Japan's occupation of China continued, the United States government began identifying people whom it believed to be foreign spies. The *Chicago Daily Tribune* reported that out of concern for a "foreign spy menace" President Roosevelt asked the State Department to reveal to the public "the names of persons or firms whose business it is to disseminate information about foreign countries in the United States." Shoji was included among the "Japanese propagandists," with his name and address published in the

Chicago Daily Tribune. There he was identified "as publicity and advertising agent for the Japanese Board of Tourist Industry and Japanese government railways."[80] Shoji had been patching together an income with some work as a photographer, some with the tea garden, and some in various capacities for Japanese interests. On November 8, 1940, he had to fill out an Alien Registration Form, and he again listed his association with the Japanese Board of Tourist Industry, which encouraged Westerners to visit Japan. He gave a concise description of the limits of his work for them: "Lending of moving picture films of Art and travel in Japan and distribution of Tourists Library books on cultural aspects of Japan, are only activities."[81]

The day after the Japanese bombed Pearl Harbor, Shoji was arrested by the FBI at his home at 11:30 p.m. He was booked in the wee hours of December 9 and detained at Fort Sheridan, Illinois.[82] Shoji's arrest occurred months before the official internment project began, and the charges against him stemmed from his ongoing alliances with Japan and his management of the tea garden, which had the performance of Japanese culture at the core of its business plan. According to historian Mae M. Ngai, 2,192 Japanese were arrested in the United States in the days immediately after Pearl Harbor, putting Shoji in an unfortunate but select group. Those arrested "comprised virtually the entire political, social, cultural, and business leadership of Japanese American communities."[83]

One government memorandum about Shoji's case, obtained under the Freedom of Information Act, spelled out the accusations against him and the considerable standing he had attained within the Japanese American community in Chicago:

> The subject...appeared before the Alien Enemy Hearing Board, Chicago, Illinois, on January 3 and January 28, 1942, accompanied by his wife. It was disclosed that the subject was a representative of the Board of Tourist Industries for the Japanese government railways. In this capacity, the investigation revealed, he contacted all of the visiting Japanese dignitaries who came to Chicago. He was also the Chicago reporter for the Nippon Publishing Company of New York. It was disclosed that the subject was a close friend of various Japanese consuls in Chicago and on several occasions had arranged free tours for outstanding American officials to Japan. The subject made the statement before the Board that he received only $350 a year in payment for his services in connection with this work. However, from several investigations conducted by the Federal Bureau of Investigation, it is apparent that the subject did a great amount of entertaining in Chicago. In explaining his income for the past several years, the subject stated that he received money for photographic work which he did and also had an income from operating the Japanese Gardens in Jackson Park, a public park in Chicago. He was paid $500 a season for this concession.[84]

Shoji's Japan-related income of $850 a year ($350 + $500) should be viewed against a context in which the bulk of American non-farm families earned under $3,000 a year in 1941.[85] In other words, Shoji was earning a very modest amount. Meanwhile, Nippon Publishing may well have put Shoji in the orbit of *Nippon,* a photojournalism magazine published from 1934 to 1944, which had the purpose of "publiciz[ing] Japanese culture to the rest of the world." *Nippon* "received support from state agencies such as the Japan National Board of Tourist Industry and the Society for International Cultural Relations."[86]

Thus Shoji Osato's ongoing ties to his homeland were clear, although none of them added up to nefarious or subversive activities. Like any immigrant in the United States, Shoji bridged cultures, and he drew on his assets as a photographer and a Japanese national to build alliances and make a living. Shoji thus appears as someone who retained commercial connections to his home country, at the same time as he posed no danger to the war effort. His arrest was a classic case of "the conflation of culture and loyalty," as Mae Ngai puts it.[87]

Yet declassified documents show that the FBI persisted in pursuing Shoji, projecting the worst possible intentions out of the tiniest details of his life by constructing damaging strings of associations. He was branded as an "alien enemy," someone who, as one official report put it, was "apprehended as being potentially dangerous to the public peace and safety of the United States."[88] The problem stemmed in part from the fact that he was not a U.S. citizen. Yet because of being from Japan he was "not eligable [*sic*] for citizenship," as another document stated starkly.[89] It was the same Catch 22 in which many Japanese nationals living in the United States found themselves after Pearl Harbor. Frances Osato worked hard to gain her husband's release. One of many reports filed during the period of his persecution—each of which contained a series of interviews with Shoji's acquaintances—bears witness to her persistence. "At the time of the subject's apprehension and temporary detention in Chicago, Illinois," one report states, "his wife visited this office daily and contacted the United States Attorney on several occasions in an effort to get him released on parole."[90]

In *Distant Dances*, Sono Osato recalled that after Pearl Harbor her father's status as an enemy alien had an immediate impact on her career, and she was forced to adapt in order to remain active professionally. For a time, she changed her last name, in response to a request from Ballet Theatre's manager, Sol Hurok:

> On December 7, 1941, I was stopped in my tracks by a news bulletin on the radio by the stage door. Japan had attacked Pearl Harbor. I ran home in a state of panic. . . . Only three hours later, I stood in the wings before the evening performance [of Ballet Theatre], still in a state of shock. How could I face the public? Having been publicized throughout my career as being half-Japanese, I feared the tragedy of Pearl Harbor would provoke an outraged American audience to an angry, possibly ugly response to me. . . . The Hurok management also feared that my presence in the company might affect the audience. They suggested that I change my name rather than risk adverse publicity on our upcoming tour. I agreed grudgingly to take my mother's name and performed for a while as Sono Fitzpatrick.[91]

In the spring of 1942, as Ballet Theatre planned a tour to Mexico, Sono received notification from the U.S. Passport Division that she was barred from leaving the country.[92] She then faced a period of several months without work, which prompted her to make an appeal to the president of Ballet Theatre, as documented in a letter to him. "As you know I have been advised from Washington, that permission cannot be granted to me to go to Mexico to join the company there," wrote Sono. "You have offered to pay me the sum of $90 in full settlement of my contract with the company, and this I accept."[93]

Ballet Theatre then had its fall season in New York City, in which Sono danced, and as the troupe prepared to go on tour once again, her problems resurfaced. In November and December 1942, the company journeyed to twenty-nine cities in the South, and Sono initially traveled with no restrictions.[94] She was listed in the program for the U.S. tour as Sono Fitzpatrick.[95] As the company prepared to head west, however, aiming for Los Angeles in early February 1943, her mobility was curtailed. "I received yet another official government notification," Sono later recalled. "This time the office of General John L. DeWitt informed me that I could not enter the state of California. Somewhat more familiar by then with the indiscriminate fear of everything Japanese that had gripped the country, I was more resigned to this notice than I had been to the earlier one."[96] Documents in the archives of Ballet Theatre confirm that on November 28, 1942, the company's president wrote to Lt. Gen. John L. DeWitt, asking how to proceed with plans to enter a "military area" when the father of a member of his company was a Japanese national. He was careful not to name Sono:

> Our organization is on a trans-continental tour of the United States and is scheduled to reach the Pacific Coast on January 16th. We have, as one of our dancers, a native born American citizen whose father is Japanese, although her mother is not. Inasmuch as such cities as Portland, Oregon; Seattle, Washington; San Francisco, Sacramento and Los Angeles, California are included in our tour, may I inquire what restrictions are now in effect as to the entry of a person of Japanese ancestry into the Pacific Coast area, and what is the extent of the area affected by such restrictions.[97]

DeWitt's office responded as follows:

> You are advised that the policy of the Commanding General, to which no exception can be made, prohibits travel to or residence within Military Area No. 1 and that portion of Military Area No. 2 lying within the State of California by persons of Japanese ancestry. These Military Areas comprise roughly all of the State of California and the western half of the states of Oregon, Washington and Arizona.[98]

As a result, Sono was closed out of the western tour. At some point during this same period, she was looking for an apartment in New York City, and "a landlord had the audacity to ask her to sign a statement saying she wasn't an enemy spy," as the *Chicago Defender* later reported.[99]

Sono's memoir dates her father's internment as occurring during the spring of 1943, but government files document it as taking place one year earlier. Whatever the case, Sono recalls visiting him while he was being held "in a large house that had formerly been a mansion on the South Side of the city, miles from our apartment."

The "mansion" might well have been at 4800 S. Ellis Avenue. Built around 1890, it was used during World War II to house detainees who were primarily German, and Sono remembered "some Germans" were jailed there when she visited her dad.[100] Surviving records show that Shoji almost got moved to one of the large Japanese relocation camps during the spring of 1942, when the camps were just being opened. That did not happen, however, and in May 1942 he was released on parole and returned to the Osato home at 455 West Webster Avenue in Chicago. From then on, he worked as a cashier at Ave & Gahan Restaurant and at the Oriental Gift Shop, owned by Teruo Mukoyama.[101] A federal order in January 1942 forcing all "enemy aliens" to "surrender to local police all portable cameras, radio transmitters, short wave receivers, and firearms" made it impossible for him to return to his work as a photographer.[102]

Meanwhile, Frances Osato moved to New York, and in October 1943, Shoji relocated to an apartment over the Chicago restaurant where he worked, staying there and in various rooming houses over the next several years.[103] He was confined to Chicago and only permitted to leave with special dispensation, which significantly circumscribed his life options. Beginning in December 1943, he made repeated appeals to change the place of his parole to New York, citing a desire to join his family. Shoji's boss at the Oriental Gift Shop was interviewed by the FBI in June 1944, and the agent reported as follows: "The witness [Shoji's boss] stated the subject appears to be very depressed over the fact that he is still on parole even though he has a son in the United States Army and a son-in-law in the United States Navy and because he has attempted to prove his loyalty to the United States in every way, possible."[104] Timothy Osato (Shoji's son) was part of the Army's 442nd Infantry, which was a segregated unit made up of *nisei*, even as his father was confined to Chicago.

The Japanese relocation program hit hardest on the West Coast, with ten isolated internment camps established in seven states, stretching from Arizona to Wyoming. Yet Japanese Americans living in the geographic center of the country— such as Shoji Osato in Chicago—could still get caught in the crossfire, with life-altering consequences. For New Yorkers, who of course were living on the opposite coast, the camps and the overall status of Japanese Americans certainly posed thorny issues, yet were removed from their everyday consciousness. Working in New York City, Sono was able to have more professional freedom than would have been the case elsewhere in the country. As a result, she kept dancing during her father's incarceration and extended parole. During Ballet Theatre's spring season of 1943 in New York, which took place right after she had been unable to travel to the West Coast, she continued to be featured in secondary roles. Tudor's *Pillar of Fire* was among the works performed that season, and John Martin praised the production yet again, calling it "superlatively cast" with "stunning performances" by Nora Kaye and Hugh Laing. He included Sono among a group of dancers who were "equally fine in slightly less rewarding roles."[105] When Tudor's *Romeo and Juliet* received its premiere that April, Sono was praised as an "excellent" Rosaline.[106]

In April 1943, Sono married Victor Elmaleh, a Moroccan-born architect and artist. Elmaleh's family, who lived in Brooklyn, maintained business ties to Morocco.

His grandfather was an Orthodox rabbi, and his family objected to his marriage to a woman who was mixed-race and not Jewish.[107] But he and Sono persisted, marrying in a simple ceremony in New York's City Hall. Soon afterward, Sono sent a letter of resignation to Ballet Theatre.[108] She was informed that her contract "stands firm until September 1, 1943," but she did not accompany the troupe on tour that summer.[109] *Oklahoma!*, with choreography by Agnes de Mille, opened that same spring (on March 31, 1943), and Sono's work as a dancer was about to shift focus, becoming part of Broadway's romance with ballet.

ONE TOUCH OF VENUS

In early September 1943, the *Chicago Daily Tribune* brought its readers up to date about one of its hometown stars, publishing a chatty segment that highlighted Sono's travel restrictions yet made no mention of her father. The opening line offered a somewhat absurd comparison:

> Two casualties of war, for different reasons, are the city of Nuremberg and the lovely little dancer Sono Osato. Osato no longer is with Ballet Theater because when the troupe went to California on tour she was not permitted, due to Japanese-American birth, to enter the military zone. Since then she has married a young French Moroccan, Victor Elmaleh, and now is rehearsing with the Kurt Weill musical, "One Touch of Venus," which has choreography by Agnes de Mille, and will have a Boston tryout the middle of the month.[110]

In fact, Osato avoided becoming a "casualty" by resourcefully searching out new professional alternatives, and *One Touch of Venus* represented a major turning point for her—an opportunity to practice her art within a commercial sphere that delivered a solid salary and the opportunity to reach a broad audience. Just as crucially, *One Touch of Venus* ultimately offered a major source of both creative ideas and dancers for *On the Town*.

When *One Touch of Venus* opened in New York City on October 7, 1943, it was a first-class production, with a score by Kurt Weill, lyrics by Ogden Nash, a book by Nash and S. J. Perelman, and choreography by Agnes de Mille. Elia Kazan directed, Maurice Abravanel conducted, and Mary Martin was the star. A musical filled with dance, *One Touch of Venus* in many ways was an important predecessor to *On the Town*, and the music historian Geoffrey Block writes that Weill "took a risk" with the show "by allowing dance to tell a story."[111] Added to that, de Mille also took a chance when she hired Osato for the role of Première Danseuse. The part involved no speaking or singing but brought high visibility. Osato "stopped the show on opening night and has all but stolen it ever since," reported New York's *PM*.[112] She was featured in three fetching ballets: "Forty Minutes for Lunch," "Foolish Heart," and the closing number, "Venus in Ozone Heights" (see page 136) At the premiere of the show, Sono's husband, Victor, her mother, and her sister, Teru, sat in the audience.[113] Her father still could not leave Chicago, and her brother was serving in the military.

Sono Osato and Peter Birch in One Touch of Venus, *1943.* Photofest Digital Archive.

Osato's mixed-race heritage did not seem to concern the culture industry of New York City. In part, acknowledgment of her race went underground for a time, as comments about her "exotic" family background diminished in the press. They did not disappear, however, and notably, the *Pacific Citizen*, a nationally distributed Japanese American newspaper, began to cover her career, often placing highlighted announcements about Sono on the front page. Osato also became increasingly involved with the Japanese American Committee for Democracy, a New York–based advocacy group. During this period, bloody fighting was under way in the Pacific, and the Allies were starting to realize some gains, albeit with heavy casualties. In February 1943, the Japanese began retreating from Guadalcanal, after an intense assault there by U.S. forces, and Allied victories slowly started to mount up in New Guinea and the Aleutian Islands.

One Touch of Venus had a slight plot, bringing a classical goddess face-to-face with the realities of modern life. Its farcical twists and turns were summarized brilliantly in *Time*, which engaged in a bit of wordplay:

> The fantasy is about an ancient statue of Venus that comes to life in the far-from-contemptible shape of Mary Martin, and pursues a timid barber whose sexual career has been sparse if not Spartan. The cutter of hair, who has a girl already, tries like the devil to keep his Greek admirer at a distance. But even

when he gets safely by her lure, he is routed by her persistence. Then, after she lands him, she discovers it means a hideous humdrum life in a joint like Ypsilanti, and scrams to her statue quo ante.[114]

Reviews were ecstatic, and Osato continued to be singled out for special praise. "Miss Osato likely is to be the toast of the autumn, for she is graceful and alive as well as being beautiful and as well as giving the impression that she, herself, is having a wonderful time," wrote Lewis Nichols in the *New York Times*.[115] In a follow-up feature, Nichols underscored his admiration: "Since the show seems to have gone in for discoveries, there also is Sono Osato....As the première danseuse in Agnes de Mille's ballets and dances she is, to be brisk about it, wonderful."[116] Note that the word "exotic" is absent from these reviews.

A ten-minute film of portions of the original production of *One Touch of Venus*, shot in 16 mm, shows Osato smiling straight into the camera at one point, and she flits by in a couple of dances.[117] The film quality is poor, but the press provided a sense of her charisma onstage. "In the first act," wrote the *New York Herald Tribune*, "she dances with a precise sharpness in every limb and a rhythmic punch that startles: she is a galvanic comedienne. In the second act she [is] glamorous, alluring...quite serious and beautiful."[118] Another critic described Osato's hairstyle, and there "exotic" reappears: "She twisted her long black satiny hair into two high knobs made secure with bone hairpins, and exotic with a knot of velvet and two flowers."[119] The "knobs," in fact, became Osato's signature in the show. "Right after Mary Martin sings *I'm a Stranger Here Myself*," reported the newspaper *PM*, "the curtain rises on *Forty Minutes for Lunch*, the first of choreographer Agnes de Mille's short ballets for the show. As the dancers, in fuchsia jerseys and short velveteen skirts, whirl their first whirl there is a stir in the audience, an audible whispering of, 'Where is she? I don't see...There! There she is. In the back row with that funny lilypad thing on her head.'"[120] "She," of course, was Sono.

Osato wrote about the difficulties of choreographing "Forty Minutes for Lunch" during Boston tryouts for *One Touch of Venus*, and the trials of shaping that segment might well have provided some inspiration for the sailors in *Fancy Free* and *On the Town*. During tryouts, de Mille proposed that Weill add a sea shanty at the end of the number, and Osato paraphrased the choreographic instructions for this new segment, as they were articulated to her by de Mille:

An American sailor will saunter in. He'll lean on the proscenium and ogle you. He'll stop you dead in your tracks. You'll go balmy over him, he'll go balmy over you and offer his arm. You'll stare at the audience thumping your foot, thinking it over. Then bolt straight up, slap your skirts, hitch your bosom, tweak your roses [in Osato's hair], and perk your head in his direction. He'll stride over to you. You give him the eye, he gives you the eye. Take his arm, bend over, do some snappy little foot patter towards the wings, and then, just before you go, lurch back with one quick take at the audience and strut off![121]

The pantomimed comedy, the notion of a sailor "saunter[ing] in" to pick up a frisky female, and the sassy self-confidence of the woman being pursued all presaged Robbins's ballet and show. He and de Mille strongly supported each other's work, in part because of shared ties to Ballet Theatre. Osato later recalled that Robbins sent well-wishes for *One Touch of Venus*: "An hour before the curtain rose, I sat at my dressing table making up...when someone handed me a handwritten note from Jerome Robbins."[122] A large number of dancers from the chorus of *One Touch of Venus* moved to *On the Town*, including Carle Erbele, Nelle Fisher, Allyn Ann McLerie, Lavina Nielsen, and Duncan Noble.[123]

Osato won the first annual Donaldson Award (a precursor of the Tony Awards) for "best dancer (female)," an achievement recognized in *Pacific Citizen*.[124] At the same time, she continued to be featured in glossy magazines. A fashion photo of her in a "Henri Bendel original" appeared during the run of *One Touch of Venus*, and photos of her joyous balletic presence appeared on the cover of the *Sunday News: New York's Picture Newspaper* and *PM's Sunday Picture News*.[125] Osato left *One Touch of Venus* in the summer of 1944 "because the strenuous schedule had worn her down and she felt the necessity of a good rest."[126]

One Touch of Venus left its mark, preparing Broadway for a Sono Osato whose racial presentation was both provocative and carefully controlled. Her flirtation with a sailor in "Forty Minutes for Lunch" brought the potential for a sense of danger at the same time as she was a nubile ingénue with pigtails. Similarly, in "Venus in Ozone Heights," she played a sinuous, sexy goddess, yet did so in the form of a fantasy figure from long ago with no threatening implications in the contemporary world. Her talent radiated powerfully in that show, yet she was not the headliner. Her presence onstage was limited to dancing, which essentially rendered her mute, and her character (Première Danseuse) was basically nameless. When Wolcott Gibbs, writing in the *New Yorker*, called her a "marvelously limber girl of cryptic nationality," he essentially articulated the ethnic assimilation of Osato that was achieved by the show.[127] One of the few exceptions occurred in the left-leaning daily *PM*, which returned to a pre–World War II journalistic practice by identifying Osato as a "24-year-old Japanese-American ballerina."[128] At the same time, her career also continued to be chronicled regularly in *nisei* publications.

HIRING *NISEI* ARTISTS: *ON THE TOWN* AND *APPALACHIAN SPRING*

With *On the Town*, Osato stepped to center stage, and the handling of her Japanese heritage became more complex now that she played a character who was simultaneously exotic and an all-American girl—or, as one newspaper profile put it, "the girl you wish lived next door."[129] Wishing for a Japanese American to move into your neighborhood was far from a common sentiment during World War II. Osato's race was both openly accepted and adroitly managed in the show, sending subtle cultural and gender signals.

Osato later recalled that Bernstein initially drew her into *On the Town*, and in an interview with me she declared, "I didn't have to audition."[130] Several weeks after she and her husband saw *Fancy Free*, Robbins introduced them to Bernstein, and the three became good friends, with Bernstein as their frequent dinner guest.[131]

At the time, Osato and Elmaleh hoped to produce a musical about King Solomon and the Queen of Sheba, and they invited Bernstein to compose the music. Even though he ultimately trained as an architect, Elmaleh had started out as a music major in college, and he had talent as an entrepreneur. "Then one night at dinner," Osato recalled, "Lenny said, 'Look, you have nothing to do until this show [about Solomon and Sheba] gets written. Why don't you do the one I'm working on right now with some friends?'" "By the time he left us that night," Osato continued, "I had agreed to join the cast of *On the Town*." As a result, Osato was an early hire for the show, before George Abbott became involved.

Osato obviously knew Robbins from their experience in Ballet Theatre. Their names appear side by side in the company's programs, including especially Massine's *Fantastic Toy Shop*, with Osato in the role of His Wife and Robbins as Their Son. They also danced together in Tudor's *Romeo and Juliet* and his *Pillar of Fire*.[132] "Jerry and I had never been close friends during my two years in Ballet Theatre," Osato later remarked. "I'd always liked him and enjoyed dancing with him.... Offstage he was reserved and seemed rather melancholy, particularly on tour."[133] When Robbins and Bernstein launched *Fancy Free* in the spring of 1944, Osato no longer danced with Ballet Theatre. But she was in the audience, and she recognized immediately that Robbins had "extraordinary talent."

Shared progressive politics inflected Osato's relationship with Robbins and Bernstein, even as attitudes toward Japanese Americans were complex, including among those who also faced racial and ethnic prejudice. Jewish advocacy groups such as the American Jewish Congress, for example, did not speak out forcefully against the injustice of the Japanese American relocation camps. At the same time, according to historian Cheryl Greenberg, Jewish organizations did join with civil rights groups, notably the NAACP, in advocating "fair treatment for individual Japanese Americans not living in militarily sensitive areas."[134] Within the realm of art and entertainment, Bernstein and Robbins took a parallel step when they reached out to Osato.

It is also intriguing to speculate how hiring Osato might have been a by-product of Bernstein's close relationship to Copland, who was then developing *Appalachian Spring* with choreography by Martha Graham. *Appalachian Spring* marked another moment when an American ballet incorporated Japanese American artists. In this case, they were Isamu Noguchi, who designed the sets for *Appalachian Spring*, and the dancer Yuriko (Yuriko Kikuchi), who performed as one of The Followers. Yuriko was the first nonwhite dancer hired by Graham.[135] She and her family had been interned at the Gila River Relocation Center, and she was released in September 1943.[136] *Appalachian Spring* had its premiere one year later, on October 30, 1944.

Like Osato, Noguchi was a highly visible artistic figure of Japanese American heritage. The luminous simplicity of his sets for *Appalachian Spring*—especially the now iconic rocking chair for Graham as The Bride—fused Shaker design with Noguchi's own Japanese-inflected modernism. At the time, Noguchi was struggling to position himself racially in the United States, and he articulated a worldview that was as syncretic as his art. "To be hybrid anticipates the future," wrote Noguchi in March 1942. "This is America. The nation of all nationalities."[137]

In May that same year, Noguchi voluntarily entered the internment camp in Poston, Arizona, where he attempted to launch an art program for detainees; he ended up staying for a short time.[138] Noguchi and Osato faced a parallel struggle in defining a strategy for carrying on their artistic work amid racist animosity. Their names repeatedly appeared side by side in *nisei* publications and activities from this period. Both were among the founders of an Arts Council established by the Japanese American Committee for Democracy in 1944, and photographs of both appeared in a promotional pamphlet published by the Japanese American Citizens League in 1945, just as the camps were closing.[139] The pamphlet was part of a campaign to demonstrate that *nisei* had contributed significantly to American culture.

ON THE TOWN AND THE ONGOING CASE OF SHOJI OSATO

By late 1944, the internment of Japanese Americans on home soil was coming under sharp scrutiny, and a cluster of major decisions about the relocation camps occurred less than two weeks before *On the Town* opened. On December 17, 1944, the War Department announced that the "mass exclusion of persons of Japanese ancestry from the West Coast States was ended . . . effective January 2," as the *New York Times* reported.[140] Yet it took well over a year to close the camps completely. The day after the order to do so, the Supreme Court handed down two conflicting decisions related to the relocation facilities. *Korematsu v. United States* had been brought by Fred Korematsu, a Japanese American who challenged the executive order that had legalized the camps. Korematsu lost in a 6–3 decision, with the court affirming the "constitutionality of the wartime regulations under which American citizens of Japanese ancestry were evacuated from Pacific Coast areas in 1942."[141] In a dissenting opinion, Justice Frank Murphy stated that the relocation of the Japanese "goes over the 'very brink of constitutional power' and falls into the ugly abyss of racism." That same day, the court handed down a unanimous opinion in favor of Mitsuye Endo, who was being held at a camp in Utah. The court ruled that since Endo's detention "was not related to espionage or sabotage, she must be released."

Government records show that Shoji Osato persisted with petitions to join his family in New York, but he was repeatedly denied and his parole extended. His associates continued to be interviewed about his loyalty, as he entered a period of transience in which deteriorating economic circumstances forced him to move from one rooming house to another. As with other Japanese Americans apprehended during the war, Shoji's career, family relationships, and sense of community had been deeply damaged. In a report from June 16, 1944, an agent from the Immigration and Naturalization Service reported on an interview with Shoji: "He felt he had done everything in his power to prove his loyalty to the United States and therefore believed he should be entitled to release from his parole." Shoji was described as asserting that "he does not belong to any [Japanese] organizations and does not read any foreign language newspapers." Purchasing war bonds was a crucial test of loyalty to the United States, and the topic came up repeatedly in Shoji's government records. Yet he could not invest in bonds "because of ill health, low salary and strained family conditions."[142] Government authorities in Chicago determined then, as they had previously, that because Shoji had "for several years [prior to his detention] maintained very close contact with various Japanese newspapers and transportation lines, . . . it is too soon to believe [that] the subject has had a complete change of ideals and is willing to sever his ties with the Japanese Government."

On December 22, 1944, a telegram was sent from Chicago to the district director of Immigration and Naturalization in New York City, reporting that Shoji had requested permission to visit New York from December 24, 1944, to January 10, 1945.[143] Although unstated in the government documents, Shoji must have been attempting to attend the debut of his daughter's Broadway show on December 28. In *Distant Dances*, Sono describes her father as "suffer[ing] a stroke that shattered his hopes of being with us on opening night." He "finally" saw the show at some point during the spring of 1945, when "he was thinner, smaller, and so feeble he walked with a cane."[144] Like the Japanese elders whom Isamu Noguchi had observed at the relocation camp in Poston, Arizona, Shoji Osato's long surveillance by the U.S. government left him with "a bitter realization of failure."[145]

RACIALIZING AND RERACIALIZING MISS TURNSTILES

Given this wartime drama, the handling of Sono Osato's race within the context of *On the Town* opens up intriguing vistas of interpretation. On one level, the role of Miss Turnstiles can simply be read as a case of lighthearted romantic comedy: Boy meets girl. Girl is gorgeous. Pursuit ensues. Boy gets girl. Yet the situation was obviously not so simple. The girl—as played by Sono—was Japanese, and the boy was Caucasian, bringing implications of miscegenation. Furthermore, the character of Ivy Smith underwent a transformation during the course of the show. Initially she appears as a guileless beauty queen, benignly plucked out of a line of coquettish contestants. Yet by Act II, Ivy is exposed in a scene titled the "The Real Coney Island" as a cooch dancer, earning a living in the Egyptian-themed Rajah Bimmy's Harum-Scarum and picking up a handkerchief with her teeth. She is a vamp. Gabey "realizes with horror" that the cooch dancer is Ivy and accidentally "pulls her skirt off"—at which point Ivy reclaims her innocence by explaining that she dances in this dive to pay her bills.[146] Not only does Gabey transgress racial boundaries, but for a brief instant he appears to be messing around with a woman of ill repute. Looked at this way, Ivy zips through stereotypes of Asian women in the course of the show. At first she is innocent and docile—a geisha girl or china doll—then she flips personas to become a predatory sex goddess.

The fundamental enigma of Miss Turnstiles as simultaneously exotic and all-American embraces an image of Sono that had already been shaped in the press and promoted by her publicist, Barry Hyams, back in 1940. When he marketed her to the *New York Post* as simultaneously representing a "cultural League of Nations" and having a "brisk American manner...as exhilarating as football weather," Hyams inspired the binary that underpinned her role in *On the Town*.[147] Yet Hyams pitched this image before Pearl Harbor, when a Japanese American dancer could still be presented to the American public as part of the country's mainstream. Three and a half years later, when the creative team of *On the Town* built on that characterization, they did so in radically different circumstances. The more a person puzzles over the nature of Miss Turnstiles—knowing that the role was written for Sono—the more racial subtleties and insinuations emerge, and Sono's mixed-race ancestry served to deepen the ambiguity.

In "Presentation of Miss Turnstiles," Sono's dress and hair are near replicas of how she looked in the first act of *One Touch of Venus*, with a kicky skirt and pigtails on the top of her head, tied with ribbons. The similarities are so close that they had to be deliberate. The lilypad (i.e., flowers) on her head in *One Touch of Venus* was replaced with a hat in *On the Town*. Yet the overall context had changed remarkably, for in "Presentation of Miss Turnstiles" Sono stands against a backdrop with the phrase "Exotic Ivy Smith" emblazoned not once but twice. In other words, this character's difference is on display. Furthermore, the photo of Ivy (aka Sono Osato) in the backdrop shows her without the hat, which emphasizes her pigtails and ribbons. The combination of the stage set and Sono's presence in front of it delivers two images simultaneously. In the portrait of her that dominates the set's backdrop, her eyes appear to be vaguely "Oriental,"

Sono Osato in front of the set for "Presentation of Miss Turnstiles"
(Act I, Scene 4). Photofest Digital Archive.

while in a photograph that captures her live onstage—that is, standing in front of that backdrop—she does not look noticeably Japanese. By 1944, Osato had years of experience in neutralizing her race through the use of makeup. While doing so can be interpreted as a controversial practice within today's standards of race pride, it was not an unusual accommodation in the first half of the twentieth century. "In the ballet I learned my own makeup," Sono recalls, "and I learned what to do with my eyes, so my eyes wouldn't look as Oriental, and little by little I got to be very good at makeup."[148] Her autobiography has even more to say about the subject. "The trick was to change the convex contours of my face to concave, more Occidental ones," Sono explained, "which I did with heavy shadowing."[149]

As Sono stands in front of the set for "Miss Turnstiles," her skill at creating a deracialized persona is clear. Yet the stage design by Oliver Smith keeps her Japanese identity intact, and it can be read as suggesting disturbing stereotypes. Not only does the word "exotic" mark Sono's identity, but the image in the background photo shows her with buck teeth. Images of the toothy "Jap" were rampant in U.S. propaganda from the period, as in a poster titled "Go Ahead, Please—Take Day Off!" issued by the Office of War Information. At the same time, the government was encouraging the U.S. culture industry to produce anti-Japanese songs and films. The popular song "You're a Sap, Mr. Jap" (1941), for example, became the basis for a 1941 Popeye cartoon of the same name, and that cartoon features a toothy Japanese caricature. In essence, the deracialized Sono who stood onstage was exposed as Japanese by the set design that hovered over her performance.

Detail of Osato's image in the stage backdrop for "Presentation of Miss Turnstiles," and "Go Ahead, Please—Take Day Off!" a propaganda poster produced by the Office of War Information during World War II. Both from Photofest Digital Archive.

Other aspects of Sono's role in *On the Town* point to yet another racialized reading in which Japanese American and African American coding overlapped suggestively. For one thing, the full name of her character—Ivy Smith—could be interpreted as having a conflated racial identity, and Sono's pigtails strengthened that link. "Smith" could certainly have suggested a nonracialized persona, since there is hardly a more ethnically neutral name in the United States. But it also could have triggered references to a string of famed African American singers, well known to audiences in the 1940s.[150] Many Smiths sang the blues, including Bessie, Mamie, Clara, and Trixie, and one particular Ivy—Ivie Anderson—made headline appearances with Duke Ellington's orchestra. Plus, Sono's pigtails, while tracing their roots to *One Touch of Venus*, also signified on well-established African American stereotypes, notably that of the pickaninny. In many ways, alluding to Sono as African American was far safer during World War II than confronting her actual identity.

Sono Osato posing in her cooch costume, together with John Battles. Unidentified clipping. Jerome Robbins Dance Division, The New York Public Library for the Performing Arts, Astor, Lenox, and Tilden Foundations.

A separate feat of reracializing occurs when Ivy is briefly revealed in "The Real Coney Island" as a Middle Eastern cooch dancer, then loses part of her costume—that is, when Gabey accidentally pulls off her skirt. In this scene, Sono reinhabits the persona of the Siren in Lichine's ballet *The Prodigal Son*, yet her sexual allure is managed adroitly. On the face of it, this is classic romantic slapstick, with Gabey's aw-shucks clumsiness generating a titillating but knee-slapping laugh. Yet a publicity photo of Sono and John Battles, now housed in a clipping file at the New York Public Library, suggests that Sono's "disnuding," as the script wackily put it, was in at least this one image being marketed quite erotically.[151] There, Ivy stands over Gabey in a skimpy two-piece costume, while he is stretched out seductively beneath her. It is a sexually charged photograph that played out fantasies of the war in the Pacific: an American soldier clearly lusts after a Japanese woman—albeit one who at the moment is playing an Egyptian—and she is thoroughly alluring. One of "our boys" is about to be bad.

In retrospect, that publicity shot appears as a preview for a secondary plot in 1949's *South Pacific*—a love affair between Liat, a Pacific Islander, and Cable, a white American soldier. *South Pacific* was not even a gleam in the eye of Rodgers and Hammerstein in 1944. But the two shows share enough traits to suggest that *On the Town* provided some degree of inspiration for its more famous successor. Notably, Liat is voiceless in *South Pacific*, and Sono too does not utter a word in "Presentation of Miss Turnstiles" (she does, however, speak lines and even sing a bit in other scenes). In both cases, their silence projects the mute innocence so familiar in stereotypes of Asian females. Liat's racial difference became an explicit part of her character's identity, a fact that is distinctly different from Ivy. But then *South Pacific* valorized a war that had ended four years earlier.

RACE AND RECEPTION

With a few notable exceptions, the mainstream white press largely ignored racial issues in covering Sono Osato's performance. At the same time, however, the historically black *Chicago Defender* published an important article about Osato, and Japanese American publications continued to cover her career. Added to that, Horace R. Cayton Jr., a black sociologist from Chicago, included in his memoir a remarkable account of attending a performance of the show.

In terms of the mainstream press, caricatures in the *New York Times* by the prominent artist Al Hirschfeld were notable in unambiguously racializing Osato. But then exaggeration is at the core of caricature. In "Mr. Hirschfeld Goes to a Rehearsal of 'On the Town,' Due Christmas Week," Robbins and Osato appear at a rehearsal of the show, surrounded by members of the cast as well as the creative and production team (see page 146).[152] There Hirschfeld rendered Osato as stereotypically Japanese, with pigtails sticking out and slits for eyes. These pigtails are definitely not African American. Rather, the hair is heavy and straight, with a pan-Asian appearance. A second Hirschfeld caricature appeared just days before the opening of the show, and it too played with race.[153] Osato again has slits for eyes, and she wears her cooch

Caricature by Al Hirschfeld of a rehearsal for On the Town, *as published in the* New York Times, *November 26, 1944.*

costume with turban and hair flowing, rendering an East Asian woman as a Middle Eastern belly dancer. In both images, Osato is at the center of the action.

Even more striking was a photo spread featuring Osato in *Life* magazine.[154] *Life* was one of the most popular mainstream publications of the day, gracing living room coffee tables in small towns and big cities from coast to coast, and it by no means had a progressive reputation when it came to race.[155] *Life* included the photograph that showed Osato in front of the set for "Presentation of Miss Turnstiles," while most of its other photos did not include the show's black dancers. This is especially notable in the shot of the Times Square scene, where *Life*'s image shows sailors dancing with girls and all appear to be white. In the final photo in *Life*, however, Ivy is pictured in "The Real Coney Island," where Gabey accidentally pulls off her skirt. There an African American dancer (Royce Wallace) appears in the crowd, second from the right.[156] Yet that bit of racial integration is so thoroughly synthesized into an otherwise white realm that a viewer could easily miss it.

Nonetheless, it was exceptional for a Japanese American woman to have her photo featured in *Life*. In March 1938, Anna May Wong had appeared on the cover of *Look*, which turned out to be a singular event in terms of cover photos of Asian American women in high-profile glossy magazines. Not until 1958 did another Asian American motion picture actress again appear on the cover of a widely distributed publication, and it was France Nuyen on the cover of *Life*—seven months after the opening of the Hollywood film of *South Pacific*, in which Nuyen played Liat.[157]

A few newspaper articles stand out for addressing Osato's family heritage. In February 1945, when her father was finally able to visit the show, a reporter from the *New York Times* interviewed both of them in her dressing room, writing a chatty feature shaped as a double profile of Sono and Nancy Walker. Remarkably, Shoji Osato was slipped into the story without a word about his internment, identified benignly as "a former photographer." The article opens with Walker in Osato's dressing room:

> She [Walker] raced back across the hall to Miss Osato's dressing room where the latter's father, Shoji Osato, a former photographer, was having a woman photographer take some shots of his famous daughter.
> "Take a picture of me with Nancy," begged Miss Osato. "We'll send it to Timothy. With us looking at his picture." She stared fondly at a snapshot of her 20-year-old brother now in Italy with the Nisei Combat Team, 442d Infantry, Seventh Army. "He was the first Japanese-American to volunteer in Chicago," said Mr. Osato proudly.[158]

How extraordinary that the *New York Times* featured this particular father and daughter so matter-of-factly! The article conveys an image of a loving Japanese American family with a son/brother as a loyal soldier, completely ignoring the traumas they faced. At this point, Shoji Osato was still on parole—a status that was not terminated until November 15, 1945, ten weeks after the Japanese surrendered.[159]

It took the black press, however, to issue a much bolder article about Osato and race: it appeared in April 1945 in the *Chicago Defender*, which was based in the city where Shoji Osato lived. The *Defender*'s article bore the headline "She's Mixed, Merry and Musical," and it put the racial politics of Japanese and African Americans side by side. "I wanted to interview Sono Osato, Japanese-Irish-French American," wrote reporter Earl Conrad, "because I believed I might find in her an embodiment and symbol of true American integration. I sought to learn what a typical 'mixture' [i.e., mixed race] personality might believe about herself, America, the Negro, and the future."[160]

Sono was exceptionally open with this reporter. Conrad had just begun writing for the *Defender*, having moved there from the progressive *PM: New York Daily*, and he interviewed Sono in her backstage dressing room, giving her star treatment, albeit with a pointed political twist.[161] "She sat before her many-mirrored dresser, applying creams to her ivory complexion, which is supposed to be 'yellow' because she is understood to look predominantly Japanese and is usually described as 'exotic,'" Conrad reported. "She has long, heavy black hair like Japanese women so often have; her eyes are large and jet black, with the whites lining the pupil in striking contrast.... Gazing at her I saw how incorrect was the conception 'exotic' for her appearance. More likely she was an American beauty of the future, a premature example of a fully-integrated type."

The article quoted Sono discussing contemporary politics, although her father's crisis was absent from this article too. Impressively articulate, she focused her remarks on racial justice and World War II. "So many people feel that what is involved in this conflict is a racial thing. But it has nothing to do with color," Sono declared. "Yet the feeling about the Japanese, the yellow race, is a deep, bitter thing, even though the white Nazis have shocked the world with their diabolical acts. Fascist savagery, whether German or Japanese, has nothing to do with color." Sono then spoke about how interactions among the racially integrated cast of *On the Town* were notably amiable, and she ardently advocated interracial marriage, which of course had been chosen by both her parents and herself. "I think it would be fine if everybody married everybody else," Sono proclaimed. "If Christian would marry Jew, if the Jew married the Finn, and the Finn married the Austrian, and the white married the black—you wouldn't have such trouble." Conrad then asserted: "Her whole attitude said, 'See, I'm mixed, I'm happy. I'm glad to be alive, glad to be what I am. If it works for me, it can work for everyone.'" Osato's outlook is strikingly similar to that in Noguchi's "I Become a Nisei" (1942), with its proclamation of Americans as "hybrid," as having a "racial and cultural intermixture" that represents the soul of the country.[162]

This feature about Osato in the *Chicago Defender* also highlighted the bond between African Americans and the *nisei* during World War II—two communities that shared an awareness of being discriminated against by the culture at large. In 1942, the Office of War Information conducted a survey in Harlem, trying to get an African American perspective on the war, and opinions about the Japanese emerged in the process. Many communicated a feeling that "these Japanese are colored people."[163] When asked "Would you be better off if America or the Axis won the war?" most blacks in the survey stated they "would be treated either the same or better under Japanese rule, although a large majority responded that conditions would be worse under the Germans."[164]

This sense of a mission shared between the *nisei* and African Americans resonates strongly, if with considerable agitation, in the memoir of the Chicago sociologist Horace R. Cayton Jr., who attended *On the Town* right after he heard about the bombing of Hiroshima, which occurred on August 6, 1945. "Our seats were good, and the theater was cool after the heat of New York," wrote Cayton.[165] He responded positively to the opening number, "New York, New York," then launched into an assessment of the racial and political complexities posed by Osato's appearance onstage at that particular moment in time. He perceived her as racially accommodating. "It was a catchy tune with cute lyrics, but when the beautiful Sono Osato, who is of Japanese descent, appeared and frolicked with the American sailors, I was filled with anger and disgust," wrote Cayton. "I care more about your people than you do, I thought, as I sat through the rest of the first act looking at the floor and wondering how soon I could escape to the bar next door."

Cayton's "anger and disgust" came from watching Osato engage directly and uncritically with white sailors. At intermission, Cayton's wife, June, who was white, said to him: "This is the first good musical I've seen in years. Isn't Sono Osato wonderful?" Cayton then recounted a tense conversation between the two of them:

"If I were half-Japanese I wouldn't be dancing with three American sailors at a time like this," I [Cayton] commented sourly.

"Why shouldn't she? She's as American as you or I." June began to warm to her subject. "She was born in this country. She's one hundred per cent American, doesn't even understand Japanese."

[Cayton replied:] "She's a Jap, I'm a nigger, and you're a white girl. Let none of us forget what we are."

Cayton's outburst comes across as a racist screed. But there is complexity to his reaction, as he expressed solidarity with other nonwhite races who were confronting the hegemonic power of Caucasians. Even though his language is disturbing, it is extraordinarily frank, conveying the era's venomous racism against the Japanese and the degree to which African Americans felt themselves to be backed against a wall during World War II. Cayton continued:

I'm torn a dozen ways. I didn't want the Japanese to win; after all, I am an American. But the mighty white man was being humiliated, and by the little yellow bastards he had nothing but contempt for. It gave me a sense of satisfaction, a feeling that white wasn't always right, not always able to enforce its will on everyone who was colored. All those fine white liberals rejoicing because we dropped a bomb killing or maiming seventy-eight thousand helpless civilians. Why couldn't we have dropped it on the Germans—because they were white? No, save it for the yellow bastards.

Those multilayered thoughts were unleashed by watching Sono Osato onstage, dancing an identity that might have been intended to portray her as all-American yet could not avoid the realities of her mixed-race heritage at a harrowing historical moment.

SONO OSATO AND POLITICAL ACTIVISM

During the war years, Sono Osato became increasingly active politically, a shift provoked by her father's detention and subsequent parole. "She feels she is first and foremost a citizen," reported the *Pacific Citizen*. "And a citizen takes an active part in politics."[166] While performing with Ballet Theatre, Osato worked alongside many who embraced left-wing politics, including not only Robbins but also Agnes de Mille, the conductor Max Goberman, and the dancer Nora Kaye. "Sono takes an active interest in outside affairs, being a decided liberal in point of view," reported a profile in *Dance Magazine* in 1945. It went on to describe her as "appearing in innumerable benefits."[167] Performing for benefits was a common activity in the 1940s for artists and celebrities connected with the left, and doing so became important to Osato, as she capitalized on her star status with *On the Town* to boost progressive causes, especially in relation to race. She also took part in war work by entertaining the troops, and she stepped forward as a spokesperson for the *nisei*.

Alliances between Japanese Americans and African Americans fueled some of these activities. Just after Osato left *One Touch of Venus*, for example, she taught ballet at the American Theatre Wing Youth Association in Harlem, where "a newly organized canteen provided the neighborhood teen-agers with facilities for after-school recreation."[168] Osato reached out to black children in an era when they were not being served by existing ballet schools. Osato told *Dance Magazine* that she came across "some unusually talented children" at the Youth Association, and a tattered clipping in a scrapbook for the Association describes a show involving Osato in which "Harlem teen-agers" were "adapt[ing] ballet to jazz."[169]

Once *On the Town* had its premiere, Osato participated actively in left-wing benefits in Harlem, which also involved others from the cast, including its African American dancers. In January 1945, Osato appeared at a "cocktail party and café show" on behalf of Sydenham Hospital, an event staged in the Orchid Room of Smalls' Paradise, one of the main nightclubs in Harlem. Osato performed there with a string of major black entertainers, including the prominent actor Canada Lee, who was honorary chairman, and the dancer Flash Riley from *On the Town*. Also on the program were the famed dancers Bill "Bojangles" Robinson and the Nicholas Brothers, the pianist Hazel Scott, and the jazz vibraphonist Lionel Hampton.[170] Sydenham was then in the process of being restructured as "an interracial voluntary hospital," and its goal, broadly construed, was to "work for the fuller integration of Negro civic leaders, physicians, nurses, and other technical and administrative staff into the organizations of other voluntary and public hospitals in New York City."[171] In June 1945, Osato also appeared at a benefit for the National Urban League. Canada Lee joined her again, together with the black actor Avon Long, the boogie-woogie pianists Albert Ammons and Pete Johnson (both of whom had performed with The Revuers at Café Society) and the white actors Zero Mostel and Margo.[172]

In September 1945, Osato got entangled in a major incident with the left-wing Spanish Refugee Appeal, which sought to aid refugees fleeing Franco, and the episode led to a period of harassment as she performed in *On the Town*. At a rally at Madison Square Garden, she joined with actors from four other Broadway shows in making a statement on behalf of Spanish refugees. The other protestors included Margo, who was starring in *A Bell for Adano*, Jean Darling from *Carousel*, David Brooks from *Bloomer Girl*, and Luba Malina from *Marinka*. "[We] all said a few words of support, then left for our respective shows at eight," Osato recalled. "Only later did we learn that more than an hour later a speech by Professor Harold J. Laski, a British Labour Party leader, referring critically to the role of the Catholic Church and the Vatican in Spain, was piped into the meeting."[173] Frank Fay, who was then starring in the show *Harvey*, launched an attack, alleging that Osato and the others had appeared at a "Communist-backed rally," that they had knowingly taken part in an affront against his religion, and that they had made their statements as official representatives of the shows in which they starred. Osato and her colleagues filed an appeal against Fay through Actors' Equity, and he was censured. "Evidence which he [Fay] has not contested," the Actors' Equity council ruled, "has proved...that these five members were not present when the disputed address was made and knew nothing about it."[174]

The incident was ugly and highly publicized, and Osato was harassed by right-wing zealots as she continued to star in *On the Town*:

Before the meeting of Equity Council took place..., the five of us experienced unbelievable repercussions....Anonymous phone calls late at night had me terribly frightened. I received letters such as, "I understand you're part Japanese. Does that yellow streak account for your anti-Catholicism? Jap or no Jap, you're distinctly un-American." These things and pickets at the various theatres unnerved me so much that I missed two performances of *On the Town*. All of our shows were threatened with boycotts, and for several weeks we needed bodyguards to escort us from our homes to our dressing rooms and back.

Before the final meeting of the Equity membership, which, after great internal furor, censured Frank Fay by a vote of 470 to 72, we were subjected to such harassment that all of our performances began to show visible strain. However, the support of the Equity membership proved that we had recourse through Democratic means.[175]

Like the reaction of Horace Cayton Jr. to viewing Osato in *On the Town*, this episode demonstrated that the presence of a Japanese American dancer and actress in a starring role on Broadway had the potential to be volatile, no matter how adroitly it was managed.

Yet even after this ugliness, Osato kept up her political activity. In March 1946, when Osato had left *On the Town* and the show was touring with Allyn Ann McLerie as Ivy, a photo of Osato carrying a picket sign appeared in the *New York Times* with the caption "Anti-Franco Demonstration Staged Here Yesterday...Members and supporters of the American Committee for Spanish Freedom and Veterans of the Abraham Lincoln Brigade outside a building housing Spanish consulate. In the center is dancer Sono Osato."[176] A few weeks later, *Pacific Citizen* again took note of Osato's political activities, stating that she "is now as well known for her social conscience as she is for her dancing and acting."[177] In 1947, Osato took part in another prominent protest—this one having to do with civil rights—when she joined illustrious colleagues, including Bernstein, Copland, and George Abbott, in signing a pledge that "they would not play or write for theatres with a Jim Crow policy."[178] Several months earlier, the Lisner Auditorium at George Washington University in Washington, D.C., had refused to admit African Americans to see *Joan of Lorraine*, starring Ingrid Bergman. The incident resulted in a boycott of both the Lisner and the National Theater by the Dramatists Guild.[179]

After *On the Town*, Osato appeared in a few more Broadway shows, starting with *Ballet Ballads*, a dance musical from 1948. Presented by the Experimental Theatre, the show was directed by Mary Hunter and choreographed by Katherine Litz, Paul Godkin, and Hanya Holm, all of whom were associated with modern dance. It consisted of three Americana dance sketches and was not a commercial success, although Osato received excellent reviews.[180] The next year she had a fling in Hollywood, appearing in *The Kissing Bandit*, a film starring Frank Sinatra and Kathryn Grayson. There she made a brief appearance, reracialized as Latina.

By the 1950s, Osato felt the squeeze of the blacklist, which she believed to have trounced her hopes for a career in television.[181] Articles in the *Chicago Daily Tribune* in 1949 document testimony by John J. Huber, "an avowed anti-communist spy" for the FBI, to the Senate's so-called McCarran Committee, which was investigating issues of national security. Huber included Osato among a list of entertainers whom he claimed to have Communist affiliations:

> "I can name Paul Draper, Larry Adler, Myrna Loy, Hester Sondergaard, Sono Osato, Canada Lee, Kenneth Spencer, Richard Dyer-Bennett, Burl Ives, Josh White, Lena Horne, Hazel Scott, Jose Ferrer, Uta Hagen, Pete Seeger, Orson Welles, Lillian Hellman, Bela Lugosi, Herman Shumlin, Margo and others."
> Huber said show people lend glamor to communism and that the Communists therefore make a special effort to attract them.[182]

In fact, many of the artists and celebrities who worked with Osato on the stage or took part with her in benefits ended up either being listed in *Red Channels* (1950), being called in to testify before HUAC or McCarthy's Senate committee, and/or simply—often mysteriously—having career opportunities disappear. Osato, too, found her options narrowing. While she had weathered the period of her father's detention during World War II, she did not navigate the subsequent years as easily.

In 1955, she returned to the theater to appear with Zero Mostel and Jack Gilford in a revue titled *Once Over Lightly*, which included comedy sketches by Mel Brooks, who was then in his late twenties. Royce Wallace, who had been among the African American dancers in *On the Town*, appeared in the same show.[183] Mostel and Gilford had also been blacklisted in the early 1950s. Dubbed an "attenuated revue" in the *New York Times*, *Once Over Lightly* was not a huge success.[184] In 1962, Mostel and Gilford made their grand-slam comeback on Broadway in *A Funny Thing Happened on the Way to the Forum*, a show directed by George Abbott. By then, Osato had stepped back from her career. She shifted her attention to raising a family, and she was approaching forty, which often represents a turning point in a dancer's career. As Osato stated toward the end of her memoir, *Once Over Lightly* marked one of "the last moments I spent on the stage for twenty years."[185]

• • •

The full measure of the risk taken in featuring Sono Osato in *On the Town* emerges most clearly against the backdrop of her family history and her experience with various manifestations of the Ballet Russe. When the Osatos first moved to Chicago, they turned Shoji's heritage to their advantage, especially in establishing the Japanese Tea Garden in Jackson Park, and they negotiated cultural boundaries as part of daily life. Once the Japanese attacked Pearl Harbor, however, their world turned upside down. As a result of Shoji's internment, then parole, his professional life and family relationships were permanently destabilized.

Meanwhile, Sono's work with the Ballet Russe de Monte Carlo made her into a first-class dancer, and it ultimately put her in New York City at a historical moment when the realms of dance and theater had become deeply transnational, in large part from absorbing so many European refugees. Coming of age with the Ballet Russe de Monte Carlo also put Sono in a profession dedicated to enacting fantasies. Exoticism represented a norm in ballet, and the transnational migrations of the troupe provided a fluid environment in which her stage persona could be in a state of constant flux. She played sirens and swans, lovers and Japanese bar boys, and with *One Touch of Venus* she started traversing genre boundaries, swapping tutus for fuchsia jerseys and short velveteen skirts.

Then she played Miss Turnstiles. Sono brought to *On the Town* all of her professional experience in the ballet, making it possible for the creative team to realize its vision of building a musical out of dance. She was a dancing actress. Or was it an acting dancer? While Sono's physical allure and celebrity had been on public display for some time, casting her as a beauty queen issued a direct challenge to social norms of the day, setting up a scenario in which audiences saw a Japanese American woman take a role onstage that was off-limits to her in real life.

5

DESEGREGATING BROADWAY
On the Town and Race
• • •

*Those were . . . the days of the swinging Big Bands. Days when the streets of Harlem
were filled with celebration every time Joe Louis knocked somebody out in the ring.
Days when we danced the Lindy at the Savoy Ballroom, and nights when new stars were
initiated on the stage of the Apollo Theater.
Yes, but those were also the days . . . of dis-possession and of protest marches. Harlem was
growing edgy. . . . There was a great turbulence growing in American society, much of it racial.*
—Ralph Ellison

*Everything we can do to fight discrimination—in any form or field—will ultimately work
toward ameliorating the musical situation.*
—Leonard Bernstein (1947)

While *On the Town* resisted racial and ethnic stage practices of the mid-1940s by
featuring Sono Osato, it also made a strong statement by hiring African American
dancers and actors to play full-fledged citizens who were portrayed equitably with
their white colleagues. The show responded to a movement on the part of civil
rights organizations to promote mixed-race casting and nonstereotyped racial
representation, and individual choices about how to deploy black actors onstage
shifted as the show took shape. African American dancers—or "colored" dancers,
as the language of the day put it—were written into draft scenarios. But racial
designations were eliminated when the script was finalized. As a result, race
played out primarily through casting and staging, all of which was implemented
with little fanfare. Four blacks appeared in the show's dancing chorus, and there
were two black singers, adding up to six African Americans out of a cast of fifty-
four—that is, 11 percent. Plus, Everett Lee, an African American violinist, played
in the pit orchestra, and nine months into the show's run he took over as conductor, marking another racial breakthrough.

On the Town's handling of race yielded a bundle of contradictions. It was bold
yet understated, progressive yet limited. By standards of the early twenty-first
century, it could be accused of tokenism, yet within the racial climate of World
War II it made a statement about racial justice. Perceptions of the show divided
starkly along race lines, and in the decades since, its mixed-race agenda has been

largely forgotten. "One of the important things in the show that was not noted was the mixed chorus," remarked Jerome Robbins forty years later. "It was pre-dominantly white, but there were four black dancers—and for the first time, they danced with the whites, not separately, in social dancing. We had some trouble with that in some of the cities we went to [on tour]."[1] Yet despite Robbins's per-ception that they were "not noted," the show's racial advances lived on in the memory of some celebrated black artists. In a chronicle of the "integration of Broadway" published in 1953, Langston Hughes listed *On the Town*, without com-ment, as having a "mixed dancing chorus."[2] And in an interview from 1958, Lena Horne recalled *On the Town* as a show with "Negro people in the chorus, young, good-looking kids." She continued, "That was the first time it had been done in a musical comedy to my knowledge—that is to say they were part of the street scene, of the people, of the play."[3]

African Americans certainly had appeared alongside whites in Broadway musi-cals before, most famously in *Show Boat* of 1927.[4] Jim Crow stage practices meant that the races occupied separate spaces onstage (this was especially the case within mixed choruses), and the characters represented by African Americans were confined to roles representing the "Eternal Menial," as one black critic de-scribed how African Americans were consistently cast as household help, labor-ers, criminals, and prostitutes.[5] In the 1940s, offensive racial formulas, which had roots extending to blackface minstrelsy of the nineteenth century, were alive and well on stage and screen. One category of the era's shows featured all-black casts in productions that were created, owned, and directed by whites, a type repre-sented most famously by *Porgy and Bess*. In such cases, the races worked together, but the power and economic structures remained deeply unequal, with whites largely controlling the narrative of the shows, as well as their production and business practices.

By contrast, *On the Town* deliberately set out to represent a desegregated world: black males donned sailor uniforms onstage, stepping high alongside their white colleagues. The workers (that is, dockworkers) who congregated onstage at the opening of the show included four African Americans, and one black singer was cast as a police officer who turned up regularly onstage, becoming a thematic thread. All this took place in a country with a contentiously segregated military, racial inequality of employment for longshoremen, and rampant police violence against African Americans. Photographs of the original production document in-terracial dancing, with men and women of both races holding hands in some of the big ensemble numbers. Antimiscegenation laws were fully enforced in many states during this era, and mixed-race dancing provoked deep anxiety, having forced the temporary closure of the famed Savoy Ballroom in Harlem the previous year. Yet, like *Porgy and Bess*, the production and creative teams of *On the Town* were thoroughly white.

The racial desegregation of *On the Town* lay at an intersection of the growing civil rights movement and the fiscal pressures of the entertainment industry. It unfolded against the backdrop of an overall challenge to racial performance conventions in New York City, whether in Broadway musicals, contemporary ballet, or the world of concert music.[6] Yet the stranglehold of Jim Crow practices applied across the spectrum of performance styles. The National Negro Congress, an organization founded in the 1930s with the intention of "arous[ing] the black masses for social and economic improvement," played an important role, undertaking an intense lobbying effort within the entertainment industry.[7] Integration of the show's cast was also boosted by the creative team's openness to merging high art and popular entertainment. Crossing race lines went hand in hand with crossing musical genres and social classes. Some of the black dancers in *On the Town* simultaneously worked in nightclubs and Broadway theaters, and Comden, Green, and Bernstein were doing the same thing.

Reconstructing racial history from this period means projecting back to a radically different world in which segregation was legal and its impact was more widespread than can easily be imagined today. This was even the case in a progressive urban center such as New York City, which avoided separate drinking fountains and many of the gross indignities of segregation in the South yet still implemented some of its ideology and practices. Most blacks lived in Harlem during the early 1940s, and Jim Crow segregation circumscribed life options. As activism grew, a language emerged for articulating the struggle. "*Segregation* and *desegregation*, terms rarely used as nouns in the 1930s, functioned as powerful rhetorical symbols during World War II," observes historian Glenda Elizabeth Gilmore, adding that the word "integration" was then rarely used.[8]

Racial segregation of the military became a flash point for igniting long-standing resentments. In early 1942, the *Pittsburgh Courier*, one of the country's major African American newspapers, launched the "Double V" campaign, calling for victory in the war abroad and in the struggle for civil rights at home.[9] Nearly one million African American men served in the U.S. armed forces during World War II, including the now-famous Tuskegee Airmen and the Army's 78th Tank Battalion. Black women also played important roles both on the home front and in military support services.[10] Yet the indignities of segregation exacted a toll. Near the end of the war, a military chaplain wrote in *The Crisis*, the official magazine of the NAACP, that during three years of active duty in the U.S. Army he had found "Negro soldiers bitterly resentful of their lot in this war."[11] In 1948, three years after the war ended, President Truman ordered desegregation of the military by issuing Executive Order 9981, which carried a clear directive mandating "equality of treatment and opportunity for all persons in the armed services without regard to race, color, religion or national origin."[12]

Four years earlier, *On the Town* became part of a movement that undertook performance-based activism to counter the degree to which second-class citizenship had been normalized for African Americans. Their quest ran parallel to that advocating for desegregation of the military. "Everybody interested in the broad struggle of people for full citizenship has felt a vital concern for the treatment accorded to Negroes on the screen and stage," declared the African American journalist Joe Bostic in a Harlem newspaper in March 1945. "Negro" was a commonly accepted term in the 1940s. Bostic continued:

> All have realized full well that the type of presentation has in reality been the most vicious sort of anti-Negro propaganda. The lazy, grinning, irresponsible

"Double V" as published on the front page of the Pittsburgh Courier, *February 7, 1942.*

men; the immoral women portrayed all have served to subtly keep alive a concept of the entire race group that prejudiced the minds of most laymen against our case for complete integration on an equal footing with the rest of the citizenry.[13]

As a result, the African American actors and dancers who leapt onto the stage of *On the Town* contributed to a transformational chapter in Broadway history, albeit one in which progress was made incrementally and fitfully over the course of decades. Here I explore *On the Town*'s racial position from a diverse series of vantage points, trying to puzzle out its cultural meaning and do so in relation to its distinctive moment in time, which was fraught but charged with opportunity. Contingencies shape the history of race, and grasping those variables helps make sense of why a largely white show with a relatively small number of African Americans could make a difference.

NOTICING RACE IN *ON THE TOWN*

Cast members from the initial production of *On the Town* share their memories with a proud sense of making history. They recall that the show's mixed-race cast was handled equitably, also that no big deal was made out of these potentially controversial actions. Although they have spoken individually, their comments shape a collective message: that they were proud to be part of a production where black performers were treated as an equal part of an interracial community. Yet as it turned out, the show's political message was subtle, and not all viewers and critics recognized that racial codes of the day had been violated. Separate strains of perception resulted, which were largely (but not entirely) divided by race.

Billie Allen, an African American dancer, director, and actress who joined the show in midrun, recalls: "It was just totally, totally an integrated experience.... No mention was made. No reference made. Our characters were just integrated so beautifully into the show."[14] Allyn Ann McLerie, the white dancer who started out in the chorus and eventually stepped into the role of Ivy, stated: "We were the first integrated show, I think. We danced black boy with white girl and vice versa, whereas usually they have black couples and white couples dancing around."[15] Everett Lee, the black violinist and conductor who initially played in the show's pit orchestra and then became music director, conveyed much the same sentiment in an interview with the *Daily Worker* in 1945. *On the Town* "has done some splendid pioneering work on Broadway," Lee declared. Beth McHenry, reporter for the *Worker*, expounded on Lee's statement:

> What he referred to particularly, he said, was the integration of Negro artists with others in the cast of On The Town, not in the usual "specialty number" category but in the regular assembly of dancers. Mr. Lee attributes this to the honest and democratic ideas and efforts of the musical's authors—Betty Comden and Adolph Green and to the cooperative efforts of the whole cast. He himself was urged to come to this show by Leonard Bernstein, the composer.[16]

Meanwhile, the white press of the day, with the notable exception of left-wing papers, ignored *On the Town*'s mixed-race casting. By and large, white journalists did not seem to have the politics of racial representation on their minds. Reviewing *On the Town*'s debut in the *New York Times*, Lewis Nichols appeared to be unaware of race, writing that "the charm of 'On the Town' is not so much in the individual performances as in the whole. The chorus and ballet numbers... are easy and graceful."[17] Perhaps with "in the whole" he was referring to the racial diversity represented by the cast overall. White newspaper coverage of the show brought many such moments in which a person could project a possible reference to race—one that is thoroughly oblique and probably not there. In writing about an out-of-town preview, for example, the *Daily Boston Globe* described the show as being "very youthful" and "seemingly designed for New York's café society trade."[18] The author might have been referring literally to Café Society (uppercase), that is, the nightclub with its mixed-race lineup of performers, or he might have been characterizing the show as hip.

PM: New York Daily was among the left-wing papers that took notice of race, albeit several months after the show opened and in the final paragraphs of an extended interview with Betty Comden and Adolph Green. The interview appeared in March 1945. *PM* was white-owned (financed by Marshall Field II) and published from 1940 to 1948. It did not include advertising, so as to remain free of ties to business.[19] "One aspect of *On the Town* had impressed us," observed the article's author, "the fact that Negroes in the chorus are not Jim-Crowed. We said so." Comden and Green were then quoted on the subject. "'We're very happy about that,' Betty said, and Adolph leaned forward earnestly to add, 'We wanted to represent the New York scene as completely as possible. The Negro people are as much a part of New York as any other group. They belong to the city, so they belonged in the show.'"[20]

In sharp contrast with mainstream white papers, the black press repeatedly pointed out the show's exceptional stance on race. Initial reports in black newspapers claimed historic precedence for *On the Town*'s avoidance of stereotyped roles, and later ones extolled the presence of an African American conductor. The fullest initial account appeared about six weeks after the show opened in *The People's Voice*, a weekly Harlem newspaper edited by Adam Clayton Powell Jr. The masthead read, "The New Paper for the New Negro," and *The People's Voice* had a reputation for being "more outspoken in castigating white practices" than other black newspapers of the day.[21] Like *PM*, *The People's Voice* represented the political left. Titled "'On the Town' Proves the Point; Negroes Cast in Normal Roles," the review was written by the African American journalist Joe Bostic, the same critic quoted earlier about the symbolic importance of racial representation in the performing arts. Bostic was a vigorous advocate for the integration of baseball, which had a history with striking similarities to that of Broadway musicals. He was also an early supporter of gospel artists in New York City, breaking the color line on radio in the mid-1940s by initiating the show *Gospel Train*.[22] Bostic's review of *On the Town* is extraordinary enough to quote at length:

> For the first time in the history of the big street a mixed cast is completely integrated in a thoroughly normal presentation of people living their lives—and having loads of fun doing it—in New York. It's the biggest, most important thing that has ever happened to Negroes in the American theatre.
>
> Six Negroes are in the cast, Glashe [*recte* Flash] Riley, Lonny Jackson, Royce Wallace, Frank Neal, Dorothy McNichols, and Melvin Howard are cast not as Negro characters but as New Yorkers, whom you'd never know were Negroes except *for the color of their skin*.
>
> ...Best of all, the producer, George Abbott, didn't make a lot of fuss about the departure from the customary policy, which we've resented for years and ranted against editorially, he just went ahead and did it.[23]

Whether or not *On the Town* represented a racial first is hard to gauge, with complex variables of casting and racial representation in the mix. Whatever the case, the claims made by Bostic suggest that *On the Town*'s efforts to counteract stereotyping were exceptional enough to be perceived as a breakthrough. Other black newspapers also covered the show, including Baltimore's *Afro-American*, the *Chicago Defender*, and Harlem's *Amsterdam News*. *Now*, a multiracial bimonthly magazine, published an article in late 1945 by the Japanese American journalist Larry Tajiri that not only highlighted Sono Osato's role in *On the Town* but also declared the production to be "one of the first Broadway shows with an unsegregated chorus line, featuring both white and Negro dancers."[24]

The other racial milestone for *On the Town* came with the appointment of Everett Lee as conductor of the pit orchestra, which occurred within an overall climate of racial exclusion in Broadway orchestras. Once again, the black press paid attention, and white papers were mostly silent, except for those on the left. "Everett Lee Sets Musical Precedent," proclaimed the *New York Amsterdam News* in September 1945, when Lee was named conductor.[25] "The assignment gives Mr. Lee the distinction of being the first Negro to wave the baton over a white orchestra in a Broadway production," reported the *Chicago Defender*.[26] "Everett Lee, First Negro Musician to Lead Orchestra in Bway Play," declared the headline in the *Daily Worker*.[27] Lee was already a violinist in *On the Town*'s otherwise all-white pit orchestra, and he was concertmaster for a time.[28]

Cast members, then, recalled *On the Town*'s stance on race as both progressive and understated. White newspapers largely ignored race, except for those aligned with the political left. So the African American press took on the task of chronicling racial developments in the show, and it rose to the challenge, noting the racial integration of the cast, the intentional depiction of the black characters as "a thoroughly normal presentation of people living their lives," and the appointment of Everett Lee as conductor.[29] *On the Town* opposed then-current racial practices in the theater, but reporting those developments—even having the fundamental capacity to notice them—was as segregated as the racialized performance practices that the show set out to challenge.

DESEGREGATING THE PERFORMING ARTS

The significance of *On the Town*'s casting decisions gain clarity when viewed in relation to an overall period of "creeping toward integration," as the theater historian James V. Hatch has put it.[30] The war years yielded a period in U.S. racial history when African Americans and their allies were increasingly emboldened, as activism on behalf of civil rights intensified. *What the Negro Wants*, an anthology of essays by prominent black writers, compiled in 1943 and published the following year, made clear that ending racial segregation was a fundamental priority. "The Negro Wants Full Equality" was the title of the contribution by Roy Wilkins, who was then editor of *The Crisis*, the official magazine of the NAACP.[31]

Within the world of stage performance overall, most performance spaces offered limited opportunities for black performers. Yet important exceptions existed, such as Town Hall, which had long been a site for political activism and often featured performers of color. Carnegie Hall also presented occasional high-profile concerts with black performers, albeit largely of jazz. At the same time, the training of black performing artists remained mostly segregated, yet exceptions occurred there too.[32] Illustrious performance institutions, notably (and notoriously) the Metropolitan Opera, maintained a refusal to feature African Americans in major roles. All the while, New York City remained "the musical center of the nation for black concert artists," according to historian Eileen Southern.[33] The same was true in dance and theater. For jazz, as the most visible performance genre employing African Americans, segregation imposed many constrictions, both in terms of where musicians could perform and who could sit in the audience.

The histories of ballet, opera, the theater, and the concert stage have been written in separate chronicles, so it is challenging to trace their shared racial trajectories. Such a perspective—one that cuts across different modes of artistic expression—is essential in order to understand the professional opportunities for *On the Town*'s performers of color, who often crossed artistic boundaries in order to stay employed. As a result, Broadway shows were in a position to hire black performers who otherwise were closed out of established institutions of classical music and dance. *Porgy and Bess* marked one notable site of opportunity, both in its original production in 1935 and in its subsequent revivals, yet the story is not clear-cut. Anne Brown and Todd Duncan, who starred in the debut, initiated a long line of trained black opera singers for whom a leading role in *Porgy and Bess* meant an exceptional professional breakthrough.[34] Yet perceptions of *Porgy and Bess* shifted over the decades, and it has often been viewed as a ghetto for black performers. That was not the case during the late 1930s and 1940s, however.

Four signal moments of mixed-race performance are offered here to provide a perspective on the racial climate in which *On the Town* emerged. They include early stagings of Marc Blitzstein's *The Cradle Will Rock* (1937–38), Katherine Dunham's work with George Balanchine on *Cabin in the Sky* (1940), Agnes de Mille's production of *Black Ritual* for Ballet Theatre (1940), and the temporary closure of Harlem's Savoy Ballroom (1943). Each in some way intersected with the experiences of *On the Town*'s creative team, and each illustrates how long-standing racial practices were being challenged step by step, in a process through which the "quantity" of black performers and the "quality" of racial representation could vary widely, as could the balance between the two.[35]

The first case of mixed-race performance focuses on early productions of Blitzstein's *The Cradle Will Rock*, which is a work known for its political passion rather than mixed-race casting. Two important aspects of the debut production of *The Cradle Will Rock* in 1937 have been noted but not highlighted: its choreographer was the African American dancer Clarence Yates, and it included an interracial chorus.[36] *The Cradle Will Rock* had no major dance ensemble, so Yates devised movements for the singing chorus. He was not given program credit, however, and that omission—which was commonly experienced by black choreographers at the time—offers a window onto the subliminal impact of race, even in a production written and staged by figures with heartfelt progressive intentions. Yates was an adaptive performer with a multifaceted career. He had studied ballet with Michel Fokine of the Ballets Russes, and he appeared in dance choruses of *Run, Little Chillun* of 1933 (a largely African American show by Hall Johnson, with choreography by the white dancer Doris Humphrey) and Irving Berlin's *As Thousands Cheer* (a mixed-race revue from the same year that featured Ethel Waters).[37] Yates was subsequently director of dance for the Federal Theatre Project's Negro Unit, and one year before *The Cradle Will Rock* he had choreographed the Negro Unit's production of *Macbeth*—the famous "Voodoo Macbeth," staged at the Lafayette Theatre in Harlem and directed by Orson Welles.

With the chorus of *The Cradle Will Rock*, it is unclear exactly how many African Americans were involved in the original production, and at this writing, few details about it are clear. However, a slim "oratorio version" of the show, produced in 1938 by the Mercury Theatre of Welles and John Houseman, included "six Negroes" in the chorus, and they were identified in a photo published in the *Amsterdam News* as "Larri Lauria, Lilia Hallums, Alma Dixon, Robert Clerk, Josephine Heathman and Eric Borroughs."[38] A total of nine performers appear to have been in the chorus, making it two-thirds black.[39] "They are a definite part of Steeltown, even if they don't have speaking parts," the *Amsterdam News* observed. "In this respect they are like Negroes in all phases of American life. They are here. And they must be seen and, we hope, soon heard." The rhetoric used by the *Amsterdam News* to describe this interracial chorus in 1938—claiming that it represented "all phases of American life"—presaged the language that greeted *On the Town* six years later.

The Federal Theatre Project, which was the initial sponsor of *The Cradle Will Rock*, played a major role in the racial desegregation of performance in the 1930s. It "crusaded openly against minority discrimination," writes historian Ronald Ross, in an account that intertwines racial activism in performance with left-wing politics.[40] Yet when the Federal Theatre Project was investigated—and subsequently closed down—by the House Un-American Activities Committee in 1939, the African American press perceived a racist agenda. "Behind all the squawking and beefing by Congressmen, Senators, and others against the spending of money to keep the WPA theatre [i.e., the Federal Theatre Project] going," wrote the *Amsterdam News*, "is seen the hand of the irreconcilables who never intend to allow the Negro to attain prominence in any given field, especially if he is placed on a par of social and economical equality with his white contemporaries."[41] Assessing the Dies Committee's assault on the Federal Theatre Project, the historian Susan Quinn writes: "The issue of race was never far from the surface." She continues: "In fact, the success of many productions of the Negro units, and the visibility they brought to blacks—not to mention the integration the project sponsored in its cast and in its audiences—were all viewed by the committee as signs of Communist influence."[42] That visibility ultimately marked a limited but crucial step toward dismantling an unspoken acceptance of segregation in performance.

A second perspective on racist practices in performance draws upon the experiences of African American dancer and choreographer Katherine Dunham, who worked together with the famed Russian American choreographer George Balanchine on the stage version of *Cabin in the Sky* (1940).[43] Dunham is almost completely absent from the narrative of Jerome Robbins's career, yet her work had a bearing on *On the Town*.[44] One member of her company, Frank Neal, danced in the show's chorus, and her collaboration with Balanchine on *Cabin in the Sky* marked a crucial moment in fusing ballet with a spectrum of African American dance idioms. In turn, Robbins's admiration for Balanchine was immense. "From the very beginning," stated a former dancer from Ballet Theatre, "Balanchine was what [Robbins] wanted to be."[45]

"Collaboration" is a fraught term to use with Dunham and Balanchine, because her choreographic contributions to the Broadway production of *Cabin in the Sky* went unacknowledged. Yet "she has a legitimate claim to be credited as co-choreographer with Balanchine," writes dance scholar Constance Valis Hill.[46] On one hand, Balanchine worked closely and respectfully with Dunham, and he featured her prominently in the show as a dancer. On the other, she was invisible as a creative and intellectual force, both to him and to the management of the show. *Cabin in the Sky* had an all-black cast, starring Ethel Waters, Dooley Wilson, and Dunham, with an extraordinary array of talent that also included Todd Duncan, Rex Ingram, and the J. Rosamond Johnson Singers. Some of the same African American artists (but not all) appeared in a 1943 film version of the show.[47] Yet *Cabin in the Sky* relied on entrenched stereotypes, "reinforcing the white culture's perception of African Americans as a fun-loving, 'rhythmic' people," as one scholar articulates it.[48] Little Joe, the lead male character, is a gambler, as played onstage by Dooley Wilson; Petunia is his mammy-inflected wife, played by Ethel Waters; and Georgia Brown is a sultry seductress, played by Dunham. With music by Vernon Duke and lyrics by John Latouche, the show revolved around the gambling escapades of Little Joe, who is stabbed and condemned to hell. Through the prayerful intercession of Petunia, he is granted extra time on earth so as to earn a place in heaven.[49] Balanchine knew Vernon Duke, the show's composer, from his days in Paris, when he danced with Serge Diaghilev's Ballets Russes.[50]

In interviews conducted decades later, Dunham expressed admiration for Balanchine, calling him "a wonderful person," saying they had "an understanding," and enthusing that she "enjoyed every minute" of working with him.[51] He had a "feeling for neglected groups," for "the deprived," Dunham stated. "You thought of him in terms of humanity."[52] She expressed no bitterness at being excluded from choreographic credits. At the same time, she outlined her creative contributions clearly. Dunham danced the central role of Georgia Brown, and her own company formed the show's dance chorus. That company, in turn, included Talley Beatty and Archie Savage, who were on the cusp of major careers in American concert dance. Dunham described the cultural disjunction that Balanchine faced as his experience in modern Russian ballet met the demands of an all-black production. "He wanted the show to open with a Russian dirge," recalled Dunham, "and have these black people singing old Russian dirges instead of spirituals."[53] She stepped in to contribute ideas from African American folklore, and she mused sympathetically about the pressures Balanchine faced. "He was staging the entire show," she continued, "and it kept him pretty busy. I think he did pretty much trust me for the choreography, especially since the company was mine."[54]

Talley Beatty remembered a far more dramatic version of events, in which Martin Beck, owner of the Martin Beck Theatre, where *Cabin in the Sky* was being staged, demanded that much of Balanchine's choreography for the show be thrown out. Beatty's story makes the choreographic process successive rather than collaborative—that is, Dunham's creative contributions were requested when Balanchine's failed. "Balanchine was doing the choreography originally," Beatty recalled, "and Mr. Martin Beck came one day and said, 'Get him [Balanchine] out of the theatre. He'll come back in here over my dead body.' Now this was a week before the previews."[55] At Beck's request, Beatty continued, "Balanchine was removed from the choreographic scene, and Dunham had to reset all of the dances. And, she did reset everything except something called 'The Hell Scene.' I think that remained [i.e., Balanchine's version]." Beatty recalled that Balanchine's rendition of the "Egyptian scene," which was subsequently rechoreographed by Dunham, "was one of the problems" and that it had attempted to modernize the representation of African Americans, yet clung to a pernicious symbol:

> Because Balanchine was so sort of "way out." You know, in that Egyptian scene. I thought it was kind of wonderful. We were sitting there—standing in the back yard with little bandanas reading the New York Times, but Dunham did all of the choreographing. As I see in the program, Balanchine takes credit for that. But he didn't choreograph it. Excepting the "Hell Scene"—which is nice. I like Mr. Balanchine.

In his review of Cabin in the Sky, John Martin, dance critic of the New York Times, recognized that not all the show's dance movements reflected Balanchine's style, although Martin offered no speculation about Dunham's creative role. "Balanchine has wisely allowed the dancers throughout to make use of great quantities of their own type of movements, many of them right out of the vocabulary of their concert repertoire," commented Martin. "Frequently, however, he has forced them into his own patterns, and in the process they have lost flavor."[56] In coded (or oblivious) language, Martin described what Beatty had recounted about the way in which the show was choreographed.

Yet despite these issues of intellectual property, Cabin in the Sky helped establish Dunham's Broadway credentials. Her dance troupe was based in Chicago, and in the years immediately surrounding Cabin in the Sky it presented a number of important performances in New York, which were mostly dance recitals.[57] Dunham also was one of the choreographers for the New Pins and Needles of 1939, for which she staged the dance movements for Bertha, the Sewing Machine Girl.[58] Then in September 1943, Dunham mounted her own show at the Martin Beck Theatre—the same Broadway house where Cabin in the Sky had played and where On the Town made its debut fifteen months later. Titled Tropical Revue, the show displayed Dunham's multilayered stylistic fusions, and it was produced by Sol Hurok, who was also manager for Ballet Theatre and Ballet Russe de Monte Carlo.[59]

A third perspective on the racial climate immediately preceding On the Town turns to the world of modern ballet and focuses on Black Ritual (Obeah), "an all-Negro Ballet," as the Amsterdam News reported, which was created by the white choreographer Agnes de Mille and debuted by Ballet Theatre on January 22, 1940.[60] "This is perhaps the first time in the history of the dance in New York," the Amsterdam News continued, "that a Negro corps de ballet has been engaged to perform with the regular ballet. Much credit is due to Agnes de Mille of the Ballet Theatre for her efforts in introducing colored dancers into the ballet."[61] The work represented a bold move on the part of both de Mille and Ballet Theatre. It was

Katherine Dunham in an undated photograph. Photofest Digital Archive.

de Mille's first ballet for the company, and Ballet Theatre was in its very first season, launching a brand-new artistic endeavor.

The score for *Black Ritual* was Darius Milhaud's *La Création du Monde* from 1922–23, which represented its own racial mix, having been written by a white European composer and inspired by African American jazz. Ballet Theatre's souvenir program described the score in a way that validated the production's cultural cachet, hailing Milhaud as "a major personality in modern French music" and *La Création du Monde* as "the most perfect of all pieces of symphonic jazz."[62] This same promotional blurb endowed the score with racial authenticity, characterizing it as having been "impregnated with the spirit of the 'blues' idiom." Alexander Smallens conducted a sixty-piece orchestra in a glamorous production at the "huge Centre Theatre" in Radio City, with celebrities including the movie star Miriam Hopkins in the audience.[63]

Black Ritual was danced by sixteen African American women. They included Lawaune Kennard, Lavinia Williams, Ann Jones, Dorothy Williams, Elizabeth Thompson, Evelyn Pilcher, Edith Ross, Valerie Black, Leonore Cox, Edith Hurd, Mabel Hart, Moudelle Bass, Clementine Collinwood, Carroll Ash, Bernice Willis, and Muriel Cook (the names are listed in the order in which they appeared in a flier for the debut).[64] They were dubbed the "Negro Unit" of Ballet Theatre, a short-lived entity that must have been modeled on similar "units" in the Federal Theatre Project. "There was going to be a Black ABT," Talley Beatty recalled. "They were going to try to shape American Ballet as a reflection of the different kinds of Americans."[65] That dream was not realized. Two of *Black Ritual*'s dancers, Lawaune Kennard and Lavinia Williams, went on to perform with Katherine

Lawaune Kennard (with wreath) and an unidentified dancer in Black Ritual (Obeah), *choreographed by Agnes de Mille for Ballet Theatre in 1940. Photograph by Carl Van Vechten. Jerome Robbins Dance Collection, New York Public Library, Astor, Lenox, and Tilden Foundations. Reproduced courtesy of the Van Vechten Trust.*

Dunham's company in *Cabin in the Sky*, which opened nine months later. Lawaune Kennard (also known as Lawaune Ingram after her marriage to actor Rex Ingram) was "a fantastic dancer," according to Beatty.[66] Both she and Lavinia Williams had studied with Martha Graham, among others, and Kennard became part of the Negro Dance Company, a largely black organization that began in the early 1940s.[67] Five dancers from *Black Ritual* also danced in the original production of *Carmen Jones* in 1943: Valerie Black, Mabel Hart, Evelyn Pilcher, Edith Ross, and Dorothy Williams.[68] None appeared in *On the Town*.

In a letter to New York's *World-Telegram*, publicists for Ballet Theatre tried to cajole the newspaper into paying attention to their programs, and they singled out *Black Ritual* as an example of Ballet Theatre's distinctive identity:

Miss de Mille, niece of William C. deMille [*recte* Cecil B. DeMille], is one of the foremost exponents of what is generally lumped under the heading of the "modern" dance. This is a far cry from some of the traditional ballets being presented in the Ballet Theatre repertoire. But this was how the Ballet Theatre was meant to be—a combination of tradition and ultra modernity. Even more startling is the fact that Miss de Mille's contribution is an all Negro ballet entitled, *Black Ritual* (Obeah). The girls who work in this ballet are absolutely unschooled in conventional choreography. Prior to their opening they rehearsed in secret and their success, as witnessed by the very favorable reviews they received, was a tribute to them and Miss de Mille.[69]

The critic John Martin called *Black Ritual* a "complete novelty for any ballet company to sponsor, and, as it turned out, an extremely interesting one."[70] Yet despite the best of intentions, the work was plagued with issues. The cast was "mostly untrained," writes dance historian Yaël Tamar Lewin—or "unschooled," as the publicist put it. Opportunities at the time for training black ballet dancers were extremely limited.[71] The black dancers were paid one-fourth of the weekly salary of white dancers in the troupe.[72] "While these debuts at the otherwise white Ballet Theatre . . . did signify progress in integrating the classical dance world," Lewin writes, "it was of a limited sort."[73] Racial representation in *Black Ritual* was also problematic. "The scenes are enacted 'vaguely somewhere in the West Indies,'" reported the *Chicago Defender*, as part of a positive review. "The story concerns a group of Race girls who have congregated to put to death one of their members whom they feel will carry their sorrows and troubles to hell. They dance and whirl and twirl with all the symptoms of that so-called voo-dooism. Finally, they dance away to the hills where they hold their primitive ceremony."[74] The word "primitive," as used by the *Defender*, probably came from the program note, which described the scenario as projecting "the psychological atmosphere of a primitive community during the performance of austere and vital ceremonies."[75] Nine extraordinary photos of *Black Ritual*'s original cast by Carl Van Vechten reveal a somber vision, draped in grief and mourning.[76]

A setting "somewhere in the West Indies" suggested a link to the work of Katherine Dunham. In her interview with Constance Valis Hill, Dunham complained about de Mille's work on *Oklahoma!* (1943), believing that some of her own ideas had been appropriated without credit. *Black Ritual* is not included in Dunham's grievance, yet its relationship to her work might have been even stronger. Looked at from another perspective, Dunham let Balanchine off the hook, but she held de Mille accountable:

Agnes and I knew each other. It has happened to me several times: people taking some of the songs I have researched—you know, popular songs—and translating them. . . . I was really annoyed with her because I think her idea came from something called the plantation dances, not in *Cabin in the Sky*, but in our concerts. . . . When I saw what she had done, I was annoyed, because it was true, there were these dances in *Oklahoma!*, and I thought, "Well, it would have been nice if she had mentioned me as a counterpart."[77]

Internal correspondence at Ballet Theatre shows that the company subsequently made plans "to have the 'Obeah' ballet redone with white dancers," as an unsigned letter of October 1940 put it.[78] Six months later, the idea was still afoot, although by the summer of 1941 it appeared to be fading.[79] The correspondence reflected no concern by either de Mille or the administration of Ballet Theatre about switching to a white cast. De Mille probably had a pragmatic goal of gaining a place for *Black Ritual* in Ballet Theatre's repertory, and the Negro Unit had been short-lived. She and her colleagues were struggling to build a brand-new dance company, with its success as their primary ambition.

A final perspective on the intersection of performance and race in the early 1940s shifts to the celebrated Savoy Ballroom in Harlem, a nightclub with a high volume of patrons, where dancers performed with dazzling virtuosity and a sense of artistic freedom. Billed as the "World's Most Beautiful Ballroom," the Savoy had an exceptionally large dance floor that was one block long.[80] It made swing dances famous, especially the jitterbug and the Lindy Hop, and those dances crossed over into greater America, becoming the rage in USO clubs and the nationwide network of Arthur Murray Dance Studios. The Savoy was known for its inclusiveness, making it "easy for people from different social classes, geographic regions, and ethno-cultural backgrounds to experience [it] ... first-hand," writes ethnomusicologist Howard Spring.[81]

In 1943, the year before *On the Town*, New York City's police closed the Savoy for five months, labeling it "a den of vice" and accusing the performance space of fostering prostitution.[82] A crisis resulted, which put mixed-race dancing in the news. Under the headline "Mixed Dancing Closed Savoy Ballroom!" the *Amsterdam News* reported:

> Persons close to the Savoy management insist that police authorities have long looked with disfavor upon the mixed dancing of those who have patronized the Savoy for the past seventeen years. It is asserted that all kinds of pressure have been brought to bear on the management, even to the extent of "suggesting" that whites be denied admittance. Over a year ago the management dropped all advertisement in white papers and stopped booking white name bands.[83]

The *Amsterdam News* quoted Mrs. Helen G. Peale, house executive of the Brooklyn YWCA, who suggested that closing the Savoy was "another of the Army's segregation stunts." She continued: "To place responsibility for venereal disease among soldiers upon Negroes, is entirely unreasonable."[84] In the formulation that Peale critiques, mixed-race dancing was likened to miscegenation, and the black member of the couple was blamed as the contaminating force. The Savoy reopened officially in late October 1943 with a gala celebration that was covered in both black and white newspapers.[85]

While no documentable link ties Robbins and Bernstein to the Savoy Ballroom, these highly publicized events were taking place as Robbins was developing *Fancy Free*. As one dance critic of the time put it, he "observed [sailors] in bars and watched them pick up girls, and in this way gathered many gestures, steps, and attitudes which he later stylized," and that same aesthetic of here-and-now realism became the ideological underpinning of *On the Town*.[86]

The Cradle Will Rock, *Cabin in the Sky*, and *Black Ritual* each highlight an interracial collaboration that mixed abundant goodwill with problematic racial representations and working relationships. Each pushed stage practices beyond blackface. Each stood out as progressive when considered in relation to the Jim Crow segregation of performance in the late 1930s and early 1940s. Each had its limits. Meanwhile, the closing of the Savoy Ballroom highlights the power of mixed-race social dancing, both in how it provided a forum for experimenting with desegregated performance and in how such violations of racial taboos were perceived as a threat. *On the Town* responded to all these worlds—to left-wing agitprop, Broadway musicals with famous choreographers, modern ballet, and the most up-to-the-minute forms of social dance.

CARMEN JONES AND ON THE TOWN

Another important predecessor of *On the Town* was *Carmen Jones*, which opened on December 2, 1943, with an "all-Negro company of 115."[87] When Jerome Robbins set out to hire black dancers for *On the Town*, he turned to that show. Dorothy McNichols, Frank Neal, J. Flash Riley, and Royce Wallace—that is, all of *On the Town*'s inaugural group of black dancers—came from that production, as did violinist/conductor Everett Lee and singer/dancer Melvin Howard. *Carmen Jones* reconceived Bizet's famous opera within the contemporary world. It retained the essence of Bizet's music, yet had a new book and lyrics by Oscar Hammerstein II and new orchestral arrangements by Robert Russell Bennett. At the helm was the white Broadway impresario Billy Rose, a theatrical producer and nightclub owner known for lavish spectacles. Bizet's opera was relocated to a parachute factory in Chicago during World War II, the character of Carmen was "transformed into a war worker," and Don José became "Joe, a military guard."[88] Given the vocal demands of a nightly performance, two contraltos—Muriel Smith and Muriel Rahn—were hired to sing Carmen at alternating performances. Eugene Loring was choreographer (Loring had previously choreographed Copland's *Billy the Kid*), and five members of *Carmen Jones*'s dance chorus had appeared in Ballet Theatre's *Black Ritual*.[89]

Carmen Jones closed on February 10, 1945, six weeks after *On the Town* opened. During the fall of 1944, as casting was under way for *On the Town*, dancers and singers from *Carmen Jones* were either signing up to go on the road or making other plans.[90] *Carmen Jones*, in turn, had hired its immense black cast with help from John H. Hammond Jr., who held auditions all over the country and was also central in booking black musicians for Café Society, where Bernstein and The Revuers performed.[91]

The relationship of *Carmen Jones* to *On the Town* offers a glimpse into how transracial networks were developing. One such case came with the decision to hire Everett Lee for *On the Town*'s orchestra. Lee recalls that he and Bernstein got to know each other through Muriel Smith, one of the women singing the role of Carmen, and Smith, in turn, knew Bernstein from the Curtis Institute of Music, where they graduated in the same class (1941).[92] Smith was reportedly the first African American to study there.[93] Her professional tie to Bernstein continued

Howard da Silva, Muriel Smith, and Leonard Bernstein, rehearsing
The Cradle Will Rock *in 1947.* Photofest Digital Archive.

well into the 1940s, and it involved political activism. The two gave a concert to-gether at the Boston Opera House in May 1944, seven months before *On the Town*. Paul Robeson also appeared at the event, although he did not sing, and Sylvia Olden Lee, Everett Lee's wife, was Smith's accompanist.[94] The concert was presented "under the auspices of the Joint Anti-Fascist Refugee Committee, Boston Chapter, and the Council on African Affairs," and Bernstein's mentor Serge Koussevitzky was the honorary chairman.[95] Then in 1947, Smith was cast as Ella Hammer when Bernstein conducted a revival of Marc Blitzstein's *The Cradle Will Rock*.[96]

Carmen Jones also marks an important moment in the ideological backdrop against which *On the Town* emerged. Being grounded in a famous European opera, conceived by a white creative team, and performed by an all-black cast and mostly white orchestra, it ran straight into progressive efforts to upgrade racial represen-tation, and it received mixed assessments in the African American press, re-flecting a transitional historical moment.[97] The show struck some as representing a racial advance, whereas others found it to be yet another case of stereotyping. The era's consciousness-raising and activism were having an effect. On the posi-tive side, Dan Burley, a regular arts critic for the *Amsterdam News*, asserted that *Carmen Jones* constituted a "major step that will probably banish 'Uncle Tom' and 'Aunt Dinah.'" He singled out the show's dancers for their extraordinary profes-sional competence. "The things Negroes are 'expected' to do in the theatre are conspicuous by their absence: there is no tap dancing, no crap games, no 'amen,

Lawd,' no hand-clapping and shouting, praying and bowing and scraping," observed Burley. "Instead there are marvelous ballets danced with precision, grace and dignity, as well as high skill by some of the best colored dancers in the country."[98] By contrast, an annual assessment of "the Negro on Broadway" by Miles M. Jefferson, published in *Phylon: The Atlantic University Review of Race and Culture*, raised pointed questions. "After you have left the theater and have time to think," Jefferson wrote, "'Carmen Jones' provokes numerous misgivings. Your eyes are opened to the fact that it is compounded of much petty (though admittedly entertaining) minstrel and 'Punch and Judy' passion."[99]

Additionally, there were complaints—especially from Joe Bostic in *The People's Voice*—about the compensation and treatment of the African American performers in *Carmen Jones*, both during the Broadway run and on the road. In November 1944, Bostic wrote of being "fed up"—in a general sense—with "the bouncing around that the [black] performers in some of the Broadway hit shows are getting in the matter of salary, billing, and exploitation." He then zoomed in on "the kids who are slaving (practically unknown) in 'Carmen Jones' and 'Anna Lucasta.'"[100] *Anna Lucasta* was an all-black drama that premiered on Broadway in 1944. In April and May 1945, Bostic was on a tirade about the low salaries and minimal billing that Rose provided, and in one article he addressed the producer directly:

> BILLY ROSE: You still don't believe that Negro performers should be paid adequately for working in a hit show. Whether you know it or not, except for three people the cast of *Carmen Jones* is generally griping over the salaries they are to receive on the road tour. So you see you didn't completely win your point by getting rid of all the "rebels" who had the guts to demand pay commensurate with their work and the prestige of the show.[101]

Carmen Jones reportedly brought in substantial revenue. In 1946, when it was about to have a return engagement at City Center, Sam Zolotow—the fact-monger of Broadway—called it "the most profitable show produced thus far by Billy Rose."[102]

In 1943–44, then, some of the same equity issues that had affected *Cabin in the Sky* were still present with *Carmen Jones*. Over the years, *Carmen Jones* remained a site of both pain and pride. In a poem from 1949, Langston Hughes wrote with bitterness:

> You put me in Macbeth and Carmen Jones
> And all kinds of Swing Mikados
> And in everything but what's about me.[103]

Yet there was no clear-cut story line to the racial saga of *Carmen Jones*. Decades later, cast members from the original production felt a strong enough tie to the experience to form a Carmen Jones Society, and in 1993 they gathered for a reunion in Astoria, Queens. There, the dancer Evelyn Pilcher—who had also been in *Black Ritual*—read from a flier to promote the gathering: "'Carmen Jones' was presented in artistic elegance that lit up Broadway. It showed what Black performers could do if given the chance."[104]

The racial issues affecting *Carmen Jones* offer a perspective on the working conditions faced by its cast. They also shed light on why the desegregation of *On the Town* made a difference. Chronicling racial history is deeply contextual business, with expectations and perceptions shifting over time, and *On the Town* was no instant panacea. Yet it offers an exceptional vision of the racial dynamics that unfolded onstage, in large part because of a wealth of documentary evidence. Details in draft scripts, stage-management documents, photographs, accounts in the black press, and interviews with surviving cast members make clear the racial choices that were implemented during the process of staging the show. Since *On the Town* posed the intermingling of races as being so commonplace that it did not need to be "mentioned," as dancer Billie Allen put it, the production essentially downplayed—even masked—the very goal it had achieved.[105] No substantial footage of *On the Town*'s original choreography survives, to my knowledge, and, as should be apparent by now, race is absent in its published script.[106]

After Joe Bostic published his initial review of *On the Town* in *The People's Voice*, he wrote a second article that suggested the show was, in part, an experiment in color-blind casting. "Flash Riley, Lonny Jackson, Royce Wallace, Frank Neal, Dorothy McNichols and Melvin Howard were hired as singers and dancers on their merit without any thought as to their racial categorization," Bostic declared.[107] In her extended interview with the *Chicago Defender*, Sono Osato essentially agreed, asserting that casting should transcend race-based considerations. "Let's not have colored people in our shows because they are colored people," Osato declared. "This [i.e., *On the Town*] depicts just people, any people, the people of New York as they live and dance and ride in subways, all intermingled."[108] Tenor Lonny Jackson, who was among those hired, told a reporter for the *Afro-American* about the audition process: "There were more than 300 contestants, both white and colored, for the 18 singing jobs in the show."[109] Jackson and Melvin Howard were the only two black singers hired, and Howard was among those who came from *Carmen Jones*. The dancers who came from that show also had to try out for *On the Town*. "An audition for Jerome Robbins led to my present engagements in 'On the Town,'" recalled dancer Royce Wallace in an interview with Baltimore's *Afro-American*.[110]

Desegregation also occurred behind the scenes of *On the Town* with the implementation of mixed-race dressing rooms. At some point during the show's run, ten males in the dance chorus, including Flash Riley and Frank Neal, signed a note to Peggy Clark requesting an electric fan for "room 10," which they shared as a group.[111] This probably took place before the show moved in June 1945 to the 44th Street Theatre, which was air-conditioned. The female dancers also shared backstage accommodations. "I love working with this bunch of kids," declared Royce Wallace in the *Afro-American*. "The treatment I get is the best. There's no discrimination at all. I think the management is very good toward the colored members of the cast."[112] The article's author then observed, "Miss Wallace shares a dressing room with several white girls and they all get along splendidly."[113] Allyn

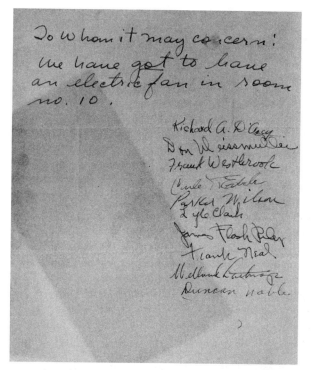

Handwritten note from the male dancers in On the Town, *requesting an electric fan in their dressing room. Flash Riley and Frank Neal signed it together with their white colleagues.* Peggy Clark Collection, Music Division, Library of Congress. © Douglas Clark.

Ann McLerie recalls: "I only remember one black girl [from the show], who was a good friend of mine, Royce Wallace. I sat next to her in the chorus room, and she was a good pal of mine."[114] In the same interview quoted earlier from the *Defender*, Sono Osato attested to forming close relationships with other cast members. "We are such a happy community here in the show. We go out together, we eat in the same restaurants," Osato said. "Why, Royce Wallace (Negro dancer) is one of the most popular people in the show."[115]

On the Town's staged vision of multiracial citizenship caught the eye of the veteran black critic Theophilus Lewis (1891–1974), who was an important force in drama criticism during the Harlem Renaissance. Lewis was writing less frequently in the 1940s, but he spoke from a position of authority, especially in having argued for some time "against the prevalence of stereotypes."[116] With *On the Town*, he perceived a breakthrough. "The average musical show would present the citizens of the town as members of a single race. Colored, especially, would be absent from the human panorama," Lewis wrote in Baltimore's *Afro-American*. He continued:

The producers of "On the Town" tailored the show to square with the facts of life, showing colored, as well as other racial elements, woven in the pattern of a cosmopolitan city.

Desegregating Broadway | 173

"On the Town" is not just a big show that includes some colored specialty acts not connected with the story. The colored characters are not dragged in for comic effect or clowning.

They are not highlighted or emphasized in any way. They are just there, a part of the human scene as they are in life.[117]

Others agreed with this interpretation of the show's racial philosophy. "Negro and white dance indiscriminately on the stage. There is no emphasis on color," wrote Earl Conrad in his portrait of Sono Osato. "There is no studied feeling of the presence of Negroes in the cast—just the natural, democratic motion of many of the scenes of great New York."[118]

All of this "democratic motion"—this vision of "the pattern of a cosmopolitan city"—added up to a political statement that was performed rather than verbalized. On the Town's creative and production teams must have worked hard to achieve such a casual sense of collective affability. They had to decide who would dance with whom, how prominent the interracial moments would be, and whether or not African Americans in the cast would have speaking lines. They also had to decide whether they would spin—or ignore—issues of race as the show was marketed to the press and the public.

In his article for the *Afro-American*, Lewis went on to give an exceptional description of details onstage, providing a framework to understand the show's racial dynamics:

As the sailors leave their ship they meet colored mechanics reporting for work on the day shift in the navy yard.

While racing about the town, they bump into colored passengers in the subway, are served by colored waiters in a café, have fun with a party of colored youngsters in an amusement park and are warned to keep within the law by a colored policemen.

When they report back to their ship the next morning, they meet colored working men leaving the navy yard after a night's work on the swing shift.

... The casting has one drawback from the reviewer's point of view. As the colored performers have no specialty numbers, it is difficult to identify them by referring to the program. Only Royce Wallace can be easily recognized, because her picture is in the foyer.[119]

This account leaves out the "Times Square Ballet," which also involved black dancers. Yet it is remarkable to learn that a photo of Royce Wallace was displayed in the lobby of the theater, at least in the period right before the release of this review in July 1945.

Early versions of the script expand on Lewis's précis, as do production flow charts drawn up by Peggy Clark, who managed the activity onstage. She also devised a separate "Scene Breakdown of Dance Personnel." By piecing together a composite portrait—which essentially reconstructs the disposition of actors onstage—it becomes clear that small details mattered a great deal in terms of race. Most crowd scenes were mixed, and early draft scripts included racial indications that were later dropped when published.

The opening scene at the Brooklyn Navy Yard included Melvin Howard, Lonny Jackson, and Flash Riley as Workers, Frank Neal as Worker & Sailor, and Dorothy McNichols as Girl.[120] These generic character names were used for all the supporting cast. No racial designations are included in this portion of the script, whether draft or published. Howard and Jackson must have performed in vocal backups for "I Feel Like I'm Not Out of Bed Yet," a number led by three workmen (all were white). "There was one black singer who opened the show that was absolutely beautiful to watch," states Jean Handy, a dancer in the show who must have been recalling Howard or Jackson. "His voice was so mellow, and what he was singing—it was always something to stop and watch."[121] There were also occasional performances when Melvin Howard took the lead, substituting for Marten Sameth.[122]

Other desegregated moments noted in the review by Lewis concur with drafts of the script and backstage documents. His description of "bump[ing] into colored passengers in the subway" must refer to both Act I, Scene 2b, when Gabey, Chip, and Ozzie take their initial ride into Manhattan, and Act II, Scene 2, when they take a subway to Coney Island. The production flow chart indicates that Howard, Neal, and Riley were all part of the subway scene—Neal as Sailor and Howard and Riley as Men. An early draft of that scene includes two black males who make a cameo appearance amid a protracted confrontation with a pesky Old Lady. The entire section must have been among those cut by Abbott, and it is fascinating. It opens with the Old Lady, then moves to the African Americans, all as a way of conveying the rapidly shifting demographics of a subway car—"the milling salt-and-pepper mob" that Ralph Ellison later described in his landmark novel *Invisible Man*.[123]

OLD LADY (brandishing umbrella furiously): Now, no back talk, young man [i.e., Gabey]—I must sit on the third cane seat from the left center going towards New York—or I get car sick.
(The three boys bow gravely and stiffly from the waist, doff their caps and move further down the car. At the same time, the music slows down, indicating the car has come to a stop. A few people exit, and two negroes, one a soldier, enters. The doors close, the music starts up again as the two negroes talk.)
NEGRO SOLDIER (to friend): Then the hostess asked me, "Will you have some corn pone—I'm sure you'll have some corn pone," and I said, "What is corn pone?"
(They exchange a puzzled look as they sit)[124]

"Corn pone"—a rural southern term for corn bread—clearly is intended to mark these soldiers as African American. At the same time, the punch line depends on grasping a twist: the two urbanized men are so remote from the culture of the South that they don't have a clue what corn pone is.

Another mixed-race scene in the show is "Presentation of Miss Turnstiles," when Sono Osato gets chosen queen of the subway. All of the female dancers appeared onstage, which meant that McNichols and Wallace were there, too.[125]

Since that scene opens with "a line of girls" who are competing to be Miss Turn-stiles, it embraces McNichols and Wallace as beauty-contest competitors within a mixed lineup, which was a radical notion for its day. No actors of color are listed in the flow chart for scenes at the Museum of Natural History or Carnegie Hall. After the museum, the "Lonely Town" scene takes place on "a busy New York City street," and it includes Howard, Jackson, McNichols, and Neal as part of the crowd.[126]

African American performers next turn up in the scene in Times Square, one of the most racially important in the entire show. There is a major role for both the vocal chorus ("Lucky to Be Me") and dance chorus ("Sailors on the Town"). At the end of the scene, as dance takes over, the published script makes a vague statement about inclusiveness: "They lock arms and plunge Gabey into a ballet depicting the teeming night life of the city . . . *all kinds of people*" (emphasis mine).[127] Bernstein articulated the scene in handwritten notes: "All the sailors in New York congregate in Times Square for their night of fun. There is communal dancing."[128] The dance critic Edwin Denby singled out this moment in the show: "I admired particularly . . . the brief strange rush of the Times Square finale."[129] "Communal" and "strange rush" captured the open-minded sense of humanity conveyed by this scene, together with the visceral thrill of witnessing virtuosic mixed-race dancers. It added up to a classic Broadway expression of community.

The papers of Jerome Robbins include a typescript dance scenario, titled "Sailor on the Town," which explicitly cites African Americans as part of the action in Times Square. (Bracketed ellipses are mine; all others appear in the original text.)

Sailors start to come on stage singing the canon? [*sic*] N.Y.N.Y. till the stage is full of sailors (full company all in sailor suits) [. . .]

As the first refrain ends, a cutout of Father Duffy's statue is brought on center and a group of sailors arrange themselves carelessly around it . . . The music becomes hot slower and intense . . . (N.Y.N.Y. march-boogie). [. . .] They're all joined by two negro couples so that now five couples are dancing together reaching to [the] height of this hot section. [. . .] The running line is formed and the crowds tear around the stage crossing upstage and down as the principals work their way across and thru them from one wing to the other.

[. . .] The lights become as if reflecting the mirrored ball and girls in awful satin long gowns come on and dance with sailors of different types . . . the heavy happy type, the slick rug cutter . . . the jitterbugger, the negro couples lindying.[130]

A "rug cutter" was a jitterbug dancer.[131] All six of the show's African American dancers were onstage during the scene, with Neal and Riley appearing in the production flow chart as Sailors. Photographs from a souvenir program give a sense of the interracial spectacle on stage, with a black serviceman on the left and two black female dancers, one at center front and another at back right. The women dance hand in hand with white sailors, and, most remarkably, the black sailor in the back, probably Flash Riley, appears to be holding hands with a

"Times Square Ballet." Photograph from the Souvenir Program for On the Town. Peggy Clark Collection, Music Division, Library of Congress.

white female dancer.[132] The photo is crowded enough so that the people on either side of Riley are not entirely clear. However, the arrangement alternates men and women throughout, and neither of the black women dancers is next to him.

Act II opens with the five principals (minus Ivy) gallivanting to three different nightclubs: Diamond Eddie's, Conga Cabana, and Slam Bang Club. Lewis cited "colored waiters in a café" as part of his litany of what black performers did in the show, and indeed Melvin Howard and Lonny Jackson are included in the production flow chart as Waiters. In the Slam Bang Club—a Harlem club—Dorothy McNichols and Flash Riley appear as Patrons.[133] Neal and Wallace were not onstage for any part of the scene. At first glance, casting Howard and Jackson as waiters appears as a lapse into stereotypes. However, Herbert Greene, a white actor, was also listed on the flow chart as a Waiter, making it a biracial representation of service employees.[134]

The subway scene of Act II then takes place, in which Gabey and his buddies head to Coney Island to search for Ivy. That segment, titled "Subway to Coney Island," was added two weeks after the show opened, and it occurs immediately before the dream ballet. It included five dancers: Royce Wallace, Allyn Ann McLerie, Frank Neal, Frank Westbrook, and Malka Farber.[135] Wallace, Neal, and Farber continued to dance that segment through the end of the Broadway run, while McLerie and Westbrook were replaced. A photograph in *Life* shows Wallace sitting on a train as part of the crowd, and a draft scenario for the dance articulates the action: "In a strange dreamlike way, a colored couple who have been sitting opposite each other rise and start to dance.... and other unrelated couples join in. It's a torchy, sexy dance."[136]

A scene called "Real Coney Island" is also racially integrated, as the sailors and their women have "fun with a party of colored youngsters in an amusement park and are warned to keep within the law by a colored policemen," as described in the *Afro-American*. The policeman was played by Lonny Jackson, who asserts authority not only over white citizens but also over white members of the military.[137] In his initial article about *On the Town*, Joe Bostic noted the black cop. His "beat is in the Times Square area," Bostic wrote. "He also bobs up as a bluecoat in Coney Island and takes a sailor into protective custody."[138]

As the production flow chart demonstrates, Jackson makes four appearances in the interracial chase interludes that end some of the scenes. In them, he assists a little old lady, who is white, as she pursues the three sailors for swiping a poster of Miss Turnstiles from a subway car. Significantly, in the final three chase segments, Jackson is joined by Roger Treat, a white actor who also played a policeman. As a result, the audience viewed a mixed-race team of cops. Like Jackson, Treat was also part of the singing chorus. In reflecting on the hiring process, Jackson pointed out that George Abbott considered masking Jackson's race, which would have created an illusion of two white cops. "After I won my spot," Jackson recalled, "Mr. Abbott, the director, asked me if I could make up 'white.' I told him I could do that, but it never came about."[139] Within the warped world of race and performance, the use of whiteface by black actors was viewed at this moment in time as a step toward equality in employment. In 1946, for example, Canada Lee famously put on whiteface in the stage play *The Duchess of*

Jitterbug from On the Town, *danced by Dorothy McNichols and Flash Riley. Photograph from the Souvenir Program for* On the Town. *Peggy Clark Collection, Music Division, Library of Congress.*

Malfi. Lee "was prepared to flip this practice [blackface] on its head to prove that black actors could and should be cast in traditionally white roles," writes his biographer.[140]

With the scene titled "Real Coney Island," Neal, Riley, Wallace, and McNichols are listed on the production flow chart with the designation "Jitterbug," and a photograph from the souvenir program captures the action.[141] The show then concludes with a vision of black and white dockworkers laboring side by side at the Brooklyn Navy Yard. As at the opening, Howard and Jackson are present as Workers, while Neal and Riley are Sailors.

In at least one other scene—"Presentation of Miss Turnstiles"—an additional segment of mixed-race dancing was contemplated, then rejected. Based on early scripts and one newspaper account, it appears that Sono Osato was slated to dance with African American jitterbuggers, and that combination would have stretched the notion of biracial performance very far for the 1940s. The jitterbug had complex racial implications. Since Neal, Riley, and Wallace are linked to that dance in "Real Coney Island," it could be viewed as black cultural expression. Yet in clubs such as the Savoy Ballroom, the jitterbug was also danced by patrons who were not African American, and often it brought the races together. In "Presentation of Miss Turnstiles," Sono Osato danced "six variations with six different boys—each one represents the ideal mate for each of her talents."[142] In all early versions of the script (but not the published text), the "mates" are described as follows, with the second one as the focus here:

Home loving type:	Boy in slippers, bathrobe with pipe.
She loves to step out:	Boy in zoot-suit outfit—jitterbugger.
She loves Army—	Boy in soldier outfit
She loves Navy—	Boy in navy outfit
Athlete—	Boy in athletic shorts with shotput.
Opera, ballet—	Boy in professorial get-up.

A zoot suit was a flashy garment, with a thigh-length jacket, wide padded shoulders, and peg trousers that tapered to narrow cuffs.[143] Like the jitterbug, it could be racially marked. The famous Zoot Suit Riots in Los Angeles in 1943, for example, pitted white sailors against Latino youths, who were known to like zoot suits.

In the flow chart for the debut production, the white dancer Lyle Clark is listed as "Jitterbug." A question remains whether casting for the jitterbugger got changed during the show's development. In *The People's Voice*, Joe Bostic described a segment that was cut because it was perceived as too racially charged. Could it have been this portion of "Presentation of Miss Turnstiles"? "For the record it might be mentioned that originally there was a scene in the show in which Frank Neal and Flash Riley did a dance routine with star Sono Osato but the director's feet developed a sudden coolness and it was taken out," reported Bostic. "He felt that New York theatregoers were not yet THAT tolerant. As it has turned out, the thoroughly bouncy show is playing to capacity audiences and there hasn't been the first unhappy repercussion to the integration of Negroes into the cast."[144] Bostic's report points up the unspoken assumption that "mixed-race dancing" within the context of *On the Town* meant either pairing white and black dancers or pairing Osato with white dancers. Within this racial framework, African American men were not coupled with a Japanese American woman.[145]

MOBILIZING RACIAL ADVOCACY IN THE ARTS

All these staging details bear witness to how *On the Town* showcased an interracial company of performers who touched and interacted with a carefully constructed sense of abandon. They also reveal moments—such as the inclusion of two black women among the contestants for Miss Turnstiles—when the show provided a model for what a desegregated citizenry could look like. Just as striking was *On the Town*'s capacity to gain the respect of black drama critics, who were ever alert to violations of civil rights within the performing arts.

Yet *On the Town*'s desegregation did not happen in a vacuum. Rather, it was fueled by the left-wing politics of its artistic leadership and by the advocacy of civil rights organizations. An article in the *Daily Worker* in late September 1945—nine months into the show's run—demonstrates how *On the Town*'s creative team had achieved a certain standing within left-wing performance circles. The *Daily Worker* announced the formation of a committee of artists, writers, and professionals, chaired by Paul Robeson, to support the reelection of Benjamin J. Davis to the city council of New York. An African American lawyer, Davis was an outspoken civil rights leader and member of the Communist Party. The group supporting his candidacy included "some of the most outstanding [figures] in the theatre, radio, motion picture, the arts."[146] Leonard Bernstein, Betty Comden, Adolph Green, Sono Osato, and Jerome Robbins were among the select group of supporters singled out. Others included Marc Blitzstein, Lena Horne, Canada Lee, Hazel Scott, and Teddy Wilson (the last two were regular performers at Café Society). "Activism" for a celebrity performer in the 1940s meant signing petitions and lending one's name to causes. It also meant appearing at left-wing benefits and banquets—activities that came back to haunt many of these performers during the McCarthy era.

Each core personality in the conception and production of *On the Town* had her or his own history of engagement with racial issues, and a loose matrix of moral convictions, ethnic and racial networks, and political affiliations connected the show with the contemporary racial struggle. For one thing, many Jews—including Bernstein, Comden, Green, and Robbins—identified strongly with the equity issues faced by people of color, and they stepped forward as activists in the struggle for civil rights, often doing so within the context of left-wing political involvement. "The Negro and the Jew," declared the *New York Amsterdam News* in 1942, "because of their race and religion, and the unsocial attitudes of the majority race toward them, are constantly under pressure and attack."[147] Jewish leaders devised an argument, according to historian Cheryl Lynn Greenberg, that "furthering black civil rights was crucial to advance the war effort," and the American Jewish Congress warned that military enemies of the United States used its race problem as a way to accuse the government of hypocrisy.[148]

In Bernstein's case, he took the initiative to appoint Everett Lee to the show's orchestra. In at least one conversation with Lee, Bernstein expressed a personal identification with the plight of African Americans, comparing the difference in opportunities open to Jews and blacks. Lee recalls that the two men talked about whether Lee should try to pass as Hispanic in order to advance his career:

> Lenny was a wonderful, fine person. Not only was he a great talent, he was a fine person. Like we talked about names and race and whatnot. And he said, "Well you and I have the same problem, only in different ways. Jews have a problem. Colored boys have a problem." And he said, "They wanted me to change my name from Bernstein to Amber or whatever else." And he [told them], "No, what's wrong with being a good Jew?"... Lenny said, "Be what you are, Everett. Just be what you're supposed to be.... The advantage that I have is I'm white."[149]

Bernstein's political activism was growing during this early stage of his career, and a key experience appeared to be his involvement with the National Negro Congress (NNC), which had been founded in 1935 to build coalitions among "a broad spectrum of groups representing black interests," including the NAACP.[150] From the beginning, the organization was tied to the American Communist Party. In their history of the party, Irving Howe and Lewis Coser identified the NNC as "the main front organization in the Negro community during the Popular Front period."[151]

The NNC appears to have entered Bernstein's scope in the fall of 1940, while he was a student at the Curtis Institute of Music in Philadelphia. Writing to his childhood piano teacher, Helen Coates, Bernstein described the possibility of leading "an all-Negro Symphony Orchestra" under sponsorship of the NNC:

> So many things are happening—all at once—but they have a habit of collecting. First of all—I have suddenly become the director of the Philadelphia People's Chorus—one that was at one time a huge and well-trained group.... They're amateurs, of course, workers, (the masses), and have a great spirit & enthusiasm.
>
> I seem to have involved myself with the proletariat in a big way; out of this have come many things. I have been asked to organize and conduct an all-Negro Symphony Orchestra! The idea excites me no end; there must be a vast field of untilled & fertile soil there; & since the organizing will be done by the Nat'l Negro Congress, I'll be only too glad to work with them. It's a great social triumph, too, if it succeeds; conquering the latest suspicion of whites among the negroes (and how justified that suspicion is!) is a large step forward.[152]

It was at Curtis that Bernstein became friends with mezzo-soprano Muriel Smith, who would soon be singing in *Carmen Jones* for Billy Rose.

In the summer of 1943—the year before *On the Town*—the National Negro Congress established a Committee for Democratic Culture that lobbied hard for equality in the hiring of musicians, dancers, and actors and for the elimination of racial stereotypes on stage and screen.[153] "Forty Cultural Figures Launch Program to Democratize Stage, Screen, Radio," reported a press release in the summer of 1943 from the NNC's cultural committee:

New York, July 28 – After hearing a ringing plea from Clarence Muse, noted film actor, forty representatives of stage, radio, movie and journalism, meeting with national and community leaders at the Hotel Theresa, launched an eight point program here today for the full integration of Negro artists into all aspects of American cultural life....A wide range of leadership was represented among those participating....The spokesman for New York's theatrical world was Mr. Jonas Rosenfield, Jr., President of the Screen Actors' Guild, who told of plans among theatrical leaders here to counteract anti-Negro propaganda.[154]

The cultural committee articulated its aims for diversity in hiring and racial representation on stage: "a) Cessation of the stereotype in stage productions, b) Production of better plays on Negro life, particularly now re war, c) Widening the opportunity for use of Negro Talent on the stage."[155] As it turned out, *On the Town* responded to those goals point by point. At the same time, the NNC's mailing lists and minutes from meetings show that its activists included some of the same journalists who were praising *On the Town*'s racial stance. They included Adam Clayton Powell Jr. and Joe Bostic of *The People's Voice*; Billy Rowe of the *Pittsburgh Courier*; and Dan Burley of the *Amsterdam News*.[156]

Nineteen forty-three was the year of race riots in Harlem and the closing of the Savoy Ballroom. It was also the year of the first Carnegie Hall concert by Duke Ellington and his Orchestra. This historic event included the debut of Ellington's ambitious extended composition *Black, Brown, and Beige*, a jazz symphony conceived as "a tone parallel to the history of the Negro in America."[157] The work's title signaled the symbolism of skin color and the impact of racial intermingling. Ellington's concert attracted a cluster of "celebrity sponsors," and proceeds from the concert went to Russian War Relief, a popular beneficiary of left-wing fund-raisers.[158] The sponsors for his concert were a mixed-race group, including celebrated African American musicians such as Count Basie, W. C. Handy, Fletcher Henderson, and Jimmie Lunceford alongside equally famous white entertainers and composers such as Jack Benny, Bing Crosby, and Bernstein's close friend Aaron Copland.[159] Although Copland's commitment to the left remained strong during this period, he generally focused less on issues affecting African Americans, channeling his energies and musical interests more toward Latin America.[160]

For Bernstein, the National Negro Congress again entered his scope in the fall of 1947—a year and a half after *On the Town* had closed—when he published an article in the *New York Times* titled "The Negro in Music: Problems He Has to Face in Getting a Start," which clearly promoted the NNC's agenda. This article illustrates how Bernstein's level of political engagement had increased. The "Cultural Division of the National Negro Congress" is cited in the lead paragraph, while Bernstein decries "the lack of the opportunity for proper training" for black artists in classical music and highlights the low representation of African Americans in Broadway pit orchestras, radio, and other major musical institutions.[161] Nora Holt, classical music critic for the *Amsterdam News*, responded immediately to Bernstein's piece. "It took more than ordinary courage for Leonard Bernstein, noted young composer and conductor of the New York City Symphony, to write

Leonard Bernstein, Ellabelle Davis, and Booker T. Washington III, published in New York Amsterdam News, *September 27, 1947.* Photofest Digital Archive.

the article, 'The Negro in Music,'" Holt declared. "He is a musician of scholarly achievements and a man of liberal views which means he measures a human being according to his qualities without odious reference to race or creed."[162] During this same period, Bernstein's appearances with black performers increased noticeably. For example, he conducted the tenor Charles Holland in the premiere of Marc Blitzstein's *The Airborne Symphony* in 1946, as well as the mezzo Marian Anderson in a concert at Lewisohn Stadium in July 1947 and the soprano Ellabelle Davis in a performance of Mahler's Second Symphony with the New York City Symphony in September 1947.[163] Twenty thousand people reportedly attended Anderson's concert.

Records of the National Negro Congress indicate that its members encompassed quite a number of artists from the personal and professional spheres surrounding *On the Town*—most notably Sono Osato. Others included the black dancer and choreographer Pearl Primus; the white dancer Helen Tamiris, who had been chief choreographer for the Federal Dance Theatre (part of the WPA); and Agnes de Mille, the choreographer of *Black Ritual*.[164] Paul Robeson and the Café Society pianist Teddy Wilson appeared repeatedly in these documents, as did *Carmen Jones*'s producer Billy Rose, record producer (and talent recruiter for *Carmen Jones*) John H. Hammond Jr., and Duke Ellington. Bernstein does not appear to have been cited in the NNC's records. Yet his involvement with the organization was clear, and it came back to plague him at the height of the Red

Scare. The NNC was among the organizations listed under his name in *Red Channels: The Report of Communist Influence in Radio and Television* (1950), and it also turned up repeatedly in his FBI files.[165]

Jerome Robbins's tie to the National Negro Congress is unknown. Yet he was allied with dancers such as Osato and de Mille, who were named in its records, and around Christmas 1943 he joined the Communist Party.[166] At the same time, however, he was very cautious about his political affiliations. His biographer Greg Lawrence argues that Robbins "appears to have kept his politics under wraps socially," exercising the same "discretion" as he did with the "gay side of his life style."[167] He definitely had ties to leftist artistic networks, however. In 1953, Robbins was called in to testify before HUAC, and it was a wrenching experience for both him and his professional associates because he took the regrettable step of naming names, becoming one of the more notorious such cases of the Red Scare.

Like Bernstein, Robbins had engaged with race before *On the Town*. In the early 1940s, before *Fancy Free*, Robbins had drafted a number of scenarios for ballets that featured racial themes. While at the left-wing Camp Tamiment around 1940, he choreographed a ballet titled *Harlem Incident*, which "showed how a party of white slummers invade the gaiety of a Harlem dive, make it surly and self-conscious and almost create a riot."[168] The following year, he drafted a scenario titled "The Story of Stack O Lee," which was submitted to Ballet Theatre but not produced.[169] "Stagger Lee" was the title of a famous African American blues song about a murder committed by Stagger Lee Shelton.[170] Other notes by Robbins for works in progress include a partial scenario titled "Negroes."[171] In these early materials, Robbins seemed to be engaging with African American themes within standard racial tropes of the day.

Once casting began for *On the Town*, Robbins was central to implementing the show's mixed-race policies, although detailed documentation is limited about individual actions in the hiring process. It was no accident, however, that four of the African Americans in the cast were dancers and that Sono Osato was Robbins's former associate from Ballet Theatre. During the early 1940s Robbins had observed his colleague Eugene Loring as he devised the choreography for *Carmen Jones*, and ultimately Robbins drew on Loring's dancers. He also had strong models, having watched Balanchine work with Dunham and Agnes de Mille stage *Black Ritual*.

Like Bernstein, Robbins maintained a long-term commitment to hiring black dancers and musicians, yet the results were not consistent. When the New York City Ballet was formed in 1948, Robbins joined Balanchine as one of the main choreographers. But it was not until 1955 that the company featured an African American dancer, Arthur Mitchell, in one of its productions. The work was *Western Symphony*, choreographed by Balanchine with music by the white composer Hershy Kay (one of the orchestrators of *On the Town*).[172] This was the same year in which the Metropolitan Opera broke through its long-resented racial barrier, featuring Marian Anderson in *Un Ballo in Maschera*.[173] Yet Robbins's dance chorus for *The King and I*, which opened in 1951, was interracial, including, for example, the Japanese Americans Michiko and Yuriko and the Dunham dancer Tommy Gomez.[174] When Robbins choreographed and directed *West Side Story* in 1957, collaborating once again with Bernstein, he appointed the African American dancer Donald McKayle as dance captain.[175] The formation of Robbins's American Theater Laboratory in 1966 was also notable, with the African American composer and conductor Coleridge Taylor Perkinson as music director.[176]

For Betty Comden and Adolph Green, desegregated performance experiences had been integral to their work with The Revuers at clubs such as the Village Vanguard and Café Society, and left-wing politics were part of the mix. Their participation in "From Swing to Shostakovich" at Carnegie Hall in April 1943 marked an important occasion when they took part in a mixed-race, mixed-genre concert, just a few months after the debut of Ellington's *Black, Brown, and Beige*. All this has already been explored within the context of the history of The Revuers. Over the years, Comden and Green maintained a firm commitment to furthering racial justice through performance. One such production was *Hallelujah, Baby!* (1967), which, as the *Chicago Defender* reported, portrayed "the American Negro's struggles from the days of slavery to contemporary times."[177] Leslie Uggams made her Broadway debut in that show.

Finally, George Abbott's attitudes about race deserve attention. Of an older generation than Bernstein, Robbins, Comden, and Green, Abbott had experimented in the late 1930s with writing and directing shows that featured African Americans. Those efforts resulted in fairly spectacular failures, which is noteworthy given his extremely successful track record in musical theater overall. In October 1936, Abbott opened *Sweet River*, a show developed as "a modern version of *Uncle Tom's Cabin*," and it lasted only five nights.[178] Yet Abbott had first-rate instincts in hiring. With *Sweet River*, he tapped Juanita Hall as choral director, and Hall of course went on to an exceptional career, especially as Bloody Mary in *South Pacific*.[179] Abbott's handling of racial representation in *Sweet River*, however, succumbed to prevailing stereotypes. Writing for the *Amsterdam News*, the esteemed black journalist Roi Ottley criticized the show for featuring "the same old Tom," while he also praised the production for "some excellent singing by Juanita Hall's choir."[180] In a short review, Ottley captured the vexing racial conundrums of the mid-1930s, where advancement was often judged in terms of how much a given show distanced itself from blackface. "A timid beginning but an important step in the American theatre was the casting of Juano Hernández as Gabe," Ottley observed. (Gabe was renamed from the character George Harris in *Uncle Tom's Cabin*.) Ottley praised Abbott for casting an African American in the role. But he expressed dismay at hiring the white actress Margaret Mullen, which meant that the role of Eliza was performed in blackface. Ottley complained of "an awkward scene" in which Hernández "makes love to his wife [as played by Mullen], but doesn't touch her, [which] probably embarrassed the whole audience."

In December 1937, Abbott unveiled *Brown Sugar*, a show with an all-black cast that stayed open for four nights (and is unrelated to *Bubbling Brown Sugar* of the 1970s). Juano Hernández appeared once again, and the show was judged as being riddled with stereotypes. "It was just another presentation of the average Broadwayite's apparent misconception of Harlem," complained the *Amsterdam News*.[181] The reviewer characterized Abbott in blunt terms, describing him as "a director who persists in the belief that Negroes are childlike, inferior beings who all talk like backwoods Georgia crackers, hold all white men in awesome respect and make their living only as entertainers, menials, or criminals." Even Brooks Atkinson in the *New York Times* shook his head over Abbott's handling of race. "After his experience with 'Sweet River' last season it appears that the sepia tones do not become him," Atkinson concluded.[182] Once again, however, Abbott made astute decisions in casting. This time he introduced Butterfly McQueen to Broadway audiences. Two years later she was to have a major role in the film *Gone with the Wind* as the maid to Scarlett O'Hara.[183]

On the Town brought Abbott a remarkably different kind of racial experience. This time there was no all-black cast, no Uncle Tom, no blackface. Rather, he collaborated with an interracial roster of young dancers and actors who aimed for socially progressive theater. While we will never fully know how racial decisions were made behind the scenes in *On the Town*, there is every sign that "the kids," as Abbott called his youthful collaborators, led the way by casting performers of color and shaping racial representation. The young creative team also hired Sono Osato, who recalls being told by Abbott that he would "never" have tapped her for the job.[184] In addition, Joe Bostic tagged Abbott as the one who vetoed the proposed dance between Osato and an African American man. Yet to his credit Abbott was open to stretching himself, even if he retained some of the bias of his generation, and he took part in enacting *On the Town*'s racial vision for a new era.

Viewing the desegregation of *On the Town* in these shifting frameworks, it becomes clear—often in quotidian detail—how the show sought to oppose prevailing racial practices onstage. Dressing rooms were shared, mixed-race personal relationships and beauty pageants were modeled, and multiracial citizenship was on full display. Yet the production was no clear-cut game-changer. Rather, it reflected the often-nebulous limitations imposed by race in New York City toward the end of an international crisis. *On the Town*'s immediate predecessors in the realm of mixed performance—whether *Black Ritual* or *The Cradle Will Rock*—offered models that alternately inspired change and perpetuated the status quo. Its decisions about what the black actors did onstage showed sensitivity about depicting a mixed citizenry but steered clear of being provocative. Its probable tie to the Cultural Division of the National Negro Congress offered a view of how an organized movement was striving to bring humanity to stage depictions but was kept in the background. And its racially divided reception was all too common at the time and somehow went unchallenged by the show's promoters.

No racially attuned tradition of performance resulted from the inaugural production of *On the Town*. That is, the focus on race in its debut was so thoroughly enacted rather than scripted—so thoroughly downplayed—that it ultimately proved to be ephemeral. The film of the show from 1949, with its all-white roster of principals surrounded by sailors who were also white, probably contributed to this racial erasure.

Ultimately, the issue of race in the first stage production of *On the Town* yields a paradox—a quirky exception when lighthearted comedy joined hands with the pursuit of social justice. Yet its enigmas open our vision to the complex questions that inflected the performance of race during World War II.

BIOGRAPHIES ONSTAGE
On the Town's Black Conductor, Dancers, and Singers
• • •

Theater has, I think, the power to change, to change an audience, to change people's lives, to make things happen, to suggest the way things can be, and to bring change and to transform people into what they really want to be and remind them of what they never want to become.
—*Billie Allen, dancer in* On the Town

Knew ev'ry step
Right off the bat.
Said, "I can do that,
I can do that."
—*"I Can Do That" from* A Chorus Line,
lyrics by Edward Kleban

Broadway shows are community spectacles in which actors, singers, dancers, and orchestra musicians fuse their artistry to pursue a common goal. Other than a few stars whose names grace the marquee, most members of the cast and crew work in near anonymity. Yet all are highly trained professionals who rank among the best in the business. Given that *On the Town* could not afford big-name stars such as Mary Martin or Ethel Merman, its box office success hinged all the more on igniting collaborative sparks throughout the production. Those collaborations reached across race lines, as is by now abundantly apparent, and the results appeared to have been largely salutary, even if large segments of the outside world did not sit up and take notice.

With this chapter, I shift from racial issues inflecting the show overall to the professional sagas of individual performers of color who were part of the team. The biographies constructed here look both backward and forward in time, offering case studies that branch out from Broadway and *On the Town.* They chart education and training, offering a vivid perspective on how a cluster of individual careers took shape, and they follow each performer into the ensuing decades to determine long-range professional destinies.

These gifted African American performing artists had come to New York City from various locations around the country, often because of *Carmen Jones*, and both it and *On the Town* involved an intensely competitive audition process. Some one hundred African American dancers reportedly auditioned for *Carmen Jones*, and some three hundred singers, including both blacks and whites, tried out for *On the Town*.[1] "Jerry [Robbins] wouldn't take you unless you were first class," recalls Everett Lee in reminiscing about *On the Town*'s dancers.[2] Some already had experience with the Federal Theatre Project. Most of the dancers were trained in ballet, and the musicians—including two singers and a violinist-conductor—also had classical training. Those facts can seem like insignificant details. But for a performer of color in the United States during the 1940s, the opportunity to obtain a first-class education was extremely limited. Change was occurring, as demonstrated by the case of Muriel Smith at the Curtis Institute of Music, but luck often determined whether or not a particular young person got the education she deserved. An aspiring artist needed to be positioned geographically and socioeconomically within the right artistic infrastructure, and savvy mentors made a difference.

The deployment of *On the Town*'s black performers onstage has already been discussed. But these actors, dancers, and musicians deserve a fresh round of introductions, bringing them to the footlights as individuals. On opening night, they included Everett Lee (violinist); Dorothy McNichols, Frank Neal, Flash Riley, and Royce Wallace (dancers); and Melvin Howard and Lonny Jackson (singers). Midway into the run, Everett Lee received his landmark promotion to the post of orchestra conductor, and a few months later Billie Allen signed on as a dancer when Royce Wallace stepped down.[3] Out of these eight figures, five of them—Lee, Neal, Riley, Wallace, and Allen—sustained lifelong careers in performance. That said, Lee and Riley did so by following a familiar pattern for African American performers: they left the United States to pursue more promising opportunities abroad. In Lee's case, he continues to live in Europe even as this book goes to press. Wallace left the country briefly as well. A network of human relationships—a professional version of family—was established in *On the Town* that continued to bind some of these performers to one another over the years, and that network was transracial, extending to Bernstein, Robbins, and other whites from the show. This is not to suggest that the careers of *On the Town*'s cast played out as a unit, but rather that an early opportunity in a mixed-race show brought long-term benefits by establishing a diverse pool of associates. Given the race-based limitations of the era, these performers quickly became able to adapt, moving nimbly from the concert hall and Broadway to films and eventually to television. That last step was significant, for after an early period of exclusion, television increasingly opened up employment for African Americans, especially by the 1970s. Along the way, *On the Town*'s performers worked with some of the best-known artists and intellectuals of the postwar era, including figures such as Maya Angelou, Harry Belafonte, Duke Ellington, James Earl Jones, Sidney Poitier, Noble Sissle, Billy Strayhorn, and Cicely Tyson.

The challenges faced by African American performers shifted as the decades passed. The hopeful desegregation of the war years persisted into the late 1940s, bringing with it a boost in hiring and equitable representation. Just as the military was being desegregated and Jackie Robinson and Larry Dobie were breaking through the color line in major-league baseball, shows such as *Beggar's Holiday* (Duke Ellington and John Latouche) and *Finian's Rainbow* (Burton Lane and E. Y. Harburg) signaled Broadway's commitment to end staged segregation. They both opened in 1946–47, and Robinson joined the Brooklyn Dodgers in 1947. Yet while the racial trajectory in baseball continued to move forward, albeit at a halting pace, employment opportunities on Broadway regressed by the early 1950s as "the musical's fling with democracy began to seem transitory," writes historian Allen Woll.[4] Racial formulas became increasingly taboo in the realm of representation, yet a new generation of roles for African Americans did not materialize in huge numbers. "We have discontinued the use of the stereotype," declared the actress Lena Horne in 1958, "but we have opened up nothing else."[5] Certain kinds of roles persisted for blacks, even if flagrant symbols of Jim Crow such as bandanas had been left behind. "I played every kind of maid, that's all I ever did," recalled the tap dancer Jeni LeGon, who performed with Bill "Bojangles" Robinson and Cab Calloway, among others. "Eventually there weren't that many roles. They were too few and far between."[6]

During the 1950s, the McCarthy and HUAC hearings disrupted the activist networks that had been promoting racial change within the theater, and the overall commercial climate on Broadway became timid. Just as the film of *On the Town* had adapted to these bracing realities, so too the careers of black performers faced radically different conditions after the optimism of World War II. "Revivals predominated," observed the critic Miles M. Jefferson in one of his annual reports about the status of African Americans on Broadway, which had begun in 1944.[7] Jefferson published these articles in *Phylon*, a journal hailed by Langston Hughes as "America's scholarly Negro quarterly."[8] In 1951, Jefferson noted "the glaring distraction of newspaper headlines forever reflecting the hysteria of the times."[9] Two years later he affirmed that "something was noticeably wrong with the theater-going public." Musing over the reasons, Jefferson conjectured that in part "it was more comfortable to sit at home with the television set, despite the comparative inferiority of that medium."[10] In 1957, with the last of his reports, Jefferson proclaimed that the 1956–57 Broadway season had produced "no new play of extraordinary stature employing the Negro as playwright or actor."[11]

Life stories of the African American dancers and singers in *On the Town* illustrate how employment in postwar theater brought exceptional challenges for those in secondary roles or choruses. During the 1950s, Broadway "substituted an integration from the top," writes Allen Woll. "Renowned entertainers from nightclubs, films, and popular recordings took center stage as proof of theatre's new racial tolerance. As a result, jobs for black secondary players, chorus members, and dancers faded as the decade progressed."[12]

Instrumentalists and conductors of color who sought work in the United States also faced "'an iron curtain of discrimination' against Negro musicians," complained the *Amsterdam News*.[13] Near the end of the 1950s, the Urban League of Greater New York published a study of the employment of black musicians by major orchestras, Broadway shows, and radio and television networks. The results were similar to what Bernstein had reported a decade earlier on behalf of the National Negro Congress. In New York's major musical ensembles—defined by the Urban League's study as the New York Philharmonic, Metropolitan Opera, Lewisohn Stadium Concert Orchestra, and Goldman Band—there were "no Negro musicians." Added to that, "a total of 14 [nonwhite] out of an estimated 650 [white] musicians had been employed in Broadway shows over the last three years." The report, which was based on interviews with some two-hundred musicians, noted the importance of networking and the "general white American blindness" to the exclusion of African Americans from the opportunities yielded by insider alliances: "Auditions for these orchestras, it was noted, are not announced, but are spread by word of mouth, thus allowing for few Negroes to apply." Actors' Equity had conducted a similar survey in 1952, with equally dispiriting results.[14]

The African American performers from *On the Town* had richly textured professional experiences and personal associations, and they mostly managed to keep working in the face of an inhospitable environment. Their individual tactics for doing so are not only fascinating—these are accomplished professionals with extensive experience onstage—but also instructive about the curves, zigzags, hurdles, and abrupt roadblocks that ultimately defined their career paths.

CONCERTMASTER AND CONDUCTOR OF *ON THE TOWN:* EVERETT LEE

When Everett Lee stepped onto the podium of *On the Town* in September 1945, he began a pattern of firsts that became a norm in his career, as he assumed the symbolic power that goes with being an orchestra conductor yet did so with racial conditions stacked against him. The visibility offered by *On the Town* and the attention paid to his exceptional appointment gave a boost to his ambitions. Yet Lee (b. 1916) consistently faced a climate of "orchestrated discrimination," as the civil rights leader Vernon E. Jordan Jr. once said of the stubbornly slow desegregation of American symphonies. Lee devised resourceful strategies to work around the system, notably by forming his own orchestra. Ultimately, he found that the best options for professional growth and employment lay outside the United States.[15] Lee's career ran in tandem with that of the conductor Dean Dixon (1915–76), who faced the same racial blockades, and Dixon also ended up as an expatriate. Conducting opera became one of Lee's specialties, and he has also had a long and distinguished career working with symphony orchestras. Along the way, he repeatedly cracked the glass ceiling. His first wife, Sylvia Olden Lee (ca. 1918–2004), built a career at the same time as her husband, and their development as musicians was deeply intertwined. She ultimately became a celebrated accompanist and vocal coach, working with African American divas such as Jessye Norman and Kathleen Battle, who were associated with the Metropolitan Opera House.

Everett Lee was the child of a middle-class black family that was dedicated to his development as a musician, and his story yields a classic example of upward mobility. The wild card was race. Born in Wheeling, West Virginia, Lee moved with his family to Cleveland in 1927 as part of the Great Migration.[16] His father, Everett Lee Sr., climbed up through the civil service, achieving leadership roles in largely white contexts. During World War II, the elder Lee became executive secretary of Ration Board 11 in Cleveland and was credited with inaugurating "a system of making the rationing program fit the individual, [which] stamped out all discrimination involving race or riches." At another point in his career, the elder Lee supervised an office of eighty-five people, "all white employees."[17] Young Everett studied violin at the Cleveland Institute of Music, a historically white conservatory, where he was awarded a Ranney Scholarship and his primary teacher was the famed violin virtuoso Joseph Fuchs.[18] He was also mentored by the famous conductor Artur Rodziński, who was then music director of the Cleveland Orchestra. They met while Lee held a job that was not unusual for people of color. "I had a little off-and-on job at a hotel, running the elevator and as a busboy—whatever I could do to help Dad put me through school. And that's how I met Rodziński," Lee recalled in an interview. "And Rodziński: somebody told him that this kid is a very promising musician, and he just asked me, 'Who are you?' and I told him, and he said, 'Well, come to my concerts.' Every Saturday I could go to the Cleveland Orchestra concerts."[19] Rodziński became central to Lee's development. "My early conducting aspirations were nurtured by him," Lee told a reporter from the *Pittsburgh Courier* in 1948. "Rodziński helped me in many ways—he would go over scores with me and give me pointers."[20]

Lee enlisted in the military in June 1943, becoming an "aviation cadet at the Tuskegee Army Air Field."[21] He was released early because of an injury and recruited for the pit orchestra of *Carmen Jones*. "To the right of renowned conductor, Joseph Littau," reported the *Amsterdam News* in late January 1944, nearly two months into the show's run, "sits the concert meister, in this particular instance a young man of comely appearance, with a face that brightens and shines when you talk about music, and probably the only Negro ever to have held that title."[22] One of his friends from Cleveland, the dancer Royce Wallace, recommended Lee for the job.[23] Very quickly Lee's talent was recognized, and he substituted as a conductor even before his debut with *On the Town*; these conducting assignments included *Carmen Jones* and a revival of *Porgy and Bess* in the spring of 1944.[24] In both cases, it meant leading all-white orchestras within the context of shows with all-black casts and white ownership. Lee recalled these early experiences on the podium as both hair-raising and career-changing. "Look what happened to me," Lee exclaimed. "Joe Littau [conductor of *Carmen Jones*] was snowed in, and I hopped on it. They said, 'Kid, can you take over tonight?' I had never conducted an opera!...Of course, I had played in the orchestra. I knew it by memory. Oh, my tempi were too fast because I was so nervous!"[25]

Thus Lee's appointment as music director of *On the Town* put him fully in charge of a Broadway pit orchestra for an extended period, and the fact that Bernstein hired him bears repeating. At the turn of the twentieth century, Will Marion Cook had conducted all-white orchestras for the production of his *Clorindy* (1896), as well as other shows, yet few if any African Americans had the same experience in the intervening years.[26]

In the mid-1940s, even as *On the Town* was still in its run, Lee was on the rise within top-flight institutions of classical music. He was one of the soloists in

Negro Conducts Broadway Show Orchestra for the First Time

Everett Lee, concert violinist, this week took over the post as conductor and musical director of the Broadway musical hit *On The Town* at the Martin Beck Theatre. The assignment gives Lee the distinction of being the first Negro to wave the baton over a white orchestra in a Broadway production.

When *On The Town* opened almost a year ago, Lee was given the spot as first violinist with the orchestra by Leonard Bernstein, composer of the music. Prior to that, he was assistant conductor of *Carmen Jones*. He was a member of the New York City Symphony Orchestra under Leopold Stokowski, and appeared as guest soloist with the orchestra last March.

Lee is just 25. He is a native of Cleveland, and was concertmaster of the Cleveland Institute of Music orchestra. He was first violinist with the great concertmaster Adolph Busch, and was soloist with the Cleveland Philhar-

Makes Theatre History. Everett Lee, young violinist, who took over the direction of the stage orchestra for "On the Town," chats with Nancy Walker, star of the show.

Announcement of Everett Lee's appointment as conductor of On the Town, *published in* The People's Voice, *September 29, 1945.*

Vivaldi's Concerto for Four Violins, performed in late February 1945 by the New York City Symphony, conducted by Leopold Stokowski. Another violinist that evening was the renowned Roman Totenberg, which signals the level of Lee's virtuosity.[27] Rodziński might have recommended Lee. Rodziński and Stokowski had a close relationship based in part on a shared Polish heritage, and Stokowski had been responsible for bringing Rodziński to the United States as his assistant in 1925.[28] Rodziński also must have provided a link between Lee and Bernstein. When Rodziński left Ohio in 1943 to become conductor of the New York Philharmonic, he hired Bernstein as his assistant conductor.[29]

Meanwhile, Bernstein and Lee continued to work together after *On the Town* closed. In the summer of 1946, both Everett and Sylvia attended Tanglewood, the summer home of the Boston Symphony Orchestra, in the Berkshires of Western Massachusetts. "Lenny talked to Koussevitzky and I got the Koussevitzky scholarship, and I was up at Tanglewood," Lee recalls, "and boy, that was a wonderful experience."[30] There Everett studied with the BSO's conductor, Serge Koussevitzky, and worked with Boris Goldovsky in the opera department.[31] Just as important, he observed Bernstein prepare the American premiere of *Peter Grimes* by Benjamin Britten. At the end of that summer, Lee wrote to Bernstein, "Once again let me say you did a tremendous job with 'Peter Grimes' and thanks again for letting me sit in the back of the pit."[32] Lee referred to a method of observing rehearsals that was standard in training conductors. The summer at

Tanglewood was equally valuable for Sylvia Lee, who served as technical assistant to Goldovsky, which meant she helped coach singers and apprenticed with one of the great opera directors of the day.[33] From late September through October 1946—right after the Tanglewood experience—Everett Lee played first violin for the New York City Symphony, which Bernstein continued to conduct (through the 1947–48 season).[34] But Lee's engagement with the orchestra was limited. "I wish I could be playing with you," Lee wrote to Bernstein, "but...it would be impossible for you to release me when my promised show comes up. Of course you understand how important that is with jobs so scarce!"[35] At some point in the late 1940s, Lee was also a staff violinist with the CBS Orchestra.

Lee faced formidable obstacles. In an interview decades later with the *New York Amsterdam News*, he recalled asking Rodziński for an audition with the New York Philharmonic. This occurred between 1943 and 1947, when Rodziński was the orchestra's music director. "He was afraid to encourage me to try because he didn't want me to be hurt," Lee told the *Amsterdam News*. "He knew that I would not be accepted into the orchestra. This was one of the factors which helped me decide to try conducting."[36] This episode offers a revealing glimpse of Lee's resilience: when told that an opportunity was closed to him, he turned around and aimed for a higher rung on the ladder.

Everett Lee in a photograph by Carl Van Vechten, 1948. Beinecke Rare Book and Manuscript Library, Yale University. Reproduced courtesy of the Van Vechten Trust.

As a result, in 1947 Lee formed the Cosmopolitan Symphony Society, an inter-racial orchestra in New York City. Other outsider (i.e., non-white-male) conduc-tors have implemented the same strategy, as Dean Dixon did in the 1930s and Marin Alsop in the 1980s. Lee's Cosmopolitan Symphony included "Americans of Chinese, Russian, Jewish, Negro, Italian and Slavic origin," as well as several female players; women were also systematically excluded from American orches-tras during this period.[37] The resounding success of the Cosmopolitan Symphony demonstrated not only Lee's musical gifts but also his organizational skill and flair for attracting an audience. The orchestra had a civil rights mission at the core of its organizational philosophy, as the *Amsterdam News* reported:

> The working together of various races for mutual sympathy and understanding has been successfully accomplished in churches, choral groups and other en-deavors, and this effort to combine highly competent musicians in a grand orchestral ensemble as a cultural venture deserves the support and good will of every faithful adherent to the principles of our democracy.[38]

"My own group is coming along fairly well, but of course there is no money in it as yet," Lee wrote to Bernstein. "I hope to make it grow into something good how-ever, and it may be the beginning of breaking down a lot of foolish barriers."[39] Musicians' Local 802 assisted the Cosmopolitan Symphony by waiving its rates for rehearsals. Lee had to pay union scale for performances, however.[40] The or-chestra rehearsed in the basement of Grace Congregational Church in Harlem through the aegis of its minister, Dr. Herbert King. Sylvia Olden Lee was organist at the same church, and her father, James Clarence Olden, was a Congregational minister in Washington, D.C. Everett recalls that James Olden provided a vital link between Grace Congregational and the Cosmopolitan Symphony.[41]

The first concert of the Cosmopolitan Symphony Society took place at the Great Hall of City College, which is located in Harlem, on November 9, 1947, play-ing to "a capacity audience" that reacted with "enthusiasm and unstinted ap-plause" to this "cultural effort which has such historic implications," reported the *Amsterdam News*.[42] The concert blended standard European symphonic literature (Beethoven's First Symphony) with an aria and recitative from *La Traviata* per-formed by the black soprano June McMechen. *Five Mosaics* by the African Ameri-can composer Ulysses Kay received its premiere, and Sylvia Olden Lee was the featured soloist for Schumann's Piano Concerto in A Minor (first movement).

The Cosmopolitan orchestra gave a notable concert on May 21, 1948, at Town Hall, the egalitarian midtown concert facility. The *New York Times* covered the event, which was unusual for the time, praising Lee as a conductor "who pos-sesses decided talent" and the orchestra as a "gifted group."[43] Like Lee's first con-cert, this one blended European classics with a new work by an African American composer (*Brief Elegy* by Ulysses Kay), and it featured black soloists. The Cosmo-politan Symphony gave a second concert at Town Hall in December that same year, this time featuring the well-known black baritone Todd Duncan.[44] Concerts by the organization continued at Harlem churches, and another at the Great Hall of City College in 1952 yielded the orchestra's "finest performance," according to

Nora Holt, classical music critic for the *Amsterdam News*. Described as "thrilling" by Holt, that event played to a "sold-out audience" of 2,100 "uptown music lovers."[45] During this period, Lee conducted elsewhere as well, including as guest conductor for the Boston Pops in July 1949, albeit as part of its "traditional Colored American Night."[46]

Navigating a career in the United States "was a struggle," Lee told me in an interview. He recounted a sobering conversation with the famed lyricist Oscar Hammerstein II:

> First as a violinist, that's how I first made my name, made a splash. Made concertmaster of two orchestras, and then getting on staff at CBS....And then I began to conduct, and naturally my name spread around like fire. And I remember when...Oscar Hammerstein had a big party, and I don't know whether it was at his home or Richard Rodgers's home. And so everybody in the musical world was there, both from the Broadway world and classical world. And so Oscar said, "Everett, come in here, I want to talk to you." He said, "Everett, we've got to explain something to you." So we went into another room, and yeah it was at Rodgers's home—apartment. He said, "You know, Dick and I"—Dick, you know, Richard—"Dick and I have talked about you, and you know we have so many big shows going. We thought to bring you in on one, but you would be the boss. We were going to, we had talked about putting you on the road, sending you on the road with one of our big shows. But you're too well known. If a colored boy is the conductor, and we go into the South, we would lose, we would not be—they would deny our coming in. But I want you to know, Everett, that we had thought about you, and we had planned one of our big shows."[47]

In other words, Lee had achieved enough success so that his name would be recognized in Jim Crow territory, and according to the warped racial logic of the day, that meant he was too accomplished and well known to be hired.

More barriers appeared. Based on the success of his Town Hall concerts with the Cosmopolitan Symphony, Lee approached Arthur Judson, the foremost concert manager of the day, hoping to get work as a guest conductor with established orchestras. Judson managed the New York Philharmonic and the Philadelphia Orchestra, as well as other major American concert organizations and virtuosi. Sylvia Lee recalled what Everett told her about the interview: "Judson turned and said, 'Oh, come in, young man. I'm reading these reviews. They are out of this world. You really have something. But I might as well tell you, right now, I don't believe in Negro symphony conductors...No, you may play solo with our symphonies, all over this country. You can dance with them, sing with them. But a Negro, standing in front of a white symphony group? No. I'm sorry.'"[48] Everett reported to Sylvia that he was "stupefied," adding that Judson told him, "I'm sorry, young man. I told the same thing to Dean Dixon." Everett responded by saying, "Yes, Dean Dixon had to *leave his country* to be a man and a musician." Judson then suggested that Everett consider going abroad.

In 1952, Everett and Sylvia Lee received Fulbright fellowships to study in France, Germany, and Italy, which ultimately marked the first stage in Everett's career in exile. They left the country that fall, and the Cosmopolitan Symphony came to an end.[49] The couple returned to the United States one year later, and Everett was guest conductor with the Louisville Orchestra in what the *New York Times* claimed to be "one of the first concerts in which a Negro has led an orchestra of white musicians."[50] Everett recalls that Sylvia's father was a key figure in setting up this opportunity: Reverend Olden was from Louisville and had recently moved back home.[51] The concert was not part of the orchestra's regular scene but rather was billed as a special event, outside the subscription series.[52]

Major breakthroughs in American opera came for both Everett and Sylvia in the early 1950s. In 1953, Sylvia was hired by the Metropolitan Opera's Kathryn Turney Long Department, and she was credited as the first African American on the Met's staff.[53] As a result, Sylvia was on hand when Marian Anderson made her Metropolitan Opera debut on January 7, 1955. Both she and Everett developed a close working relationship with Max Rudolph, a conductor and central figure in the Met's management. In 1955, Everett Lee conducted *La Traviata* at the New York City Opera, becoming "the first Negro conductor to be engaged by the company," according to the *New York Times*.[54] He went on to conduct *La Bohème* with City Opera the following fall.[55] In 1956, he signed a contract with the National Artists Corporation, one of the most influential management companies for American musicians.[56]

Yet Lee soon became an expatriate. In 1957, he and Sylvia moved to Munich, where he conducted the opera and founded the Amerika Haus Orchestra two years later.[57] That same year, Leonard Bernstein was appointed conductor of the New York Philharmonic, yielding a sharp contrast in the trajectory of their careers. In 1963 Lee became music director of the symphony orchestra in Norrköping, Sweden, southwest of Stockholm.[58] Dean Dixon had conducted the Gothenburg Symphony in Sweden from 1953 to 1960, and Lee held his Swedish post for over a decade, finding Sweden to be a place where he could make music without racial complications.

In 1965, Symphony of the New World was formed in New York City, and Lee became a central figure. An interracial orchestra, Symphony of the New World essentially picked up where the Cosmopolitan Symphony had left off. Out of eighty-eight "top musicians," it included thirty-six African Americans and thirty women.[59] Initially, Everett Lee, Henry Lewis, and James DePriest were the main conductors. DePriest was the nephew of Marian Anderson, and Lewis was then married to mezzo-soprano Marilyn Horne, with whom he collaborated professionally. Coleridge-Taylor Perkinson, who had been music director for Robbins's American Theater Laboratory, also became one of the organization's principal conductors. When Lee returned to the United States to conduct the new orchestra in 1966, the *New York Times* reported that the engagement marked "his first appearances in this country since he conducted for the New York City Opera in 1956."[60] Once again, a Harlem church provided an anchor for the orchestra—this time it was the Metropolitan Community Church—and Dorcas Neal was president of Friends of the Symphony, its fund-raising arm. Neal's husband, Frank, had been among the black dancers in the original production of *On the Town*. Clarissa Cumbo, who had been a supporter of the Cosmopolitan Symphony, was also central to the new organization.[61] Another link to the past came when John H.

Hammond Jr., who had recruited musicians and dancers for *Carmen Jones* in 1943, became vice president of the orchestra's board of directors. "Hammond will renew his friendship with guest conductor, Everett Lee, the American Negro conductor whom he first brought to New York about a generation ago," observed the *Amsterdam News*.[62]

Lee made his debut with the New York Philharmonic as a guest conductor on January 15, 1976. He was then sixty years old, and the concert took place on the birthday of Martin Luther King Jr. Similar to programming of the Cosmopolitan Symphony, the concert included Sibelius's Violin Concerto, Rachmaninoff's Third Symphony, and *Kosbro* by the African American composer David Baker. Harold Schonberg of the *New York Times* gave Lee a positive if patronizing review, stating that he "conducted a fine concert" and "made good music without bending over backward to impress." While "a Philharmonic debut can be heady stuff," Schonberg concluded sardonically, "Mr. Lee . . . refus[ed] to be drawn into the temptation to give the audience cheap thrills."[63] This breakthrough for Lee occurred during the U.S. Bicentennial, when awareness of supporting African American performers and composers was at an all-time high.[64] Bernstein was then the orchestra's laureate conductor.

In the ensuing years, Lee has continued to have a successful career working with orchestras around the world. During the 1940s and 1950s, when Lee built his reputation as a conductor and stepped onto major stages in Europe, American conductors were absent from podiums in the United States, no matter what their race. For a conductor of color, barriers defined the game. No prominent African American conductor of classical music from the generation born before 1925— not Dean Dixon, not Everett Lee—was permitted a sustained position on the playing field. Yet Lee resiliently created opportunities for himself, essentially establishing his own league.

DANCER IN *ON THE TOWN*'S SUBWAY SCENE: ROYCE WALLACE

The four black dancers in *On the Town* also had noteworthy careers, and Royce Wallace opens a journey through their individual odysseys. "Royce Wallace, who dances in and out of several scenes," enthused Joe Bostic in his review of *On the Town* for *The People's Voice*, "comes close to being the shapeliest bundle of personality to ever answer a cue on anybody's stage."[65] Like Everett Lee, Wallace (b. 1923) was recruited from Cleveland to join *Carmen Jones*. From there, she moved on to the dance chorus of *On the Town*, where she was the subject of three feature articles for black newspapers, including the *Cleveland Call and Post* (Wallace's hometown paper), Baltimore's *Afro-American*, and *The People's Voice*.[66] "Royce Wallace was an extraordinary talent," recalls Billie Allen.[67] In *On the Town*, Wallace was featured in the "Subway Scene," where she was part of a mixed-race ensemble of five dancers, including Sono Osato, Frank Neal, Frank Westbrook, and Malka Farber. Described rapturously over the years as "the beautiful tan singer," "the Negro beauty," and "luscious-looking [with] a sex-appealing figure," Wallace not only danced and acted but was also a jazz singer.[68] Although her career never resulted in high-flying success, Wallace consistently kept working, largely in secondary roles and dance choruses, and black newspapers continued to cover her career, as did the trade magazine *Variety*. After *On the Town*, she appeared in a series of productions both on Broadway and off, and eventually she moved into films and television, with appearances in a large number of individual TV episodes. Race defined the roles that came her way.

Like Everett Lee, Royce Wallace moved with her family to Cleveland as part of the Great Migration. Born in Kentucky, Wallace was an honors student, graduating in 1941 from Cleveland's Central High. At the time "nine-tenths" of its students were "members of the Race," reported the *Chicago Defender*.[69] Wallace received training as a dancer at Karamu House in Cleveland, traveling with its modern dance troupe to perform at the New York World's Fair in 1940.[70] Initially known as the Playhouse Settlement, Karamu House was a settlement house that focused on interracial theater and the arts, producing shows with mixed-race casts as early as 1917.[71] It continues to thrive in the twenty-first century. "Through personal contact with each of us as members, and with all of the members in the group, we exchanged ideas and became like a family," Wallace later recalled of her experience there. "Modern dance enriched our minds, broadened our mental outlook, and established self-confidence. We sweated, we worked, and stretched our imagination to the limit."[72] While dancing at Karamu House, Wallace had a day job as one of World War II's many "Rosie the Riveters," working as part of a team of "airplane riveters at the American Stove Company."[73] Because industry needed to expand the workforce as men headed to the battlefield, the war opened up job opportunities not only for African Americans but also for women.

In August 1943, Wallace auditioned for Eugene Loring when he traveled to Cleveland with John H. Hammond Jr. to recruit dancers for *Carmen Jones*. Loring selected Wallace together with two other dancers from Karamu House, and he "praised the Karamu dancers as the best trained modern dance group in the country."[74] Their teacher was Eleanor Frampton, a white modern dancer who had performed in early vaudeville with Martha Graham and studied at the Humphrey-Wiedeman School, one of the leading dance schools in the country.[75] After *Carmen Jones*, Wallace auditioned for *On the Town*, and her performances onstage repeatedly attracted attention. "In the show, she does interpretative ballet dancing that brings her tremendous applause," reported the *Afro-American*.[76] That same newspaper wrote of Wallace's photograph in the show's lobby.[77] "New York critics rant constantly about this former Karamu dancer, Royce Wallace," noted the *Cleveland Call and Post* with pride.[78]

After *On the Town*, Wallace had steady work for a time on Broadway, often together with others from the show. In 1946, she appeared together with Flash Riley in an all-black production of the Greek comedy *Lysistrata*. Choreography was by the white dancer Felicia Sorel, who worked both in concert dance and on Broadway, including a revival of *Run, Little Chillun* in 1943. Even though *Lysistrata* lasted only a few nights, it featured some major performers, including Rex Ingram (from *Cabin in the Sky*), Etta Moten (who played Bess in the 1943–44 revival of *Porgy and Bess*), Fredi Washington (who appeared in the original

Lysistrata, with an all-Negro cast, comes to the Belasco, Oct. 12, includes dances by Felicia Sorel. *Above:* dancers J. Flash Riley and Royce Wallace

Flash Riley and Royce Wallace in Lysistrata, *as published in* Cue, *October 5, 1946.*

Shuffle Along and in Ellington's short film *Black and Tan* of 1929), and the young Sidney Poitier. It also included Valerie Black and Mable Hart, who had been part of Agnes de Mille's *Black Ritual*.

In December that same year, Wallace joined the chorus of *Beggar's Holiday*, Ellington's mixed-race musical. Once again a number of colleagues from *On the Town* were by Wallace's side: the white dancer Malka Farber, the stage designer Oliver Smith, and the lighting designer and technical supervisor Peggy Clark. Besides being among the dancers, Wallace also had a small role as Annie Coaxer, for which she was singled out by the *Amsterdam News*.[79] *Beggar's Holiday* had ties to the political left. A preview was sponsored by the Council on African Affairs, a left-leaning anticolonial organization, and the show was covered in the *Daily Worker*.[80] While the *Worker*'s review criticized the show on artistic grounds, claiming it "promises more than it performs," it complimented the production for shaping an interracial cast "in which the Jim-crow line is dissolved."[81]

Increasingly, theater revues became Wallace's specialty, and she continued to intersect with dancers and actors from *On the Town* as she performed in both all-black and interracial casts. Noteworthy shows included *St. Louis Woman* (1946), where Wallace was an understudy for the famed Pearl Bailey, and *Inside U.S.A.: A New Musical Revue* (1948), where she joined the ballet dancer Talley Beatty, who was a close friend of *On the Town*'s Frank Neal. Beatty had of course danced with Katherine Dunham in *Cabin in the Sky* and went on to become a leading figure in American ballet, especially in his collaborations with Duke Ellington and Alvin Ailey.[82] In 1950, Wallace took part in a brief revival in the Bronx of the all-black show *Mamba's Daughters* (1953), in which Flash Riley and Billie Allen also performed, and in 1955 she had a supporting role alongside Sono Osato in *Once Over Lightly*, an interracial revue with sketches by Mel Brooks and Ira Wallach.[83]

Wallace also had been stepping forward as a singer, appearing in March 1951 at the interracial Village Vanguard. *Variety* claimed it was "her first club job" and gave her a strong review. Wallace had "an intriguing singing style," *Variety* declared. "It is her slow rhythm numbers that sell best, due perhaps to her greater familiarity with them."[84] Wallace was back at the Vanguard in November, where she appeared on a bill with Harry Belafonte and the comedian Phil Leeds. "Royce Wallace makes a stunning appearance," *Variety* reported. "Altho she's not an exciting performer, Miss Wallace is certainly an accomplished one. It's possible she might enter the former category with the acquisition of a more individualistic style and material."[85] The white dancer Allyn Ann McLerie recalled hearing Wallace sing in the dressing room of *On the Town*: "She sounded just like Billie Holiday. She was great."[86] From April through July 1952, Wallace appeared again at the Village Vanguard, where she shared the stage for a time with the white folk singer Richard Dyer-Bennet; at another point, she appeared again with Belafonte.[87] *Variety* weighed in once again, this time with a racially tinged version of its telegraphic jargon. "Miss Wallace has a relaxed, effortless manner and puts across a tune with sock effect," *Variety* observed. "At show caught, Negro chirper rated a begoff."[88]

Wallace then experimented with working abroad. In 1954, she performed at Chez Nous in Paris, also at the Mars Club in Germany, and in the fall of 1955, she got a booking in Bermuda at a nightclub called the Angels Grotto.[89] On Christmas Eve that same year she married Alexander Outerbridge, "a tall handsome aristocrat" who was a "scion of a founding family of Bermuda" and owner of the Grotto.[90] The marriage attracted a lot of press, with the *Amsterdam News* calling it "one of the most highly publicized interracial marriages in a decade."[91] Outerbridge and Wallace were flagrantly ostracized in Bermuda.[92] "Sometimes it gets really creepy around here," Wallace told a reporter; she spoke of "anonymous phone calls and letters from mysterious strangers," which were "really crazy and mixed up." The couple separated in less than a year.[93]

Wallace got back to work quickly, starring in *Nuts to You*, a revue produced by the Harlem Showcase at the YMCA Little Theatre on West 135th Street. "Royce Wallace is known to many people here and abroad," declared the *Amsterdam News*.[94] In fact, her stock seemed to be rising, as she took on more prominent roles, "heading" a "summer show" directed by Noble Sissle at Wells' Upstairs

Room (1959) and performing alongside James Earl Jones in *The Pretender* at the Cherry Lane Theatre (1960).[95]

An important break came in the early 1960s, when Wallace was cast in *Funny Girl* (1964), starring Barbra Streisand, and the network of *On the Town* continued to work its magic, with Jerome Robbins as production supervisor for the show. "He [Jerry] reached back and got me, and I had a ball. I loved that show," Wallace later told Robbins's biographer Greg Lawrence.[96] Wallace, who was then forty-one and past the age for dancing, played a named role in *Funny Girl*: Emma, the maid who worked for Fanny, the role played by Streisand. "Wallace has a wonderfully warm role," reported the *Pittsburgh Courier*, using language that echoed the reception of *On the Town* twenty years earlier. "The production is deliciously mixed from orchestra pit to stage," the newspaper continued. "For the first time the chorus, boys and girls, and the show girls are a mixture of all the races. . . . *Funny Girl* . . . will give all a brilliant opportunity to see democracy in action on the broad expanse of the Broadway stage."[97] Wallace continued to play maids, including in the films *Goodbye, Columbus* (1969) and *Funny Lady* (1975), which also starred Streisand.

Beginning in the 1960s, the bulk of Wallace's work shifted to television, with appearances in more than fifty shows that stretched from *East Side/West Side* (1963) to *The Fresh Prince of Bel-Air* (1992) and *Sirens* (1993).[98] With television, she found steady employment over a thirty-year period. Wallace played Minnie in the first two episodes of the famous television series *Roots* (1979), and she appeared in some of the best-known shows of the 1970s and 1980s, including *The Bill Cosby Show* (1971), *The Waltons* (1973), *Kojak* (1975), *Good Times* (1976), *Sanford and Son* (1972–76), *Barnaby Jones* (1975–77), *Hill Street Blues* (1982), and *Roseanne* (1989). In 1993, when the cast reunion for *Carmen Jones* took place in New York City, Wallace was there.[99]

Royce Wallace proved to be a flexible performer, shifting from dancing to singing to acting, from stage to nightclubs to films to television. It is fascinating to track such an extended and durable career that did not have the benefit of a breakout success. Wallace maintained strong connections to performers from *On the Town*, working consistently with members of the show. Most of her employment over the years either came from all-black productions, especially in the early stages of her career, or involved playing racially marked characters, especially maids. In the 1950s, when she was achieving some success as a singer, her forward momentum was interrupted by her interracial marriage and the tabloid publicity that ensued. When Wallace returned to New York City, she did so as a stage actress, and the number of her appearances on television is noteworthy.

SAILOR FROM *ON THE TOWN*, DUNHAM DANCER, AND VISUAL ARTIST: FRANK NEAL

Remembered by Sono Osato as a "very good ballet dancer, very graceful," Frank Neal was featured with Royce Wallace in the "Subway Scene" of *On the Town*.[100] Neal (ca. 1915–1955) reorients the story to Chicago, where he was raised within the energetic ambitions of the city's African American arts culture. He danced with Katherine Dunham's company, and he was equally active as a theater designer and a painter, with his art featured in prominent exhibitions over the years. Neal had a gift for surrounding himself with intriguing people. In Chicago, his extended circle encompassed Dunham as well as the composer Margaret Bonds, the poet Gwendolyn Brooks, the sociologist Horace Cayton, the soprano Etta Moten, the painter Charles W. White Jr., and the writer Richard Wright.[101] When Neal moved to New York City, appearing first in *Carmen Jones* then in *On the Town*, he remained close to Chicago friends who had also relocated, including Talley Beatty and the painter Charles Sebree. The *Chicago Defender* amply covered Neal's career, and a striking number of his artistic associates from Chicago were interviewed in their later years, offering rich insights about the artistic milieu in which he was raised.

Yet another child of the Great Migration, Frank Neal was born in Palestine, Texas, and moved with his family to Chicago as a child.[102] His mother, Alice J. Neal, was a well-known educator in Chicago and one of the founders in 1928 of the Chicago DuSable League, which was "dedicated to the preservation and dissemination of the history and culture of Chicago's first permanent non-Native-American settler, Jean Baptiste Pointe DuSable, a Black man."[103] Frank studied for six years at the School of the Art Institute of Chicago, where he received a first-prize scholarship in painting, and he also attended the Lewis Institute (now the Illinois Institute of Technology).[104]

Neal's youth in Chicago centered around African American community and art centers on the South Side, and many of his friends were exploring both the visual arts and performance. That neighborhood yielded "a lot" of young artists, with "a lot going on," recalled John Carlis, a South Side designer and painter of Neal's generation.[105] Neal was a member of the Art Crafts Guild, a club of young black artists who "met every Sunday afternoon in each other's homes," according to artist Margaret Goss Burroughs. In 1935, he exhibited work in a show of "27 race artists" that was sponsored by the Art Crafts Guild, and he was also deeply tied to the South Side Community Art Center.[106] Like many African American artists in Chicago during the Depression, Frank Neal was mentored by George Neal (1906–1938; no relation), who also both painted and danced.[107]

Frank Neal's training as a dancer began in the mid-1930s with Sadie Bruce (ca. 1908–1993), a successful African American dancer in Chicago's theaters and clubs who ran a South Side dancing school for over fifty years.[108] There Neal learned both tap and theater styles. Remarkably, he also danced with the Chicago Civic Opera Ballet, where he received classical training under the white dancer Ruth Page.[109] Neal's path to the Chicago Civic Opera Ballet was probably the same as that of Charles Griffin, another black Chicagoan around Neal's age. As a kid, Griffin later recalled, he performed in a production of *Heaven Bound*, an influential black folk drama that was staged at his church on the South Side, and recruiters from the Chicago Opera Company were in the audience:

> I had been in a play at our church, Albert Baptist Church. They used to, once a month, give musicals there, and they gave this musical called "Heaven Bound." . . . Some people were—some guests—were there from the Chicago

Opera Company. So, they asked me if I was interested in dancing or ballet.... So the chance to dance, and dance with the Opera Company was something.... But many of the people—dancers—that came out of Chicago at that time, they worked with [Ruth] Page at the Chicago Opera Company.[110]

Talley Beatty recalled being discovered through the same route. He was also in *Heaven Bound* "at the Baptist church ... and they asked me if I'd like to work with the Chicago Opera Company."[111] In November 1936, Neal performed with Ruth Page's dance company in *An American in Paris*, a ballet starring the white tap dancer Paul Draper that was choreographed to the score by George Gershwin. The performance took place at Chicago's Civic Opera House.[112]

As the 1930s progressed and Neal moved into his twenties, his artistic ambitions remained multifaceted, and Chicago continued to be his home. In the fall of 1938, he was art director of *Don't You Want to Be Free?* by Langston Hughes, produced by the Negro People's Theatre. It encompassed a remarkable group of artists. Margaret Bonds was music director, Charles Sebree joined Neal as art director, and Etta Moten, who later starred in the early 1940s revivals of *Porgy and Bess*, was also involved.[113] The Negro People's Theatre had ties to the Young Communist League and to churches on the South Side.[114] Neal was also helping produce the annual Artist and Models Ball, which was an elaborate artistic and theatrical spectacle sponsored by the South Side Community Art Center and held at Chicago's Savoy Ballroom. Artist William McBride later recalled that "one of the great balls" was produced by Etta Moten and that Frank Neal was a leading figure.[115] In 1941, the theme was "Pan-Americana," and Neal designed "the dedication number."[116] Katherine Dunham was honored at the event, which also included an exhibit of sculptures by the African American artist Augusta Savage.[117] During this period in Chicago, Neal and his wife, Dorcas, who was also a dancer, had a salon for local artists, as McBride stated.[118]

While Neal was dancing with Dunham's company, his colleagues included Talley Beatty and Janet Collins, who later made history as the first African American prima ballerina hired by the Metropolitan Opera House. Dunham's company did not have the resources to rehearse throughout the year, as Beatty later recalled, but "perseverance" kept them together. "We would do three performances a year," Beatty remembered. "All of the rest of the year there was practically no company. But when Dunham would announce that she was going to do the concerts, then people would come back."[119] The troupe's performances in Chicago took place at the Abraham Lincoln Center on the South Side. Neal traveled with Dunham and her dancers to Los Angeles in 1941 and to Iowa in 1942, as programs attest.[120] Dorcas Neal "danced with the group, too," recalled McBride.[121] Numerous biographical profiles of Frank Neal over the years—mostly included in theater programs—claimed that he performed with Dunham in the film *Stormy Weather* in 1943; many of Dunham's dancers in that film, including Neal, are not credited, however.[122] Late that same year Neal opened in the dance chorus of *Carmen Jones*.[123]

Neal's friendship with Talley Beatty was central both professionally and personally. While Neal gravitated toward Broadway shows, Beatty focused on concert dance, with only occasional work in theater.[124] "Talley was a very delicate, dashing type of person," stated McBride. "He had a lot of finesse and he and Frank Neal

"Frank Neal and the Beauteous Mable Curtis are shown in the number 'Convoy to Rio' to be presented at the Artists and Models Ball October 24th, Saturday, at the Savoy Ballroom, sponsored by the South Side Community Art Center. This year's ball excels all previous year's record-breaking productions in its sensational, breath taking dances and choreography." *Photograph probably dates from 1941 and includes the caption.* William McBride Jr. Papers, Harsh Research Collection, Chicago Public Library.

looked a little alike. They used to wear these sombreros from Mexico in the summertime, have them real straight and stiff and be wearing white shoes."[125] When *On the Town* was in development, Beatty was invited by Robbins to join the dance chorus, but, as he recalled, "I didn't take the job."[126] Robbins's papers include an undated roster of dancers for the show, and Beatty's name appears there. Male dancers are listed in one column and female in another. In each case, a pair of African Americans is notated separately at the bottom: Neal and Beatty in the left column, McNichols and Wallace on the right.[127] This suggests that Neal and Beatty were initially hired together, which means that Flash Riley probably replaced Beatty. "I was so crazy then," Beatty later recalled, adding that he also did not accept a spot in *Finian's Rainbow* and rejected work on the film version of that show.[128]

With the stage production of *Finian's Rainbow* in 1947, not only did Frank Neal take the offer, but he became dance captain of an interracial dance chorus.[129] It was a noteworthy appointment, putting Neal in charge of white colleagues. Flash Riley was also in the dance chorus, as was the white dancer Cyprienne Gableman, both from *On the Town*.[130] The plot of *Finian's Rainbow* delivered a lighthearted homily about racial tolerance. It "makes a huge joke of racial stereotypes, and lightly caricatures some of the more stalwart defenders of white supremacy," observed the *Pittsburgh Courier*.[131]

During this entire period, Neal continued to paint, and coverage of his achievements as both dancer and visual artist shifted from the *Chicago Defender* to the *New York Amsterdam News* and, notably, the *New York Times*. In the 1940s his work appeared in New York City at an exhibit "by a group of Negro artists" at the McMillen Gallery on East 55th Street and also at an interracial exhibit at the International Print Society on West 57th Street, which had been founded as a forum for nonwhite artists.[132] Charles Sebree and Romare Bearden also participated in the McMillen show. While *Finian's Rainbow* was in midrun, Neal won a $300 prize for his painting "Oppression," which was exhibited at Atlanta University's sixth annual Exhibition of Paintings, Sculpture and Prints by Negro Artists.[133] He also turned to interior design and began painting lamp shades, screens, and window shades.[134]

At some point in the 1940s, Neal and his wife, Dorcas, established an artistic circle in New York City, informally dubbed the Neal Salon.[135] It was a version of the social sphere they had enjoyed in Chicago. Talley Beatty and Charles Sebree participated, as did Billy Strayhorn, creative amanuensis of Duke Ellington. "This group was a breeding ground for a certain group of artists at a certain time when they had nowhere else to go," observed Dorcas Neal in an interview with Strayhorn's biographer David Hajdu. She continued:

> It was like Bloomsbury. In this group, these people could be the artists they were and be dealt with like artists. They all faced a lot of the same problems and a lot of the same questions regarding their careers and their place in the world, which really was a white world at the time. Together, I think they were able to answer many of those questions for each other and solve those problems and become successful in the world. . . . Really, the group was mostly people who were black and gay—but not everybody, mind you. I guess you could say this was a safe place to be.[136]

Talley Beatty and Billy Strayhorn were both gay, and Frank Neal's sexual orientation is unknown (he and Dorcas had two daughters). Others in the Neal Salon included the composers John Cage and Lou Harrison, the singer Harry Belafonte, and the writer James Baldwin.[137]

Beatty shared vivid memories of evenings spent with the Neals, recalling "animated" conversations. "Everything was criticized [and] no one came away unscathed," Beatty remembered. It was "a black gathering, very sociopolitical," he continued.

We had all worked with prominent white people—myself, with Jerome Robbins—and we had done well with them, up to a point. At the salon, we could discuss our observations and frustrations together and argue about them, which is what inevitably happened. I had been reviewed in the *New York Times*, and I said, "This should be worth about fifty thousand dollars. But look at me—I can't get a job!"[138]

Frank Neal's work on Broadway continued with *Peter Pan*, a mixed-race show that opened in April 1950, and once again Flash Riley joined him. A version of the famous children's story with music and lyrics by Bernstein, this show had quite a long run but was eclipsed four years later by a completely separate version starring Mary Martin.[139] In the *Peter Pan* of 1950, Neal and Riley played "Indians" (Neal was listed in the program as Fred Neal).[140] When the show went on the road, Neal took the role of the dog, Nana. "The part, which is played entirely in pantomime, requires the dexterity of a trained dancer," reported the *Pittsburgh Courier* about Neal's new role, "and that is just what Frank turns out to be."[141]

Neal kept painting. The glossy magazine *Jet* reported in 1952 that he had "recently made a big sale of a choice painting to movie director Vincent Minelli [*sic*]" and that he "soon will have a one-man show in Hollywood."[142] He designed costumes for the Talley Beatty Dance Group (formed in 1952), and he also designed sets for the American Negro Theatre.[143] In 1953, he started to sell hand-painted trays, as the *Chicago Defender* announced.[144]

All this activity and talent screeched to a halt in May 1955, when Neal died in a car accident on the Grand Central Parkway in New York.[145] He was forty. An impressive number of obituaries appeared in publications such as the *Chicago Defender*, *New York Times*, *Amsterdam News*, *New York Herald Tribune*, and *Variety*.[146] Emerging from the racial and artistic consciousness-raising of interwar Chicago, Neal had structured an unusual career, with accomplishments both onstage and in the visual arts, and *On the Town* provided him with an opportunity to pivot from all-black to interracial productions. The shift turned out to be definitive, for all of his subsequent work in the theater took place in top-flight integrated shows. Yet by the early 1950s, Neal was facing the same diminished opportunities that affected black performers overall. At the same time, he was approaching middle age, which can signal a difficult transition for dancers. Neal did not live long enough to participate in the major victories for black dance that lay just around the corner, especially the founding of the Alvin Ailey Dance Company (1958) and the Dance Theatre of Harlem (1969).

JITTERBUGGER FROM *ON THE TOWN* AND VERSATILE ACTOR: FLASH RILEY

Flash Riley (1916–1988) danced alongside Frank Neal as a Sailor in *On the Town* and was among the jitterbuggers in the "Real Coney Island" scene. Rather than emerging from the worlds of ballet or modern dance, as was the case with Neal and Wallace, Riley had a different background, which lay in acting onstage and dancing in nightclubs.[147] His name appeared as James Flashe Riley in the opening-night program for *On the Town*, and he was most often called "Flash Riley" by friends and colleagues. Over the years, he performed under a string of related names, including J. Flash(e) Riley, Flash(e) Riley, Jay Riley, Jay Flash Riley, Jay J. Riley, Joe Flash Riley, James Riley, and Jay Merriman Riley.[148] Extending through the early 1950s, Riley worked in a series of interracial shows, and he was among those who maintained strong ties to *On the Town*'s network of performers. Mostly, however, his employment came from all-black productions. Some—notably Richard Wright's *Native Son* and Jean Genet's *The Blacks: A Clown Show*—had a political edge, and Riley capitalized on the resurgence of black entertainment during the U.S. Bicentennial, including revivals of *Carmen Jones* and *Mamba's Daughters*. Like Everett Lee, Riley relocated to Europe for a considerable stretch of time—in his case, for much of the 1960s and 1970s—where he ran successful touring productions of *Bubbling Brown Sugar* and *Trumpets of the Lord*. In an interview with the *Los Angeles Times* in 1977, Riley discussed race openly, and he was exceptionally articulate on the subject. "I'd left New York [for Rome] with lots of Broadway credits under my belt—'Finian's Rainbow,' 'On the Town,' 'Carmen Jones,'" Riley observed, "but I was black and in those days black was not beautiful."[149] Over the course of a long career, Riley kept in touch with Robbins and to a lesser extent with Bernstein, with letters from him preserved in their archives. In 1981 the jazz scholar Eddie Determeyer interviewed Riley at length in Holland.

When members of the original cast of *On the Town* hear Riley's name, they chuckle with delight. He was "a character," exclaimed Billie Allen. "He was larger than life—flamboyant...He was a wonderful talent...and ridiculous. And he would try anything and therefore [was] so accessible as a performer because he was open." She perceived him as gay. "I remember...he got distracted during a lift and dropped me. It was funny, because it was like, 'What were you thinking?' I think some beautiful man must have walked in the room."[150] Allyn Ann McLerie responded with similar exuberance. "Flash Riley! He was great," McLerie recollects. "He was a character. He was funny, and he was crazy, and kind of wild and wonderful."[151] According to Jean Handy, "I laugh because he was a big ham. And he was tall and thin. And I got to dance with him a little at one point."[152] Sono Osato remembers, "He was tall, gangly, had a marvelous smile, kind of crooked. He was just—he had a terrific personality, and he was not as refined as Frank [Neal]."[153]

Flash Riley spent his childhood in Scranton, Pennsylvania, and recalled getting hooked on theater when he attended a traveling performance of *The Chocolate Dandies*. A successor to *Shuffle Along*, this all-black revue by Eubie Blake and Noble Sissle was on tour during 1924–25. Thus for Riley, early all-black shows were not just the stuff of newspaper accounts but rather a real-life force that captured his imagination as a child. Riley remembered:

My father worked in the Hotel Casey, which is a big hotel [in Scranton]. This black troupe came through called "The Chocolate Dandies," Eubie Blake's show

... There was no place for blacks to stay; they weren't allowed in the hotel. So they asked the waiters could they put up somebody, and [my segregated neighborhood] put up all the people in the show—Miss Jenkins next door [to our family] and myself... And they gave us a pass to the show and I went to see it. The show was absolutely sensational. It had horses on the stage, galloping on a treadmill. [*Makes horse sounds*]...I was 8 or 7 or something, and I was amazed. I never got over it. I couldn't sleep that night. I thought, you can make a living doing that!... And then the next year, my father, who was West Indian, and [my family], we moved to New York.[154]

In New York City, Riley made good on his family's investment by pursuing a career in the theater. As a young adult, he appeared in *Swing It*, yet another show by Eubie Blake, which was produced in 1937 by the Federal Theatre Project's Vaudeville Unit at Harlem's Lafayette Theatre. A review of *Swing It* captured the visceral energy of his performance. "Miss [Frances or Francine] Everett... teamed with a wild, spirited dancer, James (Flash) Riley, in an African jungle scene of superb staging and novel costuming," enthused the *Chicago Defender*. "In this glamorous, colorful situation, Francis and 'Flash' turn on the heat in a wild, fantastic 'love dance.'"[155] Years later, Riley recalled this production in a letter to his close friend Lorenzo Tucker: "I did a sensational dance routine that opened the second act with pretty Francine Everette [*sic*]."[156] Tucker was an accomplished actor best known for lead roles in the early black films of Oscar Micheaux.

According to his own account, Riley spent 1938–40 in vaudeville, and then he found work on Broadway.[157] Remarkably, he was in the cast of *Native Son*, a stage adaptation of the black protest novel by Richard Wright, which opened in 1941. Riley took the role of Jack, a friend of Bigger Thomas, the main character played by Canada Lee. The play was directed by Orson Welles and produced by him and John Houseman.[158] "I didn't do comedy. I wanted to be a serious actor," Riley later stated in the interview with Determeyer. "Of course there were no jobs for blacks in the theater. There was *Green Pastures* and *Porgy* (not *Porgy and Bess*)....You had to dance in those days to make a living, and I had big long arms."[159] He also claimed to have a photographic memory. So Riley worked mostly as a dancer, performing in the dance chorus of *Carmen Jones*, where he was dubbed "one of the dancing geniuses."[160] At the same time, he was also dancing in nightclub shows, working with a string of top-flight musicians including Duke Ellington, Billie Holiday, Jimmie Lunceford, Red Norvo, and Fats Waller.[161] A fabulous photo from the *Amsterdam News* in 1944 shows Riley wearing an elaborate headpiece for an appearance at Smalls' Paradise, a well-known Harlem club.[162]

Then came *On the Town*. When the show reached the final leg of its run and took to the road, Riley got upgraded from the dance chorus to a program listing as a Sailor.[163] In Chicago, he was also included in the dance ensemble for "Carried Away," the wacky number sung by Claire and Ozzie.[164] After *On the Town*, Riley's career often ran in tandem with those of other black dancers from the show. In 1946, he joined Royce Wallace in the all-black production of *Lysistrata*.[165] Riley then worked with Frank Neal in *Finian's Rainbow* and Bernstein's *Peter Pan*. Except for a revival of *Finian's Rainbow* at City Center in 1955, Riley's career during the 1950s and early 1960s was increasingly tied to all-black productions, and he performed frequently in road tours. In early 1952, he was in an all-black touring production of the play *Harvey*, which included his friend Lorenzo Tucker as well as Butterfly McQueen and Dooley Wilson.[166] Then in 1953, Riley appeared with Royce Wallace and Billie Allen in *Mamba's Daughters*, an all-black show revived by Equity Community Theatre in the Bronx.[167]

Work on Broadway was hard to get, and in 1954 Riley set out on an American tour of *Carmen Jones* in a cast that initially included Muriel Rahn and Avon Long. *Variety* offered an illuminating perspective on audience demographics, reporting that around the same time, Dick Campbell, the African American manager of the tour, launched two other black touring productions. He anticipated the shows would perform for "about 90 percent Negro audiences," describing tours on the so-called Chitlin' Circuit, which targeted black audiences, especially in the South.[168] Campbell published an extended article in the *Chicago Defender* describing the stress of traveling across the country under Jim Crow restrictions. Flash Riley was part of the story. For much of the *Carmen Jones* tour, Campbell managed to avoid the problems of hotel segregation "by playing [historically black] colleges where housing was always available, and large southern towns where fine colored homes were open."[169] One night, however, the cast got tired on a drive from Alabama to Chicago, and they needed to stop. The bus pulled over at a hotel in Terre Haute, Indiana, and Campbell, who was light-skinned, went to the desk alone, successfully obtaining rooms. Once the hotel's managers realized they had rented to twelve African Americans, they tried to evict the cast. Campbell threatened to contact the press, and he won the battle, declaring that "Jim Crow just lost a round."

The late 1950s yielded an up-and-down period for Flash Riley. In February 1958, he pitched an idea to Jerome Robbins for "a very exciting Caribbean version of 'Macbeth' with the text virtually intact, with all the roaring melodrama contained, but the locale moved to a Negro Kingdom such as 'Haiti' in the early nineteenth century." Riley appealed directly to Robbins's ego: "It takes one with the ingenuity and inventiveness that you possess to work this into a great masterpiece of the American Theatre."[170] Nothing came of the idea. That December, Riley's career was at a low point when he worked as Santa Claus at Blumstein's Department Store on West 125th Street.[171] The next year he won an Ira Aldridge–Rose McClendon Memorial Scholarship "for Negro actor students," permitting him to study at the Paul Mann Actors Workshop in New York, which was an influential site for Method Acting.[172] The following year, Riley was back on his feet, appearing with Royce Wallace in off-Broadway productions of Langston Hughes's *Shakespeare in Harlem* and James Weldon Johnson's *God's Trombones*.[173]

Riley's most notable acting engagement of this period came with the successful and historically important off-Broadway production of the French avant-garde play *The Blacks: A Clown Show* by Jean Genet, which opened in the spring of 1961.[174] Talley Beatty was choreographer, and the cast included such luminaries as Maya Angelou, Cicely Tyson, and James Earl Jones. The production ran through September 1964, becoming something of a cult classic. The black actor and director Arthur French went "every night" to watch the production. "I must have seen the play at least one hundred times," he later told an interviewer. "Those people were amazing."[175] *The Blacks: A Clown Show* was a strident and controversial play. "A group of colored players," summarized the *New York Times*, "enact before a jury of white-masked Negroes...the ritualistic murder of a white of which they have been accused."[176] Flash Riley did a comedy routine as part of the play, which Maya Angelou recalled in her memoir. "His face and body jumped and skittered and his eyes opened and shut in rhythm," Angelou wrote; "his lines were funny and unexpected, so the boys beside me howled in appreciation."[177]

From the mid-1960s stretching well into the 1970s, Riley went into exile in Europe, at first settling in Rome. He appeared among the massive cast of *Cleopatra*, which was filmed in Rome in 1963, although his name is not on the official cast list.[178] He cited the film on his resume, and Wilbur Bradley, a Dunham dancer who was also involved with the film, told an interviewer: "I believe every Negro in Europe was in the movie. Among them was Flash Riley."[179] While living in Europe, Riley produced a revival of *Trumpets of the Lord*, a gospel musical that had originally opened in New York in 1963, and that production sustained Riley for a number of years.[180] "I'm up to my neck in producing but it's dull work," Riley reported to the *Amsterdam News* in 1965. "I'd much rather be up on the stage making noises. But still it's a long way from playing Santa Claus in Blumstein's on 125th Street."[181] The show was a big success. "Paris gave an enthusiastic reception tonight to 'Trumpets of the Lord,'" reported the *New York Times* in 1967: "This entertainment from New York's Circle in the Square is representing the United States at the Théâtre des Nations Festival. It was received with such overwhelming enthusiasm at its premiere and has evoked such high praise from French critics that an extra Saturday matinee has been added."[182]

Riley looked back on these years as rewarding. "I formed my own company of black actors that toured the Continent, playing most of the major cities in Western Europe," he told the *Los Angeles Times*. "The experience was a mind-blower. For the first time in my life, I was completely accepted without regard for race or color."[183] When casting *Trumpets of the Lord*, Riley posted a call for black actors in the *Amsterdam News*: "He says if there are any Negro artists who anticipate being in Europe this summer they should send him their photos and resumes."[184] "When I was in Rome," declared the actress Jane White, "this crazy man Jay 'Flash' Riley heard that my husband and I had arrived there, and he said, . . . 'I've got this package of Trumpets of the Lord, based on James Weldon Johnson's God's Trombones.' He had been touring it throughout Europe, and people loved it. Any Black actor who came through Rome, he grabbed and put them into it."[185] By November 1965, Riley was reported as having "a new deluxe Volkswagen Camper-Land Yacht which substitutes as a traveling hotel for part of the cast and carries all of the scenery."[186] A year later, Riley had "been bouncing like a yo-yo around Europe with his 'Trumpets of the Lord' company."[187] All these reports came from the *Amsterdam News*, which clearly viewed Riley as important enough to keep track of his whereabouts.

Bubbling Brown Sugar, which opened on Broadway in 1976, offered another major wave of work for Riley. A nostalgia show, *Bubbling Brown Sugar* was set in a Harlem nightclub between the wars and paid tribute to the history of black jazz, including music by Count Basie, Eubie Blake, Duke Ellington, and Fats Waller. Riley was not in the original Broadway cast. Rather, he was part of a "second cast touring production," playing the central role of Checkers Clark. "Vernon Washington, Mable Lee, and Jay Flash Riley caper in the roles performed here last autumn by Avon Long, Thelma Carpenter, and Joseph Attlee," reported the *Chicago Tribune*. "The talent is just as dedicated and delightful as it was eight months ago."[188] Starting in June 1977, Riley was a replacement in *Bubbling Brown Sugar*'s Broadway production.[189] During this same period Riley also took part in *The Wiz*, another major black musical that opened on Broadway in 1975. There too he had a replacement role, in this case as the Cowardly Lion.[190]

Other than *Bubbling Brown Sugar*, Riley's work in the United States remained erratic. In 1975, he appeared in individual episodes of the black television series *Sanford and Son* and *Good Times*.[191] In 1977, he was reported as having "resettled" in Los Angeles.[192] As it turned out, though, he continued to be peripatetic. In the fall of 1979, he was staying at the Times Square Motor Hotel while doing "a couple of auditions for B'way shows," he wrote to Lorenzo Tucker.[193] "Did final audition today," he reported a couple of weeks later. "*Not so hot*. Maybe returning to Calif. Next week."[194] In 1981, he appeared in an episode of the television show *The White Shadow*.[195] Two years later, Riley was back in Europe, starring in a production of *Bubbling Brown Sugar*, which brought him briefly back in contact with Bernstein. At some point during this period, when Riley and Bernstein were both in Amsterdam, Riley sent a note backstage: "Mr. Leonard Bernstein, With fond memories of 'On the Town'—'44. Jay Flash Riley will be paying you homage tonight. In attendance, Flash. May I pop in, after?"[196] The note was written on stationery for "Bubbling Brown Sugar in Europe."

For several years, *Bubbling Brown Sugar* was Riley's main source of employment. "Experienced leadership comes from ... J. Flash Riley (old style comic and jazz singer)," reported *The Stage and Television Today*. "Indeed, the cast are now probably better than their show," the review continued. "This is essentially a team production by a versatile company who can deliver all the black music there ever was from hot gospel through ragtime, jazz, blues, and scat to forties swing, and pitched true—sung, not shouted."[197] The touring company of *Bubbling Brown Sugar* gave "command performances" for Queen Beatrix of Holland and Prince Harald and the royal family of Norway.[198] It traveled to England and Germany, among other countries.[199] After the tour ended, Riley settled in Amsterdam, opening an office there for the American Negro Festival Theatre, and he directed *Trombones*, "a new version of 'God's Trombones' with SOUND & Light," as he reported to Lorenzo Tucker.[200] In 1987, he was back in Los Angeles, where he appeared in the television movie *A Gathering of Old Men*, as well as in an episode of *Frank's Place*. Riley died in Los Angeles in 1988.[201] A program for his memorial service appears among Jerome Robbins's papers, together with a note that Robbins had "sent flowers."

The career of Flash Riley offers a transgenerational odyssey in black musical theater. Starting with a childhood experience of watching Eubie Blake's *The Chocolate Dandies*, then launching his career in *Swing It*, *Native Son*, and *Carmen Jones*, Riley succeeded within the world of black entertainment, right up through *The Blacks: A Clown Show*, *Bubbling Brown Sugar*, and black shows on television. At the same time, Riley constantly tried to maneuver more widely and flexibly within a business with rigid constraints. Would he have moved beyond secondary roles without Jim Crow? That was the $64,000 question for American blacks of Riley's generation, and it makes assessments of careers such as Riley's deeply problematic.

REPLACEMENT DANCER IN *ON THE TOWN* AND DISTINGUISHED DIRECTOR: BILLIE ALLEN

As *On the Town* moved to the end of its Broadway run and then took to the road, the cast shifted. Allyn Ann McLerie replaced Sono Osato, Don Miller replaced Cris Alexander, and in the dance chorus Billie Allen replaced Royce Wallace. Allen (b. 1925) went on to an influential career as dancer, actress, and director, consistently disrupting the color line and fusing performance with social activism. She managed to negotiate the black-performance logjam of the 1950s and 1960s more successfully than any other black cast member from the show. Allen was hired as a model at a time when modeling agencies were largely closed to African Americans, and she broke through race barriers in television commercials in the 1950s. Not only has Allen's career been amply covered in both the black press and mainstream media, but she has also been interviewed repeatedly over the years, especially for her starring role in the first production of Adrienne Kennedy's controversial play *Funnyhouse of a Negro*.[202]

Wilhelmina "Billie" Allen was a twenty-year-old dancer in New York City as *On the Town* moved into its extended run. Thus she was five to ten years younger than the show's already youthful cast, which placed her in a slightly different position in relation to the unfolding of the civil rights movement. Raised in an upper-middle-class family in Richmond, Virginia, Allen got the job with *On the Town* through contacts in the world of black dance.[203] "I met these friends—Frank Neal," Allen states. "And he said, 'You should audition for this, because we're replacing people. . . . We are looking for dancers to end the Broadway run and for the national tour.' So I did, and I got into the show, and I was very excited because [of] Jerome Robbins. And because I had seen *Fancy Free* . . . It was just such a high. . . . I remember Glenn Tetley was also in the company that went in when I did—and he became a very, very celebrated ballet dancer and choreographed for ballet companies all over the world."[204] Allen had attended the Hampton Institute, a historically black college in Virginia, and she studied dance in New York City during the summers, while her mother worked on a doctorate at Columbia University's Teachers College. Allen describes her mother as "politically active." "When I was a little girl," Allen states, "she would take me to hear James Jackson. . . . He was organizing the tobacco workers into a union, and that was very dangerous, very dangerous. He later became editor in chief of *The Daily Worker* and secretary of the Communist Party, and my mother sometimes took me to Camp Unity."[205]

In the years immediately after *On the Town*, Allen balanced dance, theater, and professional modeling. She appeared in the short-lived show *Caribbean Carnival*

Billie Allen dancing with Alan Dixon in a dance act called "Alan and Angel," 1944 or 1945.
Personal collection of Billie Allen; reproduced courtesy of Billie Allen Henderson.

(1947), a "calypso musical" that included the well-known black dancer Pearl Primus, and she also danced with Claude Marchant's Afro-Cuban Dance Company.[206] At the same time, Allen started to work for the Brandford Modeling Agency, one of the first black modeling firms, which was founded in 1946 to reach a growing black middle-class market.[207] Allen at first appeared in magazine and newspaper ads, then on television. In 1949, she was listed as part of a group of "Negro models" who were to be employed in ads for Colgate Dental Cream. "The Negro market is accounting for a steadily increasing portion of American purchasing power," the *Philadelphia Tribune* reported.[208]

Allen also remained active onstage, initially through dance and musical comedy. Then she branched out into dramatic acting, working with a series of distinguished theatrical figures. In 1950, she appeared in *Head of the Family*, a "new Negro comedy," together with Etta Moten, Fred O'Neal, Avon Long, and Harry Belafonte.[209] Two years later she was among the lead dancers—together with Louis Johnson and Arthur Mitchell—in the revival of *Four Saints in Three Acts*, which opened on Broadway, and the following year she appeared in *Mamba's Daughters* in the Bronx, in the same performance as Royce Wallace and Flash Riley.[210] Around the same time, Allen auditioned for Tennessee Williams's *Camino Real*, which opened in 1953. While she did not get the role, she caught the attention of director

Elia Kazan, who arranged a scholarship so she could study Method Acting with Lee Strasberg.[211] From then on, she was cast in an important series of theatrical shows, such as *Reuben Reuben*, a musical by Marc Blitzstein (1955), and *Take a Giant Step*, a "touching drama about a Negro boy" that appeared off-Broadway (1957).[212] According to one theater historian, *Take a Giant Step* helped "prepar[e] the way for Lorraine Hansberry's triumph, *A Raisin in the Sun*" (1959). With the latter, Billie Allen was again on the scene, as an understudy and replacement in the role of Beneatha Younger.[213]

One of Allen's most important roles was in Adrienne Kennedy's experimental play *Funnyhouse of a Negro*, playing the lead character Sarah.[214] A racially charged work from 1964 that has become a landmark in African American literature, the play explores Sarah's inner struggles over her racial identity. "Adrienne Kennedy delves into the black psyche," Allen stated in an interview, "exposing our universal demons to the scrutiny of the light."[215] "It's completely surrealistic," Allen explained in a separate conversation. "It's happening in Sarah's mind, in her nightmares, in her dreams."[216] Many people found *Funnyhouse of a Negro* to be "horrifying," Allen recalls. "People could not understand this groundbreaking play," she continues. "Black people were very upset about putting our business and tightly held secrets in the street."

Allen also pushed past the color barrier on television. She played a WAC named Billie on *The Phil Silvers Show*, doing so in an era with few integrated television shows. A successful Jewish comedian, Silvers was praised by the black press for producing "one of the few national programs that presents an interracial cast regularly."[217] Allen appeared in thirty-six episodes of the show between 1955 and 1959, although often without credit.[218] Allen had another breakthrough in 1963, when she and the actress Vinnie Burrows made a television commercial for Oxydol, becoming, as the *Amsterdam News* reported, "the first network commercial seen on television done around a Negro." The article continued, "It is taped straight and, what's more, is not a 'Negro' product aimed at 'Negroes.'"[219] Then Allen broke yet another color barrier by appearing on the soap opera *Flame in the Wind* in 1965.[220] "ABC Steps Up Integration on Daytime Soapers," declared a front-page headline in *Variety*. She had "a key role...portraying an apartment house confidante to one of the serial's stet characters newly arrived in Manhattan."[221] Allen had outstripped the history of black actresses playing maids.

In 1962 Allen made another bold move in joining Juanita Poitier (wife of Sidney Poitier) to form "a theatrical brokerage firm" that was designed "to raise money from backers."[222] "Not many women have tried to be brokers for a Broadway production, and certainly no Negro women," reported the *Amsterdam News*. During these same years, Allen was in the supporting cast of *Black Like Me* (1964), a film about a white newspaperman who posed as African American and traveled through the deep South, documenting egregious racism. Based on a book by John Howard Griffin, it was "filmed entirely on location, in secrecy, in Maryland, Virginia, Washington, D.C., and on the West Coast of Florida with an interracial cast and crew," the *Amsterdam News* reported. "The working title 'No Man Walks Alone' was used to protect the location company and to avoid interference from or violence by extremist groups."[223]

In the 1980s, Allen stepped forward as a director. "Billie Allen believes you can do anything if you want it enough," declared the *New York Amsterdam News* in 1982. "In her show business career, Billie has danced, has been an actress for fifteen years, and has taught at Nassau Community College. Now she's directing."[224] A notable early production was a revival of *Funnyhouse of a Negro* at the Tisch School of the Arts at New York University in 1984.[225] "I remember Jerry [Robbins] came to see the play," Allen recalls of the NYU production, "and [he] thought it was kind of a ballet."[226] Thus her work as a dancer became part of the sensibility that Allen brought to directing, and just as for Royce Wallace and Flash Riley, her tie to Robbins remained vital. Allen has directed many other works, ranging from *The Brothers* by Kathleen Collins, which was mounted as part of the Women's Project at the American Place Theatre (1982), to *St. Lucy's Eyes*, starring Ruby Dee at the Cherry Lane Theatre (2001).[227] Plays confronting the issues of black women are her special focus. "I treat actors with a great deal of caring and respect," Allen declares. "I'm interested in people who are willing to take chances; willing to make mistakes and be outrageous to achieve something meaningful. Life is like that. You can't just play it safe. You have to take risks."[228]

FORESHORTENED CAREERS: LONNY JACKSON, MELVIN HOWARD, AND DOROTHY MCNICHOLS

The careers of the remaining African Americans from the original cast of *On the Town* appear to have peaked with the show. Lonny (also Lonnie) Jackson was the Policeman in *On the Town*, a "handsome young tenor" and "eye arresting cop" who wandered across the stage in the interstitial chase episodes and performed in the show's chorus.[229] Jackson captured critics' attention in two profiles published in the spring of 1945: one (very brief) in *The People's Voice* and another (more extensive) in Baltimore's *Afro-American*. Jackson's "greatest ambition," the *Afro-American* reported, was "to sing the role of 'Othello' in one of the major opera houses." "I know singing in the Metropolitan Opera is impossible at present because of my color but I may yet get the chance with the Chicago Opera Company," Jackson confided with the idealism of youth. "I believe this country is becoming more democratic every day, and I have my hopes."

Born in Brownwood, Texas, around 1914, Jackson attended three Texas schools: Howard Payne College, Sam Houston College (both historically white), and Wiley College (historically black).[230] In 1933, Jackson earned front-page coverage in the student newspaper of Howard Payne College for an event that inspired a rapturous reception. "The colored evangelical singer," the *Yellow Jacket* reported, "received more real applause than almost any performer that has appeared in chapel." Jackson was "the only negro ever to receive training in the Howard Payne Voice Department," and he was scheduled to perform in a quartet at the Chicago World's Fair (1933), "in order to raise funds for the endowment of one of the colleges of which he is a graduate."[231]

Jackson kept winning scholarships and capitalizing on new opportunities for voice study. He moved to Chicago at some point in the late 1930s, after receiving "a scholarship to the Chicago Musical College," and he aimed for a career in classical music.[232] When the Chicago Negro Choral Club gave a performance of Handel's oratorio *Samson* in Chicago's Orchestra Hall in the spring of 1938, Jackson was one of the soloists, and he placed third among tenors in the interracial Chicagoland Music Festival a few months later.[233] Jackson was "the people's choice" in the Chicagoland contest, reported the *Chicago Daily Tribune*. "He sang twice, easily and with a graciousness that brought his listeners to their feet cheering." At the time, he was earning a living as a waiter. The next year, Jackson had a lead role (Nanki-Poo) in a Chicago production of *Swing Mikado,* which went on tour.[234] He then served in the army for a little over two years. "I was quartered at Camp Wheeler, Ga., where I sang and entertained the men," Jackson told the *Afro-American*. "I also acted as representative for our group whenever any prominent entertainers performed for us. I received my honorable discharge and came to New York eight months ago."[235]

That interview was published in May 1945, suggesting that Jackson had been brand-new to the city when he auditioned for *On the Town* in the fall of 1944. Immediately after *On the Town*'s Broadway run was over, Jackson studied at the Institute of Musical Art (now known as the Juilliard School), where he earned diplomas in the Voice Program and the Extension Division.[236] In 1947 he was among contestants for the Marian Anderson Award in New York City, but did not win.[237] He also auditioned to perform at Café Society, although the result is not known. It appears that Lonny Jackson then abandoned his hopes for a career as a professional musician.

Dorothy McNichols was another performer whose career did not extend very far beyond *On the Town*. "Dorothy McNichols was an African American woman," recalls Billie Allen. "I think she was from the Bronx, because she was so unusual—she had a real Bronx accent. And it was unusual seeing an African American woman—hearing her with this Bronx accent."[238] McNichols danced in *Carmen Jones*. In an interview with Robbins's biographer Greg Lawrence, McNichols discussed the racial difficulties encountered when *On the Town* went on tour:

> We had trouble all over the road, being the first integrated show. We left New York and went to Baltimore, Maryland, and they wouldn't let me in backstage to work. They said we weren't in the show, and my picture was out front! Oh, and then we had to send for Jerry, and Jerry gave them a few choice words, you know, swore at them. He said, "If you keep any of my people out of this theater, you're gonna lose your jobs." There were all sorts of stories. In Pittsburgh, they wouldn't serve us between shows for dinner. In Chicago, we were put out of a hotel. They said all of the sudden they had a convention. It was terrible. Jerry had a conscience, you see, because he had to struggle because of the prejudices.[239]

In 1948, McNichols joined a number of white dancers from the *On the Town*—including Atty Van Den Berg, Frank Westbrook, and Nelle Fisher—in the first production of Theatre Dance, Inc., a new ensemble that performed at the 92nd Street Y.[240] After that point, newspaper coverage ends. Over the years, McNichols remained friends with Jean Handy, a fellow dancer from *On the Town*, and Handy recalls that McNichols moved with her husband to California and became a teacher.[241] "We have kept in touch all these years," says Jean Handy, "and about two or three years ago she died. But her family lives on the West Coast...She knew some of the dancers, and kept in touch with them in New York."[242] McNichols was among the dancers who participated in the *Carmen Jones* reunion in 1993.[243]

Melvin Howard (b. 1914) was also in the singing chorus of *On the Town*. A native of South Carolina, he enlisted in 1941 at Camp Upton Yaphank, New York.[244] Howard then appeared in *Carmen Jones*.[245] After *On the Town*, his name appears a few times in black newspapers in connection with nightclub dates and social events during the 1940s.[246] He too seems to have given up on the entertainment business.

* * *

All in all, the African Americans in the original cast of *On the Town* added up to a diverse and capable group of young professionals—each brimming with talent, each poised as a twentysomething to seize the opportunities and face the challenges that lay ahead. Collectively, their biographies disclose the racial barriers faced by performing artists of color after World War II. They also demonstrate how a key opportunity such as dancing in *On the Town* or conducting its pit orchestra could launch or enhance a career—or not.

The odysseys of the African American performers in *On the Town* unfolded alongside a fraught but accelerating civil rights movement and the repressions of the Red Scare. In chronicling the experience of jazz artists in pursuing racial justice during this same period, Ingrid Monson writes of the "racial fault lines around which individual artists negotiated their careers."[247] Indeed, the African Americans in *On the Town* danced, conducted, and acted in a landscape that was deeply unstable, and they did so with varying degrees of success. Most became artistically versatile as they pursued careers in a business that was notoriously rough, even without race in the mix. "Until the last weeks of the season ending with the breezes and buds of May," wrote Miles M. Jefferson in his report on the 1951–52 season, "the Negro hardly participated at all in activity which, even for the Caucasian, was the most dismal in several decades on Broadway."[248] And Jefferson was chronicling only one moment in time. Performers of color consistently faced inhibiting constraints, and the career narratives of those involved with *On the Town* demonstrate how an employment gap opened in the 1950s between the stereotyped roles so common in early black performance and the attainment of equitable racial representation and color-blind casting. As opportunities in mixed-race shows diminished, all-black entertainment became a haven, and for a time in the early 1950s, those shows were largely revivals. Furthermore, even though none of *On the Town*'s black performers had sufficient celebrity to be targeted by HUAC or the McCarthy Committee, they had to contend with the repercussions of a broad-based attack on progressive impulses in the American entertainment industry. As a result, artistic organizations became more cautious, and fear restrained left-wing advocacy. Yet another variable for *On the Town*'s black performers came with the rise of television, which was racially restrictive in the

1950s yet extended new employment possibilities during the 1970s with the emergence of all-black sitcoms and television specials.

Racial bias is insidious and slippery to track. Yet when a whole segment of the population is denied access to a particular area of employment, the resulting exclusions are not so subtle. Such was certainly the case with both opera and symphony orchestras in the 1940s and 1950s—two areas of American classical music with the highest cultural prestige and largest operating budgets. Two of *On the Town*'s black performers, Everett Lee and Lonny Jackson, worked on Broadway even though classical music was their real passion. While Jackson abandoned his ambition of singing at a major American opera house, Everett Lee built a successful career by being entrepreneurial, at first through forming his own orchestra in Harlem, with a black church as his base of support. Along the way, Lee had a significant series of guest appearances at illustrious American performance institutions, doing so at auspicious historical moments. This was the case when Lee became the first African American to conduct the orchestra of the New York City Opera in 1955, the same year Marian Anderson stepped to the footlights at the Metropolitan Opera. And it was also the case when he conducted the New York Philharmonic on the birthday of Martin Luther King Jr. in 1976, eight years after the civil rights leader had been assassinated.

Almost every performer of color in *On the Town* had a family history shaped by the Great Migration, and several were raised in the vibrant black artistic communities of Chicago, Cleveland, and New York. Collectively these figures participated in shaping the major trends in black entertainment after World War II. In the late 1950s and early 1960s, the civil rights movement created a climate in which racially charged dramas began to appear. Flash Riley (in *The Blacks: A Clown Show*) and Billie Allen (in *Funnyhouse of a Negro*) both stepped into that performance space with professional success. Then the U.S. Bicentennial ushered in a new wave of employment possibilities, whether through featuring black conductors such as Everett Lee in the programs of high-ranking American musical institutions, through television series such as *Roots* in which Royce Wallace joined a celebrated exploration of African American history, or through a new generation of black musicals in which Flash Riley appeared as a legacy figure, conjuring up a golden age of black entertainment. Exile to Europe became another means of career survival, and it was achieved through study abroad, government-subsidized travel, working for European musical organizations, or independently producing shows that toured the continent.

When all was said and done, *On the Town* opened its stage and orchestra pit to the exhilarating virtuosity of a group of African American performers, making it possible to oppose racial segregation publicly, even if only for an evening's entertainment. No revolution occurred, but for at least a few gifted performers, new opportunities came into view.

MUSICAL STYLE

7
CROSSOVER COMPOSITION
The Musical Identities of
On the Town

• • •

Although On the Town *is largely about contemporary young people, and is lighthearted and fanciful, even at times surreal, its score has a symphonic texture unlike that of any musical comedy before or since.*
—*Betty Comden and Adolph Green*

The glittering world of musical theater is an enormous field that includes everything from your nephew's high-school pageant to Götterdämmerung.
—*Leonard Bernstein, in "American Musical Comedy" telecast*

Leonard Bernstein liked to shape an argument in which Broadway musicals existed on a "continuum," as he stated in an *Omnibus* television broadcast in 1956, with "the variety show at one end and the opera at the other." In this formulation, Minsky's Burlesque stood on a par with *Götterdämmerung*, with musical comedies seizing an egalitarian "middle ground," as he put it. Rather than being defined by how they conformed to the parameters of a well-established genre, musicals were characterized by their capacity for flexibility, especially in relation to high-low qualities. While Bernstein posed this argument to characterize musical comedy in general, he was also articulating a framework for his own compositional style. In a sense, he was validating the cultural status of an aspect of his artistic life that was disdained by many of his classical-music colleagues. When Bernstein offered a list of the composers who provided his primary models, as he did in this *Omnibus* broadcast, he singled out those whose works hovered in a liminal artistic space, unfettered by traditional genre definitions. First came Marc Blitzstein with *The Cradle Will Rock*, "his odd, original opera."[1] Then Kurt Weill with *Lady in the Dark*, which "brought his whole German training to Broadway." And finally George Gershwin with *Porgy and Bess*, which "had invaded the opera house." Aaron Copland, whose voice had been powerfully resonant in *Fancy Free*, was nowhere in sight.

On the Town emulated the crossover aspirations of Blitzstein, Gershwin, and Weill, and as Bernstein's first Broadway show, it set in place a compositional philosophy and artistic style that defined much of his future work in the theater. *On the Town*'s music was thoroughly accessible to listeners, yet it was also often complex and unconventional, making it a challenge to perform. With it, Bernstein established aesthetic diversity as central to his compositional identity, and he found he was most comfortable in creative environments filled with surprising juxtapositions. He devised a recognizable voice, working within established norms yet most often challenging and even disrupting them. "From Lenny I learned to approach theater music more freely and less squarely," wrote composer Stephen Sondheim. He continued with an exceptionally insightful assessment of Bernstein's somewhat out-of-the-box style:

> I had been brought up to think of Broadway songs in terms of four- and eight-bar phrases, as Berlin and Porter and Rodgers and Kern—even Gershwin— did. Lenny taught me by example to ignore the math. Four bars may be expected, but do you really need them all? How about three bars? And why have the same number of beats in every bar? How about varying the meter? I was used to this in contemporary concert music, but I had never experienced it on Broadway until *On the Town* had exploded on me.[2]

This tendency to "ignore the math" by devising asymmetric phrase lengths and an unorthodox handling of Broadway forms became a defining trait of Bernstein's mature writing. Although other composers had employed related practices before, especially Blitzstein in *The Cradle Will Rock*, Bernstein turned a strategy that had been atypical into a signature aspect of his musical style.[3]

This chapter begins with the show's opening scene, which combines a spiritual-inflected number for vocal ensemble—one deeply indebted to Gershwin— with a razzle-dazzle Broadway anthem. The music of the show is then divided into three different types: ballads, which provide the vocal tunes at the core of any musical's identity; comedic vocal numbers, which in *On the Town* played a significant role in upending the power balance between men and women; and symphonic writing for the show's extended segments of ballet, which set *On the Town* apart from most of its contemporaries.

Bernstein as composer moves to center stage in this chapter, as selected segments of *On the Town* are explored in terms of musical style, dramatic and choreographic function, and process of revision. The last emerges through close readings of existing manuscripts for the score and script, combined with programs, ephemera, and correspondence documenting various stages of the show. The experience of reading this chapter will be greatly enhanced by listening to recorded excerpts, as listed in the discography in the Appendix. Various iterations of the show's script are central to the discussion, including the version published in 1997.[4] Some of the draft scripts are composites—that is, they splice together segments that appear to be of different vintages. For the music, the published piano-vocal score is the principal text, together with the orchestral score (now available through rental).[5] Bernstein's papers include sketches for some numbers, and piano-vocal scores prepared by copyists also enter the discussion.[6]

When the curtain rose, the audience attending the original production of *On the Town* witnessed the Brooklyn Navy Yard at dawn, with Workmen and Girls milling about as they waited for the newest shipload of sailors to disembark. "The movement is all slow and quiet—but there is an air of expectancy—of a day about to begin," states the published script.[7] Music opens the show when three Workmen and a male quartet sing "I Feel Like I'm Not Out of Bed Yet." The scene then segues immediately into "New York, New York," sung by Chip, Gabey, and Ozzie. The two interlinked numbers, which fill the entire scene, announce a show that pushed the boundaries of a standard Broadway musical by overflowing with music, and they introduced the creative style of a brand-new songwriting team. From the first sounds, it is clear that young Bernstein—the composer on that team—owed a debt to the work of George Gershwin. It was also clear that at twenty-five he had already established a signature compositional voice, which capitalized on his deep love for both the classical and popular worlds. This emerging composer identified with earlier creative figures on Broadway who leaned toward opera and operetta, as well as with those who crossed race lines, absorbing musical tropes of urban black America into their compositions.[8]

"I Feel Like I'm Not Out of Bed Yet" fits into a lineage that I term "Broadway spirituals"—that is, songs from musicals that were written by white composers and lyricists and emulate African American spirituals. It incorporates call-and-response, with blue notes and melismas that almost seem improvised, and it conjures up the sound world of "Summertime" from Gershwin's *Porgy and Bess*, which Bernstein knew very well. "Summertime" was also an opening number, and it mentioned a baby. While a teenager in Boston in 1935, Bernstein had attended out-of-town previews for *Porgy and Bess*, initiating his exceptionally close relationship to the work, and in 1942, not long before *On the Town*, he had conducted two scenes from the opera as assistant to Serge Koussevitzky at the Tanglewood Music Festival.[9] He had other models as well. "Ol' Man River" from *Show Boat* (Jerome Kern and Oscar Hammerstein II, 1927) stood at the head of a lineage of Broadway spirituals. *Show Boat* also takes place on a dock, albeit on the Mississippi rather than in New York Harbor. The lineage also extended beyond *On the Town* to include, for example, "Thousands of Miles" in the show *Lost in the Stars* (Kurt Weill and Maxwell Anderson, 1949). In the case of "I Feel Like I'm Not Out of Bed Yet," its opening lyric also vaguely recalled an actual African American spiritual, "I Feel Like a Motherless Child," and a link to the Christian heritage of spirituals appeared in an early draft, where "Sleep, sleep in your lady's arms" had been "Sleep, sleep in Jesus' arms."[10]

In many ways, "I Feel Like I'm Not Out of Bed Yet" announces *On the Town* as a mixed-race show, yet it does so with caution. Production flow charts reveal that while the show opened with both black and white Workers onstage, whites were at the center of the action. The white singer Marten Sameth took the solo for Workman I, and the other members of the trio were Frank Milton (Workman II) and Herbert Greene (Workman III), both of whom were white. The following members of the dancing and singing chorus were onstage for "I Feel Like I'm Not Out of Bed Yet," as listed in production flow charts. African American performers are indicated with an asterisk:

Singers (all listed as Workers):

Sam Adams
*Melvin Howard
*Lonny Jackson
Robert Lorenz
Milton Taubman
Roger Treat
Benjamin Trotman

Dancers:

Carle Erbele (St[reet] Sweeper)
Jean Handy (Worker)
*Frank Neal (Worker & Sailor)
*James Flash Riley (Worker)[11]

Performers from the singing chorus handled backup vocals, taking the part of the Men's Quartet, and it is unclear whether the dancers also sang. Thus an opening number written by a team of whites with music coded as black—albeit within a white lineage of Broadway spirituals—was performed by a white trio with mixed-race background vocals.

Quietly and unpretentiously, "I Feel Like I'm Not Out of Bed Yet" announced the arrival of a new composer who worked within contemporary theater tradi-

Table 7.1. "I Feel Like I'm Not Out of Bed Yet": Overall Structure

First stanza: "free and flowing"

A	mm. 3–10 (8 bars)	Workman I
B	mm. 11–16 (6 bars)	Workman I
B¹	mm. 17–20 (4 bars)	Men's Quartet + Workmen II and III (spoken)

Second stanza: waltz rhythm in accompaniment

A	mm. 21–28 (8 bars)	Workman I
B	mm. 29–36 (8 bars)	Workman I
B¹	mm. 37–40 (4 bars)	Men's Quartet + Workmen II and III (spoken)

Third stanza: returns to opening accompaniment

A	mm. 41–48 (8 bars)	Workman I
B	mm. 49–54 (6 bars)	Workman I
B¹	mm. 55–57 (3 bars)	Men's Quartet + Workmen II and III (spoken)

tions yet traded on imaginative handling of those norms. It divides into three stanzas, each of which falls into three internal sections of unequal lengths (see Table 7.1). Within a musical realm where 8-bar phrases were the norm, Bernstein immediately signals his tendency to "ignore the math," as Sondheim put it.[12]

Two aspects of "I Feel Like I'm Not Out of Bed Yet" deserve to be singled out. First, the vocal writing is demanding, with Workman I traversing down the interval of a thirteenth (essentially one and a half octaves) in the first half of the A section (Example 7.1, mm. 2[pickup]–6). Then he leaps up an octave plus flat seventh (m. 7) and finishes the initial phrase with a bluesy vocalise. This is the opening salvo of an overall tendency in *On the Town* to draw upon tropes from opera and operetta—especially with strategic placements of high notes—and fuse them with then-current modes of popular songwriting, often with a blues-based edge. Second, the handling of rhythm in "I Feel Like I'm Not Out of Bed Yet" also exhibits aspects of stylistic fusion. Designated "free and flowing" at the opening, the number combines the fluidity of imitating African American vocal improvisation with that of an operatic recitative. In the first stanza, the B section changes to duple meter (at the words "Oh the sun is warm"), then back again to triple (at "Sleep, sleep") to achieve this sense of free-flowing suppleness. Harmonically, the first stanza unfolds over a sustained F in the bass, and it is unresolved, even slightly unstable, until the stanza's final chord, which resolves to an F-major tonic triad with added seventh.

"I Feel Like I'm Not Out of Bed Yet" was written early in the process of developing the show, and it changed little along the way. "Gosh!" exclaimed Jerome Robbins in an interview with Lehman Engel in which he discussed the opening scene overall. "Almost every show I have worked on has had—some problems with the opening. Not *On the Town*. That was very clear."[13] Even though the number was indeed stable from early versions of the script and score, pencil notes in the papers of Comden and Green show its embryonic emergence. The pencil draft includes three male sailors clumsily named "Gable, Denny & Mitch," and the basic concept of the lyric was in place. Otherwise its "tra la la's" had little connection with Broadway spirituals, instead signaling Gilbert and Sullivan. Here is the first stanza from this very early draft. When compared with the final version, it shows a considerable gap between initial ideas and a well-shaped final lyric:

"I Feel Like I'm Not Out of Bed Yet"

Draft Lyric—Opening	Final Lyric—Opening
I feel like I still was in bed yet	I feel like I'm not out of bed yet. Oh—
I'm feeling o.k. but I'm sleepy as hell	Oh, the sun is warm,
I'm feeling quite well	But my blanket's warmer.
But sleep is so swell.	Sleep, sleep in your lady's arms.
But I'm up & tra la la la la la la[14]	[Men's Quartet] Sleep in your lady's arms.[15]

An early sketch for the melody of what was initially titled "Prologue" also reveals that the song became more bluesy—more Gershwin-like—as it progressed. Of special interest is a draft of the opening phrase of the melody (transcribed in Example 7.2a), which includes none of the blues-based inflections of the final version. At this early stage of development, it is also simpler and easier to sing. It shares a basic architecture with the final score, however, with downbeats on the same pitches in the first and second measures (compare to Example 7.2b). Yet it is intriguing to see how other pitch choices in this early attempt were far less interesting.

Example 7.2. *Comparison of manuscript and published versions for the opening melody of "I Feel Like I'm Not Out of Bed Yet."*

Ex. 7.2a. *Transcription of the manuscript version, mm. 1–4, with pickup. Bernstein Collection B26/F10.*

I feel like I'm not out of bed yet.

Ex. 7.2b. *Published version, mm. 3–6, with pickup.*

I feel like I'm not out of bed yet.

"I Feel Like I'm Not Out of Bed Yet" leads immediately into the second half of the opening scene, featuring "New York, New York," which became the best-known song of the show—largely from its performance by Frank Sinatra, Gene Kelly, and Jules Munchin in the 1949 film of *On the Town*.[16] Sono Osato later described "New York, New York" as a "paean of syncopated song and patter," declaring it to be "a song that made swing almost classical."[17] It was a brilliant observation, capturing the show's irrepressible energy and its essence of cultural mergers. Heralding the action onstage as three sailors walk off the ship, "New York, New York" is scored for full theater orchestra with a brassy swagger. "Enter three sailors" is given as the stage direction for the sailors' initial appearance, providing a direct link to *Fancy Free*, where the opening movement used that same phrase as its title.[18] In the lingo of swing, "New York, New York" is up-tempo.

"New York, New York" takes bolder compositional steps than "I Feel Like I'm Not Out of Bed Yet." At the very beginning, tone clusters herald the beginning of a new day (Example 7.3), replicating sounds of urban activity, whether car horns or train whistles. This musical trope was familiar from movie scores and orchestral works like Gershwin's *An American in Paris*. Bernstein's love of asymmetry is immediately apparent, with unpredictable placement of the clusters, shifting accents, and a freewheeling metrical scansion (see arrows in Example 7.3).

The initial vocal trio for the three sailors establishes the sonic identity of the show with an exhilarating 5-bar sound bite. The melody leaps up an octave, and the sailors sing in counterpoint (Example 7.4).[19] Throughout "New York, New York," there is a balance of popular-song conventions with disruption of their norms. The vocal segments of the number divide into three stanzas, each with the semblance of a verse and chorus and with internal patterns that fall into 2- and 4-bar cells.[20] None of that is unusual. Yet the verse and chorus fuse into a single entity, and each component has equal weight, defying the usual practice of establishing the chorus as the core of the tune.[21] Plus, the verse-like portion is longer than the so-called chorus, and its final phrase is unusual, ending with a one-measure interjection that changes from the first stanza to the second (compare Example 7.5a to 7.5b).

Example 7.3. "New York, New York," opening, mm. 1–8.

The lyric, meanwhile, announces the main themes of the show in the first stanza:

CHIP
We've got one day here, and not another minute
To see the famous sights!
OZZIE
We'll find the romance and danger waiting in it
Beneath the Broadway lights.[22]

Furthermore, that same stanza makes it clear that gendered characterizations and frank articulations of sexual desire are central to the thematic mix:

Example 7.4. "New York, New York," initial vocal tag, mm. 45–50, with pickup.
Voices only.

GABEY
New York, New York,_____

CHIP
New York, New York,_____

OZZIE
New York, New York,_____

Meno mosso

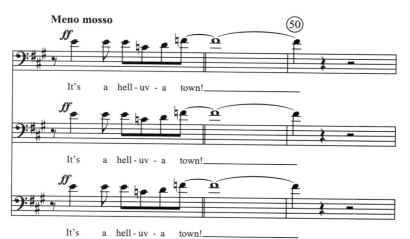

It's a hell-uv-a town!_____

It's a hell-uv-a town!_____

It's a hell-uv-a town!_____

GABEY, CHIP, OZZIE
But we've hair on our chest,
So what we like the best
Are the nights!
CHIP
Sights!
OZZIE
Lights!
GABEY
Nights!

"New York, New York" was written early in the process of creating the show, and it remained largely intact, although some of the lyrics were changed.

Example 7.5. "New York, New York":

Ex. 7.5a. Conclusion of verse in Stanza 1 (m. 62).

Ex. 7.5b. Conclusion of verse in Stanza 2 (m. 98, with pickup).

One deleted verse has interesting aspects. It opens by identifying Chip and Ozzie as looking for "pickups," which then rhymes with "hiccups"—a wacky rhyme that traces its roots to The Revuers. It ends with an ardent proclamation from Gabey that he wants to find "a girl of my own" and do so "in just one day":

GABEY
You guys are looking for just a bunch of pickups
But I don't feel that way
All you'll wind up with is just a case of hiccups
But what I want today
Is a girl of my own
Who will be mine alone
Come what may
In just one day
(The others do a take at this strange desire)[23]

"New York, New York" also provides the first of many links in *On the Town* to parodies of Gilbert and Sullivan by The Revuers. A number titled "Three Little Psychopaths Are We" parodied "Three Little Maids" from *The Mikado*, and it includes the following lines, which presage the first stanza of "New York, New York":

"Three Little Psychopaths" by The Revuers

You'll find our queer actions explained in some high sounding jive
At physical prowess we're not at our best
We've got baby faces, no hair on our chest

Chip, Gabey, and Ozzie in "New York, New York"

But we've hair on our chest,
So what we like the best
Are the nights![24]

Also, "New York, New York" involved a trio—the same number of characters as in "Three Little Maids" but with their gender reversed. As a teenager, Bernstein directed *The Mikado* during the summer of 1935, organizing neighborhood kids near his family's summer home in Sharon, Massachusetts. Bernstein sang the role of Nanki-Poo, and his sister, Shirley, was Yum-Yum.[25] "I think the bane of my family's existence was Gilbert and Sullivan," Bernstein later reminisced, "whose scores we [i.e., Leonard and Shirley] would howl through from cover to cover."[26] Added to that, in the summer of 1937 Bernstein and Adolph Green produced *The Pirates of Penzance* at Camp Onota in the Berkshires.

"New York, New York," then, announced a bold new musical voice—a composer who understood the expectations of Broadway, swing, and the commercial music industry, at the same time as he loved the chestnuts of classical composition and operetta. For Bernstein, Broadway norms were not an end in themselves but rather fuel for a creative odyssey that challenged the boundaries dividing musical genres and stylistic affinities.

In the 1940s, ballads were the soul of a Broadway show, and *On the Town* boasted some beautiful exemplars of the genre, including "Lonely Town," "Lucky to Be Me," and "Some Other Time." Defined as "slow, sentimental love-song[s]," "generally cast in 32-bar song form," ballads yielded the takeaway segments—the tunes that got hummed by the audience as they spilled onto the street after a night in the theater.[27] There were also medium- and up-tempo ballads. "The tunes themselves...make or break a show score," Bernstein later acknowledged, and there was a rich lineage of show tunes that gained a huge following.[28] "Someone to Watch over Me" came from Gershwin's *Oh, Kay!*, "Bewitched" from *Pal Joey*, and "People Will Say We're in Love" from *Oklahoma!*—to cite a few examples among a genre of song that often climbed to the top of the sales charts. Audiences eagerly anticipated the next infectious new number, and shows were judged in part by how they delivered the goods. Ballads also served as an important marketing tool and revenue generator, with airtime on the radio and mass distribution via sheet music and recordings. A select group of successful ballads was embraced by jazz musicians, becoming known as "standards"—that is, tunes that routinely became the basis for jazz improvisation. "Popular songs" (or "pop songs") was another rubric that subsumed ballads and jazz standards. Whatever the terminology, these songs were united in their formal structure, which at its most conventional featured a 32-bar "chorus" divided into four equal parts with two contrasting sections that most commonly fell into the following pattern: A (8 bars), A (8 bars), B (8 bars, often called a bridge or release), A (8 bars).[29]

Broadway was tightly aligned with the commercial music industry in producing successful ballads. In his introduction to Alec Wilder's *American Popular Song*, the cultural historian and critic James Maher ruminated at length about why the theater had been "far more receptive to innovation in popular song than the marketplace-oriented music publishing companies."[30] Maher believed that Broadway "permitted song writers a latitude they could not find elsewhere," and his conviction emerged from surveying "some seventeen thousand pieces of sheet music." Bernstein turned out to be just such a figure, a composer who was inspired by working in collaborative theatrical environments and who produced songs that have turned out to be among the best-known and most beloved of American musical theater. Several of his later ballads from *West Side Story* became stratospherically famous, including "Somewhere," "I Feel Pretty," "Tonight," and "One Hand, One Heart."

With *On the Town*, Bernstein was a beginner, and song composing presented a challenge. It put him in direct competition with some of the great pop-song writers of his day—from George Gershwin and Eubie Blake to Harold Arlen, Irving Berlin, Duke Ellington, Jerome Kern, Cole Porter, and Richard Rodgers—and it required a set of skills different from those needed to compose symphonies, art songs, or ballets. Given *On the Town*'s strong focus on dance, Bernstein was able, in part, to work within his comfort zone, producing much more orchestral music than was the norm in a Broadway show. Furthermore, when his growing fame as a symphony conductor was thrown into the mix, audiences expected "long-haired" music from him, as an article stated right before the Boston preview.[31] Yet Bernstein also had experience composing popular songs, especially during his year as an arranger and songwriter for Harms-Witmark. His papers at the Library of Congress include manuscripts for a number of songs written during that early period.[32]

In composing ballads for *On the Town*, then, Bernstein faced the task of devising a melody so magical that it could take flight as soon as it crossed the footlights. It needed to do so within well-established Broadway norms, yet have an identity all its own. He expressed ambivalence about this aspect of writing a show. "A song is a melodic line, and it's the melody that I've tried to develop in the music for *On the Town*," Bernstein told an interviewer around the time of the show's premiere. At the same time, the writer noted that Bernstein felt "too many popular songs have banal melodies dressed up in fancy harmonies."[33] By 1947, Bernstein was blatantly critical—even disdainful—of the tradition of American popular song. In an article for *Esquire*, which he published alongside a parallel statement from the jazz drummer Gene Krupa, Bernstein addressed the question of whether jazz had "influenced the symphony," and his position was harsh:

> The "popular song" has had, and can have, no influence whatsoever on serious music. It is created for money, sung for money, and dies when the money stops rolling in. It is imitative, conventional, emotionless. This has nothing to do with the fact that there are many such songs of which I am very fond. I wish I had written *I Get a Kick Out of You*; but I must insist that Mr. Porter has no influence on serious music. I love a Gershwin or a Rodgers tune; but the same truth still holds.[34]

With *On the Town*, then, Bernstein was contributing to the very tradition about which he had mixed feelings. In varying degrees, the three major ballads in the final version of the show—"Lonely Town," "Lucky to Be Me," and "Some Other Time"—were among its more traditional numbers, and they formed the core of the sheet-music folio published in 1945.[35] Early versions of *On the Town* had even more ballads, a few of which exist only as a lyric. They include "Lonely Me," which gave birth to "Lonely Town"; "Another Love"; I'm Afraid It's Love"; and "Say When."[36] "Lucky to Be Me" initially had a different lyric and was called "Nicest Time of Year." A reviewer for the *Boston Herald*, writing about the show as it emerged in previews, captured a sense of how much these signature ballads mattered, as well as how the creative team was writing and adjusting up until the last minute. "The songs most likely to be remembered," noted the Boston critic Elinor Hughes, "[are] 'Lonely Town' and 'Lucky to Be Me,' though there are definite possibilities in 'Some Other Time' not yet realized."[37]

* * *

"Lonely Town" is sung by Gabey in Act I, Scene 7, which takes place on "A Busy New York City Street." It comes at a point in the plot when Gabey is forlorn because his attempts to locate Ivy have been fruitless, and it is essentially a torch song, that is, a ballad lamenting unrequited love. Reviews singled out "Lonely

Town" as representing "strict Broadway" and as a prime candidate for being "voted the most likely in its class to succeed."[38] Perhaps reflective of pride in this number, Bernstein gave the sheet music to his father, inscribing it "To Dad with love, Lenny."[39] Remarkably, the solo song and an accompanying ballet fill the entire scene, which includes only a few words of dialogue. Early versions of the script and music reveal that the "brow" level of the scene was raised as revisions progressed.[40]

"Lonely Town" fits into the scene as follows. First Gabey performs the song as a solo. A brief intervening orchestral number titled "High School Girls" comes next. Then follows the "Lonely Town Pas de Deux," which in the original production was danced by Nelle Fisher and Richard D'Arcy. The ballet, observed Sono Osato, was "beautiful," and the symphonic writing climaxes passionately, as the primary theme of the song enflames a transient tryst.[41] A brief segment from "Lonely Town" is then sung by "Passersby," and Gabey joins them to conclude the scene. Bernstein and Robbins thus expanded a ballad into balletic-symphonic proportions, yet did so within Broadway parameters, with no individual segment exceeding three minutes. The scene fuses poetic lyrics with a haunting melody, rich chromatic harmonies, striking orchestration, and sexually charged choreography.

"Lonely Town" is a gorgeous song, with a lyric that serves a dual function. The musicologist Paul Laird ranks it as "one of Bernstein's finest Broadway ballads."[42] On one hand, the lyric fits into the plot of *On the Town*, describing a seaport that can feel desolate "when you pass through," that is, an unfamiliar location where a sailor takes a break from the disorienting violence of war. This targeted meaning was essential in the era of the integrated musical, with high value placed on the dramatic correlation of words, music, and choreography. On the other hand, "Lonely Town" can also convey a more generalized sense of isolation in the midst of a crowd.[43] That kind of solitude—even alienation—had the potential to affect sailors and citizens alike, and the lyric's dual implications gave the song potential for a life beyond the show.

Bernstein's tendency to synthesize practices from pop songs and classical music is clear from the very beginning of "Lonely Town." The verse functions as a ruminative recitative, with the text spinning forward in a continuous narrative. In the copyist score, it is marked "freely recit," but that designation was eliminated in the published version.[44] Recitative is common in opera, defined as "a type of vocal writing, normally for a single voice, with the intent of mimicking dramatic speech in song."[45] The verse to "Lonely Town" opens with two measures of the tune "Gabey's Comin'," echoing a fragment of the upbeat swing number heard in Scene 3 (Example 7.6). It becomes melancholic as Gabey realizes: "But once on shore, / It's not such a snap. / You get the cold shoulder, / The old runaround, / You're left with no one but you." While the verse conveys a sense of spontaneity, it is built of patterns that repeat, adopting a common stylistic trope from popular song. In this case, the patterns are handled asymmetrically, and the verse closes with a return to the initial 2-bar unit. Harmonically, the verse is rich and unstable from the outset, modulating at the midpoint without ever establishing a firm key center.

Example 7.6. "Lonely Town," first half of verse, mm. 27–32.

With the chorus of "Lonely Town," the tempo picks up to "Fast, with urgency," even as high-low fusions continue alongside harmonic slippage between major and minor. The chorus is modeled on standard popular-song form, yet it ignores the usual 8-bar phrase lengths. It includes five internal sections, not four, and one of them (the third A section) is performed by the orchestra, integrating vocal and instrumental writing. The chorus attains its core character—simultaneously forlorn and sensuous—through the use of extended harmonies, with the A section progressing from minor to major (see Example 7.7, m. 57). The B section carries the bulk of the chromatic load, as is traditional in pop-song ballads. Incorporating the dramatic intensity of operatic high notes, the bridge rises to the highest pitches, ultimately culminating the number overall. "High School Girls" then follows. A brief instrumental interlude, it too is built of selected snippets from "Gabey's Comin'." It has a pert quality, especially in comparison to the ardent outcry of "Lonely Town," and it offers an unflattering depiction of teenage girls as "sniggering" and "cheap, petty, dishy, with a sexual awareness," according to a draft scenario for the ballet.[46]

Example 7.7. *"Lonely Town," first A-section of the chorus, mm. 47–58.*

The sumptuous "Lonely Town Pas de Deux" then wafts in, which is a full-blown ballet with orchestral accompaniment. In his scenario, Robbins gave an extended narrative for this dance section, which featured a "lone girl" and a single sailor. It is quoted in part here, and the ellipses come from the original. Note the description of a "hot dance," "honest lust," and "hot embrace." Also note that the sailor "is kissing her" as "his hand caresses her body." This is a passionate segment of dance that enacts a pickup:

One sailor has come on later than the rest, and has stopped to light a cigarette. He watches the preceding action taking in the lone girl. He is shrewd, calculating and dirty in an attractive sailor way...he is slick and scheming. He allows everyone to leave and then innocently boyishly saunters over to the bench the girl is on and sits dejectedly, and lonely-like too. She is very conscious of the sailor sitting there, and he plays her for all she is worth. He manages to engage her into what finally becomes a hot dance in which she really gives herself to him...he very well knowing how to manage her, when to show affection and when he can really come out with his honest lust when it is too late for her to back off. The dance ends up with them sitting in a hot embrace on the bench and while he is kissing her his hand caresses her body. When they separate she looks hard at him for a moment, he sort of smirks and she buries her head in her hands embarrassed and ashamed. He lights another cigarette, and leans back on the bench happy.[47]

The critic Edwin Denby singled out "Lonely Town Pas de Deux," marveling over the choreography as "fresh, neat, direct and sincere." Denby also emphasized how a simple, well-placed gesture could have magical results. "I admired particularly the end of the 'Lonely Town' number," Denby wrote, "and the way the singer's one nod completes a dance."[48] Sono Osato recalled a similar moment when Robbins performed in an earlier ballet, *Three Virgins and a Devil*, choreographed by Agnes de Mille. Osato perceived Robbins's flair for simple movements as a key to his comedic sense. "He gave the chaste girl a knowing nod, tipped his hat, and sauntered offstage again with a bobbing gait," Osato recalled of *Three Virgins and a Devil*. "With just those few gestures he never failed to make an audience chuckle or titter with glee."[49] With an adjustment for a different story line—including a girl who was not so chaste—this same observation fit "Lonely Town."

Musically, "Lonely Town Pas de Deux" does not simply orchestrate the song. Rather, thematic elements from "Lonely Town" are shaped into a compact new composition, with the main tune of the song at times fractured into cells. "Lonely Town Pas de Deux" falls into a loose three-part structure, and its melancholic cast comes from a low range and richly colored orchestrations by Hershy Kay.[50] The number opens with a distinctive pairing of clarinet and bass clarinet, with the melody assigned to muted trumpet. The reeds form an undulating riff that is built of triplets with offbeat emphases (Example 7.8), and that riff infuses the entire pas de deux in one way or another, moving from the accompaniment of the opening section to the foreground of the middle section. In his study of Broadway orchestrators, Steven Suskin suggests that Bernstein selected Kay for the show's ballet numbers because he "apparently wanted[ed] his ballets to sound more symphonic than the typical Broadway score."[51] Like Bernstein and the conductor Max Goberman, Kay had also studied at the Curtis Institute of Music, and this was his first arranging assignment for Broadway.

Manuscript sources show that the song "Lonely Town" involved substantial rewriting and that, as the process unfolded, it was increasingly permeated with compositional traits from the classical world. The song's roots lay in "Lonely Me," which exists in a copyist's score and had a completely different musical setting than

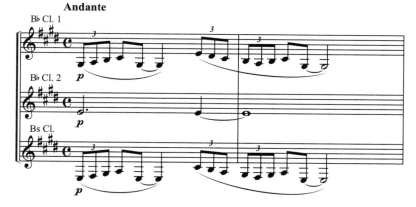

Example 7.8. "Lonely Town Pas de Deux," clarinet and bass clarinet, mm. 1–2.

did "Lonely Town."[52] It is bluesy and written in a straightforward 32-bar song form with a brief tag at the end, and it has neither the compelling melodic and harmonic richness nor the deviations from standard song form of "Lonely Town." There is no ballet at this stage of development, and the scene is jam-packed with dialogue.

The lyric for "Lonely Town" also evolved in fascinating ways, offering another inside view of the show's development process (see Table 7.2). "Lonely Me" in Version A of the draft script is a conventional love song: boy yearns for girl and confronts the frustration of a love "that wasn't meant to be." "Lonely Town," by contrast, has much shapelier and more evocative language. Yet some of its images trace their roots to "Lonely Me." For example: "Through this sea of empty faces" ("Lonely Me") becomes "A million faces pass before your eye" ("Lonely Town"). "Or find an empty memory" ("Lonely Me") initially becomes the somewhat clunky "The world's an empty world" (Version B of "Lonely Town"), then the more compelling "The world's an empty place" (Version D of "Lonely Town").

● ● ●

"Lucky to Be Me" (Act I, Scene 11) is another ballad in *On the Town* that features Gabey, and it stands in stark contrast to the overt sensuality of "Lonely Town." The song is thoroughly chaste, portraying Gabey as a straightforward American guy, and it expresses "sheer joyousness," as the *Christian Science Monitor* observed.[53] In wartime America, it was meaningful to hear a handsome young sailor sing, "What a day, fortune smiled and came my way," and the song mirrored the exultant affirmation of "Oh, What a Beautiful Mornin'" from Rodgers and Hammerstein's *Oklahoma!* After Gabey's solo, the vocal ensemble repeats the chorus in a statement of communal optimism. Within minutes of the number's conclusion, however, Gabey's dreams are dashed by Madame Dilly, Ivy's drunken voice teacher, who arrives to say Ivy has stood him up.

Table 7.2. Versions of the lyric to the chorus of "Lonely Town"

"Lonely Me"	"Lonely Town"	"Lonely Town"
On the Town script, Versions A¹ and A², p. 1-4-6	*Version B, p. 1-4-4 (much the same in Version C, p. 1-4-20)*	*Version D, p. 1-7-**36***
Lonely Me in search of you—	A town's a LONELY TOWN	A town's a LONELY TOWN
I don't know where to begin—or what to do	When you pass through	When you pass through
I keep on looking everywhere	And know that no one's waiting there for you	And there is no one waiting there for you
And hope that somehow you'll be there.	It's a LONELY TOWN.	Then it's a LONELY TOWN.
Suddenly—my hopes are high	You wander up and down	You wander up and down—
When I think that I might meet you passing by—	The crowds rush by	The crowds rush by
Then I get feeling so low	A million faces pass before your eye	A million faces pass before your eye—
We might be close and never know—	Yet it's a LONELY TOWN.	Still it's a LONELY TOWN.
Can it be that there's no way	Unless there's love	Unless there's love
Through this sea of empty faces	A love that's shining like a harbor light	A love that's shining like a harbor light—
Lonely me—is this the day	You're lost in the night	You're lost in the night
When I'll turn around and find you there with me		
Or find an empty memory	Unless there' [*sic*] is love	Unless there's love—
Of love that wasn't meant to be	The world's an empty world	The world's an empty place
	Where you must roam	
	And know your heart has never found a home	
	Then it's an empty world	
For Lonely Me.	And every town—is a LONELY TOWN.	And every town's—a LONELY TOWN.

In keeping with its clean-cut demeanor, "Lucky to Be Me" exhibits few of the irregularities in pop-song practice that were otherwise common to Bernstein's style. The chorus is written in F major with quarter-note rhythms in the melody and no syncopation. The number's most adventuresome sections are the verse, which shares with "Lonely Town" some of the free-flowing quality of a recitative, and the bridge of the chorus, which employs a melody that ascends the chromatic scale. The chorus has a tempo marking of "Gently" in the published version, signaling that Gabey is not a cocky dude but rather young and innocent. The clarity of the number continues when the vocal ensemble enters for the second stanza, singing the first two A sections in unison. In the bridge, the ensemble croons in close harmony. Gabey joins the ensemble for the final A section, and Broadway tradition steps in when the key is jacked up (in this case from F major to A-flat major).

In drafts of the show, "Lucky to Be Me" started out with a lyric in Bernstein's hand titled "The Nicest Time of Year," which probably dated back to his early songwriting efforts.[54] Its various versions show how changes in the show's overall structure were made along the way. "The Nicest Time of Year" was originally sung toward the end of Act I in a "Theatre Lobby," then reprised in Act II in a "Tunnel of Love."[55] In the Boston preview, both scenes still existed but the number had been retitled "Lucky to Be Me"; the reprise in Act II was then sung by the characters Lucy Schmeeler and Pitkin.[56] When the show opened in New York, the structure had been tightened: the scenes in the "Theatre Lobby" and "Tunnel of Love" had been cut, and "Lucky to Be Me" was sung by Gabey in the "Times Square" scene. The reprise was gone.[57]

* * *

"Some Other Time" stands alongside "New York, New York" as one of the best-known numbers of the show. A song with deep emotional resonance, "Some Other Time" can be viewed as a precursor to "Somewhere" from *West Side Story*. Both acknowledge the limits of the present moment, expressing a utopian faith in the unknown possibilities of the future. "Some Other Time" was a number that the creative team of *On the Town* especially loved. Bernstein called it "my favorite song from the show," and Comden declared it to be a "special song."[58] Phyllis Newman, who played Claire in the 1971 revival of the show and was the wife of Adolph Green, concurs. The song has "a universal feeling, and it's done in such a subtle, non-sentimental way," she states. "And just his intervals. Lenny's . . . They're just not like anything else. That's my favorite."[59] Those intervals caught the ear of jazz pianist Bill Evans, making their way onto Miles Davis's famous recording *Kind of Blue* in 1959 and becoming part of the song's long-range history.

"Some Other Time" appears in Act II, Scene 4, which is set on "The Coney Island Subway Express." The song functions as a reality check within the overall hilarity of the plot, as the young couples suddenly realize that the clock is chipping away at their day of freedom. Its lyric is specific to the show's plot, opening with "Twenty-four hours can go so fast / You look around, the day has passed." At the same time, it makes a broadly applicable statement about life and love as fleeting. The song opens with Claire, then Hildy, then Ozzie, and ends with a vocal quartet that also includes Chip. "Some Other Time" first appeared in the Boston previews. Since there was no protracted compositional process, no paper trail exists of various sources, and the earliest version appears to be a copyist's score with block chords in the accompaniment.[60] "Some Other Time" was not singled out much by critics when the show opened in New York.

"Some Other Time" is thoroughly compelling, poised emotionally between the charming simplicity of "Lucky to Be Me" and the desolation of "Lonely Town." It fits neatly into a standard AABA song form and has a bluesy cast, which effectively enhances the poignancy of the lyric. The secret to a well-crafted popular song lay in subtle details, and this one is tightly written, with many inspired moments. The verse is a mere 8 bars, compared to 12 bars in "Lucky to Be Me" and 19 bars in "Lonely Town," and it opens with a triplet that is among the song's key markers, uniting the verse and chorus as it assumes shifting incarnations. In the verse, the triplet descends by half steps (Example 7.9, m. 3). While at the start of the chorus it reverses direction to ascend with a pattern of a half and whole step (Example 7.10). At "we'll catch up" (m. 16) and "other time" (m. 17), the triplet morphs into a rhythm of short-short-long. Within the rhythmic suppleness of jazz performance, these variations on the triplet have more to do with notational differences than with performed sound. Another signature gesture is the phrase "Oh well," which opens the second half of each A section and employs a descending offbeat octave (m. 15). The bridge is unusual, opening in exactly the same way as the A section, yet doing so in a flat key a third lower.

Example 7.9. "Some Other Time," opening of verse, mm. 3–4.

The full arrangement of "Some Other Time," as performed in the show, ends with a vocal quartet, offering an early foray into the ensemble numbers that would become one of Bernstein's signatures, notably "Conversation Piece" from *Wonderful Town*, the "Quartet Finale" from *Candide*, and the "Tonight Quintet" from *West Side Story*. The ensemble section of "Some Other Time" is much simpler and shorter than those later ventures. All four voices perform the first half of the bridge in unison (mm. 59–62), and the second half of the phrase is taken up

Example 7.10. "Some Other Time," opening of chorus, mm. 11–17.

by the orchestra, as though the pain of parting has rendered the young couples speechless (mm. 63–66). Ozzie concludes that section, which overlaps with a coda (mm. 67–73). Claire and Hildy initially sing in counterpoint, harmonized by the men (mm. 73–76), and the number concludes with close vocal harmonies in a manner reminiscent of the concluding ensemble segment of "Lonely Town." Looking ahead to Bernstein's future vocal ensembles, it is the very brief section of counterpoint in "Lonely Town" that provided a seed for growth.

Another instantly recognizable aspect of "Some Other Time" is its two-chord ostinato at the opening (e.g., m. 1), which oscillates like the pendulum of a clock. Its chords are jazz-based, first C major with an added sixth, then G minor seventh. That ostinato had a fascinating life outside of the show, charting a path through Bill Evans to Miles Davis. Sheet music for "Some Other Time" was published in 1945, and over the years it became a jazz and pop standard, with memorable performances by Tony Bennett, Bill Charlap, Blossom Dearie, Maureen McGovern, and Marian McPartland. Most notable were the renditions of the jazz pianist Bill Evans, who made "Some Other Time" one of his staples. Evans first recorded it with his trio in 1958 on *Everybody Digs Bill Evans*, and he then did so ten more times.[61] On that same album, Evans released "Peace Piece," which was inspired by the opening ostinato of "Some Other Time," and "Peace Piece" in turn became the basis of the first ostinato in "Flamenco Sketches," which was the closing track on Miles Davis's *Kind of Blue*, recorded in 1959.[62] Evans was the pianist on that highly revered album of modal jazz, which became one of the best-selling jazz records of all time. By that point, "Some Other Time" had traveled across historical eras and performance genres.

GENDER-BENDING COMEDY

While the ballads in *On the Town* aimed to satisfy contemporary expectations for a memorable take-home tune, the comedy numbers needed to produce laughs night after night. All those numbers involved Hildy, Claire, or Ivy, either alone or in a duet with male partners, and they provided a means to foreground female power in a show that appeared to be about male sailors. The women usually had the last word in these songs, as they vigorously—sometimes raucously—breached the gender norms of their day. Stacy Wolf, a feminist scholar of musical theater, posits an "act-1-finale-of-female-self-assertion" as a prominent song type in shows after 1950.[63] These numbers often produced a "terrifying and enthralling display of confidence," Wolf observes, as in "Everything's Coming Up Roses" from *Gypsy* or "Don't Rain on My Parade" from *Funny Girl*. *On the Town* predates that convention and has none of its "terrifying" capacities. But the comedy numbers of *On the Town* certainly fit into a lineage of "self-assertion," presenting the women onstage as stunningly capable and thoroughly comfortable about expressing their desires. These characters could easily have been perceived as a threat, but instead they became an ebullient source of jocular energy. The comedy segments of *On the Town* provided a prototype for later Bernstein numbers such as "One Hundred Easy Ways to Lose a Man" in *Wonderful Town*, which again had a lyric by Comden and Green, and "Gee, Officer Krupke" from *West Side Story* (lyric by Stephen Sondheim). In the latter, juvenile delinquents catalogue various forms of deviancy that included cross-dressing.

The female comedy numbers in *On the Town* include "Come Up to My Place" (sung by Hildy and Chip), "I Can Cook Too" (Hildy alone), "Carried Away" (Claire and Ozzie), and "Carnegie Hall Pavane" (Ivy, Madame Dilly, and women's chorus). The songs involving Hildy or Claire were dubbed by *Variety* as "carry[ing] the show," and they had strong ties to the lightning-quick verbal exchanges and unexpected plot twists of screwball film comedy.[64] *On the Town* pushed farther than screwball films permitted, however. While screwball was self-consciously chaotic, with smart female characters and elegant writing, it "downplayed the female lead's physical sexuality to the point of ignoring (or sublimating) it," notes one scholar, focusing instead on "love companionship"—a perspective on sexuality that was influenced in part by the restrictions of Hollywood's Production Code.[65] That is precisely what sets apart the comedy writing in *On the Town*: far from being downplayed, the sexuality of Hildy and Claire is outsized, omnivorous, even overwhelming, and it gets expressed in song. Defying conventional norms of propriety, these two women pursue their guys aggressively, and they are often downright raunchy, incorporating an element of burlesque. With Betty Comden central to the creative team, a woman's voice participated in shaping these hilarious feminist anthems.

Many of the comedy numbers went through substantial revisions, replacing sober predecessors. In other words, their process of conception showed how comedy was added to the show as it was being developed.

* * *

"Come Up to My Place" is the first of *On the Town*'s female comedy numbers. It is the centerpiece of Act I, Scene 5, in which Hildy meets Chip, and the two sing a duet. The scene opens with Hildy getting fired for sleeping (literally) on the job. She declares "philosophically": "Might as well make this last fare a good one," as she starts assessing potential riders as sexual prospects. One is "too small," another "too big." A woman steps up, and Hildy naughtily "shouts": "NO GIRLS!!"[66] Then she notices Chip. Thus rather than a standard setup in which a male driver hits on a female passenger, a woman is at the wheel, and she solicits the male passenger's business, with all possible sexual implications brazenly flaunted.

"Come Up to My Place" is an action number that takes up half the scene, delivering dialogue between Hildy (the comedian) and Chip (the straight man). Hildy steals the attention and controls the message. The number is sung in her cab as she drives wildly, narrowly avoiding collisions, and Chip pedantically lists tourist sites he would like to visit, even though every single location has since been torn down, moved, or trumped by a newer development. First he wants to see the Hippodrome, which got demolished in 1939. Next he asks to go to the Forrest Theater to see *Tobacco Road*, which opened in December 1933. Then he proposes the New York Aquarium in Battery Park, only to be told it moved to the Bronx in 1941. Finally, he wants to visit the Woolworth Tower, believing it to be the "city's highest spot," and Hildy informs him that the Empire State Building is newer and taller. While Hildy repeatedly and abrasively corrects his outdated information, she also makes a pitch for him to forget about sightseeing and "come up to my place." The intensity of her requests builds over the course of the number, exploding in a riotous final "shout chorus," as musicologist Katherine Baber aptly terms it.[67] Such a device was standard at the conclusion of hard-driving swing arrangements.

Stylistic fusions are once again central to the work's conception, and "Come Up to My Place" positions itself, in part, in relation to the list and patter songs of comic opera, operetta, and musical theater. On the highbrow end, its theme of sexual conquest and its technique of delivering comedy through reciting a list recall the famous "Catalogue Aria"—"Madamina, il catalogo è questo"—from Mozart's *Don Giovanni*, in which the servant Leporello lists absurdly huge numbers of women who have been seduced by his master. "Come Up to My Place" simply flips the gender roles. *On the Town*'s taxi number also emulates the accelerating hilarity of *The Marriage of Figaro*, in which lecherous schemes of a predatory nobleman unfold over the course of a tightly packed day. *On the Town* is a "one-day" show too. "Come Up to My Place" also connects to the tradition in operetta of patter songs—fast-paced songs in which the text is set syllabically, as in "When You're Lying Awake" from Gilbert and Sullivan's *Iolanthe*.

And the number also traces its roots to the list songs of musical comedy, such as Cole Porter's famous "Let's Do It, Let's Fall in Love" (from the musical *Paris*, 1928).

On the surface, the rapid pace, syllabic text setting, and pattern-based construction of "Come Up to My Place" can seem quite unremarkable. But when a person looks closely, a tight conception emerges. The terms "verse" and "chorus," as usually understood in connection with popular songs, do not apply here, and there is no central melodic idea plus a bridge. Rather, the stanza-based construction of operetta's patter songs provides the most salient model. "Come Up to My Place" has four stanzas, each of which uses the same musical setting and centers around one tourist location on Chip's itinerary.

Each stanza divides into three large sections, and the melodies are constructed from closely interrelated pitch cells. Asymmetry of rhythmic patterns and phrasing is a consistent force. In the opening section, Chip introduces a new tourist site, Hildy queries it, and Chip doggedly stands by his goal (mm. 7–18). The accompaniment consists of a chordal vamp, mimicking the sounds of traffic.[68] In the middle section, Hildy asks Chip to repeat the location, and Chip does so (mm. 19–26). Just as he starts to restate the name of the place, Hildy hits the brakes to express her shock at his ignorance. (In the first stanza, for example, Chip states "Hip"—for "Hippodrome"—when the brakes screech.) The final segment has a lead-in that builds progressively from one stanza to the next. It playfully scrambles language à la Gilbert and Sullivan, which assists in the rhyme scheme, and Chip delivers the material. "Hey, what did you stop for?" in the first stanza (m. 27 with pickup) is rearranged in the second as "Hey what for did you stop?" (m. 63). Next it is "Did you stop for what, hey?" (m. 99). And finally "Did you stop for hey what?" (Example 7.11, m. 135). Hildy then sassily winds up those sections with a string of bluesy thirds, destroying Chip's outdated blunders. In spoken dialogue performed over a vamp between stanzas, Hildy propositions Chip, as in this text after the first stanza, where she goes ballistic with the word "seats" after first using it to describe the audience capacity of the Hippodrome:

HILDY
Give me a chance, kid. I haven't got 5,000 seats, but the one I have is a honey! Come up to my place.[69]

In the final out-chorus of the number, Hildy and Chip compete to dominate the conversation, with their interchanges rising in intensity as the pace becomes ever more compressed and frantic. At the end, Hildy gets the last word when she screams, "My place!" followed by emphatic punctuation in the orchestra.

"Come Up to My Place" was in the script from early drafts, where it was blandly titled "My Father Said," drawn from the opening line of an early lyric.[70] A particularly racy stanza about Minsky's Burlesque on 42nd Street ended with a high-low quip about Billy Rose, the famed producer of *Carmen Jones*. It traded in part on a mispronunciation of "burlesque," dividing "lesque" into two syllables to fit the rhythm of the melody and complete the rhyme. This distorted syllabification had roots in The Revuers' mangling of word rhythms for comic effect:

Example 7.11. *"Come Up To My Place," mm. 134–38.*

"Come Up to My Place": Deleted Stanza

CHIP
No! No!
42nd Street!
Mother told me with a frown
There's one thing that I mustn't do
But Poppa told me where it was—
So off to Minsky's Burles-que

HILDY
The Burles-que

CHIP
The Burles-que

HILDY
(double take)
Hold the phone Joe—
Did you mention burles-que?

CHIP
I'm still ringing—
Yes I mentioned—burl—
(brake)

CHIP
Did what for stop hey you

HILDY
The burles-que is through
Cause Billy Rose got smart
And now they call it art.
Come up to my place![71]

Also note that this deleted stanza includes yet another word-order arrangement of the line related to "Hey, what did you stop for?" and it ends with Comden and Green taking a shot at Billy Rose—and entertainers like themselves—who try to raise the cultural status of their work.

* * *

Hildy's other main comedy number is "I Can Cook Too," which appears in Act I, Scene 10, set in her apartment. With tempo indications of "Hot and Fast" and "Swing," "I Can Cook Too" is even more energetic and sexually explicit than "Come Up to My Place." This time it is a solo, with Hildy completely in control of belting out the message. Whereas "Come Up to My Place" traced its roots to opera and operetta, "I Can Cook Too" embraced the blues.

Chip turns up at Hildy's door with a bag of groceries, and he meets Hildy's roommate, Lucy Schmeeler, who sneezes prodigiously from a cold. Once Hildy succeeds in getting Lucy to leave, the following spoken dialogue leads into the song:

HILDY   Well, now what?
CHIP   We eat, huh?
HILDY   Sure, we can do that first.
CHIP   You claim you can cook.
HILDY   That's often been considered one of my strongest points.
CHIP   Yeah? What's the specialty of the house?
HILDY   Me!!

Then comes "I Can Cook Too," where the spices of sex and cooking mingle pro-vocatively. Like Bernstein's "Big Stuff" from *Fancy Free* and "It's Gotta Be Bad to Be Good," which was cut from *On the Town*, "I Can Cook Too" shows a com-poser-lyricist team completely at home with the blues. The song's theme of cooking opens the door to sexualized imagery standard in the blues, whether "my sugar's the sweetest aroun'," "my oven's the hottest you'll find," or "my chickens just ooze, my gravy will lose you your mind."[72] Overall, it is a case of linking "jazz to feminine power," which Jeffrey Magee observes in shows by Irving Berlin.[73]

In the chorus of "I Can Cook Too," the harmonic motion of the blues domi-nates, with a strong attraction to the subdominant. Yet its form is again irregular, consisting of three (not four) 8-bar sections (ABA). In between two iterations of the chorus, there is a 16-bar vocal section that feels like a verse (even though it is not heard at the opening of the song). In the copyist score, this section is labeled "Patter."[74]

"Come Up to My Place" and "I Can Cook Too" were originally conceived as a pair, appearing in the same scene in early versions of the script. At this initial stage of conception, Chip tries to sneak off after "Come Up to My Place," and Hildy "grabs him":

HILDY Awwwwww no ya don't—Listen, Chip—<u>I'm</u> unattached—
(MUSIC goes into introduction of "I CAN COOK")
I'm talented—I'm free—I'm perfect—Pull up a hydrant and sit down.[75]

Then follows "I Can Cook Too." In this early version, the number functions as a tag to "Come Up to My Place"—as an extended out-chorus, delivered after the singer has taken in a huge gulp of air and goes for broke. By the final version of the show, these two numbers were divided between the taxi scene and the scene in Hildy's apartment.

*   *   *

"Carried Away" is a comedy number sung by Claire and Ozzie, and it plays an im-portant role in establishing Claire's character as a well-educated, oversexed female professional. The number appears in Act I, Scene 6, set in the Museum of Natural History, where Claire works as an anthropologist. Ozzie turns up there by acci-dent, as he combs the city to help Chip find Ivy Smith. When Claire enters the scene, she is described as moving "briskly": "She is a handsomely attractive, smartly dressed girl, and seems to be of the cool and poised school."[76]

Claire notices Ozzie immediately, labeling him "a Pithecanthropus Erectus—in a sailor suit," and as they chat, she tells him that she is in the middle of writing a book titled *Modern Man—What Is It?* As part of the research, she wants to take both his photo and his measurements, and the latter sets up sexualized slapstick. Claire informs Ozzie that she is engaged to marry Judge Pitkin W. Bridgework, saying he "is the finest man I've ever known": "We have a purely intellectual relationship. It was Pitkin who made me study anthropology. I made a clean breast to him of all my past and he understood. He said, 'Claire, I understand. Just make a scientific study of man and know them objectively, and you'll get them out of your system.'"[77] Ozzie asks, "Well did it work?" Claire responds, "Almost completely." She then "makes a lunge for him. . . . and bends him over her knee in a passionate kiss," adding: "Of course, sometimes I get carried away." Then follows the number built on that line, which becomes an anthem for both rampant sexual desire and obsessive-compulsive behavior. This is a chatty scene, with lots of comic patter between Ozzie and Claire.

In terms of both musical style and social class, "Carried Away" joins "I Understand," which is sung later in the show by Pitkin, in parodying operatic practice. Both numbers musicalize Claire and Pitkin as being of a higher socioeconomic status than anyone else in the show. With "Carried Away," Claire and Ozzie share the same musical material, although she leads the way. They sing with elevated elocution, employing a sung equivalent of the mock-stentorian mode of delivery used in radio shows by The Revuers. The song opens with a 7-bar verse shaped as recitative (Example 7.12), and the copyist score is clear about its operatic lineage, indicating "Recit., freely."[78] "Carried Away" includes lots of dramatically emphatic high notes, especially in the 4-bar tag that ends each of the internal sections. In the final tag, Claire and Ozzie both hurtle to high notes, parodying an operatic trope as a way of seeming totally out of control (Example 7.13).

Throughout, the language and subject matter of the lyrics match the elevated signifiers in the music—all as a means of getting a good laugh. In the first chorus, Claire gives an example of her problem with self-control—that is, she continually gets "carried away"—and she does so by evoking a scene at a concert of classical music, where she seizes power from the conductor, who presumably is male:

> When I sit and listen to a symphony,
> Why can't I just say the music's grand?
> Why must I leap upon the stage hysteric'lly?
> They're playing pizzicato,
> Then ev'rything goes blotto,
> I grab the maestro's stick and start in leading the band![79]

The operatic delirium of "Carried Away" is especially sharp in performances on the studio cast recording, where Comden and Green ham it up to the max, as though strutting on the stage of La Scala.[80] At times, the lyric employs a stilted word order to generate a rhyme, emulating Gilbert and Sullivan via The Revuers. An example follows from the second stanza, as sung by Claire; the segment with stylized word order is underlined. Note, too, the use of "golly" within this parody of elevated speech:

Example 7.12. "Carried Away," verse, mm. 1–8.

Example 7.13. "Carried Away," final tag, mm. 89–94.

And when I go to see my friends off on a train,
Golly, how I hate to see them go,
For then my love of traveling I can't restrain.
The time has come for parting,
The train's already starting,
I hop a freight and in a flash I'm off to Buffalo![81]

An early version of the script included "Another Love" in the spot later filled by "Carried Away." It is sober and completely lacks the wacked-out comedy of the final number: "Well—there was just one love affair after another—and at the end—nothing to look forward to—but the next one."[82] "Carried Away" appeared in Version B of the show, where the scene includes many handwritten changes.[83]

* * *

"Carnegie Hall Pavane" (Act I, Scene 8), a duet by Ivy Smith and her drunken singing teacher, Madame Dilly, offers yet another female comedy number, and it

Madame Dilly (played by Susan Steell) takes a swig of booze while Ivy (Sono Osato) stands on her head to sing "Carnegie Hall Pavane." Photofest Digital Archive.

stands out because it is the only time in the show when Ivy sings. A women's swing chorus and big-band instrumentals are also included, yielding jazz-vocal writing. Written for Sono Osato, who had no experience singing onstage, Ivy's vocal lines are largely supported by Madame Dilly or the ensemble, and Ivy stands on her head while she delivers them. The character of Madame Dilly was based on Osato's real-life singing teacher, Susan Steell, who initially played the part. "Susan's hilarious audition for the role of Mme. Maude P. Dilly, a vocal coach prone to hitting the bottle during her classes," Osato recalled, "had just the screwy quality they wanted and won her the part hands down."[84] On another occasion, Osato called the number a "burlesque."[85] Interestingly, Cole Porter's *Kiss Me, Kate* (1948) included "Pavane: Why Can't You Behave?"

"Carnegie Hall Pavane" spoofs the power center of American classical music, parodying solfège and the tedious practice routines that were staples for classical musicians. The number might be viewed as a forerunner of "Do-Re-Mi" in *The Sound of Music* (1959), but its overall message is radically different. "Do-Re-Mi" serves in the plot as a means of teaching children and conveys a sense of innocence. "Carnegie Hall Pavane," by contrast, provides a riotous flash point for the high-low fusions that define *On the Town*, invading the sacred space of "Carnegie Hall" with rousing swing rhythms and bluesy harmonies. Including "pavane" in the title sharpened the number's parody of high art. A courtly dance of the Renaissance period, the pavane (or pavanne) was described by the sixteenth-century composer and theorist Sir Thomas Morley as "a kind of staid music, ordained for grave dancing," and beloved works such as Ravel's *Pavane pour une infante défunte* (1899) had brought the dance's sobriety into the modern era.[86] "Carnegie Hall Pavane" flips that dignified aura as Madame Dilly nips at a bottle of liquor and natters on about the importance of sexual abstinence for singers: "Love life must go, / If you'd be a nightingale instead of a crow" (Example 7.14, mm. 8–10).

Bernstein once again shapes an idiosyncratic structure in "Carnegie Hall Pavane," devising a compactly crafted composition, using two alternating sections that again draw upon popular-song conventions and deploy them in unusual ways. The opening section divides into three 4-bar units, and Ivy's lyrics initially are made up of solfège syllables (Example 7.14, mm. 3–14). A "swing" section follows, which Ivy kicks off with a new syncopated pattern (mm. 15–18). The melodic ideas are built of slightly asymmetric phrases, yet they unfold in clusters of 2- and 4-bar cells that trace their roots to the opening material, albeit with constant transformation of the two initial melodic cells (mm. 3 and 4), which are presented straight out, inverted, expanded, and reorganized. "Carnegie Hall Pavane" traces its roots to the scalar melody and accompaniment of the closing number of "World of Music," a skit by The Revuers. The opening line of that skit's lyric, as discussed in Chapter 2, is "Benny Goodman, shake hands with Brahms." There, however, the scales are rhythmically square, with none of Bernstein's inventive patterns and phrasings.

During the development of *On the Town*, "Carnegie Hall Pavane" went through an extensive evolution. Version A of the script includes the basic concept of the scene, and Gabey sings an ardent number titled "I'm Afraid It's Love."[87] In this early scenario, Ivy does not vocalize, but the stage instructions contain seeds of what eventually became "Carnegie Hall Pavane":

Example 7.14. *"Carnegie Hall Pavane," mm. 1–18.*

Example 7.14. (Continued)

DANCE. IVY starts a scale, starts walking to it. Orchestra picks up music of the scale and she starts to dance to the music of all the practicing noises of Carnegie Hall. At the end of it—winds up standing on her hands again, doing a scale.[88]

An early incarnation of Madame Dilly is included there, although she was then named "Maud P. Smead." There is also a character named Pinchy Terkle, who is a "cheap small time agent"; he was deleted by Version B of the script.[89]

Example 7.14. (Continued)

Smead is a "blowsy voice teacher," who is "huge," with "a broken contralto," but she is not yet a drunk.[90] At that early stage, Smead sings "I'm a Little Prairie Flower," a well-known number from radio performances in the 1930s.[91] In Version B, Maud P. Smead hits the bottle. She has a "cultured" voice, and there is a hilarious (and sad) description of her sitting "at the piano—vocalizing—and taking huge swigs out of a wicked looking booze bottle...A gin-soaked charlatan."[92] There, Smead and Ivy sing solfège syllables in the same patterns that were to be used in "Carnegie Hall Pavane": "Do—do re do—do re mi do." The solfège segments are brief, however, and no full-fledged song is indicated. Meanwhile, a scenario amid Robbins's papers describes a dance built around solfège, surrounded by the sounds of people "practicing." Ellipses are in the original, except for those in brackets:

CARNEGIE HALL...IVY SMITH'S DANCE.
SMEADE [*sic*] leaves IVY in her studio alone and looking dejectedly after her. Ivy heaves a sigh and determinedly starts her vocalese [*sic*]. Do, do re do, do re mi do, do re mi fa do, etc. It doesn't sound so good even to her. She starts walking around the room rather bored. [...] She continues marking out the steps [of] the music which leads into a casual dance...this is Ivy trying and playing at dancing, sometimes very lovely and lyrically, and sometimes finding herself too carried away and becoming gawky. [...] One long whirl lands her outside in the hall. Here the noises of other people practicing floods up and she dances to the various sounds she hears...a violin practicing Flight of the Bumble Bee, a soprano's Je Suis Titania, a horn's Siegfried's Call, etc. Finally there is a concerted climax when all the instruments work together and Ivy cuts loose.[93]

During the Boston preview, this number was labeled "Pavanne, Danced by Sono Osato," suggesting there was no singing.[94] Osato recalled in an interview that at this point the scene in Carnegie Hall bombed with audiences. "When we were already playing [in the Boston preview], and he [Robbins] had devised a very ordinary, trivial kind of solo for me, which took place in Carnegie Hall," Osato states. "But it was no good; it was *so* no-good that when I left the stage it was [she claps slowly and reluctantly]. And I remember thinking, 'Oh, something has to be better than this!' And anyway, so he disappeared, he went back to New York."[95] A copyist score titled "Carnegie Hall Pavane" fits with this memory. It is completely instrumental and winds up with a brief vocalise.[96] The Carnegie Hall scene yielded a crisis for the show because Robbins left Boston without a word. "He was too untried in commercial theater," Osato continues, "to not be terrified of all these different things." The impasse finally ended. "Then Jerry reappeared after the third day," she states. "And I remember he came to the dressing room, and I said, 'We'll do anything you say. We can work until three in the morning, but you can't leave.' Because it was just like bringing the curtain down on everything." The number was then completely reworked.[97]

SYMPHONIC IDEALS

On the Town's symphonic ambitions were central to its identity, and the show includes an exceptional number of extended instrumental segments, totaling well over a half hour of running time. All the instrumental numbers accompany dance, with a heavy concentration in the second act. The main instrumental numbers for dance in Act I include "Presentation of Miss Turnstiles," "Lonely Town Pas de Deux," and "Times Square Ballet." Those in Act II are "Subway Ride and Imaginary Coney Island," "The Great Lover Displays Himself," "[Imaginary Coney Island] Pas de Deux," and "The Real Coney Island." In addition, there are orchestral components standard to a Broadway score, including overture, entr'acte, and finale. Once again, there were substantial revisions as the show was being shaped, and the second act was the focus of an exceptional amount of rewriting. The nightclub scenes were reworked vigorously (as will be discussed in the concluding chapter), and much of the dance was added or revised. As a result, On the Town's symphonic dimensions grew considerably.

Composer Stephen Sondheim recalled the strong impact of hearing On the Town's orchestra: "Well, I saw it when I was fourteen, and I remember being exhilarated by the sound coming out of the orchestra pit, which was unlike any other pit orchestra that I've ever heard."[98] Critics of the mid-1940s often noticed that On the Town's orchestral writing was unusual for the Broadway stage, and they did so by recognizing how Bernstein challenged traditional categories and cultural hierarchies. "Leonard Bernstein's music is smart and, for ballet purposes, socko, but it is not exactly show music," declared Variety.[99] "Leonard Bernstein has written a score of which no musician need be ashamed artistically," wrote the Musical Courier: "The musical numbers are built by someone who knows his craft."[100]

In 1945, Bernstein extracted "The Great Lover Displays Himself," "Lonely Town: Pas de Deux," and "Times Square: 1944" and published them as On the Town: Three Dance Episodes.[101] "I believe this is the first Broadway show ever to have as many as seven or eight dance episodes in the space of two acts," Bernstein wrote in a program note for the first performance of the Episodes. He added, "The essence of the whole production is contained in these dances."[102] Besides claiming historical precedent for the dance numbers within the musical repertory for Broadway, Bernstein also noted how the orchestral writing was devised so that it did not call attention to itself: "That these are, in their way, symphonic pieces rarely occurs to the audience actually attending the show, so well integrated are all the elements."

Such an exceptional amount of orchestral music brought risks. It demanded a top-notch set of players, which in turn required additional resources, as Bernstein later acknowledged:

> What I was very much afraid of was cutting a lot of the so-called symphonic music—which was quite long and complicated and would entail a lot of extra rehearsal time and a slightly larger and more expensive orchestra....[Mr. Abbott] used to make sort of friendly fun of some of my music by calling it "that Prokofieff stuff." I was afraid all "that Prokofieff stuff" would go, but it didn't—not a bar of it.[103]

Bernstein also mused about the show's overall hybrid aesthetic, pinpointing its symphonic sections as a key component in giving the work a veneer of being "serious":

We were very much influenced by our masters, our teachers—people like Koussevitzky, Lucia Chase [co-director of Ballet Theatre] and others who were trying to goad us into doing more serious things; serious in the sense of being non-Broadway, because as Jerry pointed out, shows on Broadway then were in very low estate. What we accomplished was a happy and moving show about wartime, in the lightest possible vein but with the most serious esthetic means.[104]

In her biography of Bernstein, Meryle Secrest writes of how his "determination to democratize the symphony" began around 1943, and indeed his work as a symphonic composer during this formative period fused mightily with his ties to the commercial music industry, including Broadway.[105] When he set out to compose *On the Town*, Bernstein had one major symphony behind him: his Symphony No. 1 (*Jeremiah*), and his other major work for orchestra was *Fancy Free*. Composed beginning in 1942, the *Jeremiah* symphony was premiered by the Pittsburgh Symphony Orchestra on January 28, 1944, and in New York City that March, just months before the premiere of *Fancy Free* and the start of *On the Town*. The *Jeremiah* symphony had a dramatic strain, with dark colors and a brooding atmosphere. Bernstein addressed his Jewish identity in the work, with melodies derived from synagogue chant and inspiration from the story of the prophet Jeremiah as told in the Book of Lamentations.[106] The second movement of the symphony includes a melody that Bernstein would adapt into "Maria" from *West Side Story*. While *Jeremiah* largely represents a distinct sphere from *On the Town*, the two works share a love for the expressive capacities of orchestral "sound," delivering the kind of visceral pleasure that affected the young Sondheim.

The discussion here focuses on "Presentation of Miss Turnstiles," especially in relationship to *Fancy Free*. "Times Square Ballet" shifts the perspective to racial representation; and the web of orchestral numbers beginning with "Subway Ride and Imaginary Coney Island" gain meaning in connection with the vogue for dream ballets. The orchestrations for all of these ballet sections were done by Hershy Kay.

* * *

The first major orchestral and ballet segment of *On the Town* appears in "Presentation of Miss Turnstiles" (Act I, Scene 4), where dance and the sounds of an orchestra fill a scene with nearly seven minutes of music. A ballet-pantomime, the scene enacts the beauty pageant in which Ivy Smith is chosen Miss Turnstiles. Ivy twirls through a now-familiar series of episodes, first being crowned as Miss Turnstiles, then doing a brief pas de deux with a string of male admirers: Home-Loving Type, Playboy, Soldier, Sailor, Aesthete, and Athlete. While Ivy is at the center of these encounters in terms of the narrative conception, the musical characterizations focus on the men, recalling *Fancy Free*'s analogous fixation. Ivy's flirtation with celebrity is then shattered as the Announcer intones a reminder that after a month she will be replaced by a new queen of the subway.

Sono Osato later reminisced about the bold comedy produced in this scene, and she expressed admiration for the orchestral score, especially for its diversity of emotional, dramatic, and musical expression:

Selected from the masses by a spotlight resting on my fanny...I emerged to perform the Miss Turnstiles variations. This music-and-dance portrait of the All-American Girl was one of the most innovative of its kind ever seen on the Broadway stage. Lenny's music was brash, bold, frantic, and funny, capturing the pulse of New York life. It was symphonic, jazzy, atonal and operatic. It was low-down, honky-tonk, and "hot."[107]

"Presentation of Miss Turnstiles" is indeed highly varied and sectional, with rapidly changing moods. Employing a montage structure similar to *Fancy Free*, it mimes the shape and gestures of some of the great ballet classics, with strong roots in Tchaikovsky, together with vaudeville, cartoons, and European-modernist titans of the ballet. An early script describes the concluding dance between Ivy and all the men as "a gay dance with all six of them in which she is TOSSED from one to the other in the manner of those 'Miss Schmaltz and Boys' numbers of the Twenties. This reaches a mad pitch."[108] (Miss Schmaltz was likely a reference to the character of that name in the *Moon Mullins* comic strip, which began in 1923.)[109] As a result, the overall conception of "Presentation of Miss Turnstiles" is closely related to *Fancy Free*, even though it does not quote directly from that earlier ballet. This is not only the case in its montage of different styles but also in its use of generic character names, its reliance on pantomime, its parody of gender conventions, and its tie to cartoons.[110] At times, the musical renditions appear to be asserting a homosexual thread into the characterizations. In sharp contrast to *Fancy Free*, however, the internal sections of "Presentation of Miss Turnstiles" are supershort, leaving quick impressions but offering little opportunity to savor individual ideas, and Ivy remains the center of attention, even if the guys get caught up in themselves. The quick pace of the ballet serves as a reminder that it was written for Broadway, not for the old Metropolitan Opera House. Taking one segment of the score at a time, however, makes it possible to grasp the number's rich detail and its many parodies.

The orchestra is principally used in "Presentation of Miss Turnstiles" to illustrate the action and provide caricatures of the admirers. The opening of the scene is melodramatic, with suspenseful tremolo chords, illustrating the tension that builds up to the announcement of the pageant's winner. "Allegretto di 'Ballet Class'" introduces Ivy (Example 7.15). She is sketched *à la française*, presenting her as an elegant and refined ballerina. The Parisian modernism of the French Les Six, whose composers often wrote for ballet, is parodied through the section's exceptionally spare texture, 5/4 meter (which toward the end of the section alternates with 3/4), wrong-note writing (e.g., m. 30, beat 3; m. 34), and focus on woodwinds, with the flute, oboe, and clarinet taking turns with the melody. In the next segment, "Tempo di Valse Lent," the orchestration shifts suddenly to the lush and thoroughly consonant world of Tchaikovsky (mm. 41–57). The Announcer sings a description of Ivy as she is crowned, accompanied by a waltz with resonating strings.

From that point on, the number is essentially a theme and variations, albeit with disruptions. The theme is the melody sung by the Announcer. As the variations unfold, Bernstein writes phrases of irregular lengths (the theme itself is 11

Example 7.15. "Presentation of Miss Turnstiles," mm. 28–31.

Allegretto di "Ballet Class"

bars). Since each variation depicts one of the male characters—and those characters represent types rather than individuals—it lampoons clichéd musical signifiers. Gendered parody rules. "Allegretto giusto [Home-loving man]," the first variation, starts off by poking fun at musical tropes of masculinity (Example 7.16). The first half caricatures a regular sort of guy, with the melody in the bass clarinet and a rhythm that is squarely duple, emphasized by steady pizzicato chords in the accompaniment (mm. 58–65). In the second half, the melody moves up an octave to clarinet and viola, while the bass clarinet cavorts contrapuntally below (mm. 66–72). A cartoonish parody emerges, with the delicacy of the texture suggesting an oafish person on tiptoe (or *en pointe*), Plus the solidity of the rhythm is destabilized in the second phrase by shifting to triple meter. These musical devices render the "home-loving man" as effeminate, and they intensify in the second half of the variation by shifting the melody to a higher range and adding elegant counterpoint. This variation foretells the gendered caricature of The Wreck in "Pass the Football" from *Wonderful Town*, where in an early version The Wreck was lampooned as a campy clod pirouetting to a waltz.[111] The next variation, "Playboy," swings with a bluesy E-flat clarinet (mm. 73–86, with phrases of 8 + 6 bars). This is the character who had been conceived of in earlier drafts as a jitterbugger. A parody of masculinity continues, in part through the abrupt and farcical shift from the gracefulness of the first variation. Borrowing a technique from *Fancy Free*, the orchestra simulates a big band, with a saucy clarinet solo. It divides into brass, reed, and rhythm sections and includes a rumba rhythm in the bass. This admirer prances and preens, with a sense of abandon encoded in hot jazz.

"Soldier" announces the character's identity through the use of brass and snare drums. Since the tempo is "twice as fast," this variation zips past in a blink. The next section, "Sailor," is longer than the other variations and once again emulates

Example 7.16. "Presentation of Miss Turnstiles," mm. 58–61, with pickup.

the jazzy style and instrumentation of *Fancy Free*. The first half is essentially a 12-bar blues, delivered via solo jazz piano, and this standard presentation of a vernacular form brilliantly disrupts the irregular phrase lengths that surround it. The second half unites the worlds of classical music and jazz: the orchestra articulates the theme, followed by a response from jazz piano. "Athlete" grows directly out of "Sailor"—enough so that it is difficult to hear a break between the two sections without the score in hand. Lush orchestral writing with standard duple meter abruptly eclipses the sounds of jazz, and the section builds in intensity, with a sense of being transitional. When "Aesthete" begins, the frenzy breaks. In Version A[1] of the script, the character is designated as "Opera, ballet" and described as "Boy in professorial get-up."[112] In Version B, he is "a flowing tie poetic type."[113] The rhythm shifts to a lumbering waltz, echoing the queer-inflected parody in "Home-Loving Man." There is once again spare voicing, with a waltz rhythm in the bass clarinet and double bass and an elegant melodic variation in the violin.

After the individual admirers have all been caricatured, the variations continue, with the final segments culminating in a dance between Ivy and the group of men. References to famed ballets of the Romantic era appear in grand articulating chords (e.g., the downbeats of mm. 167 and 169), and handwritten notes by Robbins describe "a brief, triumphal coda with all the boys in which she is being carried around the stage."[114] The published script describes the scene's sad conclusion, as Ivy ceases being a celebrity and once again joins the working masses:

> The ADMIRERS all disappear. IVY waves a sad farewell to them. Her picture, an enlargement of the subway advertisement, which has been on display at the rear of the stage, disappears. She waves goodbye to that. The same line

of GIRLS appears again, sidling on with their backs to the audience. IVY disconsolately resumes her place in line and sidles off with the rest as the Curtain closes.[115]

After a fling with fame, Ivy is back in the chorus line. Musically, the culminating sections intensify the stylistic montage, as they continue to narrate the action. "Tempo I" brings back the scurrying sixteenth-note patterns from the opening of "Presentation of Miss Turnstiles" and the melody first associated with Ivy (mm. 201–17, which refers back to "Allegretto di 'Ballet Class'"). Here, however, the melody is caricatured through wrong-note dissonances that convey how Ivy's fate has turned. The scene concludes with three crisp diatonic triads, again echoing tropes from Tchaikovsky.

An extraordinary feat of delivering comic caricature through musical composition, "Presentation of Miss Turnstiles" cuts, pastes, fuses, and parodies, and it pokes fun at masculinity, succinctly sharpening the action onstage.

* * *

Act I climaxes with "Times Square Ballet," a scene notable for its racial integration. The ballet depicts a teeming crowd in Times Square, a location that served as a transnational hub during the war. An early script describes the stage design more specifically than the published script:

> There is a Nedicks—on stage—through which the scene is seen. At the right of it is a photographer's shop unlit until the end. And stage Left is the corner the Nedicks is on—with the Times Building in the background—with the sign lit. Passersby are walking on the street corner—and on the street in front of the Nedicks (upstage) and seen through the Nedicks window.[116]

Focusing on Nedick's, with the scene viewed through its window, parallels the use of the bar in *Fancy Free*. In both, a commercial public location offers a social space for sailors to mingle with civilians (Nedick's was a fast-food chain located throughout New York City). Another realistic aspect of the scenario came with the "sign" referred to in this early description—that is, the electric billboard outside the New York Times tower at Broadway and 42nd Street, which was an iconic image during World War II, delivering the latest news from the battlefield.

"Times Square Ballet" lasts four minutes, and the score is sectional, although less extremely so than "Presentation of Miss Turnstiles." It is built of riffs that spin off of "New York, New York."[117] There are once again parallels to *Fancy Free*, imitating a big band within the instrumental resources of a full theater orchestra. The big band sections of "Times Square Ballet" achieved a kind of racial détente, with swinging clarinet and saxophone solos conjuring up a style performed by musicians on both sides of the color line. The opening clarinet, for example, could trace its roots to African American performers, such as Barney Bigard of the Duke Ellington Orchestra, or to white musicians, such as Benny Goodman or Ross Gorman (Gorman famously performed the opening clarinet solo at the premiere of Gershwin's *Rhapsody in Blue*). Each of those musicians, like Bernstein, was working within a racially hybrid musical sphere.

With "New York, New York" as the core melodic material of "Times Square Ballet," the city is the star. The overall musical structure alternates an A section that replicates a big band (mm. 1–14), with a B section written for more conventional theater orchestration (mm. 15–48). In the middle of the ballet, a C section appears (mm. 122–59), which is super-kitschy and evokes the world of cartoons, complete with xylophone, slide whistle, woodblock, and ratchets for special effects. It must have accompanied "Penny Arcade Boy," which is listed in programs as part of the ballet.[118]

The number's opening clarinet solo delivers the "verse" of "New York, New York" as a 12-bar blues chorus (Example 7.17). The orchestration is lean, with clarinet and rhythm section (percussion, piano, and bass); woodwind harmonies punctuate the final measure of each of the first two phrases, which is a classic big-band scoring technique. The final phrase of the A section extends the verse of "New York, New York," adding two measures to a standard blues form and enhancing the work's

Example 7.17. "Times Square Ballet," mm. 1–4, orchestral score.
Sounding instruments only.

sense of giddiness. In the second A section, a sultry alto saxophone takes the solo, with a riff of bass clarinet, brass, and rhythm section. And the final iteration of that section begins with a trumpet solo, then alto sax, and finally flute, clarinet, and alto sax—all accompanied by riffs in the brass and rhythm section. Throughout, the piano plays a central role in helping the rhythm section drive the band.

The big-band segments alternate with a B section that features full orchestra with strings, generating the kind of razzle-dazzle excitement that is standard at the conclusion of a first act in the theater. Its initial melodic material comes from the opening chordal riff in "New York, New York." Thus in a larger structural sense, "Times Square Ballet" rounds off the first act by recalling thematic ideas from the opening scene of the show, returning to the song that is at the core of the show's identity. Yet "Times Square Ballet" is no rehash of the opener. Rather, it rearranges and recomposes melodic ideas from "New York, New York," playing up their bluesy qualities.

"Times Square," as a location and a concept, existed in the earliest scripts for the show as a conclusion to Act I, and the scene's concluding ballet took shape as the show was being developed. At first, the scene did not include "Lucky to Be Me," and there was no ballet. In Version A[1] of the script, the scene begins with a choral number, where the crowd recites the news as they read it from the Times building sign. Stage directions appear in parentheses:

CROWD
(to music, reading)
The time is now—10:57.
(as headline comes around they follow the letters)
All-eye-yad trow-opps feig-but vvye-cut-ore-es-us bat-tul-lee
Allied troops fight victorious battle—!...[119]

Version B of the script ends with a dance, but it does not yet have the grandeur of the title "Times Square Ballet." Rather, the conclusion of the scene is described quite generally: "Dance and excitement starts. They dance in and out of the crowd—The excitement builds."[120] Version C is much the same, but Version D includes a full-blown "Times Square Ballet."[121] The semantic shift to "ballet" is significant, reflecting how the final dance of Act I was expanded in length and elevated in status. Late completion of the ballet is confirmed in copyist scores for "Times Square," which are shorter than the final version. Notably, both of them lack most of the opening section with the clarinet solo, and the two scores differ somewhat, bearing witness to a multilayered process of revision.[122]

●　●　●

Orchestral music and ballet are central to much of Act II, accompanying *On the Town*'s version of a dream ballet, which fills three numbers over the course of two scenes. Even though separate titles are listed for each component of the dream ballet, one flows into another, yielding a continuous, multimovement work. The segments include:

Act II, Scene 2: "Subway Ride and Imaginary Coney Island"
Act II, Scene 3: "The Great Lover Displays Himself"
　　　　　　　　"Pas de Deux"[123]

Sono Osato was the star of the entire dream ballet, and Ray Harrison joined her to dance "The Great Lover Displays Himself" and "Pas de Deux," while John Battles stepped to the side.

"Subway Ride and Imaginary Coney Island," which initiates the dream ballet of *On the Town*, is an extended number in which Gabey gets drawn into a lover's reverie. Merging the aspirations of a ballet with a setting on the subway—the most common mode of transportation for average New Yorkers—"Subway Ride and Imaginary Coney Island" built its narrative premise on high-low mergers, and Bernstein's music supported that mission. As in the other ballet music discussed here, "Subway Ride and Imaginary Coney Island" relies on montage and crossover; pop-song form and blues harmonies join with impassioned orchestral writing. Once again, its segments of full-blown orchestral sound conjure up the great Romantic-era ballets, and the number as a whole thrives on unexpected juxtapositions.

In "Subway Ride and Imaginary Coney Island," Gabey falls asleep on the subway, and a doll in his lap comes to life as Ivy, who dances the role of an enchantress, seducing him into a "dream" Coney Island. Gabey sits throughout the scene as a spectator, and production flow charts indicate that "Dream Subway" included five dancers in addition to Ivy and Gabey: two were African American (Frank Neal and Royce Wallace) and three were white (Malka Farber, Allyn Ann McLerie, and Frank Westbrook).[124] With "Imaginary Coney Island," more dancers are added. The published script describes the scene in detail (ellipses are from the original):

> The subway train to Coney Island. GABEY is seated, his doll in his hand. TWO COUPLES are in the car. A GIRL passes through, fishing in her pocketbook. GABEY's head drops, he is asleep, and in his dreams...
>
> The IMAGINARY CONEY ISLAND BALLET begins. The swaying of the PEOPLE in the car becomes rhythmic. The music picks up and the PEOPLE dance to it, in a trance-like movement, their eyes closed, their movements detached. Suddenly, IVY appears from one end of the subway, dressed as the doll now lying in GABEY's lap. She comes toward GABEY, who looks up. The dance becomes wilder, and she motions him to come into the resplendent world which is now visible through the car windows—the Dream Coney Island of GABEY's imagination. IVY leads him invitingly to the center doors of the subway car, which open. The entire car splits in two, rolls off to either side of the stage, and IVY and GABEY step into the dream world.[125]

The music for "Subway Ride and Imaginary Coney Island" is sultry and sensuous, even containing the indication "sexily" when the alto saxophone enters with the main melody. Once again, Benny Goodman meets Tchaikovsky, although this time strings are present throughout, akin to Gershwin's symphonic jazz. The structure of "Subway Ride and Imaginary Coney Island" is straightforward, relying, like "Times Square Ballet," on two main sections that alternate. The model of swing bands is again employed, with the solo in the A section taken up by a different instrument each time it appears. Its melodic material presages the verse of "Some Other Time," which is sung after the dream ballet concludes. The phrase lengths are again irregular, and the ballet is essentially constructed as a modified popular-song form.

"The Great Lover Displays Himself" then follows without a break. It is a dance in which male power and sexuality preen audaciously. In it, the real Gabey moves to the side, while his "Dream Counterpart" steps in, with his prowess as a lover articulated in part through the sounds of swing. The published script describes the ballet as follows:

> The Dream Coney Island. A limitless void of blue. In the distance soar the myriad lights of Coney Island—deeper, richer, higher, more exotic than the real place. The Dream continues with the DREAM BALLET. GABEY is conscious of motion around him—a swirl of skirts, the scuffling of passing feet. The lights slowly come up and he realizes where he is—a wonderful, suspended, fluid and dreamy, sophisticated place for rich people. Suave, well-groomed MEN and lovely, unattainable WOMEN dance by easily and coldly, with a great impersonal quality about them. IVY is seized by the MEN and they carry her off over GABEY's head. There is great excitement. The real GABEY goes off to one side to see his DREAM COUNTERPART enter. TWO GIRLS carry on a poster, advertising "Gabey The Great Lover."
>
> The stage is a swirl of excitement as his DREAM SELF enters. They all watch as the GREAT LOVER dances for them—a jazzy, slick, ingratiating, torchy, sexy dance. He finishes with a bang. There is a fanfare. The MASTER OF CEREMONIES from Diamond Eddie's enters.[126]

The "impersonal quality" of the "unattainable women" in *On the Town* gestures back to the dream ballet of *Oklahoma!*, where "dance-hall girls" enacted "the Police Gazette pictures" of prostitutes that were pinned on the walls of the lurid smokehouse where the sinister character Jud lives.[127] *On the Town*'s women are similarly cold in this dance, almost like female automatons, offering another instance in which Robbins learned from watching de Mille.

The title "The Great Lover Displays Himself" signals the exhibitionistic maleness of the scenario, and the number has a tempo indication of "Allegro pesante" (essentially meaning "fast but heavy"), which indicates a cartoonish representation. It again employs a sectional structure (basically the same as "Subway Ride and Imaginary Coney Island"). This movement passes very quickly, lasting just over a minute and a half. Various parallels to "Presentation of Miss Turnstiles" are present. The trombone solo at the opening, which falls sturdily on the beat, recalls the "Home-Loving Man," musicalizing heteronormative masculinity as a way of poking fun at it. The first section of the piece provides a jazzy edge, especially with syncopated trumpet interjections. Another parallel with "Presentation of Miss Turnstiles" occurs in the B sections, which include meter changes and offbeat accents to generate a modernist veneer (mm. 41–48).

"Pas de Deux," the final segment of the dream ballet, is launched by a Master of Ceremonies, who announces "the main event of the evening": "Gabey the Great Lover versus Ivy Smith!"[128] At that point, the scenario takes a bizarre twist, pitting a pair of potential lovers against each other in a boxing ring:

> With much ceremony, a prize ring is set up, a fight light comes down, and IVY enters the ring. The match begins. IVY starts toward the GREAT LOVER with soft, voluptuous movements—and the attacking feints of the GREAT LOVER become

slow motion movements, until finally they are caresses rather than punches. She lures him into unwrapping her turban. Suddenly, in her grasp, the length of red cloth becomes a rope with which she proceeds to ensnare the GREAT LOVER, until he is helpless in its coils. He is overcome, and IVY is lifted to receive the plaudits of the multitude in triumph. The real GABEY, who has watched horror-struck, is brushed away, and he glides rapidly backward off-stage.

In this face-off, the woman emerges triumphant. The scene unfolds in front of a spectacular set design by Oliver Smith, which features a roller coaster (prede-cessor of the Coney Island roller coaster under which the childhood home of Alvy Singer stood in Woody Allen's now-iconic 1977 film *Annie Hall*).

"Pas de Deux" is a three-and-a-half-minute number that again employs big-band scoring with strings. The orchestration is exceptionally full and rich, as befits the culminating portion of this trilogy. Like the previous two ballet seg-ments, the formal structure is compact and fairly regular, with a song-form shape using 12-bar phrases. The A section refers to melodic fragments of "Lonely Town," and the bridge once again conjures up the dry textures of French modernism, with lean counterpoint and woodwinds.

"Some Other Time" (Act II, Scene 4) comes immediately after the dream ballet, and "The Real Coney Island" fills the next scene. Partly danced, partly sung, it takes place in "a gaudy honky-tonk sort of place." This is where Ivy is exposed as a cooch dancer, and it completes the extended arc of dance that is a centerpiece of the second act.[129]

According to Sono Osato's memoirs, the choreography for "Pas de Deux" was finalized several days before the Boston tryouts:

> Jerry showed up at rehearsal with a huge grin on his face and a length of red jersey in his hand. "I've *got* it!" he announced. He flipped one end of the fabric to Ray Harrison, who was my partner as the Dream Gabey, and gave me the other end. Next, with a slight shove, he set me turning into its length until I was wound into Ray's arms. It worked. Then we spent hours experimenting, winding the jersey around my waist, chest, and neck until it finally ended up as a turban on my head.[130]

Yet even after that point, the dream sequence continued to undergo revision, ex-tending beyond opening night. By the time of the Boston previews, the ballet se-quence had been divided into scenes titled "Gabey in the Playground of the Rich" and "Coney Island."[131] But not until January 14, 1945, two weeks after the show opened, was "Subway to Coney Island" added to the dream sequence.[132] All these changes went hand in hand with the addition of "Some Other Time" during Boston tryouts.

Bernstein's instrumental writing in the three components of the dream ballet consistently fulfilled a narrative function by enhancing the drama, conjuring up sexual fantasies, and delivering comedy, often through gendered parodies. A structural montage with fast-paced juxtapositions is his main compositional device. Once he developed a distinctive style for composing orchestral music to accompany dance, he stuck with it, employing segments that simulated swing bands within an overall framework that divided the orchestra into different types of ensembles. He also relied on popular-song form, consistently altering standard phrase lengths, and he composed for the physicality of dance. "There was all this music that had been so finely orchestrated that you could just—you could just listen to the music," recalls the dancer Billie Allen. "Every time my body hears the music it SO responds after all these years kinesthetically to that ballet and to that experience."[133]

● ● ●

In the course of writing his first Broadway show, Bernstein developed the musical voice that would carry through his subsequent works for the stage. High-low fusion was a key marker of the language that emerged, as was a flexible attitude about how to utilize an orchestra. His ballads intermingled operatic high notes, recitative-based verses, patter from operetta, popular-song form, and blues-based harmonies. His comedy numbers employed those same devices to lampoon traditional gender roles and the musical tropes that animated them on stage and screen. They were often raunchy, pushing the boundaries of respectability and using humor to proclaim liberation from social norms. And his symphonic writing signified equally on famous ballet scores and swing-dance orchestras, essentially offering a kind of musical diplomacy that put the golden age of European ballet on a par with the dance halls of wartime New York. Furthermore, the American sounds that he chose to feature were fundamentally transracial and commercial, thus deploying the politics of compositional choice to push back against the largely white high-art values that defined both his education and the expectations for his career. Bernstein delighted in manipulating traditional musical materials, doing so with equity across genres and styles, and parody was one of his most potent tools. He snipped apart fragments of seemingly dissimilar sound worlds, then lampooned them and spliced the results into a montage. All these imaginative choices emerged from the collaborative energy of working with like-minded colleagues. When composing the music for *On the Town*, Bernstein might have been in the driver's seat, but he did so with collaborators who were musically attuned, devising lyrics and choreography that Bernstein animated with an irrepressible urban sound.

8

ON THE TOWN AFTER DARK
The Nightclub Scene
• • •

Nightlife, gay and glamorous,
Nightlife, loud and clamorous,
Nightlife starts at half past eight.
Broadway, 52nd Street,
Harlem, hear those dancing feet,
Hurry or you'll be late.
—From "Nightlife"
by The Revuers (1940)

If a single segment of *On the Town* brought the creative team full circle, it was the nightclub scene that opened Act II. Five of the show's principal characters (minus Ivy) visit Diamond Eddie's Nightclub, an old-fashioned and largely white club with an opulent floor show. They then go to the Congacabana, a hip Latin location, and they conclude with the Slam Bang Club, a black swing joint. Each site gets "progressively louder and less inhibited," as a Boston critic put it during previews.[1] The scene recalled *Fancy Free*'s setting at night in a bar, and it reflected the formative nightclub experiences of Comden, Green, and Bernstein. Not only did the fictional venues of the nightclub scene come straight out of environments in which The Revuers had performed, but the scene progressed from reading like a string of Revuers' skits to taking shape as a well-edited work for the theater. At the same time, the skit-like quality remained. Women's sexual desires were once again flaunted, and comedy again provided a means for challenging gender stereotypes. The creative team's passion for Gilbert and Sullivan was also fully on display. Race was carefully managed in the scene, with initial intentions getting scaled back during the revision process. In short, *On the Town*'s nightclub scene provides a concise opportunity to round up the myriad issues that animated the show overall, including the degree to which it sought a realistic depiction of New York City during World War II.

Scenes featuring excursions to late-night clubs had a long history in Broadway musicals, which meant that *On the Town* offered an updated version of a well-worn trope. In club scenes, the main characters, who were most often white, visited a site marked with racial, ethnic, or socioeconomic difference in a city that was otherwise thoroughly familiar. One such case was George M. Cohan's *The Rise of Rosie O'Reilly* (1923), in which the principals headed to the "slums" of Brooklyn to hear Rosie sing. These outings "offered the upper-class visitor unparalleled excitement in the form of a range of novel exotic and modern stimuli, from jazz music to chop suey, topped off with a whiff of danger," writes historian Elizabeth Craft.[2] *On the Town*'s nightclub scene did not re-create the trope of "danger." Rather, it essentially parodied a tried-and-true theatrical tradition.

In the 1940s, the synergy between nightclubs and Broadway was especially strong. "As a training for the theatre," Betty Comden wrote in 1944, "there is no sterner teacher than a few smoke-filled years in the nightclubs."[3] Some entertainers got their "training" in clubs, as happened with Comden and Green, while others turned to them as a collateral source of employment and a means of promoting new Broadway productions. Among *On the Town*'s African American dancers, Flash Riley worked in nightclubs, and other Broadway figures were doing the same thing. A few cases exemplify this symbiotic relationship. When Café Zanzibar opened in 1943 at 49th and Broadway, Ethel Waters appeared there.[4] By that point, she had *As Thousands Cheer*, *Mamba's Daughters*, and *Cabin in the Sky* to her credit. Around the same time, Celeste Holm, who was then playing Ado Annie in *Oklahoma!*, also appeared nightly in the Persian Room of the Plaza Hotel on Fifth Avenue and Central Park South. Her schedule sounded grueling, with shows beginning at 12:15 a.m., not long after the curtain had fallen on that evening's Broadway appearance.[5] Another case involved Zero Mostel, who in the early months of 1944 performed at La Martinique on West 57th Street, where he was described by the *New York Times* as a "zany comedian" who was making his "first public appearance since returning to civilian life after an abbreviated military career."[6] Comden, Green, and Bernstein took part in this same performance culture when they used a club date at Le Ruban Bleu to try out material from *On the Town*. That evening, reported one observer, "the theater, the arts and letters were all well represented in the crowd that filled the room."[7]

Over the course of developing *On the Town*, the nightclub scene went through substantial rewriting as manuscripts demonstrate, and those rewrites tell a story that connects narrative threads in the show with life in New York City (see Table 8.1). The scene dated back to the earliest sketches for the show, and it was retained during a revision process in which other segments, such as those in night court and the Tunnel of Love, hit the cutting-room floor. Yet significant changes were still made along the way. Although racial identities were inscribed directly into early drafts, they had mostly been obscured or eliminated by the show's final version. All in all, the nightclub scene signified on The Revuers' penchant for creating comic satire out of issues, places, and personalities of the moment, and it bore witness to how the creative team faced choices about racial representation. Through and through, the nightclub scene traded on broad physical comedy.

Table 8.1. Nightclub Scene: Revisions in Draft Scripts

	Scene Divisions:	
1-A: Diamond Eddies	*1-B: The Congacabana*	*1-C: The Slam-Bang Club*
Version A¹ (Comden and Green B6/F6) and Version A² (Robbins B63/F10)		
"So Long"(includes "At the Midnight Jamboree") "Parody on Things Always Happen That Way"	"La Passa-Outa" "Ya Got Me"	"Ain't Got No Tears Left"
Version B (Comden and Green B6/F5)		
"So Long"(includes "At the Midnight Jamboree") "It's Gotta Be Bad to Be Good"	"It's Gotta Be Bad to Be Good" (sung in Spanish)	"It's Gotta Be Bad to Be Good" "Ain't Got No Tears Left"
Version C (Robbins B63/F11)		
"So Long"(includes "At the Midnight Jamboree") "It's Gotta Be Bad to Be Good"	"It's Gotta Be Bad to Be Good" (sung in Spanish) Hildy starts "I Can Cook Too"	"It's Gotta Be Bad to Be Good" "Tender Night"
Version D (Robbins B63/F9)		
"So Long" (trimmed down) "I'm Blue"	"I'm Blue" (sung in Spanish) "Ya Got Me"	"Do-Re-Do" (recap snippet) "I Understand"
Published Script		
"So Long" "I'm Blue"	"I'm Blue" "Ya Got Me"	"Do-Re-Do" (recap snippet) "I Understand"

DIAMOND EDDIE'S NIGHTCLUB: *ON THE TOWN* CELEBRATES ENTERTAINMENT FOR THE MASSES

Each club in *On the Town* was based on an actual site in New York City, starting with Diamond Eddie's Nightclub, the first stop on the tour for Gabey and his friends. Diamond Eddie's poked fun at large establishments with cheesy chorus lines: that is, joints that attracted huge crowds at rock-bottom prices. The club's name represented "a composite," as early scripts put it, of two "large cheap" clubs in New York City, which were "gaudy [and] popular."[8] The first was the Diamond Horseshoe, a lavish operation run by Billy Rose, the same flamboyant producer who staged *Carmen Jones* in 1943, and the second was Leon and Eddie's, a well-known vaudeville club. These establishments were largely white, and production flow charts for *On the Town* reveal that their demographic was replicated onstage. To produce the bustling activity of a large club, thirty-seven members of the cast took part in the scene at Diamond Eddie's, and only two of them were African American: Melvin Howard and Lonny Jackson. Both played waiters; this was the spot where a white waiter was also included to create a mixed-race service staff.[9]

The Diamond Horseshoe, which was located in the Hotel Paramount on West 46th Street, had opened in late 1938 as a "spectacle" show, as the *New York Times* reported, and its purpose was nostalgic, looking back at the Gay Nineties.[10] There, Billy Rose "pushed female nudity to new levels of prominence," observes Burton Peretti in his study of New York clubs.[11] The Diamond Horseshoe was "immensely profitable," according to Peretti, and it had a populist impulse. Rose "consciously embraced the egalitarian ideology of the New Deal," creating a nightclub for the masses. From its perch in the heart of Broadway, the Diamond Horseshoe featured an old-fashioned chorus line, complete with "winsome young ladies," according to the *New York Times*.[12] By December 1944, on its sixth anniversary, the club had brought in more than three million customers.[13] The shows were "fast, colorful, a blend of reminiscence and brasses."[14] These were elaborate productions, with costumes by the theater designer Raoul Pène du Bois, an American of French descent who hailed from Staten Island. Pène du Bois specialized in "dramatic dresses."[15] He had designed costumes and sets for the Ziegfeld Follies, for Billy Rose's opulent Aquacade at the New York World's Fair in 1939, and for a string of Broadway shows that included *Carmen Jones*. The Diamond Horseshoe featured a high-kicking chorus of dancers modeled on the Ziegfeld Follies, and it showcased stars of yesteryear, such as Gilda Gray, a Ziegfeld headliner known for her signature shimmy.[16]

While the Diamond Horseshoe largely presented white entertainers, there was at least one exception: the band led by African American composer, lyricist, and singer Noble Sissle. The group had been performing at the Diamond Horseshoe since it opened, according to one source.[17] Sissle had famously joined with Eubie Blake to produce the all-black show *Shuffle Along* in 1921, and the Diamond Horseshoe had strong ties to musical theater in general. It also presented blackface entertainment. In 1943, Rose started a traveling vaudeville show that replicated the club's offerings in New York, and he hired Aunt Jemima as emcee. A female blackface singer and comedian, Aunt Jemima (aka Tess Gardella) had played Queenie in the original production of *Show Boat* in 1927 and was also a well-known presence on radio. As part of Rose's show, she concluded performances with "a medley of George Gershwin's hymns," reported *Billboard*, including three songs from *Porgy and Bess*.[18] Notably, Comden and Green did not include blackface in their script for the nightclub scene. They did, however, feature an emcee, and they might well have been inspired by a Billy Rose production titled "Mrs. Astor's Pet Horse," which revolved around "a tour of night spots popular a decade or so ago" and included "a neat ballerina routine."[19] That skit ran simultaneously in both the road show with Aunt Jemima and in the New York club.[20]

Leon and Eddie's on West 52nd Street—the other club parodied in the Diamond Eddie's segment of Act II—was also white and also featured a variety show with chorines. The club was operated by Leon Enkin and Eddie Davis, and *Billboard* covered its acts with regularity. "Talent policy: Floorshows at 8, 10, 12 and 2. Dancing, continuous," reported the trade magazine in June 1944.[21] "Opener is a hoofer...Joan Summers, who does a fair to middling tap routine....her abbreviated costume shows her good figure off to advantage." That same show included a singer named Sherry Britton whose voice apparently was not too impressive. The audience's response improved, however, when she started "peeling" her clothes. "Line [i.e., chorus line] has a few more lookers than the previous one. Routines are simple and don't call for any talent."

On the Town's sequence at Diamond Eddie's parodies the tacky, highly produced extravaganzas of these white clubs. The final (published) script opens with "So Long, Baby," a step-and-kick number performed by "six girls," which offers a frenetic lampoon of an old-fashioned chorus line.[22] According to Peggy Clark's "Scene Breakdown of Dance Personnel," all the "So Long girls" were white, specifically indicating that Wallace and McNichols, the two African American women, were not part of the group.[23] An early version of the script concurs, calling the dancing chorus "a cheap line of girls—all blond."[24]

The orchestral introduction to "So Long, Baby" is exaggeratedly dramatic, marked "Moderato pomposo" (medium tempo with a grandiose affect), with brasses blaring and a six-bar anticipatory trill in the reeds and strings, much like the razzle-dazzle pageantry conjured up at the opening of "Presentation of Miss Turnstiles." When the dancing girls enter, the tempo shifts to "fast and corny," and the number uses a pop-song form that is exceptionally commonplace for Bernstein.[25] The lyrics mimic chorine tunes, with a singsong melody and a coquettish "oo" predominating. Here is the first half of the chorus:

GIRLS
So long, I'm on the loose again.
So long, I counted up to ten.
Bye, bye, baby, I got wise.
Too long you made a fool of me.
Too long you had me up a tree,
Now you get the booby prize.

FIRST GIRL
So you cry: boo hoo hoo,
And you feel oh so blue.
It's no use, now I'm leaving you.[26]

Musically and textually, "So Long" parodies the nostalgic motifs of Billy Rose's Diamond Horseshoe, and it does so by mocking showgirl tunes in which the "oo" sound was a staple. One example was "I'd Like to See a Little More of You," subtitled "The Peek-a-boo Sextette," which appeared in the Ziegfeld Follies of 1906.

Its sheet-music cover showed a chorus girl undressing behind a screen, with a man trying to catch a glimpse. The lyric concludes:

What can a fellow do
In this game of peek-a-boo
Won't you tell me, tell me, pray
When you have nothing on some day.
For I'd like to see a little more of you.
Yes I'd like to see a little more of you.[27]

The cartoon figure Betty Boop, with her simpering sexuality, was another contemporary case of the character type being mocked.

In the final version of the show, "I'm Blue" is the second number performed at Diamond Eddie's. It is sung by a lowbrow lounge lizard named Diana Dream, who is introduced as "star of the [radio] networks."[28] The white singer Frances Cassard, who was blond, delivered the tune.[29] Like so many others in the cast of *On the Town*, Cassard had a career that encompassed more than one performance domain—in her case, both opera and Broadway—and she was at midcareer when the show opened.[30]

"I'm Blue" is also titled "I Wish I Was Dead," drawing on the final line of the lyric, and the number relates to material by The Revuers.[31] While the name Diana Dream recalls Lamar Lamour in the skit "The Girl with the Two Left Feet," "I'm Blue" trades on the torch-song parody of "The World's Fair Is Unfair," performed by

John Battles, Adolph Green, Betty Comden, Cris Alexander, and Nancy Walker with
Frances Cassard, who sings the role of Diana Dream at Diamond Eddie's Nightclub.
Photofest Digital Archive.

Example 8.1. *"I'm Blue" (also known as "I Wish I Was Dead"), mm. 1–7.*

Judy Tuvim. "I'm Blue" delivers two phrases of a "slow blues" (the tempo indication in the published score), and the script states that Diana Dream should perform it "with stylized gestures."[32] The number calls for maxed-out camp. The melodic line is wild and wailing, with an ungainly leap of a minor ninth, followed by a downward swoop of a seventh (Example 8.1, mm. 3–4). Overall, it exaggerates the contours of the blues by gyrating through a series of chromatic cells. Hildy cuts off the lugubrious song in midstream with a hyperbolic exclamation: "I'm sorry, I'm very sorry. This is too depressing. I've got a friend over there who's dyin'!"[33]

Example 8.2. Manuscript of "It's Gotta Be Bad to Be Good," first page.
Bernstein Collection B21/F9.

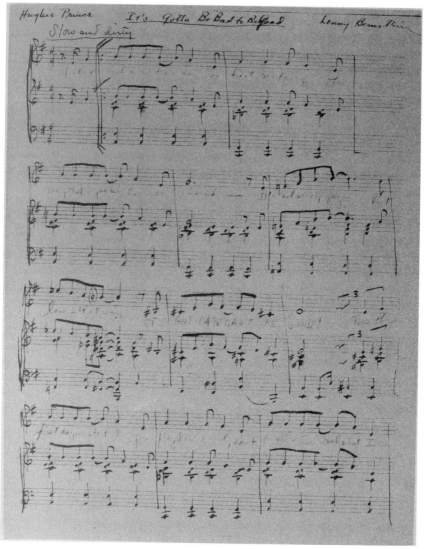

"I'm Blue" was added late in the creative process, first appearing in the Boston preview.[34] In an early script, "SONG: Parody on 'Things Always Happen That Way'" appears in that same spot, and it was clearly a placeholder.[35] The next tune destined for the slot was "It's Gotta Be Bad to Be Good," and this time a fully developed piece existed: a blues by Bernstein that dated back to 1942. It lasted through two versions of the script.[36] "It's Gotta Be Bad to Be Good" relates closely to "Big Stuff" from *Fancy Free*—the song written with Billie Holiday in mind. Both are blues-based pop songs, composed and performed within an interracial context. Both appeared on an early to-do list for *On the Town*, in which Bernstein itemized what had already been written. At that point, "Big Stuff" was also on its way to being included in the show.[37]

If "It's Gotta Be Bad to Be Good" had been retained for the final version of the show, it would have meant a more straightforward evocation of a nightclub performance. "Vocalist steps in front of bandstand," instructs the draft script. Then "orchestra plays mournful bluesy introduction and torch singer sings."[38] "It's Gotta Be Bad to Be Good" represents a fairly standard pop song of the era; it uses minor mode, altered harmonies, and a melody with blue notes (Example 8.2). The lyrics are identified as being by Hughie Prince, a Hollywood and Broadway writer whose most famous song was "Boogie Woogie Bugle Boy of Company B," a wartime hit for the Andrews Sisters.[39]

When "I'm Blue" replaced "It's Gotta Be Bad to Be Good," it ramped up the level of camp. When all was said and done, "It's Gotta Be Bad to Be Good" bequeathed to "I'm Blue" a grounding in urban blues, and "I'm Blue" parodied those traits to deliver over-the-top satire of cheap white nightclub entertainment. It was a twisted racial journey.

CONGACABANA: THE LATIN CRAZE

The next stop for the club-hoppers of *On the Town* was the Congacabana. "A large palm tree stands in the center of the stage," instructs the published script, while "the PATRONS are indulging in a Conga line." Hildy is part of that line, and she gets "completely knocked out and has to be assisted back to the table."[40] The two main musical numbers are "I'm Blue" and "Ya Got Me," both of which are rearranged from earlier scenes. Latin beats undulate throughout, as the sailors and women enter into the world of contemporary Latin bands, such as Xavier Cugat and His Orchestra, or Machito and His Afro-Cubans. Parody and camp join hands with exoticism. At the same time, the Congacabana segment links to the "Danzón" of *Fancy Free*. Like the scene in Diamond Eddie's Nightclub, Congacabana went through a series of major changes. On one hand, those revisions resulted in a more concise text. On the other, they made the scene safer and more contained.

Betty Comden later recalled *On the Town*'s Congacabana as a "Spanish-ish nightclub," a description that aptly fit both the musical style and the fabricated club.[41] This was an era when a commercial form of Latin music had emerged in the United States that represented "a confused jumble of musical styles with influences from Spain, Mexico, Argentina, Brasil, and of course the United States, in addition to Cuba," writes ethnomusicologist Robin Moore.[42] The name Congaca-bana, while not explained in scripts for the show, was most likely a conflation of La Conga and Copacabana, two of the best-known Latin nightclubs in New York.

La Conga, the first of those actual clubs, had opened in 1937, and even though it was billed as Cuban, it became a major venue for a wide range of entertainers from diverse locations south of the border. "Ever since Desi Arnaz began thump-ing the Conga drum at La Conga and Diosa Costello gave her first exhibition of uninhibited Latin behavior," the *New York Times* reported in 1940, "the Fifty-first Street basement premises have been filled nightly with the town's conga-rhumba devotees."[43] Director George Abbott was among the regular patrons of the club, with one New York newspaper describing him as "a great rumba fan" and "a nightly visitor."[44] In 1939, Abbott directed Arnaz and Costello in *Too Many Girls*, a Latin musical.[45] The Copacabana, the second club referenced in *On the Town's* Congacabana, had opened in 1940 and was named for a famous neighborhood in Rio de Janeiro. The Copacabana had a pseudotropical atmosphere, and one of its most celebrated headliners was the Brazilian singer Carmen Miranda—the same star who appeared with Comden and Green in *Greenwich Village*.[46]

The segment in *On the Town's* Congacabana opens with a high-spirited orches-tral number. It has a classic conga rhythm—one, two, three, kick—and its percus-sive pattern and trumpet riff later became the basis for "Conga" in *Wonderful Town*. After the conga line concludes, part of "I'm Blue" is wailed out again. This time the accompaniment takes on a Latin beat, punctuated with blaring brass and a percus-sion section with piano. The character performing "I'm Blue" is Señorita Dolores Dolores, and she is essentially a reincarnation of Diana Dream as Latina. That role—labeled as the Spanish Singer in the opening-night program—was sung by the contralto Jeanne Gordon.[47] Like Frances Cassard, Gordon was an opera singer. She was older than Cassard, however, and her age probably heightened the exag-gerated quality of the scene, making it seem a bit tawdry, even over the hill.[48]

In early versions of the script, two different numbers appeared in the spot ul-timately filled by the Latinized version of "I'm Blue." Initially, the number planned for the scene was "La Passa Outa," which was to have been accompanied by "fan-tastic contortions," according to an early version of the script.[49] Decades later, an interviewer asked Bernstein if he had composed a tune for "La Passa Outa," and Comden also chipped in with her recollections:

> COMDEN: Where did you find that [i.e., reference to "La Passa Outa"], in some museum version of the show? It must have been in an early version of the book, some number in a night club.
> BERNSTEIN: When the sailors were touring the night clubs, one of the stops was a sort of Copacabana. They were introducing a great new Latin Ameri-can bombshell number, "The Passa Outa."
> COMDEN: Never got as far as Mr. Abbott. We cut that ourselves.[50]

"La Passa Outa" might have been modeled on Diosa Costello, La Conga's star, who was known for performing with extremely exaggerated physical movements. She delivered "torrid singing of Latin numbers" and did so with "reverse bumping all around the ringside," observed a critic in the *New York World-Telegram*.[51]

Revisions continued, and Version B of the script placed "It's Gotta Be Bad to Be Good" where "La Passa Outa" had been indicated. The performance instructions for this recap of "It's Gotta Be Bad to Be Good" are similar to the ones that eventually accompanied "I'm Blue": "Sings—It's Gotta Be Bad To Be Good—in Spanish—doing the title line in English with an accent. (It goes on gloomily for a chorus)."[52] This version of the scene begins with "Music loud... Latin rhythm... violent rhythm playing." It overflows with "broken English," as stage directions put it, and the Latin singer is named "Fasquita Menzales," perhaps parodying the character Fasquita from *Carmen*. Blues-based writing merged with Latin rhythms and orchestrations, in a parallel to contemporary works for Latin jazz such as "Rhapsody in Rhumba" or "Chili Con Conga" of Cab Calloway. Once again, the goal was a hyped-up, campy performance.[53]

In the final version of the show, as performed in both the Boston preview and New York opening, the Congacabana segment culminates riotously with "Ya Got Me." Hildy launches the number, which becomes an ensemble performance also involving Claire, Chip, and Ozzie, all of whom sing it to Gabey as part of their campaign to boost his spirits. Hildy's opening verse recalls the racy lyrics of "Come Up to My Place" and "I Can Cook Too," which is a bit strange.[54] Hildy directs the number to Gabey, who is a friend but not a potential lover, yet her lyrics suggest much more. Note the rhymes of "share"/"spare" and "ample"/"sample":

HILDY
I'm eager to share
My love and devotion,
It's deep as the ocean.
I've plenty to spare
And since it's so ample
I'll throw you a sample.[55]

The roots of this sexualized language lay in an early version of the script, where Hildy instead sings the number to Chip (not Gabey), whom she spent the entire first act trying to seduce.[56] After Gabey became the target, the lyric does not quite make sense. But somehow that detail gets finessed through highly energized bravado. "Ya Got Me" becomes an anthem about mobilizing a friend—about the importance of human connections—and a series of klutzy rhymes continue, with a flagrant grammatical infraction that uses "he," "she," and "we" before delivering the tag line of the song:

CLAIRE, HILDY, CHIP, OZZIE
You got her whole reservoir of passion
To fill your need,
And it's free, Gabey,
Without fee, Gabey,
Can't you see, Gabey?

It's all free!

CLAIRE AND HILDY
Ya got he!

CHIP AND OZZIE
Ya got she!

CLAIRE, HILDY, CHIP, OZZIE
Ya got we!!

CLAIRE, HILDY, CHIP, OZZIE
Ya got me!!!

The music deliciously enhances the humor in the lyric. It employs Latin rhythms and melodic formulas, and it has swinging orchestrations by Elliott Jacoby.[57] In its broadest outlines, "Ya Got Me" joins components typical of Latin big bands with the popular-song structure of a Broadway show. Latin swing, as defined by ethnomusicologist John Storm Roberts, included a "head" with a basic theme, a "montuno section during which the *coro* (chorus) began its unvarying refrain," and "a section of contrasting riffs for brass and reeds, which was to come to be called the 'mambo' section."[58] "Ya Got Me" merges that format with the verse and chorus structure of Broadway.

"Ya Got Me" opens with a high-energy 4-bar head (or riff) that immediately codes the number as Latin (Example 8.3). Ethnic markers appear throughout, from the opening instrumental glissando to the underlying rhythm of 3 + 3 + 2 and the prominence of brass. The melody of the verse is also riff-based, with 1-bar syncopated cells. The verse breaks at the midpoint when three gleaming brass chords land on the beat (m. 12). When the chorus begins, the key shifts abruptly from B-flat minor to B-flat major, one of many such moments when a change of key ramps up energy (m. 21). The opening of the bridge is punctuated by a chromatic upward-sweeping burst in the brass (m. 29).

The most Latin part of the number comes with an instrumental break before the final vocal ensemble, which functions like a mambo section. The brass leads the way into this instrumental revelry, with hard-driving percussion. At the bridge, the piano breaks into a segment labeled "Boogie Woogie" (Example 8.4). A rhythmic shift in the third trombone articulates this new beat, as does the rhythm section. There is a steady eighth-note pattern marked "Swing," and the section is pared down to a Latin-jazz combo. Mario Bauza, who in the 1940s was musical director for Machito and His Afro-Cubans, describes the mix of styles that made up Latin jazz, recalling how he wanted "to bring Latin music up to the standard of the American orchestras" and "brought a couple of the guys that arranged for Calloway and Chick Webb."[59] Bauza and other band leaders aimed to "blend [the] Cuban rhythm section and repertoire with a trumpet and sax frontline that played the most powerful of black swing voicings," according to John Storm Roberts.[60] The mambo section of "Ya Got Me" produces just this sort of fusion, although it zips by so fast that it is hard to pick up the details. "Ya Got Me" ends with another key change, and the rumba rhythm leads into the final chorus, producing a high-voltage conclusion.

Example 8.3. "Ya Got Me," mm. 1–8.

Example 8.4. "Ya Got Me," orchestral score, mm. 143–47

From start to finish, "Ya Got Me" has an infectious sense of swing, trading on what the dance critic Edwin Denby obliquely dubbed "monkeyshines," which he called "the most striking moment of all" in the many details that he admired in the show's choreography.[61] He was probably referring to the clowning around that accompanied "Ya Got Me." The entire number was choreographed, and in 1988 the movements were reenacted in *Jerome Robbins' Broadway*, a show that featured highlights from Robbins's career. To reconstruct the original, Robbins gathered together Comden, Green, Nancy Walker, and Cris Alexander, and Comden published an account of their process of choreographic recovery:

> Jerry remembered how quickly it ["Ya Got Me"] had fallen into place that first time, how spontaneous it had been, how inevitably right every move he invented turned out to be. We had gathered around a table on the stage of the Colonial Theatre in Boston and in a short time, through Jerry's wizardry, it was all there. This time—in 1988—we again took our places around a table.... Gabey had sat downstage of the table, with his head on it. Or had he sat somewhat to the side so we could perform at him better? And we were couples. Chip (Chris) with Hildy the cab driver (Nancy), and Ozzie (Adolph) with Claire de Loone the anthropologist (me). Wouldn't the couples have sat side by side? But we changed places a lot during the number, jumping from chair to chair and winding up in the perfect spot for each to sing his separate message of cheer and devotion to Gabey. How did we do that?[62]

Journeying through memories, Comden recalled how the music was deeply kinetic. "The words of my chorus of this song from 'On the Town' plus the attendant wild gestures," Comden wrote, "have recently taken up residence inside my head and body and they refuse to move out." She then described the movements that made up those "wild gestures" (ellipses appear in the original):

> YA GOT ME, BABY, YA GOT ME! (ba-bumbum-bum! while clapping hands over head and stamping feet)
>
> YA GOT MY EXTENSIVE KNOWLEDGE OF ANATOMY... (while outlining undulating body with rippling hands)
>
> YA GOT MY WHO-O-O-OLE INTEREST IN MANKIND OF EVERY BREED (while extending arms in generous gesture of giving)
>
> AND IT'S FREE, BABY, IT'S ALL FREE! IT'S ALL FREE! IT'S ALL FREE! IT'S ALL FREE! (while dancing to new position)[63]

Comden also recalled the choreography for the orchestral mambo section, which she called the "tango part":

> Chris remembered there was a place where we all "made like an accordion." It was in the tango part where Gabey danced with all of us at once, one lined up behind the other, and we spread apart as far as we could, still holding on, and then folded back together in a tight clump. And JR [Robbins] recalled that at one point we had all sat on Gabey's lap, one on top of the other. Adolph

remembered his mad bit of "bullfight" solo, and flung himself into it, astonishing all the dancers in the room.

"Ya Got Me," then, was a razzle-dazzle ensemble number, and its pantomimed antics were central to both Jerome Robbins's choreography and Adolph Green's shtick.

SLAM BANG CLUB: AFRICAN AMERICAN SWING

In the final segment of *On the Town*'s nightclub scene, the women and sailors move to the Slam Bang Club, a site where, as Claire declares, "the music's primitive, the atmosphere primeval."[64] It was a black club, as early versions of the script attested, and its character was defined by its small size and musical style. "The music changes from Latin to good swing music," states Version A of the script.[65] A "colored girl" launches into "Ain't Got No Tears Left," which, like "Big Stuff" and "It's Gotta Be Bad to Be Good," was a preexisting song by Bernstein, plugged into a new context.[66] Once again, the number was ultimately replaced. In Version C of the script, "Tender Night" replaced "Ain't Got No Tears Left," and it must have been a placeholder. The real change—one that was thoroughly radical—came on opening night in New York, when "I Understand," performed by Pitkin, culminated the scene.[67]

Thus the segment at the Slam Bang Club went from showcasing black jazz—and explicitly indicating an African American singer—to featuring Pitkin, the white comic cuckold. In the final script, the only remnant of the segment's black origins was "Slam Bang Blues (Dixieland)," an 8-bar instrumental arrangement of "I'm Blue," which serves as a transition from the Congacabana Club and is scored for a small jazz ensemble of rhythm section (including piano), trumpet, trombone, and clarinet.[68] In the show's staging, a residue of the segment's black origins appeared in the presence of two black patrons at the Slam Bang Club: Dorothy McNichols and Flash Riley.[69] All of the other five patrons were white. This meant that the Slam Bang Club was represented as mixed-race, much like the places where Comden and Green had been performing.

Although draft scripts do not link the Slam Bang Club with an actual New York site, its name probably represented a takeoff on the Ubangi Club, a famous Harlem venue that opened in 1936 in the former premises of Connie's Inn. The Ubangi Club moved with considerable fanfare in late 1941 or early 1942 to W. 52nd Street.[70] "Broadway has accepted the new Ubangi Club on Broadway at 52nd Street as it did the old Cotton Club and other cabaret revues featuring colored entertainment," reported the *Amsterdam News* in January 1942, "mainly because Broadway knows that the Gay White Way would not be truly gay without a major Negro vehicle of fun."[71] At the Harlem location, there had been a drag component to the club, which could have enhanced its appeal for some on the creative team of *On the Town*. Gladys Bentley, a black lesbian entertainer, was regularly featured there, and her well-known floor show "attracted an interracial audience of literati and entertainers, including many gay men and lesbians," writes historian George Chauncey. The *Amsterdam News* reported that "during her sojourn at Ubangi,"

Adolph Green, Betty Comden, and Robert Chisholm, in the scene where Pitkin sings "I Understand" for the first time. He does so while serving champagne to his fiancée and her new boyfriend, and he wears an apron that matches his tie (Act I, Scene 9). Photofest Digital Archive.

Bentley "held the reputation of having brought more Park Avenue notables and International celebrities to Harlem than any other entertainer."[72] She delivered raunchy lyrics, heading up "a revue that included a pansy chorus line composed entirely of female impersonators."[73] The article described her as a "talented pianist," and her choice of music appealed to an audience of broad-ranging backgrounds: "Her versatility is not only confined to entertainment, but she is an excellent linguist and composer. Her songs in French, Spanish, Yiddish and the like are a sensation."[74] By the time the Ubangi Club moved downtown, Bentley had relocated to Los Angeles. At the new Ubangi, the band of jazz violinist Stuff Smith performed regularly "before a packed house of Naval officers and colored and white patrons," as the *Amsterdam News* observed—the very demographic represented in *On the Town*.[75]

"Ain't Got No Tears Left," which in early scripts for *On the Town* was to be delivered by a black singer, was yet another number that dated back to Bernstein's songwriting period in 1943. A lead sheet titled "I've Got No Tears Left" exists in the composer's hand, and the number was revamped for incorporation in *On the Town*, as documented in a copyist's score. There, a second A section was added after the bridge, and the lyric was revised, presumably in conjunction with Comden and Green.[76] The tempo on the lead sheet is "Slow and Blue or Slow and Dirty." The song joins "Big Stuff" and "It's Gotta Be Bad to Be Good" in fusing the style of a 16-bar blues with a fairly standard popular song form.

No documentation exists to show whether a singer was selected to deliver "Ain't Got No Tears Left." Since Robbins had a score for the number, it is clear he was working with the song, and casting might have taken place. If so, Royce Wallace would have been a likely candidate. Had the scene in the Slam Bang Club been retained as originally conceived, it would have enacted a common experience in wartime New York, with sailors and their dates hanging out at clubs that featured black performers and catered to mixed-race audiences. Showcasing a black performer as a nightclub singer was also a standard trope in Broadway shows and Hollywood films that were otherwise white.

OPERETTA DISPLACES SWING: "I UNDERSTAND"

Once the experience of listening to the blues was dropped from the Slam Bang Club, "I Understand" culminated the scene, and it appeared very late in the development process. The new number was sung by Pitkin, also known as Judge Pitkin W. Bridgework, who begins the song in a state of abject emasculation because of Claire's infidelities. Over the course of four stanzas, he progresses to a triumphal assertion of his manhood. In parodying both gender and high-art culture, Pitkin's character came straight out of operetta via The Revuers. Pitkin first had sung one stanza of "I Understand" in Act I, Scene 9, when he discovered Claire's shenanigans with Ozzie, and he turned up again at the tail end of the nightclub segments at Diamond Eddie's and the Congacabana. Each time, Claire stuck him with the bill and waltzed off with Ozzie. Like a wimp, Pitkin paid the check, affirming his docility with a four-note tag, "I Understand." At the end of the Slam Bang segment, however, he finally wakes up, declaring, "I hereby do not understand." Comedy results both from a gendered portrayal of Pitkin and also from a racial bait-and-switch. Rather than including a blues-based number, which would have fit comfortably in a swing club, "I Understand" suddenly—jarringly—preens as a parody of Gilbert and Sullivan, without a syncopation or rumba rhythm in sight. The key to the humor in "I Understand"—and it is one of the funniest songs in the show—comes in part from the abrupt racial turnabout.

The lyric for "I Understand" is remarkable. Pitkin uses each of the first three stanzas to recall an absurd episode in which he was played for a fool, and in the final stanza he recoups his masculinity. The key to the lyric's success lies in its details. In the second line of each stanza, for example, the message of the first line is restated with inverted word order (e.g., "My lollipop stole he"), employing a technique also used in "Come Up to My Place." In the third and fourth lines, awkward rhymes occur on the final words (e.g., "hide" and "I'd"). And in the last word of the fifth line (which needs to rhyme with "understand"), the rhyme carries across all the stanzas, as underlined below.

[Stanza 1]
When I was five my brother stole my lollipop.
My lollipop stole he!
But I didn't mutter "Damn your hide,"
He needed candy more than I'd
So instead of biting off his <u>hand</u>,
I just said "Goo! I understand!"

[Stanza 2]
When I was ten my mother trounced me with a mop.
With a mop troun-cèd she me!
But I didn't mutter "Damn your eyes,"
I knew she needed exercise,
So instead of joining a gypsy <u>band</u>,
I just said "Mom, I understand."

[Stanza 3]
At thirty a man in a car ruthlessly ran me down.
He ruthlessly down ran me!
But I didn't mutter "Damn your spleen,"
For a man's a man but a car's a machine.
So instead of stripping him of his <u>land</u>,
I just said "Jack—I understand."

[Stanza 4]
Now I'm forty-five and I've met Claire, we're engaged to wed.
Engaged to wed are we!
But tonight I tell you "Damn you Claire!"
You played me evil, and that's not fair!
So instead of remaining calm and <u>bland</u>,
I hereby do not understand!!![77]

Bernstein's musical setting accentuates the highbrow parodies of the text. Marked "Moderato, lugubriously," "I Understand" is essentially a recitative cloaked in the garb of a popular song. Each stanza is sixteen bars—that is, half as long as the norm. The number's main goal, as with any recitative, is to deliver a story, and the accompaniment drops to the background, reduced to the kind of oompah chords that were common with The Revuers. In each stanza, the most tactically deployed high note falls on the last word of the fifth line (that is, the text underlined in the lyric on page 288). In the final line of the first three stanzas, Pitkin surrenders to his fate as a wimp by dropping an octave and a half to proclaim, "I understand" (Example 8.5). In the final stanza, however, he suddenly rebukes Claire and soars to his liberation in part through melodic range, ending on an exultant high note, with rhythmic pacing that enhances the dramatic effect (Example 8.6).

Comparing "I Understand" with an excerpt near the opening of *The Pirates of Penzance* offers yet another example of how Comden and Green reprocessed Gilbert and Sullivan. For one thing, both lyrics use a six-line stanza. For another, they playfully distort the pronunciation of words to produce ungainly rhymes. "Hide" and "I'd," as just discussed in "I Understand," are absurd in a similar way to "gyrate" and "pirate" in the excerpt from *The Pirates of Penzance*. Both also employ

Example 8.5. "I Understand," piano-vocal score, mm. 13, with pickup – 18.

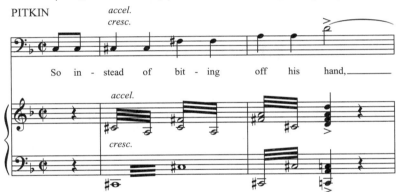

Example 8.6. "I Understand," piano-vocal score, mm. 64, with pickup – 69.

illogical juxtapositions, with innocent idiocy often producing dire results. Pitkin's episodes with the lollipop and the mop bear a relationship to actions of the child's nurse in Gilbert and Sullivan's *The Pirates of Penzance*, who makes the unfortunate mistake of confusing a "pilot" with a "pirate" because she is "hard of hearing":

The Pirates of Penzance

I was a stupid nurserymaid,
On breakers always steering,
And I did not catch the word aright,
through being hard of hearing;
Mistaking my instructions,
Which within my brain did gyrate,
I took and bound this promising boy
Apprentice to a pirate.
A sad mistake it was to make
And doom him to a vile lot.

I bound him to a pirate—you—
Instead of to a pilot.[78]

The Revuers' parody "Three Little Psychopaths Are We" also had resonances in Pitkin's song, as it had with "New York, New York." Conceived as a spoof on "Three Little
Maids" from *The Mikado*, "Three Little Psychopaths" poked fun at a "sordid" childhood, while ghoulishly mocking violence in children. With much more verbiage,
"I Understand" basically does the same thing, with Pitkin looking back at himself
as a five-year-old and recalling that he contemplated "biting off" his brother's hand:

"Three Little Psychopaths"

Our childhood was blighted by matters both sordid and dark,
At the ripe age of two, our nurses we slew in the park.[79]

"I Understand"

When I was five my brother stole my lollipop.
. . .
So instead of biting off his hand,
I just said "Goo! I understand!"

Even as Pitkin was a character straight out of operetta, he was also a classic figure
within the tradition of nightclub scenes: an upper-class white who suddenly
found himself in an intoxicating but nefarious world of scantily clad chorines and
lowbrow divas belting out tunes drenched in rumba rhythms and the blues.

* * *

Over the course of its three brief segments, the nightclub scene contributed to
the intentional hyperactivity of *On the Town*, as the principal characters barely
finished a drink in one club before they dashed off to another. Each segment of
the scene zipped by in a hyped-up flurry. Having passed the Cinderella hour in
their single day of freedom, the sailors were watching time evaporate. Songs were
partly sung and scenarios interrupted as they pursued a good time with increasing desperation. If the original concept of the scene had been enacted and the
final version had included two blues-based popular songs together with an African American vocalist, the work's overall commitment to black performers would
have been sharpened. Yet as substantial streamlining took place, especially during
the major rehabilitation in Boston, editorial concision and dramatic effectiveness
overwhelmed political goals. By that point, George Abbott was at the controls.

Yet even with diminished attention to race, the final version of the nightclub
scene had a great deal to say about the character of New York City during World War
II. Diamond Eddie's Nightclub evoked entertainment intended to attract crowds of
white middle- and working-class patrons, enticing them through nostalgic cues to a
world that was slipping away. It traded on spectacle and splashy production numbers, on memory, and on constructing a cultural comfort zone with people just like
oneself. The Congacabana broadened the geographic lens to represent solidarity
with Latin cultures in the era of the Good Neighbor Policy, when the Western

Hemisphere formed a phalanx of morality against fascism and military aggression in Europe and Asia. The segment also tipped its hat to the campy onstage antics of performers such as Carmen Miranda and to Latin jazz, which was gaining an enthusiastic audience via recordings and radio. Finally, the Slam Bang Club gestured ever so slightly to the intense interplay between black swing clubs in Harlem and those in the neighborhood of Broadway. For some in the audience, it also triggered reminders of drag entertainment in the same locations.

By the end of the nightclub scene, when the bulky basso Pitkin stood at center stage, the world of Gilbert and Sullivan trumped all else, delivering laughs through gendered stereotypes, word inversions, operatic high notes, and unadulterated whiteness. Whether intentionally or not, ideals about providing a showcase for African Americans had been scaled back, at the same time as the racial groups that did remain in the scene—meaning whites and Latinos—were subjected to a campy lampoon. At its most fundamental level, the nightclub scene demonstrated how an omnivorous consumption of contemporary culture was central to the comedy style of *On the Town*.

EPILOGUE
Beyond *Fancy Free* and
On the Town

● ● ●

The presence of Sono Osato as a star on Broadway, playing the unlikely role of an all-American beauty queen, represented one of the more remarkable moments in American performance during World War II. With messages more understated than explicit, *On the Town* and *Fancy Free* found ways to challenge the era's restrictions on personal freedoms, modeling interracial fellowship and signaling the presence of gay culture. For their part, The Revuers devised skits that showed empathy for the working class, and they practiced their politics by appearing in mixed-race venues. All this was achieved through lighthearted comedy and performed virtuosity, with music, lyrics, and dance rising out of a shared aesthetic. With these early works, Bernstein, Robbins, Comden, and Green developed ways of using their art to blur boundaries, finding themselves equally at home in nightclubs and in concert halls, in live performances or on the radio. They crossed over aesthetically, and they also did so racially. Ultimately, they moved beyond conceptual frameworks that embedded division, as they strove for a middle ground of open-minded integration, where long-standing categories of all sorts could be erased. They found artistic satisfaction in that place. "I like middle," the American writer John Updike once declared in an interview. "It is in middles that extremes clash, where ambiguity restlessly rules."[1]

On the Town, *Fancy Free*, and The Revuers ultimately appear as part of a process in which American creative and performing artists sought to express not only their individual identities but also those of a multifaceted nation. Compelled by the power of African American music and dance and the growing diversity of the country's population, Bernstein and his collaborators challenged the domination of the European high-art tradition, even as they deeply loved its music, literature, and classical ballets. Yet far from endorsing a highbrow bias that deemed Art with a capital *A* to be good while dismissing commercial entertainment as lightweight, they shaped a fluid definition of themselves and the work they created, finding liberation in the combination of seemingly disparate realms. "Every time I do a show I'm known as the ballet choreographer, and every time I do a ballet I'm known as the Broadway choreographer," Robbins once declared.[2] Taking a more provocative stance, Bernstein told a reporter right before the opening of *On the Town* that he liked to do "anything that's fun," asserting that he gained equal pleasure from composing for the commercial theater and a symphony orchestra. "I'm very promiscuous that way," he declared, "and I like all music if it's good."[3]

Those values continued to resonate over the decades, and *West Side Story* of 1957 was a striking outgrowth. Recognized today as one of the landmarks in American music and theater, *West Side Story* brought together some of the same collaborators as *On the Town*, including Bernstein, Robbins, the set designer Oliver Smith, and the conductor Max Goberman. The rich complexity of a city-scape again provided a conceptual core. Broadway conventions again merged with contemporary jazz, opera, and operetta. And minorities again were represented as part of the community. A fascination with Latin music and culture also resurfaced, expanding to fuel an entire show. While the male gangs of *West Side Story* are larger than the group of three sailors in *Fancy Free*, they too navigated the stage in tightly compressed packs, achieving cartoon-like synchrony, and those gangs can be read as embodying gay subjectivity within an overall plot that is heterosexual. Furthermore, like *On the Town*, *West Side Story* showcased per-formers of color, including the African American soprano Reri Grist as Con-suela, Donald McKayle as dance captain, and a number of Latinos: Chita Rivera as Anita, Tony Mordente as A-Rab, Jamie Sanchez as Chino, and Carmen Guti-errez as Teresita. As a result, *West Side Story* reconfigured a wartime focus on swing, youth culture, and a segregated military to address issues of the 1950s, especially new Puerto Rican immigrants and teen violence in New York's bar-rios. The political message of *West Side Story* might have been more brazenly stated than in *On the Town*, but it was still encased in beautiful melodies, daz-zling choreography, and compelling entertainment. In the intervening decade, the civil rights movement had gained considerable momentum, with the forced integration of Little Rock Central High School taking place the day before *West Side Story* opened.[4]

In the decades after *On the Town* and *Fancy Free*, Bernstein continued to build on the compositional aesthetic of montage, with a delight in simulating the music of others. By incorporating this intentional cut-and-paste effect, he often found himself accused of writing conductor's music, meaning that his head was filled with so many sounds originating with other people that it compromised his crea-tivity. These criticisms reflected a high-modernist ideology that valued a notion of pure originality.

With the passage of time, however, the sampling and postmodern quotation of the twenty-first century offer new ways of understanding Bernstein's aes-thetic, and fresh perceptions of his music are emerging. Reviewing a performance of Bernstein's *Mass* that took place in the fall of 2008, for example, Anthony Tom-masini of the *New York Times* addressed these shifting attitudes. In 1971, when *Mass* first appeared, it fused rock, jazz, and sacred choral traditions, and it was judged as iconoclastic and wrongheaded, even chaotic, for doing so. "A lingering criticism of 'Mass,'" Tommasini wrote three decades later, "is that with his brash mixing of pop and classical styles, Bernstein came across as just too hip. But the evocations are expertly done. And today such blending of styles is commonplace.

Young composers, who disdain categories, borrow from any style they care to."[5] String quartets now play in clubs, and jazz has a home at Lincoln Center.

Many aspects of *Mass* that were once perceived as audacious traced their lineage to *Fancy Free* and *On the Town*. *Mass* incorporated diverse instrumental ensembles, including a standard orchestra, a rock band, and an ensemble of steel drums and percussion—a technique related to Bernstein's flexible deployment of a pit orchestra in the 1940s. *Mass* also drew upon a mixed-race cast, with choreography by the famed African American dancer Alvin Ailey, and it addressed social crises of its day, especially with its antiwar message. Archival documents show that as Bernstein conceived the work, he envisioned a protest against violence and genocide by contemplating the composition of "4 Lullabies for Martyrs," including "JFK, RFK, MLK, MX, and 6,000,000 (1,000,000 children)"—that is, an ecumenical list of those who had been murdered because of race or political conviction, including John F. Kennedy, Robert F. Kennedy, Martin Luther King Jr., Malcolm X, and victims of the Holocaust.[6]

Back in the 1940s, as a commitment to racial desegregation informed the work of Bernstein and his colleagues in deeply meaningful ways, it affected both the political ideology underlying their art and the nature of the art itself, contributing to a strong sense of collaboration and community. In reviewing the debut production of *On the Town*, the dance critic Edwin Denby marveled at how the "originality" of the show came from the "spirit" of the dancing. "Spirit": what an apt word to describe not only *On the Town* but also this cluster of World War II productions overall! "All of them, chorus as well as principals," Denby continued, "give you the sense of a happy co-operation with the piece and with each other, a cordial glow that they share, newcomers and experienced dancers alike."[7] As it turns out, that "cordial glow" was no accident. It came from valorizing differences of race and gender, from forging "a happy community," as Osato once characterized social interactions among *On the Town*'s cast.[8] And it defined membership in that community in broad-minded terms. "Participate as citizens of the United States and as citizens of the world," Robbins advised his fellow choreographers when *On the Town* was in the midst of its run.[9] At a fundamental level, he and his collaborators were intent on mixing art with responsible citizenship, as they challenged the artistic, social, and cultural boundaries that constricted who could enjoy the full benefits of living in the United States. They aimed for art that would help make a better world, and *Fancy Free* and *On the Town* launched an enduring commitment to stage those very ideals.

APPENDIX
Selected Discography and Videography for The Revuers, *Fancy Free*, and *On the Town*
Compiled by Elizabeth Titrington Craft

Note: This discography includes all known recorded material of The Revuers. Audio recordings of *Fancy Free* and *On the Town*, as listed here, include all complete recordings and some major releases of selections from those works. Single numbers and arrangements are omitted. The discography includes selected online resources, available as of late 2012, though the details of their contents are frequently unverifiable. Listed video recordings of *Fancy Free* and *On the Town* include commercially available complete recordings and known footage of the original productions. Recordings are listed in chronological order by release date.

THE REVUERS
Audio Recordings

The Girl with the Two Left Feet/Joan Crawford Fan Club (1940). The Revuers with Leonard Bernstein, piano. 78 rpm. Musicraft records 1133, 1134, and 1135. Reissued on *Leonard Bernstein, Wunderkind* (1998), CD, 2 discs, Pearl GEMS 0005.

"The Magazine Stand," "Nightlife," "20th Anniversary of Radio," "The World's Fair," "The World of Music," and "WSM's 15th Anniversary" from the NBC radio series *Fun with the Revuers* (1940). http://otrrlibrary.org, *Old Time Radio Researchers Group Library*, streaming.

"Tin Pan Alley" in "Command Performance—Episode 101 2/3" (1944). YouTube video, 9:36. From a performance recorded January 15, 1944, broadcast in the radio series *Command Performance, USA!*, produced by the Radio Section of the Bureau of Public Relations under the War Department. Posted by OTRNut, April 28, 2009, http://www.youtube.com/watch?v=QJFsEbt55rQ.

"The Reader's Digest," "Baroness Bazooka," and "Movie Ads" in *A Party with Betty Comden and Adolph Green* (1958), original Broadway cast, recorded live. LP, Capitol SWAO-1197. Reissued (1993) as CD, Angel 764773.

"The Reader's Digest," "The Screen Writers," "The Banshee Sisters," and "The Baroness Bazooka" in *A Party with Betty Comden and Adolph Green* (1977), Broadway cast, recorded live at Arena Stage, Washington, D.C., May 1, 1977. LP, Stet S2L-5177. Reissued (1996) as CD, DRG 5177.

"Tin Pan Alley" and "The Magazine Sellers" on *Judy Holliday: A Legacy of Laughter* (1984). LP, AEI 2118.

Video Recordings

Greenwich Village (1944). The Revuers are part of the "musical ensemble." Directed by Walter Lang. DVD, Twentieth Century Fox 2252003.

FANCY FREE (BALLET, 1944)
Audio Recordings

Ballet Theatre Orchestra (1946). *Fancy Free.* Conducted by Leonard Bernstein. Recorded June 2, 1944, and March 13, 1946. 78 rpm, 4 discs, Decca DA-406. Reissued on *Leonard Bernstein, Wunderkind* (1998), CD, 2 discs, Pearl GEMS 0005.

Boston Pops Orchestra (1947). *Music from the Ballet Fancy Free.* Includes "Galop," "Waltz," and "Danzón." Conducted by Arthur Fiedler. Recorded June 5, 1946. 78 rpm, Victor 11-9386. Reissued on *On the Town: Original Cast Recording* (2010), CD, Naxos 8.120889.

Philadelphia Pops Orchestra (1952). *William Walton: Four Dances from "Facade"; Leonard Bernstein: Three Dances from "Fancy Free."* Includes "Galop," "Waltz," and "Danzón." Conducted by Alexander Hilsberg. Recorded January 3, 1952. LP, Columbia AAL-17.

Ballet Theatre Orchestra (1953). *Bernstein: Fancy Free; Copland: Rodeo.* Conducted by Joseph Levine. Recorded 1952. LP, Capitol P-8196. Reissued for streaming and download as Naxos Classical Archives 9.80305.

Boston Pops Orchestra (1953). *Slaughter on Tenth Avenue and Other Ballet Selections.* Includes "Galop," "Waltz," and "Danzón." Conducted by Arthur Fiedler. Recorded June 25, 1952. LP, RCA LM-1726.

Columbia Symphony Orchestra (1956). *Bernstein: Fancy Free; Copland: El Salón Mexico; Milhaud: La Création du Monde.* Conducted by Leonard Bernstein. Recorded July 13, 1956. LP, Columbia CL-920. Reissued on *Bernstein: Prelude, Fugue and Riffs, On the Town (Three Dance Episodes), Fancy Free, Serenade After Plato's Symposium* (1998), CD, Sony 60559.

Boston Pops Orchestra (1959). *Rodgers: Slaughter on Tenth Avenue.* Includes "Galop," "Waltz," and "Danzón." Conducted by Arthur Fiedler. Recorded June 18, 1958. LP, RCA LM-2294/LSC-2294. Reissued (1997) as CD, RCA 68550.

New York Philharmonic (1965). *Bernstein Conducts Bernstein.* Conducted by Leonard Bernstein. Recorded June 11, 1963. LP, Columbia ML-6077/MS-6677. Reissued on *Bernstein: Candide Overture, Symphonic Dances from West Side Story, On the Waterfront Symphonic Suite, Fancy Free Ballet* with extra tracks and remastered (2004), CD, Sony Classical Masterworks 92728.

Concert Arts Orchestra (1967). *The Story of Great Music: The Music of Today.* Conducted by Robert Irving. Recorded 1966. LP, 4 discs, Time-Life TL-145/STL-145. Reissued on *Copland & Bernstein* (2001), CD, EMI Seraphim 74503.

Israel Philharmonic Orchestra (1979). *Leonard Bernstein: Serenade, Fancy Free.* Conducted by Leonard Bernstein. Recorded October 23, 1978, Frederic R. Mann Auditorium, Tel Aviv. LP, Deutsche Grammophon 2531 196. Reissued on *Bernstein Conducts Bernstein* (2003), CD, 7 discs, Deutsche Grammophon 000001402.

Saint Louis Symphony Orchestra (1986). *Leonard Bernstein: Candide—Facsimile—Fancy Free—On the Town.* Conducted by Leonard Slatkin. Recorded October 1985 and April 1986. LP, Angel DS-37358. Reissued (1997) as CD, EMI 72091.

National Philharmonic Orchestra (1986). *A Salute to America.* Includes "Danzón," "Waltz," and "Galop," conducted by Eric Hammerstein. CD, Menuet 160003-2.

Bournemouth Symphony Orchestra (1991). *Bernstein: Symphony No. 2, Candide Overture, Fancy Free.* Conducted by Andrew Litton. Recorded July 1990, Wessex Hall, Poole Arts Centre, Dorset. CD, Virgin Classics 7 91433-2. Reissued as *Leonard Bernstein:*

Overture—Candide; Fancy Free; Symphony No. 2, "The Age of Anxiety" (2008), CD, EMI Classics 34461.

Baltimore Symphony Orchestra (1997). *Bernstein: West Side Story Symphonic Dances, Candide Overture, Fancy Free, Facsimile.* Conducted by David Zinman. Recorded on February 3 and 4, 1996 at Joseph Meyerhoff Symphony Hall, Baltimore, Maryland. London/Decca 452 916-2.

Jena Philharmonic Orchestra (1997). *Leonard Bernstein: Overture to Candide, Symphonic Dances from West Side Story, Symphonic Suite from On the Waterfront, Fancy Free.* Conducted by David Montgomery. Recorded July 30, 1996, Volkshaus Jena, Germany. CD, Arte Nova Classics 74321 43321 2. Reissued (2006) as CD, Arte Nova 433210.

Royal Philharmonic Orchestra (1999). *Bernstein: Overture to Candide; Symphonic Dances from West Side Story; Symphonic Suite from On the Waterfront.* Includes "Galop," "Waltz," and "Danzón." Conducted by Carl Davis. Recorded 1996. CD, Platinum 2878. Reissued (2010) as CD, RPO 28780.

Nashville Symphony (2006). *Fancy Free; Dybbuk.* Conducted by Andrew Mogrelia. American Classics. Recorded principally May 14–16, 2005, Blair Hall, Nashville, Tennessee. CD, Naxos 8.559280.

Video Recordings: Original Production

American Ballet Theatre (194-?). *Jerome Robbins collection [of] Fancy Free 8 mm scenes.* Footage of (supposed) original *Fancy Free*, from the balcony. DVD, transferred from Digital Betacam cassette. Available at the New York Public Library, MGZIDVD 5-6092.

Ballet Theatre (1944). *[Ballet Theatre—Excerpts].* Performed by John Kriza, Jerome Robbins, and Janet Reed. Excerpts from Ballet Theatre productions. Chapman collection of ballet films. DVD, available at the New York Public Library, MGZIDVD 5-6031.

Ballet Theatre (1944–45). *Fancy Free [Excerpts].* Performed by Harold Lang, John Kriza, Janet Reed, Muriel Bentley, Richard Reed, Paula Lloyd, Norma Vance, Eric Braun, Zachary Solov, and Paul Godkin. Filmed in performances at the Civic Opera House, Chicago, 1944–45, by Ann Barzel. VHS. Available at the New York Public Library, MGZIA 4-6076 JRC.

Ballet Theatre (1944–45). *Fancy Free/Ballet Theatre; choreography by Jerome Robbins.* Performed by the original cast: Jerome Robbins, John Kriza, Harold Lang (Sailors), Janet Reed, Muriel Bentley, Shirley Eckl (Passersby), and Rex Cooper (Bartender). Filmed in performance. Gift of American Ballet Theatre. VHS. Available at the New York Public Library, MGZIA 4-5120.

Jerome Robbins: Something to Dance About (2009). Includes some footage from original production, with Harold Lang, John Kriza, and Jerome Robbins. Written by Amanda Vaill, produced and directed by Judy Kinberg. Originally broadcast on PBS on February 18, 2009, as an episode of the television program *American Masters.* DVD, Kultur D4454.

ON THE TOWN (MUSICAL, 1944)
Audio Recordings

Studio production (1945). *On the Town.* Victor Chorale conducted by Robert Shaw and "On the Town" Orchestra conducted by Leonard Bernstein. Includes "Lonely Town," "Times Square," "Dance of the Great Lover," "Dream in the Subway," "I Feel Like I'm Not Out of Bed Yet/New York, New York," "Some Other Time," and "Lucky to Be Me." Recorded February 3, 1945. 78 rpm, 4 discs, RCA Victor M/DM 995. Reissued on *Leonard Bernstein, Wunderkind* (1998), CD, 2 discs, Pearl GEMS 0005.

Studio production with members of the original cast (1946). *Selections from Oliver Smith and Paul Feigay's On the Town.* Conducted by Lyn Murray, Camarata, and Leonard Joy. With Nancy Walker, Betty Comden, and Adolph Green from the original production and Mary Martin. Recorded February 1 and 6, 1945, and September 14, 1945. 78 rpm, 3 discs, Decca A-416. Reissued on *On the Town: Original Cast Recording* (2010), CD, Naxos 8.120889.

Film soundtrack with additional songs by Roger Edens, Betty Comden, and Adolph Green (1949). *On the Town & Dancing Co-Ed.* Conducted by Lennie Hayton. With Frank Sinatra, Gene Kelly, Jules Munshin, Ann Miller, Betty Garrett, Vera-Ellen, and Alice Pearce. LP, Caliban 6023.

Performances by Betty Comden and Adolph Green (1955). *Comden and Green.* Includes "New York, New York," "Lonely Town," "Taxi Song," "Some Other Time," and "Carried Away." LP, Heritage 0057. Reissued on *Comden and Green Perform Their Own Songs* (1998), CD, DRG 5247.

Studio production of the film (1959). *On the Town.* Conducted by Geoff Love. With Fred Lucas, Dennis Lotis, Lionel Blair, Shane Rimmer, Noele Gordon, and Stella Tanner. LP, Music for Pleasure MFP 1010. Reissued (1980) as LP, Stet DS-15029.

Studio production/"First Full-Length Recording" (1961). *On the Town.* Orchestra conducted by Leonard Bernstein. With original cast members Cris Alexander (Chip), Adolph Green (Ozzie), Nancy Walker (Hildy), and Betty Comden (Claire). Cast also includes Michael Kermoyan (Workman), John Reardon (Gabey), George Gaynes (Pitkin), and Leonard Bernstein (Barker at Coney Island). Recorded May 31, 1960. LP, Columbia Masterworks OS 2028. Reissued (1998) with bonus material as CD, Columbia Broadway Masterworks SK 60538.

London production (1963). *On the Town.* Conducted by Lawrence Leonard. With Elliott Gould, Don McKay, Franklin Kiser, Carol Arthur, Gillian Lewis, and Meg Walter. LP, CBS APG-60005.

Concert recording (1993). *On the Town.* Conducted by Michael Tilson Thomas. With Frederica von Stade (Claire), Tyne Daly (Hildy), Marie McLaughlin (Ivy), Evelyn Lear (Madame Dilly), Cleo Laine (The Nightclub Singer), Thomas Hampson (Gabey), Kurt Ollmann (Chip), David Garrison (Ozzie), Samuel Ramey (Pitkin/First Workman/Announcer), London Voices, and the London Symphony Orchestra. Recorded live, Barbican Centre, London, June 1992. CD, Deutsche Grammophon 437 516-2.

Studio production/"First complete recording" (1996). *On the Town.* National Symphony Orchestra. Conducted by John Owen Edwards. With Gregg Edelman (Chip), Tim Flavin (Ozzie), Ethan Freeman (Gabey), Kim Criswell (Hildy), Judy Kaye (Claire), Louise Gold (Dolores/Cabaret Singer), Valerie Masterson (Dilly), and Tinuke Olafimihan (Ivy). Recorded at Abbey Road Studios on May 9, 10, and 11, 1995. CD, 2 discs, Jay 1231.

Video Recordings

MGM film production (1949). *On the Town.* Directed by Gene Kelly and Stanley Donen. Produced by Arthur Freed. DVD, Warner Home Video 65092.

[On the Town (excerpts)] (1988). Compilation of clips from the original Broadway production. Performers include Allyn Ann McLerie (Ivy), Nancy Walker (Hildy), Betty Comden (Claire), Adolph Green (Ozzie), John Battles (Gabey), Robert Chisholm

(Pitkin), Cris Alexander (Chip), Nanette Fabray (Sara Longstreet), and Jack McCauley (Henry Longstreet). Filmed in performance at the Martin Beck Theatre, New York City, in 1945. VHS, available at the New York Public Library, The Jerome Robbins Collection, MGZIA 4-6069 JRC.

Concert performance (1993). *On the Town.* Conducted by Michael Tilson Thomas. With Betty Comden and Adolph Green (narrators), Frederica von Stade (Claire), Tyne Daly (Hildy), Marie McLaughlin (Ivy), Evelyn Lear (Madame Dilly), Cleo Laine (The Nightclub Singer), Thomas Hampson (Gabey), Kurt Ollmann (Chip), David Garrison (Ozzie), Samuel Ramey (Pitkin/First Workman/Announcer), London Voices, and the London Symphony Orchestra. Videotaped at the Barbican Centre, London, June 1992. VHS and laser disc, Deutsche Grammophon Video 440 072 297-1.

NOTES

ABBREVIATIONS FOR FREQUENTLY CITED SOURCES

B = Box; F = Folder

NYPL	New York Public Library for the Performing Arts, Lincoln Center, New York, NY
ABT Records	American Ballet Theatre Records, Jerome Robbins Dance Division, NYPL
American Memory, LC	American Memory, The Library of Congress, http://memory.loc.gov/ammem/index.html, accessed September 21, 2013. This resource includes selected items from the collections of Leonard Bernstein and Aaron Copland.
Ancestry.com	www.ancestrylibrary.com
Bernstein Collection	Leonard Bernstein Collection, Music Division, Library of Congress, Washington, DC
Bernstein Scrapbooks	Leonard Bernstein Collection Scrapbooks, Washington, DC: Library of Congress Preservation Microfilming Program, 1999.
Black Thought and Culture	Black Thought and Culture, Alexander Street Press, http://alexanderstreet.com/products/black-thought-and-culture.
Burton	Humphrey Burton. *Leonard Bernstein*. New York: Doubleday, 1994.
Clark Collection	Peggy Clark Collection, Music Division, Library of Congress, Washington, DC
Comden-Green Papers	Betty Comden and Adolph Green Papers, Billy Rose Theatre Division, NYPL
Comden Score Collection	Betty Comden Scores, Music Division, NYPL
Copland Collection	Aaron Copland Collection, Music Division, Library of Congress, Washington, DC
Engel Collection	Lehman Engel Collection, Irving S. Gilmore Music Library, Yale University, New Haven, CT
Grove Music Online	*Grove Music Online*. Edited by Deane Root. www.oxfordmusiconline.com.
HTC	Harvard Theatre Collection, Houghton Library, Harvard University, Cambridge, MA
IBDB	Internet Broadway Database, begun in 2001. New York: The Broadway League. www.ibdb.com/index.php.
IMDb	Internet Movie Database, begun in 1990. www.imdb.com.
Jowitt	Deborah Jowitt. *Jerome Robbins: His Life, His Theater, His Dance*. New York: Simon & Schuster, 2004.
Lawrence	Greg Lawrence. *Dance with Demons: The Life of Jerome Robbins*. New York: G. P. Putnam's Sons, 2001.

NNC Papers	*Papers of the National Negro Congress* [1933–1947], Schomburg Center for Research in Black Culture, New York Public Library. Microfilm: Frederick, MD: University Publications of America.
On the Town, Colonial Theatre Program	"December 13 to 23rd, Oliver Smith & Paul Feigay Present 'On the Town,'" Colonial Theatre, Boston, [1944], HTC.
On the Town Program, December 28, 1944	"Adelphi Theatre . . . Beginning Thursday, December 28, 1944, *On the Town*," NYPL Theater Programs.
On the Town, Souvenir Program	"Oliver Smith & Paul Feigay Present *On the Town*," Souvenir Program, [1945], Bernstein Scrapbooks.
On the Town, Souvenir Program for Road Tour	"On the Town" [Souvenir Program], undated, NYPL Programs.
On the Town, Copyist score (Comden)	Betty Comden Scores, Series XII, B6/F1
On the Town, Copyist score (Robbins)	Jerome Robbins Collection Papers, Series I, B64
On the Town, Piano-vocal score	Leonard Bernstein. *On the Town: A Musical Comedy in Two Acts*, book and lyrics by Betty Comden and Adolph Green. New York: Leonard Bernstein Music Publishing Company and Boosey & Hawkes, 1997.
On the Town, Orchestral score	Leonard Bernstein. *On the Town*, June 1992 edition. New York: Jalni Publications and Boosey & Hawkes, 1992. Rental score.
On the Town, Published script	*The New York Musicals of Comden & Green: The Complete Book and Lyrics: On the Town, Wonderful Town, Bells Are Ringing*, foreword by Mike Nichols. New York: Applause Books, 1997.

On the Town, Draft scripts. Versions A and B are compilations of various segments of text, and the chronology of these versions is not clear:

On the Town script, Version A[1]	Comden-Green Papers, Series I, B6/F6
On the Town script, Version A[2]	Jerome Robbins Papers, Series I, B63/F10
On the Town script, Version B	Comden-Green Papers, Series I, B6/F5
On the Town script, Version C	Jerome Robbins Papers, Series I, B63/F11
On the Town script, Version D	Jerome Robbins Papers, Series I, B63/F9
On the Town script, Version E	"The Ron Field Production of ON THE TOWN" [1972]. Comden-Green Papers, Series I, Comden-Green Collection, B6/F7.
"*On the Town* Symposium"	Leonard Bernstein, Betty Comden, Adolph Green, Arthur Laurents, Jerome Robbins, and Oliver Smith. "Projects Committee Introduces Its Landmark Series of Symposia: *On the Town*." *Dramatists Guild Quarterly* 18, no. 2 (1981): 11–24.

Osato Clippings NYPL	Sono Osato, Clipping Files (*MGZR), Jerome Robbins Dance Division, NYPL
Osato Programs NYPL	Sono Osato, Program Files (*MGZB), Jerome Robbins Dance Division, NYPL
RobbinsPP	Jerome Robbins Personal Papers, 1923–2000, Jerome Robbins Dance Division, NYPL
RobbinsCP	Jerome Robbins (Collection) Papers, 1930–2001, Jerome Robbins Dance Division, NYPL
Schomburg Center	Schomburg Center for Research in Black Culture, NYPL
Shoji Osato USCIS Records	U.S. Department of Homeland Security, USCIS Genealogy Program, U.S. Citizenship and Immigration Services, Washington, DC, Case Number CMT-1100601350
Tucker Collection	Lorenzo Tucker Collection, Schomburg Center
Vaill	Amanda Vaill. *Somewhere: The Life of Jerome Robbins*. New York: Broadway Books, 2006.

INTRODUCTION

1. Jerome Robbins, quoted in Tobi Tobias, "Bringing Back Robbins's 'Fancy,'" *Dance Magazine* 54, no. 1 (January 1980): 76.

2. Betty Comden, "Jerome Robbins Gets a Little Help from His Friends," *New York Times*, December 4, 1988.

3. James A. Huston, "Selective Service in World War II," *Current History*, June 1, 1963, 346–48.

4. Allan Bérubé discusses policies "to disqualify homosexuals" in *Coming Out Under Fire: The History of Gay Men and Women in World War Two* (New York: Free Press, 1990), 9 (see Chapter 1, "Getting In," 8–33).

5. For more about Sinatra's draft exemption and the controversy that ensued, see James Kaplan, *Frank: The Voice* (New York: Doubleday, 2010), 186–89.

6. Bernstein, Letter to Copland, written from Sharon, Massachusetts, "1941" added in pencil, Copland Collection B247/F1.

7. This account comes from Jowitt (49; 524), who was told this story in an interview with Brian Meehan. She writes it is not an "actual quote" from Robbins.

8. Re Green: Will Holtzman describes Green as being "exempt from service" in *Judy Holliday* (New York: G. P. Putnam's Sons, 1982), 75. I have obtained Green's draft registration card, which does not include his exemption. It is dated October 16, 1940, gives his employer as the National Broadcasting Co., and states that he is a resident of the Bronx, which means he was still using his parents' address (Adolph Green, Registration Card, October 16, 1940, National Archives, National Personnel Records Center, St. Louis). Re Steve Kyle: "Siegfried Schutzman," U. S. World War II Army Enlistment Records, 1938–1946, Ancestry.com, accessed March 28, 2013.

CHAPTER 1: YOUTHFUL CELEBRITY AND PERSONAL FREEDOM

Epigraphs: Sono Osato, Interview with the author, New York City, February 28, 2009; John Martin, "The Dance: 'Fancy Free' Does It," *New York Times*, April 23, 1944.

1. Bernstein, quoted in Arthur Berger, "Notes on the Program: Three Variations from Fancy Free," New York City Symphony, January 21, 1946, Bernstein Collection B71/F11.

2. John Martin, "'Fancy Free' Still Sparkling Dance," *New York Times*, October 10, 1944.

3. "Black & Blue Ballet," *Time*, May 22, 1944.

4. Edwin Denby, "The American Ballet," *The Kenyon Review* 10, no. 4 (Autumn 1948): 638.

5. Caption to an unlabeled color photo of Robbins taking a leap in *Fancy Free*, RobbinsPP, Series I, B40/F7.

6. *Fancy Free*, Ballet Theatre Orchestra, conducted by Leonard Bernstein, Decca Records DA-406, 1946.

7. In the 1949 production, Robbins, Lang, and Reed returned to their original roles, and Donald Saddler took the part of the Bartender. Saddler later choreographed *Wonderful Town* (W.T., "'Fancy Free' Is Danced by First Cast at Center" [no newspaper named], May 12, 1949, *Fancy Free* Clippings, NYPL).

8. Anne Searcy, "Soviet and American Ballet Exchanges in the Cold War, 1958–1962," Ph.D. dissertation, Harvard University, in progress.

9. Clive Barnes, "Dance: An Anniversary Audience for 'Fancy Free,'" *New York Times*, January 25, 1974, and Clive Barnes, "City Ballet's 'Fancy Free,'" *New York Post*, February 1, 1980. Both in *Fancy Free* Clippings, NYPL.

10. Major writings about *Fancy Free* include: Beth Genné, "'Freedom Incarnate': Jerome Robbins, Gene Kelly, and the Dancing Sailor as an Icon of American Values in World War II," *Dance Chronicle* 24, no. 1 (2001): 83–103; Lawrence, *Dance with Demons*; Jowitt, *Jerome Robbins*; Marshall Berman, *On the Town: One Hundred Years of Spectacle in Times Square* (New York: Random House, 2006); Peter Stoneley, *A Queer History of the Ballet* (London: Routledge, 2007).

11. Maureen Honey, *Creating Rosie the Riveter: Class, Gender, and Propaganda during World War II* (Amherst: University of Massachusetts Press, 1984), 5.

12. George Amberg, *Ballet in America: The Emergence of an American Art* (New York: Duell, Sloan and Pearce, 1949), 140.

13. Agnes de Mille, "'Fancy Free' in Review," liner-note essay, Decca DA-406.

14. For an account of Bernstein's activities that summer, see Ryan Raul Bañagale, "'Each Man Kills the Thing He Loves': Bernstein's Formative Relationship with *Rhapsody in Blue*," *Journal of the Society for American Music* 3, no. 1 (2009): 54–57.

15. In the sketches for *Fancy Free*, the Hawkins title was crossed out, and the paper was reused. The sheets that followed it include "Green Piece/Ballet on a Theme by Adolph Green," Bernstein Collection B15/F9.

16. This sum is given in an early profile of Bernstein: Mark A. Schubart, "Triple-Note Man of the Music World," *The New York Times Magazine*, January 28, 1945. The relative value of $25 (from 1942–43) is $345 in 2011; www.measuringworth.com/uscompare/relativevalue.php, accessed February 9, 2013.

17. Shirley Bernstein, Letter to Leonard Bernstein, written from 86 Park Avenue, Newton, MA, n.d., Bernstein Collection B60B. The letter was probably written during 1940, while Bernstein was studying at Curtis, because Shirley refers to "your woodwind pieces," presumably the unpublished *Four Studies* for two bassoons, two clarinets, and piano (dated 1940). WEEI is a Boston station, and Scott broadcast

from the Bermuda Terrace of the Hotel Brunswick in Boston (David Goldin, "Raymond Scott and His Orchestra," http://radiogoldindex.com/cgi-local/p2.cgi?ProgramName=Raymond+Scott+and+His+Orchestra, accessed February 9, 2013).

18. Bernstein, Letter to Aaron Copland, written from "15 W 52/NYC," 1943, Copland Collection B247/F1.

19. Bernstein, "A Career as an Orchestra Conductor," *1948 Book of Knowledge Annual*, ed. Holland Thompson (New York: The Grolier Society, 1948), 255–56, Bernstein Collection B71/F29.

20. "Young Aide Leads Philharmonic, Steps in When Bruno Walter Is Ill," *New York Times*, November 15, 1943.

21. Robbins, quoted in Tobi Tobias, "Bringing Back Robbins's 'Fancy,' " *Dance Magazine* 54, no. 1 (January 1980): 69.

22. Robbins, quoted in Tobias, 69. Also, Jowitt discusses Robbins's work at Camp Tamiment (26–34).

23. Robbins, Interview with Clive Barnes, 1973; typed draft transcript, RobbinsPP, Series I, B21/F7. This interview served as the basis for Barnes's article, "The 'Fancy' That Made History: Dance 'Fancy Free,' " *New York Times*, February 3, 1974.

24. Robbins, Interview with Clive Barnes.

25. Jowitt, 40.

26. Selma Jeanne Cohen and A. J. Pischl, *The American Ballet Theatre: 1940–1960*, in *Dance Perspectives* 6 (Brooklyn: Dance Perspectives, 1960), [5].

27. Irving Kolodin, "Fifteen Years of Ballet Theatre," *Saturday Review*, April 15, 1955, 30.

28. Amberg, *Ballet in America*, 99.

29. John Martin, "The Dance: Honor Roll—Some Artists of Less than Stellar Rank Who Belong Among Season's Assets," *New York Times*, June 15, 1941.

30. In Ballet Theatre's production of *Petrushka*, Robbins started out dancing "one of the vigorous little coach boys" and advanced to being an understudy to the lead, as recounted in Jowitt, 63–64.

31. Robbins, Interview with Clive Barnes.

32. Robbins, Interview with Clive Barnes.

33. de Mille, " 'Fancy Free' in Review." Jowitt provides a chronology and framework for the conception of *Fancy Free* (74–87).

34. Robbins, quoted in Tobias, 70.

35. Notebook for *Fancy Free*, RobbinsPP, Series II, B40/F3. A separate sheet in Robbins's hand lists "poss. Musicians for F.F.," including [Gershon] Kingsley, Persichetti, [Alec] Wilder, "Siesse" [handwriting is unclear], [Louis] Alter, Gould, Dello Joio, and [?Les] Baxter (RobbinsPP, Series II, B40/F6).

36. de Mille, " 'Fancy Free' in Review."

37. In a letter to Copland, Bernstein wrote: "I accompany dancers" (September 1, 1942, Copland Collection B247/F1).

38. Robbins, quoted in Tobias, 70.

39. Notebook for *Fancy Free*, Robbins PP, Series II, B40/F3.

40. The article stated in part, "Jerome Robbins will begin work about January 1 on his first assignment as a choreographer.... Its music, in the jazz idiom, is being composed by Leonard Bernstein" (John Martin, "The Dance: On Broadway," *New York Times*, November 14, 1943).

41. Bernstein, Letter to J. Alden Talbot, November 11, 1943, ABT Records B8/F524.

42. Bernstein, *Fancy Free*, manuscript short score, date in pencil at the bottom of the first page of music (Bernstein Collection B15/F8), and Bernstein, *Fancy Free* (New York: G. Schirmer, 1950, 1968), 151.

43. "Itinerary: Ballet Theatre/November & December, 1943," typescript, RobbinsPP, Series II, B40/F6.

44. Robbins, Draft scenario for *Fancy Free*, June 1943, RobbinsPP, Series II, B40/F6.

45. Burton, 127. The Bernstein Office in New York City owns recordings of a work-in-progress from this period, but most of the music is from *On the Town*, not *Fancy Free*.

46. A negative copy exists of a contractual letter from J. Alden Talbot (President of Ballet Theatre) to Robbins, 57 Hudson Place, Weehawken, NJ, April 4, 1944 (RobbinsPP, Series I, B14/F10). The dollar equivalent in 2010 was $124, using the Consumer Price Index; www.measuringworth.com/calculators/uscompare/result.php. This sum did not change over the years, according to Robbins (Tobias, 76).

47. Dorothy Barret, "Jerome Robbins," *Dance Magazine*, May 1945, 13.

48. de Mille, "'Fancy Free' in Review." On the day of the premiere, de Mille sent a handwritten note to Robbins expressing confidence in his new work: "I have a feeling tonight is going to be important to everyone who loves dancing and to everyone who loves you. And as I belong to both categories I give you something a little more durable than a yellow slip of paper—as a commemoration." Agnes de Mille to Robbins, April 18, 1944, RobbinsPP, Series III, B84/F8.

49. Edwin Denby, "Fancy Free," *New York Herald Tribune*, April 19, 1944. Reprinted in *Edwin Denby: Dance Writings*, ed. Robert Cornfield and William Mackay (London: Dance Books, 1986), 218.

50. Bernstein to Copland, "Friday," on stationery for "The Philharmonic-Symphony Society of New York," Copland Collection B247/F1. The contents of the letter date it as April 1944, although "1943(?)" is written in pencil at the top. Also, "Season Is Extended by Ballet Theatre," *New York Times*, April 27, 1944.

51. "Black & Blue Ballet," *Time*.

52. Francis A. Coleman, "Composer Teams with Choreographer: Leonard Bernstein," *Dance Magazine*, May 1945, 12. Twenty years later, Clive Barnes wrote an article chronicling the development of ballet in America: "Probably no choreographer has ever made such an explosive debut as was achieved by Jerome Robbins with 'Fancy Free.' The more I think of it, the more I am convinced that this was one of the most remarkable and definitive debuts in ballet history. No one could look at 'Fancy Free' and not notice that something had happened" ("Dance: Retracing Some First Steps," *New York Times*, December 5, 1967).

53. Amberg, *Ballet in America*, 132. Harold Lang went on to have a successful career in musical theater, including a major role in *Kiss Me, Kate* (1948) and the lead in a revival of *Pal Joey* (1952).

54. Lincoln Kirstein, *Four Centuries of Ballet: Fifty Masterworks* (New York: Dover, 1970, 1984), 235. Originally published as *Movement and Metaphor* (New York: Praeger, 1970).

55. *Fancy Free/Ballet Theatre; choreography by Jerome Robbins*, videocassette, 26 minutes, 1944–45, Jerome Robbins Dance Division, NYPL. The catalogue entry states: "Ballet Theatre production, filmed in performance."

56. Robbins, quoted in Tobias, 76.

57. In *Black and Tan Fantasy*, the five dancers—known as the Five Hotshots—are featured approximately three minutes into the film (www.youtube.com/watch?v=oy4CL2Loon0, accessed July 12, 2013). Thanks to Jeffrey Magee for pointing this out.

58. Robbins, Notes for *Fancy Free*, RobbinsPP, Series II, B40/F3.

59. These three solos appear in a different order on the 1946 Decca recording: "Waltz Variation," "Danzón Variation," and "Galop Variation." Plus "Scene at the Bar" and "Enter Two Girls" are fused into one movement.

60. Ballet Theatre [program], *Fancy Free*, April 18, 1944, NYPL Clippings.

61. The text of the scenario was lightly edited for Amberg's *Ballet in America* (132–39), and Robbins's scenario for the sailors' solos was published in Barret, "Jerome Robbins" (14, 40). A scenario also appears in de Mille's liner notes for the first recording of *Fancy Free*, but it appears to have been written by her, not Robbins.

62. Robbins, quoted in Tobias, 69, and Robbins, Interview with Clive Barnes. Also, Kirstein, *Four Centuries of Ballet*, 234.

63. For a full description and analysis of the controversy, see Richard Meyer, "A Different American Scene: Paul Cadmus and the Satire of Sexuality," in *Outlaw Representation: Censorship and Homosexuality in Twentieth-Century American Art* (New York: Oxford University Press, 2002), 33–93. After the painting's censorship, it hung above the fireplace of the Alibi Club in Washington, DC, for more than forty years. It is now owned by the Naval Historical Center in Washington, DC.

64. As quoted in "Bans CWA Picture as Insult to Navy; Swanson Bars Cadmus Study from Exhibit, but Holds It Is 'Right Artistic';... Painting of 'Sordid Brawl' by Men on Leave Is Declared 'Untrue' to Navy Life," *New York Times*, April 19, 1934.

65. Lincoln Kirstein, *Paul Cadmus* (New York: Imago, 1984), 21. Historian Allan Bérubé calls Riverside Park one of the famous "cruising parks where men had been picking up other men long before the war" (*Coming Out Under Fire: The History of Gay Men and Women in World War Two* [New York: Free Press, 1990], 110).

66. Kirstein, *Paul Cadmus*, 21.

67. Weinberg, "Cruising with Paul Cadmus," *Art in America* (November 1992): 103–4. George Chauncey discusses the symbolism of blonde hair (*Gay New York: Gender, Urban Culture, and the Makings of the Gay Male World, 1890–1940* [New York: Basic Books, 1994], 52, 54). Other important studies engage with *The Fleet's In!*, including Jonathan Weinberg, *Speaking for Vice: Homosexuality in the Art of Charles Demuth, Marsden Hartley, and the First American Avant-Garde* (New Haven, CT: Yale University Press, 1993), and Marshall Berman, *On the Town*.

68. Meyer, "A Different American Scene," 42.

69. Meyer, 54. Also, Weinberg, *Speaking for Vice*, 43–44.

70. Kirstein, *Paul Cadmus*.

71. Lincoln Kirstein, *Blast at Ballet: A Corrective for the American Audience* (1937), reprinted in *Three Pamphlets Collected* (Brooklyn, NY: Dance Horizons, 1967), 45–46.

72. de Mille, "'Fancy Free' in Review."

73. Dance historian Peter Stoneley offers an analysis of the ties between *Fancy Free* and *The Fleet's In!*, building on earlier scholarship. His conclusions are fascinating, but he and I differ in our assessments of the degree to which *Fancy Free*'s gay allusions were legible.

Stoneley recognizes that the ballet has a gay identity, yet he characterizes it as being "relentlessly heterosexual in its narrative logic." At the same time, he acknowledges that the "small, heterosexual figures that we see on the stage seem to cast huge, queer shadows." Stoneley's focus is on dance, not on the music (Stoneley, *A Queer History*, 109, 110).

74. Robbins, in Amberg, *Ballet in America*, 133.

75. Robbins, in Amberg, *Ballet in America*, 133. Robbins's undated draft scenario uses slightly different language, which emphasizes the mens' relationship even more: "The three of them are very close friends. One should feel their inter-dependence.... that they are used to each others company, that they have bummed around together and know each others habits, kidding, and guff.... one should feel the natural affection and security between them" (RobbinsPP, Series II, B40/F6).

76. Robbins, in Amberg, 137.

77. Robbins, in Amberg, 137.

78. Chauncey, *Gay New York*, 78. Beth Genné writes: "The sailors that Robbins so closely studied on the streets of New York were erotic objects for him as well as research material for his new ballet" (94).

79. Bérubé, *Coming Out Under Fire*, 33.

80. Bérubé, *Coming Out Under Fire*, 109. The remaining quotations in this paragraph come from this same book (113, 105, 114, 115).

81. Janet Reed, quoted in Tobias, 72, 74.

82. Gore Vidal, *Palimpsest: A Memoir* (New York: Random House, 1995), 131, as cited in Lawrence, 63.

83. Janet Reed, Interview with Lawrence, August 17, 1999, quoted in Lawrence, 63.

84. Robbins, quoted in Tobias, 77.

85. Lawrence, xv.

86. Robbins, Letter to unknown recipient, written on stationery from the Hotel Whitcomb in San Francisco, [1943], RobbinsPP, Series II, B40/F6. Since this letter is housed with Robbins's papers, it either was not sent, or it was returned to him by the recipient.

87. Notebook for *Fancy Free*, RobbinsPP, Series II, B40/F3.

88. Oliver [Smith] to Jerry [Robbins], RobbinsPP, Series IV, B115/F5.

89. Lawrence does not cite Oliver Smith as a lover of Robbins, however.

90. Shaun O'Brien, Interview with Lawrence, May 18, 1999, quoted in Lawrence, 64.

91. Janet Reed, Interview with Lawrence, August 17, 1999, quoted in Lawrence, 64.

92. Richard D'Arcy, Interview with Lawrence, July 28, 1999, quoted in Lawrence, 63.

93. Burton, 108. Correspondence added to the Bernstein Collection in 2011 includes many letters with Bernstein's lovers. See Mark Horowitz, "Letters Shed New Light on Bernstein Era," *Prelude, Fugue & Riffs* (Fall-Winter 2011–2012): 1–4.

94. Harold Lang to Bernstein, May 23, 1944, Bernstein Collection B60H/F16.

95. Lang to Bernstein, undated, written from the Hollywood-Roosevelt Hotel, June or July 1944, Bernstein Collection B60H/F16.

96. The correspondence of Bernstein and Copland is discussed in Vivian Perlis, "Dear Aaron, Dear Lenny: A Friendship in Letters," *Aaron Copland and His World*, ed. Carol J. Oja and Judith Tick (Princeton: Princeton University Press, 2005), 151–78.

97. Two examples of intimate letters: Bernstein, Letter to Copland, [1939?], Copland Collection B247/F1; and Copland, Letter to Bernstein, May 26, 1942, Bernstein Collection B60C/F3.

98. Copland, Letter to Bernstein, undated (probably early 1940s), Bernstein Collection B60C/F3.

99. Copland, Letter to Bernstein, July 3, 1943, Bernstein Collection B60C/F3. I silently removed "the" before "while."

100. Robbins, in Amberg, *Ballet in America*, 132–33. Berman (63–65) pursues "the street" and "ordinary people" as important themes in *On the Town*.

101. Amberg, 140.

102. Lang, quoted in Tobias, 69.

103. Reed, quoted in Tobias, 69.

104. Robbins, quoted in Tobias, 71, 69.

105. Bentley, quoted in Tobias, 69.

106. John Martin, "The Dance: 'Fancy Free' Does It."

107. Denby, "Fancy Free," 219.

108. Chrystelle Trump Bond, "Homefront Heroes: Jitterbugging in Wartime Baltimore," *Maryland Historical Magazine* 88, no. 4 (Winter 1993): 462.

109. Joy Richards, "Dance and War," *Dance* (September 1942): 20, 29; quoted in Bond, "Homefront Heroes," 462.

110. Denby, "Fancy Free," 219.

111. Robbins, quoted in Tobias, 71.

112. A typescript itinerary for Ballet Theatre's tour in November and December 1943 is contained in RobbinsPP, Series II, B40/F6.

113. Robbins, quoted in Tobias, 71.

114. Janet Reed, quoted in Tobias, 69.

115. de Mille, "'Fancy Free' in Review." In critical reception of *Fancy Free*, a tight link was consistently stressed between the shaping of characters and the original cast.

116. Robbins, Scenario for *Fancy Free*, quoted in Barret, 40. This text also appears in Amberg, *Ballet in America*, 136, with slight edits.

117. Robbins, quoted in Tobias, 71.

118. Robbins, quoted in Barret, 40.

119. Robbins, quoted in Tobias, 71.

120. Robbins, quoted in Barret, 40.

121. Robbins, quoted in Tobias, 71.

122. Sono Osato, *Distant Dances* (New York: Alfred A. Knopf, 1980), 229.

123. Bentley, Reed, and Robbins, quoted in Tobias, 71.

124. Robert LaFosse, Interview for the "Jerome Robbins Celebration" at the New York City Ballet, 2008, www.youtube.com/watch?v=JbmyH_dysd4 (accessed March 24, 2013). LaFosse was once principal dancer with the New York City Ballet and is separate from the Broadway choreographer Bob Fosse.

125. Amberg, *Ballet in America*, 130, 140.

126. Robbins, "Thoughts on Choreography: Jerome Robbins as told to Selma Jeanne Cohen," typescript, RobbinsPP, Series I, B5/F8.

127. John Martin, "The Dance: 'Fancy Free' Does It."

128. Bernstein's "Big Stuff" is published in the back of the orchestral score: *Fancy Free (Ballet)* (New York: Amberson Enterprises and G. Schirmer, 1950, 1968), 152–53; the quotations that follow are taken from this imprint. A note at the bottom of the first page of the orchestral score states that "a jukebox" will play "Big Stuff." But the silent film of the first production of *Fancy* shows a turntable on the counter of the bar

(*Fancy Free/Ballet Theatre*, videocassette), while de Mille says "Big Stuff" is played from a "radio" (de Mille, "'Fancy Free' in Review").

129. These lyrics come from the published version of "Big Stuff" and are slightly different from those in Example 1.1.

130. Burton, 127.

131. David Margolick calls Holiday's performances of "Strange Fruit" at Café Society a "nightly ritual," in *Strange Fruit: The Biography of a Song* (New York: HarperCollins, 2001), 4.

132. As quoted in Margolick, *Strange Fruit*, 5.

133. Barney Josephson and Terry Trilling-Josephson, *Café Society: The Wrong Place for the Right People* (Champaign: University of Illinois Press, 2009), 9. See also Michael Denning, *The Cultural Front: The Laboring of American Culture in the Twentieth Century* (New York: Verso, 1996), 325.

134. Re The Revuers at Café Society: Alice M. Robinson, *Betty Comden and Adolph Green: A Bio-Bibliography*, Bio-Bibliographies in the Performing Arts, No. 45 (Westport, CT: Greenwood Press, 1994), 4–6. Re Blitzstein and Bernstein: Josephson and Trilling-Josephson, *Café Society*, 40.

135. These memories come from the filmmaker Richard Leacock, who was a friend of Bernstein at Harvard (Leacock, Interview with Drew Massey, Harvard University, October 14, 2006, http://isites.harvard.edu/icb/icb.do?keyword=bernstein&tabgroup id=icb.tabgroup47656).

136. David W. Stowe, "The Politics of Café Society," *Journal of American History* 84, no. 4 (March 1998): 1394.

137. Dorothy Bird and Joyce Greenberg, *Bird's Eye View: Dancing with Martha Graham and on Broadway* (Pittsburgh: University of Pittsburgh Press, 2002), 156.

138. Mike Lubbers, "Billie Holiday Discography," www.billieholiday.be, accessed March 25, 2013; "Fancy Free," Decca Records DA-406.

139. Bernstein, *Fancy Free*, 1.

140. Jump is defined as "a style of jazz related to swing. It developed around 1937 and flourished during the 1940s.... In a general sense the word 'jump' described the compelling energy of the dance music played by the big bands." See Howard Rye and Barry Kernfeld, "Jump," *Grove Music Online*, accessed March 25, 2013.

141. My analysis builds on the work of Paul Laird, who discusses Bernstein's "eclecticism" and offers an important assessment of Bernstein's musical style in *Fancy Free* (Paul R. Laird, *Leonard Bernstein: A Guide to Research*, Routledge Music Bibliographies [New York: Routledge, 2002], 13–15, 32–37). Katherine A. Baber also addresses eclecticism, although I gained access to her fine dissertation when my book was in production: "Leonard Bernstein's Jazz: A Musical Trope and Its Cultural Resonances," Ph.D. dissertation, Indiana University, 2010.

142. Montage and pastiche have both been explored in relation to early film music, notably in Daniel Goldmark, *Tunes for 'Toons: Music and the Hollywood Cartoon* (Berkeley: University of California Press, 2005).

143. Kirstein, *Four Centuries of Ballet*, 234.

144. John Martin, "The Dance: 'Fancy Free' Does It."

145. The "big band" segments of the score consist of a brass section (3 trumpets and 3 trombones), a reed section (2 clarinets), and a rhythm section (string bass, piano, snare drum, bass drum, and suspended cymbal). Significantly, there are no saxophones.

146. de Mille, "'Fancy Free' in Review."

147. As used here, "riff" follows a standard definition in jazz: "a short melodic ostinato which may be repeated either intact or varied to accommodate an underlying harmonic pattern" (J. Bradford Robinson, "Riff," *Grove Music Online*, accessed March 25, 2013).

148. Bernstein, *Fancy Free*, manuscript short score, bottom of the first page (Bernstein Collection B15/F8).

149. Robbins, in Amberg, *Ballet in America*, 134.

150. I have often included measure numbers, even when there is no musical example. Unless otherwise indicated, all references are to the published score, cited earlier.

151. Robbins, in Amberg, *Ballet in America*, 134. "Juke Box" is written at the head of sketches for this section (Sketches for *Fancy Free*, Bernstein Collection B15/F9).

152. Robbins, in Amberg, *Ballet in America*, 134.

153. Robbins, in Amberg, *Ballet in America*, 135.

154. Copland, Letter to Bernstein, "Tuesday" [April or May 1944], Bernstein Collection B16/F45.

155. Bernstein to Copland, September 1, 1942, written from New York City, 158, W. 58 Street, Copland Collection B247/F1.

156. Bernstein to Copland, 1942, written from New York City, Copland Collection B247/F1.

157. Arthur Berger, *Aaron Copland* (New York: Oxford University Press, 1953), 70.

158. "Lento Molto" from *Two Pieces for String Quartet* is one of many possible models for the "Copland sound" in *Fancy Free*. Another is the first movement of Copland's Piano Sonata (1941), which opens with a three-chord descending motive.

159. Robbins, in Amberg, *Ballet in America*, 133.

160. Bernstein, *Fancy Free*, manuscript short score, VII-8.

161. Robbins, in Amberg, *Ballet in America*, 137. When Ballet Theatre took *Fancy Free* on tour in the fall of 1944, as Robbins worked on the choreography for *On the Town*, the role of Third Sailor was taken by Alberto Alonso, a dancer from Cuba (Program, "Philadelphia All Star Concert Series Presents Ballet Theatre," Academy of Music, November 9, 1944, RobbinsPP, Series I, B40/F8).

162. Maurice Zolotow, "South of the Border—On Broadway," *New York Times*, February 18, 1940.

163. [Agnes de Mille], " 'Fancy Free': Scenario of the Records." This plot summary follows the essay, " 'Fancy Free' in Review."

164. Robbins, quoted in Tobias, 71.

165. Bernstein, quoted in Arthur Berger, "Notes on the Program: Three Variations from Fancy Free."

166. In Act II of *Nutcracker*, a string of national dances accompany a celebration of sweets from around the world: "Spanish Hot Chocolate Performers," "Arabian Coffee Performers," "Chinese Tea Performers," "Russian Candy Cane Performers," and "Danish Marzipan Shepherdess Performers."

167. Here is a formal diagram for "Danzón," including the number of measures in each section:

Introductory riff (mm. 737–744): 8 bars
A (mm. 745–754): 10 bars

A^1 (mm. 755–769): 15 bars
Introductory riff (mm. 770–775): 6 bars
A^2 (mm. 776–787): 12 bars
B (mm. 788–799): 12 bars
B^1 (mm. 800–809): 4 + 6 bars
Introductory riff (mm. 810–15): 6 bars
A (mm. 816–830): 15 bars

168. Rolando Antonio and Pérez Fernández, *La binarización de los ritmos ternarios africanos en América Latina* (Havana, Cuba: Casa de las Américas, 1987), 113 (example 1-E). Thanks to Marc Gidal for help with understanding the traditional *danzón*.

169. Jean Dickson, "Orquesta típica," *Grove Music Online*, accessed March 25, 2013.

170. Aaron Copland and Vivian Perlis, *Copland: 1900 through 1942* (New York: St. Martin's Press, 1984), 338.

171. Bernstein, Letter to Copland, October 20, 1938, Copland Collection B247/F1; published in Vivian Perlis, "Dear Aaron, Dear Lenny," 161. Clifford Odets was a famed leftist playwright of the day, perhaps best known for *Waiting for Lefty* (1935).

172. Aaron Copland, *El Salón México*, arranged for solo piano by Leonard Bernstein (New York: Boosey & Hawkes, 1941); two-piano arrangement by Bernstein published by Boosey & Hawkes in 1943.

173. Copland and Perlis, *Copland*, 367. Laird, *Leonard Bernstein*, 36, also connects Bernstein's "Danzón" to Copland's *Danzón Cubano*.

174. "By the early 1940s," writes Copland's biographer Howard Pollack, "the romance between Copland and Kraft had begun to unravel, with Copland, Kraft, and Bernstein embroiled in a muddled affair" (*Aaron Copland: The Life and Work of an Uncommon Man* [New York: Henry Holt, 1999], 241).

175. Copland, Letter to Bernstein, undated ["April 1941" added at the top], from Havana, Bernstein Collection; online in American Memory, LC (also quoted in Pollack, *Aaron Copland*, 228). Copland's "South American Diary" dates this trip as August to December 1941 (Copland Collection B243/F15).

176. Letter, Copland to Bernstein, n.d. ["1941? April–May?" added at top], from Havana (Bernstein Collection, online in American Memory, LC).

177. Copland, Postcard to Bernstein, April 13, 1941, postmarked Key West, Florida; Bernstein Collection LC; online in American Memory, LC.

178. Burton, 95, dates Bernstein's time in Key West by citing a letter written from there on August 28, 1941.

179. Bernstein, quoted in Mel Gussow, "Theater, 'West Side Story': The Beginnings of Something Great," *New York Times*, October 21, 1990.

180. The "jukebox" tie among "Conch Town," *Fancy Free*, and the Drugstore Scene of *West Side Story* is fascinating. Mark Horowitz's entry for "Conch Town" in his inventory of music manuscripts in the Bernstein Collection states: "*Conch Town* sketches . . . ballet dated '1940?'; according to the envelope, 'Conchtown' refers to Key West (locals) where LB spent time in 1940 or 1941, the ms. was in the Dakota for LB to peruse 1989–90; the score includes significant musical material that became 'America' in *West Side Story* and the Third Sailor's *Danzon* in '*Fancy Free*'" ("Music Holographs," typescript, [2004]; Entry for B9/F14). Burton recognized its links to "America" from *West Side Story* (95–96).

181. Burton states that Bernstein listened to Radio Havana while in Key West.

182. Ned Sublette, *Cuba and Its Music: From the First Drums to the Mambo* (Chicago: Chicago Review Press, 2004), 369, 435, 437.

183. *The WPA Guide to Florida: The Federal Writers' Project Guide to 1930s Florida* [1939], new introduction by John I. McCollum (reprint, New York: Pantheon Books, 1984), 197.

CHAPTER 2: FROM NIGHTCLUBS TO BROADWAY

Epigraph: "20th Anniversary of Radio," from the series "Fun with The Revuers," aired on NBC, November 3, 1940. "I like The Revuers" is sung by Judy Tuvim. Audio transcript streamed at http://otrrlibrary.org/f.html, starting at 8:29, accessed April 11, 2013. In my transcription, I did not include Tuvim's barely audible interjections at the end of some lines.

1. Theodore Strauss, "News of Night Clubs," *New York Times*, June 18, 1939.

2. Kyle Crichton, "Musical Express," *Colliers Weekly* 104 (November 25, 1939), 19.

3. Milton Meltzer, "A 'Little Revue' That Does Big Things: Vanguard Group Hits New High in Social Satire," *Daily Worker*, April 13, 1939.

4. Betty Comden, "10,000 Easy Ways to Get into the Theater," *Mademoiselle*, October 1944, 149; Bernstein Scrapbooks.

5. A full list of the group's original members appears in Strauss, "News of Night Clubs," June 18, 1939.

6. Re Comden, Frank, and Vaughn as pianists: Crichton, "Record of The Revuers," 76. Re Heywood: "Dan Burley's Back Door Stuff: Zero Hour in the House Without Chairs," *New York Amsterdam Star-News*, May 17, 1941. Roger Vaughn appears to have become a television producer ("Vaughn Joins Harvey Stewart," *Back Stage*, October 8, 1976, 1W).

7. Biographical sources for Comden include: Alan Ackerman, "Betty Comden," *Jewish Women: A Comprehensive Encyclopedia*, http://jwa.org/encyclopedia/article/comden-betty, accessed April 11, 2013; "Betty Comden and Adolph Green," *Current Biography: Who's News and Why* 1945, ed. Anna Rothe (New York: H. W. Wilson, 1945), 117–19; Alice M. Robinson, *Betty Comden and Adolph Green: A Bio-Bibliography*, Bio-Bibliographies in the Performing Arts, No. 45 (Westport, CT: Greenwood Press, 1994). In the 1920 census, Comden is listed as Baswa [*sic*] Cohen, age 2; in the 1930 census, she is Betty Cohen (listed under her father, Leo Cohen, in 1920 and 1930 United States Federal Census; in Ancestry.com).

8. Comden, in "Betty Comden and Adolph Green," *The Art of the American Musical: Conversations with the Creators*, ed. Jackson R. Bryer and Richard A. Davison (New Brunswick, NJ: Rutgers University Press, 2005), 52.

9. Green, quoted in "The Success Story of B. Comden and A. Green," *PM: New York Daily*, March 11, 1945. I silently added "of" to Green's quotation. Biographical information about Green comes from "Betty Comden and Adolph Green," *Current Biography*; and Robinson, *Betty Comden and Adolph Green*.

10. Jonathan Krasner, "The Interwar Family and American Jewish Identity in Clifford Odets's *Awake and Sing!*" *Jewish Social Studies: History, Culture, Society* 13, no. 1 (Fall 2006): 25.

11. Daniel Green is listed in the United States Federal Census from 1910, 1915, 1920, and 1930. His birth year is variously given as "about" 1883, 1884, 1885, and 1887. In the 1910

census, his date of immigration is cited as 1903. His draft registration card for World War I states his occupation as "machinist" (dated September 2, 1918). All in Ancestry.com.

12. Green, in "The Success Story of B. Comden and A. Green."

13. Meltzer, "A 'Little Revue' That Does Big Things." Also Green, in *The Art of the American Musical*, 52.

14. Green, in *The Art of the American Musical*, 52.

15. Phyllis Newman, Interview with the author, April 27, 2007, New York City.

16. Arthur and Barbara Gelb, "'On the Town' with Comden & Green," *New York Times*, December 11, 1960.

17. Green, in *The Art of the American Musical*, 52.

18. Re A.S.U.: Meltzer, "A 'Little Revue' That Does Big Things." Re switchboard: Max Gordon, *Live at the Village Vanguard*, introduction by Nat Hentoff (New York: St. Martin's Press, 1980), 33.

19. Meltzer, "A 'Little Revue' That Does Big Things."

20. Milly S. Barranger, *Unfriendly Witnesses: Gender, Theater, and Film in the McCarthy Era* (Carbondale, IL: Southern Illinois University Press, 2008), 11.

21. "Judy Holliday," IMDb, accessed April 13, 2013.

22. Meltzer, "A 'Little Revue' That Does Big Things."

23. "Alvin Hammer," IMDb, accessed April 13, 2013.

24. Re "highly talented": Theodore Strauss, "Notes on Night Clubs," *New York Times*, March 26, 1939. Re "seedling": Strauss, "News of Night Clubs," June 18, 1939.

25. Strauss, "Notes on Night Clubs," March 26, 1939.

26. Meltzer, "A 'Little Revue' That Does Big Things."

27. Comden, in *The Art of the American Musical*, 53.

28. Adolph Green, Letter to Bernstein, from Hotel Astor, NYC, [May 1939], Bernstein Collection B60E/F1.

29. Comden, quoted in "The Success Story of B. Comden and A. Green."

30. Comden, quoted in "The Success Story."

31. Green, Letter to Bernstein, [May 1939]. Harvard's production of *The Cradle Will Rock* opened May 27, 1939 (Program, Harvard University Archives). See Drew Massey, "Leonard Bernstein and the Harvard Student Union: In Search of Political Origins," *Journal of the Society for American Music* 3, no. 1 (2009): 67–84.

32. Adolph Green, Interview with Humphrey Burton, undated; quoted in Burton, 57.

33. Green, Letter to Bernstein, [May 1939]. In this letter, Green includes Claman as part of the subletting plan.

34. See Trudi Ann Wright, "Labor Takes the Stage: A Musical and Social Analysis of *Pins and Needles* (1937–1941)," Ph.D. dissertation, University of Colorado, 2010.

35. Michael L. Greenwald, "Actors as Activists: The Theatre Arts Committee Cabaret, 1938–1941," *Theatre Research International* 20, no. 1 (Spring 1995): 19.

36. Greenwald, "Actors as Activists," 22.

37. Judy Holliday, as paraphrased in Max Gordon, *Live at the Village Vanguard*, 33.

38. Otis Ferguson, "Vanguard Underground," *The New Republic*, August 30, 1939, 104.

39. Strauss, "Notes on Night Clubs," March 26, 1939.

40. Crichton, "Musical Express," 19.

41. Ferguson, "Vanguard Underground." Ferguson made a career for himself in the 1930s and early 1940s as a progressive entertainment critic, with a special affinity for jazz. Malcolm Cowley described Ferguson's writing: "Much of it dealt with swing

bands or unpretentious, well-crafted films and, by extension, with the revival of popular culture during the 1930s." In *The Otis Ferguson Reader*, ed. Dorothy Chamberlain
and Robert Wilson (Highland Park, IL: December Press, 1982), ix.

42. Ferguson, "Vanguard Underground."

43. Strauss, "News of Night Clubs," June 18, 1939.

44. Barnaby Hotchkiss, "In the Vanguard: A Witty, Waggish Revue in New York's
Greenwich Village," *New Masses*, August 8, 1939, 31.

45. Strauss, "News of Night Clubs," *New York Times*, September 10, 1939.

46. Green, Introduction to "The Reader's Digest," in *A Party with Comden and Green*,
Capitol SWAO-1197, 1958; CD Angel 764773, 1993.

47. Gelb, " 'On the Town' with Comden & Green."

48. Green, Letter to Bernstein, [May 1939].

49. Gelb, " 'On the Town' with Comden & Green."

50. They appeared on March 5 and April 9, 1940; then weekly broadcasts began
on April 23. Robinson consulted NBC files at the Library of Congress, and she provides
a valuable list of the programs (*Betty Comden and Adolph Green: A Bio-Bibliography*,
211–14).

51. Otis Ferguson, "Review of Revuers," *The New Republic*, April 14, 1941, 500.

52. Robert Coleman, " 'Revuers' Click Here After Tough Going," *New York Mirror*,
February 16, 1945, Bernstein Scrapbooks.

53. Shirley Bernstein, Letter to Leonard Bernstein, November 27, 1939, written
from 86 Park Avenue in Newton, Bernstein Collection B60B/F3-5. I have not located a
listing for this radio broadcast, which precedes The Revuers' regular show on NBC.

54. Re 1939 show: Robinson, *Betty Comden and Adolph Green: A Bio-Bibliography*,
215. Re 1940 show: "Ray of Hope Seen for Television," *New York Times*, June 16, 1940,
and Robinson, 215. Bernstein is not named in the *Times* listing; rather, his involvement is chronicled in Burton, 71–72.

55. Ferguson, "Review of Revuers," April 14, 1941.

56. Howard Taubman, "Records: Lower Prices," *New York Times*, May 26, 1940. See
Appendix for discographic information.

57. Bernstein might have been a late addition to the recording. A letter from Adolph
Green to Bernstein (undated, yet clearly written in 1939) reports on the recording ses-
sions, and Bernstein doesn't seem to be involved at this point: "We recorded for 3 hours
over at Musicraft. Everything including 2 Left Feet—a bit of a mess but Musicraft like
it. Will know soon whether the deal goes through. Musicraft recording methods are
lousy." Green, Letter to Bernstein, written on the stationery of William Morris Agency,
Rockefeller Center, [1939], Bernstein Collection B60E/F1.

58. Shirley Bernstein, Letter to Leonard Bernstein, no date, from 68 Park Avenue,
Newton, Bernstein Collection B60B/F3-5.

59. Marc Blitzstein, *The Cradle Will Rock*, Musicraft 1075-1081, 1938.

60. A brief history of Musicraft emphasizes its jazz releases: Mark Gardner, "Musicraft," *Grove Music Online*, accessed April 16, 2013. The eclecticism of its catalogue is
documented in Steve Abrams and Tyrone Settlemier, "Musicraft 78rpm numerical
listing discography—200 through 600," in *The Online Discographical Project*, http://
78discography.com/Musicraft200.htm, accessed April 26, 2014.

61. Re Maplewood, NJ: "Piscator Acquires New Lewis Play," *New York Times*, September 13, 1940. Re Radio City Music Hall: [Ad] "Radio City Music Hall," *New York*

Times, October 30, 1940. Re Village Vanguard: "The Night Clubs During January," *New York Times*, January 4, 1941.

62. Green, in *The Art of the American Musical*, 53.

63. Green, Postcard to Bernstein, August 14, 1941, New York, Bernstein Collection B60E/F1.

64. Bernstein, Letter to Copland, September 1, 1942, Copland Collection B247/F1.

65. "Of Local Origin," *New York Times*, July 5, 1943.

66. "Betty Comden and Adolph Green," *Current Biography*, 118.

67. Green, Letter to Bernstein, undated [September 1943], Bernstein Collection B60E/F1. The remaining citations in this paragraph and the next one come from this same letter. Green congratulates Bernstein on his appointment as assistant conductor of the New York Philharmonic, which had just been announced ("U.S. Conductor Gets Philharmonic Post," *New York Times*, September 9, 1943). The Re-vuers' agent, Kurt Frings, was German (not Austrian) and worked with major actors, including Elizabeth Taylor and Audrey Hepburn. Deborah Greenhut, "Ketti Frings Adapts Look Homeward Angel for a Pulitzer Prize," *Playwrights & Stage Actors @ Suite101*, http://suite101.com/article/ketti-frings-adapts-look-homeward-angel-for-a-pulitzer-prize-a364053#ixzz22Dbf7mgF, accessed April 16, 2013.

68. Betty Comden, "10,000 Easy Ways to Get into the Theater."

69. Bosley Crowther, "'Greenwich Village,' with Carmen Miranda, Comes to Roxy," *New York Times*, September 28, 1944.

70. Joseph Foster, "Films of the Week," *New Masses*, October 10, 1944, 30.

71. The Revuers' appearance on Armed Forces Radio was recorded January 15, 1944: www.youtube.com/watch?v=45FeHwZOfS8, accessed September 13, 2013.

72. Adolph Green, "The Magic of Fred Astaire," *American Film* 6 (April 1981): 38.

73. Olin Downes, "Composers' Tribute: Dinner for Koussevitzky Was a Gesture of Gratitude from American Musicians," *New York Times*, May 21, 1944.

74. "Nightclubs: United States of America," *Grove Music Online*, accessed April 16, 2013.

75. "Dan Burley's Back Door Stuff: Zero Hour in the House Without Chairs," *New York Amsterdam Star-News*, May 17, 1941. By "grey act," Burley must have been indicating a mixed-race group, since The Revuers were accompanied by an African American jazz trio. This stretch of performance dates for The Revuers is chronicled through the *New York Times* and the *Amsterdam News*: "The Night Clubs During January," *New York Times*, January 4, 1941; "The Night Clubs During February," *New York Times*, February 1, 1941; "The Hotels and Night Clubs During April," *New York Times*, April 5, 1941; and "Dan Burley's Back Door Stuff."

76. Max Gordon, *Live at the Village Vanguard*, 40.

77. "Betty Comden and Adolph Green," *Current Biography*, 118.

78. Theodore Strauss, "News of Night Clubs," *New York Times*, April 23, 1939.

79. Green, Letter to Bernstein, [May 1939].

80. It is difficult to document all of Bernstein's appearances at Café Society because he was most often there to accompany The Revuers, hence not a headliner. One known instance was in the fall of 1942 (Burton, 102–3).

81. Re "American Committee": Henry F. Srebrnik, "An Idiosyncratic Fellow-Travel-ler: Vilhjalmur Stefansson and the American Committee for the Settlement of Jews in

Birobidzhan," *East European Jewish Affairs* 28, no. 1 (1998): 41–47. Re "composed of Jewish residents": "Jews Make War Aid Gifts," *New York Times*, December 5, 1941.

82. "Benefit, The Ambijan Committee for Emergency Aid to the Soviet Union . . . Café Society Concert" [program], April 11, 1943, Carnegie Hall, Archives and Museum of Carnegie Hall.

83. Scott's performance is discussed in Karen Chilton, *Hazel Scott: The Pioneering Journey of a Jazz Pianist from Café Society to Hollywood to HUAC* (Ann Arbor: University of Michigan Press, 2008), 86.

84. Golden Gate Jubilee Quartet, "Stalin Wasn't Stallin," Okeh Records 78–6712, released 1943.

85. Howard Taubman, "Swing Features Soviet Benefit," *New York Times*, April 12, 1943.

86. "Reporters Frolic Tonight," *New York Times*, March 8, 1941; Bill Chase, "All Ears: Mother Thisa and Thata," *New York Amsterdam Star-News*, May 9, 1942; [Advertisement] "Tonight—Carnegie Hall—8:30; Stars for Democracy, presented by Allied Votes Against Coudert," *New York Times*, October 21, 1942.

87. Carol Smith et al., "The Struggle for Free Speech at CCNY, 1931–42," Learning/ American Social History Project, The Graduate Center, CUNY, www.vny.cuny.edu/ gutter/panels/panel15.html, accessed April 16, 2013.

88. Betty Comden, "10,000 Easy Ways to Get into the Theater."

89. Comden and Green, "Notes for 'ON THE TOWN' Album," typescript,1; Comden-Green Papers B16/F18.

90. Gordon, *Live at the Village Vanguard*, 67.

91. Louis Calta, "News of Night Clubs: A New Club, The Blue Angel, Will Make Its Broadway Debut on April 14," *New York Times*, April 4, 1943.

92. "Music: Caf," *Time*, April 26, 1943.

93. Lorraine Gordon, as told to Barry Singer, *Alive at the Village Vanguard* (Milwaukee: Hal Leonard, 2006), 109, 112.

94. Bernstein, Letter to Copland, [Spring] 1943, from 15 W. 52 NYC, Copland Collection B247/F1.

95. Copland, Letter to Bernstein, May 6, 1943, Bernstein Collection B16/F44.

96. There was a history to Copland's advice. In 1939, he wrote to Bernstein, "Glad Tin Pan Alley was a flop. That's not where you belong" (Letter, August 1, [1939], Bernstein Collection B16/F44). The letter dates from 1939 because Copland responded to news that Bernstein had missed the application deadline to study conducting at Juilliard.

97. Green, Letter to Bernstein, undated [September 1943].

98. Comden, in *The Art of the American Musical*, 53. Jerome Robbins does not appear to have been part of that visit to the Blue Angel. Comden does not mention him, and he is not included in an earlier account of this story ("Betty Comden and Adolph Green," *Current Biography*, 118).

99. I have compiled an informal list of nearly forty skits. Sixteen scripts are included in the Comden-Green Papers, Series I, B4/F5-20.

100. Gelb, " 'On the Town' with Comden and Green."

101. Untitled sheet of handwritten notes in pencil, with "Conductor" at the top, Comden-Green Papers, Series II, B16/F18.

102. The opening gambits of The Revuers had slight variations from one performance to another. This version comes from "The World of Music," in the series

"Fun with The Revuers," June 18, 1940, NBC radio; lyrics transcribed from http://otrrlibrary.org/f.html, accessed April 20, 2013.

103. "20th Anniversary of Radio," in the series "Fun with The Revuers," http://otrrlibrary.org/f.html, accessed April 20, 2013.

104. Comden and Green, "The Reader's Digest," from *A Party with Betty Comden and Adolph Green*. Lyrics are transcribed from that recording.

105. W. S. Gilbert and Arthur Sullivan, *Vocal Score of The Mikado, or, The Town of Titipu*, arrangement for pianoforte by George Lowell Tracy (New York: Wm. A. Pond, [1885]), 50, 128. Another example of The Revuers' fascination with *The Mikado* is the number "Three Little Psychopaths Are We," which was a parody of "Three Little Maids from School Are We" ("The Movie Villains," in "Fun with The Revuers, WJZ, April 23, 1940, 9:30–10:00 p.m.," typescript, inserted between pages 6 and 7; Comden-Green Papers, Series I, B4/F7).

106. It is hard to hear what Comden calls out before she shouts "The End!" It might be "oy," a common Yiddish exclamation.

107. "The Girl with the Two Left Feet," Musicraft 1133-35, 1940; reissued on *Leonard Bernstein: Wunderkind*, Pearl CD, 1998.

108. The audio quality makes it hard to decipher the male voices.

109. "The Girl with the Two Left Feet," transcription starts at 4:29.

110. Because of the audio quality, I am not sure if this character name is correct.

111. "The Girl with the Two Left Feet," transcription starts at 10:55.

112. "The Girl with the Two Left Feet," transcription starts at 18:45.

113. "The Girl with the Two Left Feet," transcription starts at 21:19.

114. "Nightlife," in the series "Fun with The Revuers," http://otrrlibrary.org/f.html, accessed April 21, 2013.

115. "World's Fair," radio transcript available at http://otrrlibrary.org/f.html, accessed April 21, 2013; "Ray of Hope Seen for Television."

116. Gordon, *Live at the Village Vanguard*, 36.

117. "Joan Crawford Fan Club," *Leonard Bernstein: Wunderkind*, transcription from the opening of the number.

118. "The World of Music," http://otrrlibrary.org/f.html, transcription starts at 3:26.

119. "The World of Music," http://otrrlibrary.org/f.html, transcription starts at 26:23.

120. Gordon, *Live at the Village Vanguard*, 36.

121. Comden, quoted in Jerry Tallmer, "Comden and Green," *Playbill* 93, no. 4 (April 1993).

122. Bernstein, Interview with Lehman Engel, January 19, 1980, Engel Collection B1/F21.

123. "What a Waste," *Wonderful Town* in *The New York Musicals of Comden & Green* (New York: Applause Books, 1997), 117–18. Book by Joseph Fields and Jerome Chodorov.

CHAPTER 3: CREATING A BROADWAY MUSICAL

Epigraphs: "The Ballet Really Comes to Town," *PM: New York Daily*, May 14, 1944; Betty Comden, in *The Art of the American Musical: Conversations with the Creators*, ed. Jackson R. Bryer and Richard A. Davison (New Brunswick, NJ: Rutgers University Press, 2005), 54.

1. Betty Comden and Adolph Green, "When N.Y. Was a Helluva Town," *New York Times*, October 31, 1971.

2. Lewis Nichols, "The Play," *New York Times*, December 29, 1944.

3. Henry Simon, "Musical Diary: Broadway Music," *PM: New York Daily*, January 7, 1945, Bernstein Scrapbooks.

4. Comden and Green, "When N.Y. Was a Helluva Town."

5. Jeffrey Magee, *Irving Berlin's American Musical Theater* (New York: Oxford University Press, 2012), 214.

6. Tina Olsin Lent, "Romantic Love and Friendship: The Redefinition of Gender Relations in Screwball Comedy," in *Classical Hollywood Comedy*, ed. Kristine Brunovska Karnick and Henry Jenkins (New York: Routledge, 1995), 327.

7. Oliver Smith, Interview with Lehman Engel, February 24, 1978, Engel Collection B6/F179.

8. Sam Zolotow, "'On the Town' Run Will End on Feb. 2," *New York Times*, January 11, 1946.

9. These touring locations come largely from accounting sheets in Comden and Green's papers (Comden-Green Papers B16/F11).

10. Arthur Gelb, "Revival: 'On the Town' 14 Years Later," *New York Times*, January 16, 1959.

11. Clive Barnes, "Theater: 'On the Town' Bernstein's 1944 Musical," *New York Times*, November 1, 1971.

12. Important accounts of the writing and production of *On the Town* include Burton, 129–37; Jowitt, 88–99; Lawrence, 71–85; and Vaill, 103–15.

13. Betty Comden and Adolph Green, "A Pair of 'Bookmakers' Tell All: 'On the Town' Authors Recount the Story of their Hit," *New York Times*, February 18, 1945.

14. Ruth Sulzberger, a female driver during World War II, wrote: "Men hackies accept women cab drivers now as something a little out of the ordinary but nothing to get excited about." "Adventures of a Hackie (Female)," *New York Times*, November 28, 1943.

15. Re "objective": "Notes" [typewritten], Comden-Green Papers B16/F18. Re "unruly woman": Kathleen Rowe writes of this comedy type: "She is not a 'nice girl.' She *is* willing to offend and be offensive..... [She] creates disorder by dominating, or trying to dominate, men." In "The Unruly Woman: Gender and the Genres of Laughter," in *Understanding Inequality: The Intersection of Race/Ethnicity, Class, and Gender*, ed. Barbara A. Arrighi (Lanham, MD: Rowman & Littlefield, 2001), 273.

16. Hildy's full name is spelled as "Bruennhilde" in Comden and Green, "A Pair of 'Bookmakers' Tell All: 'On the Town' Authors Recount the Story of Their Hit," *New York Times*, February 18, 1945. Comden and Green's fascination with the operas of Wagner turns up in a draft lyric for "Say When," which was cut from the final version of *On the Town*:

> I've learned a lot about the science of drinking
> From doing lots and lots of scientific thinking,
> Now take Isolde, when Tristan wouldn't sin,
> To make him bolder, she simply slipped him some gin.
> (*On the Town* script, Version C, I-9-61.)

17. *On the Town*, Published script, 11. The dialogue quoted in the remaining part of this paragraph comes from the same page.

18. This occurs in Act I, Scene 5, when Chip gets into Hildy's taxicab.

19. Leonard Bernstein, *American Musical Comedy*, telecast October 7, 1956; transcript reprinted in *The Joy of Music* (New York: Simon & Schuster, 1959), 163–66, 168. Thanks to Jeffrey Magee for pointing out this lineage.

20. Leonard Bernstein, Interview with Lehman Engel, January 19, 1980, Engel Collection B1/F21.

21. Bernstein, in "*On the Town* Symposium," 15.

22. Comden, in "*On the Town* Symposium," 22.

23. Adolph Green, quoted in "Putting It All Together: The Synthesis of a Musical as a Work of Art," in *Musical Theatre in America: Papers and Proceedings of the Conference on the Musical Theatre in America*, ed. Glenn Loney (Westport, CT: Greenwood Press, 1984), 344.

24. Comden, in Comden and Green, Interview with Lehman Engel, March 17, 1978, Engel Collection B2/F37. In the same interview, Green added: "No one said let's do an extension of FANCY FREE [that is, into *On the Town*]. That was never the original discussion."

25. Smith, in "*On the Town* Symposium," 13.

26. Seymour Peck, "*PM* Visits 'On the Town's' Tunesmith," *PM: New York Daily*, December 27, 1944.

27. Bernstein, in "*On the Town* Symposium," 24.

28. Comden and Robbins, in "*On the Town* Symposium," 13.

29. Comden, Interview with Lehman Engel.

30. "On the Town—With Some Youngsters," *Cue*, December 2, 1944, Bernstein Scrapbooks.

31. Oliver Smith, quoted in Elinor Hughes, "Theater and Screen," *Boston Herald*, December 13, 1944, Bernstein Scrapbooks.

32. "Contract," June 2, 1944, RobbinsCP, B63/F13. The contract stipulates the division of royalties as Green 1.5 percent, Comden 1.5 percent, Robbins 1 percent, and Bernstein 2 percent.

33. Re "a group": "Young Talents Map Broadway Musical," *Variety*, June 7, 1944. Re "will be placed": Sam Zolotow, "Bernstein Music for 'On the Town'—New Show is Due Late in the Summer—Jerome Robbins to Stage the Choreography," *New York Times*, June 7, 1944. Both in Bernstein Scrapbooks.

34. Sam Zolotow, "Kaufman Doubling on 'George Apley,'" *New York Times*, July 3, 1944. Burton reports that "Robbins had wanted Arthur Laurents to write the book and John La Touche for the lyrics but Bernstein insisted on bringing in his friends Comden and Green" (129). Jowitt (90) states the same, although neither gives their source.

35. "Rhapsody," IBDB, accessed January 11, 2013.

36. Comden and Green, "A Pair of 'Bookmakers' Tell All."

37. "Broadway Gazette" [newspaper identification unclear], June 10, 1944, Bernstein Scrapbooks. A later article refers to the hospitalization: Mona Gardner, "Triple-Threat Man," *Collier's*, October 13, 1945.

38. Oliver Smith, Letter to Robbins, August 8, 1944, RobbinsPP, Series I, B115/F5.

39. Leonard Bernstein, Letter to Helen Coates, Bernstein Collection B13/F4.

40. Betty Comden, Draft for telegram, Comden-Green Papers B16/F18.

41. Leonard Bernstein, Letter to Copland, August 16, [1944], Copland Collection B247/F1.

42. Oliver Smith, Letter to Robbins.

43. Comden and Green, "A Pair of 'Bookmakers' Tell All."

44. Smith, in "*On the Town* Symposium," 13.

45. George Abbott, "*Mister Abbott*" (New York: Random House, 1963), 199. Abbott had an extraordinarily long life: 1887–1995.

46. Sam Zolotow, "He Likes the Kids," *New York Times*, October 4, 1944.

47. Comden, Interview with Lehman Engel.

48. Smith, Interview with Lehman Engel.

49. Smith, in "*On the Town* Symposium," 13.

50. Sam Zolotow, "News of the Stage: Some Ample Financing," *New York Times*, October 11, 1944. Much of the information about the funding for *On the Town* comes from Zolotow, who was legendary for pursuing hard data about Broadway shows; Glenn Collins, "Sam Zolotow, a Theater Reporter for Many Decades, Is Dead at 94," *New York Times*, October 23, 1993.

51. Re funders: Sam Zolotow, "'On the Town' Progressing," *New York Times*, October 12, 1944. Re de Cuevas: "Marquis de Cuevas Dead at 75; Impresario of Ballet Company," *New York Times*, February 23, 1961.

52. Joseph X. Dever, "Society Today: Some Leave Gotham as Others Move In," *Palm Beach Daily News*, December 27, 1963. http://news.google.com/newspapers?nid=1961&dat=19631211&id=uYohAAAAIBAJ&sjid=IZcFAAAAIBAJ&pg=6870,4678137, accessed January 12, 2013.

53. Zolotow, "'On the Town' Progressing." An article in the *Jewish News*, a Detroit publication, stated that Bernstein was "under contract with Warner Brothers for all his future compositions, many of which will be used in forthcoming motion pictures" (William B. Saphire, "Leonard Bernstein...Composer," August 25, 1944, Bernstein Scrapbooks).

54. Peck, "*PM* Visits 'On the Town's' Tunesmith."

55. "The Success Story of B. Comden & A. Green," *PM: New York Daily*, March 11, 1945.

56. Green, quoted in Loney, "Putting It All Together," 359–60. Draft scripts for *On the Town* include a "night court" scene (e.g., *On the Town* script, Version A²).

57. George Abbott, Interview with Lehman Engel, September 8, 1978, Engel Collection B1/F1. Ellipses in interview transcript.

58. [George Abbott?], [Typed suggestions for *On the Town*], n.d., Comden-Green B16/F18. Ellipses in the original.

59. Peck, "*PM* Visits 'On the Town's' Tunesmith."

60. Robbins, in "*On the Town* Symposium," 17.

61. "Singers Wanted," *New York News*, October 19, 1944, Bernstein Scrapbooks; and Sam Zolotow, "'On the Town' Gets a Broadway House," *New York Times*, November 13, 1944.

62. Allyn Ann McLerie, Interview with the author, February 15, 2009.

63. Zolotow, "'On the Town' Gets a Broadway House." The International (formerly Park Theatre) reopened October 30, 1944 (IBDB, accessed January 16, 2013).

64. Sam Zolotow, "Myerberg Owner of the Mansfield." The Adelphi was re-named the George Abbott Theatre in 1965, then demolished in 1970 by the Hilton Hotel chain (IBDB, accessed January 16, 2013).

65. [Untitled], *Amsterdam Recorder*, November 25, 1944, Bernstein Scrapbooks.

66. Al Hirschfeld, "Mr. Hirschfeld Goes to a Rehearsal of 'On the Town,'" *New York Times*, November 26, 1944.

67. Bernstein, Unlabeled sketches for *On the Town* ["Starr on Whiteman" in top left corner], Bernstein Collection B26/F10.

68. Bernstein, Letter to Koussevitzky, December 4, 1944, Bernstein Collection, American Memory, LC.

69. Peck, "*PM* Visits 'On the Town's' Tunesmith."

70. Bernstein and Comden in "*On the Town* Symposium," 23. Bernstein also stated in this interview: "I got some severe slaps from Serge Koussevit[z]ky, . . . who was my great master and could not believe I was going to take all those months off to write a Broadway show."

71. "He worked on the mural 'Alice in Wonder Bread Land' and on the Hall of Pharmacy's 'Sorcery to Science,' which showed the march of medicine from the days of witchcraft to the days of World War II" (Lucy Greenbaum, "Producers with a Philosophy," *New York Times*, May 26, 1946).

72. There were direct ties between the New Opera Company and Ballet Theatre. Not only did George Balanchine choreograph some of NOC's productions, but in 1941, the *New York Times* announced: "The first two weeks [of Ballet Theatre's New York season] will be sponsored by the New Opera Company at the Forty-fourth Street Theatre" (John Martin, "The Dance: Miscellany," *New York Times*, October 19, 1941).

73. "Rosalinda," IBDB, accessed January 16, 2013. Also John Pennino, "The New Opera Company: What Did It Accomplish?" *Opera Quarterly* 16, no. 4 (Autumn 2000): 589–610.

74. Greenbaum, "Producers with a Philosophy."

75. Paul Feigay, "The Dance on 'Omnibus,'" *Dance Magazine*, March 1955, 23–27, 83.

76. John Chapman, "'On the Town' Is Not as Carefree and Gay as Its Title Hopes It Is," *Daily News*, December 29, 1944, Clark Collection B99/F2.

77. Greenbaum, "Producers with a Philosophy."

78. Jack Anderson, "Oliver Smith, Set Designer, Dead at 75," *New York Times*, January 25, 1994.

79. Two examples of high praise for Goberman and the orchestra are: Burton Rascoe, "'On the Town' Is Lively, Tuneful and Good Fun," *New York World-Telegram*, December 29, 1944, Bernstein Scrapbooks; and S. L. M. Barlow, "Music and Dancing on Broadway," *Modern Music* 22, no. 2 (January-February 1945): 131.

80. Goberman conducted the Gotham Little Symphony under WPA sponsorship in 1936 ("Programs of the Week," *New York Times*, July 19, 1936). In 1937, he performed in a concert connected with the American League Against War and Fascism, which had been founded by the American Communist Party ("For Anti-War Music: Group Is Formed to Present Peace Compositions," *New York Times*, May 10, 1937). That same year, he conducted a concert sponsored by the International Coordinating Committee for Aid to Republican Spain ("Concert Aids Refugees," *New York Times*, July 2, 1937).

81. Goberman's obituary in *Variety* states that he was musical director of Ballet Theatre for five seasons, yet reviews in the *New York Times* make it clear that he continued to conduct for the organization into the 1950s. Perhaps he became a guest conductor ("Max Goberman," *Variety*, January 16, 1963, 86).

82. Testimony alleging Goberman's affiliation with the Communist Party came from the pianist Seymour Levitan (Russell Porter, "Witness Pictures Red Rule in

Union," *New York Times*, April 13, 1957). Goberman died unexpectedly while in the midst of a project to record all of Haydn's 104 symphonies; he had apparently completed recordings of 40 of them. See biography of Goberman in Steven Suskin, *The Sound of Broadway Music: A Book of Orchestrators and Orchestrations* (New York: Oxford University Press, 2009), 140–41.

83. Arthur Gell, "Director Signed for Wouk's Play," *New York Times*, July 8, 1957.

84. *On the Town*, Souvenir Program.

85. Peggy Clark, Sketches for *On the Town*'s Stage Designs, Clark Collection B100/F3.

86. *On the Town*, Colonial Theatre Program.

87. *On the Town* Program, December 28, 1944.

88. "'Stage Door Canteen' on the Air," *PM's Daily Picture Magazine*, August 2, 1942, Clark Collection B158/F16.

89. Brooks Atkinson, "Curtain's Up at the Stage Door Canteen," *New York Times*, March 3, 1942.

90. There were concerns about "white chorus girls and actresses dancing with colored soldiers," as one article put it, but largely the Stage Door Canteen maintained its policy of desegregation ("Mixed Dancing at N.Y. Canteen for All Service Men," *New Journal and Guide*, May 30, 1942). See also James V. Hatch, "Creeping Toward Integration," in Errol G. Hill and James V. Hatch, *A History of African American Theatre* (Cambridge: Cambridge University Press, 2003), 336.

91. David Johnson, "40 Years of Broadway Theatre Design," *Back Stage*, December 15, 2000, A38. Clark's first engagement as lighting designer appears to have been *Beggar's Holiday*, which was directed by Nicholas Ray and opened in December 1946 (IBDB, accessed January 18, 2013).

92. Tharon Musser quoted in Tish Dace, "Designing Women," *Back Stage*, March 20, 1998, 30.

93. Lucy Greenbaum, "Two Who Help Make 'The Town,'" *New York Times*, February 4, 1945.

94. Peggy Doyle, "'On the Town' Rich Treat for Devotees of Ballet," *Boston American*, December 16, 1944, Bernstein Scrapbooks.

95. Comden and Green, "A Pair of 'Bookmakers' Tell All." A program for the show recounts this story from Walker's perspective: "While on the Coast she encountered her friends, Leonard Bernstein, Betty Comden and Adolph Green who were up to their ears in the score and book of 'On the Town.' They wanted her for their show and so did the producers—and after hearing some of it, she wanted to be in it too" (*On the Town*, Souvenir Program). The early appointments of Walker and Osato were confirmed in cast announcements made in October (Zolotow, "'On the Town' Progressing").

96. Sono Osato, *Distant Dances* (New York: Alfred A. Knopf, 1980), 232.

97. Walker's height is given in Seymour Peck, "'On Town's' Lady Cabbie," *PM: New York Daily*, January 9, 1945, Clark Collection B99/F2. Biographical information for Walker comes from her obituary in the *New York Times* (James Barron, "Nancy Walker, 69, of 'Rhoda' and TV Commercials, Is Dead," *New York Times*, March 27, 1992), and *On the Town*, Souvenir Program. Walker's birth year is variously given as 1921 and 1922.

98. Nichols, "The Play."

99. Greenbaum, "Two Who Help Make 'The Town.'"

100. Abbott, *"Mister Abbott,"* 199–200.

101. "Showlog," *Billboard*, July 21, July 28, August 4, and August 11, 1945. Comden and Green had been at Pike, N.H., and Holly Harris and Johnny Stearns substituted for them in the show.

102. Battles's involvement in these two shows is not documented in IBDB, which might suggest that he was not part of the original cast. Rather, the information appears in his biography in the opening night program for *On the Town*, where it states that Battles left *Follow the Girls* "when after one audition, he was offered his present part in this musical" (*On the Town* Program, December 28, 1944).

103. Brooks Atkinson, "The New Play in Review," *New York Times*, October 11, 1947.

104. The letters from Battles to Bernstein are not dated, but their contents place them within the first ten days of February 1945. In one, Battles mentions that friends are going to see *Carmen Jones*, which means the letter was written before the show's closing date of February 10, 1945. The other two refer to Bernstein conducting in St. Louis, which he did in February 1945 (Burton, 139). All in Bernstein Collection B60A/F10.

105. "Chatter: Paris," *Variety*, June 17, 1953, 62.

106. Stephen E. Long, "Cris Alexander," in *The Gay and Lesbian Theatrical Legacy: A Biographical Dictionary of Major Figures in American Stage History in the Pre-Stonewall Era*, ed. Billy J. Harbin, Kim Marra, and Robert A. Schanke (Ann Arbor: University of Michigan Press, 2005), 24.

107. John Battles, Letter to Bernstein, [early February 1945].

108. Joseph Dalton, "'On the Town' Actor/Photographer Cris Alexander Dies," *Albany Times Union*, March 21, 2012, and Margalit Fox, "Shaun O'Brien, Dancer Known for Character Roles, Dies at 86," *New York Times*, February 27, 2012.

109. Zolotow, "'On the Town' Progressing."

110. J. Brooks Atkinson, "The Play," *New York Times*, December 1, 1927.

111. "Robert Chisholm," *The Stage*, November 17, 1960.

112. Chisholm's career is chronicled in Frank van Straten, "'A Bachelor Gay': Australia's Forgotten Musical Star," paper expanded from a presentation at Australasian Sound Recordings Association Conference, 2007.

113. Bernstein, Interview with Lehman Engel. George Abbott recalled, "The inexperienced managers had allowed only two weeks for the tryout in Boston. This was much too brief by all normal standards, and the problem was further aggravated by the snowstorm which delayed the scenery's arrival" (*"Mister Abbott,"* 200).

114. "Tickets on Sale for 'On the Town,'" *Boston Traveler*, December 4, 1944, and "Musical's Cast Due Tomorrow," *Boston American*, December 9, 1944, Bernstein Scrapbooks.

115. Natalie Gordon, "Preview Tribute Paid Bernstein," *Boston Traveler*, December 14, 1944, Bernstein Scrapbooks. The *New York Times* reported the delay as having to do with "a shortage of stagehands" (Sam Zolotow, "Anderson to Stage Max Gordon Show," *New York Times*, December 14, 1944).

116. L. A. Sloper, "New Musical by Bernstein and Robbins," *Christian Science Monitor*, December 22, 1944, Bernstein Scrapbooks.

117. Carol J. Oja and Kay Kaufman Shelemay, "Leonard Bernstein's Jewish Boston: Cross-Disciplinary Research in the Classroom," *Journal of the Society for American Music* 3, no. 1 (February 2009): 3–33.

118. "'On the Town' at the Colonial," *Jewish Advocate*, December 14, 1944, Bernstein Scrapbooks.

119. Warren Storey Smith, "Leonard Bernstein: Score of Broadway Show, 'On the Town' Latest Musical Work of Roxbury Maestro," *Boston Post*, December 24, 1944, Bernstein Scrapbooks.

120. G. Y. Loveridge, "Bernstein: Boy Wonder of Podium: 26-Year-Old Musical Phenomenon Steers Symphonies with Bare Hands," *Providence Journal* [RI], November 19, 1944, Bernstein Scrapbooks. The concert took place during the week of November 19: "Bernstein at Symphony," *Daily Boston Globe*, November 19, 1944.

121. Jules Wolffers, "Music in Review: Bernstein Conducts Symphony," *Jewish Advocate*, December 7, 1944, Bernstein Scrapbooks.

122. Gordon, "Preview Tribute Paid Bernstein."

123. Alison Arnold, "Modern Art Institute Plans Another First-Night Benefit," *Boston Herald*, December 8, 1944, Bernstein Scrapbooks. An invitation for this benefit also appears in the scrapbooks.

124. Bernstein's involvement in this committee is chronicled in Barry Seldes, *Leonard Bernstein: The Political Life of an American Musician* (Berkeley: University of California Press, 2009), 33.

125. Jules Wolffers, "Music in Review," *Jewish Advocate*, December 21, 1944, Bernstein Scrapbooks.

126. Natalie Gordon, "Gracious Ladies," *Boston Traveler*, December 13, 1944, Bernstein Scrapbooks.

127. Re "aura" and "rhythmic": Cyrus Durgin, "The Stage: Colonial Theatre: 'On the Town,'"*Daily Boston Globe*, December 16, 1944. Re "brilliant": L. A. Sloper, "Bernstein-Robbins Musical Seen at Colonial Theater," *Christian Science Monitor*, December 16, 1944. Both Bernstein Scrapbooks.

128. Elliot Norton, "Jolly New Comedy at Colonial; 'On the Town,' Rich in Music, Action, Laughter," *Boston Post*, December 16, 1944, Bernstein Scrapbooks.

129. Sloper, "New Musical by Bernstein and Robbins."

130. One early script of the show (*On the Town* script, Version B) includes two versions of the "Lobby" scene.

131. Comden, quoted in Tony Vellela, "Comden Is Back in 'Town,'" *Christian Science Monitor*, December 5, 2003.

132. "On the Town—With Some Youngsters." Green referred specifically to the New York opening.

133. Peck, "*PM* Visits 'On the Town's' Tunesmith."

134. "News of the Theater," *New York Herald Tribune*, December 18, 1944, Bernstein Scrapbooks.

135. Al Hirschfeld, "Glorifying the Twenty-Four-Hour Pass and Saluting American Song," *New York Times*, December 24, 1944.

136. Many clippings from advance publicity appear in Bernstein's scrapbooks: Danton Walker, "Broadway Beat," *New York News*, December 27, 1944 (announcing that Shirley Burton, who sang in the show's chorus, was "Leonard Bernstein's kid sister"); photo of Comden and Green, *Brooklyn Eagle*, December 24, 1944.

137. Sam Zolotow, "'On the Town' Set for Debut Tonight: Musical Comedy Opening at Adelphi with Backing of Two Film Companies," *New York Times*, December 28, 1944. The relative value of these ticket amounts in terms of purchasing power in 2011 is: $1.20 (1944) = $15.30 (2011); $6.00 (1944) = $76.70 (2011); $12 (1944) = $153 (2011); www.measuringworth.com, accessed January 25, 2013.

138. Nichols, "The Play."

139. "Big Time in the Big Town," *Newsweek*, January 8, 1945; "Four Way Flash," *Time*, January 15, 1945; "On the Town," *Life*, January 15, 1945; Kate Sproehule, "Theatre," *Mademoiselle*, March 1945; all in Bernstein Scrapbooks.

140. By August 1945, one critic assessed that the "capacity audience" included "a larger number of non-New Yorkers," so the local audience had been largely saturated at that point (George Freedley, "The Stage Today—'On the Town' Still Holds Its Own as Finest Musical on Broadway," *New York Telegraph*, August 24, 1945, Bernstein Scrapbooks).

141. Hal Prince, Interview with the author, April 29, 2009.

142. Re "air-cooled": "Broadway Showlog," *Billboard*, April 28, 1945, 32. Re "more convenient": Clark, Letter to "Dott," May 14, 1945, Clark Collection B172/F12.

143. The dates for each theater come from IBDB. One detail: "Showlog" states that the show moved to the 44th Street Theater on June 5 (not June 4) ("Showlog," *Billboard*, June 9, 1945, 34).

144. "Publicity's Pay Dirt Tricks; P.S.'s Seek New Avenues to Hypo Clients' Box Office," *Billboard*, May 4, 1946, 4.

145. "Showlog," *Billboard*, January 13, 1945, 31, and February 3, 1945, 31. The "Showlog" citations that follow are all taken from *Billboard*.

146. "Showlog," January 13, 1945, 31, and February 24, 1945, 38.

147. Re Fisher on radio: "Showlog," August 25, 1945, 35. Re Osato's vacation: "Showlog," September 8, 1945, 37. Even after radio coverage had diminished, Osato appeared on a radio show on May 18 ("Showlog," May 19, 1945, 33).

148. Abbott, Letter to Peggy Clark, February 2, 1945.

149. "Showlog," February 3, 1945, 31, and February 10, 1945, 31.

150. Henry Sherwood took over the role. "Showlog," January 27, 1945, 29.

151. George Abbott, Letter to Peggy Clark, February 28, 1945, Clark Collection B99/F3.

152. Clark, "Understudies."

153. Eric Salzman, "Song Recital Given by Marten Sameth," *New York Times*, October 20, 1959. Sameth appeared in *The Golden Apple* in 1954 (IBDB).

154. George Abbott, Letter to Peggy Clark, February 2, 1945, Clark Collection B99/F3.

155. Robbins's appearances in the show took place on February 28, "as a warm-up for [his] forthcoming Met appearance [with Ballet Theatre]" ("Showlog," March 10, 1945, 30), and on March 27 ("Showlog," April 7, 1945, 33). Harrison is mistakenly listed as "Rex" on April 7.

156. Re "artist": "Showlog," February 3, 1945, 31. Re "current": "Showlog," February 17, 1945, 31.

157. "Showlog," June 23, 1945, 34.

158. "Showlog," June 30, 1945, 35, and July 7, 1945, 38.

159. "Showlog," September 29, 1945, 40, and February 9, 1946, 41.

160. Elizabeth Morgan, Letter to Charles Harris, January 2, 1945. The date of *On the Town*'s performance is given in a second letter, Morgan to Clark, January 23, 1945. Both Clark Collection B99/F3.

161. Re orchestra: Clark, "Stage Door Canteen—Feb. 8," handwritten list; includes Max Goberman, Clark Collection B99/F6. Re "entertainment": "Showlog," February 24, 1945, 38.

162. Re "abridged version": Clark, "Company Call Canteen Show—Thursday, June 14th," handwritten (this folder contains various agendas for that day's performance).

Re orchestra: Clark, "June 14—Stage Door Canteen, Cond. Frank Nowicki"; the list includes the names of 21 musicians. Both in Clark Collection B99/F6.

163. Re March 11: Clark, "On the Town, St. Alban's [sic] Naval Hospital, Sunday, March 11, 1945"; this performance was cited in "Showlog," *Billboard*, March 24, 1945, 31. Re May 6: Clark's "Running Order" for the appearance at Halloran Hospital carefully indicates a few cuts (typescript, May 6, 1945). Both in Clark Collection B99/F6. Re June 24: Mitchel (spelled with one "l") Field was on Long Island (Clark, Letter to "Dott").

164. Clark, Letter to "Dott."

165. "9 Shows to Make Bows This Month," *New York Times*, February 2, 1946.

166. These dates are not definitive. Comden and Green's papers include business correspondence with dates for the tour, although I have adjusted a few of them based on newspaper reports (Comden-Green Papers B16/F11). The closing date in Philadelphia is approximately March 2 ("4 Stage Shows Hold Over," *Philadelphia Record*, February 25, 1946); and the closing date in Chicago comes from "Stage Notes," *Chicago Daily Tribune*, April 23, 1946 (both articles in Bernstein Scrapbooks). There appears to have been a two-week break between closing in Pittsburgh and opening in Detroit.

167. Osato left the show on December 1, 1945 (Sam Zolotow, "News of the Stage," *New York Times*, December 3, 1945).

168. Norman Clark, "'On Town,' Musical Hit from Broadway, Is Now at Ford's," *The Baltimore News-Post*, February 5, 1946, Bernstein Scrapbooks.

169. Sam Zolotow, "'Duchess' Arriving After Day's Delay," *New York Times*, February 13, 1946. In terms of the performance networks that sustained the show, Xenia Bank had been in the chorus of *Rosalinda*, the remake of *Die Fledermaus* by the New Opera Company, for which Paul Feigay had been Associate Stage Manager (IBDB).

170. "'Whitman Avenue' to Open on May 8," *New York Times*, April 20, 1946.

171. E. B. Rea, "Encores and Echoes," *Afro-American*, February 9, 1946.

172. Allen, Neal, and Riley are profiled in Chapter 6. The African American dancer Dorothy McNichols also went on tour, so Hilda Seine was perhaps a replacement in Baltimore only. Seine is mentioned as a "member of the cast of 'On the Town'" and being from British Guinea (Lula Jones Garrett, "Gadabouting in Baltimore," *Afro-American*, February 23, 1946).

173. Elsie Graves Lewis, "Richmond Hears Dr. L. P. Jackson on Negro in Politics in Virginia," *New Journal and Guide* [Norfolk, VA], February 23, 1946. The article continued, "'Billie,' another young miss, and three young men were the only Negro artists in the play which was given for a week in Baltimore's leading theatre."

174. Al Monroe, "Swinging the News," *Chicago Defender*, April 20, 1946.

175. Claudia Cassidy, "'On the Town' Catches on Gaily at Great Northern," *Chicago Daily Tribune*, April 7, 1946.

176. Paul Feigay, Letter to Bernstein, April 17, 1946, Bernstein Collection B21/F16. A copy of this same letter was also addressed to Comden (Comden-Green Papers B16/F12).

177. The closing date appears in "Stage Notes," *Chicago Daily Tribune*, April 23, 1946, and Sam Zolotow, "'Apple of His Eye' to Close on May 18," *New York Times*, April 23, 1946.

178. Re *Victor Record News*: "On the Town" [cover], *Victor Record News*, May 1945. An article one month earlier stated that the recording was "soon to be released"

("Leonard Bernstein: Career in Four Keys," *Victor Record Review*, April 1945). Re *PM*: Dan Keleher (photographer), "Music for the Mayor," *PM: New York Daily*, May 9, 1945. That article states "the album will be available at record stores in a week or 10 days." Both in Bernstein Scrapbooks.

179. See, for example, Paul Crowell, "Mayor Protests Japanese in East: He Opposes Shifting of Former Pacific Coast Residents—Sees Military Peril Here," *New York Times*, April 27, 1944.

180. The recording of *Porgy and Bess* featured Anne Brown, Todd Duncan, and other performers from the premiere, conducted by Alexander Smallens (Decca DA 145). The recording of *This Is the Army* (DA 340) included the show's original New York Cast, conducted by Milton Rosenstock (Decca B0000831-02).

181. *Oklahoma!* appeared on Decca (DA 359) in 1943. Tim Carter, *Oklahoma! The Making of an American Musical* (New Haven, CT: Yale University Press, 2007), 227.

182. One such example appeared as an ad in the *Daily Boston Globe*: "Arcade Music Shop presents DECCA RECORDS," *Daily Boston Globe*, May 23, 1946.

183. See Appendix for full recording information.

184. Bernstein, Symphony No. 1, *Jeremiah*, Nan Merriman, mezzo-soprano; St. Louis Symphony Orchestra; Leonard Bernstein, conductor; recorded February 14, 1945; Victor DM 1026.

185. IMDb dates the New York City release as December 8, 1949, and the "USA" release as December 30 ("On the Town," IMDb, accessed January 27, 2013). This concurs with the *New York Times* review: Bosley Crowther, "'On the Town' Yuletide Picture at Radio City, Is Musical to Please the Family," December 9, 1949.

186. The IMDb entry for *On the Town* is exceptionally rich with information, including a list of filming locations.

187. IMDb lists these uncredited choreographic assistants.

188. The chase segments in the film are related to brief chase interludes between scenes in the stage script, which got whittled down from longer versions in early drafts (e.g., *On the Town* script, Versions A^1 and A^2).

189. Burton states, "MGM bought [Bernstein's] approval to change the score with a five-thousand-dollar consultation fee" (193).

190. Gene Kelly, Letter to Charles Harmon of the Leonard Bernstein office, March 11, 1991, Bernstein Collection B31/F47. In this letter, Kelly expresses regret at losing documents in a house fire, including some related to his work with Bernstein. Burton states that "Kelly had been at the opening night of *On the Town* in December 1944" (192).

191. IMDb gives a "Soundtrack Listing," citing all of Roger Edens's tunes as "uncredited" in the film, www.imdb.com/title/tt0041716/soundtrack, accessed January 28, 2013.

192. Betty Comden and Adolph Green, in *The Art of the American Musical*, 53.

193. Nelson Lansdale, "Talent On the Town," *Theatre Arts* 34, no. 7 (July 1950): 46.

194. Edwin Schallert, "'On the Town' Sprightly, Amusing Film Musical," *Los Angeles Times*, December 30, 1949.

195. Crowther, "'On the Town,' Yuletide Picture at Radio City, Is Musical to Please the Family."

196. A clip of "New York, New York" from the 1949 film can be viewed on YouTube, www.youtube.com/watch?v=x7CIgWZTdgw, accessed January 28, 2013. The lyric from

the stage show, "New York, New York, it's a helluva town" was changed to "wonderful town" to satisfy the Hollywood production code. Also, "New York, New York" from *On the Town* should not be confused with a theme song from the film *New York, New York* (1977), which was directed by Martin Scorsese, with music for the song by John Kander and lyrics by Fred Ebb. Frank Sinatra frequently performed the Kander and Ebb song, sometimes introducing it with a fragment of the tune from *On the Town* (www.youtube.com/watch?v=Mo_S62E2ylY, accessed January 28, 2013).

197. Donald Bogle, *Toms, Coons, Mulattoes, Mammies, & Bucks: An Interpretive History of Blacks in American Films*, 4th ed. (New York: Continuum, 2001), 158, 144. Another important study of race and Hollywood musicals is: Arthur Knight, *Disintegrating the Musical: Black Performance and American Musical Film* (Durham, NC: Duke University Press, 2002).

198. Comden and Green, "When N.Y. Was a Helluva Town."

CHAPTER 4: A JAPANESE AMERICAN STAR DURING WORLD WAR II

Epigraph: Sono Osato, quoted in Earl Conrad, "American Viewpoint: She's Mixed, Merry and Musical," *Chicago Defender*, April 14, 1945.

1. Jerome Robbins, Interview with Clive Barnes, 1973; typed draft transcript, RobbinsPP, Series I, B21/F7. This interview served as the basis for Barnes's article, "The 'Fancy' That Made History," *New York Times*, February 3, 1974.

2. Everett Lee, Interview with the author, March 25, 2009.

3. Greg Robinson, "Nisei in Gotham: The JACD and Japanese Americans in 1940s New York." *Prospects: An Annual of American Cultural Studies* 30 (2005), 585. I am grateful to Greg Robinson for generously offering leads to a number of *nisei* newsletters and other sources from World War II.

4. Wong played the character of "Minn Lee"—a "loyal Chinese jade"—in *On the Spot*, a crime spoof (J. Brooks Atkinson, "The Play," *New York Times*, October 30, 1930).

5. Sono Osato, Interview with the author, February 28, 2009; Sono Osato, *Distant Dances* (New York: Alfred A. Knopf, 1980), 243.

6. *On the Town*, Published script, 12. The quotations that follow from this scene are taken from pages 18 and 12.

7. Brackets and upper-case appear in the published script.

8. *On the Town* (excerpts), filmed in performance at the Martin Beck Theatre, New York City, 1945, NYPL. Length: 7 minutes.

9. Edwin Denby, "Dancing in Shows," *New York Herald Tribune*, January 21, 1945; reprinted in *Edwin Denby: Dance Writings*, ed. Robert Cornfield and William Mackay (London: Dance Books, 1986).

10. Edward Barry, "Osato—Born to Dance," *Chicago Daily Tribune*, February 28, 1937.

11. Lucy Greenbaum, "Two Who Help Make 'The Town,'" *New York Times*, February 4, 1945.

12. The word "exotic" will be explored later in this chapter. Here is one occasion when it was used: Walter E. Owen, "Sono Osato," *Dance Magazine*, February 8, 1945.

13. Information about "Miss America" comes from "People & Events: Breaking the Color Line at the Pageant," webpage accompanying the television episode "Miss America" from *American Experience*, PBS Online/WGBH, www.pbs.org/wgbh/amex/missamerica/

peopleevents/e_inclusion.html, accessed February 18, 2013. See also Sarah Banet-Weiser, *The Most Beautiful Girl in the World: Beauty Pageants and National Identity* (Berkeley: University of California Press, 1999).

14. Ann Bayer, "Token Women," *New York Magazine*, March 29, 1976, 45.

15. Jerry Bullard, "Miss Subways Contest," blog post to "Brooklyn Memories," February 11, 2010, http://bklynmemories.blogspot.com/2010/02/miss-subways-contest.html, accessed February 18, 2013.

16. Comden, quoted in Bayer, "Token Women," 46.

17. Melanie Bush, "Miss Subways, Subversive and Sublime," *New York Times*, October 24, 2004.

18. In *Distant Dances* (4), Sono says her father was in San Francisco for the 1906 earthquake and that he came to the United States at age nineteen. Shoji Osato's "Alien Registration Form" (filled out in Chicago on November 8, 1940) gives his birthdate as March 11, 1885, and dates his arrival in the United States as April 1905, making him twenty when he arrived (Shoji Osato USCIS Records), and a genealogist at USCIS gives the same date (Lynda K. Spencer, Letter to author, June 9, 2010).

19. Osato, *Distant Dances*, 4.

20. Frances Osato's birthdate: July 8, 1899. Included in "Information for Travel Purposes; Sono Osato," Questionnaire for Ballet Theatre (early 1940s, ABT Records B11/F1014). Frances was listed in the 1920 census as age 20 (U.S. Bureau of the Census, "Fourteenth Census of the United States: 1920, Ward 10, Precinct 9 and 10, Omaha, Nebraska; Ancestry.com, accessed February 19, 2013). Re "daringly modern": Osato, *Distant Dances*, 5.

21. Osato, *Distant Dances*, 5.

22. "Blackstone Hotel," City of Omaha Landmarks, City of Omaha; this website states "architect unknown": www.cityofomaha.org/planning/landmarks/alphabetical-listing/blackstone-hotel, accessed February 19, 2013.

23. Osato, *Distant Dances*, 5.

24. Nancy F. Cott, "Marriage and Women's Citizenship in the United States, 1830–1934," *American Historical Review* 103, no. 5 (December 1998): 1461, 1464. In 1931, the Cable Act was amended so that women were no longer penalized for marrying "aliens," and Frances might have regained her citizenship then (Martha Mabie Gardner, *The Qualities of a Citizen: Women, Immigration, and Citizenship, 1870–1965* [Princeton, NJ: Princeton University Press, 2005], 146).

25. SS *Homeric*, September 25, 1929; Ancestry.com, accessed February 19, 2013.

26. Osato, *Distant Dances*, 14.

27. Barry, "Osato—Born to Dance."

28. "Sono Osato," *Current Biography: Who's News and Why 1945*, ed. Anna Rothe (New York: H. W. Wilson, 1946), 440.

29. Re taking a Russian name: Osato, *Distant Dances*, 30. Re "Osatchka": "Sono Osato," *Current Biography*, 440.

30. Re "notable picture": Greg Robinson, "The Great Unknown and the Unknown Great: Jun Fujita, a Brilliant Chicago Photographer and Poet," *Nichi Bei Times Online: Japanese American News*, August 21, 2008; www.nichibeitimes.com/e/dates/080821.html, accessed July 18, 2010 (no longer available online as of May 2013). Re Hansen: Oskar J. W. Hansen, *Chien-Mi-Lo: A Satirical Prose Fantasy with Interpretative Sculpture* (Chicago: Nordic Press, 1927).

31. Shoji Osato, "Bit of Michigan Avenue," photograph, *Chicago Evening Post's Magazine of the Art World*, July 6, 1926, Art and Artist Files, Smithsonian American Art Museum/National Portrait Gallery Library.

32. Ruth De Young, "A Cup of Tea Is Ceremony to Japanese," *Chicago Daily Tribune*, July 15, 1933.

33. Judith Cass, "Japanese Tea Will Reopen 1893 Gardens," *Chicago Daily Tribune*, June 4, 1936.

34. "Japanese Gardens to Be Opened to Public Today," *Chicago Daily Tribune*, June 16, 1936. Tragically, Teru Osato died at twenty-six of cancer (Osato, *Distant Dances*, 249–50). Although Teru's name is given as "Tera" in the caption to this photo, it was a typo; Sono Osato consistently spells it as "Teru" in *Distant Dances*.

35. Cass, "Japanese Tea Will Reopen 1893 Gardens."

36. "Head of Japanese Flower School Will Be Guest in City," *Chicago Daily Tribune*, July 13, 1939.

37. "Russian Troupe to Arrive: Monte Carlo Ballet Russe Begins Engagement Here December 18," *New York Times*, November 11, 1933.

38. Peggy Wright, "Sono Osato," *PM's Sunday Picture News*, December 5, 1943.

39. Wright, "Sono Osato."

40. [Sheet of notes about Osato], clipped to: Barry Hyams (Associate Press Representative), Letter (carbon) to Marion Bussang (*New York Post*), November 19, 1940, Osato Clippings, NYPL. In *Distant Dances*, Osato said that she played "a Chinese barboy" (36). *Union Pacific* told the story of building America's first trans-continental railroad in 1869, a task that was largely completed by Chinese workers. A photo of Osato in *Union Pacific* can be found at: Maurice Seymour [photographer], Portrait of Marian Ladre and Sono Osato in costume for *Union Pacific*, Ballets Russes [*sic*], Chicago, [between 1930–1939], Geoffrey Ingram Archive of Australian Ballet, Digital Collections Pictures, National Library of Australia, http://nla.gov.au/nla.pic-vn3414642, accessed March 2, 2013.

41. The date for *Union Pacific* appears in the memoirs of Sol Hurok, who managed the Ballet Russe de Monte Carlo: *S. Hurok Presents: A Memoir of the Dance World* (New York: Hermitage House, 1953), 114.

42. Osato, *Distant Dances*, 36.

43. John Gruen, "Sono Osato," in *The Private World of Ballet* (New York: Viking Press, 1975), 71.

44. Osato, *Distant Dances*, 41.

45. "Five Americans Members of Ballet Russe Troupe," *Los Angeles Times*, January 3, 1937, and "Ten American Dancers Due with Ballet Russe," *Los Angeles Times*, January 2, 1938. This is out of a total of 150 dancers, as stated in these same articles. The dance scholar Lynn Garafola has questioned the numbers as being "suspiciously high" (Personal correspondence, August 6, 2010).

46. T. Essington Breen, ed., "The Ballet in Australia," in *Balletomane's Art Book: Pictorial Parade of Russian Ballet 1940* (Sydney: London Book Company, 1940), unpaginated; Digital Collections Books & Serials, National Library of Australia, www.nla.gov.au/apps/cdview?pi=nla.aus-vn3016378-s4-e, accessed March 2, 2013.

47. Osato, *Distant Dances*, 149.

48. John Martin, "The Dance: Ballet Russe; De Basil Troupe to Replace Monte Carlo Company in Fall Season Plans," *New York Times*, September 8, 1940.

49. "Music: Sur les Pointes," *Time*, November 1, 1937.

50. Osato, *Distant Dances*, 135, 141.

51. "Sono Osato's Letter Tells of Chase by Sub," *Chicago Daily Tribune*, March 17, 1940. See also "Ballets Russes in Australia, Our Cultural Revolution: A Timeline," National Library of Australia, www.australianballet.com.au/res/pdfs/Ballet_Russes_timeline.pdf, accessed March 2, 2013.

52. Isabel Morse Jones, "'Eternal Struggle' Ballet Philharmonic Feature," *Los Angeles Times*, October 16, 1940. This Los Angeles premiere is also listed in Kathrine [*sic*] Sorley Walker, "[Appendix]: Productions," in *De Basil's Ballets Russes* (New York: Atheneum, 1983), 266–67.

53. Edward Barry, "Ballet Russe Opens 5 Days' Shows Tonight," *Chicago Daily Tribune*, October 28, 1940.

54. *Les Fils Prodigue*, Inside front cover to Theatre Royal [Australia] program for Covent Garden Russian Ballet, December 30, 1938, through January 5, 1939, Digital Collections: Books & Serials, National Library of Australia, www.nla.gov.au/apps/cdview/?pi=nla.aus-vn143713-2-2-3-7-s2-v, accessed March 4, 2013.

55. The ballet had initially been choreographed by George Balanchine, with a score by Sergei Prokofiev; David Lichine completely redid the choreography because Balanchine would not release the rights ("The Prodigal Son (Australian context)," Trove, National Library of Australia, http://trove.nla.gov.au/list?id=1143, accessed April 9, 2013).

56. Review quoted in Osato, *Distant Dances*, 163–64.

57. John Martin, "'The Prodigal Son' Danced by Lichine," *New York Times*, November 27, 1940. During the troupe's 1941 spring season in New York, Martin again singled out Osato as among the "season's best" for "her stunning performance of the temptress in David Lichine's 'The Prodigal Son'" (John Martin, "The Dance: Honor Roll—Some Artists of Less than Stellar Rank who Belong Among Season's Assets," *New York Times*, June 15, 1941).

58. Hurok, *S. Hurok Presents*, 142.

59. Osato, quoted in Gruen, "Sono Osato," 71–72.

60. Walker, *De Basil's Ballets Russes*, 37.

61. Hurok, *S. Hurok Presents*, 137–38.

62. Hyams, Letter (carbon) to Marion Bussang. Osato's memory of the Yokohama earthquake came from a family trip to Japan in 1923 (Osato, *Distant Dances*, 5–7). Hyams was a "former Broadway producer and publicist": "Barry Hyams, 78, Producer and Publicist," *New York Times*, September 4, 1989.

63. Shirley Jennifer Lim, *A Feeling of Belonging: Asian American Women's Public Culture, 1930–1960* (New York: New York University Press, 2006), 58, 63.

64. "Ballet on the Wing," *New York Times*, November 17, 1940; "Accent on Action," *New York Times*, March 23, 1941.

65. George Platt Lynes, *Portrait: The Photographs of George Platt Lynes, 1927–1955*, foreword by Lincoln Kirstein (Santa Fe, NM: Twin Palms, 1994), [unpaginated book].

66. Nancy Grove, *Isamu Noguchi: Portrait Sculpture* (Washington, DC: Smithsonian Institution Press, 1989), 96–97.

67. I am grateful to Lynn Garafola for pointing out this connection between the School of American Ballet and dancers from the Ballet Russe (Personal correspondence).

68. John Martin, "The Dance: Russe and Near Russe," *New York Times*, August 31, 1941.

69. Hurok, *S. Hurok Presents*, 153. Vaccination certificate: "To Whom It May Concern," on stationery of Dr. Miron Silberstein, New York City, October 10, 1941; ABT Records B17/F1772. A questionnaire in the same folder is titled "Information for Travel Purposes"; it was filled out by Osato and is undated. In response to the question "Where and when did you last enter the United States," she wrote: "Laredo Texas, November 9, 1941," which was when Ballet Theatre returned from its trip to Mexico.

70. "Season Opens November 12 for Ballet Theatre," *New York Times*, November 4, 1941. See also display ad, *New York Times*, November 9, 1941.

71. John Martin, "The Dance: Third Season," *New York Times*, December 21, 1941.

72. Agnes de Mille, *America Dances* (New York: MacMillan, 1980), 131.

73. John Martin, "Ballet Premiere of 'Pillar of Fire,'" *New York Times*, April 9, 1942. A program for the premiere is included in Osato Programs, NYPL.

74. John Martin wrote: "'Princess Aurora' revealed once more what a really superior company this is, with Nora Kaye, Rosella Hightower, Sono Osato, ... and a dozen others besides the ranking stars" ("Ballet Theatre Opens Its Season," *New York Times*, October 7, 1942). The ballet was sometimes performed under the title *Aurora's Wedding* ("Aurora's Wedding" in *Library of Congress: Name Authority File*, http://id.loc.gov/authorities/names/n97820364.html, accessed April 29, 2013).

75. Two examples appear in a photo caption in the *Chicago Daily Tribune* (Barry, "Osato—Born to Dance") and a review of Osato in *The Prodigal Son* (Martin, "'The Prodigal Son' Danced by Lichine").

76. Osato on cover of *Peacock Alley*, plus inside photo and caption, April 1942 (Osato Clippings, NYPL). According to "WorldCat," *Peacock Alley* was also published under the title "Waldorf-Astoria Promenade Magazine," and it appeared between July 1940 and September 1947 (entry 19921016).

77. Unlabeled photo, Osato Clippings, NYPL. The same dress, with long sleeves, appears in a photo spread titled "New All-American Fashions," where Pattullo Modes was among several featured designers: *Life*, November 18, 1940, [61].

78. Lim, *A Feeling of Belonging*, 75.

79. Alice Murata, *Japanese Americans in Chicago* (Charleston, SC: Arcadia, 2002), 11.

80. Willard Edwards, "Foreign Agent Files Fail to Unmask a Spy: State Department Makes Records Public," *Chicago Daily Tribune*, October 11, 1938.

81. Shoji Osato, Alien Registration Form.

82. "Data Required for Reporting Detentions Under Special Orders: Shoji Osato," stamped December 9, 1941, Shoji Osato USCIS Records.

83. Mae M. Ngai, *Impossible Subjects: Illegal Aliens and the Making of Modern America* (Princeton, NJ: Princeton University Press, 2004), 175–76.

84. Samuel M. Chaimson, Immigrant Inspector, "RE: SHOJI OSATO," November 20, 1943, Shoji Osato USCIS Records.

85. Albert Gailord Hart and Julius Lieblein, "Family Income and the Income Tax Base," in *Studies in Income and Wealth*, Conference on Research in Income and Wealth (Ann Arbor, MI: UMI, 1946), 239. According to statistics given there, some 20 percent of Americans earned $2,000 a year or less in 1941, and some 70 percent earned $3000 a year or less.

86. Gennifer S. Weisenfeld, "Touring Japan-as-Museum: NIPPON and Other Japanese Imperialist Travelogues," *Positions: East Asia Cultures Critique* 8, no. 3 (Winter 2000): 753.

87. Ngai, *Impossible Subjects*, 179.

88. Francis Biddle, Attorney General, "In the Matter of SHOJI OSATO Alien Enemy; ORDER," February 14, 1942, Shoji Osato USCIS Records.

89. "United States Department of Justice, Application for Certificate of Identification (Aliens of Enemy Nationalities)," form filled out by Osato on June 1, 1942 (date unclear), Shoji Osato USCIS Records.

90. Richard F. Plzak, Immigrant Inspector, Alien Control Division; Memorandum to Andrew Jordan, District Director, Chicago 7; June 16, 1944, Shoji Osato USCIS Records.

91. Osato, *Distant Dances*, 187.

92. Osato, *Distant Dances*, 196.

93. Sono Osato, Letter (handwritten) to Harry M. Zuckert, June 4, 1942, ABT Records B17/F1772.

94. John Martin, "The Dance: Travel Notes," *New York Times*, January 3, 1943.

95. "S. Hurok Presents, The Ballet Theatre, Coast to Coast Tour 1942–1943," New York: Program Publications, [vii]; Programs, Jerome Robbins Dance Division, NYPL.

96. Osato, *Distant Dances*, 198.

97. H.M.Z. [Harry M. Zuckert], Letter (carbon) to Lt. Gen. John L. DeWitt, November 28, 1942, ABT Records B17/F1772.

98. Ray Ashworth, Major, U.S. Army, Chief of Regulatory Branch, Western Defense Command and Fourth Army; Letter (copy) to Harry M. Zuckert, December 4, 1942, ABT Records B17/F1772.

99. Conrad, "American Viewpoint." General John L. DeWitt, who sent the notification to Sono, was stationed in San Francisco, where he was a central architect of the relocation of Japanese Americans from the West Coast to inland "relocation camps" ("John Lesesne DeWitt [1880–1962]," *Virtual Museum of the City of San Francisco*, www.sfmuseum.org/bio/jldewitt.html, accessed April 29, 2013).

100. Osato, *Distant Dances*, 199. In an interview with me, Osato said her father was detained in "a big stone house" (February 28, 2009). See also "4800 Ellis Avenue, Chicago, Illinois" in "Temporary Detention Facilities," *German American Internee Coalition*, www.gaic.info/camp_temporary.htm#chicago, accessed March 11, 2013. Thanks to Karen Kanemoto, archivist at the Japanese American Service Committee in Chicago, for locating this link.

101. Re restaurant and gift shop: Plzak, Memorandum to Andrew Jordan, June 16, 1944. Most of Osato's USCIS records spell Mukoyama's last name as "Nukoyama." However, a biography of him establishes "Mukoyama" as the correct spelling: "Teruo Mukoyama, an Issei resident of Chicago for 16 years, owns his Trading Company in the Garfield Park section of Chicago. Mr. Mukoyama has several resettled employees in his prosperous gift shop. He is also Chicago correspondent for the Utah Nippo and has written many articles on evacuee problems." Photograph caption, courtesy Bancroft Library, University of California, Berkeley, available online through Online Archive of California, www.oac.cdlib.org/ark:/13030/ft7j49p18x/?docId=ft7j49p18x&brand=oac4&layout=printable-details, accessed March 11, 2013.

102. "Enemy Aliens Must Give Up Radios Monday: Guns and Cameras Also to Be Collected," *Chicago Daily Tribune*, January 2, 1942.

103. Multiple documents chronicle Osato's moves, including Shoji Osato, Authorized Change of Address or Change of Employment, Alien Registration Division, October 2, 1943, Shoji Osato USCIS Records.

104. Plzak, Memorandum to Andrew Jordan, June 16, 1944. This statement referred to Teruo Mukoyama (Shoji's boss), Shoji's son Timothy, and his son-in-law
Victor Elmaleh, who was in the navy.

105. John Martin, "Russian Ballet Opens Its Season," *New York Times*, April 2, 1943.

106. John Martin, "Premiere Offered by Ballet Theatre: Tudor's 'Romeo and Juliet,'
with Setting by Berman, Given at Metropolitan," *New York Times*, April 11, 1943. Osato
also took part that spring in a repeat performance of *Princess Aurora*: Martin, "Old-
Time Ballets at Metropolitan," *New York Times*, April 13, 1943.

107. "Victor Elmaleh—94," Interview, October 25, 2011, posted in *Old New York
Stories*, http://oldnewyorkstories.com/post/11666572720/victor-elmaleh-94, accessed
September 21, 2013.

108. Osato, *Distant Dances*, 206.

109. Ballet Theatre, Inc., Letter to Miss Sono Osato, April 23, 1943; carbon in ABT
Records B17/F1772.

110. Claudia Cassidy, "'Kiss and Tell' a Smashing Box Office Success," *Chicago Daily
Tribune*, September 5, 1943.

111. Geoffrey Block, *Enchanted Evenings: The Broadway Musical from "Show Boat" to
Sondheim*, 2nd ed. (New York: Oxford University Press, 2009), 135.

112. Wright, "Sono Osato."

113. Osato, *Distant Dances*, 220.

114. "New Musical in Manhattan," *Time*, October 18, 1943.

115. Lewis Nichols, "The Play: 'One Touch of Venus,' Which Makes the Whole World
Kin, Opens at the Imperial," *New York Times*, October 8, 1943.

116. Lewis Nichols, "'One Touch of Venus,'" *New York Times*, October 17, 1943.

117. Ralph Du Bois [filmmaker], *One Touch of Venus (excerpts)*, filmed at the Imperial Theater in New York City, 1943, videocassette copied from 16mm film, Theatre on
Film and Tape Archive, NYPL.

118. Unidentified quotation from *New York Herald Tribune*; quoted in Wright,
"Sono Osato."

119. Julia McCarthy, "'Foolish Heart' Ballet Star Knows Answers," *New York Sunday
News*, November 21, 1943, Osato Clippings, NYPL.

120. Wright, "Sono Osato."

121. de Mille, as paraphrased by Osato in *Distant Dances*, 218–19.

122. Osato, *Distant Dances*, 220.

123. "One Touch of Venus," IBDB, accessed April 29, 2013.

124. "'Voice of Turtle' Wins New Award," *New York Times*, July 4, 1944; "Sono Osato
Cited as Best Dancer of Broadway Season," *Pacific Citizen*, July 15, 1944, 3.

125. Bendel photo in unidentified magazine. Cover photos: *PM's Sunday Picture
News*, December 5, 1943, and *Sunday News: New York's Picture Newspaper*, January 16,
1944 (all in Osato Clippings, NYPL).

126. Owen, "Sono Osato," 9. The *New York Times* reported that Osato had "turned
in her notice to take effect July 8" (Sam Zolotow, "Premiere Tonight of 'Broken
Hearts,'" *New York Times*, June 12, 1944).

127. Wolcott Gibbs, "Pygmalion and Mary Martin," *New Yorker*, October 16, 1943.

128. Wright, "Sono Osato."

129. Greenbaum, "Two Who Help Make 'The Town.'"

130. Osato, Interview with the author, February 28, 2009.

131. All Osato quotations in this paragraph from *Distant Dances*, 230–31.

132. "Metropolitan Opera House: S. Hurok Presents the Ballet Theatre" [programs] April 3, 1942, April 14, 1943, and May 21, 1943, Osato Programs, NYPL.

133. Osato, *Distant Dances*, 229. The next quotation comes from the same source.

134. Cheryl Greenberg, "Black and Jewish Responses to Japanese Internment," *Journal of American Ethnic History* 14, no. 2 (Winter 1995): 4.

135. Yuriko Kikuchi and Emiko Tokunaga, *Yuriko: An American Japanese Dancer: To Wash in the Rain and Polish with the Wind* ([New York]: Tokunaga Dance Ko., 2008), 82; and Joyce Nishioka, "Yuriko Coaches Ballet San Jose Silicon Valley for Company Premiere," *AsianWeek*, October 10, 2003, www.asianweek.com/2003/10/10/yuriko-coaches-ballet-san-jose-silicon-valley-for-company-premiere, accessed March 21, 2013.

136. Natalie Davis, "Introducing to Our Mayor a Japanese-American Girl: Yuriko Amemiya Is an Answer to His Move to Bar Loyal Citizens," *PM: New York Daily*, May 3, 1944.

137. Isamu Noguchi, "I Become a Nisei," manuscript, 1942, 1; Isamu Noguchi Foundation Archives and Museum, Long Island City, NY; quoted in Amy Lyford, "Noguchi, Sculptural Abstraction, and the Politics of Japanese American Internment," *Art Bulletin* 85, no. 1 (March 2003): 141.

138. Lyford, "Noguchi, Sculptural Abstraction," 142.

139. "Arts Council Organized," *JACD Newsletter* 3, no. 2 (February 1944); and "They Work for Victory: The Story of Japanese Americans and the War Effort" [Illustrated promotional pamphlet], 1945, Collection of Material about Japanese American Internment, 1929–1956, Charles E. Young Research Library, University of California at Los Angeles, Series 3, B3, F20.

140. Lawrence E. Davies, "Ban on Japanese Lifted on Coast," *New York Times*, December 18, 1944.

141. Lewis Wood, "Supreme Court Upholds Return of Loyal Japanese to West Coast," *New York Times*, December 19, 1944. The remaining quotations in this paragraph come from the same article.

142. Plzak, Memorandum to Andrew Jordan, June 16, 1944. The next quotation in this paragraph comes from the same source.

143. Andrew Jordan, District Director, Chicago, "Confirmation of Telegram," to District Director, Immigration and Naturalization Service, New York City, December 22, 1944, Shoji Osato USCIS Records.

144. Osato, *Distant Dances*, 246. However, one feature article about Osato, published while *On the Town* was running, quotes Sono as saying, "Dad was here to see me in the show's opening, but he went back to the Middle West for a while to rest" (Julia McCarthy, "'On the Town' Star Product of Melting Pot," unidentified newspaper, Osato Clippings, NYPL).

145. Isamu Noguchi, "Trouble Among Japanese Americans," *New Republic* 108 (February 1, 1943), 142.

146. *On the Town*, Published script, 81.

147. Hyams, Letter (carbon) to Marion Bussang. An article in the *New York Post* picked up on Hyams's pitch about Osato. It presented Sono as a multicultural bundle, "exotic" yet talking "in a crisp Midwestern accent, between chews [of gum]" ("Name, Sono; Eyes, Oriental; Accent, Omaha; Place, Ballet Russe," *New York Post*, November 27, 1940, Osato Clippings NYPL).

148. Osato, Interview with the author, February 28, 2009.

149. Osato, *Distant Dances*, 65.

150. I am grateful to Tamar Barzel for suggesting the possible link between Ivy Smith and blues singers.

151. Osato, *Distant Dances*, 82.

152. Al Hirschfeld, "Mr. Hirschfeld goes to a rehearsal of 'On the Town,' due Christmas week," *New York Times*, November 26, 1944. Geoffrey Block's *Enchanted Evenings* reproduces many caricatures by Hirschfeld, demonstrating the artist's fascination with Broadway musicals. See, for example, Marc Blitzstein (113) and Rodgers and Hammerstein (196).

153. Al Hirschfeld, "Glorifying the Twenty-Four-Hour Pass and Saluting American Song," *New York Times*, December 24, 1944.

154. "On the Town," *Life*, January 15, 1945, 49–51. Also, a photo-essay about the Broadway season overall featured a photo of Osato as cooch dancer ("Big Season: Broadway Shows, Good and Bad, Pack Them In," *Life*, April 9, 1945, 80).

155. In 1942, 0.4 percent of the total coverage in *Life* related to issues affecting African Americans. In 1947, it was 0.3 percent (Mary Alice Sentman, "Black and White: Disparity in Coverage by Life Magazine from 1937 to 1972," *Journalism Quarterly* 60, no. 3 [Autumn 1983]: 505).

156. "On the Town," *Life*, 51.

157. Wong's cover photo bore the caption "World's Most Beautiful Chinese Girl," *Look*, March 1, 1938; France Nuyen, Cover of *Life*, October 6, 1958. Both cited in Lim, 48.

158. Greenbaum, "Two Who Help Make 'The Town.'"

159. "Shoji Osato, United States Department of Justice...Detention, Deportation, and Parole Section, Chicago Illinois, Report of Alien Enemy," December 7, 1945, Shoji Osato USCIS Records.

160. Conrad, "American Viewpoint."

161. A squib in *Time* gave information about the article's author: "Earl Conrad is free, white and 36, a Hearstwhile reporter who became a Negro expert for Manhattan's race-conscious *PM* [the New York daily paper]" ("The Press: White on Black," *Time*, March 12, 1945). According to this article, the *Defender* also had a Japanese American reporter on its staff.

162. Noguchi, "I Become a Nisei."

163. William Pickens, Letter to Peter H. Oddgood, [no date given], William Pickens Papers, Schomburg Collection, NYPL, as cited in Lee Finkle, "The Conservative Aims of Militant Rhetoric: Black Protest during World War II," *Journal of American History* 60, no. 3 (December 1973): 702. An African American journalist, Pickens worked for the U.S. Department of Treasury during World War II.

164. Finkle, "The Conservative Aims of Military Rhetoric," 701.

165. Horace R. Cayton, *Long Old Road* (New York: Trident Press, 1965), 272–73. The quotations that follow are from 273 and 275. Many thanks to Greg Robinson for pointing out this important memoir to me.

166. "Sono Osato: Ballet Dancer with Brains," *Pacific Citizen*, December 20, 1947, 53.

167. Owen, "Sono Osato," 9.

168. Osato, *Distant Dances*, 227–28.

169. Owen, "Sono Osato," 9; "Harlem Teen-Agers Plan Show,...to Adapt Ballet to Jazz," unlabeled newspaper, October 17, 1944; American Theatre Wing Youth Association Dance Scrapbook, NYPL.

170. "Sydenham Party Plans Continue for Big Affair," *New York Amsterdam News*, January 27, 1945.

171. "First Annual Report of the Trustees of Sydenham Hospital to the Organization Committee for an Interracial Voluntary Hospital in the Harlem Area," *Journal of the National Medical Association* 37, no. 2 (March 1945): 73; available at www.ncbi.nlm.nih.gov/pmc/articles/PMC2616080, accessed March 26, 2013.

172. "At League Benefit," *New York Amsterdam News*, June 2, 1945. Names of headliners at this benefit also come from: "Benefit Party of Urban League Has Its Usual Success," *New York Amsterdam News*, June 16, 1945.

173. Osato, *Distant Dances*, 267. The next quotation comes from this same source.

174. "Fay Reprimanded by Equity Council," *New York Times*, October 21, 1945.

175. Osato, *Distant Dances*, 267–68.

176. "Anti-Franco Demonstration Staged Here Yesterday," *New York Times*, March 3, 1946.

177. "Vagaries, Sono Osato," *Pacific Citizen*, March 23, 1946, 6.

178. "The Negro's Status in the Theatre (Summary of material presented to the Theatre Panel of the Conference called March 16, 1947, at the Murray Hill Hotel)," NNC Papers, Reel 34. Other signatories included Maxwell Anderson, Irving Berlin, Ira Gershwin, Oscar Hammerstein II, and Moss Hart ("Artists Vote Boycott of Restricted Theatres," *Afro-American*, November 23, 1946).

179. "Bergman to Keep Role: Actress Agreed to Part Before Learning of Racial Bias," *New York Times*, October 28, 1946.

180. John Martin, "Ballet 'Ballads' a New Venture," *New York Times*, May 10, 1948; and John Martin, "The Dance: 'Ballads'; Experimental Theatre in Choreographic Mood," *New York Times*, May 2, 1948.

181. Osato, *Distant Dances*, 266.

182. William Moore, "Tells How Reds Used Girls to Lure GIs in War," *Chicago Daily Tribune*, December 21, 1949.

183. "Once Over Lightly" [program], Barbizon-Plaza Theatre, no date; Osato Programs, NYPL.

184. Brooks Atkinson, "Theatre: Little Revue: Mr. Zero Plays It Low in 'Once Over Lightly,'" *New York Times*, March 16, 1955.

185. Osato, *Distant Dances*, 275.

CHAPTER 5: DESEGREGATING BROADWAY

Epigraphs: Ralph Ellison, "Bearden [Memorial Address for Romare Bearden]," *Callaloo* 36 (Summer 1988): 418; Leonard Bernstein, "The Negro in Music: Problems He Has to Face in Getting a Start," *New York Times*, November 2, 1947.

1. Robbins, in *"On the Town* Symposium," 19.

2. Langston Hughes, "Federal Theatre Led the Way to Plenty of Integration on Broadway," *New York Age* (May 2, 1953): 10.

3. "An Interview: Lena Horne," *Equity* 43 (May 1958): 4–5.

4. See Todd Decker, *"Show Boat": Performing Race in an American Musical* (New York: Oxford University Press, 2013).

5. Miles M. Jefferson, "The Negro on Broadway—1944," *Phylon* 6, no. 1 (1945): 43.

6. To date, the history of desegregation in performance has placed a special focus on jazz. See Ingrid Monson, *Freedom Sounds: Civil Rights Call Out to Jazz and Africa* (New York: Oxford University Press, 2007); Burton W. Peretti, *Nightclub City: Politics*

and *Amusement in Manhattan* (Philadelphia: University of Pennsylvania Press, 2007); and David W. Stowe, *Swing Changes: Big-Band Jazz in New Deal America* (Cambridge: Harvard University Press, 1994).

7. Robert L. Harris Jr., "Introduction," NNC Papers, v.

8. In keeping with the language of the era, I mostly use the term "desegregation," recognizing that usage was not consistent. Glenda Elizabeth Gilmore, *Defying Dixie: The Radical Roots of Civil Rights, 1919–1950* (New York: W. W. Norton, 2008), 347.

9. The *Pittsburgh Courier* first displayed the "Double V" symbol on its masthead on February 7, 1942.

10. Important histories of African Americans in World War II include: Ulysses Lee, *The Employment of Negro Troops* (Washington, DC: United States Army, 1966); Mary Penick Motley, *The Invisible Soldier: The Experience of the Black Soldier, World War II* (Detroit: Wayne State University Press, 1975); and Christopher Moore, *Fighting for America: Black Soldiers, the Unsung Heroes of World War II* (New York: One World, 2005).

11. Grant Reynolds, "What the Negro Soldier Thinks About this War," *The Crisis* 51, no. 9 (September 1944): 289.

12. Harry Truman, "Executive Order 9981," 1948; text at www.trumanlibrary .org/9981a.htm.

13. Joe Bostic, "Headline/Footlights," *The People's Voice*, March 24, 1945.

14. Billie Allen, Interview with the author, August 10, 2008.

15. Allyn Ann McLerie, Interview with the author, February 15, 2009.

16. Beth McHenry, "Everett Lee, First Negro Musician to Lead Orchestra in Bway Play," *Daily Worker*, October 13, 1945.

17. Lewis Nichols, "The Play," *New York Times*, December 29, 1944.

18. Cyrus Durgin, "The Stage; Colonial Theatre, 'On the Town,'" *Daily Boston Globe*, December 16, 1944, Bernstein Scrapbooks.

19. See Paul Milkman, *PM: A New Deal in Journalism, 1940–1948* (New Brunswick: Rutgers University Press, 1997).

20. "The Success Story of B. Comden & A. Green," *PM: New York Daily*, March 11, 1945.

21. Richard Robbins, "Counter-Assertion in the New York Negro Press," *Phylon* 10, no. 2 (1949): 126.

22. Re Bostic and baseball: Leslie A. Heaphy identifies Bostic as being "among the real reporters of the Negro Leagues" and writes of his role as an advocate for the desegregation of baseball, in *The Negro Leagues, 1869–1960* (Jefferson, NC: McFarland, 2003), 132, 194–95. Re Bostic and gospel: Dexter Allgood calls Bostic "the most celebrated of all gospel promoters" and writes that "by the mid-forties he was broadcasting gospel's first radio show, Gospel Train," in "Black Gospel in New York City and Joe William Bostic, Sr.," *The Black Perspective in Music* 18, nos. 1–2 (1990): 106–7.

23. Joe Bostic, "'On the Town' Proves the Point: Negroes Cast in Normal Roles," *The People's Voice*, February 17, 1945. There are many different versions of the name of Flash Riley, as will be discussed in Chapter 6. Here, the spelling "Flash" is used consistently, unless it appears differently within a quotation.

24. Larry Tajiri, "Who Can't Be Assimilated?" *NOW*, First Half December 1945; reprinted in *Pacific Citizens: Larry and Guyo Tajiri and Japanese American Journalism in the World War II Era*, edited with an introduction by Greg Robinson (Urbana: University of Illinois Press, 2012), 104.

25. "Everett Lee Sets Musical Precedent," *New York Amsterdam News*, September 22, 1945. Lee was first listed as "Musical Director" in a program for the week of September 16, 1945 ("On the Town/Martin Beck Theatre," Beginning Sunday, September 16, 1945, NYPL Programs).

26. "Negro Conducts Play, On the Town," *Chicago Defender*, September 22, 1945.

27. McHenry, "Everett Lee, First Negro Musician to Lead Orchestra in Bway Play." In terms of precedents for Lee's breakthough, Lee himself had been a substitute conductor for *Carmen Jones* (Annegret Fauser, " 'Dixie Carmen': War, Race, and Identity in Oscar Hammerstein's *Carmen Jones* [1943]," *Journal of the Society for American Music* 4, no. 2 [2010]: 164).

28. In an interview with me, Lee said that he wasn't sure if he was "concertmaster or second concertmaster" (interview, March 25, 2009); he had previously been concertmaster in *Carmen Jones* (see Fauser). Members of the pit orchestra were not listed in programs for *On the Town*, and it appears that Lee was promoted from second chair violin to first chair at some point during the first six months of the show's run. Two different lists of orchestra players, drawn up by Peggy Clark as technical director, reveal Lee's change in status. On February 8, 1945, Samuel Gardner is cited as first chair, and Lee is second. On June 14, 1945, Lee is first chair. In a third list, which is undated, he is second chair (Clark Collection B99/F6). At least two contemporaneous articles identified him as concertmaster: "[Photo caption:] Talented Violinist," *The People's Voice*, March 31, 1945, and E. B. Rea, "Encores and Echoes," *Afro-American*, September 1, 1945.

29. Bostic, " 'On the Town' Proves the Point."

30. James V. Hatch, "Creeping Toward Integration," in *A History of African American Theatre* by Errol G. Hill and Hatch (Cambridge: Cambridge University Press, 2003), 335.

31. Roy Wilkins, "The Negro Wants Full Equality," in *What the Negro Wants*, ed. Rayford W. Logan (Chapel Hill: University of North Carolina Press, 1944), 113. The fraught publication history of this volume is discussed in Gilmore, *Defying Dixie*, 378–80.

32. The training of black performing artists yields a huge story. In the realm of music conservatories, there were schools such as Oberlin, the New England Conservatory, the Boston Conservatory, and the now defunct National Conservatory of Music in New York that had been accepting black students since the 1860s. See Josephine Wright, "Black Women and Classical Music," *Women's Studies Quarterly* 12, no. 3 (Fall 1984): 19. Eileen Southern also points to schools such as Eastman, Juilliard, and the Curtis Institute (all established during the 1920s), arguing that "from these schools would come the most celebrated black musicians of the mid-century period." See Eileen Southern, *The Music of Black Americans: A History*, 3rd ed. (New York: W. W. Norton, 1997), 406–7.

33. Southern, *The Music of Black Americans*, 418.

34. In the 1950s, Leontyne Price was another black opera singer whose career was launched through *Porgy and Bess*. She emerged at a moment in the struggle for civil rights when opportunities for exceptional black performers were appearing. In 1952, Price debuted as St. Cecilia in Virgil Thomson's *Four Saints in Three Acts* at the International Arts Festival in Paris. Ira Gershwin then cast Price as Bess in the 1952 revival of *Porgy and Bess*. In 1961, Price made her debut at the Metropolitan Opera. See Elizabeth Amelia Hadley, "Leontyne Price: Prima Donna Assoluta," in *Black Women and*

Music: More than the Blues, edited by Eileen M. Hayes and Linda F. Williams (Urbana: University of Illinois Press, 2007), 199–202.

35. Brandi Wilkins Catanese raises the issues of "quantity and quality" in the opening salvo of: *The Problem of the Color[blind]: Racial Transgression and the Politics of Black Performance* (Ann Arbor: University of Michigan Press, 2011), 1.

36. The interracial chorus is noted in Pollack, *Marc Blitzstein*, 173. Eric A. Gordon also points it out in *Mark the Music: The Life and Work of Marc Blitzstein* (New York: St. Martin's Press, 1989), 137. Blitzstein later stated that with the production of *The Cradle Will Rock* "back in 1937," he had "discovered for the first time the immense versatility and adaptability of Negro singers and actors" (Corp. Marc Blitzstein, "Mr. Blitzstein Reports: Now in the Army, He Tells of His Music and His Negro Singers," *New York Times*, October 3, 1943).

37. Biographical information about Yates comes primarily from Susan Manning, *Modern Dance, Negro Dance: Race in Motion* (Minneapolis: University of Minnesota Press, 2004), 95.

38. Re "oratorio version": Pollack, *Marc Blitzstein*, 180. Re "six Negroes": E.B., "'The Cradle Will Rock' Presents Small Industrial Town at Its Worst: Negroes Contribute Excellent Music to Mercury Production," *New York Amsterdam News*, March 26, 1938.

39. IBDB lists nine chorus members for the Mercury Theatre's production, as does a program for the week beginning January 3, 1938. However, the program for the week beginning February 28, 1938, gives the black singers as the whole group (that is, when the names are collated with those listed in the *Amsterdam News*, March 26, 1938). The sources give varied spellings for the dancers' names, as when the programs list Robert Clark instead of Clerk ("Cradle Will Rock," Theater Programs, NYPL).

40. Ronald Ross, "The Role of Blacks in the Federal Theatre, 1935–1939," *The Journal of Negro History* 59, no. 1 (January 1974): 42.

41. Showboat [author pseudonym], "WPA Stage End Blamed on the Race Question: See Hostility of Project Based on Social Angle of Federal Theatre," *New York Amsterdam News*, July 29, 1939.

42. Susan Quinn, *Furious Improvisation: How the WPA and a Cast of Thousands Made High Art Out of Desperate Times* (New York: Walker, 2008), 247.

43. *Cabin in the Sky* ran for a little over four months, opening October 25, 1940, and closing March 8, 1941.

44. Jowitt has two listings for Dunham in the index; Lawrence has none; and Vaill has one.

45. Isabel Brown (Mirrow), quoted in Jowitt, 144.

46. Constance Valis Hill, "Collaborating with Balanchine on *Cabin in the Sky*: Interviews with Katherine Dunham," in *Kaiso!: Writings By and About Katherine Dunham*, ed. VèVè A. Clark and Sara E. Johnson, in Studies in Dance History (Madison: University of Wisconsin Press, 2005), 235.

47. Duncan, who was the original Porgy, played The Lawd's General in *Cabin in the Sky*, and Rex Ingram, who had been in *Sing Out the News*, played Lucifer Jr. In the film, the Hall Johnson Choir replaced the J. Rosamond Johnson Singers.

48. James Naremore, "Uptown Folk: Blackness and Entertainment in *Cabin in the Sky*," in *Representing Jazz*, ed. Krin Gabbard (Durham: Duke University Press, 1995), 170. Naremore writes about the film, not the stage production, but the two shared their scenario and racial representation.

49. Plot summary drawn from "Notes on *Cabin in the Sky*," as part of Selections from the Katherine Dunham Collection at the Library of Congress, http://lcweb2.loc.gov/diglib/ihas/html/dunham/dunham-notes-cabininthesky.html, accessed July 19, 2013.

50. Sally Banes, "Balanchine and Black Dance," *Choreography and Dance* 3, no. 3 (1993): 65.

51. Dunham, quoted in Hill, "Collaborating with Balanchine," 245.

52. Dunham, quoted in Hill, "Collaborating with Balanchine," 237.

53. Dunham, quoted in Hill, "Collaborating with Balanchine," 236–37.

54. Dunham, quoted in Hill, "Collaborating with Balanchine," 245.

55. Talley Beatty, Interview with Zita Allen, in *Artists and Influences* (New York, NY: Hatch Billops Collection, 1981), 11–12; available online in "Black Thought and Culture." The remaining quotations in this paragraph come from the same interview. Beatty recalled that Beck yelled out his demands from the "back of the house." After declaring, "over my dead body," Beck "was dead a week later." Beatty's chronology is a tiny bit off, but not by much. *Cabin in the Sky* opened October 25, 1940, and Martin Beck died on November 16. Beck's obituary states that he "had a financial interest" in *Cabin in the Sky* ("Martin Beck Dies; Theatre Veteran," *New York Times*, November 17, 1940).

56. John Martin, "The Dance: Elysian Jazz: Katherine Dunham and George Balanchine Swing 'Cabin in the Sky,'" *New York Times*, November 10, 1940.

57. Dunham's New York performances began in 1937, when her company appeared at the YMHA on 92nd Street. See "Special Presentation: Katherine Dunham Timeline," in "Selections from the Katherine Dunham Collection at the Library of Congress," http://lcweb2.loc.gov/diglib/ihas/html/dunham/dunham-timeline.html, accessed December 28, 2012.

58. Newspaper accounts detail Dunham's role in *New Pins and Needles*, including "Dunham Dances Sunday," *New York Amsterdam News*, March 9, 1940, and "Plymouth Theatre: 'New Pins and Needles,'" *Daily Boston Globe*, October 15, 1940. Talley Beatty recalled that Dunham's company performed a skit titled "Sammy, Listen to Your Mammy" for *Pins and Needles* (Beatty, 8).

59. See Vèvè A. Clark, "Katherine Dunham's Tropical Revue," *Black American Literature Forum* 16, no. 4 (Winter 1982): 147–52.

60. "Negro Ballet at Centre: New Epoch Hailed in the American Dance Field," *New York Amsterdam News*, January 20, 1940.

61. "Negro Ballet at Centre."

62. [Souvenir program] "Advanced Arts Ballets, Inc., Presents The Ballet Theatre, America's First Ballet Theatre … First Season—1940," Ballet Theatre Programs 1940, NYPL.

63. "Ballet Dance at Center Draws Unstinted Praise," *Chicago Defender*, February 3, 1940. Information about the performance is found in Selma Jeanne Cohen and A. J. Pischl, *The American Ballet Theatre: 1940–1960*, Dance Perspectives, 6 (Brooklyn, NY: Dance Perspectives, 1960), 13.

64. "The Ballet Theatre Announces Agnes De Mille … in Antony Tudor's 'Judgment of Paris' (American Premiere) … and The World Premiere … of 'Obeah' West Indian Ritual" [flier], Ballet Theatre Programs 1940, NYPL. Note that in this flier, the work does not yet have its final title of "Black Ritual (Obeah)." A list of the members of Ballet Theatre's "Negro Unit," which formed the cast for *Black Ritual*, also appears in Cohen and Pischl, 8. Many of the names are spelled differently there, with a few additional variations in "Ballet Dance at Center Draws Unstinted Praise."

65. Beatty, 13. Beatty tried to register at the School of American Ballet in 1940, where a secretary informed him "we don't have colored children at the school." Balanchine apparently intervened and gave Beatty a scholarship (Mindy Aloff, "Talley Beatty—A Biography," 3; this essay was available at www.alvinailey.org; as of November 2012, it appears to have been removed). John Perpener states: "Agnes de Mille created *Black Ritual* (1940) in an attempt to make the American Ballet Theatre's plans for a Negro wing a reality" (*African-American Concert Dance: The Harlem Renaissance and Beyond* [Urbana: University of Illinois Press, 2005], xiv).

66. Beatty, 13. Kennard's marriage to Ingram is mentioned in E. B. Rea, "Encores and Echoes," *Afro-American*, May 19, 1945.

67. Re study with Graham: Jennifer Dunning, "Lavinia Williams, 73, a Dancer," *New York Times*, August 10, 1989, and Beatty, 13. Re Negro Dance Company: John Martin, "The Dance: Growing Up," *New York Times*, December 13, 1942.

68. Information about *Carmen Jones* is from IBDB.

69. Letter carbon, Peter Kalischer of the Irving Hoffman Office, to Elmer Roesner, Feature Editor, *New York World-Telegram*, January 24, 1940, ABT Records, Series II, B8/F637.

70. John Martin, "De Mille Ballet Seen as Novelty: 'Black Ritual' Has Premiere at the Center Theatre in Two Settings," *New York Times*, January 23, 1940.

71. Yaël Tamar Lewin, *Night's Dancer: The Life of Janet Collins* (Middletown: Wesleyan University Press, 2011), 115. John Martin was harshly critical of the dancers, calling them "manifestly inexperienced" ("De Mille Ballet Seen as Novelty").

72. Lewin, *Night's Dancer*, 115. Lewin's book includes a useful appendix listing "Black Dancers in Ballet" (315–17). A context for the wages paid to Ballet Theatre's black dancers appears in an FBI report from 1942 about wages in New York City: "The Negro earns about one-half the amount earned in one year by the average in the poorer half of the White population." In Robert A. Hill, ed., *The FBI's RACON: Racial Conditions in the United States During World War II* (Boston: Northeastern University Press, 1995), 176.

73. Lewin, *Night's Dancer*, 116.

74. "Ballet Dance at Center Draws Unstinted Praise," *Chicago Defender*, February 3, 1940.

75. Martin, "De Mille Ballet Seen as Novelty."

76. Carl Van Vechten, Photographs of *Black Ritual*, in Agnes de Mille, Photographic Scrapbooks, volumes 3 and 4, NYPL.

77. Dunham, quoted in Hill, 242–43.

78. [Unsigned carbon], Letter to Agnes de Mille, October 12, 1940, ABT Records, Series II, B8/F637.

79. Agnes de Mille, Letter to George Ewing, President Ballet Theatre, March 3, 1941 (de Mille talks of being offered a kill fee of $50 if *Black Ritual* was not programmed); Eugene Langston, Letter to de Mille, March 7, 1941 (writes of *Black Ritual* as "not having been done"); and de Mille, Letter to Lucia [Chase], "June? 1943" written in pencil at the top ("I suggested to Hurok that we revise 'Black Ritual' since this would cost nothing but my fee and could be done quickly.... Let's do 'Ritual.'... It had the makings of a swell ballet and the décor was so very extraordinary"). All in ABT Records, Series II, B8/F637.

80. Barbara Engelbrecht, "Swinging at the Savoy," *Dance Research Journal* 15, no. 2 (Spring 1983): 3.

81. Howard Spring, "Swing and the Lindy Hop: Dance, Venue, Media, and Tradition," *American Music* 15, no. 2 (Summer 1997): 185.

82. Russell Gold writes: "The documentary evidence suggests that the Savoy was closed for almost five months." He calls the length of time it was shut down "problematic" (Russell Gold, "Guilty of Syncopation, Joy, and Animation: The Closing of Harlem's Savoy Ballroom," *Of, By, and For the People: Dancing on the Left in the 1930s*, in *Studies in Dance History* 5, no. 1 [Spring 1994]: 53).

83. "Mixed Dancing Closed Savoy Ballroom!" *New York Amsterdam News*, May 1, 1943. Russell Gold quotes Charles Buchanan, manager of the Savoy, as writing that "about half the people at the Savoy were white and half colored. The cops used to hate it" (53).

84. "Indignation Grows Over Savoy Case," *New York Amsterdam News*, May 15, 1943.

85. "Savoy Ballroom Opens Friday Night with Cootie Williams Band, Sultans," *New York Amsterdam News*, October 23, 1943.

86. Dorothy Barret, "Jerome Robbins," *Dance Magazine*, May 1945, 14.

87. Sam Zolotow, "Opening Tonight of 'Carmen Jones,'" *New York Times*, December 2, 1943.

88. Zolotow, "Opening Tonight of 'Carmen Jones.'"

89. Fauser reveals that when Hammerstein first began developing *Carmen Jones* in 1942, he discussed "with Hollywood agent Elizabeth A. Shaw the involvement of the African American dance star Katherine Dunham" ("'Dixie Carmen,'" 135).

90. For example, *The People's Voice* reported plans for *Carmen Jones*'s road show on December 16, 1944 ("Odds and Ends").

91. Fauser, "'Dixie Carmen,'" 141. There were also auditions for *Carmen Jones*: "Well over 100 Negro performers turned up at the Nola Studios at a call for dancers for Billy Rose's forthcoming production of *Carmen Jones*" ("Billy Rose Picks Dancers for 'Carmen Jones,'" *PM: New York Daily*, August 6, 1943).

92. Everett Lee, Interview with the author, March 25, 2009.

93. Stephen Bourne, "Muriel Smith," *Oxford Dictionary of National Biography* (New York: Oxford, 2004); online at www.oxforddnb.com/view/article/73747, accessed January 7, 2013.

94. "An Evening with Paul Robeson, Leonard Bernstein, Muriel Smith" [program], Boston Opera House, May 14, 1944, Bernstein Scrapbooks.

95. "Robeson-Bernstein Evening on May 14th," *Boston Herald*, April 19, 1944, Bernstein Scrapbooks. Smith and Bernstein also gave a benefit concert for the Victory Lodge of B'nai B'rith Hillel Foundation in New York on March 17, 1945 ("In a Reflective Mood," *New York Amsterdam News*, March 17, 1945).

96. Marc Blitzstein, "Opera's History: Blitzstein Recalls Career of a Work Now In Its Fourth Production," *New York Times*, November 23, 1947.

97. Fauser says there were "at least" five black musicians in the orchestra for *Carmen Jones*, including the drummer Cozy Cole, who appeared both on stage and in the pit ("'Dixie Carmen,'" 164).

98. Dan Burley, "All-Negro Opera, 'Carmen Jones,' Scores in Philly Premiere," *New York Amsterdam News*, October 30, 1943.

99. Miles M. Jefferson, "The Negro on Broadway—1944," 47.

100. Joe Bostic, "Headlines, Footlights," *The People's Voice*, November 11, 1944. *Anna Lucasta* was initially staged by the American Negro Theatre in Harlem; then it moved to Broadway, opening August 30, 1944.

101. Joe Bostic, "Headlines, Footlights: Short Memos to Several Well Knowns," *The People's Voice*, May 12, 1945. Theater historian James Hatch describes Billy Rose's treatment of Muriel Rahn as "disgraceful" ("Creeping Toward Integration," in *A History of African American Theatre*, 343).

102. Sam Zolotow, "'3 to Make Ready' Booked at Adelphi," *New York Times*, February 22, 1946.

103. Hughes, quoted in James V. Hatch, "A White Folks Guide to 200 Years of Black & White Drama," *The Drama Review: TDR* 16, no. 4 (Black Theatre Issue) (December 1972): 5–6. Hughes is referring to the so-called Voodoo Macbeth, staged by Orson Welles under the WPA.

104. Mel Tapley, "Original 'Carmen Jones' Cast Stages Reunion at Astoria Manor Sunday," *New York Amsterdam News*, April 17, 1993.

105. Billie Allen, Interview with the author.

106. However, the script includes one photo of the "Times Square Ballet" (reproduced here on page 177, which shows the mixed-race cast on stage (*On the Town*, Published script, 58–59).

107. Joe Bostic, "Headlines, Footlights," *The People's Voice*, March 24, 1945.

108. Osato, quoted in Earl Conrad, "She's Mixed, Merry and Musical," *Chicago Defender*, April 14, 1945.

109. Lonny Jackson, quoted in R. Dier, "Youthful Cop in New Broadway Musical Yearns for Chance to Sing Grand Opera," *Afro-American*, May 19, 1945. Another feature piece about Jackson says that he "won his present spot in the Betty Comden piece in a competitive audition" ("Broadway Who's Who: Lonny Jackson," *The People's Voice*, March 3, 1945).

110. Royce Wallace, quoted in R.R.D. [R. Dier], "No Discrimination in 'Town,' Says Ballerina," *Afro-American*, June 9, 1945.

111. "To Whom It May Concern," undated note from Richard A. D'Arcy, Don Weissmuller, Frank Westbrook, Carle Erbele, Parker Wilson, Lyle Clark, James Flash Riley, Frank Neal, Welland Lathrop, and Duncan Noble; Clark Collection B99/F5. Clark also drew up a list of dressing-room assignments: "Girl Dancers and Singers" were on the second floor, and "Men Dancers" were on the third floor ("Final OK," handwritten list "from Peggy Clark," no date, Clark Collection B99/F8).

112. Royce Wallace, quoted in R.R.D., "No Discrimination in 'Town.'"

113. R.R.D., "No Discrimination in 'Town.'"

114. Allyn Ann McLerie, Interview with the author.

115. Osato, quoted in Conrad, "She's Mixed, Merry and Musical."

116. Johanna L. Grimes-Williams, "Theophilus Lewis," in *The Concise Oxford Companion to African American Literature*, edited by William L. Andrews, Frances Smith Foster, and Trudier Harris (New York: Oxford University Press, 2012 online version).

117. Theophilus Lewis, "Broadway Musical Gives True Picture of N.Y. Life," *Afro-American*, July 7, 1945.

118. Conrad, "She's Mixed, Merry and Musical."

119. Lewis, "Broadway Musical Gives True Picture of N.Y. Life."

120. There are two sources for this information: (1) "On the Town: Scene Breakdown of Dance Personnel," one-page typescript, Clark Collection B99/F8 (abbreviation used hereafter: Scene Breakdown of Dance Personnel), and (2) "On the Town" [this document is an oversized flow chart for the production], Clark Collection B99/F6 (hereafter "production flow chart").

121. Jean Handy, Interview with the author, February 16, 2009.

122. Howard is listed as Workman in *On the Town* program, Week of September 16, 1945, NYPL-Theatre Division.

123. Ralph Ellison, *Invisible Man* (New York: Vintage Books, 1952), 155.

124. *On the Town* script, Versions A^1 and A^2.

125. "All girls (except [Jean] Handy)" in Scene Breakdown of Dance Personnel. The production flow chart for this scene lists McNichols, Wallace, and the white female dancers as Girls.

126. All four are listed in the production flow chart. However, McNichols and Neal are not included for this scene in the Scene Breakdown of Dance Personnel.

127. *On the Town*, Published script, 61.

128. Bernstein, Handwritten draft of an introduction to *On the Town: Three Dance Episodes* (published version: New York: Amberson Enterprises, 1968), Bernstein Collection B71/F12.

129. Edwin Denby, "Dancing in Shows," *New York Herald Tribune*, January 21, 1945; reprinted in *Edwin Denby: Dance Writings*, edited by Robert Cornfield and William Mackay (London: Dance Books, 1986).

130. "Sailor on the Town," typescript scenario, RobbinsCP B63/F18. I have corrected silently the typographical errors in this document. The scenario is much longer than what is quoted here, and it is a goldmine for anyone wanting to reconstruct Robbins's choreography. That said, it is not clear if this scenario is a final version.

131. A definition of "rug-cutter" appears in *Webster's Third New International Dictionary, Unabridged* (online), accessed November 22, 2012.

132. These photos come from: "On the Town" [souvenir program, undated]; NYPL-Theatre Division. Allyn Ann McClerie was then playing Ivy, so this program dates from late in the Broadway run and might have been used on the road.

133. Under "Night Club," the Scene Breakdown of Dance Personnel states: "All other girl dancers at tables (except Wallace, McNichols)." This might have referred, however, to the first segment in Diamond Eddie's Nightclub.

134. Herbert Greene is another interesting figure connected with *On the Town*. He ended up as a music director for Broadway shows, winning a Tony for *The Music Man*. While in the chorus of *On the Town*, he caught Bernstein's attention, working for a time as musical director of the show ("Herbert Greene Dead: A Director of Musicals," *New York Times*, September 27, 1985).

135. The subway scene of Act II first appeared in *On the Town*'s program on January 14, 1945, Clark Collection B99/F6, and the dancers named here appear on both the scene breakdown and the production flow chart.

136. Re photo in *Life*: "On the Town [photo]," in "Big Season: Broadway Shows, Good and Bad, Pack Them In," *Life*, April 9, 1945, 80. Re draft scenario: "Ballet...Act II," typescript scenario, RobbinsCP B63/F13.

137. See James I. Alexander, *Blue Coats, Black Skin: The Black Experience in the New York City Police Department Since 1891* (Hicksville, NY: Exposition Press, 1978).

138. Joe Bostic, "'On the Town' Proves the Point: Negroes Cast in Normal Roles."

139. Jackson, quoted in R. Dier, "Youthful Cop in New Broadway Musical Yearns for Chance to Sing Grand Opera."

140. Mona Z. Smith, *Becoming Something: The Story of Canada Lee* (New York: Faber and Faber, 2004), 219.

141. Jowitt (92) states that Dorothy McNichols and Flash Riley "did an eye-catching jitterbug" as part of the Times Square Ballet. In the production flow chart, however, the four black dancers are given the designation "Jitterbug" for "The Real Coney Island," and the photo from the souvenir program matches that scene. A jitterbug might have been included in both.

142. This text, with slight editorial variations, appears in *On the Town* script, Version A^1 (1-4-9) and is essentially retained through Version C (1-3-14). The following list of "boys" also comes from these same early versions.

143. "Zoot suit," in *Webster's Third New International Dictionary, Unabridged* (online), accessed November 22, 2012. A slightly different version of the list, which appears to be the earliest, describes the second fellow—the "jitterbugger"—as "a smooth dresser in top hat" (*On the Town* script, Version B [Act I, Scene 3A]).

144. Bostic, "Headlines/Footlights," *The People's Voice*, March 24, 1945.

145. By the time the script was published in 1997, the jitterbugger was neutralized as a "playboy"; and "Army" and "Navy" became "soldier" and "sailor" (*On the Town*, Published script, 18).

146. "Thousand Artists, Writers Back Davis," *Daily Worker*, September 25, 1945.

147. Article from *New York Amsterdam Star News*, August 22, 1942, quoted in Louis Harap and L. D. Reddick, *Should Negroes and Jews Unite?*, Race and Culture Series, No. 1 ([New York]: Negro Publication Society of America, 1943), 23. This booklet featured two essays: "Anti-Negroism Among Jews" and "Anti-Semitism Among Negroes," with responses from the black press.

148. Cheryl Lynn Greenberg, *Troubling the Waters: Black-Jewish Relations in the American Century* (Princeton, NJ: Princeton University Press, 2006), 99, 97.

149. Everett Lee, Interview with the author, March 28, 2009.

150. Robert L. Harris Jr., "Introduction," NNC Papers, v. Barry Seldes mentions the NNC in passing in *Leonard Bernstein: The Political Life of an American Musician* (Berkeley: University of California Press, 2009), 26, 43.

151. Irving Howe and Lewis Coser, *The American Communist Party: A Critical History* (New York: Praeger, 1962), 356; quoted in Lawrence Wittner, "The National Negro Congress: A Reassessment," *American Quarterly* 22, no. 4 (Winter 1970): 883. Wittner argues that the NNC collapsed in 1940; yet the cultural activities chronicled here continued with intensity after that date.

152. Bernstein, Letter to Helen Coates, November 11, 1940, Bernstein Collection B13/F2; quoted in Burton, 87.

153. The cultural committee's title changed over time. This initial name appears in "Proposal for the Establishment of a Committee for Democratic Culture" [1943], NNC Papers, Series II, Reel 1.

154. "National Negro Congress News: Clarence Muse Calls for Democracy in Film Industry," July 30, 1943, NNC Papers, Series II, Reel 1. The *Daily Worker* picked up this press release: "Cultural Leaders Call for Full Participation of Negro Artists," August 4, 1943.

155. "National Negro Congress News."

156. These names turn up repeatedly in NNC documents. One example is a sign-up sheet titled "Cultural Meeting, Hotel Theresa, July 28, 1943," NNC Papers, Series II, Reel 1.

157. The program for Ellington's Carnegie Hall concert is reproduced in Mark Tucker, ed., *The Duke Ellington Reader* (New York: Oxford University Press, 1993), 161–64.

158. Comden and Green, together with Avon Long, were part of a benefit for Russian War Relief in May 1942, as discussed in Chapter 2.

159. "Celebrities Back Duke Ellington's Carnegie Hall Concert," *New Journal and Guide*, January 9, 1943.

160. Howard Pollack makes this point in comparing Blitzstein and Copland, and Bernstein allied with Blitzstein in his focus on civil rights' issues (Pollack, *Marc Blitzstein*, 259).

161. Leonard Bernstein, "The Negro in Music." According to a handwritten annotation on a typescript of the essay among Bernstein's papers, the article "was originally drafted by Paul Secon, publicity director for the National Negro Congress. It was revised and mostly rewritten by Leonard Bernstein, October 26, 1947," Bernstein Collection B72/F32.

162. Nora Holt, "Music," *New York Amsterdam News*, November 8, 1947.

163. "Tenor Wins Coveted Role," *Pittsburgh Courier*, March 30, 1946 (Holland was "personally selected for the role by Marc Blitzstein"); Billy Rowe, "20,000 Acclaim Marian Anderson in NY Concert: Public, Critics Bless Contralto's Top Performance," *Pittsburgh Courier*, July 5, 1947); and "Sings Here," *New York Amsterdam News*, September 20, 1947.

164. Re de Mille, Primus, and Tamiris: "Mailing List for Cultural Meeting" (together with documents from the summer of 1943), NNC Papers, Series II, Reel 1; also Elizabeth Cooper, "Tamiris and the Federal Dance Theatre 1936–1939: Socially Relevant Dance Amidst the Policies and Politics of the New Deal Era," *Dance Research Journal* 29, no. 2 (Autumn 1997): 23–48. Re Osato: Handwritten list of names "For Dorothy," April 15, [1944], NNC Papers, Series II, Reel 2.

165. "Leonard Bernstein," in *Red Channels: The Report of Communist Influence in Radio and Television* (New York: Counterattack, 1950), 17.

166. Jowitt, 80.

167. Lawrence, 57.

168. "The Ballet Really Comes to Town," *PM: New York Daily*, May 14, 1944. Jowitt dates "Harlem Incident" as 1940 (31).

169. "The Story of Stack O Lee," Scenario [by] Jerome Robbins, Narration [by] Horton Foote, typescript, December 1941, RobbinsPP, Series I, B61/F8. A note in the file says this scenario was submitted to B.T. [Ballet Theatre] in 1942.

170. Robbins described the music that he envisioned for his ballet, just as he was to do with *Fancy Free*: "The overture music is loud, bright and gay—and suggests all of the color of Stack's life and time. Parts of the can-can, the escape theme, and the boogie-woogie are brought in. The music winds up in the best large scale overture style and there is a pause. Now a very plaintive sad sighing melody is picked up by the saxes or some low sobbing instrument. This mournful tune is played against a background of faint honky-tonk and bar-room music. This is the Devil's theme music" ("The Story of Stack O Lee," 2).

171. These notes are filed among materials from 1943 (RobbinsPP, Series I, B40/F3).

172. John Martin, "Ballet: A Homecoming," *New York Times*, November 9, 1955. Martin wrote about Mitchell: "A casting novelty and a debut was the appearance of the talented young Negro dancer, Arthur Mitchell."

173. Black critics repeatedly decried the Metropolitan Opera Company's refusal to feature black singers. Anderson gave a concert at the old Metropolitan Opera House in

April 1945—a concert that was presented without the opera company's sponsorship—and Joe Bostic made the following statement: "Neither Miss Anderson nor any other Negro artist has ever sung an operatic role there with the Metropolitan opera company because that organization subscribes to the thoroughly un-American policy of exclusion of a whole segment of American citizens from its artistic ranks for no other reason except that they are Negroes" (Joe Bostic, "Headlines, Footlights: The Opera Goers Are Getting Shortchanged," *The People's Voice*, April 21, 1945).

174. *The King and I*, IBDB.

175. Perpener, *African-American Concert Dance*, 193.

176. Allen Hughes, "For Black Conductors, A Future? Or Frustration?" *New York Times*, March 15, 1970. Robbins's American Theater Lab was intended as an experimental "playground," where professionals could explore "fusions of drama, music, and dance that didn't conform to any commercial model" (Jowitt, 369). The actor Morgan Freeman was among the performers involved (Jowitt, 370), as was the director Robert Wilson (Lawrence, 364). The American Theater Lab did not permit the press to review its workshops.

177. "Theater Wing," *Chicago Defender*, April 15, 1967.

178. George Abbott, *"Mister Abbott"* (New York: Random House, 1963), 178.

179. The *Amsterdam News* announced that in *Sweet River* Hall "plans to grasp this opportunity to try some new ideas she has worked into her arrangements." "To Harmonize on Rialto," *New York Amsterdam News*, August 29, 1936.

180. R.O. [Roi Ottley], "Uncle Tom Redressed," *New York Amsterdam News*, October 31, 1936.

181. S.T.B., "Entertainment," *New York Amsterdam News*, December 11, 1937. The next quotation comes from this same review.

182. Brooks Atkinson, "The Play: Dark Town Melodrama," *New York Times*, December 3, 1937.

183. In a profile of McQueen, Nora Holt credited McQueen's "small part" in *Brown Sugar* as providing her big break ("Butterfly McQueen, 'Gone with the Wind' Star Styles Comedy Like Bert Williams," *New York Amsterdam News*, November 17, 1945).

184. Osato, Interview with the author, February 28, 2009. In his memoir, Abbott spent a full page discussing how "all my associates in this venture were Jews" ("except for Oliver Smith"), and his attitudes offer a glimpse of how someone born in the late nineteenth century viewed racial difference (Abbott was born in 1887). Abbott professed to identify intensely with Jews and made a number of essentializing statements, such as "Jewish people are warm, have deep feelings and seem to give more of themselves" (Abbott, *"Mister Abbott,"* 200–201).

CHAPTER 6: BIOGRAPHIES ONSTAGE

Epigraphs: Billie Allen, Interview with the author, August 10, 2008; Edward Kleban, lyrics (Marvin Hamlisch, music), "I Can Do That," *A Chorus Line* (1975) (New York: Hal Leonard, 1977).

1. Re *Carmen Jones*: "Billy Rose Picks Dancers for 'Carmen Jones,'" *PM: New York Daily*, August 6, 1943. Re *On the Town*: R. Dier, "Youthful Cop in New Broadway Musical Yearns for Chance to Sing Grand Opera," *Afro-American*, May 19, 1945.

2. Everett Lee, Interview with the author, March 25, 2009.

3. "Nancy Walker in On the Town" [program], Shubert Great Northern Theatre [Chicago], beginning Monday evening, April 1, 1946, NYPL Programs.

4. Allen Woll, *Black Musical Theatre: From Coontown to Dreamgirls* (Baton Rouge: Louisiana State University Press, 1989), 216.

5. "An Interview: Lena Horne," *Equity* 43 (May 1958): 4–7, quoted in Woll, 220.

6. Bruce Weber, "Jeni LeGon, Singer and Solo Tap-Dancer, Dies at 96," *New York Times*, December 16, 2012.

7. Miles M. Jefferson, "The Negro on Broadway 1951–1952—Another Transparent Season," *Phylon* 13, no. 3 (1952): 206. Jefferson's first report was "The Negro on Broadway—1944," *Phylon* 6, no. 1 (1945): 42–52.

8. Langston Hughes, "The Written Word and the Negro Race: The Pen Is Mightier Than the Sword," *Chicago Defender*, January 1, 1955.

9. Miles M. Jefferson, "Empty Season on Broadway, 1950–1951," *Phylon* 12, no. 2 (1951): 133.

10. Miles M. Jefferson, "The Negro on Broadway, 1952–1953: Still Cloudy: Fair Weather Ahead," *Phylon* 14, no. 3 (1953): 268.

11. Miles M. Jefferson, "The Negro on Broadway, 1956–1957," *Phylon* 18, no. 3 (1957): 286.

12. Woll, *Black Musical Theatre*, 218.

13. James Booker, "Urban League Hits Bias in Orchestra Hiring Policy," *New York Amsterdam News*, November 22, 1958. The remaining quotations in this paragraph come from the same article.

14. Jefferson, "The Negro on Broadway 1951–1952—Another Transparent Season," 199–200.

15. Vernon E. Jordan Jr., "Orchestrated Discrimination," *New Pittsburgh Courier*, December 7, 1974.

16. Much of the biographical information in this paragraph comes from: Joseph M. Goldwasser, "Where There's A Will, There's Everett Lee and Family," *Cleveland Call and Post*, November 10, 1945.

17. Goldwasser, "Where There's a Will."

18. Lee's scholarship is mentioned in many newspaper articles, including "Give Reception for Newlyweds," *Chicago Defender*, February 26, 1944. (The fellowship name is spelled "Ranny" in this article and appears to be an error.)

19. Lee interview, March 25, 2009.

20. "Everett Lee to Conduct Symphony: Town Hall Concert on May 21 Awaited," *Pittsburgh Courier*, May 8, 1948.

21. "Pilot's Wings are Sought by Violinist," *Chicago Defender*, June 19, 1943.

22. Nora Holt, "Everett Lee, First Negro Concert Meister, Soloist in 'Carmen Jones,'" *New York Amsterdam News*, January 29, 1944.

23. Lee interview, March 25, 2009.

24. Re Lee in *Carmen Jones*: "Violinist in 'Carmen' Hits for Another," *Chicago Defender*, May 13, 1944; "Billy Rowe's Notebook," *Pittsburgh Courier*, May 20, 1944; Sam Zolotow, "Stewart to Direct New Melodrama," *New York Times*, May 29, 1944; and "Everett Lee Youngest Conductor on Broadway," *Pittsburgh Courier*, June 3, 1944. Lee's work with *Carmen Jones* is discussed in Annegret Fauser, "'Dixie Carmen': War, Race, and Identity in Oscar Hammerstein's *Carmen Jones* (1943)," *Journal of the Society for American Music* 4, no. 2 (2010): 164. Re Lee and *Porgy*: Lee was reported as conducting the orchestra of *Porgy* "last week," in Constance Curtis, "New Yorker's Album," *New York Amsterdam News*, April 8, 1944.

25. Everett Lee, Interview with the author, March 28, 2009.

26. Marva Griffin Carter, *Swing Along: The Musical Life of Will Marion Cook* (New York: Oxford University Press, 2008), 40.

27. "Events in the World of Music," *New York Times*, February 25, 1945; and "Stokowski Offers Concert Novelties," *New York Times*, February 27, 1945.

28. Michael Steinberg, "Rodziński, Artur," *Grove Music Online*, edited by Deane Root, accessed January 18, 2013.

29. The *New York Times* stated that Bernstein heard Lee conducting *Carmen Jones* "and engaged him to conduct his musical, 'On the Town'" (Ross Parmenter, "The World of Music: Season's Start," *New York Times*, August 31, 1947). Also, an article in the *Pittsburgh Courier* (May 8, 1948) credited Rodziński with having "helped him [Lee] make useful contacts in the musical world" ("Everett Lee to Conduct Symphony: Town Hall Concert on May 21 Awaited").

30. Lee interview, March 25, 2009.

31. Wallace McClain Cheatham and Sylvia Lee, "Lady Sylvia Speaks," *Black Music Research Journal* 16, no. 1 (Spring 1996): 201–2. This interview was also published in *Dialogues on Opera and the African-American Experience*, ed. Wallace McClain Cheatham (Lanham, MD: The Scarecrow Press, 1997), 42–67. That same volume includes a terrific interview with Everett Lee (24–42).

32. Everett Lee, Letter to Leonard Bernstein, undated, "1946" written on the back, Bernstein Collection B35/F15; Lee interview, March 25, 2009.

33. "Violinist, Wife in Joint Recital," *Chicago Defender*, June 22, 1946.

34. Lee is listed as first violin in programs from the week of September 30, 1946, through the week of October 28 (*The Program-Magazine of the New York City Center*, April 4–9, Bernstein Collection B335/F3). Names of the players are listed in alphabetical order, so the seating is not apparent.

35. Lee, Letter to Bernstein (perhaps in 1947), Bernstein Collection B35/F15.

36. Raoul Abdul, "Reading the Score: Conversation with Everett Lee," *New York Amsterdam News*, October 8, 1977.

37. Re "Americans of Chinese": "Everett Lee to Present Mixed Symphony Group," *New York Amsterdam News*, October 25, 1947. Re female players: N.S. [Noel Straus], "Symphony Group in Formal Debut," *New York Times*, May 22, 1948.

38. N.S. [Noel Straus], "Everett Lee to Present Mixed Symphony Group."

39. Although this letter is undated, it appears to refer to the period when Lee was conducting the Cosmopolitan Symphony (Lee, Letter to Bernstein, Bernstein Collection B35/F15).

40. The "cooperation" of Local 802 is noted in "Everett Lee Organizes Interracial Symphony," *New York Amsterdam News*, August 30, 1947. Also Lee explained his arrangement with the union in an interview with me: "I asked the musician's union if I could just get a bunch of musicians together. The union gave me permission to rehearse these people. And of course with stipulations, there was no recordings, and if I were to have a concert, then I would have to, naturally they would have to be paid" (March 28, 2009).

41. Lee interview, March 28, 2009.

42. "Cosmopolitan First Concert Wins Acclaim," *New York Amsterdam News*, November 15, 1947.

43. N.S. [Noel Straus], "Symphony Group in Formal Debut."

44. "Negro Symphony Goes Back to Town Hall," *Chicago Defender*, December 25, 1948, and Noel Straus, "Everett Lee Leads Cosmopolitan Unit," *New York Times*, December 27, 1948.

45. Nora Holt, "Cosmopolitan Symphony in Its Finest Performance: Sold-Out Audience of 2,100 Acclaims Lee's Production," *New York Amsterdam News*, March 8, 1952.

46. "Guest Conductor for Boston Concert," *Chicago Defender*, July 2, 1949.

47. Lee interview, March 28, 2009.

48. Everett Lee, as paraphrased by Sylvia Olden Lee, in "Dialogue with Sylvia Olden Lee," *Fidelio Magazine* 7, no. 1 (Spring 1998), www.schillerinstitute.org/fid_97-01/fid_981_lee_interview.html, accessed January 18, 2013. The remaining quotations in this paragraph come from the same interview. Thanks to Annegret Fauser for sending me this link.

49. "Plan 'Bon Voyage' Affair for Everett Lee and Wife," *New York Amsterdam News*, September 13, 1952.

50. "Negro to Direct in South: Everett Lee Will Conduct White Musicians in Louisville Concert," *New York Times*, September 19, 1953.

51. Lee interview, March 28, 2009; "Dialogue with Sylvia Olden Lee."

52. This information comes from the program for the Louisville concert, as conveyed by Addie Peyronnin, Operations Assistant, Louisville Orchestra (email to the author, March 18, 2009).

53. Sylvia Lee recalled that the Kathryn Turney Long Department did not allow women to work there during the main opera season, so Lee was employed for six weeks before the season and six weeks afterwards (Cheatham and Lee, "Lady Sylvia Speaks," 202).

54. "City Opera Engages Two Conductors," *New York Times*, February 10, 1955.

55. "New York City Opera Chores," *New York Times*, September 22, 1955.

56. "Conductor," *New York Times*, April 29, 1956.

57. "To Conduct UN Concert at Philharmonic Hall," *New York Amsterdam News*, October 15, 1966.

58. Ross Parmenter, "The World of Music," *New York Times*, July 8, 1962.

59. Sara Slack, "Symphony of the New World a Truly Integrated Group," *New York Amsterdam News*, March 5, 1966.

60. Re three main guest conductors: "New World Symphony Will Play," *New York Amsterdam News*, April 17, 1965. Re "his first appearance": Raymond Ericson, "Two Elek(c)tras Come to Town," *New York Times*, October 23, 1966. In 1974, Lee became head conductor of the orchestra (Donal Henahan, "'New and Newer Music' Begins Its Fourth Season," *New York Times*, January 29, 1974).

61. Frank Neal's biography will be explored in the pages ahead. See Clarissa and Marion Cumbo, compilers, "In Retrospect...The Symphony of the New World," *The Black Perspective in Music* 3, no. 3 (Autumn 1975): 312–30.

62. "Hammond Named VP of Symphony," *New York Amsterdam News*, September 3, 1966. Others on the interracial board were the choral conductor Hall Johnson, the actors Zero Mostel and Frederick O'Neal, and "some ministers" ("Arts Council Refuses Symphony Support," *New York Amsterdam News*, October 15, 1966).

63. Harold C. Schonberg, "Everett Lee Leads Philharmonic in Debut," *New York Times*, January 16, 1976. Schonberg's review did not place Lee's appearance within a racial context. His condescension extended to Baker's *Kosbro*. After calling it "a lively

and at times tumultuous piece," Schonberg concluded: "The materials are thin. But, then again, Mr. Baker did not start out with an intention of rivaling the Ninth Symphony. He seemed primarily interested in composing a fun piece."

64. For example, Columbia Records issued its important "Black Composers Series" between 1974 and 1979.

65. Joe Bostic, "'On the Town' Proves the Point; Negroes Cast in Normal Roles," *The People's Voice*, February 17, 1945.

66. Bob Williams, "Ex-Karamu House Star Makes Debut in Gotham Play," *Cleveland Call and Post*, February 24, 1945; R.R.D. [R. Dier], "No Discrimination in 'Town,' Says Ballerina," *Afro-American*, June 9, 1945; and "Broadway Who's Who: Royce Wallace," *The People's Voice*, May 5, 1945. The article in *The People's Voice* was brief.

67. Billie Allen interview.

68. Quotes describing Wallace come from: "Royce Wallace Flees Her Blueblood Groom," *New York Amsterdam News*, November 3, 1956; "Masco Young's They're Talking About," *Daily Defender*, May 31, 1960; Alvin "Chick" Webb, "'The Year Round' Should Run Even Longer," *New York Amsterdam News*, May 9, 1953.

69. "Graduate 112 from Central Hi, Cleveland," *Chicago Defender*, February 1, 1941. A birth certificate for "Royse A. Wallace" appears in Ancestry.com and gives her place of birth as Garrard County, Kentucky. A brief biography of Wallace appears in Edward Mapp, *Directory of Blacks in the Performing Arts* (Metuchen: Scarecrow Press, 1978); as found in *World Biographical Information System (WBIS) Online*.

70. Wallace, quoted in R.R.D., "No Discrimination in 'Town,' Says Ballerina."

71. "Karamu House," *The Encyclopedia of Cleveland History* (Cleveland: Case Western Reserve University and the Western Reserve Historical Society), http://ech.case.edu/cgi/article.pl?id=KH, accessed January 19, 2013.

72. Royce Wallace, quoted in Marjorie Witt Johnson, "Positive Group Work Experiences with African-American Adolescents 1935–1945: An Afrocentric Retrospective Analysis," in *Social Group Work Today and Tomorrow: Moving from Theory to Advanced Training and Practice*, ed. Benjamin L. Stempler, Marilyn S. Glass, and Christine M. Savinelli (New York: Haworth Press, 1996), 52. This book is a sociological study of the impact of experiences at the Playhouse Settlement (later renamed Karamu House) upon those who were trained there.

73. "Six Karamu Dancers Picked by Billy Rose for 'Carmen,'" *Cleveland Call and Post*, August 28, 1943.

74. Loring's visit to Cleveland was reported in "Six Karamu Dancers Picked by Billy Rose for 'Carmen.'" While this article lists six dancers from Karamu House who were chosen for *Carmen Jones*, only three of them appear in IBDB. Besides Royce Wallace, they were Roger Mae Johnson (whose stage name was Rhoda Johnson) and Erona Harris.

75. See Wilma Salisbury, "Eleanor Frampton, 1964 Cleveland Arts Prize for Dance," Arts Prize Cleveland, http://clevelandartsprize.org/awardees/eleanor_frampton.html, accessed January 19, 2013.

76. R.R.D., "No Discrimination in 'Town,' Says Ballerina."

77. Theophilus Lewis, "Broadway Musical Gives True Picture of N.Y. Life," *Afro-American*, July 7, 1945.

78. Williams, "Ex-Karamu House Star."

79. A small notice in the *Amsterdam News*, published when the show was in tryouts and still called "Twilight Alley," advises: "Don't overlook the beautiful Royce Wallace"

("Duke's 'Twilight Alley' to Star Pretty Girls," *New York Amsterdam News*, November 23, 1946).

80. "Preview Performance of 'Beggar's Holiday,'" *Daily Worker*, December 19, 1946.

81. Samuel Sillen, "Beggar's Holiday," *Daily Worker*, January 3, 1947.

82. Re *St. Louis Woman*: Untitled biographical snippet, with "Happy as Larry" written in pencil on the side (Theatre Clippings, NYPL). Beatty was initially slated to appear in *On the Town*, then withdrew—as will be discussed in the next section about Frank Neal.

83. Re *Mamba's Daughters*: Brooks Atkinson, "At the Theatre: 'Mamba's Daughters' Put on by Equity Community Troupe at De Witt Clinton in the Bronx," *New York Times*, March 21, 1953. Re *Once Over Lightly*: Louis Calta, "Intimate Musical Will Bow Tonight," *New York Times*, March 15, 1955; and untitled clipping, with a penciled-in annotation, "Once Over Lightly, 15 March '55," Theatre Clippings, NYPL.

84. "Village Vanguard, New York," *Variety*, March 10, 1951.

85. June Bundy, "Night Club-Vaude Reviews: Village Vanguard, New York," *Variety*, November 17, 1951.

86. Allyn Ann McLerie, Interview with the author, February 15, 2009.

87. Listings in *Variety* for this particular appearance by Royce Wallace at the Village Vanguard extend from April 23, 1952 ("Cabaret Bills"), to July 2, 1952 ("Variety Bills").

88. Holl., "Village Vanguard, N.Y.," *Variety*, June 11, 1952.

89. Re Paris and Germany: Mapp, "Royce Wallace," *Directory of Blacks in the Performing Arts*. Also, Wallace's name appears on a list of passengers arriving from France, July 19, 1954, Ancestry.com, accessed December 12, 2012. Re Angels Grotto: Al Wagstoff, "Bermuda," *Variety*, September 21, 1955.

90. "White Bermudan Marries Girl Singer from Harlem, Shunned," *New York Amsterdam News*, January 21, 1956.

91. "Royce Wallace Flees Her Blueblood Groom." The *Amsterdam News* published a number of articles about Wallace's marriage to Outerbridge.

92. Elsie Wisner, "Bermuda Shuns Socialite for his Mixed Marriage," *Daily Mirror*, stamped January 23, 1956, Theatre Clippings, NYPL. Same source for the next quotation.

93. When Wallace left Outerbridge, she claimed both mental and physical cruelty ("Royce Wallace Flees Her Blueblood Groom").

94. "'Nuts to You' Opens Saturday Night at YMCA," *New York Amsterdam News*, June 1, 1957.

95. "Singing Uptown—Royce Wallace [photo caption]," *New York Amsterdam News*, July 4, 1959; "Masco Young's They're Talking About."

96. Royce Wallace, Interview with Greg Lawrence, April 26, 2000, quoted in Lawrence, 331.

97. "Izzy Rowe's Notebook," *Pittsburgh Courier*, September 26, 1964.

98. IMDb lists over sixty titles for Royce Wallace in both films and television. Most valuably, it gives the dates of individual television episodes on which she appeared: www.imdb.com/name/nm0908847, accessed January 20, 2013.

99. Mel Tapley, "Original 'Carmen Jones' Cast Stages Reunion at Astoria Manor Sunday," *New York Amsterdam News*, April 17, 1993.

100. Sono Osato, Interview with the author, February 28, 2009.

101. The painter Charles White recounted the members of this Chicago group in "African American Artist: Charles W. White, Jr.," *Info of Artist Biography*, http://american-biography.blogspot.com/2011/02/african-american-artist-charles-w-white.html, accessed January 20, 2013.

102. The 1930 census gives Neal's birth date as 1915 (ancestrylibrary.com, accessed December 17, 2012).

103. "Chicago DuSable League," www.artic.edu/~apalme/duslea.htm, accessed January 20, 2013.

104. "Dancer Wins $300 Art Prize," *New York Times*, April 8, 1947, and "Frank Neal Rites Today: Service to be Held for Artist and Dancer Killed in Crash," *New York Times*, May 11, 1955.

105. John Carlis, "Interview of John Carlis by James V. Hatch, October 30, 1988," in *Artist and Influence* 9 (1990), 13; available online in *Black Thought and Culture*.

106. Margaret Goss Burroughs, "Chicago's South Side Community Art Center: A Personal Recollection," *Illinois Women Artists Project*, http://iwa.bradley.edu/ChicagoCommunityArtCenter, accessed January 20, 2013. See also Bill V. Mullen, "Artists in Uniform: The South Side Community Art Center and the Defense of Culture," in *Popular Fronts: Chicago and African-American Cultural Politics, 1935–46* (Urbana: University of Illinois Press, 1999), 75–105.

107. Charles White separates Frank from George in an interview quoted in "African American Artist: Charles W. White, Jr."

108. "Sadie Bruce Glover, Noted Dancer, Actress," *Chicago Sun-Times*, March 23, 1993. Frank Neal is listed among the performers in "Sadie Bruce's Pupils Get Plenty Hot on Regal Stage," *Chicago Defender*, May 30, 1936.

109. Neal's work with Ruth Page and the Chicago Civic Opera Ballet was mentioned repeatedly over the years, including "Frank Neal, Noted Artist, Dancer Dies," *New York Amsterdam News*, May 14, 1955, and "Frank Neal Dies in NYC Auto Crash," *Chicago Defender*, May 21, 1955.

110. Charles Griffin, "Interview of Charles Griffin by Camille Billops, 1981," in *Artists and Influences* (1981), 138; available online in *Black Thought and Culture*. Griffin was an actor with the American Negro Theater.

111. Talley Beatty, "Interview of Talley Beatty by Zita Allen, James Hatch, and Arthur Smith, 1981," *Artists and Influences* (1981), 18; available online in *Black Thought and Culture*.

112. "Success Story Has Its Climax on Opera Stage," *Chicago Daily Tribune*, November 14, 1936.

113. Consuelo C. Young, "Preface," *Chicago Defender*, October 8, 1938. The article spells Sebree's name as "Seabry." Dorcas Neal (Frank's wife) later told the writer David Hajdu that Sebree was among the Neals' closest friends; he too worked with Katherine Dunham in Chicago (David Hajdu, Interview with Dorcas Neal, October 10, 1993; transcription courtesy of Hajdu); also, "Charles Sebree," *Answers.com: Black Biography*, www.answers.com/topic/charles-sebree, accessed January 20, 2013.

114. For more about the fusion of left-wing politics and support from black churches, see Melissa Barton, "'Speaking a Mutual Language': The Negro People's Theatre in Chicago," *The Drama Review: TDR* 54, no. 3 (Fall 2010): 54–70.

115. William McBride, Interview with Carol Adams, October 31, 1988, transcription at the Archives of American Art, Smithsonian Institution, 51.

116. "'Chi' Awaits Parade of Beauty at 4th Annual Artists', Models' Ball Scheduled for October 25th," *Philadelphia Tribune*, October 11, 1941. Neal also designed costumes for the ball the next year (Elizabeth Galbreath, "Artists' and Models' Ball Attracts Large Crowd," *Chicago Defender*, October 31, 1942).

117. Re Dunham: "'Chi' Awaits Parade of Beauty at 4th Annual Artists', Models' Ball." Re Augusta Savage: Burroughs, "Chicago's South Side Community Art Center," accessed January 21, 2013.

118. McBride interview, 24. John Carlis also recalled parties at the home of Frank and Dorcas Neal (Carlis Interview, 21). According to the 1940 census, Frank and Dorcas Neal lived with Charles Thompson, who was the uncle of Dorcas (ancestrylibrary.com, accessed December 22, 2012).

119. Beatty interview, 8.

120. Re Los Angeles: Yaël Tamar Lewin, *Night's Dancer: The Life of Janet Collins* (Middletown: Wesleyan University Press, 2011), 75. Re Iowa: "Katherine Dunham and Her Dance Company" [program], Davenport [Iowa] Hotel, June 9, 1942 (Katherine Dunham Museum, East St. Louis, IL).

121. McBride interview, 78.

122. Neal is not listed for *Stormy Weather* in IMDb. Here is an example of including that film in his standard biography: "Frank Neal in 'Peter Pan' at Nixon Show," *Pittsburgh Courier*, October 13, 1951.

123. "Billy Rose Presents Carmen Jones," program, The Broadway Theatre, for week beginning December 2, 1943 (NYPL).

124. Beatty recalled, "It was crazy. But you know how that is. I wasn't interested in shows" (Beatty interview, 20).

125. McBride interview, 22. As of this writing, a full sense of Neal's work with Dunham is not available. His wife later said that Frank "worked with Dunham for a long time" (Dorcas Neal interview). In two of his obituaries, Neal was described as "one of the original members of the Katherine Dunham troupe": "Obituaries: Frank Neal," *Variety*, May 11, 1955, and "Frank Neal, Noted Artist, Dancer Dies." An important study about Dunham: Joanna Dee Das, "Choreographing a New World: Katherine Dunham and the Politics of Dance," Ph.D. dissertation, Columbia University, 2014.

126. Beatty interview, 19.

127. Jerome Robbins, untitled and undated typescript list of dancers, RobbinsCP, B63/F18.

128. Beatty interview, 19.

129. "Neal to Lead 'Finian' Dancers," press release from Samuel J. Friedman/42 West 48th Street, undated (Theatre Clippings, NYPL). IBDB also lists Neal as dance captain.

130. IBDB lists "Cyprionne Gabel" for *Finian's Rainbow*, and I assume this is another form of the name "Cyprienne Gableman" from *On the Town*.

131. Izzy, "Reviewer Tabs 'Finian's Rainbow,'" *Pittsburgh Courier*, January 18, 1947.

132. Re McMillen Gallery: "News and Notes of Art," *New York Times*, September 26, 1941. Re International Print Society: Howard Devree, "From a Reviewer's Notebook," *New York Times*, October 8, 1944, and Ramona Lowe, "N.Y. Inter-Racial Gallery Presents Best of Flourishing New Negro Art," *Chicago Defender*, May 19, 1945.

133. "Thespian Wins Painting Prize," *Chicago Defender*, April 12, 1947; also, "Dancer Wins $300 Art Prize."

134. "Picture Item" [about handicraft shops], *PM: New York Daily*, August 4, 1946 (Theatre Clippings, NYPL). This article discusses Neal's work as a painter.

135. David Hajdu, *Lush Life: A Biography of Billy Strayhorn* (New York: Farrar Straus Giroux, 1996), 114.

136. Dorcas Neal interview; partly quoted in Hajdu, *Lush Life*, 115.

137. Hajdu, *Lush Life*, 114–15.

138. Talley Beatty, quoted in Hajdu, *Lush Life*, 116.

139. The 1954 version of *Peter Pan* had a score by Mark Charlap and Julie Styne, with some lyrics by Comden and Green; Jerome Robbins was director and choreographer.

140. "Peter Pan," IBDB, accessed January 21, 2013. While Neal is listed in the opening night cast in IBDB, his name does not appear in the initial review (Flash Riley's is there, however, as "Jay Riley"): Brooks Atkinson, "First Night at the Theatre: Jean Arthur and Boris Karloff in an Excellent Version of Barrie's 'Peter Pan,'" *New York Times*, April 25, 1950.

141. "Frank Neal in 'Peter Pan' at Nixon Show," *Pittsburgh Courier*, October 13, 1951. Neal is cited as a replacement in Louis Calta, "'Gioconda Smile' Arrives Tonight," *New York Times*, October 7, 1950.

142. "Society: New York," *Jet*, July 24, 1952.

143. "Frank Neal Rites Today." The founding date of Talley Beatty's dance company comes from Allison X. Miller, "Talley Beatty," *Encyclopedia of African-American Culture and History*, Volume 1, edited by Jack Salzman, David Lionel Smith, and Cornel West (New York: Macmillan, 1996), 298. The American Negro Theatre was founded in 1940 in Harlem and lasted into the mid-1950s.

144. "Chicago Artists in New York," *Chicago Defender*, May 2, 1953. Neal had formed a company called Tray House, which was located in Merchantville, NJ ("Frank Neal Rites Today").

145. "12 Die, 15 Hurt in Mishaps on Wet Highways," *New York Daily Mirror*, May 9, 1955 (Theatre Clippings, NYPL).

146. "Frank Neal Dies in NYC Auto Crash," *Chicago Defender*, May 21, 1955; "Frank Neal Rites Today: Service to be Held for Artist and Dancer Killed in Crash," *New York Times*, May 11, 1955; [Frank Neal], *New York Herald Tribune*, May 11, 1955 (Theatre Clippings, NYPL); "Frank Neal," *Variety*, May 11, 1955; "Frank Neal, Noted Artist, Dancer Dies," *New York Amsterdam News*, May 14, 1955.

147. Riley's dates appear on a program for his memorial service (RobbinsCP B527/F24), and in "Jay F. Riley," Social Security Death Index, Ancestry.com.

148. The many versions of Riley's name are confusing. In IBDB, for example, there are separate entries for "James Flash Riley" and "Jay Riley."

149. Riley, quoted in Ruth L. Carter, "Resettle in L.A.: Expatriates Say 'Ciao' to Rome," *Los Angeles Times*, May 1, 1977.

150. Billie Allen interview.

151. Allyn Ann McLerie interview.

152. Jean Handy, Interview with the author, February 16, 2009.

153. Sono Osato interview.

154. Flash Riley, Interview with Eddy Determeyer, November 5, 1981, Groningen, The Netherlands; thanks to Mr. Determeyer for providing me with a tape. In this interview, Riley talked about *Hot Chocolates*, but he meant to say *The Chocolate Dandies*, and I have silently corrected his error in the quotation here. *Hot Chocolates* dated from

1930 and was composed by Fats Waller and Harry Brooks, not by Eubie Blake. It also does not fit into the chronology laid out by Riley. He and his family moved to New York City before 1927, because he remembered attending a parade there to celebrate Lindbergh's flight across the Atlantic. Instead, Riley meant to describe his experience with *The Chocolate Dandies*, a show by Blake that had an extended run in Philadelphia in late 1924, then took to the road ("Philadelphia Ready to Welcome Big Musical Hit, The 'Chocolate Dandies,'" *Pittsburgh Courier*, November 22, 1924). *The Chocolate Dandies* included "an exciting horse race in which three real 'Blue Ribbon' equines participate," which was also part of Riley's recollection ("Looking 'Round the Corner at 'The Chocolate Dandies,'" *Philadelphia Tribune*, November 15, 1924).

155. "'Swing It' A Hit at Harlem's Lafayette," *Chicago Defender*, October 2, 1937.

156. Riley, Letter to Lorenzo Tucker, envelope dated May 7, 1978, Tucker Collection. Francine [Frances] Everett went on to star in a series of race movies, but her career collapsed after World War II. She is reported to have refused stereotyped roles. Everett eventually ended up working at a clerical job at Harlem Hospital (Mel Watkins, "Francine Everett, Striking Star of All-Black Movies, Is Dead," *New York Times*, June 20, 1999).

157. Riley, Letter to Lorenzo Tucker, [1978], Tucker Collection.

158. Riley as "Jack" appeared in Marvel Cooke, "Orson Welles Conducts 'Native Son' Rehearsal," *New York Amsterdam Star-News*, March 22, 1941.

159. Riley interview.

160. "Dan Burley's Back Door Stuff: Hit That Jive, Jack," *New York Amsterdam News*, September 16, 1944.

161. Eddy Determeyer, *Rhythm Is Our Business: Jimmie Lunceford and the Harlem Express* (Ann Arbor: University of Michigan Press, 2006), 55; also, Riley interview.

162. "So Is Flash," *New York Amsterdam news*, October 7, 1944. Verneda LaSalle, Riley's dance partner at the nightclub Smalls' Paradise, appeared in *On the Town* for a time as a substitute ("Dan Burley's Back Door Stuff," *New York Amsterdam News*, September 22, 1945).

163. *On the Town* [programs]; Riley is first listed as Sailor in the Broadway program dated "week beginning September 30, 1945," and he stayed in that position at least through a program for a Chicago performance on April 1, 1946 (NYPL Programs).

164. "Nancy Walker in On the Town" [program], Shubert Great Northern Theatre, Chicago, NYPL Programs.

165. D. B. [Dan Burley?], "'Lysistrata' Due at the Belasco Saturday Night," *New York Amsterdam News*, October 12, 1946.

166. Ted Yates, "I've Been Around New York," *Chicago Defender*, February 23, 1952.

167. Brooks Atkinson, "At the Theatre: 'Mamba's Daughters' Put On by Equity Community Troupe at De Witt Clinton in the Bronx," *New York Times*, March 21, 1953.

168. Re Muriel Rahn: Alvin Chick Webb, "Footlights and Sidelights," *New York Amsterdam News*, November 7, 1953. Re "90 percent": "2 Negro Legiters Set for Fall Tours," *Variety*, June 18, 1952.

169. Dick Campbell, "Tells How Jim Crow Lost a Round to Cast of Touring 'Carmen Jones,'" *Chicago Defender*, January 30, 1954.

170. Flash Riley, Letter to Jerome Robbins, February 15, 1958, RobbinsCP B527F31.

171. George Barner, "Santa Claus Greets Kids at Blumstein's," *New York Amsterdam News*, December 6, 1958.

172. "Negro Stage Scholarships Won," *New York Times*, October 9, 1959.

173. Jesse H. Walker, "Theatricals," *New York Amsterdam News*, January 30, 1960.

174. "The Blacks: A Clown Show," Lortel Archives: The Internet Off-Broadway Database, www.lortel.org/lla_archive/index.cfm?search_by=show&id=2814, accessed January 24, 2013.

175. Arthur French, "Interview of Arthur French by Henry Miller, March 21, 2004," *Artist and Influence* 23 (2004), 27; available online in *Black Thought and Culture*.

176. As quoted in Lewis Funke, "News of the Rialto: Herbert Swope Jr. Planning Return to Broadway—Genet Play Listed," *New York Times*, March 19, 1961; the source of the quotation is not clear, but it might be the director Gene Frankel.

177. Maya Angelou, *The Heart of a Woman* (New York: Bantam Books, 1981), 76.

178. Riley is not listed among the "uncredited" actors for *Cleopatra* in IMDb.

179. "Jay Flash Riley," undated resume (the latest item listed is 1985), RobbinsCP B31/F13, and Louise P. Dumetz, "Talented Wilbur Bradley Describes European Career," *Chicago Defender*, March 1, 1966.

180. The European production of *Trumpets of the Lord* was staged by the "Jay Flash Riley Company," and Riley's resume (*op. cit.*) lists the dates as "1966/1967/1971."

181. Flash Riley, quoted in Jesse H. Walker, "Theatricals," *New York Amsterdam News*, December 11, 1965.

182. The production took place at the Théâtre de France: "The audience…sat in rapt and amused attention as Jay Riley and Lex Monson as clergymen preached on the Creation, the Flood, the Hebrew Exodus from Egypt and Judgment Day" (Thomas Quinn Curtiss, "'Trumpets of the Lord' A Triumph in Paris," *New York Times*, June 1, 1967).

183. Riley, quoted in Carter, "Resettle in L.A.: Expatriates Say 'Ciao' to Rome."

184. Jesse H. Walker, "Theatricals," *New York Amsterdam News*, February 13, 1965.

185. Jane White, "Interview of Jane White by Delilah Jackson, April 17, 1993," in *Artist and Influence* 12 (1993), 193; available online in *Black Thought and Culture*.

186. Jesse H. Walker, "Theatricals," *New York Amsterdam News*, November 27, 1965.

187. Cathy W. Aldridge, "P.S.," *New York Amsterdam News*, April 16, 1966.

188. William Leonard, "'Sugar' Bubbles Over with Nostalgia," *Chicago Tribune*, June 25, 1976.

189. "James Flash Riley," in IBDB.

190. "Jay Flash Riley," undated resume.

191. "Joe 'Flash' Riley," in IMDb.

192. Carter, "Resettle in L.A.: Expatriates Say 'Ciao' to Rome."

193. Riley, Postcard to Tucker, September 9, 1979, Tucker Collection.

194. Riley, Postcard to Tucker, September 21, 1979, Tucker Collection.

195. "Joe 'Flash' Riley," in IMDb.

196. Flash [Riley], Note to Bernstein, undated [Amsterdam, June 2], Bernstein Collection B47/F33.

197. Peter Spalding, "Gospel, Ragtime, Jazz and Blues," *The Stage and Television Today*, April 28, 1983.

198. "Jay Flash Riley," undated resume.

199. Re England: Spalding, "Gospel, Ragtime, Jazz and Blues." Re Germany: E. Durrell Echols, "Munich Offers Cultural Variety," *New York Amsterdam News*, June 16, 1984.

200. Riley, Postcard to Lorenzo Tucker, undated; sent from Amsterdam, Tucker Collection.

201. [Flash Riley obituary], *Variety*, October 5, 1988, 159.

202. Billie Allen today goes by the name Billie Allen Henderson, having taken the last name of her second husband, composer and arranger Luther Henderson. Also, her niece Candace Allen has written a provocative memoir and cultural critique: *Soul Music: The Pulse of Race and Music* (London: Gibson Square, 2012).

203. Allen told an interviewer that her mother graduated from Spelman College in Atlanta: "In fact, my family goes back over four generations of women who have graduated from Spelman.... My great-grandmother was in the first graduating class" (Billie Allen, in Philip C. Kolin, "Revisiting *Funnyhouse*: An Interview with Billie Allen," *African American Review* 41, no. 1 [2007]: 167).

204. Allen interview with the author. Glenn Tetley (1926–2007) appears in the Chicago program for *On the Town*'s national tour. As Billie Allen states, Tetley became a renowned choreographer. His standard biography gives his first Broadway experience as *Kiss Me Kate* (1948), for which he was dance captain; but his work in *On the Town* predates that experience ("Glenn Tetley," American Ballet Theatre, www.abt.org/education/archive/choreographers/tetley_g.html, accessed January 29, 2013).

205. Allen interview with the author. James Jackson (1914–2007) was also from Richmond. In addition to his early work organizing tobacco workers and his stint with the *Daily Worker*, he was known as "a civil rights activist" and "former official of the American Communist Party" (Dennis Hevesi, "James Jackson, Rights Activist, Dies at 92," *New York Times*, September 7, 2007). Camp Unity was a Communist-run interracial camp in upstate New York.

206. Gladys Graham, "Caribbean Carnival Off to Good Start in New York City," *New Journal and Guide*, December 20, 1947.

207. "Bon Voyage: Fashion Editor Off to Paris to Attend Fashion Show," *New Journal and Guide*, August 14, 1948. See also Elspeth H. Brown, "Black Models and the Invention of the US 'Negro Market,' 1945–1960," in *Inside Marketing: Practices, Ideologies, Devices*, edited by Detlev Zwick and Julien Cayla (New York: Oxford University Press, 2011), 186, 195–96.

208. "Colgate Dental Cream Opens Advertising Campaign," *Philadelphia Tribune*, March 8, 1949.

209. "Etta Moten, Fred O'Neal in Comedy," *Chicago Defender*, September 23, 1950.

210. The dancers are listed in "'4 Saints in 3 Acts' Opens in B'way Theatre," *Pittsburgh Courier*, April 26, 1952. Allen's photo appears in "Scenes from Two Productions on the Broadway Playbill This Week," *New York Times*, April 13, 1952, and Brooks Atkinson, "At the Theatre: 'Mamba's Daughters' Put on by Equity Community Troupe."

211. "Billie's First Break Came in an Elevator," *New York Amsterdam News*, June 5, 1965.

212. Re *Reuben Reuben*: "Izzy Rowe's Notebook: Short and to the Period," *Pittsburgh Courier*, October 15, 1955. Re *Take a Giant Step*: Brooks Atkinson, "Theatre Audit at Mid-Season," *New York Times*, February 24, 1957.

213. Re "prepar[ed] the way": James V. Hatch, "Creeping Toward Integration," in *A History of African American Theatre* by Errol G. Hill and Hatch (Cambridge: Cambridge University Press, 2003), 369. Re original cast of *Raisin in the Sun*: IBDB.

214. Howard Taubman, "Adrienne Kennedy Play Opens at East End," *New York Times*, January 15, 1964.

215. Allen, quoted in Paul K. Bryant-Jackson and Lois More Overbeck, "An Interview with Billie Allen," in *Intersecting Boundaries: The Theatre of Adrienne Kennedy*, edited by Paul K. Bryant-Jackson and Lois More Overbeck (Minneapolis: University of Minnesota Press, 1992), 223.

216. Allen, quoted in Kolin, "Revisiting *Funnyhouse*," 167. The next quotation comes from 169.

217. "The Phil Silvers Show," *Chicago Daily Defender*, March 19, 1956.

218. "Billie Allen," IMDb. Of the thirty-six episodes of *The Phil Silvers Show* in which Allen appeared, nineteen are listed as "uncredited."

219. Dave Hepburn, "In the Wings: The Power of a Woman," *New York Amsterdam News*, February 23, 1963. Allen later did a commercial for Pampers diapers (Philip H. Dougherty, "The Negro Makes a Start in Commercials," *New York Times*, October 13, 1968).

220. Jesse H. Walker, "Theatricals," *New York Amsterdam News*, April 24, 1965.

221. "ABC Steps Up Integration on Daytime Soapers," *Variety*, April 14, 1965. "Stet" is another case of *Variety*'s insider jargon, perhaps indicating "standing."

222. The first two quotes come from Dave Hepburn, "Raising Money for B'way Show Is Easy, Say Girls," *New York Amsterdam News*, December 15, 1962. The final quote is from: Dave Hepburn, "In the Wings: The Power of a Woman."

223. "'Black Like Me' Opens Next Week," *New York Amsterdam News*, May 16, 1964.

224. Barbara Lewis, "'Brothers' Defies Stereotypes About Black Women: Interview with Billie Allen," *New York Amsterdam News*, April 17, 1982.

225. In 2006, Allen directed another production of the show at the Classical Theatre of Harlem. Kolin, "Revisiting *Funnyhouse*," 165.

226. Allen, quoted in Bryant-Jackson and Overbeck, "An Interview with Billie Allen," 217.

227. Barbara Lewis, "'Brothers' Defies Stereotypes About Black Women."

228. Allen, quoted in Lewis, "'Brothers' Defies Stereotypes." See Allen's profile for more of her credits as a director: http://americantheatrewing.org/biography/detail/billie_allen.

229. Re "handsome": Dier, "Youthful Cop in New Broadway Musical." Re "eye arresting": "Broadway Who's Who: Lonny Jackson," *The People's Voice*, March 3, 1945.

230. Jackson's birth date comes from the 1940 census, Ancestrylibrary.com, accessed January 6, 2013.

231. "Noted Negro Tenor Appears on BSU Program," *Yellow Jacket* (Brownwood, Texas), May 4, 1933. http://texashistory.unt.edu/ark:/67531/metapth102208/m1/1, accessed January 29, 2013.

232. Dier, "Youthful Cop in New Broadway Musical."

233. Cecil Smith, "Concert Turns Spotlight on 3 Chicago Artists," *Chicago Daily Tribune*, May 23, 1938, and "Close Contests Open Festival Voice Tourney," *Chicago Daily Tribune*, August 5, 1938. The quotations that follow come from the second of these articles.

234. This production was separate from the Federal Theatre Project's *Swing Mikado*, and one reviewer called it "far from being equal" to that better-known production (David W. Kellum, "Comedians Spoil 'Mikado in Swing': Introduce Georgia Minstrel Jokes in Comic Opera," *Chicago Defender*, April 8, 1939). It was also separate from the *Hot Mikado*, which was produced at the 1939 World's Fair in New York.

235. Jackson, quoted in Dier, "Youthful Cop in New Broadway Musical."

236. Jeni Dahmus, Archivist, Juilliard School, Email to author, January 7, 2013.

237. "Philadelphia Girl Wins Marian Anderson Award," *Philadelphia Tribune*, October 11, 1947.

238. Billie Allen, Interview with the author.

239. Greg Lawrence, Interview with Dorothy McNichols, June 3, 1999, quoted in Lawrence, 84.

240. "The Week's Programs," *New York Times*, May 21, 1948. In connection with *On the Town*, Van Den Berg's name is spelled "Vandenberg."

241. Jean Handy, Email to author, March 15, 2009.

242. Jean Handy, Interview with the author. Deborah Jowitt interviewed McNichols in connection with her book on Jerome Robbins (92).

243. Mel Tapley, "Original 'Carmen Jones' Cast Stages Reunion at Astoria Manor Sunday," *New York Amsterdam News*, April 17, 1993.

244. Melvin R. Howard, U.S. World War II Army Enlistment Records, 1938–1946, Ancestry.com. Howard's "civil occupation" is listed as "showmen" [*sic*].

245. John O. Perpener III, *African-American Concert Dance: The Harlem Renaissance and Beyond* (Urbana: University of Illinois Press, 2005), 73.

246. George Palmer, "Tavern Topics," *New York Amsterdam News*, October 8, 1949.

247. Ingrid Monson, *Freedom Sounds: Civil Rights Call Out to Jazz and Africa* (New York: Oxford University Press, 2007), 64.

248. Miles M. Jefferson, "The Negro on Broadway 1951–52—Another Transparent Season," 199.

CHAPTER 7: CROSSOVER COMPOSITION

Epigraphs: Betty Comden and Adolph Green, "Preface," *On the Town*, Published script, 2; Leonard Bernstein, "American Musical Comedy," telecast October 7, 1956; transcript reprinted in *The Joy of Music* (New York: Simon & Schuster, 1959), 152. The quotations in the opening paragraph come from pages 152–53, 157, and 173, respectively.

1. Bernstein recognized *The Cradle Will Rock* as unusual from his first acquaintance with it. In the spring of 1939, as he prepared to direct the work in a student production at Harvard, he described the score as "incredible—much more complex than I thought—much more an opera" (Bernstein, Letter to Copland, written from Eliot [House] E07 [at Harvard], "Spring 1938? (39)," Copland Collection B247/F1; the letter definitely dates from 1939).

2. Stephen Sondheim, *Finishing the Hat: Collected Lyrics (1954–1981) with Attendant Comments, Principles, Heresies, Grudges, Whines and Anecdotes* (New York: Alfred A. Knopf, 2010), 28.

3. "Croon Spoon," for example, divides up the sections as A (7 bars), A (7), B (14), A (11). Another song with an asymmetric phrase length was Richard Rodgers's "Ship Without a Sail." Gershwin's "Wintergreen for President" from *Of Thee I Sing* offers yet another case of a number that pushed past convention (see Larry Starr, *George Gershwin* [New Haven, CT: Yale University Press, 2011], 103–4). Thanks to Geoffrey Block for pointing this out.

4. Betty Comden and Adolph Green, "On the Town," in *The New York Musicals of Comden & Green* (New York: Applause Books, 1997), 1–84. It bears repeating that unlike most shows of its day, *On the Town* did not have its book published at the time of its premiere.

5. Piano-vocal score: Leonard Bernstein, *On the Town: A Musical Comedy in Two Acts*, book and lyrics by Betty Comden and Adolph Green, book based on an idea of Jerome Robbins (New York: Boosey & Hawkes, 1997). This edition is labeled "First publication for sale 1997, USA" (copyright page), and it includes the following annotation:

"The engraving of this score is based on Leonard Bernstein's conducting score for his 1960 Columbia recording of *On the Town*, and the score and orchestra material used in the 1992 Deutsche Grammophon recording under Michael Tilson Thomas, which was prepared with the participation of Betty Comden and Adolph Green" ([iii]). Also, *On the Town*, Orchestral score.

6. "Copyist score (Comden)" is housed in the Comden Score Collection (separate from the Comden-Green Papers), and it includes piano-vocal scores for individual numbers, which are gathered together loosely in a binder titled "Director's Score of On the Town" (Series XII, B6/F1). "Copyist score (Robbins)" is in the Robbins Collection and includes individual numbers from *On the Town* in separate folders (Robbins CP, Series I, B64). These two scores are often duplicates of one another, but not always. Most measure numbers relate to in-text musical examples; at times, however, they refer to the published score, with no example given.

7. *On the Town*, Published script, 8.

8. In "Berlin's Jazz," Jeffrey Magee offers an insightful analysis of how Berlin, a predecessor of Bernstein on Broadway, worked jazz into his shows (*Irving Berlin's American Musical Theater* [New York: Oxford University Press, 2012], 129–44).

9. Leonard Bernstein, Letter to Helen Coates [summer 1942], quoted in Burton, 99.

10. Leonard Bernstein, "Prologue," *On the Town* Sketches, in pencil, Bernstein Collection B26/F10.

11. *On the Town*, Production flow chart, Clark Collection B99/F6. In the flow chart, the actors on stage for "I Feel Like I'm Not Out of Bed Yet" and "New York, New York" are listed in the same column, under the caption "Navy Yard." Here, I have included only those listed as workers, since the sailors came on stage in the second half of the scene.

12. Sondheim, *Finishing the Hat*, 28.

13. Jerome Robbins, Interview with Lehman Engel, February 28, 1978, Engel Collection B6/F157.

14. Betty Comden and Adolph Green, Pencil Notes for "Scene I: Gable, Denny & Mitch," Comden-Green Papers B16/F18. The remaining quotations in this paragraph come from the same document.

15. *On the Town*, Published script, 8–9.

16. It is easy to confuse *On the Town*'s "New York, New York" with a song by John Kander and Fred Ebb, which has the same name and was also made famous by Frank Sinatra. This later hit was written for the Martin Scorsese film *New York, New York* (1977).

17. Sono Osato, *Distant Dances* (New York: Knopf, 1980), 240.

18. *On the Town*, Piano-vocal score, 13.

19. A "tag" is a common device in jazz, defined as "a phrase (usually of a few bars, sometimes no more than a motif) added to the end of a theme, a chorus, or (most often) an entire piece....A frequent practice is to repeat (once, twice, or a few times) the last two or four bars of the final chorus" ("Tag," *The New Grove Dictionary of Jazz*, 2nd ed., ed. Barry Kernfeld, in *Grove Music Online*, accessed May 2, 2013).

20. Helen Smith offers interesting perspectives on what she terms Bernstein's "intervallic composition," comparing him to Stravinsky. Helen Smith, *There's a Place for Us: The Musical Theatre Works of Leonard Bernstein* (Surrey, England: Ashgate, 2011), see especially 15–22.

21. Overall structure of the first vocal stanza: opening tag (mm. 45–49); verse-like section (mm. 51–62); chorus-like section, which builds on the tag (mm. 63–71).

22. *On the Town*, Published script, 9. The next segment of text comes from this same source.

23. *On the Town* script, Version B, Act I-1-2 to I-1-3, and in the copyist's score in Robbins Collection.

24. "The Movie Villains," in "Fun with The Revuers, WJZ, April 23, 1940, 9:30–10:00 p.m.," typescript, inserted between pages 6 and 7, Comden-Green Papers B4/F7. Although this script is not titled, it might be "Magazine Page" (listed in "Rumshinksy Opens Bureau," *New York Times*, August 23, 1939).

25. Burton, 23. In 2006, Shira Brettman made a short documentary about Bernstein's teenage productions in Sharon, including *The Mikado*. She did so as part of a seminar at Harvard taught by me and Kay Kaufman Shelemay. The documentary can be viewed at the website "Leonard Bernstein's Boston Years: Team Research in a Harvard Classroom," http://isites.harvard.edu/icb/icb.do?keyword=bernstein&pageid=icb.page178512, accessed May 3, 2013.

26. Leonard Bernstein, "A Career as an Orchestra Conductor," *The Book of Knowledge Annual* (New York: The Grolier Society, 1948), 256.

27. Robert Witmer, "Ballad," *The New Grove Dictionary of Jazz*, 2nd ed., in *Grove Music Online*, accessed May 3, 2013.

28. Bernstein, "American Musical Comedy," 173.

29. Related formal patterns included ABAC and ABAB.

30. James T. Maher, Introduction to Alec Wilder, *American Popular Song: The Great Innovators, 1900–1950*, ed. Maher (New York: Oxford University Press, 1972), xxx. All the quotations in this paragraph come from this same source.

31. Mary X. Sullivan, "Two on the Aisle," *Boston Advertiser*, December 3, 1944, Bernstein Scrapbooks.

32. For a fascinating analysis of Bernstein's early ventures writing popular songs, see Lars Helgert, "The Songs of Leonard Bernstein and Charles Stern in 1942: Toward the Origins of Bernstein as a Dramatic Composer," *American Music Research Center Journal* 21 (2012): 41–66.

33. Seymour Peck, "*PM* Visits: 'On the Town's' Tunesmith," *PM: New York Daily*, December 27, 1944, 255.

34. Leonard Bernstein, "Jazz Forum: Has Jazz Influenced the Symphony?" [Article in the form of a debate with Gene Krupa], *Esquire*, February 1947, 153. An undated handwritten draft of the segment quoted here exists in the Bernstein Collection B71/F17.

35. The other numbers issued in sheet music were "New York, New York," "Ya Got Me," and "I Can Cook Too." Individual folios were issued by M. Witmark & Sons of New York, 1945.

36. Lyrics for "Lonely Me" and "Another Love" appear in Version A of the script, 1-4-6 and 1-6-6, respectively. "I'm Afraid It's Love" is in Version A as well, 1-7-6 to 1-7-7; and it was set to music by Bernstein (Copyist score, Robbins). "Say When" is also in Version A, 1-8-6.

37. Elinor Hughes, "The Theater," *Boston Herald*, December 16, 1944, Bernstein Scrapbooks.

38. Lewis Nichols, "The Play," *New York Times*, December 29, 1944, and L. A. Sloper, "Bernstein-Robbins Musical Seen at Colonial Theater," *Christian Science Monitor*, December 16, 1944. Both Bernstein Scrapbooks.

39. "Lonely Town" [sheet music] (Witmark, 1945); Bernstein Collection B26/F7.

40. In using the term "brow level," I borrow from David Savran. See his important book: *Highbrow/Lowdown: Theater, Jazz, and the Making of the New Middle Class* (Ann Arbor: University of Michigan Press, 2009).

41. Osato, *Distant Dances*, 234. Jowitt describes this ballet as expressing "the darker side of shore-leave pickups" (95). Nelle Fisher had been in *One Touch of Venus*; in *On the Town* she was also an understudy for Osato (see Saul Goodman, "Nelle Fisher," *Dance Magazine*, December 1954, 36–37).

42. Paul R. Laird, "Leonard Bernstein's Musical Style," in *Leonard Bernstein: A Guide to Research*, Routledge Music Bibliographies (New York: Routledge, 2002), 64. Laird's chapter provides a foundational overview of Bernstein's music.

43. The published sheet music for "Lonely Town" includes an entirely different verse (in both lyric and melody), which opens with a fragment of "New York, New York" ("Lonely Town" [sheet music] [New York: M. Witmark & Sons, 1945], Bernstein Collection B26/F7).

> New York, New York
> Or a village in Ioway;
> The only diff'rence is the name.
> If you're alone
> Whether on Main Street or on Broadway
> If you're alone they are both the same.

44. "Lonely Town," Copyist score (Robbins).

45. Dale E. Monson with Jack Westrup, "Recitative," *Grove Music Online*, accessed May 4, 2013.

46. Robbins, "Lonely Me" [Ballet Scenario], typescript, RobbinsCP B63/F18. Note that the scenario is titled "Lonely Me," not "Lonely Town."

47. Robbins, "Lonely Me" [Ballet Scenario].

48. Edwin Denby, "Dancing in Shows," *New York Herald Tribune*, January 21, 1945; reprinted as "'On the Town'; 'Sing Out, Sweet Land'; 'Song of Norway,'" in *Edwin Denby: Dance Writings*, ed. Robert Cornfield and William Mackay (London: Dance Books, 1986), 281–82.

49. Osato, *Distant Dances*, 229.

50. "No. 6B—Lonely Town—Pas de Deux, orch. Hershy Kay," in *On the Town*, Orchestral score, 177–83.

51. Steven Suskin, *The Sound of Broadway Music: A Book of Orchestrators and Orchestrations* (New York: Oxford University Press, 2009), 498; Suskin summarizes Kay's career, 48–54.

52. "Lonely Me," Copyist score (Robbins). The number was always sung by Gabey. Initially "Lonely Me" appeared in Scene 4, and the number "Gabey's Comin'" was part of the same scene.

53. E. C. Sherburne, "'On the Town': New Musical Comedy Hailed in Premiere at the Adelphi," *Christian Science Monitor*, December 29, 1944, Bernstein Scrapbooks.

54. "The Nicest Time of Year," lyric in Bernstein's hand (Bernstein Collection B71/F2). A copyist score for *On the Town* includes a melody with the same lyric (Robbins).

55. *On the Town* script, Versions A¹ and A², 1-8-14 and 2-4-4; also in Versions B and C. Version D includes the final version, with the lyric "Lucky to Be Me."

56. *On the Town*, Colonial Theatre Program.

57. *On the Town* Program, December 28, 1944.

58. Leonard Bernstein, Interview with Lehman Engel, January 19, 1980, Engel Collection B1/F21. Betty Comden, quoted in Tony Vellela, "Comden Is Back in 'Town,'" *Christian Science Monitor*, December 5, 2003.

59. Phyllis Newman, Interview with the author, New York City, April 27, 2007.

60. "Some Other Time" first appears in Version D of the script; see also "Some Other Time," Copyist score (Comden).

61. "Bill Evans Discography" on Nobuaki Togashi, Kohji "Shaolin" Matsubayashi, and Masayuki Hatta, JAZZDISCO.org, www.jazzdisco.org/bill-evans/discography, accessed May 7, 2013.

62. The connection between "Some Other Time," "Peace Piece," and "Flamenco Sketches" is made by Ashley Kahn in *Kind of Blue: The Making of the Miles Davis Masterpiece* (New York: Da Capo Press, 2000), 133–34.

63. Stacy Wolf, *Changed for Good: A Feminist History of the Broadway Musical* (New York: Oxford University Press, 2011), 4. The next quotation comes from this same source.

64. "Play Out of Town: On the Town," *Variety*, December 20, 1944, Bernstein Scrapbooks.

65. Tina Olsin Lent, "Romantic Love and Friendship: The Redefinition of Gender Relations in Screwball Comedy," in *Classical Hollywood Comedy*, ed. Kristine Brunovska Karnick and Henry Jenkins (New York: Routledge, 1995), 320, 314.

66. *On the Town*, Published script, 19.

67. Katherine A. Baber, "Leonard Bernstein's Jazz: A Musical Trope and Its Cultural Resonances," Ph.D. dissertation, Indiana University, 2010, 156.

68. "Vamp" usually refers to an improvised segment of accompaniment. Clearly, the musical material in *On the Town* was all notated. Yet there are sections of accompaniment that employ repeated patterns and simulate the concept of a "vamp."

69. *On the Town*, Published script, 22.

70. The tune was titled "My Father Said" in all draft scripts before Version D.

71. *On the Town* script, Version A¹, 1-5-5 to 1-5-6.

72. *On the Town*, Published script, 53–54.

73. Magee, *Irving Berlin's American Musical Theater*, 140.

74. "I Can Cook Too," Copyist scores (both Comden and Robbins).

75. *On the Town* script, Version A¹, 1-5-8.

76. *On the Town*, Published script, 27.

77. *On the Town*, Published script, 31. The next quotation comes from 31–32.

78. "Carried Away," Copyist scores (both Comden and Robbins).

79. *On the Town*, Piano-vocal score, 64–65.

80. *On the Town*, "First full-length recording," Columbia Masterworks OS 2028 (for a full citation see Appendix).

81. *On the Town*, Piano-vocal score, 70–72.

82. *On the Town* script, Version A¹: the lyric for "Another Love" is found on 1-6-6, and the quotation (beginning "Well—there") comes from 1-6-5.

83. Re Version B: *On the Town* script, Version B, Act I, Scene 6, 6. This lyric for the verse ends with Claire singing "True," instead of "I do," as it appears in the published score. The same is the case in Copyist score (Robbins).

84. Osato, *Distant Dances*, 234.

85. "*On the Town*'s Osato—Dancer into Actress," *Cue*, January 13, 1945, 7.

86. Alan Brown, "Pavan," *Grove Music Online*, accessed May 9, 2013.

87. *On the Town* script, Version A^1, 1-7-7. A copyist's score for the song reveals a fairly traditional pop song: "I'm Afraid It's Love," Copyist score (Robbins).

88. *On the Town* script, Version A^1, 1-7-4.

89. "Pinchy Terkle" is listed in "Cast of Characters," *On the Town* script, Version A^1, [3].

90. Re "blowsy": "Maude P. Smead" is listed in "Cast of Characters," *On the Town* script, Version A^1, [3]. Re "huge": *On the Town* script, Version A^1, 1-7-2.

91. "I'm a Little Prairie Flower" was performed on the radio in the 1930s by the British comedy team of The Two Leslies (i.e., Leslie Sarony and Leslie Holmes).

92. Re "cultured": *On the Town* script, Version B, "Act 1-Scene 7-Carnegie Hall-1." Re "at the piano": "Act I, Scene 7, page 2." The published script is toned down considerably. The next quotation comes from the second citation above.

93. Jerome Robbins, "Carnegie Hall" in *On the Town*, Set and script notes, 1944, RobbinsCP B63/F18.

94. *On the Town*, Colonial Theatre Program.

95. Sono Osato, Interview with the author, February 28, 2009. The quotations below come from the same interview.

96. "Miss Turnstiles: Carnegie Hall Pavane," Copyist score (Robbins).

97. "Carnegie Hall Pavane" exists from the very beginning of the New York run, although the title in the program is "Do, Re, Do."

98. Stephen Sondheim, Interview with the author, June 13, 2005.

99. "Play Out of Town," *Variety*.

100. Henry W. Levinger, "A Music Critic Looks at Broadway," *Musical Courier*, March 15, 1945, Bernstein Scrapbooks.

101. Leonard Bernstein, *On the Town: Three Dance Episodes* (New York: Amberson Enterprises, G. Schirmer, and H. Witmark, 1945).

102. Leonard Bernstein, "Three Dance Episodes from *On the Town*," program note for the San Francisco Symphony Orchestra, Bernstein conducting, February 13, 1946, Bernstein Scrapbooks. The next quotation is from the same source.

103. Leonard Bernstein, quoted in "*On the Town* Symposium," 18.

104. Bernstein, quoted in "*On the Town* Symposium," 24.

105. Meryle Secrest, *Leonard Bernstein: A Life* (New York: Alfred A. Knopf, 1994), 137.

106. Jack Gottlieb, "Prefatory Note," in Bernstein, *Jeremiah: Symphony No. 1* (New York: Jalni, Boosey & Hawkes, 1992), [i–ii].

107. Osato, *Distant Dances*, 240.

108. *On the Town* script, Version B, Act I Scene 3A.

109. I have also wondered if Miss Schmaltz might have been a figure from Yiddish theater, vaudeville, or early films.

110. Helen Smith raises useful comparisons between *Fancy Free* and "Presentation of Miss Turnstiles," and I am pushing the argument further here. See Smith, *There's a Place for Us*, 35–36.

111. I have explored this characterization of The Wreck in "Bernstein's *Wonderful Town* and McCarthy-Era Politics," paper delivered at the annual meeting of the American Musicological Society, Quebec City, November 3, 2007; abbreviated version published as "*Wonderful Town* and McCarthy-Era Politics," *Prelude, Fugue & Riffs*, Spring-Summer 2007, 8.

112. *On the Town* script, Version A¹, 1-4-9.

113. *On the Town* script, Version B, "Act I Scene 3A."

114. Robbins, Handwritten notes in *On the Town* script, Version A², 1-4-9.

115. *On the Town*, Published script, 18.

116. *On the Town* script, Version A¹, [1-9-1].

117. The first full-length recording of "Times Square Ballet" appeared on *On the Town*, Columbia Masterworks OS 2028, 1961.

118. "Penny Arcade Boy" is listed under "Musical Numbers," in *On the Town* Program, December 28, 1944.

119. *On the Town* script, Version A¹, [1-9-1].

120. *On the Town* script, Version B, "TIMES SQUARE" [no page number].

121. *On the Town* script, Version D, 1-13-67.

122. Copyist scores (both Comden and Robbins).

123. *On the Town*, Piano-vocal score, 6.

124. *On the Town*, Production flow chart.

125. *On the Town*, Published script, 76.

126. *On the Town*, Published script, 77.

127. Dream Ballet from *Oklahoma!*, in Richard Rodgers and Oscar Hammerstein II, 6 *Plays by Rodgers and Hammerstein* (New York: The Modern Library, [1955?]), 49–51.

128. *On the Town*, Published script, 77. The next quotation comes from the same page.

129. *On the Town*, Published script, 81.

130. Osato, *Distant Dances*, 235.

131. *On the Town*, Colonial Theatre Program.

132. *On the Town* Program, January 14, 1945.

133. Billie Allen, Interview with the author, August 10, 2008.

CHAPTER 8: *ON THE TOWN* AFTER DARK

Epigraph: "Nightlife," from the series "Fun with The Revuers," aired on NBC, September 29, 1940; audio transcript streamed at http://otrrlibrary.org/f.html, accessed May 5, 2013.

1. Peggy Doyle, "'On the Town' Rich Treat for Devotees of Ballet," *Boston American*, December 16, 1944, Bernstein Scrapbooks.

2. Elizabeth Craft, "'You Can't Deny You're Irish': The Irish American Experience in *The Voice of McConnell*, *Little Nellie Kelly*, *The Rise of Rosie O'Reilly*, and *The Merry Malones*," in "Becoming American Onstage: Broadway Narratives of Immigration Experiences in the United States," Ph.D. dissertation, Harvard University, 2014.

3. Betty Comden, "10,000 Easy Ways to Get into the Theater," *Mademoiselle*, October 1944.

4. Louis Calta, "News of the Night Clubs," *New York Times*, February 13, 1944; "Zanzibar," in "Nightclubs and Other Venues," *New Grove Dictionary of Jazz*, 2nd ed., ed. Barry Kernfeld, in *Grove Music Online*, accessed May 5, 2013.

5. Louis Calta, "News of the Night Clubs," *New York Times*, February 13, 1944.

6. Louis Calta, "Night Clubs Here and There," *New York Times*, January 2, 1944.

7. Untitled clipping, *Amsterdam Recorder*, New York, November 25, 1944, Bernstein Scrapbooks.

8. Re "large": *On the Town* script, Version B, "Act 2, Scene 1," [1]. Re "gaudy": Version A, [2-1-1].

9. "On the Town," Production flow chart, Clark Collection B99/F6.

10. Bruno, "News of Night Clubs: Being a Note on the Decline and Fall of Those Spectacle Shows," *New York Times*, February 11, 1940; Theodore Strauss, "Night Club Notes," *New York Times*, October 23, 1938.

11. Burton W. Peretti, *Nightclub City: Politics and Amusement in Manhattan* (Philadelphia: University of Pennsylvania Press, 2011), 192. The next quotations come from this same source, 208.

12. Theodore Strauss, "Around the Night Clubs: The Past Recaptured, Being an Interim Report on the Diamond Horseshoe," *New York Times*, July 23, 1939.

13. "Diam. Horseshoe in 6th Year," *Billboard*, December 30, 1944, 14.

14. "News of Night Clubs: The Diamond Horseshoe Opens a New Show—Ditto the Cotton Club," *New York Times*, May 12, 1940.

15. Benjamin Welles, "Raoul Pène du Bois: A Note or Two on the Scene and Costume Designer Extraordinary," *New York Times*, September 8, 1940.

16. "News of Night Clubs: The Diamond Horseshoe Opens a New Show—Ditto the Cotton Club."

17. "A Job at Billy Rose's Diamond Horseshoe is Equal to a Career," *Variety*, March 18, 1942. Sissle's orchestra was resident at Rose's club from 1938 to 1942 and again from 1945 to the mid-1950s ("Diamond Horseshoe," in "Nightclubs, United States of America," in *Grove Music Online*).

18. Caskie Stinnett, "Billy Rose's 'Diamond Horseshoe Revue' (Reviewed at Capitol, Washington, Thursday, May 13)," *Billboard*, May 22, 1943. The Gershwin medley included "Ain't Necessarily So," "I Got Plenty of Nuttin,'" and "Summertime" from *Porgy and Bess*, as well as "Strike Up the Band."

19. Caskie Stinnett, "Billy Rose's 'Diamond Horseshoe Revue.'"

20. "Rose Sets 'Horse' Dupe for Vaude," *Billboard*, September 19, 1942.

21. Bill Smith, "Night Club Reviews: Leon & Eddie's, New York," *Billboard*, June 17, 1944, 22, 25. The remaining quotations in this paragraph come from the same article.

22. *On the Town*, Published script, 64.

23. "On the Town: Scene Breakdown of Dance Personnel," Clark Collection B99/F8.

24. *On the Town* script, Version A, [2-1-1].

25. "So Long," *On the Town*, Piano-vocal score, 142.

26. "So Long," *On the Town*, Published script, 64.

27. Will Cobb and Gus Edwards, "I'd Like to See a Little More of You" (New York: Gus Edwards Music Publishing Company, 1906), sheet music available at Library of Congress, Performing Arts Encyclopedia, http://lcweb2.loc.gov/diglib/ihas/loc.natlib .ihas.100005126/default.html, accessed May 16, 2013. The lyric quoted here comes from the final segment of the song.

28. *On the Town*, Published script, 65.

29. *On the Town* Program, December 28, 1944. Cassard is described as a "blonde" in "Music Hall, N.Y.," *Variety*, November 26, 1941.

30. Cassard was trained at Oberlin and Union Theological Seminary in New York. She was an opera singer in Italy until 1941 ("U.S. Singer in Italy Says Crisis Canceled Her Jobs,"

New York Times, May 19, 1941). After returning to the United States, she starred in *Tosca* at the City Center, and she also performed at Radio City Music Hall ("City Center 'Tosca,'" *New York Times*, November 16, 1944; "Music Hall, N.Y.," *Variety*, November 26, 1941).

31. "I'm Blue" is the title given in *On the Town* Program, December 28, 1944. "I Wish I Was Dead" appears in *On the Town*, Piano-vocal score, 147.

32. *On the Town*, Published script, 65.

33. *On the Town*, Published script, 65.

34. "On the Town, Colonial Theatre," December 13–23, 1944. With draft scripts of *On the Town*, "I'm Blue" first appears in Version D, 2-1A-4.

35. *On the Town* script, Version A, 2-1-4.

36. A typed lyric for "It's Gotta Be Bad to Be Good" appears on stationery for "Advanced Music Corporation... Rockefeller Center," with "Lyric '42" handwritten in blue pencil in the corner, Bernstein Collection B71/F2. In scripts for *On the Town*, "It's Gotta Be Bad to Be Good" first appears in the scene at Diamond Eddie's in Version B of the script (2-1-3). It also appeared in Version A (1-8-1), although there it was sung in a different scene: the one in Claire's apartment.

37. Bernstein, "Key West Piece," in *On the Town* sketches, Bernstein Collection B26/10. The first column of titles includes: "Lonely Night; Nicest Time of Year; Gotta Be Bad to Be Good; I Can Cook Too; Hep March; Big Stuff and Riobamba."

38. *On the Town* script, Version B, 2-1-3.

39. "It's Gotta Be Bad to Be Good," ink piano-vocal manuscript, Hughie Prince (lyric), Lenny Bernstein (music), Bernstein Collection B21/F9. When "It's Gotta Be Bad to Be Good" was submitted for copyright, however, Bernstein was listed as both composer and lyricist. Copyright records: "It's Gotta Be Bad to Be Good: [from] On the Town," music and words Leonard Bernstein, Copyright Numbers PA0000111151 and PA0000111153, United States Copyright Office, Public Catalog, http://cocatalog.loc.gov/cgi-bin/Pwebrecon.cgi?DB=local&PAGE=First, accessed May 24, 2013.

40. *On the Town*, Published script, 68.

41. Betty Comden, "Jerome Robbins Gets a Little Help from His Friends," *New York Times*, December 4, 1988.

42. Robin Moore, "The Commercial Rumba: Afrocuban Arts as International Popular Culture," *Latin American Music Review/Revista de Música Latinoamericana* 16, no. 2 (1995): 179.

43. Theodore Strauss, "News of Night Clubs," *New York Times*, January 28, 1940.

44. Robert W. Dana, "Tips on Tables: Desi and Diosa Rock Roof at the Harem," *New York World-Telegram*, March 23, 1948.

45. Costello was also a replacement for Juanita Hall as "Bloody Mary" in the original production of *South Pacific* (Diosa Costello, in IBDB).

46. Kristin Baggelaar, *The Copacabana* (Charleston, SC: Arcadia Publishing, 2006), 11.

47. *On the Town* Program, December 28, 1944. The character is identified as "Señorita Dolores Dolores" in the published script, 68.

48. Gordon debuted at the Metropolitan Opera in 1919 and retired from the company in 1928 ("Obituaries: Jeanne Gordon," *Variety*, February 27, 1952, 63).

49. *On the Town* script, Version A, 2-1-6.

50. Comden and Bernstein, "*On the Town* Symposium," 22.

51. Dana, "Tips on Tables: Desi and Diosa Rock Roof at the Harem."

52. *On the Town* script, Version B, 2-1-8.

53. "Chili Con Conga" was recorded in 1939, and "Rhapsody in Rhumba" in 1940 ("Recordings" in "Cab Calloway Orchestra Home Page," www.cabcalloway.cc/recordings.htm, accessed May 24, 2013).

54. Before "Ya Got Me" entered the script, a brief segment of "Cook Again," as it was dubbed, was included in the script, immediately after "It's Gotta Be Bad to Be Good" (*On the Town* script, Version B, 2-1-9). As a result, the verse of "Ya Got Me" must have grown out of this reprise.

55. *On the Town*, Published script, 68.

56. *On the Town* script, Version A, 2-1-8.

57. Jacoby appears to have had a limited career on Broadway. He orchestrated three shows and composed the music for *Edna His Wife* (1937) ("Elliott Jacoby, Composer, Orchestrator," IBDB). Before *On the Town*, Jacoby conducted the orchestra on the Rudy Vallee Hour ("Elliott Jacoby, Led the Orchestra on Rudy Vallee Hour, 1932–41," *New York Times*, March 29, 1977).

58. John Storm Roberts, *The Latin Tinge: The Impact of Latin American Music on the United States*, 2nd ed. (New York: Oxford University Press, 1999), 102.

59. Mario Bauza, quoted in John Storm Roberts, 101.

60. Roberts, 101.

61. Edwin Denby, " 'On the Town'; 'Sing Out, Sweet Land'; 'Song of Norway,' " *New York Herald Tribune*, January 21, 1945; reprinted in *Edwin Denby: Dance Writings*, ed. Robert Cornfield and William Mackay (London: Dance Books, 1986), 282.

62. Comden, "Jerome Robbins Gets a Little Help from His Friends." The remaining quotations in this section come from the same source.

63. This quotation and the next one come from a draft of the 1988 article for the *New York Times*, which Comden sent to Robbins for approval; there was substantial rewriting of this segment before the article was published (Betty Comden, "1944–1988," typescript, May 10, 1988, RobbinsPP, Series IV, B79/F2).

64. *On the Town*, Published script, 71.

65. Version A, 2-1-12. Version B (2-1-10) calls the group a "swing trio" and says the music is "very hot."

66. Version A, 2-1-13.

67. "On the Town, Colonial Theatre," December 13–23, 1944, and *On the Town* Program, December 28, 1944.

68. *On the Town*, Orchestral score, 393.

69. *On the Town*, Production flow chart.

70. "Crime Smear Sends Ubangi to Broadway," *New York Amsterdam News*, December 20, 1941, and "Nightclubs, United States of America," in *Grove Music Online*, accessed May 24, 2013.

71. Dan Burley, "Ubangi Club Revue Scores Big Hit on Broadway," *New York Amsterdam News*, January 10, 1942.

72. "Gladys Bentley Opened Thursday at Tondayleyos," *New York Amsterdam News*, September 30, 1944. See also Billy J. Harbin, Kim Marra, and Robert A. Schanke, "Gladys Bentley," *The Gay and Lesbian Theatrical Legacy: A Biographical Dictionary of Major Figures in American Stage History in the Pre-Stonewall Era* (Ann Arbor: University of Michigan Press, 2005), 56–59. Also, I am grateful to Sarah Hankins for an unpublished paper, "Double-Guise: Manipulating Sex and Race in Early Male Impersonation," Harvard University, December 2009.

73. George Chauncey, *Gay New York: Gender, Urban Culture, and the Making of the Gay Male World, 1890–1940* (New York: Basic Books, 1994), 252–53.

74. "Gladys Bentley Opened Thursday at Tondayleyos."

75. Dan Burley, "Jackie Mabley Wows Broadway in Initial Appearance There: Female Comedienne Breaks Up Ubangi Club's Hot Show," *New York Amsterdam News*, January 17, 1942.

76. Leonard Bernstein, "I've Got No Tears Left," Bernstein Collection B21/F14; "Ain't Got No Tears Left," copyist's score, Robbins Collection B64/F3.

77. *On the Town*, Published script, 74–75.

78. W. S. Gilbert and Arthur Sullivan, *The Pirates of Penzance, or, The Slave of Duty*: Libretto PDF, 2; Paul Howarth and Jim Farron, curators, "Gilbert and Sullivan Archive," http://math.boisestate.edu/gas/pirates/html/index.html, accessed May 24, 2013.

79. "The Movie Villains," in "Fun with The Revuers, WJZ, April 23, 1940, 9:30–10:00 p.m.," typescript, inserted between pages 6 and 7; Comden-Green Papers, Series I, B4/F7.

EPILOGUE

1. John Updike, quoted in Christopher Lehmann-Haupt, "John Updike, a Lyrical Writer of the Middle-Class Man, Dies at 76," *New York Times*, January 28, 2009.

2. Robbins, "*On the Town* Symposium," 23.

3. Bernstein, quoted in "Bernstein Writes Musical Comedy," *New Britain Herald* [CT], December 12, 1944, Bernstein Scrapbooks. This is a United Press article, which appeared in a number of different papers.

4. I explore the relationship of *West Side Story* to events in the Civil Rights Movement in "*West Side Story* and *The Music Man*: Whiteness, Immigration, and Race in the U.S. During the late 1950s," *Studies in Musical Theatre* 3, no. 1 (2009): 13–30.

5. Anthony Tommasini, "Youthful Choristers Imparting New Life," *New York Times*, October 27, 2008. This review covered a performance of *Mass* in Harlem, conducted by Marin Alsop.

6. Bernstein, "4 Lullabies for Martyrs," reproduced at www.leonardbernstein.com/mass_notes.htm.

7. Edwin Denby, "Dancing in Shows," *New York Herald Tribune*, January 21, 1945; reprinted in *Edwin Denby: Dance Writings*, ed. Robert Cornfield and William Mackay (London: Dance Books, 1986), 281.

8. Sono Osato, quoted in Earl Conrad, "American Viewpoint: She's Mixed, Merry and Musical," *Chicago Defender*, April 14, 1945.

9. Robbins, quoted in Dorothy Barret, "Jerome Robbins," *Dance Magazine*, May 1945, 40.

PERMISSIONS

SELECTED BIBLIOGRAPHY

BOOKS AND ARTICLES

Abbott, George. *"Mister Abbott."* New York: Random House, 1963.

Amberg, George. *Ballet in America: The Emergence of an American Art.* New York: Duell, Sloan and Pearce, 1949.

Baber, Katherine A. "Leonard Bernstein's Jazz: Musical Topic and Cultural Resonance." Ph.D. diss., Indiana University, 2011.

Banes, Sally. "Balanchine and Black Dance." *Choreography and Dance* 3, no. 3 (1993): 59–77.

Barret, Dorothy. "Jerome Robbins." *Dance Magazine,* May 1945, 13–14, 40.

Berman, Marshall. *On the Town: One Hundred Years of Spectacle in Times Square.* New York: Random House, 2006.

Bernstein, Burton, and Barbara B. Haws, eds. *Leonard Bernstein: American Original.* New York: Collins, 2008.

Bernstein, Leonard, Betty Comden, Adolph Green, Arthur Laurents, Jerome Robbins, and Oliver Smith. "Projects Committee Introduces Its Landmark Series of Symposia: On the Town." *Dramatists Guild Quarterly* 18, no. 2 (1981): 11–24.

Bérubé, Allan. *Coming Out Under Fire: The History of Gay Men and Women in World War Two.* New York: Free Press, 1990.

Block, Geoffrey. *Enchanted Evenings: The Broadway Musical from "Show Boat" to Sondheim,* 2nd ed. New York: Oxford University Press, 2009.

Bryer, Jackson R., and Richard A. Davison, eds. *The Art of the American Musical: Conversations with the Creators.* New Brunswick, NJ: Rutgers University Press, 2005.

Burton, Humphrey. *Leonard Bernstein.* New York: Doubleday, 1994.

Carter, Tim. *Oklahoma! The Making of an American Musical.* New Haven, CT: Yale University Press, 2007.

Chauncey, George. *Gay New York: Gender, Urban Culture, and the Makings of the Gay Male World, 1890–1940.* New York: Basic Books, 1994.

de Mille, Agnes. "'Fancy Free' in Review." Liner note essay, Decca DA-406, 1946.

Decker, Todd. *"Show Boat": Performing Race in an American Musical.* New York: Oxford University Press, 2013.

Fauser, Annegret. "'Dixie Carmen': War, Race, and Identity in Oscar Hammerstein's *Carmen Jones* (1943)." *Journal of the Society for American Music* 4, no. 2 (2010): 127–74.

Garafola, Lynn, ed. *Of, By, and For the People: Dancing on the Left in the 1930s.* In *Studies in Dance History* 5, no. 1 (1994).

Garafola, Lynn, and Eric Foner, eds. *Dance for a City: Fifty Years of the New York City Ballet.* New York: Columbia University Press, 1999.

Garafola, Lynn, and Nancy Van Norman Baer, eds. *The Ballets Russes and Its World.* New Haven, CT: Yale University Press, 1999.

Genné, Beth. "'Freedom Incarnate': Jerome Robbins, Gene Kelly, and the Dancing Sailor as an Icon of American Values in World War II." *Dance Chronicle* 24, no. 1 (2001): 83–103.

Gilmore, Glenda Elizabeth. *Defying Dixie: The Radical Roots of Civil Rights, 1919–1950*. New York: W. W. Norton, 2008.

Gottlieb, Jack, ed. *Leonard Bernstein: August 25, 1918–October 14, 1990: A Complete Catalogue of His Works*. New York: Leonard Bernstein Music Publishing Company, 1990.

Greenberg, Cheryl. "Black and Jewish Responses to Japanese Internment." *Journal of American Ethnic History* 14, no. 2 (1995): 3–37.

Greenberg, Cheryl. *Troubling the Waters: Black-Jewish Relations in the American Century*. Princeton, NJ: Princeton University Press, 2006.

Hill, Errol G., and James V. Hatch. *A History of African American Theatre*. Cambridge: Cambridge University Press, 2003.

Hubbs, Nadine. *The Queer Composition of America's Sound: Gay Modernists, American Music, and National Identity*. Berkeley: University of California Press, 2004.

Jowitt, Deborah. *Jerome Robbins: His Life, His Theater, His Dance*. New York: Simon & Schuster, 2004.

Knapp, Raymond. *The American Musical and the Formation of National Identity*. Princeton, NJ: Princeton University Press, 2005.

Knapp, Raymond. *The American Musical and the Performance of Personal Identity*. Princeton, NJ: Princeton University Press, 2006.

Knight, Arthur. *Disintegrating the Musical: Black Performance and American Musical Film*. Durham, NC: Duke University Press, 2002.

Laird, Paul R. *Leonard Bernstein: A Guide to Research*. Routledge Music Bibliographies. New York: Routledge, 2002.

Lawrence, Greg. *Dance with Demons: The Life of Jerome Robbins*. New York: G. P. Putnam's Sons, 2001.

Lewin, Yaël Tamar. *Night's Dancer: The Life of Janet Collins*. Middletown, CT: Wesleyan University Press, 2011.

Lim, Shirley Jennifer. *A Feeling of Belonging: Asian American Women's Public Culture, 1930–1960*. New York: New York University Press, 2006.

Loney, Glenn (moderator), and David Black, Betty Comden, Adolph Green, Joe Layton, Oliver Smith, Charles Strouse, and Gwen Verdon (panelists). "Putting It All Together: The Synthesis of a Musical as a Work of Art." In *Musical Theatre in America: Papers and Proceedings of the Conference on the Musical Theatre in America*, edited by Glenn Loney, 339–75. Westport, CT: Greenwood Press, 1984.

Magee, Jeffrey. *Irving Berlin's American Musical Theater*. New York: Oxford University Press, 2012.

Manning, Susan. *Modern Dance, Negro Dance: Race in Motion*. Minneapolis: University of Minnesota Press, 2004.

Meyer, Richard. *Outlaw Representation: Censorship and Homosexuality in Twentieth-Century American Art*. New York: Oxford University Press, 2002.

Mikotowicz, Thomas J. *Oliver Smith: A Bio-Bibliography*. Westport, CT: Greenwood Press, 1994.

Monson, Ingrid. *Freedom Sounds: Civil Rights Call Out to Jazz and Africa*. New York: Oxford University Press, 2007.

Most, Andrea. *Making Americans: Jews and the Broadway Musical*. Cambridge, MA: Harvard University Press, 2004.

Murata, Alice. *Japanese Americans in Chicago*. Chicago: Arcadia, 2002.

Oja, Carol J. "Bernstein's Musicals: Reflections of their Time." In *Leonard Bernstein: American Original*, edited by Burton Bernstein and Barbara B. Haws, 59–75, 80–83. New York: Collins, 2008.

Oja, Carol J. "Bernstein's *Wonderful Town* and McCarthy-Era Politics." Paper delivered at the American Musicological Society, Quebec City, November 3, 2007. Summary published in *Prelude, Fugue & Riffs*, Spring-Summer 2007, 8.

Oja, Carol J. "*West Side Story* and *The Music Man*: Whiteness, Immigration, and Race in the US During the Late 1950s." *Studies in Musical Theatre* 3, no. 1 (2009): 13–30.

Oja, Carol J., and Kay Kaufman Shelemay. "Leonard Bernstein's Jewish Boston: Cross-Disciplinary Research in the Classroom." *Journal of the Society for American Music* 3, no. 1 (2009): 3–33.

Osato, Sono. *Distant Dances*. New York: Alfred A. Knopf, 1980.

Peretti, Burton W. *Nightclub City: Politics and Amusement in Manhattan*. Philadelphia: University of Pennsylvania Press, 2007.

Perlis, Vivian. "Dear Aaron, Dear Lenny: A Friendship in Letters." In *Aaron Copland and His World*, edited by Carol J. Oja and Judith Tick, 151–78. Princeton, NJ: Princeton University Press, 2005.

Peterson, Bernard L., Jr. *A Century of Musicals in Black and White: An Encyclopedia of Musical Stage Works By, About, or Involving African Americans*. Westport, CT: Greenwood Press, 1993.

Peyser, Joan. *Bernstein: A Biography*. New York: Beech Tree Books, 1987.

Phillips, Kimberley L. *War! What Is It Good For? Black Freedom Struggles & the U.S. Military from World War II to Iraq*. Chapel Hill: University of North Carolina Press, 2012.

Pollack, Howard. *Aaron Copland: The Life and Work of an Uncommon Man*. New York: Henry Holt, 1999.

Pollack, Howard. *Marc Blitzstein: His Life, His Work, His World*. New York: Oxford University Press, 2012.

Robinson, Alice M. *Betty Comden and Adolph Green: A Bio-Bibliography*. Westport, CT: Greenwood Press, 1994.

Robinson, Greg. "Nisei in Gotham: The JACD and Japanese Americans in 1940s New York." *Prospects: An Annual of American Cultural Studies* 30 (2005): 581–95.

Savran, David. *Highbrow/Lowdown: Theater, Jazz, and the Making of the New Middle Class*. Ann Arbor: University of Michigan Press, 2009.

Schiff, David. *The Ellington Century*. Berkeley: University of California Press, 2012.

Secrest, Meryle. *Leonard Bernstein: A Life*. New York: Alfred A. Knopf, 1994.

Seldes, Barry. *Leonard Bernstein: The Political Life of an American Musician*. Berkeley: University of California Press, 2009.

Simeone, Nigel. *Leonard Bernstein, West Side Story*. Farnham, Surrey, UK: Ashgate, 2009.

Smith, Helen. *There's a Place for Us: The Musical Theatre Works of Leonard Bernstein*. Farnham, Surrey, UK: Ashgate, 2011.

Stempel, Larry. *Showtime: A History of the Broadway Musical Theater*. New York: W. W. Norton, 2010.

Suskin, Steven. *The Sound of Broadway Music: A Book of Orchestrators and Orchestrations*. New York: Oxford University Press, 2009.

Tobias, Tobi. "Bringing Back Robbins's 'Fancy.'" *Dance Magazine* 54, no. 1 (January 1980): 60–77.

Vaill, Amanda. *Somewhere: The Life of Jerome Robbins*. New York: Broadway Books, 2006.

Walker, Kathrine Sorley. *De Basil's Ballets Russes*. New York: Atheneum, 1983.

Weinberg, Jonathan. "Cruising with Paul Cadmus." *Art in America* 80, no. 11 (November 1992): 102–5, 108–9.

Weinberg, Jonathan. *Speaking for Vice: Homosexuality in the Art of Charles Demuth, Marsden Hartley, and the First American Avant-Garde*. New Haven, CT: Yale University Press, 1993.

Wells, Elizabeth. *"West Side Story": Cultural Perspectives on an American Musical*. Lanham, MD: Scarecrow Press, 2011.

Wolf, Stacy. *Changed for Good: A Feminist History of the Broadway Musical*. New York: Oxford University Press, 2011.

Woll, Allen. *Black Musical Theatre: From Coontown to Dreamgirls*. Baton Rouge: Louisiana State University Press, 1989. Reprint, New York: Da Capo, 1991.

INTERVIEWS CONDUCTED BY THE AUTHOR

Allen, Billie. Telephone interview, August 10, 2008; and New York City, April 21, 2013.

Handy, Jean. Telephone interview, February 16, 2009.

Lee, Everett. Telephone interviews, March 25 and 28, 2009.

McKenzie, Ada Bard. Telephone interview, November 5, 2012.

McLerie, Allyn Ann. Telephone interview, February 15, 2009.

Newman, Phyllis. New York City, April 27, 2007.

Osato, Sono. New York City, February 28, 2009, January 18, 2010, and December 13, 2012.

Prince, Harold. New York City, April 28, 2009.

Sondheim, Stephen. Telephone interview, June 13, 2005.

DIGITAL RESOURCES

Of the links given below, only the American Memory Project and the Harvard site are open-source websites. All of the others require access through subscription, usually via libraries.

American Memory. Library of Congress. http://memory.loc.gov/ammem.

Ancestry.com. Provo, UT.

Black Thought and Culture. Alexander Street Press. http://alexanderstreet.com/products/black-thought-and-culture.

Grove Music Online. Edited by Deane Root. http://www.oxfordmusiconline.com.

Oja, Carol J., and Kay Kaufman Shelemay, eds. *Leonard Bernstein's Boston Years: Team Research in a Harvard Classroom,* compiled and edited by Elizabeth Craft and Liza Vick. http://isites.harvard.edu/icb/icb.do?keyword=bernstein.

ProQuest Historical Newspapers. Ann Arbor, MI: ProQuest. http://www.proquest.com/en-US/catalogs/databases/detail/pq-hist-news.

Entertainment Industry Magazine Archive. Ann Arbor, MI: ProQuest. http://www.proquest.com/en-US/catalogs/databases/detail/eima.

INDEX

Page numbers in **bold** indicate photos, *italics* indicate musical examples or tables.

Index | 391

White, Josh, 152
The White Shadow, 211
whiteface, 178–79
Wilder, Alec, 16, 232
Wiley College (Texas), 215
Wilkins, Roy, 160
William Morris Agency, 58
Williams, Dorothy, 165–66
Williams, Gwen, 69
Williams, Johnny, 64
Williams, Lavinia, 165–66
Williams, Mary Lou, 62
Williams, Tennessee, 49, 213
Willis, Bernice, 165
Wilson, Dooley, 163, 209
Wilson, Teddy, 34, 59, 63, 180, 183
The Wiz, 211
Woetzel, Damian, 12
Wolf, Stacy, 243
Wolfe, George C., 85
Wolffers, Jules, 103
Woll, Allen, 189
Women's Project, 215
Wonderful Town, 4, 61, 79, 97, 100,
    241, 243, 261, 279, 306n9
Wong, Anna May, 115, 124, 127,
    129, 147

Woolworth Tower, 244
Works Progress Administration,
    21, 97
World Federation of Democratic
    Youth, 56
"The World of Music" (The
    Revuers), 77–78, 253
World War II
    African Americans and *nisei*,
        148–49
    bombings of Hiroshima and
        Nagasaki, 115, 148
    Bundles for Britain, 5–6
    European exiles, 5, 65,
        125, 153
    Good Neighbor Policy, 45, 291
    Guadalcanal, 136
    Japanese detainment and
        internment, 3, 6, 85, 115,
        131, 133–34, 139, 140, 141
    and *nisei*, 115, 120–23, 128, 134,
        138, 140, 147, 148, 150
    propaganda, **143**
    racial climate in U.S., 160, 180
    "Rosie the Riveter," 198
    Selective Training and Service
        Act of 1940, 5

Tripartite Pact, 128
    U.S. military segregation, 4–5,
        85, 155–56
"The World's Fair Is Unfair" (The
    Revuers), 76, 275, 277
Wright, Richard, 202, 207, 208

"Ya Got Me" (*On the Town*), 89, 111,
    272, 278, 280–85, 282, 283
Yates, Clarence, 161–62
Yellow Jacket newspaper (Howard
    Payne College, Texas), 215
YMCA Little Theatre, 200
"You're a Sap, Mr. Jap," 143
"You're Awful" (*On the Town*,
    film), 113
Young Communist League, 203
"Young Man with a Kazoo" (The
    Revuers), 58
Your Hit Parade, 111
Youth Theatre, 56
Yuriko. *See* Kikuchi, Yuriko

Zanuck, Darryl, 60
Ziegfeld Follies, 273–75
Zolotow, Sam, 171
Zoot Suit Riots, 179